DATE

DEC 1 7 2010	
RECEIVED	
DEC 1 7 2010	

A Song of Power and the
Power of Song

Sources for Biblical and Theological Study

General Editor:
David W. Baker
Ashland Theological Seminary

1. *The Flowering of Old Testament Theology: A Reader in Twentieth-Century Old Testament Theology, 1930–1990*
   edited by Ben C. Ollenburger, Elmer A. Martens, and Gerhard F. Hasel

2. *Beyond Form Criticism: Essays in Old Testament Literary Criticism*
   edited by Paul R. House

3. *A Song of Power and the Power of Song: Essays on the Book of Deuteronomy*
   edited by Duane L. Christensen

A Song of Power and the Power of Song

Essays on the Book of Deuteronomy

edited by
Duane L. Christensen

Eisenbrauns
Winona Lake, Indiana
1993

Library of Congress Cataloging-in-Publication Data

A Song of power and the power of song : essays on the book of Deuteronomy
/ edited by Duane L. Christensen.
   p.   cm.—(Sources for biblical and theological study ; 3)
Includes bibliographical references and indexes.
ISBN 0-931464-74-9
   1. Bible. O.T. Deuteronomy—Criticism, interpretation, etc.
I. Christensen, Duane L., 1938– .
BS1275.2.S66 1993
222′.1506—dc20   93-6413
                                     CIP

CONTENTS

SERIES PREFACE

Old Testament scholarship is well served by several recent works which detail, to a greater or lesser extent, the progress made in the study of the Old Testament. Some survey the range of interpretation over long stretches of time, while others concern themselves with a smaller chronological or geographical segment of the field. There are also brief *entrés* into the various subdisciplines of Old Testament study included in the standard introductions as well as in several useful series. All of these provide secondary syntheses of various aspects of Old Testament research. All refer to, and base their discussions upon, various seminal works by Old Testament scholars which have proven pivotal in the development and flourishing of the various aspects of the discipline.

The main avenue into the various areas of Old Testament inquiry, especially for the beginner, has been until now mainly through the filter of these interpreters. Even on a pedagogical level, however, it is beneficial for a student to be able to interact with foundational works firsthand. This contact will not only provide insight into the content of an area, but hopefully will also lead to the sharpening of critical abilities through interaction with various viewpoints. This series seeks to address this need by including not only key, ground-breaking works, but also significant responses to these. This allows the student to appreciate the process of scholarly development through interaction.

The series is also directed toward scholars. In a period of burgeoning knowledge and significant publication in many places and languages around the world, this series will endeavor to make easily accessible significant, but at times hard to find, contributions. Each volume will contain essays, articles, extracts, and the like, presenting in a manageable scope the growth and development of one of a number of different aspects of Old Testament studies. Most volumes will contain previously published material, with synthetic essays by the editor(s) of the individual volume. Some volumes, however, are expected to contain significant, previously unpublished works. To facilitate access to students and scholars, all entries will appear in English and will be newly typeset. If students are excited by the study of Scripture and scholars are encouraged in amicable dialogue, this series would have fulfilled its purpose.

DAVID W. BAKER, *series editor*
Ashland Theological Seminary

EDITOR'S PREFACE

Selecting and compiling essays that cover a wide range of issues and the entire span of modern critical scholarship, for a book as central in importance as Deuteronomy, has been no simple task. The bibliography of available works on Deuteronomy is overwhelming, even to the specialist. By its very nature the book attracts the attention of anyone who takes a serious look at almost any Old Testament topic of substance in terms of both biblical theology and the questions engendered by the historical-critical method. Moreover, many of the more important works are not available in the English language, and efforts to obtain permission to reprint certain essays were not always successful.

Two primary factors governed the choice of materials selected for this volume. The first objective was to assemble representative essays for each of the four major division of this book, namely, issues that deal with the study of Deuteronomy as a whole and with specific texts within the three subdivisions of material that reflect the editor's understanding of the literary structure of the book (see introduction). The second goal was to include as many as possible of the major scholars currently involved in Deuteronomy research. This latter decision resulted in the translation from German of recent essays by Norbert Lohfink and Georg Braulik, which appear here for the first time in English.

It was not possible to include the work of many scholars who have made significant contributions to the study of Deuteronomy within this volume, such as: A. Alt, C. I. Begg, A. Bertholet, J. Blenkinsopp, P. Buis, C. Carmichael, H. Cazelles, A. Cholewínski, R. E. Clements, R. Clifford, D. Daube, S. R. Driver, J. Dus, O. Eissfeldt, F. García López, J. Halbe, W. Harrelson, J. Hempel, H. Junker, P. Kleinert, S. A. Kaufman, D. Knapp, E. König, J. Levenson, J. L'Hour, S. Loersch, J. Lust, D. J. McCarthy, J. G. McConville, R. P. Merendino, J. Milgrom, S. Mittmann, R. D. Nelson, E. Nielsen, M. Noth, T. Oestreicher, B. Peckham, L. Perlitt, J. G. Plöger, H. D. Preuss, G. von Rad, M. Rose, U. Rüterswörden, G. Seitz, G. A. Smith, D. E. Skweres, J. J. Stamm, W. Staerk, C. Steuernagel, J. A. Thompson, G. M. de Tillesse, J. J. Tigay, G. Vanoni, A. C. Welch, R. Westbrook, J. Wijngaards, and G. E. Wright.

A fifth section of the book, "New Directions in Recent Research," is included to suggest that we may be on the verge of opening a new chapter of research in Deuteronomy, one that will not be easily integrated into what has taken place before. All three of the essays in this section focus primarily on the received Masoretic Text and the information it provides the careful reader, information that has largely been ignored in prior research. Making use of Russian Formalist and Structuralist theory, Polzin offers a close reading of the Hebrew text of Deuteronomy, with specific attention to the phenomenon of reporting speech in an "attempt to uncover the various points of view that make up its compositional structure" (p. 355). Labuschagne's concept of *Zahlenkomposition* ('numerical composition') suggests that the ancient scribes who redacted the biblical text were well versed in basic mathematical concepts and may well have played rather complex "mathematical games" with the shaping of sacred tradition. My own study of the Masoretic accentual system in Deuteronomy suggests that those same scribes were also musicians and that musical structure is an essential part of the received tradition. The implications for understanding the so-called *Numeruswechsel* are of particular importance. In short, the book of Deuteronomy is a work of literary art in poetic form, subject to the restraints of the musical media to which it was originally composed.

I would like to take this opportunity to express profound gratitude to Georg Braulik and Norbert Lohfink for sharing so generously their extensive bibliography on the book of Deuteronomy. The initial selection of articles for this volume was made at the University of Vienna in April of 1989 and final decisions during a return visit in August of 1990. All told, I was able to spend five weeks in Vienna, working in what I consider a "scholar's paradise," so far as Deuteronomy is concerned. It was a joy to have at one's fingertips, so to speak, virtually all of the literature on the subject. This volume could not have been compiled without that base on which to build.

DUANE L. CHRISTENSEN
*American Baptist Seminary of the West
and Graduate Theological Union*

ABBREVIATIONS

General

A.T.	*Alten Testament* (Old Testament)
CH	Code of Hammurapi
D	Deuteronomy (Pentateuchal source)
D(eu)t(n)	Deuteronomy
D(eu)tr	deuteronomistic
dtc	deuteronomic
E	Elohist (Pentateuchal source)
EA	El-Amarna
E.T.	English translation
EVV	English Versions
FS	Festschrift
HL	Hittite Laws
IOSOT	International Organization for the Study of the Old Testament
J	Yahwist (Pentateuchal source)
LE	Laws of Eshnunna
LXX	Septuagint (Greek translation of Old Testament)
MAL	Middle Assyrian Laws
MT	Masoretic Text
NEB	New English Bible
NJPS	New Jewish Publication Society Version
NT	New Testament
OT	Old Testament
P	priestly source (Pentateuchal)
RSV	Revised Standard Version
SBJ	La Sainte Bible, Jerusalem
YHWH	Yahweh

Books and Periodicals

AASF	Annales Academiae Scientiarum (Fennicae, Helsinki)
AB	Anchor Bible
ABR	*Australian Biblical Review*
AfO	*Archiv für Orientforschung*

xi

AICL	A. Phillips, *Ancient Israel's Criminal Law: A New Approach to the Decalogue*
AJSL	*American Journal of Semitic Languages and Literature*
AnBib	Analecta Biblica
ANET	J. B. Pritchard (ed.), *Ancient Near Eastern Texts Relating to the Old Testament*
AOAT	Alter Orient und Altes Testament
AOS	American Oriental Series
ASTI	*Annual of the Swedish Theological Institute*
ATD	Das Alte Testament Deutsch
AT(h)ANT	Abhandlungen zur Theologie des Alten und Neuen Testaments
BA	*Biblical Archaeologist*
BASOR	*Bulletin of the American Schools of Oriental Research*
BBB	Bonner biblische Beiträge
BET(h)L	Bibliotheca ephemeridum theologicarum lovaniensium
BEvT	Beträge zur evangelischen Theologie
BFChrTh	Beiträge zur Förderung christlicher Theologie
BGBE	Beiträge zur Geschichte der biblischen Exegese
Bib	*Biblica*
BiblOr	*Bibliotheca orientalis*
BibOr	Biblica et Orientalia
BK(AT)	Biblischer Kommentar: Altes Testament
BL	J. C. Miles, *The Babylonian Laws*, 2 vols.
BN	*Biblische Notizen*
BO	*Bibbia e oriente*
BTB	*Biblical Theology Bulletin*
BWANT	Beiträge zur Wissenschaft vom Alten und Neuen Testament
BZ	*Biblische Zeitschrift*
BZAW	Beihefte zur ZAW
CB(ib)	Cambridge Bible
CB.OTS	Coniectanea Biblica, Old Testament Series
CBQ	*Catholic Biblical Quarterly*
CTA	A. Herdner (ed.), *Corpus des tablettes en cunéiformes alphabétiques*
DBS	*Dictionnaire de la Bible, Supplément*
DJD	Discoveries in the Judaean Desert of Jordan
DSD	Dead Sea Scrolls: Manual of Discipline
ET(h)L	*Ephemerides theologicae lovanienses*
EvT(heol)	*Evangelische Theologie*
FRLANT	Forschungen zur Religion und Literatur des Alten und Neuen Testaments

GCS	Griechischen christlichen Schriftsteller
GHAT	Göttinger Handkommentar zum Alten Testament
HAT	Handbuch zum Alten Testament
HKAT	Handkommentar zum Alten Testament
HSM	Harvard Semitic Monographs
HT(h)R	*Harvard Theological Review*
HUCA	*Hebrew Union College Annual*
IB	*Interpreter's Bible*
ICC	International Critical Commentary
IDBSup	*Interpreter's Dictionary of the Bible, Supplementary Volume*
IEJ	*Israel Exploration Journal*
Int	*Interpretation*
IOS	*Israel Oriental Studies*
JANES	*Journal of the Ancient Near Eastern Society of Columbia University*
JAOS	*Journal of the American Oriental Society*
JBC	R. E. Brown et al. (eds.), *Jerome Biblical Commentary*
JBL	*Journal of Biblical Literature*
JCunSt	*Journal of Cuneiform Studies*
JETS	*Journal of the Evangelical Theological Society*
JJS	*Journal of Jewish Studies*
JNES	*Journal of Near Eastern Studies*
JPOS	*Journal of the Palestine Oriental Society*
JRAS	*Journal of the Royal Asiatic Society*
JSOT	*Journal for the Study of the Old Testament*
JSOTSup	Journal for the Study of the Old Testament, Supplement Series
JTS	*Journal of Theological Studies*
KAT	Kommentar zum Alten Testament
KEHAT	Kurzgefasste exegetische Handbuch zum Alten Testament
KHAT	Kurzer Hand-Commentar zum Alten Testament
KHC	Kurzer Hand-Commentar zum Alten Testament
KlSchr	*Kleine Schriften*
LCL	Loeb Classical Library
MIO(r)	*Mitteilungen des Instituts für Orientforschung*
MRS	Mission de Ras Shamra
MVAG	Mitteilungen der Vorder-asiatisch-ägyptischen Gesellschaft
NCB(C)	New Century Bible Commentary
NICOT	New International Commentary on the Old Testament
OTS	*Oudtestamentische Studiën*

PEQ	*Palestine Exploration Quarterly*
PRU	*Le Palais royal d'Ugarit*
RB	*Revue biblique*
RHPR	*Revue d'histoire et de philosophie religieuses*
RIDA	*Revue internationale des droits de l'antiquité*
RSP	L. R. Fisher (ed.), *Ras Shamra Parallels*
SANT	Studien zum Alten und Neuen Testament
SB	Sources bibliques
SBL	Society of Biblical Literature
SBLDS	Society of Biblical Literature Dissertation Series
SBL.MS	Society of Biblical Literature Monograph Series
SBM	Stuttgarter biblische Monographien
SBS	Stuttgarter Bibelstudien
SBT	Studies in Biblical Theology
SOTS	Society for Old Testament Study
STAT	Suomalaisen Tiede Akatemian
TAik	*Teologinen Aikakauskirja*
THAT	E. Jenni and C. Westermann (eds.), *Theologische Handwörterbuch zum Alten Testament*
ThB	Theologische Bücherei
T(h)LZ	*Theologische Literaturzeitung*
T(h)S(t)	*Theologische Studiën*
ThW	*Theologische Wissenschaft*
T(h)WAT	G. J. Botterweck and H. Ringgren (eds.), *Theologisches Wörterbuch zum Alten Testament*
ThZ	*Theologische Zeitschrift*
TRE	*Theologische Realenzyklopädie*
TR(u)	*Theologische Rundschau*
UF	*Ugarit-Forschungen*
UT	C. H. Gordon, *Ugaritic Textbook*
VS	Verbum salutis
VT	*Vetus Testamentum*
VTS(up)	Vetus Testamentum Supplements
WMANT	Wissenschaftliche Monographien zum Alten und Neuen Testament
WTJ	*Westminster Theological Journal*
WUS	Joseph Aistleitner, *Wörterbuch der Ugaritischen Sprache*
ZAW	*Zeitschrift für die Alttestamentliche Wissenschaft*
ZDMG	*Zeitschrift der deutschen morgenländischen Gesellschaft*
ZDPV	*Zeitschrift des deutschen Palästina-Vereins*
ZKT	*Zeitschrift für katholische Theologie*
ZTK	*Zeitschrift für Theologie und Kirche*

Introduction

Deuteronomy in Modern Research: Approaches and Issues

Duane L. Christensen

Major Impulses in the Study of Deuteronomy

Though the book of Deuteronomy has been of central concern throughout the entire period of modern critical research on the biblical text, a number of problems remain unresolved, including the basic question of genre. The book contains a collection of laws, but it is clearly not a law code in its received literary form. And though Deuteronomy has affinities to international treaty texts of the ancient Near East, it is not the text of a covenant treaty as such, as M. Weinfeld in particular has shown.[1] It may be correct, with von Rad, to see the book as being shaped by Levitical preaching and put in the form of a cult liturgy, a series of sermons from the lips of Moses shortly before his death.[2] But once again the model of the sermon is less than adequate to explain this remarkable literary work. And though the book is clearly a repository for ancient traditions, the concept of an archive, as suggested by N. Lohfink, is simply too pedantic to describe adequately a work of such remarkable literary quality.[3] A new model is needed to explain the nature and function of this work of extraordinary literary coherence and political sophistication.

W. M. L. de Wette's 1805 dissertation laid the cornerstone for the edifice of pentateuchal literary criticism of the nineteenth century. The

---

1. M. Weinfeld, *Deuteronomy and the Deuteronomic School* (Oxford: Clarendon, 1972) 146–57; reprinted (Winona Lake, Ind.: Eisenbrauns, 1992).

2. G. von Rad, *Deuteronomy* (OTL; Philadelphia: Westminster, 1966) 23–27.

3. N. Lohfink, *Lectures in Deuteronomy* (Rome: Pontifical Biblical Institute, 1968) 7; and earlier, P. Kleinert, *Das Deuteronomium und der Deuteronomiker* (Bielefeld and Leipzig: Velhagen & Klasing, 1872).

book of Deuteronomy was identified with the scroll found in the temple in Jerusalem under the reign of Josiah and became the focus of cultic centralization in Jerusalem. Starting from this one fixed point of departure, the familiar JEDP documentary theory of pentateuchal criticism took shape within the mainstream of European scholarship. The Jahwist (J), Elohist (E), and Priestly (P) sources of the "Tetrateuch" (Genesis through Numbers) were set over against Deuteronomy (D).

The history of pentateuchal criticism has been recounted many times and will not be repeated in detail here. Though there were numerous precursors to the nineteenth-century movement, it was the dating of Deuteronomy to the seventh century B.C.E. that enabled the so-called Reuss-Graf-Kuenen-Wellhausen hypothesis to emerge triumphant by the last quarter of the nineteenth century. In particular, J. Wellhausen's *Prolegomena to the History of Ancient Israel,*[4] which appeared in its first German edition in 1878, summed up the scholarly contributions of previous generations with the "assured results" of literary criticism in a compact and persuasive fashion. His conclusions are often summarized by the scholarly "tetragrammaton" JEDP. J and E were narrative sources dating to the ninth and eighth centuries B.C.E. respectively. The combination of these two sources into JE took place by the seventh century, when D was composed. P was written after the Exile, and the final editing of the Pentateuch took place ca. 400 B.C.E. From a stimulating modern restatement of the matter that takes into account the research of the century since Wellhausen, see R. E. Friedman, *Who Wrote the Bible?*[5]

Though analysis from the point of view of source documents had produced a consensus of opinion regarding the formation of the Pentateuch as a whole by the turn of this century, that approach had not succeeded in drawing a convincing picture of the literary structure of source D, as such. Working independently of each other, C. Steuernagel and W. Staerk each posited a "redactional" model to explain the growth of Deuteronomy on the basis of the so-called *Numeruswechsel,* the frequent change in the form of address between second-person singular and plural forms. Both men's works appeared in 1894.[6] They argued for an older stratum, which used the singular pronoun, and a

---

4. J. Wellhausen, *Prolegomena to the History of Ancient Israel* (reprinted, Cleveland: Meridian, 1957).

5. R. E. Friedman, *Who Wrote the Bible?* (New York: Summit, 1987).

6. C. Steuernagel, *Der Rahmen des Deuteronomiums: Literarcritische Untersuchungen über seine Zusammensetzung und Entstehung* (Halle a.S.: J. Krause, 1894; 2d ed., 1923); and W. Staerk, *Das Deuteronomium—Sein Inhalt und seine literarische Form: Eine kritische Studie* (Leipzig: Hinrichs, 1894).

later one, which used the plural. Since there are a number of places in Deuteronomy where one can say with some certainty that the plural passage was apparently inserted into the singular context, many critical scholars still continue this line of research (see the essay below by T. Veijola in particular, pp. 137–46). On the other hand, the detailed analysis presented by Steuernagel in his *Kommentar* has found relatively few followers. His assumption of several parallel "editions" of the original Deuteronomy, each with its own parenetic introduction, seems improbable, and the so-called "plural edition" he extracted probably never existed by itself. In my personal estimation, the incisive comments of G. von Rad, which appeared as early as 1929 in *Das Gottesvolk in Deuteronomium*,[7] may well mark the beginning of the end for this methodological approach, which is sometimes referred to as "stratigraphical" study of the biblical text.

The third major impulse in the study of Deuteronomy during the modern era flows from the theory of M. Noth (1943). In his view, Deuteronomy 1–3 (4) and 31–34 are the introduction to the deuteronomic historical work (Joshua through 2 Kings).[8] Steuernagel had regarded Deuteronomy 1–3 as the introductory address of one edition of Deuteronomy. Noth's theory undermines the basic assumptions of that earlier one and carries subsequent discussion in new directions. Later F. M. Cross (1968) argued for a two-stage process in the composition of the "Former Prophets" (Joshua through 2 Kings): a deuteronomic edition (Dtr[1]) in the time of Josiah and a deuteronomistic redaction (Dtr[2]) during the Babylonian Exile.[9] A. D. H. Mayes is building on that model in his discussion of Deuteronomy 4 in relation to its larger literary context (see his essay reprinted below, pp. 195–224).

At the same time that M. de Tillesse published his essay on the so-called *Numeruswechsel*,[10] which championed the basic redactional theory of Steuernagel, another major impulse in the modern study of

7. G. von Rad, *Das Gottesvolk in Deuteronomium* (BWANT 47; Stuttgart: Kohlhammer, 1929).

8. M. Noth, *The Deuteronomistic History* (trans. J. Doull et al.; JSOTSup 15; Sheffield: JSOT Press, 1981). This volume is a translation of *Überlieferungsgeschichtliche Studien* (2d ed.; Tübingen: Niemeyer, 1957) 1–110. The first edition appeared as "Schriften der Königsberger Gelehrten Gesellschaft," *Geisteswissenschaftliche Klasse* 18 (1943) 43–266.

9. F. M. Cross, Jr., "The Themes of the Book of Kings and the Structure of the Deuteronomistic History," in *Canaanite Myth and Hebrew Epic* (Cambridge: Harvard University Press, 1973) 274–89, published originally in *Perspectives in Jewish Learning* 3 (Annual of the College of Jewish Studies, 1968) 9–24.

10. G. M. de Tillesse, "Sections 'tu' et sections 'vous' dans le Deutéronome," *VT* 12 (1962) 29–87.

Deuteronomy was taking shape in the work of W. L. Moran and his student N. Lohfink. Lohfink's doctoral dissertation turned to "stylistics" as the primary focus of attention.[11] The new approach tended to find unity in the received text, in spite of the apparent diversity in surface form, which had led Steuernagel and others after him to posit complex theories of redactional growth.

Meanwhile another lesson from the history of research in Deuteronomy was making its mark as well. Contrary to what de Wette and others had said, the search for the original Deuteronomy must ignore the account of 2 Kings 22–23 almost completely (see the essay below by N. Lohfink, pp. 36–61). Even if Deuteronomy did influence history at the time of Josiah, it is not to be assumed that it had its full effect at that time. It can be argued that Josiah may have gone well beyond Deuteronomy in his measures. Moreover, the assumption that the original Deuteronomy is to be found only within chapters 12–26 must be rejected, for that section cannot be designated as the real "codex," as opposed to the "introduction" (chapters 6–11), since both of the sections share the same characteristic signs (*Numeruswechsel*, parenetic style, etc.).

The zeal for literary analysis of Deuteronomy along lines suggested by the so-called documentary hypothesis has flagged in recent years. The realization is growing that the method of purely literary-critical analysis in the traditional sense will unveil the complexity of the history of the Hebrew text of Deuteronomy only to a limited degree, because the strata that are present point not to literary processes but rather to a preliterary process of slow enrichment of the original mass of tradition. The time seems right for a new model of analysis that will account for the unity of the text within the context of diversity of traditions. That model will need to build on the work of M. Noth, who saw the canonical function of Deuteronomy within the context of what D. N. Freedman has called the "Primary History" (Genesis through 2 Kings in the Hebrew Bible).[12] It will also need to take into account the older impulse of form criticism as it entertains new possibilities for understanding the genre of Deuteronomy within the canonical process in ancient Israel. But its primary motive force will come from new areas of interdisciplinary concern, especially from the field of epic and narrative poetry within the context of musical performance of texts in antiquity.

Music and poetry are a common medium for transmitting cultural tradition among virtually all so-called preliterate peoples. In light of

11. N. Lohfink, *Das Hauptgebot: Eine Untersuchung literarischer Einleitungsfragen zu Dtn 5–11* (AnBib 20; Rome: Pontifical Biblical Institute, 1963).
12. See D. N. Freedman's article, "Canon of the OT," in *IDBSup* (Nashville: Abingdon, 1976) 130–36.

this fact some missionaries and administrators of mission agencies are beginning to ask new questions about the translation of the Bible into previously unwritten languages. The model of the Wycliffe Bible translator has been seriously challenged in recent years, from within the very ranks of some of these translators themselves, as the most effective means of communicating the "Word of God" in such situations. Should an individual scholar give virtually a lifetime to the tedious task of reducing such a language to written form in order to translate the Bible into one more of the 2,000 such languages existing to the present time? Where this has been done, the Bible often remains an external artifact that never really becomes a vital part of the cultural tradition of the tribal group. Would it not be better to translate the Bible into media already present in such societies for the transmission of culture, namely into their own forms of music? Recent experiments with the oral communication of scripture in sub-Sahara Africa, as reported by H. Klem, suggest a positive answer to this question.[13] Moreover, it may well be that these experiments themselves provide a closer analogue to the actual historical situation in ancient Israel than any of the models advanced in recent years within the mainstream of the academic study of the Bible.

As Bishop Robert Lowth noted more than 200 years ago, the law codes throughout the Mediterranean world were sung at the festivals in antiquity.[14]

It is evident that Greece for several successive ages was possessed of no records but the poetic: for the first who published a prose oration was Pherecydes, a man of the Isle of Syrus, and the contemporary of king Cyrus, who lived some ages posterior to that of Homer and Hesiod: somewhat after the time Cadmus the Milesian began to compose history. The laws themselves were metrical, and adapted to certain musical notes: such were the laws of Charondas, which were sung at the banquets of the Athenians: such were those which were delivered by the Cretans to the ingenuous youth to be learned by rote, with the accompaniments of musical melody, in order that by the enchantment of harmony, the sentiments might be forcibly impressed upon their memories. Hence certain poems were denominated *nomoi* which implied convivial or banqueting songs, as is remarked by Aristotle; who adds, that the same custom of chanting the laws to music, existed even in his own time among the Agathyrsi.

13. H. Klem, *Oral Communication of the Scriptures: Insights from African Oral Art* (Pasadena: W. Carey Library, 1982).
14. R. Lowth, *Lectures on the Sacred Poetry of the Hebrews* (trans. G. Gregory; London: Buckingham, 1815) 54–55; from Latin, 2d ed., 1763 (first published in 1753).

The law book we call Deuteronomy was in the hands of the Levites
(Deut 17:18), who were commanded by Moses to proclaim it at the
feast of booths (Deut 31:9). Though we do not know the precise nature
of this proclamation of the law, which was handed down within levitical
circles, it is likely that it was sung and that this greater "Song of Moses"
(i.e., the entire book of Deuteronomy) was taught to the people.

J. Lundbom apparently intuited at least part of the picture in his
suggestion that it was the "Song of Moses" (Deuteronomy 32), rather
than the entire book of Deuteronomy as such, that was found in the
Temple in Jerusalem during the reign of Josiah.[15] As perhaps the most
archaic material in the book of Deuteronomy, this official "Song of
Moses" dates from the premonarchic era of ancient Israel in essentially
its present form (see the essay by G. Mendenhall below, pp. 169–80).
But that song was imbedded in a much larger "Song of Moses," which
we now call the book of Deuteronomy. For generations that song was
recited in levitical circles as a primary means of religious education.
Eventually it was put in written form and promulgated in Jerusalem as
part of a reform movement in the days of Josiah. Within that movement, Deuteronomy became the center of a canonical process that
eventually produced the Hebrew Bible as we now know it. That canonical text was recited within the musical tradition of the Second Temple
in Jerusalem. The memory of that ancient performance is still reflected in the Masoretic accentual system of the Hebrew Bible.

When J. van Goudoever commented that Deuteronomy is "the most
liturgical book of the Bible," he described the function of the book
within a larger cultic pattern in ancient Israel.[16] The book of Deuteronomy is presented as the Testament of Moses, to be read in preparation for the Passover in Joshua 5. In short, the Torah itself is a Passover
story that is made up of three Passovers: in Egypt (Exodus 12), in the wilderness at Sinai (Numbers 9), and in the promised land (Joshua 5). This
tradition of three Passovers is the basis of the "Poem of the Four Passovers," known within both Jewish and Samaritan tradition. This observation bears witness to the memory of the original form and function of
the book of Deuteronomy, which is captured by the descriptive phrase
"A Song of Power and the Power of Song" in ancient Israel.[17]

15. J. Lundbom, "The Lawbook of the Josianic Reform," *CBQ* 38 (1976) 293.

16. J. van Goudoever, "The Liturgical Significance of the Date in Dt 1,3," in *Das
Deuteronomium: Entstehung, Gestalt und Botschaft* (BETL 68; Louvain University Press, 1985)
145–48.

17. This phrase is borrowed from Michael Lannon, one of my students, who used it
as the title of a term paper in my course on Deuteronomy during the spring semester of
1985 in the Graduate Theological Union.

The Five-Part Concentric Design of Deuteronomy

Deuteronomy is often outlined as a series of three discourses, followed by three short appendices. The three discourses are: Deut 1:1–4:43, a historical review of God's dealings with Israel, recounting the chief events in the nation's experience from Horeb to Moab and concluding with an earnest appeal to be faithful and obedient and in particular to keep clear of all forms of idolatry; 4:44–26:19, a hortatory résumé of Israel's moral and civil statutory rulings; and 27:1–31:30, a predictive and minatory section that begins with a ritual of covenant blessings and curses and concludes with Moses' farewell charge to Israel and his formal commission of Joshua as his successor following the renewal of the covenant in Moab. Three appendices close the book: the "Song of Moses" (chap. 32), which the great lawgiver taught the people; the "Blessing of Moses" (chap. 33), which forecasts the future of the various tribes; and an account of Moses' death and burial (chap. 34).

The structure of the book may also be described in terms of a five-part concentric design, as follows:

A—THE OUTER FRAME: A Look Backwards (Deuteronomy 1–3)
  B—THE INNER FRAME: The Great Peroration (4–11)
    C—THE CENTRAL CORE: Covenant Stipulations (12–26)
  B′—THE INNER FRAME: The Covenant Ceremony (27–30)
A′—THE OUTER FRAME: A Look Forward (31–34)

The two parts of the "Outer Frame" (chaps. 1–3 and 31–34) may be read as a single document, tied together by the figure of Joshua, who appears only in chapters 3, 31, and 34. The two parts of the "Inner Frame" (chaps. 4–11 and 27–30) may also be read as a single document, joined together by the reference to blessings and curses connected with a cultic ceremony on Mount Gerizim and Mount Ebal (11:26–32 and 27:1–14), which are mentioned only in these two contexts within the book of Deuteronomy. At the center of this construction lies the "Central Core" (chaps. 12–26), which is the primary body of instruction in the culture of ancient Israel, sometimes called the deuteronomic law code. As S. D. McBride has noted, this block of material is in turn arranged in "a remarkably coherent five-part structure," which is also organized concentrically.[18] Each of these five major sections may in turn be analyzed into somewhat similar concentric structures.[19]

18. S. D. McBride, "Polity of the Covenant People: The Book of Deuteronomy," *Int* 41 (1987) 239. This article is reprinted below (pp. 62–77).
19. See my article, "Form and Structure in Deuteronomy 1–11," in *Das Deuteronomium: Entstehung, Gestalt und Botschaft* (BETL 68; Louvain: Louvain University Press, 1985)

Concentric structural features are characteristic of liturgical expression, from so-called primitive peoples to the celebration of the Roman Catholic mass. Such structuring of ritual activity is sometimes explained by reference to the superstitious belief that the ritual will be nullified if the worshiper does not exit from the experience in the reverse order of his or her entry.

It should also be noted that concentric structures are common to both musical composition and epic literature in general. A striking example of such structures in music is a recent symphony by A. Panufnik, which was commissioned by the Boston Symphony Orchestra as part of its centennial celebration. The composer explained in detail in the program for that occasion an intricate concentric design based on the number eight, since this was his eighth symphony.[20] Such structuring devices are one of the means of achieving the feeling of balance and symmetry that is an essential aspect of making art appear beautiful to both the ear and the eye. The astute observer of modern cinematography is struck with the way some modern filmmakers have mastered this same technique in the composition of an art form for popular consumption.

I have argued elsewhere that the book of Deuteronomy is much more than what is commonly conveyed in the term *Kunstprosa* or artistic prose.[21] The book is written in rhythmic language, individual "verses" and groups of metrical units being in turn arranged into larger, sometimes rather elaborate, concentric structures. This architectural/structural design of the book may be delineated by means of a careful analysis of the received Masoretic Text's system of prosodic scansion, which combines the "counting of morae" (a unit of length in time) and "syntactic accentual stresses" (a unit of rhythm or metrical beat). This particular approach is described briefly in the essay that concludes this particular volume: "The *Numeruswechsel* in Deuteronomy 12" (pp. 394–402).

The presence of carefully balanced structures at virtually all levels of analysis within the book of Deuteronomy suggests a rather different model for explaining the form and function of the book from what is often assumed. Such structures are common in works of art, both from antiquity and in the present, particularly in the fields of epic poetry

---

135–44; and my commentary, *Deuteronomy 1–11* (Word Biblical Commentary 6A; Dallas: Word, 1991).

20. See my article, "Andrzej Panufnik and the Structure of the Book of Jonah: Icons, Music and Literary Art," *JETS* 28 (1985) 133–40.

21. See my article, "Prose and Poetry in the Bible: The Narrative Poetics of Deuteronomy 1,9–18," *ZAW* 97 (1985) 179–89.

and music. The reason for the similarity is apparently the simple fact that in its essential nature the book of Deuteronomy is itself a work of literary art in poetic form, subject to the restraints of the musical media for which it was originally composed in ancient Israel.

Introduction to the Essays in This Volume

The essays reprinted in this volume are arranged in five sections. The first section contains seven essays that deal with the book of Deuteronomy as a whole. Though originally published more than twenty years ago, M. Weinfeld's assessment of the "Present State of Inquiry" remains apropos (pp. 21–35). His discussion of the history of research focuses primarily on the work of W. M. L. de Wette, G. von Rad, and G. Mendenhall, with particular interest in the impulse generated by "form criticism." Weinfeld traces the history of the birth of von Rad's theory about the Levites and Deuteronomy to as early as 1934, noting that it reached its full expression in his *Studies in Deuteronomy*, published in 1947. But it was Mendenhall's study of the Hittite treaties in 1954 that marked the decisive change so far as form-critical study of Deuteronomy was concerned. Weinfeld looks to wisdom circles within the royal court in ancient Jerusalem, from the time of Hezekiah through Josiah, to explain the literary form of Deuteronomy and its connection with certain aspects of the ancient international treaty documents.

N. Lohfink's essay "Recent Discussion of 2 Kings 22–23" was the introductory address at the international colloquium on Deuteronomy held at the University of Louvain in 1983 (pp. 36–61). His essay and that of Georg Braulik (pp. 313–35) from the same scholarly event appear here for the first time in English translation. Lohfink argues that the present situation regarding identifying the book of Deuteronomy with the scroll that was found in the Temple of Jerusalem during the reign of Josiah remains problematic. In some respects we are back to the state of affairs in the 1920s, and the "Archimedian point" of Wellhausen's system of pentateuchal criticism must be rejected.

S. Dean McBride's essay on "The Polity of the Covenant People" (pp. 62–77) demonstrates that the book of Deuteronomy is a work of extraordinary literary coherence and political sophistication. Taking a fresh look at the reflections of Josephus at the end of the first century C.E., he argues that the book preserves in essence the national "constitution" of ancient Israel. Moreover, its impact continues to the present time through its influence on modern western constitutionalism.

Though E. W. Nicholson's essay "Covenant in a Century of Study since Wellhausen" (pp. 78–93) does not focus primarily on the book of

Deuteronomy as such, it is a useful summary of the course of scholarly debate regarding evidence from the study of ancient Near Eastern suzerainty treaties and the concept of covenant in the Hebrew Bible. In some respects that discussion has come full circle. According to Nicholson, the resemblances between Deuteronomy and the treaty form, as presented by G. Mendenhall and others, "are more apparent than real" (p. 86). The works of L. Perlitt and E. Kautsch, in particular, have vindicated the position of J. Wellhausen. It is not possible to trace the origins of covenant language back any further than the period of the prophets in ancient Israel.

The next three essays were selected as representative studies of major areas of inquiry that deal with Deuteronomy as a whole in relation to both central issues and new impulses in comparative data from the ancient Near East. G. J. Wenham, in his essay on "Deuteronomy and the Central Sanctuary" (pp. 94–108), takes issue with the time-honored conclusion that "Deuteronomy demands centralization of all worship at a single sanctuary, and therefore that its composition must be associated with Josiah's attempt to limit all worship to Jerusalem" (p. 94). As J. N. M. Wijngaards has argued, Deuteronomy does not envisage centralization of worship at Jerusalem but rather in a series of sanctuaries in the early history of Israel, particularly at Shechem. He argues that the book was written sometime during the united monarchy or earlier.[22] P. Craigie's essay on "Deuteronomy and Ugaritic Studies" (pp. 109–22) demonstrates the value of comparative study of relevant documents from the ancient Near East. The Ugaritic texts "have proved to be invaluable in clarifying our knowledge of the text and in increasing our knowledge of the ancient world" (p. 121). Nonetheless, as he notes, "the use of Ugaritic in the study of the Hebrew text is not without difficulties of a practical nature" (p. 121). In his essay on "Wisdom Influence in Deuteronomy" (pp. 123–34), C. Brekelmans builds on the work of M. Weinfeld while rejecting the latter's conclusion that Deuteronomy is to be ascribed to the circle of scribes at the royal court in ancient Jerusalem. Though wisdom certainly exerted an influence on the book of Deuteronomy, "thus far no real method for the study of these problems has been worked out" (p. 134).

The collection of five essays in Part II: The Outer Frame: Deuteronomy 1–3 and 31–34 deals with central issues for this particular section of the book. T. Veijola (see pp. 137–46) rejects what he calls "new literary approaches" to the study of Deuteronomy, and the recent "rhetorical

---

22. J. N. M. Wijngaards, *The Dramatization of Salvific History in the Deuteronomic School* (OTS 16; Leiden: Brill, 1969).

analysis" of R. Polzin in particular (see Polzin's essay below, pp. 355–74). He favors the retention of traditional literary criticism, which he then illustrates within the framework of what N. Lohfink describes as the "Smend orientation" (see Lohfink's essay on "Recent Discussion on 2 Kings 22–23" below, pp. 36–61). Veijola's study also illustrates the more traditional interpretation of the most conspicuous problem inherent to the study of Deuteronomy, namely, the matter of the so-called *Numeruswechsel.* Following the lead of Steuernagel and Staerk, he attempts to explain the frequent change between second-person singular and second-person plural forms in the Hebrew text by recourse to a redactional theory of the growth of the text in ancient Israel. My own brief concluding essay, "The *Numeruswechsel* in Deuteronomy 12" (pp. 394–402), presents an alternate reading of the evidence.

The older essay by W. L. Moran, "The End of the Unholy War and the Anti-Exodus" (pp. 147–55), argues for the dependence of Deuteronomy on older sources within the tradition of "holy war" in ancient Israel and the "Song of Moses" of Exodus 15 in particular. The essays on the "Song of Moses" in Deuteronomy 32 by P. W. Skehan, "The Structure of the Song of Moses in Deuteronomy (32:1–43)" (pp. 156–68), and G. E. Mendenhall, "Samuel's 'Broken *Rîb*': Deuteronomy 32" (pp. 169–80), are representative examples from the extensive secondary literature on this important chapter, which also functions as a primary source within the book of Deuteronomy itself, in parallel with the other "Song of Moses" in Exodus 15. Skehan focuses on the external structure of the poem, which he argues "consists of 69 verses, or 3 x 23; that is: three times the number of letters in the Hebrew alphabet from *aleph* to *taw*, with the letter *pe* added again at the end to close the cycle" (p. 164). He compares the metrical form to that of the book of Proverbs but argues that the date of the poem may well predate 1000 B.C.E. Mendenhall is more specific concerning actual date in his arguments for the prophet Samuel as the author. Though influenced by the earlier study of G. E. Wright who argued that the poem reflects the form of the "covenant lawsuit," Mendenhall concludes that it is not a "lawsuit" at all. "It is a prophetic oracle essentially concerned with the interpretation of history past, and appealing for public opinion that would make the future more palatable" (pp. 178–79). The essay by G. Coats, "Legendary Motifs in the Moses Death Reports" (pp. 181–91), makes use of methodology from the study of folklore to take a fresh look at the report of Moses' death in Deut 34:1–12. He sees particular importance here for biblical theology: "For in these legends may lie a vision of man valuable for an age devoid of confidence in man and a hedge on the power of men who violate the legendary image by presenting themselves as gods" (p. 191).

The five essays in Part III: The Inner Frame: Deuteronomy 4–11 and 27–30 focus on two aspects of the academic study of Deuteronomy: (1) the redactional history of the growth of the biblical text, particularly in light of the "double redaction" theory, as advanced by F. M. Cross and R. D. Nelson;[23] and (2) the relation of the covenant ceremony, with its cultic blessings and curses, to the treaty texts of the ancient Near East. In his essay (pp. 195–224), A. D. H. Mayes builds on the work of both G. Braulik (1978) and F. M. Cross (1973),[24] arguing for the unity of the Hebrew text of Deuteronomy 4, which he maintains belongs to the deuteronomistic edition of Deuteronomy. He would see the following passages as additions to the book made during the Babylonian Exile: Deut 6:10–19; 7:4–5, 7–15, 25–26; 8:1–6, 11b, 14b–16, 18b–20; 10:12–11:32; 26:16–19; 27:9–10; 28:1–6, 15–19; and 29:1–30:20 (or 29:1–31:1). For him the change of address between second-person singular and plural forms (*Numeruswechsel*) is to be explained on stylistic grounds, since it does not support his conclusions concerning the two primary strata in the Hebrew text.

A. Phillips (pp. 225–46) distinguishes between crimes and torts in the legal tradition of ancient Israel and argues that the Decalogue in an original short form constituted Israel's criminal law in the preexilic period. For him the Decalogue derives from Israel's earliest times and plays a formative role in the structure of the book of Deuteronomy: "It was the Decalogue which both created Israel as a distinct community, and, though from time to time reinterpreted and remoulded, secured her survival from the earliest days of the settlement until exile in Babylon" (p. 226).

The essays by F. C. Fensham (pp. 247–55) and E. Bellefontaine (pp. 256–68) explore the blessings and curses of Deuteronomy in relation to the covenant treaty tradition in the ancient Near East. While Fensham concludes that "there is a close connection in form between the Near Eastern vassal-treaties and the Old Testament covenant" (p. 255). Bellefontaine demonstrates the unique features of the tradition as preserved in Deuteronomy 27. The curse list here is firmly rooted in the legal traditions of early Israel. "Every act which is made the object of a curse is condemned in one way or another elsewhere in the biblical tradition. In all cases a prohibitive foundation can be demonstrated for the accursed deed" (p. 267).

23. See R. D. Nelson, *The Double Redaction of the Deuteronomistic History* (JSOTSup 18; Sheffield: JSOT Press, 1981).

24. G. Braulik, *Die Mittel deuteronomischer Rhetorik* (AnBib 68; Rome: Pontifical Biblical Institute, 1978). On the work of Cross ("Themes of the Book of Kings"), see note 9 above.

In another essay from the international colloquium at Louvain in 1983 (pp. 269–80), A. Rofé makes a strong case for both the covenant-concept and covenant-ritual in ancient Israel, which he dates to late premonarchical times. In opposition to L. Perlitt, and R. Smend, Rofé insists "that the origins of the Covenant of the Land of Moab go back to an ancient ritual, moulded by the Israelites after the pattern of political vassal treaties of the Second Millennium" (p. 279). As he put it, "Just as old pieces of furniture are likely to be found in basements and attics, so the old treaty-pattern does not show in the main body of Deuteronomy, but appears where one should expect to find it—in the appendix to Deuteronomy, ch. 29 and 30" (pp. 278–79).

Four representative essays in Part IV: The Central Core: Deuteronomy 12–26 explore the structure and function of the laws of Deuteronomy. M. Greenberg's seminal essay, "Some Postulates of Biblical Criminal Law" (pp. 283–300), discusses the biblical law corpora within the context of the various collections of cuneiform law from the ancient Near East. Divergent underlying principles account for the rather sharp contrasts between the Bible and these other legal systems, particularly in the matter of homicide. The divergence reflects a basic difference in assumptions, namely "the unique worth of each life that the religious-legal postulate of man's being the image of God brought about" (p. 299).

Though the essay by P. D. Miller on "The Deuteronomic Portrait of Moses" (pp. 301–12) concerns much more than the so-called "central core" of Deuteronomy, it has been included to suggest the integral nature of this material in relation to both the rest of the book of Deuteronomy and the deuteronomic history as a whole. His discussion of Moses as prophet in relation to Deut 18:15–22 and his comments on Moses as transmitter and teacher of the Torah are of particular importance in reflection on the question of Mosaic authorship of Deuteronomy within the canonical process in ancient Israel.

The essay by G. Braulik (pp. 313–35) demonstrates that the ten commandments, as presented in Deuteronomy 5, function as the structuring principle for the collection of laws in Deuteronomy 12–26. This is particularly true of chaps. 19–25 in relation to the fifth through the tenth commandments of the Decalogue. Within the collection of laws in Deuteronomy 12–26, the central ones are the "law of the king" (Deut 17:14–20) and the "law of the prophet" (Deut 18:9–22), which are part of the larger complex of laws in Deut 16:18–18:22 that concern offices of authority in ancient Israel. The significance of this block of ancient legal tradition to modern political structures, and to Roman Catholic canon law in particular, is explored in a provocative essay by

N. Lohfink, "Distribution of the Functions of Power: The Laws Concerning Public Offices in Deuteronomy 16:18–18:22" (pp. 336–52).

The texts on the "law of the king" and the "law of the prophet" not only stand at the center of the book of Deuteronomy, they also function as primary sources in shaping the text of the Former Prophets (Joshua through 2 Kings in the Hebrew Bible). This is particularly true in the series of key chapters that deal with the transition of political leadership between the three charismatic leaders: Joshua (Joshua 23), Samuel (1 Samuel 12), and Elijah (1 Kings 19); and in a second series of key chapters, dealing with the relationship of kingship to prophecy and the question of true and false prophets in ancient Israel. Such chapters include: 2 Samuel 7 (Nathan's promise regarding the "house" of David), 1 Kings 8 (the dedication of Solomon's dynastic temple), 1 Kings 13 (prophetic conflict), 1 Kings 18 (Elijah against the prophets of Baal on Mount Carmel, 1 Kings 19 (Elijah as the prophet like Moses on Mount Horeb), 1 Kings 22 (Micaiah against the "false" prophets of Yahweh), 2 Kings 17 (peroration over the fall of Samaria), and 2 Kings 23 (Josiah's reform). It is quite likely that these texts were constructed as a "midrash" of sorts on the "law of the king" (Deut 17:14–20) and the "law of the prophet" (Deut 18:9–22) during the canonical process in ancient Israel.

The three essays of Part V: New Directions in Recent Research represent examples of current studies, which are in tension with the historical-critical methodology as it has developed since the days of de Wette (1805). The reaction of Veijola (p. 139) to R. Polzin's new "literary criticism" (pp. 355–74) illustrates the tension. His summary dismissal of Polzin's work, which Veijola insists "can only be the last step in the multiphase exegetical work" (p. 139), is a bit too hasty. Polzin's choice to study the text of Deuteronomy in terms of a methodology derived from modern Russian formalist literary theory is a bold one (pp. 356–62). That particular approach makes little sense as merely "the last step in the multiphase exegetical work," as Veijola has put it. Rather, it is quite independent of the historical-critical method as such. It presupposes the integrity of the final form of the text, whereas the historical-critical method attempts to get behind that text into a presumed historical process within ancient Israel. Polzin is asking a new set of questions of the text, which stand alongside those generated by the historical-critical method.

C. J. Labuschagne's approach (pp. 375–93) also focuses on the received Hebrew text, which he handles in a rather mechanical fashion—counting words and noting patterns that seem to defy the laws of probability, so far as chance occurrence is concerned. Once again his method is in obvious tension with the presuppositions on which the historical critical enterprise is based, but the tension in this case may prove to be illusory. Labuschagne's evidence is more objective in nature and may simply point the way to a more detailed understanding of the final stages of the canonical process within ancient Israel. It would appear that the Hebrew text of Deuteronomy may have been altered deliberately by scribes in antiquity who brought an elaborate theological agenda with them to the task at hand, namely the preservation of a canonical form of the sacred tradition. In that process they apparently chose to apply their skills in mathematics to code esoteric information within the text.

My own study of the accentual system of the received Masoretic tradition (pp. 394–402) has led to the conclusion that this system represents a complex set of musical notations to which the text of Deuteronomy was "sung" or chanted within some liturgical setting. The question is whether this setting may have been original to the text itself within the context of the so-called Second Temple in ancient Jerusalem. The Masoretes themselves were not musicians. They merely fixed a once-living tradition onto paper, so as to preserve it for all time.[25] In so doing, they may have provided another clue to help us in the quest to describe the canonical process in ancient Israel, perhaps as early as the time of the Second Temple. Rather than seeing the frequent change of second-person forms between singular and plural as evidence for a process of redaction behind the received Hebrew text, it is also possible to see the phenomenon as part of the complex set of signals for rhythmic boundaries within the context of the musical performance of that text in ancient Israel.

25. See Paul E. Kahle, *The Cairo Geniza* (2d ed.; New York: Praeger, 1959) 82–86 and 103. The word *ṭeʿāmîm*, according to Moses ben Asher who took it from the "Elders of Bathyra" (sages living during the first century C.E.), had a wide range of meanings, including: taste, intelligence, command, reason or cause, sense of meaning, accent, or intonation. I am indebted to John Wheeler for this reference. Kahle was aware of the fact that the meaning of the verbal root behind this word includes 'to sound, resound, proclaim, or celebrate'.

Part 1

Basic Issues and
the Book as a Whole

Deuteronomy: The Present State of Inquiry

MOSHE WEINFELD

[[249]] The sole concern of the pentateuchal literature, as is well known, is with the period preceding the conquest of Canaan; thus any direct reference to an historical event of the later periods would be sought in it in vain. Even after different sources were distinguished in the Pentateuch no criterion was yet available for establishing the date of the composition of these sources. The first scholar to find this criterion was W. M. L. de Wette.[1] It was he who raised the theory that Deuteronomy reflects the reform of Josiah, a theory which was considered a great discovery and was used as a key to understand the process of the composition of the Pentateuch.[2]

The main argument in the thesis of de Wette was that Deuteronomy reflects the centralization of the cult. For according to the historical traditions of Israel, stemming from the times before Hezekiah-Josiah, sanctuaries and high places were not only existent and tolerated but were even considered indispensable for the religious life of Israel. Thus,

Reprinted with permission from *Journal of Biblical Literature* 86 (1967) 249–62.

1. *Dissertatio critico-exegetica* etc. 1805. That the book discovered in the temple was Deuteronomy was already surmised by Jerome (*Comm. in Ezech.* 1, 1), but that this book reflects a new historic religious reality from the time of Hezekiah-Josiah was for the first time suggested by de Wette.

2. De Wette himself considered D the last source of the Pentateuch, but the Graf-Kuenen-Wellhausen school placed the P source after D, a supposition which gained general acceptance but has been recently strongly questioned by Y. Kaufmann (see the first volume of his *Toledot haʾemunah hayisreʾelit*, 1937; and in English: Y. Kaufmann, *The Religion of Israel*, tr. by M. Greenberg, 1960, 175ff.). Kaufmann's arguments, plus the new light which has been spread on the institutions of P by comparative evidence from the ancient Near East, do not allow us any longer to take the lateness of P for granted.

21

we hear Elijah the prophet complaining bitterly about the destroying of altars of Yahweh in Israel by the followers of Baal, a crime which is mentioned by him in one breath with the slaying of the prophets of Yahweh.[3] The first we hear about abolishing legitimate altars is in the time of Hezekiah[4] and in a more radical way in the time of Josiah.[5] As the demand for an exclusive center of worship is raised within the pentateuchal [[250]] literature only in Deuteronomy, there is no escaping the conclusion that this book reflects the reform, in other words, that this book was the outcome of the reform movement flourishing in the times of Hezekiah and Josiah.

The theory of de Wette stood firm and unshaken during a period of over 100 years. In the twenties of this century, for the first time, voices were raised against the theory. The objection came from two different directions. A group of scholars represented by Oestreicher[6] and Welch[7] tried to disconnect Deuteronomy from the reform by arguing that the book of Deuteronomy does not demand centralization of cult at all. In order to prove their point which was very revolutionary, they had to resort to all kinds of doubtful and forced interpretations. So, for example, in the phrase which expresses the idea of centralization: המקום אשר יבחר ה׳ באחד שבטיך, which means literally "the place which Y. shall choose in one of your tribes," they attempted to demonstrate that not "one place" is meant here but "*any place*," so that Y. could choose several places where he would establish his name. Where the evidence for centralization was too obvious to be misinterpreted, as Deut 12:5–7, where we read מכל שבטיכם ("from all your tribes"), they did away with it by suggesting it was a late addition.[8] Another faction represented by Hölscher[9] denied the very fact of centralization of worship in the time of Josiah. This was done by deleting verses in 2 Kings 23[10] and by the very radical and extreme theory that Deuteronomy is a utopian product of the second commonwealth.

Neither this theory nor the other has gained real support in biblical scholarship. A sort of account settling with these dissident opinions

---

3. 1 Kgs 19:10, 14.

4. 2 Kgs 18:4, 22.

5. 2 Kgs 23:8–9.

6. Th. Oestreicher, *Das deuteronomische Grundgesetz*, 1923.

7. A. C. Welch, *The Code of Deuteronomy*, 1924; idem, *Deuteronomy, The Framework to the Code*, 1932.

8. Cf. Welch, *Code*, 57ff. and his article in *ZAW* 42 (1925) 250ff.

9. G. Hölscher, "Komposition und Ursprung des Deuteronomiums," *ZAW* 40 (1923) 161–255.

10. Verses 8a, b.

was done in a symposium on the problem of Deuteronomy which was published in *JBL* in 1928.[11]

In the twenties the controversy about de Wette's thesis was limited to the question of centralization of worship which was, in fact, the point of departure for de Wette. However, in the course of time, the question of the style of Deuteronomy turned out to be not less but even more important than centralization of cult for dating Deuteronomy. Style such as we have in Deuteronomy is not to be found in any of the historical and prophetical traditions before the seventh century B.C. Conversely, from the seventh century onwards almost all of the historical, [[251]] prophetical,[12] and even psalmodic literature[13] is permeated with this style. Indeed arguments of style and form are characteristic of the new stage in the research in the book of Deuteronomy. This new stage is a direct outcome of the new trend in biblical criticism, the so-called "history of form." By this new constructive approach in biblical research we were taught to look for the social circumstances which produced the pattern of a piece of literature rather than for the time of its composition. Instead of asking about the historical background of a certain composition by examining its contents, the answer to which may be sometimes very subjective, we ask about the sociological background of the composition—the "Sitz im Leben"—by considering its style and forms of expression. Thus problems in biblical criticism were shifted from the question of "when" to the question of "where" and "who." This was the way Gunkel investigated the Psalms, Alt the law, and von Rad Deuteronomy. And dealing with Deuteronomy one must say that thanks to von Rad the problem of Deuteronomy has undergone important changes in the last thirty years. Let us, then, glance at the theory of von Rad and survey briefly its main points.

As early as 1938 G. von Rad was struck by the peculiar structure of the book of Deuteronomy: homily, laws, sealing of covenant, blessings and curses.[14] He rightly observed that such a strange combination of different literary genres could hardly be invented. He assumed therefore that the complex literary structure must have been rooted in a cultic ceremony in which God's laws were recited by clergy. Traces of an old cultic ceremony could indeed be found in Deuteronomy 27, and traditions connected with Shechem in Joshua 24. According to

---

11. See the articles of Bewer, Paton, and Dahl, 305–79.

12. So Jeremiah, Ezekiel, and Second Isaiah, but the deuteronomic style is especially marked in the prose sermons in Jeremiah.

13. Cf. the historic Psalms 105 and 106.

14. *The Problem of the Hexateuch and Other Essays* (tr. by E. W. J. Dicken), 1966, 26–40.

von Rad Deuteronomy renews the cultic tradition of the old Shechem amphictyony, a theory which fits well the prevalent opinion about the affinities of Deuteronomy to northern traditions.[15] As a matter of fact, already in the nineteenth century A. Klostermann[16] had conjectured that the preaching style of Deuteronomy reflects a public recital, but he could not yet, of course, base his thesis on form-critical observations as did von Rad, and therefore did not connect it with the cult.

In 1947 von Rad[17] went a step further and identified the reciters of the law with the Levites and moreover recognized them as the actual [[252]] spokesmen of the deuteronomic movement. This supposition he based mainly on Neh 8:7, where we read about the Levites instructing the people in law. One would shrink from such a reconstruction based upon a late text which, as von Rad himself admitted, is heavily overloaded and may be interpolated by the chronicler who was specially interested in levitical duties. But nevertheless he says that it is hard to believe that this procedure of law reading is an invention of the second commonwealth.

Now, it seems that of the two problems which von Rad tried to solve—the problems of the "where" and "who" of Deuteronomy—the solution to the problem of the "where," i.e., the cult as the life setting of Deuteronomy, has a more objective basis than does that of the "who," viz., the Levites. For the hypothesis of a cultic covenant ceremony solves at least the problem of the peculiar structure of the book, while the second hypothesis about the Levites not only lacks any objective basis but has much against it.

First of all, it is inconceivable that the Levites, who were deprived of their office through the centralization of the cult and as a result of which are considered in Deuteronomy as a part of the *personae miserabiles*,[18] could be identified with the circle which stands behind Deuteronomy. The Levites as composers of Deuteronomy would be comparable to one cutting off the branch upon which he sits. Von Rad saw this difficulty[19] but tried to do away with it by arguing that the demand for centralization in Deuteronomy rests upon a very narrow basis and could be considered a late stratum in the book. Such an answer seems hardly satisfactory;

---

15. See, for example, A. Alt, *Die Heimat des Deuteronomiums*, Kleine Schriften II, 250–75.

16. *Der Pentateuch*, N.F., 1907, 154ff.

17. *Studies in Deuteronomy* (tr. by D. Stalker), 1953.

18. Deuteronomy is the only book which adds the Levite to the *personae miserabiles* known from the Tetrateuch: the poor (עני), the resident alien (גר), the orphan, and the widow. The rise of this new social stratum in Deuteronomy comes without doubt as a result of the abolishment of the provincial cult rites.

19. *Studies in Deuteronomy*, 67.

after all, centralization serves as the guiding principle for chs. 12–19, the nucleus of the code, and therefore cannot be simply discounted.[20]

One can even trace the history of the birth of von Rad's theory about the Levites. In 1934, analyzing the sermons in the book of Chronicles,[21] von Rad came to the conclusion that these sermons reflect the instruction of the Levites of the postexilic period who built their sermons on quotations from ancient authoritative texts. Asking himself about the "situation in life" of the Levitic sermon style, he said that it would be conceivable that the Levites who had been deprived of [[253]] office through the centralization of the cult found a new sphere of activity in religious instruction.[22] This means, then, that the Levite sermon is the outcome of the reform while, as we already indicated, in his *Studies in Deuteronomy* in 1947 he considers the Levites a religious order from old times, responsible for the composition of Deuteronomy. This change of attitude was caused apparently by von Rad's discovery, in the meantime, i.e., in 1938, of the covenantal structure of Deuteronomy; for if Deuteronomy really reflects a cultic ceremony, then it is sensible to suppose that the clerics taking part in the ceremony stand behind the book.

But the whole problem was changed when attention was drawn to the structural form of treaties in the ancient Near East. Mendenhall in 1954 was the first to see the similarities between the Hittite treaties and the Israelite covenant.[23] After the treaties of Esarhaddon with his eastern chieftains were published in 1958[24] and after the relationship between the ancient Near Eastern treaties and the covenant in the OT was more intensively investigated,[25] it became evident that a treaty pattern with a common basic structure—historical introduction,[26] stipulations, blessings and curses—was prevalent in the ancient Near East for a period of over a thousand years. Von Rad's question of the peculiar structure of

---

20. The laws about sacrifices, tithes, firstlings, holidays, and the cities of refuge, incorporated in this collection, are based on the principle of centralization and reflect clearly the change these institutions underwent following the reform; see below 258ff.

21. See "The Levitical Sermon in I and II Chronicles" in *The Problem of the Hexateuch*, 267–80.

22. *Ibid.*, 279.

23. G. E. Mendenhall, "Covenant Forms in Israelite Traditions," *BA* 17 (1959) 49–76.

24. D. J. Wiseman, "The Vassal Treaties of Esarhaddon," *Iraq* 20 (1958) 1–99.

25. Cf. D. J. McCarthy, "Treaty and Covenant," *Analecta Biblica* 21 (1963).

26. The lack of this component in the Assyrian treaty does not necessarily indicate a change in the general pattern prevalent in the first millennium B.C. but could rather be explained as originating in Assyrian political mentality. The Assyrian emperor who pretended to be the king of the world did not feel it necessary, and would even be humiliated, to justify his demand for loyalty through referring to his gracious acts for the vassal as the Hittites used to do. This was indicated by A. Goetze during a private conversation.

Deuteronomy could now be answered in a different way. Now it can be said that the structure of Deuteronomy follows a literary tradition of covenant writing rather than imitating a periodical cultic ceremony which is still unattested. And if it is unnecessary to assume a cultic ceremony for understanding the structure of Deuteronomy, then the assumption about the Levites preserving this cultic tradition becomes dubious too, for if a literary pattern lies behind the form of Deuteronomy, then it would be much more reasonable to assume that a literary circle which was familiar with treaty writing—in other words, court scribes—composed the book of Deuteronomy. I refer to the scribes of the period of Hezekiah-Josiah, a period which should be marked as one of religious revival.[27] This hypothesis of mine, to which [[254]] I devote a comprehensive study about scribes/wise men as composers of Deuteronomy, could explain another question of von Rad, namely, the question about the strange combination of cultic and national-political institutions which we find in Deuteronomy, a fact which led von Rad[28] to assume a connection between the Levites and the עם הארץ, the full citizens of Judah, which group constituted the national military movement in Judah.[29] But if we see the scribes of Hezekiah-Josiah as responsible for the crystallization of Deuteronomy, the problem is much more simple, because only scribes who deal with literary and written documents and who have access to the court could have assembled so variegated a collection of documents as are encountered in Deuteronomy and the whole deuteronomic composition.[30] Especially instructive from this point of view is a series of maledictions in Deuteronomy 28 which can be proved to have been transposed directly from Assyrian contemporary treaties into the book of Deuteronomy.[31] Frankena's supposition[32] that Josiah's covenant with God was considered a substitution for the former treaty with the king of Assyria, thereby expressing vassal-

27. This atmosphere of revival was felt in this period all over the Near East; cf. W. F. Albright, *From the Stone Age to Christianity*, 314–19.

28. *Studies in Deuteronomy*, 60ff.

29. See especially E. Würthwein, *Der ᶜamm haᵓareṣ in A.T.*, 1936.

30. A. Bentzen (*Die Josianische Reform und ihre Voraussetzungen*, 1926) who raised before von Rad the thesis that Deuteronomy derives from the country Levites (a thesis unknown to von Rad while writing his *Studies*; see his note on p. 68) regarded the Levites as the authors of all deuteronomic literature, whereas von Rad does not allude to the rôle of the Levites in the composition of deuteronomic historiography. His failure to investigate the question of the deuteronomist's identity is strange, as the Levites, in his opinion, functioned as instructors from pre-exilic days until the restoration; therefore, it would be natural for him to regard them as playing an influential rôle in all deuteronomic literature.

31. Cf. M. Weinfeld, "Traces of Assyrian Treaty Formulae in Deuteronomy," *Biblica* 46 (1965) 417–27.

32. R. Frankena, "The Vassal Treaties of Esarhaddon and the Dating of Deuteronomy," *Oudtest. Studiën* 14 (1965) 152–54.

ship to Yahweh instead of vassalship to the king of Assyria, is very plausible and accounts for the similarities between the various Assyrian-Aramean treaty formulae from the eighth-seventh centuries B.C. and the covenant formulations in Deuteronomy.[33] Deuteronomy surely preserves [[255]] motives of the old covenant tradition, but those were reworked and adapted to the covenant type prevalent in the eighth and seventh century B.C.[34]

An analysis of the orations in deuteronomic literature[35] leads us to a similar conclusion. It is in the many and diverse rhetorical addresses

33. The similarity between the covenant form of the book of Deuteronomy and ancient Near Eastern treaties lies not only in their external structure but also in their basic mode of formulation. The stipulation requiring exclusive allegiance to the God of Israel in Deuteronomy is formulated in the conventional manner of state treaties and documents demanding political allegiance to the suzerain. Mark for instance the expressions in Deuteronomy "to love" (= *ra²āmu*) in the sense of loyalty (cf. W. L. Moran, "The Ancient Near Eastern Background of Love of God in Deuteronomy," in *CBQ* 25 [1963] 77ff.); "with all your heart" (= *ina kul libbi, ina gammurti libbi*; see references cited by Moran, *op. cit.*, n. 35); "to go after" (*alāku arki*), meaning to serve (El Amarna 136:11ff.; 149:46, 280:20); "to fear the Lord" (= *palāḫu*; see, e.g., Wiseman, *op. cit.*, line 396); "to hearken to his voice," "to do as he commands" (Wiseman, lines 194–96: *ammar iqabbūni lâ tašammâni kî pîšu la têppašāni*); "to act in complete truth . . . sincerely . . . with him" (Wiseman, lines 96–99; cf. Deut 18:13 and 1 Kgs 3:6, 9:5). The warnings against treason and inciting treason met with in Deuteronomy 13 closely resemble those found in Hittite, Aramean, and Assyrian treaties. The depiction of the covenant scene in Deut 29:9ff. also coincides with the description of the treaty scene in the Esarhaddon treaties and in Assyrian and Aramean treaties of the eighth and seventh century B.C. Basic evidence for all these covenantal images is to be presented in my forthcoming study on Deuteronomy and the deuteronomic school [[published as *Deuteronomy and the Deuteronomic School* (Oxford: Clarendon, 1972; repr. Winona Lake, Ind.: Eisenbrauns, 1992)]].

34. Treaties of the second millennium B.C. were made valid through ritual ceremonies. Thus in the Mari documents covenant is made by killing an ass, in Alalaḫ by slaughtering a sheep (D. J. Wiseman, *JCunSt* 12 [1957] 127f.; *Archives Royales de Mari* 2, no. 32) and similarly in the old covenant depicted in Exodus 24. In the treaties of the first millennium B.C., however, the oath constituted the principal feature, while the ritual, in the event that we meet with one, is of secondary importance and has only a symbolic significance (cf. the treaty of Ašurnirari V with Mati²ilu, *Arch. für Orientforschung* 8 (1932) 17ff.). For the primary rôle of the oath in the late treaties as opposed to its secondary rôle in the early treaties cf. J. Gelb, *BiblOr* 19 (1962) 162.

35. Distinction should of course be made between Deuteronomy and the deuteronomic literature which includes the historiography in the former prophets and the editorial part of Jeremiah. But these three literary strands have a common theological outlook and identical stylistic features and therefore must be considered as a product of a continuous scribal school. In my opinion this school is to be connected with the family of Shaphan the scribe who took an active part in the discovery of the book in the time of Josiah. The scribal activity at court of this family persisted until after the destruction (Gedaliah the son of Ahikam, the son of Shaphan, Jeremiah 40ff.). A. Jepsen has also suggested that scribes from this family sitting in Mizpah were responsible for the deuteronomic historiography; see A. Jepsen, *Die Quellen des Königsbuches*, 1956.

in deuteronomic composition (the valedictory address,[36] the prophetic,[37] liturgical,[38] and military orations[39]) that the specific literary
technique [[256]] of the author manifests itself. Like the ancient Greek
historians, the Judean scribes of the seventh and sixth centuries also
employed programmatic orations to present their ideological views.
Thus they put on the lips of such prominent natural figures as Moses,
Joshua, David, Solomon, and the various prophets, orations which
gave expression to their views and aims.

The book of Deuteronomy and deuteronomic historiography reveal a positive attitude towards monarchy, a fact which also informs us
of the character of the circle which is responsible for deuteronomic
composition. The law corpus of Deuteronomy is designed to serve as a
national constitution. The situation reflected by the law code is that of
an ideal political regime in which such institutions as the monarchy,
the military, the judiciary, the priesthood, and the prophetic guild,
which characterize the Israelite monarchic regime, act in harmonious
conjunction (Deut 16:18–20:20). The law of the king reflects a positive
attitude toward the monarchic institution which is given articulation in
the closing verse of the law which expresses the hopes that the king
"may continue long in his kingdom, he and his children, in Israel"
(17:20).[40] The deuteronomic historian also exhibits a positive attitude
toward the monarchy; he regards the Davidic dynasty as the ideal
model of the desired social regime, which is difficult to comprehend
unless he held a positive view of the monarchic institution.

36. These appear at the crossroads of the major periods in Israelite history. The period of Exodus and desert wanderings ends with the valedictory sermon of Moses, which
is congruent with the book of Deuteronomy; the period of conquest ends with the farewell speech of Joshua (Joshua 23); and the speech of Samuel in 1 Samuel 12 marks the
end of the period of Judges (1 Samuel 12 contains ancient material but was reworked
and put into its present place by the deuteronomist). Where there is no opportunity to
put the sermon in the mouth of a national leader, the writer offers his own summary of
the period in the form of a speech (Judg 2:11ff., 2 Kgs 17:7ff.); see M. Noth, *Überlieferungsgeschichtliche Studien*, 1943, 5f.

37. 1 Kgs 11:32–39; 14:7–11, 13–16; 16:2–4; 21:20b–26; 2 Kgs 9:7–10, 21:11–15,
22:16–17; and the prosaic sermons of Jeremiah.

38. A classic liturgic sermon is to be found in the mouth of Solomon in 1 Kgs 8:15ff.
Liturgic addresses which bear the character of a "credo" occur in Deut 6:21–25; 26:5–10,
15, and in other parts of the deuteronomic literature; as 2 Sam 7:22b–29, 2 Kgs 19:15–
19, Jer 32:17–22.

39. Cf. Deut 7:17–24, 9:1–6, 11:22–25, 20:3–8, 31:2–6. Concerning these speeches
see G. von Rad, *Studies in Deuteronomy*, 51f.

40. The kernel of the law is ancient (cf. v. 14b with 1 Sam 8:5, 6; v. 16 with Hos
8:13b, 9:3b), but the law in its present form comes without doubt from a deuteronomic
hand.

Now we shall analyze the method employed by those scribes, which reflects a connection with Wisdom.[41] The means which the deuteronomic circle used to foster its aims are identical with those employed by Israelite wisdom teachers and by wisdom teachers of other ancient Near Eastern peoples. Like the sapiential teachers and pedagogues, the author of Deuteronomy also places great stress on the education of children. The author of the book repeatedly emphasizes that children must be taught the fear of God and that this is to be done by inculcation (6:7), that is to say, by formal methods of education. The book of Deuteronomy does indeed contain a wealth of didactic idioms which are not encountered in any other of the pentateuchal books, such for example, as the use of the verbs הדח [['to thrust away']], יסר [['to discipline']], למד [['to study']], or the expression סור מהדרך [['to turn from the way']], terms which constitute part and parcel of the vocabulary of sapiential literature which, to be sure, was composed with a pedagogical view in mind. It need hardly be said that deuteronomic historiographical work is a pedagogical-didactic work whose purpose was to draw an historical lesson from Israel's past errors. [[257]]

Like the wisdom teachers, the author of Deuteronomy holds wisdom in esteem and sets it above other spiritual qualities. This becomes particularly evident when we compare the traditions concerning the Mosaic appointment of judges in Exodus 18 and Deuteronomy 1. According to Deuteronomy (1:13) the essential traits characterizing the judge and leader must be wisdom, understanding, and knowledge (דעת, בינה, חכמה), that is to say, the same intellectual traits possessed by the scribes, and not other personal characteristics or social standing (e.g., the אנשי־חיל [['warriors']] as in Exod 18:21. The particular esteem with which the deuteronomic circle regarded wisdom explains the presence of exhortations in Deuteronomy which have a sapiential character and formulation[42] and also enables us to trace the origin of the humanistic laws of Deuteronomy.[43] Wisdom has been styled "the humanism of the Ancient East," and it is due to its impact that humanistic laws, which have no counterpart in any other of the pentateuchal books, found their way into the book of Deuteronomy.

41. See my article, "The Dependence of Deuteronomy upon Wisdom," *Kaufmann Jubilee Vol.*, 1960, פט-קה (Hebr.).

42. Compare especially Deut 8:5 with Prov 3:11–12; Deut 6:7–8 and 11:19–20 with Prov 6:20–22; Deut 20:1–4 with Prov 21:31; Deut 4:2 and 13:1 with Prov 30:5–6 and Eccl 3:14; Deut 19:14 with Prov 22:28; Deut 25:13–16 with Prov 20:10 and 23; Deut 24:22–24 with Eccl 5:1–5 and Prov 20:5; Deut 23:16 with Prov 30:10.

43. Cf. my article "The Origin of the Humanism in Deuteronomy," *JBL* 81 (1961) 241–47.

Like the wise teacher who stresses the material benefits that accrue from proper behavior, the author of Deuteronomy makes repeated references to the good fortune that will be the lot of those who observe God's commandments. The principal deuteronomic inducement to observe the Torah is, as in the wisdom literature, material retribution. In no other book of the Pentateuch does the concern for material welfare occupy so great a place as in the book of Deuteronomy. Life, good fortune, longevity, large families, affluence and satiety, the eudemonistic assurances which constitute an essential part of wisdom teaching— these constitute the primary motivation for the observance of God's laws (Deuteronomy 5, 16, 30 etc.).[44] In other pentateuchal contexts and notably in the holiness code the motivation is a theocentric one: "You shall keep my commandments and do them: I am the Lord." Divine authority is enough to obligate the observance of God's commandments. In Deuteronomy, on the other hand, it is the welfare of the individual that serves as the motivation for the observance of the laws.

Finally we shall point out the religious program of the circle. Deuteronomy constitutes a great turning point in the religion and culture of Israel. The three foundations of Israelite religion: faith, the cult, and the law, have been refined in Deuteronomy and made more abstract, [258] apparently through the inspiration of the scribes who left their impress upon the book.

1. *Faith.* The concept of cult centralization, which is one of the fundamental tenets of the book of Deuteronomy and of deuteronomic historiography, brought with it a new religious orientation. The abolition of the high places and provincial sanctuaries led to the purification of the cult from its syncretistic elements and, moreover, severed the daily religious life of the Israelite from its ties to the cultus and paved the way for abstract religious worship dominated by a book and liturgy of torah. The Israelite religion thus underwent a profound transmutation: a cultic religion had been transformed into a religion of a book. E. Meyer[45] is justified in asserting that the reform of 621 was of decisive significance for world history and that the event was the basis of the three great religions: Judaism, Christianity, and Islam. If it were not for the abolition of the high places, who knows whether monotheistic believers might not be still offering sacrifice and pouring libations?

The turning point that occurred in the wake of cult centralization also included a new and more abstract conception of the Divinity. The

44. See M. Weinfeld, "The Source of the Idea of Reward in Deuteronomy," *Tarbiz* 30 (1960) 8–15 (Hebr. with Engl. summary).

45. *Geschichte des Altertums,*[2] III/2,158.

idea underlying the reform of cult centralization is that the sanctuary was chosen by God to cause his *name* to dwell there. The object of this notion, which appears in its most uniform formulation in the book of Deuteronomy—"the place which the Lord will choose to cause his name to dwell there"—is to repudiate the notion propagated by the priestly-conservative circles that the sanctuary is the domicile of God (Exod 25:8, 29:45–46; cf. Isa 8:18).[46] According to deuteronomic ideology God dwells in heaven[47] and is only *represented* by the temple to which he has given his name, and thus the ark, which according to early popular conception and in the priestly document constituted the seat of the Divinity, is nothing more than a depository in which the tables of the covenant are laid.

2. *The cult.* Laws and institutions which have a substantially sacro-ritual character have in the book of Deuteronomy undergone a process of rationalization. Following the elimination of the provincial sanctuaries, [[259]] the judiciary, which was closely associated with the sanctuary, was freed of its sacred ties and took on a more secular aspect.[48] The cities of asylum which were previously temple cities (= levitical cities) and served as sacral places of refuge for the accidental homicide[49] henceforth became secular cities whose exclusive function was to protect the manslayer from blood vengeance.[50] The military, which was

---

46. Cf. G. E. Wright, *BA* 6 (1944) 75; F. M. Cross, *BA* 10 (1947) 67f.; G. von Rad, *Studies*, 37ff. It is not for nothing that in an identical context Deuteronomy uses only שָׁכֵּן ("causes to dwell") while the priestly code uses only שָׁכַן ("dwells").

47. Deut 26:15 and similarly in the deuteronomic liturgy in 1 Kgs 8:15ff. where the word בשמים ("in heaven") is consistently appended to the expression מקום שבתך or מכון שבתך ("your dwelling place") to inform us that it is heaven which is meant and not the temple as the ancient song that precedes the deuteronomic prayer (vv. 12–13) implies. In actual fact, however, the term "dwelling place of the Lord" in the early sources (cf., for example, Isa 4:5) as well as in Solomon's Song always denotes the sanctuary; it is the deuteronomist who here attempted to alter this meaning and thereby wrests the song from its natural sense.

48. Cf. Exod 21:6 with Deut 15:17. Provincial sanctuaries performed also judicial functions (Exod 22:7, 10; 1 Sam 2:25; Prov 16:33) and the abolition of the sacral sites naturally created a judicial vacuum which the law by providing for the appointment of state judges in every city (Deut 16:18–20) was designed to fill.

49. See M. Greenberg, "The Biblical Conception of Asylum," *JBL* 78 (1959) 125–32.

50. The premise underlying the laws of asylum is that the accidental manslayer must also atone for the shedding of innocent blood (cf. M. Greenberg, *op. cit.*) and must presumably undergo the punishment of forced residence at a sacral domicile until the death of the high priest. Deuteronomy, however, which demands the abolition of provincial altars and sanctuaries, has removed the institution of asylum from sacerdotal jurisdiction. The assignment of cities of refuge is no longer dependent upon sacral factors (= temple cities) but is decided by rational and geographic considerations. The land must be measured and subdivided equally into three sections, and cities of refuge assigned at equidistant locations, so that the fleeing manslayer may reach the place of asylum with the maximum speed.

previously subject to severe sacral discipline, also underwent a process of secularization, and the *ḥerem*, which heretofore had the character of taboo, was now rationalized and given an educational motive: "that they teach you not to do after all their abominations" (Deut 20:18).

The sabbath and holy seasons in Deuteronomy are also severed from their early sacral background. The sabbath is disassociated from its mythical origin and is given an historico-religious and social rationale. It is not God's primeval rest from his creative labors which serves as the basis of the sabbath law, but man's rest and the rest of his slave and bondwoman (Deut 5:14). God ordained the sabbath rest not because he ceased from his labors on the seventh day of creation (Exod 20:11) but because he freed the Israelites from Egyptian bondage (Deut 5:15); thus they must all permit their servants to rest from their daily toil.

The festivals and holy seasons were also freed in the book of Deuteronomy from their mytho-ritual setting. According to the JE and P documents the paschal sacrifice is a domestic celebration which is accompanied by apotropaic rites of an animistic nature; the paschal blood is daubed upon the lintel and doorposts (Exod 12:7, 22); the lamb must be roasted together with its head, legs, and inner parts (v. 9); it may not be removed from the house; no bone may be broken (v. 46); and so forth. In the deuteronomic law, however, not the slightest reminiscence of these magical prescriptions has been preserved. The paschal ritual has instead been converted into a communal sacrifice which must be [[260]] offered at the central sanctuary like all other sacrifices. The paschal offering—which is the most ancient sacrifice in Israel's tradition and which apparently originates from Israel's former nomadic life—succeeded in preserving its early primitive character until it was here divested of its original import and recast in a form more consistent with the spirit of the times. Even the earliest features of the sacrifice, such as the requirement that it be selected only from sheep or goats, or that it be roasted by fire—which attest to a distinct nomadic setting of the paschal ritual—have been completely obscured by the deuteronomic law. The new provision allows the Israelite to select the animal from the herd as well as from the flock (Deut 16:2) and permits it to be cooked like any other ordinary sacrifice (v. 7).

The feast of unleavened bread and the feast of weeks marked in old times the season of the harvest and first fruits, during which the first yield of the fields was brought to the sanctuary. At the beginning of the harvest season every farmer was obligated to bring his first sheaf to the priest, together with a male lamb which was to be sacrificed as a burnt offering to the Lord (Lev 23:10–14). At the close of the season he was required to present two loaves of bread baked from new wheat and two male lambs which were "holy to the Lord for the priest" (vv. 15–21). By means of these gifts the farmer secured the blessing for his crops and permission to enjoy them (v. 14).

The season of the ingathering of crops was also characterized before the days of Josiah by religious ceremonies consisting of festive processions, with fruits and decorative plants (Lev 23:40). These took place at neighboring sanctuaries located at not too great a distance from the booths in which the celebrants resided during the seven-day period of the festival (v. 42: cf. Hos 12:10). This, indeed, was the season for merry days of rejoicing (הלולים, Judg 9:27; cf. Lev 19:24) when the Israelites were wont to bring their vintage crops and wines to the house of God. The booths were, apparently, set up in the vineyards (cf. Isa 1:8) where festal dances took place (Judg 21:19–22).

Such ceremonies were possible only at provincial sanctuaries situated in the neighborhood of the fields and vineyards of the celebrants. It is hard to believe that the first of the harvest sheaves or the two loaves of bread were brought from settlements separated from the capital city by a journey of three or more days. It is likewise absurd to assume that the farmer was required to bring willows and decorative flora which might easily wither during the journey from areas located at a considerable distance from the chosen city.

The book of Deuteronomy, which proclaims the law of cult centralization, ignores all these rituals whose very implementation predicates the existence of provincial sanctuaries and reestablishes the festivals on the exclusive basis of ceremonial rejoicing and votive offerings. It does not [[261]] prescribe a sheaf-waving ceremony or the donation of loaves of bread and offerings of lambs nor does it contain any allusion to the four species of flora or to the festal purpose of the booths, notwithstanding the odd fact that the very name of the festivals: *weeks* (שבעות) and *booths* (סכות), are reminiscent of these rites. The author of Deuteronomy has, to be sure, preserved the festivals themselves and their prescribed times of celebration, but he has stripped them of their original sacral content.

The sacral donations also assume an anthropocentric character in the book of Deuteronomy. The Deity and his ministrants, the priests, who generally take the lion's share of the sacrificial offering, are here supplanted by the donors and the indigent elements of Israelite society dependent upon them. The firstlings and the tithes, which heretofore went to the Deity and his ministrants (Exod 22:28–29; Num 18:15–18, 21), are according to deuteronomic law to be consumed only by the donor (14:22–29, 15:19–23), whereas the laws concerning the human first-born and the firstlings of unclean animals are entirely omitted.

3. *The law.* Laws governing human relations appear in the book of Deuteronomy in a more humane light than their analogues in earlier sources. Thus, for example, Deuteronomy prescribes the same law for male and female slaves, who are, moreover, not regarded as the property of their master (cf. Exod 21:21) but as his kinsmen and normal Israelite citizens. Hence deuteronomic law makes no mention of supplying the slave with a wife to increase the master's slaveholdings or of the bondswoman as serving as the master's or his son's concubine, as does the slave law in the book of the covenant. The law governing the injury of slaves, which is given ample space in the book of the covenant (Exod 21:20–21, 26, 27), is completely lacking in the deuteronomic law code, though this latter also contains slave legislation, because in the deuteronomic view the Israelite slave is regarded as his master's "brother" and all injuries suffered by him entail the same legal penalty as those suffered by the free Israelite.

The book of Deuteronomy does, indeed, mark the transition from the narrow casuistic and statutory law corpus to the humanistic law code. Laws concerning civil damages which make up almost the entire bulk of the casuistic section of the book of the covenant (Exod 21:18–22:16) and which figure prominently in ancient Near Eastern legislation, are entirely lacking in the book of Deuteronomy. These laws deal with the protection of property (i.e., compensation for injury, property damages, theft, etc.) and are not, therefore, the concern of the deuteronomic legislator. His purpose was not to produce a civil lawbook like the book of the covenant, treating of pecuniary matters, but to set forth a code of laws securing the protection of the individual and particularly of those persons in need of protection. It is in keeping with this purpose that the author of Deuteronomy incorporated in his legal corpus laws concerning [[262]] the protection of the family and family dignity (22:13–19) which are, significantly enough, not found elsewhere in the Pentateuch.

Indeed, the author of Deuteronomy appears to sermonize no less than the teacher in wisdom literature, and the exhortations and ordinances of the former read more like a parenetic address than a pronouncement of law. The laws enjoining generous lending (Deut 15:7–11), bestowing on the manumitted slave gifts and sending him off without complaint (vv. 14, 15, 18), joining the impecunious in the festive celebrations (16:11–12, 14), and the like are not laws in the usual sense of the word but moral discourse directed to the conscience of the individual.

In sum it may be said that the scribes of the courts of Hezekiah and Josiah achieved a religio-national ideology which was inspired by the sapiential-didactic school. Thus they freed the Israelite faith from its mythical character, religious worship from its ritual stress, and the laws of the Torah from their strict legalistic character. One may argue that the scribes of Deuteronomy could be identified with any religious clerical circle and must not be considered a separate circle defined as wise men. Since, however, it is just in this period that we definitely hear about the distinction between the three classes constituting the so-called intelligentsia of Judah, namely, the priest, the prophet and the wise (Jer 18:18; Ezek 7:26), and since Jeremiah mentions the scribes/wise men in connection with the written Torah in 8:8, we would not be amiss in saying that it is the scribes/wise men who are responsible for the composition of Deuteronomy.

Trying to summarize the development of the deuteronomic problem since de Wette, we may say that to the criterion of centralization of cult, which was used as the first key for understanding the book, two other criteria were added: the stylistic criterion and the ideological one. Both of these criteria give additional support to de Wette's hypothesis but with one important reservation: one can no longer speak of a new book written in the time of Josiah but about compiling old traditions and reworking them in the spirit of a new historical and social reality.

Recent Discussion on 2 Kings 22–23: The State of the Question

NORBERT LOHFINK

When we planned this colloquium[1] three years ago, Joseph Coppens was still with us, and the choice of subject was primarily determined by his wishes. It was only later that I discovered that, especially in 1927–28, the first year of his professorship here in Louvain, he had done some very basic work on 2 Kings 22–23.[2] In 1928 he published his article, "La

Translated and reprinted with permission from "Zur neuren Diskussion über 2 Kön 22–23," in *Das Deuteronomium: Entstehung, Gestalt und Botschaft* (ed. Norbert Lohfink; Bibliotheca ephemeridum theologicarum lovaniensium; Louvain: Louvain University Press, 1985) 24–48. Translated by Linda M. Maloney.

1. This essay was the introductory lecture at the conference [Colloquium Biblicum Lovaniense 33 (17–19 August 1983)]. I had quickly abandoned any attempt to give an introduction to Deuteronomy research as a whole and restricted myself to the subject described in the title. This was made easier by the fact that we now possess the largest bibliography on Deuteronomy thus far published: H. D. Preuss, *Deuteronomium* (Erträge der Forschung 164; Darmstadt: Wissenschaftliche Buchgesellschaft, 1982) 203–43. It is well arranged, provided with many cross-references, and contains an author index (pp. 245–58) and an index of biblical references (pp. 259–69). The introduction to the state of research, which precedes the bibliography (pp. 1–201), contains a number of additional titles. On the whole book, see my review in *TLZ* 108 (1983) 349–53.

[Final editing of this essay was completed in the fall of 1983, and the English translation was done in the fall of 1986 by Dr. Linda M. Maloney. No literature that appeared in 1983 or later has been added. It should simply be noted that the question of the expansion of Josiah's kingdom to the northward (pp. 39–43) is once again wide open, since in the meantime a new dating of the royal seals has rendered questionable the argument based on them.]

2. The university library at Louvain was kind enough to give me information from its archives showing that in the second semester of that academic year J. Coppens lectured Fridays and Saturdays on "Le Deutéronome." The examination questions from the years

Réforme de Josias: L'Objet de la réforme de Josias et la loi trouvée par Helcias," in the *Ephemerides Theologicae Lovanienses*.[3] This article seems to me to be highly suggestive for the history of biblical scholarship within the Catholic context. It can be compared at all points with Walter Baumgartner's article, "Der Kampf um das Deuteronomium," which appeared in the following year, 1929, in the new series of the *Theologische Rundschau*.[4] While Baumgartner's article represents a kind of summation and last word on the violent discussions of the 1920s over the interpretation of 2 Kings 22–23 and the dating of Deuteronomy, Coppens's contribution was the first to draw to the attention of Catholic exegetes, who at that time were quite out of the picture, the existence of a controversy. It also suggested solutions that differ from those of Baumgartner only in detail.[5] It is a pleasure to be able to connect my remarks with this initial work of the respected founder of the *Colloquium Biblicum Lovaniense*.

It was in 1928–29 that the tide of the "Battle over Deuteronomy" slowly began to ebb. The two most famous champions had been Östreicher and Hölscher.[6] Theodor Östreicher of Bethel had again given serious consideration to the Chronicler's version of the Josiah story, whose historicity had been called into question since de Wette,[7] and this in turn had suggested to him the presence in 2 Kings 22–23 of two originally unrelated *Vorlagen*: a report of the discovery of a book[8] and a reform account.[9] In this way he was able to make Josiah's cultic reforms independent of the discovery of the book of the law. They were carried out in stages, in a sense as signs of the gradually successful liberation

---

1928–30, which refer to these lectures, show that in them he discussed the problems of the origins and age of Deuteronomy.

3. Joseph Coppens, "La Réforme de Josias: L'Objet de la réforme de Josias et la loi trouvée par Helcias," *ETL* 5 (1928) 581–98.

4. Walter Baumgartner, "Der Kampf um das Deuteronomium," *TR*, n.s., 1 (1929) 7–25.

5. On the rejection of the opinions of his teacher and predecessor A. Van Hoonacker, see J. Lust's essay in this volume 〚*Das Deuteronomium: Entstehung, Gestalt und Botschaft*, pp. 13–23〛.

6. For individual titles including the works of Östreicher and Hölscher, see Baumgartner's report on research, "Der Kampf," 7–8.

7. 2 Chronicles 34–35. Cf. W. M. L. de Wette, *Kritischer Versuch über die Glaubwürdigkeit der Bücher der Chronik mit Hinsicht auf die Geschichte der Mosaischen Bücher und Gesetzgebung* (Beiträge zur Einleitung in das Alte Testament 1; Halle, 1806; repr. Hildesheim: Olms, 1970) 56–57, 67–73, 106, 115–16; cf. also 168–79.

8. 2 Kgs 22:3–23:3, 16–18, 20–24.

9. 2 Kgs 23:4–14, 15, 19.

from Assyrian domination. It was then no longer so important to know what the newly discovered book contained. For Östreicher this was no longer simply the book of Deuteronomy, which he was able to regard for other reasons as a very old book. Thus he deprived Wellhausen's system of its Archimedean point.

Gustav Hölscher in Marburg had achieved the same result in a completely different way. His analysis of Deuteronomy had shown that it constituted a postexilic utopian program. He also saw in the books of Kings an exilic and postexilic work that was far removed both in time and in content from the events there described. Josiah and Deuteronomy were still related, but only on the literary level.

These two main figures were surrounded by a wide variety of allies and go-betweens. Others remained as observers, content to hold for the time being to de Wette and Wellhausen. There was neither winner nor loser; the end result for all was simply exhaustion.[10]

A new generation decided to push the text in 2 Kings 22–23 out of the center of the argument over the question of Deuteronomy and the history of Josiah and to concentrate on other source materials and new ways of looking at the problem. Historians like Albrecht Alt sought new types of sources, such as texts that could be interpreted in the context of territorial history or the results of archeological excavations. Exegetes like Gerhard von Rad raised new questions about the content of Deuteronomy itself and developed form-critical systems of inquiry.[11]

Around 2 Kings 22–23 all was quiet. How quiet is apparent from Ernst Jenni's 82-page report on research, "Zwei Jahrzehnte Forschung über Josua bis Könige," in the *Theologische Rundschau* in 1961.[12] On the very last page he was able to include *just* two authors who, he said, had treated these two chapters in their own publications during the period on which he was reporting: Alfred Jepsen and Rudolf Meyer.[13] He was mistaken, of course, but the numbers cannot be increased by much.[14]

---

10. In addition to Baumgartner's report, "Der Kampf," the following accounts of the history of research can be recommended: S. Loersch, *Das Deuteronomium und seine Deutungen* (SBS 22; Stuttgart: Katholisches Bibelwerk, 1967) 50–68; W. Dietrich, *Josia und das Gesetzbuch (2 Reg. XXII), VT* 27 (1977) 13–35, esp. 13–18; H. Spieckermann, *Juda unter Assur in der Sargonidenzeit* (FRLANT 129; Göttingen, Vandenhoeck & Ruprecht, 1982) 18–24.

11. See details in Spieckermann, *Juda unter Assur*, 24–26.

12. Ernst Jenni, "Zwei Jahrzehnte Forschung über Josua bis Könige," *TR* 27 (1961) 1–32, 97–140.

13. R. Meyer, "Auffallender Erzählungsstil in einem angeblichen Auszug aus der 'Chronik der Könige von Juda,'" in *Festschrift Friedrich Baumgärtel zum 70. Geburtstag* (Erlanger Forschungen A 10; Erlangen: Universitätsbibliothek, 1959) 114–23; A. Jepsen, "Die Reform des Josia," ibid., 97–108.

14. Z. Karl, "Die Auffindung der Tora in den Tagen Josias" [Hebrew], *Tarbiz* 22 (1950–51) 129–35; D. W. B. Robinson, *Josiah's Reform and the Book of the Law* (London:

New figures, however, show how the situation has changed. By my reckoning, which is certainly incomplete, there have been about fifty publications since 1960 on 2 Kings 22–23, on individual passages and topics drawn from those chapters, and on Josiah.[15] Of course, in the last two decades many works dealing primarily with other subjects have also discussed 2 Kings 22–23, Josiah, and the question of the origins of Deuteronomy. What happened? I would say that all the unanswered questions of the 1920s, and almost all the different ways of approaching the questions at that time, have arisen again. It was of no use to leave them lying around without answers. Or perhaps it was, at least to some extent and in some areas.

For example, it seems in the meantime to have become fairly clear how far Josiah expanded the borders of his kingdom northward in the last years of his rule: not very far at all.[16] He seems rather to have advanced westward to the sea. The broad consensus on this matter is based on the stratigraphic and geographic distribution of royal seals found on storage jars, now numbering about 1000, and on newer excavations, especially in Meṣad Ḥašavyahu.[17]

Tyndale, 1951); F. M. Cross and D. N. Freedman, "Josiah's Revolt against Assyria," *JNES* 12 (1953) 56–58. These are all I can add.

15. See below, n. 60.

16. P. Welten, *Die Königs-Stempel: Ein Beitrag zur Militärpolitik Judas unter Hiskia und Josia* (Wiesbaden: Harrassowitz, 1969); D. Lance, "The Royal Stamps and the Kingdom of Josiah," *HTR* 64 (1971) 315–22; A. Malamat, "Josiah's Bid for Armageddon: The Background of the Judean-Egyptian Encounter in 609 B.C.," *JANES* 5 (Gaster FS; 1973) 267–79; M. Cogan, *Imperialism and Religion: Assyria, Judah and Israel in the Eighth and Seventh Centuries B.C.E.* (SBLMS 19; Missoula, Mont.: Scholars, 1974) 71; M. Rose, *Der Ausschliesslichkeitsanspruch Jahwes: Deuteronomische Schultheologie und die Volksfrömmigkeit in der späten Königszeit* (BWANT 106; Stuttgart: Kohlhammer, 1975) 156–59; E. Würthwein, "Die Josianische Reform und das Deuteronomium," *ZTK* 73 (1976) 395–423; H. Barth, *Die Jesaja-Worte in der Josiazeit: Israel und Assur als Thema einer produktiven Neuinterpretation der Jesaja-überlieferung* (WMANT 48; Neukirchen-Vluyn: Neukirchener Verlag, 1977) 255–60; G. S. Ogden, "The Northern Extent of Josiah's Reforms," *ABR* 26 (1978) 26–34; H. Cazelles, "La Vie de Jérémie dans son contexte national et international," in *Le Livre de Jérémie: Le Prophète et son milieu, les oracles et leur transmission* (BETL 54; Louvain: Peeters, 1981) 21–39, esp. 29–31; Spieckermann, *Juda unter Assur*, 114–18. Among these authors only Cogan still assumes a full expansion of the kingdom northward. Rose takes the evidence of the royal seals as indicative only of the limits of the civil authority within whose jurisdiction troops were maintained from the crown lands. Nothing can be concluded from this about the extension of military occupation to the northward. Malamat argues that Megiddo passed directly from Assyrian to Egyptian control. Cazelles thinks that in the period after 622 there was a division of territory between Egypt and Judah by mutual agreement: Egypt held Megiddo, Judah the hill country. Otherwise Welten's position has gained general acceptance.

17. For a summary of information see: *Encyclopedia of Archaeological Excavations in the Holy Land* (4 vols.; London: Oxford University Press, 1975–78) 3:872–73; O. Keel and

Archaeological findings[18] have also aided in progress in the question of the historical beginnings of cult centralization, especially Yohanan Aharoni's excavations of Arad and Beersheba.[19] It is true that Aharoni's original opinion, that he would be able to synchronize the non-reestablishment of the altar in the Yahweh sanctuary at Arad with a centralization of sacrifice under Hezekiah, and the non-rebuilding of the whole sanctuary with a radical destruction of all holy places except the Temple at Jerusalem under Josiah, has proved untenable on the basis of stratigraphy. But the decision not to rebuild the shrine at Arad can now be placed before Josiah's time.[20] One can thus no longer regard the destruction of Yahweh shrines as something that first occurred under Josiah. Moreover, Ruth Amiran may have uncovered some sacrificial mounds that were desacralized by Josiah in the area of present western Jerusalem.[21]

As late as 1980 Hans-Detlev Hoffmann sought to show that the Huldah oracle was a postexilic construction by positing that at the time of Josiah there was no new city (*mišneh*) corresponding to that in which Huldah was supposed to have lived according to 2 Kgs 22:14.[22] There-

---

M. Küchler, *Orte und Landschaften der Bibel* (Zürich: Benziger/Göttingen: Vandenhoeck & Ruprecht, 1982) 2:32–33.

18. Still the best introduction: E. Stern, "Israel at the Close of the Period of the Monarchy: An Archaeological Survey," *BA* 38 (1975) 26–54.

19. See his own articles: Y. Aharoni, "Arad," *BA* 31 (1968) 2–32; "Israelite Temples in the Period of the Monarchy," *Proceedings of the Fifth World Congress of Jewish Studies* (Jerusalem: World Union of Jewish Studies, 1969) 1:69–74; "The Horned Altar of Beer-sheba," *BA* 37 (1974) 2–6. On this last, in more detail, see Z. Herzog, A. F. Rainey, and S. Moshkovitz, "The Stratigraphy at Beersheba and the Location of the Sanctuary," *BASOR* 225 (1977) 49–58. On the excavations at Arad and Beersheba cf. Keel and Küchler, *Orte und Landschaften*, 2:209–33 and 185–209. A very cautious report on these is found in D. Conrad, "Einige (archäologische) Miszellen zur Kultgeschichte Judas in der Königszeit," in *Textgemäss: Aufsätze und Beiträge zur Hermeneutik des Alten Testaments* (FS E. Würthwein; Göttingen: Vandenhoeck & Ruprecht, 1979) 28–32.

20. See, from a fellow-excavator, V. Fritz, *Temple und Zelt: Studien zum Tempelbau in Israel und zu dem Zeltheiligtum der Priesterschrift* (WMANT 47; Neukirchen-Vluyn: Neukirchener Verlag, 1977) 41, n. 5. On another serious difficulty with Aharoni's thesis see F. M. Cross, "Two Offering Dishes with Phoenician Inscriptions from the Sanctuary of ARAD," *BASOR* 235 (1979) 75–78.

21. R. Amiran, "The Tumuli West of Jerusalem," *IEJ* 8 (1958) 206–27; interpretation as Yahweh-mounds destroyed by Josiah: Y. Elitzur, "The Josiade Reform in the Light of Jerusalem Archaeology" [Hebrew], *Proceedings of the Fifth World Congress of Jewish Studies* (Jerusalem: World Union of Jewish Studies, 1969) 1:92–97. But the situation is not absolutely unambiguous. Cf. Fritz, *Tempel und Zeit*, 73.

22. H.-D. Hoffmann, *Reform und Reformen: Untersuchungen zu einem Grundthema der deuteronomistischen Geschichtsschreibung* (ATANT 66; Zürich: TVZ, 1980) 199, n. 30. His archaeological authorities do not extend beyond Ms. Kenyon.

fore I want to point out emphatically that, in the excavation of the Jewish quarter of Jerusalem in 1969–71, N. Avigad established that the southwest hill of Jerusalem has been inhabited since the eighth century. At the earliest in the time of Hezekiah,[23] and at least since the time of Josiah,[24] this new city was also protected by a wall, part of which can be viewed by every tourist at the present time.

In addition, the broader course of political and military events, the individual phases of the collapse of Assyrian power, the role of Babylon on the one hand and of Egypt on the other, can be much more accurately determined now than they could be half a century ago.[25] But still more important is the fact that there has been more thorough research done on the Assyrian techniques of conquest and control in the territories assimilated to their empire as provinces or associated with it as vassal states.[26] The techniques of control and economic exploitation have been investigated, but also, in particular, the question of the extent of religious pressure. A whole series of extensive works on this subject appeared in the past decade. While John William McKay (1973) was more inclined to credit Assyria with generosity toward subject peoples in the matter of religion,[27] Morton Cogan painted a far darker picture as early as 1974, while still maintaining that there was a sharp difference between areas that became provinces in the Assyrian Empire and

23. So N. Avigad himself in *Jerusalem Revealed: Archaeology in the Holy City 1968–1974* (ed. Y. Yadin; Jerusalem: Israel Exploration Society, 1976) 44.

24. So E. Otto, *Jerusalem—die Geschichte der Heiligen Stadt: Von den Anfängen bis zur Kreuzfahrerzeit* (Urban-Taschenbücher 308; Stuttgart: Kohlhammer, 1980) 68.

25. In the last two decades, A. Malamat in particular has repeatedly published on the subject of the history of the period of Josiah, and his works are a good source for further literature. I will mention the following: "The Historical Background of the Assassination of Amon, King of Judah," *IEJ* 3 (1953) 26–29; "The Last Kings of Judah and the Fall of Jerusalem," *IEJ* 18 (1968) 137–56; "Josiah's Bid for Armageddon"; "Megiddo, 609 B.C.: The Conflict Re-Examined," *Acta antiqua academiae scientiarum hungaricae* 22 (1974) 445–49; "The Twilight of Judah: In the Egyptian–Babylonian Maelstrom," *Congress Volume, Edinburgh 1974* (VTSup 28; Leiden: Brill, 1975) 123–45. See further M. Elat, "The Political Status of the Kingdom of Judah within the Assyrian Empire in the 7th Century B.C.," in *Investigations at Lachish: The Sanctuary and the Residence* (ed. Y. Aharoni; Lachish 5; Tel Aviv, 1975) 61–70; Barth, *Jesaja-Worte*, 242–50; B. Otzen, "Israel under the Assyrians: Reflections on Imperial Policy in Palestine," *ASTI* 11 (1977–78) 96–110; S. Bulbach, "Judah in the Reign of Manasseh as Evidenced in Texts during the Neo-Assyrian Period and in the Archaeology of the Iron Age" (Ph.D. diss., New York, 1981); Cazelles, "La Vie de Jérémie," 29ff.; Spieckermann, *Juda unter Assur*, 139–43 and passim.

26. Cogan, *Imperialism and Religion*; G. Begrich, "Der wirtschaftliche Einfluss Assyriens auf Südsyrien und Palästina" (Ph.D. diss., Berlin, 1975). Cf. the notes that follow.

27. J. W. McKay, *Religion in Judah under the Assyrians* (Studies in Biblical Theology 2/26; London: SCM, 1973), esp. 28–44.

those that remained vassal states.[28] Hermann Spieckermann's very
broadly conceived and precisely documented 1982 monograph, *Juda
unter Assur in der Sargonidenzeit*, has also questioned this latter distinction in a number of ways.[29] One must take into account the fact that
the Assyrian cults were influential in Jerusalem and Judah, not just as a
result of cultural pressure, but, especially in Jerusalem itself, were even
officially imposed. Judging by Assyrian practice there is every reason to
suppose that Josiah's cultic reforms consisted to a great extent of the
abolition of Assyrian religious forms, even though the biblical texts
tend to give Canaanite names to the divinities in question.[30]

Spieckermann's book is especially important as well because it
shows that Assyria's sudden collapse at the time of Josiah of Judah can
be attributed, in the final analysis, to a deep religious identity crisis in
Assyria that could not be resolved by an increasingly intensive elaboration of divination and ritual.[31] One could wish, in this connection, for
a similarly thorough investigation of the prominent role of oaths and
obligations within the ever-more-precarious maintenance of Assyria's
inner consistency,[32] since certain aspects of Deuteronomic language
and theology could very well have been influenced by this.[33] At all
events, there have been a great many individual studies in this connection, especially those of Moshe Weinfeld.[34]

---

28. Cogan, *Imperialism and Religion*, esp. 42–86.

29. Spieckermann, *Juda unter Assur*, esp. 200–225 and 307–72.

30. H. Gressmann ("Josia und das Deuteronomium: Ein kritisches Referat vom
Herausgeber," *ZAW* 42 [1924] 313–37, esp. 321–27) had already noted this.

31. Spieckermann, *Juda unter Assur*, 227–306.

32. Cf., for the present, Cogan, *Imperialism and Religion*, 42–44. Both aspects of the
attempt at preservation, intensifying of religion and swearing of oaths, coincide at the
point where "contractual" obligations toward the divinity itself were sworn. For evidence
of these, see N. Lohfink, "Gott im Buch Deuteronomium," in *La Notion biblique de Dieu*
(BETL 41; Louvain: Peeters, 1976) 101–26, esp. 115, n. 52 (covenant between the god
Assur and the people of Assyria in favor of Asarhaddon, mediated by the goddess Ishtar);
Z. Zevit, "A Phoenician Inscription and Biblical Covenant Theology," *IEJ* 27 (1977) 110–
18, esp. 114–18 (covenant of a group with the god Assur, the "sons of God," and the "chief
of the assembly of all the saints"), if this inscription is genuine. On Preuss's report on this
matter in *Deuteronomium* (see n. 1 above), cf. my review, 352.

33. Cf. N. Lohfink, "Culture Shock and Theology: A Discussion of Theology as a
Cultural and a Sociological Phenomenon Based on the Example of Deuteronomic Law,"
BTB 7 (1977) 12–22. The two most influential monographs in Old Testament "covenant
theology" within the period of this report seem to take too little account of these connections: L. Perlitt, *Bundestheologie im Alten Testament* (WMANT 36; Neukirchen-Vluyn:
Neukirchener Verlag, 1969); E. Kutsch, *Verheißung und Gesetz: Untersuchungen zum sogenannten "Bund" im Alten Testament* (BZAW 131; Berlin: de Gruyter, 1972). But cf. the
positive, if brief, discussion at the very end of Perlitt's book, pp. 282–83.

34. The most fundamental account of the whole matter is that of D. J. McCarthy,
Treaty and Covenant: A Study in Form in the Ancient Oriental Documents and in the Old Testament

So we cannot say that, in dealing with the text of 2 Kings 22–23, we find everything just as it was in the 1920s. We know quite a bit more about the context in which the events in these two chapters took place.[35] The factual events, the material culture, the major political events, the social and ideological shifts—all these are much more clearly delineated. Nevertheless, 2 Kings 22–23 is a text. The new insights into its historical context may prevent our freely-wandering fantasy from pursuing certain directions of interpretation. But in the final analysis the text must first be understood and classified as a text. And besides, it remains our principal source for the epoch and the region of Judah, so that, again, much of our historical insight depends finally on its interpretation. For 2 Kings 22–23 as a text, the unanswered questions of the 1920s have, despite everything, arisen again.

Indeed, in many respects they have become more complicated. For in the meantime Martin Noth's theory of the "Deuteronomic History," applied to the larger textual context of the biblical books from Deuteronomy to 2 Kings, has come on the scene.[36] In the discussion of this

---

(3d ed., completely rewritten; AnBib 21A; Rome: Pontifical Biblical Institute, 1981). The most recent notes on literature are in D. J. Wiseman, "'Is it Peace?'—Covenant and Diplomacy," *VT* 32 (1982) 311–26. At the outset the discussion was too much restricted to a comparison with Hittite vassal treaties; in fact, with treaties per se. M. Weinfeld's service has been precisely on the subject of the broadening of the historical point of view in various directions. See, for example, his "Covenant of Grant in the Old Testament and in the Ancient Near East," *JAOS* 90 (1970) 184–203; *Deuteronomy and the Deuteronomic School* (Oxford: Clarendon, 1972; repr. Winona Lake, Ind.: Eisenbrauns, 1992); "Covenant Terminology in the Ancient Near East and Its Influence upon the West," *JAOS* 93 (1973) 190–99; "Bᵉrit: Covenant vs. Obligation," *Bib* 56 (1975) 120–28; "The Loyalty Oath in the Ancient Near East," *Ugarit-Forschungen* 8 (1976) 379–414.

35. In two questions scarcely any new point of view seems to have appeared. (1) Did Josiah's cultic reforms begin before the book was found, or were they first occasioned by its finding? Here authors who, like de Wette and Wellhausen, trust only the books of Kings, are arrayed against others who, like Östreicher, see a tiny kernel of truth in the reconstruction found in the books of Chronicles. I cannot discover any really new arguments. (2) Was the book that was found Deuteronomy and, if so, in what sense? The consensus continues to point to Deuteronomy in some form or other. The only exceptions are J. Maier, "Bemerkungen zur Fachsprache und Religionspolitik im Königreich Juda," *Judaica* 26 (1970) 89–105, esp. 101–5 (a book "in the line of the tradition of the priestly writings"); and J. R. Lundbom, "The Lawbook of the Josianic Reform," *CBQ* 38 (1976) 292–302 ("the lawbook is the song of Moses in Deut 32"). Of further interest is M. Rose, "Bemerkungen zum historischen Fundament des Josia-Bildes in 2 Reg 22f," *ZAW* 89 (1977) 50–63, esp. 56, n. 26, where from 2 Kgs 22:19, *dibbartî*, he concludes that at that time Deuteronomy was not yet "stylized as a speech of Moses" but "as a speech of Yahweh."

36. Martin Noth's theory developed in *Überlieferungsgeschichtliche Studien: Die sammelnden und bearbeitenden Geschichtswerke im Alten Testament* (2d ed.; Tübingen: Niemeyer, 1957).

theory our two chapters form a strategic point. And this discussion
continues to be quite lively.

It is certainly true that in the 1920s there was division about the
source structure of the books of Kings, but everyone was agreed about
their Deuteronomistic redaction. After Abraham Kuenen,[37] who himself
was following Heinrich August Ewald, there was also general assent to a
differentiation between two phases of this redaction: a preexilic phase
ending with Josiah or Jehoiakim, and a supplementary, exilic redaction
extending beyond the fall of Jerusalem. This doubling of the redaction,
however, was called into question by Hölscher's[38] theory, which located
the whole work, and even its principal sources, in the exilic and postexilic periods. In view of this constellation of theories in the 1920s, at
least one of Martin Noth's lines of descent is clearly evident. Not only
did he make a genuine "author" out of the Deuteronomistic "redactors"[39]—a fact that he himself clearly emphasized—and separate that
author's work as a self-contained entity from the Tetrateuch, which was
to be evaluated quite differently;[40] more than that, he, together with
Hölscher, consistently pushed the Deuteronomistic literary production
beyond the fall of Jerusalem[41]—though Noth did not locate the work
quite so late as did Hölscher and also took into account the possibility
of preexilic source material for his Deuteronomist. Although Noth displayed great confidence in this theory, it is really a dangerously unstable
balancing act. If one looks carefully at the footnotes in the *Überlieferungsgeschichtliche Studien* it quickly becomes clear that he was able to maintain his *single* Deuteronomist, only because he accounted for a great
number of inconsistencies either by attributing them to discrepancies in
the source material used or by positing a considerable number of later
additions.

37. Abraham Kuenen, *Historisch-Kritische Einleitung in die Bücher des Alten Testaments
hinsichtlich ihrer Entstehung und Sammlung* 1/2 (Leipzig: Reisland, 1890) 90–96. R. D. Nelson (*The Double Redaction of the Deuteronomistic History* [JSOTSup 18; Sheffield: JSOT Press,
1981] 14–19) gives a brief sketch of the principal proponents of the theory of a double
redaction of the books of Kings.

38. On Hölscher's predecessors in the French- and English-speaking worlds, cf.
Spieckermann, *Juda unter Assur*, 18, n. 17, as well as J. Lust's essay in this volume [*Das
Deuteronomium: Entstehung, Gestalt und Botschaft*, pp. 13–23].

39. See, for example, the text printed in spaced type in Noth, *Überlieferungsgeschichtliche Studien*, 11.

40. Ibid., 180–216.

41. Ibid., 91–95 and 110, n. 1. Noth himself seems not to have been fully conscious
of the age and weight of the theory of a double redaction of the books of Kings. At any
rate, he says (p. 91, n. 1) that some such idea had "recently" been popular. He would
scarcely have written that if he had been aware that Kuenen and Wellhausen had upheld
the theory.

Noth's colleagues were amazingly slow in reacting critically to his thesis, with the exception of some friends of the older way of thinking[42] and Gerhard von Rad. The latter was wide awake to the situation at once but formulated his remarks so politely and judiciously that his dissent was scarcely noticeable.[43] Noth's "Deuteronomistic History" was almost unanimously accepted.[44] It was only in the last two decades that a genuine discussion of the theory began, and it is still in full flood.[45] Two directions have developed, which at first attempted to solve the same problems in different ways and without any communication with one another. It seems best once again to link each of them with a single name, although this is really an oversimplification. We can speak of a "Cross orientation" and a "Smend orientation."

Rudolf Smend[46] and his students[47] hold to Noth's starting point at the Exile but bring Noth's footnotes, to a degree, into the text in the

42. It is noteworthy that it was especially the authors of commentaries and introductions who were inclined to be cautious toward Noth's work, apparently because they were more strongly attuned to the importance of previous research and, at least in part, had probably already begun their work before Noth's theory became known. Among the commentaries, cf. J. A. Montgomery and H. S. Gehman, *A Critical and Exegetical Commentary on the Books of the Kings* (ICC; Edinburgh: Clark, 1951) and J. Gray, *I & II Kings: A Commentary* (OT Library; London: SCM, 1964). For introductory texts, cf. R. H. Pfeiffer, *Introduction to the Old Testament* (rev. ed.; London: Black, 1948); O. Eissfeldt, *Einleitung in das Alte Testament* (3d rev. ed.; Tübingen: Mohr, 1964); G. Fohrer, *Einleitung in das Alte Testament: Begründet von Ernst Sellin* (10th ed.; Heidelberg: Quelle & Meyer, 1965). Eissfeldt reacted first in a monograph: *Geschichtsschreibung im Alten Testament: Ein kritischer Bericht über die neueste Literatur dazu* (Berlin, 1948). Details concerning the early reaction to Noth's theory can be found in Jenni's article, "Zwei Jahrzehnte Forschung," 97–118.

43. Gerhard von Rad, "Die deuteronomische Geschichtstheologie in den Königsbüchern," in his *Deuteronomium-Studien* (FRLANT 58; Göttingen: Vandenhoeck & Ruprecht, 1947) 52–64.

44. We may take as typical the sympathetic description in G. Minette de Tillesse, "Martin Noth et la Redaktionsgeschichte des livres historiques," in *Aux grands carrefours de la révélation et de l'exégèse de l'Ancien Testament* (ed. Charles Hauret; Recherches Bibliques 8; Bruges: Desclée de Brouwer, 1967) 51–75, or the review of research by A. N. Radjawane, who was completely convinced by Noth's theory: "Das deuteronomistische Geschichtswerk: Ein Forschungsbericht," *TR* 38 (1974) 177–216.

45. For the latest example, see R. Rendtorff, *Das Alte Testament: Eine Einführung* (Neukirchen-Vluyn: Neukirchener Verlag, 1983) 194–99. Rendtorff favors the theory of two major redactions, one in Josiah's time and one during the Exile.

46. R. Smend, "Das Gesetz und die Völker: Ein Beitrag zur deuteronomistischen Redaktionsgeschichte," in *Probleme biblisher Theologie: Gerhard von Rad zum 70. Geburtstag* (Munich: Kaiser, 1971) 494–509. In this essay he developed a second Deuteronomistic stratum in Joshua and Judges, which he called DtrN. In his textbook, *Die Entstehung des Alten Testaments* (Theologische Wissenschaft 1; Stuttgart: Kohlhammer, 1978), he essentially adopted the hypotheses of his students, who worked mainly in the area of Samuel and Kings.

47. Cf. primarily W. Dietrich, *Prophetie und Geschichte: Eine redaktionsgeschichtliche Untersuchung zum deuteronomistischen Geschichtswerk* (FRLANT 108; Göttingen: Vandenhoeck

sense that they presume a series of Deuteronomistic redactional layers, one atop the other. They use symbols like "DtrH," "DtrP," and "DtrN" for the Deuteronomistic historical writer, the prophetic Deuteronomist, the nomistic Deuteronomist.[48] Frank Moore Cross[49] and his students[50] have followed up on Gerhard von Rad's critique. The latter had countered Noth's interpretation of the work as essentially a justification of the catastrophe that had overtaken Israel, devoid of any hope for the future, by pointing to the hope-filled role of the promises to David in the books of Kings. Cross combines this tension between two different proclamations (which seems built into the work as it now stands) with the old theory of two redactions: One that is preexilic and hopeful, culminating in the person and work of Josiah; and one that is exilic and supplementary, offering a new interpretation in light of the fall of Jerusalem. In contrast to the older interpretation, however, and in agreement with Noth's concept, Cross concedes much more credit for genuine authorship to his Josianic Deuteronomist. Other positions

---

& Ruprecht, 1972); T. Veijola, *Die ewige Dynastie: David und die Entstehung seiner Dynastie nach der deuteronomistischen Darstellung* (STAT 193; Helsinki: Suomalainen Tiedeakatemia, 1975); idem, *Das Königtum in der Beurteilung der deuteronomistischen Historiographie* (STAT 198; Helsinki; Suomalainen Tiedeakatemia, 1978); Spieckermann, *Juda unter Assur.* Cf. also L. J. Hoppe, "The Origins of Deuteronomy" (Ph.D. diss., Northwestern University, 1978) 325–26; C. Levin, *Der Sturz der Königin Atalja: Ein Kapitel zur Geschichte Judas im 9. Jahrhundert v. Chr.* (SBS 105; Stuttgart: Katholisches Bibelwerk, 1982); R. Stahl, *Aspekte der Geschichte deuteronomistischer Theologie: Zur Traditionsgeschichte der Terminologie und zur Redaktionsgeschichte der Redekompositionen* (Jena: Habilitationsschrift, 1982).

48. There are a number of discrepancies in detail within the school (still more in cases where the starting-points are only loosely accepted). It would be well, at some point, to examine the degree tò which the theory of A. Jepsen, *Die Quellen des Königsbuches* (Halle: Niemeyer, 1953) gave impetus to the whole school.

49. "The Structure of the Deuteronomic History," in *Perspectives of Jewish Learning* (Annual of the College of Jewish Studies; Chicago: College of Jewish Studies, 1968) 3:9–24; reprinted as "The Themes of the Book of Kings and the Structure of the Deuteronomistic History" in his *Canaanite Myth and Hebrew Epic: Essays in the History of the Religion of Israel* (Cambridge: Harvard University Press, 1973) 274–89.

50. R. D. Nelson, "The Redactional Duality of the Deuteronomistic History" (Th.D. diss., Union Theological Seminary in Virginia, 1973), pub. with minor revisions as *The Double Redaction of the Deuteronomistic History* (JSOTSup 18; Sheffield: JSOT Press, 1981); J. D. Levenson, "Who Inserted the Book of the Torah?" *HTR* 68 (1975) 203–33; R. E. Friedman, "From Egypt to Egypt: Dtr¹ and Dtr²," in *Traditions in Transformation: Turning Points in Biblical Faith* (FS F. M. Cross; ed. B. Halpern and J. D. Levenson; Winona Lake, Ind.: Eisenbrauns, 1981) 167–92, included in his *Exile and Biblical Narrative: The Formation of the Deuteronomistic and Priestly Works* (Harvard Semitic Monographs 22; Chico, Cal.: Scholars Press, 1981); Rendtorff, *Das Alte Testament* (see above, n. 45). From Nelson, see also "Josiah in the Book of Joshua," *JBL* 100 (1981) 531–40.

similar to Cross's, but independent of his work, have been proposed, for example, by Wolfgang Richter[51] and Helga Weippert.[52]

Attempts to bring the two schools into confrontation and to develop a compromise between their different stances have only just begun. The first of any size is the recent book by Andrew D. H. Mayes, *The Story of Israel between Settlement and Exile.*[53] This means that for the interpretation of the text in 2 Kings 22–23, which is key to both positions, one is almost necessarily drawn into more general problem fields and runs the risk of deciding individual exegetical questions on some basis outside themselves.

This is, of course, equally the case if one works simply on the basis of Noth's concept. The latter is, by the way, being in a certain sense radicalized along its own line at the present time. In his book *Reform und Reformen,* Hans-Detlev Hoffmann accuses Noth of not having held consistently enough to his own theory of a genuine Deuteronomistic "author."[54] He then tries to do this himself by practically abandoning the question of recoverable sources and, taking Hölscher's line, conceiving the entire Deuteronomistic work as a single project of the postexilic period. One must recognize here a third line of development of Martin Noth's work that is just now beginning to articulate itself fully.[55]

51. Wolfgang Richter, *Die Bearbeitungen des "Retterbuches" in der deuteronomistischen Epoche* (BBB 21; Bonn: Hanstein, 1964).

52. Helga Weippert, "Die 'deuteronomistischen' Beurteilungen der Könige von Israel und Juda und das Problem der Redaktion der Königsbücher," *Bib* 53 (1972) 301–39; see also W. B. Barrick, "On the 'Removal of the "High-Places"' in 1–2 Kings," *Bib* 55 (1974) 257–59; E. Cortese, "Lo schema deuteronomistico per i re di Giuda e d'Israele," *Bib* 56 (1975) 37–52; Nelson, *Double Redaction,* 31.

53. Andrew D. H. Mayes, *The Story of Israel between Settlement and Exile: A Redactional Study of the Deuteronomistic History* (London: SCM, 1983). Mayes had previously, and apparently still independently of Cross, come to accept a first, preexilic redaction: cf. his *Deuteronomy* (New Century Bible Commentary; Grand Rapids, Mich.: 1979) and the prepublication extract from the introduction to this commentary, "King and Covenant: A Study of 2 Kings Chs 22–23," *Hermathena* 125 (1978) 34–47, esp. 37. My own line of thinking tends toward a Josianic composition based on preliminary stages of the exilic DtrG but more likely in small units than in a single work. The exilic DtrG could have had a number of revisions, including the DtrN detected by Smend in Joshua and Judges. Cf. most recently N. Lohfink, "Kerygmata des deuteronomistischen Geschichtswerks," in *Die Botschaft und die Boten* (FS H. W. Wolff; Neukirchen-Vluyn: Neukirchener Verlag, 1981) 87–100.

54. Hoffmann, *Reform und Reformen,* 17–21. He refers to his own program, then, as "consistent tradition-historical analysis" (p. 21).

55. Cf. especially O. Kaiser's introductory manual, *Einleitung in das Alte Testament: Eine Einführung in ihre Ergebnisse und Probleme* (Gütersloh: Mohn, 1969) in its several editions. Already in the first edition there is a preference for the theory—with all its consequences for the Deuteronomistic work as a whole (cf. p. 140)—that "Deuteronomy originated in the time when the Jewish community in Palestine was being consolidated"

It can, of course, only be carried through if one works with an extremely "broad definition of Deuteronomism"[56] whereby the differences and tensions that disturb other scholars no longer pose any
problem, and if one can maintain the plausibility of the displacement
of the entire historical work to such a late period.[57]

Hoffmann's book in fact contains one of the most extensive and
original analyses of 2 Kings 22–23 that has thus far been written (101
pages).[58] There is really only *one* other that is comparable in scope and
exhaustiveness: Spieckermann's, just published in his book *Juda unter
Assur in der Sargonidenzeit* (130 pages).[59] This one should be classified
within the Smend school. There is unfortunately no comparable analysis from the Cross school. In what follows, therefore, I would like to describe these two authors briefly and interpret them in light of their
individual achievements and their limitations. They can serve as representative for the literary work on 2 Kings 22–23 that has enjoyed such
a strong revival in the last two decades.[60]

(p. 109). For a long time now a similar proposal, connected with the idea of the purely literary character of the Deuteronomic law, has been offered to readers in numerous book
reviews by J. Becker. He sees a time coming when, in biblical studies, "the Deuteronomist
work, including Deuteronomy, will take its exclusive place in the exilic and post-exilic restoration" (review of F. I. Andersen and D. N. Freedman, *Hosea*, in *Bib* 63 [1982] 583–87,
esp. p. 585). For concrete application to a partial text, see Würthwein, "Die josianische
Reform." Cf. also Hoppe, *Origins*; C. Levin, "Noch einmal: Die Anfänge des Propheten
Jeremia," *VT* 31 (1981) 428–40, esp. 434, n. 9 (on 2 Kings 22–23: here "the period of the
second Temple" is already "reflected").

   56. So Spieckermann's critical remark in *Juda unter Assur*, 119.

   57. For me this lacks plausibility because the conclusion of the work in 2 Kgs 25:27–
30 is much more likely to be the last event that can still be reported than the narrative
conclusion, chosen from a distant perspective, to a work that consciously seeks to describe an earlier epoch and not to continue the story up to the time of the author. In addition, those few texts that envision an end to the Exile (I think especially of Deut 4:1–40
and 30:1–10) appear more like the last highlights added to a work that is in itself quite
differently conceived, even if, in them, the key word *return* has its basis in older strata of
the work (on this, see the basic work of H. W. Wolff, "Das Kerygma des deuteronomistischen Geschichtswerks," *ZAW* 73 [1961] 171–86). The future hope of the "Deuteronomists" who composed the book of Jeremiah is just barely achieved here through a last
exertion of effort. And even this seems to me to be still entirely exilic, and not postexilic.
On the relationship of the conclusion of DtrG to the book of Jeremiah, cf. most recently
K. F. Pohlmann, "Erwägungen zum Schlusskapitel des deuteronomistischen Geschichtswerks. Oder: Warum wird der Prophet Jeremia in 2 Kön 22–25 nicht erwähnt?" in
Textgemäss: Aufsätze und Beiträge zur Heremeutik des Alten Testaments (FS E. Würthwein; Göttingen: Vandenhoeck & Ruprecht, 1979) 94–109.

   58. Hoffmann, *Reform und Reformer*, 169–270.

   59. Spieckermann, *Juda unter Assur*, 30–160.

   60. It is unfortunately quite impossible in this context to discuss all the writing since
1960 on these two chapters or passages from them. I will simply summarize (without making

I will begin with Hoffmann. It seems to me, taking an outsider's view, that two things are typical for him. For one thing, although his analysis of 2 Kings 22–23 is central to his interest, it was preceded by a number of other studies. He has already examined the way in which the books of Kings tend, as a general rule, to construct the history of

---

any claims to completeness) the titles not yet mentioned with full citation and the others with short title. As the works are seldom related directly to one another, an alphabetical listing should prove more practical. J. Alonso Diaz, "La muerte de Josias en la redacción deuteronomica del libro de los reyes como anticipo de la teología del libro de Job," in *Homenaje a J. Prado* (Madrid, 1975) 167–77; O. Bächli, *Israel und die Völker: Eine Studie zum Deuteronomium* (ATANT 41; Zürich: Zwingli, 1962) 208ff.; K. Baltzer, *Das Bundesformular* (WMANT 4; Neukirchen-Vluyn: Neukirchener Verlag, 1960) 60–62; G. Braulik, "Gesetz als Evangelium: Rechtfertigung und Begnadigung nach der deuteronomischen Tora," *ZTK* 79 (1982) 127–60, esp. 131–35; W. E. Claburn, "The Fiscal Basis of Josiah's Reform," *JBL* 92 (1973) 11–12; M. Delcor, "Les cultes étrangers en Israël au moment de la réforme de Josias d'après 2R 23," in *Mélanges bibliques et orientaux en l'honneur de M. Henri Cazelles* (AOAT 212; Kevelaer: Butzon & Bercker/Neukirchen-Vluyn: Neukirchener Verlag, 1981) 91–123; idem, "Reflexions sur la pâque du temps de Josias d'après 2 Rois 23,21–23," *Henoch* 4 (1982) 205–19; Dietrich, "Josia und das Gesetzbuch"; S. B. Frost, "The Death of Josiah: A Conspiracy of Silence," *JBL* 87 (1968) 169–82; Y. M. Grintz, "The Josianic Reform and the Book of Deuteronomy," in *Studies in Early Biblical Ethnology and History* (Hakibbutz hameuchad, 1969) 222–41; A. H. J. Gunneweg, *Leviten und Priester* (FRLANT 89; Göttingen: Vandenhoeck & Ruprecht, 1965) 118ff.; Hoffmann, *Reform und Reformen*, 169–270; H. Hollenstein, "Literarkritische Erwägungen zum Bericht über die Reformmassnahmen Josias 2 Kön xxiii 4ff.," *VT* 27 (1977) 321–36; Hoppe, *Origins*, 322–28; C. D. Isbell, "2 Kings 22:3–23:4 and Jeremiah 36: A Stylistic Comparison," *JSOT* 8 (1978) 33–45; Levin, "Die Anfänge," 434, n. 9; J. Lindblom, *Erwägungen zur Herkunft der josianischen Tempelurkunde* (Lund: Gleerup, 1971); N. Lohfink, "Die Bundesurkunde des Königs Josias (Eine Frage an die Deuteronomiumsforschung)," *Bib* 44 (1963) 261–88 and 461–98; idem, "Die Gattung der 'Historischen Kurzgeschichte' in den letzten Jahren von Judah und in der Zeit des babylonischen Exils," *ZAW* 90 (1978) 319–47; J. Lundbom, "Lawbook"; B. Z. Luria, "Joshua, Governor of the City, and the High Places of the Gates," *Beth Mikra* 23 (1977–78) 136–38; Maier, "Fachsprache und Religionspolitik"; Mayes, "King and Covenant"; idem, *Story of Israel* (see n. 53) 128–31; J. W. McKay, "Further Light on the Horses and Chariot of the Sun in the Jerusalem Temple (2 Kings 23.11)," *PEQ* 105 (1973) 167–69; R. P. Merendino, "Zu 2 Kön 22,3–23,15: Eine Erwiderung," *BZ* 25 (1981) 249–55; Nelson, "Josiah"; idem, *Double Redaction* (see n. 37) 76–85; E. W. Nicholson, "The Centralisation of the Cult in Deuteronomy," *VT* 13 (1963) 380–89; idem, "II Kings XXII 18: A Simple Restoration," *Hermathena* 97 (1963) 96–98; idem, "Josiah's Reforms and Deuteronomy," *Transactions of the Glasgow University Oriental Society* 20 (1965) 77–84; idem, *Deuteronomy and Tradition* (Oxford: Blackwell, 1967) 1ff.; G. Odasso, "La familiglia di Shafan e la funzione di 'aser al habbayit'" (Ph.D. diss., Universitas S. Thomae Aquinae, Rome, 1978); M. Or, "I Have Found the Book of the Law in the House of the Lord," *Beth Mikra* 23 (1977–78) 218–20; Perlitt, *Bundestheologie*, 8–12; G. Pfeifer, "Die Begegnung zwischen Pharao Necho und König Josia bei Megiddo," *MiOr* 15 (1968) 297–307; D. Plataroti, "Zum Gebrauch des Wortes *mlk* im Alten Testament," *VT* 28 (1978) 286–300; N. Poulssen, *König und Tempel im Glaubenszeugnis des Alten Testaments* (SBM 3; Stuttgart: Katholisches Bibelwerk,

individual kings.[61] He has also described the motifs and motif com-
plexes that extend through all the reports on the kings' actions regarding the cult and thus establish an extensive network of relationships.[62]
Finally, he has analyzed the way in which the foundation for the cultic
policy is laid in the descriptions of Solomon, Jeroboam, and Rehoboam, and the individual model instances of cultic reform in the representation of the remaining royal period until Josiah.[63] He thus
comes to the analysis of 2 Kings 22–23 armed with the results of a thorough investigation of what readers of this text bring with them in the
way of knowledge, opinion and expectation.[64] Secondly, in his analysis
of the text, Hoffmann refers repeatedly in the notes to a very extensive
appendix, which offers a statistical investigation of "Deuteronomic-
Deuteronomistic cult language."[65] Here are lists that offer a substantial

---

366–68; H. Reviv, "The Pattern of the Pan-Tribal Assembly in the Old Testament," *JNES*
8 (1980) 85–94; Rose, *Ausschliesslichkeitsanspruch*, 163–65; idem, "Bemerkungen"; L. Rost,
"Josias Passa," in *Theologie in Geschichte und Kunst* (FS W. Elliger; Witten: Luther, 1968)
169–75; idem, "Zur Vorgeschichte der Kultusreform des Josia," *VT* 19 (1969) 113–20;
J. Sharbert, "Jeremia und die Reform des Joschija," in *Le Livre de Jérémie: Le Prophète et son
milieu, les oracles et leur transmission* (BETL 54; Louvain: Peeters, 1981) 40–57, esp. 48–49;
M. Sekine, "Beobachtungen zu der josianischen Reform," *VT* 22 (1972) 361–68; R. Smend,
Die Bundesformel (TS 68; Zürich: TVZ, 1963) 8–10; E. J. Smit, "Death and Burial Formulas
in Kings and Chronicles Relating to the Kings of Judah," in *Biblical Essays: Proceedings of the
Ninth Meeting of Die Ou Testamentiese Werkgemeenskap in Suid-Afrika* (Potchefstroom, S. Af-
rica: Pro Rege Pers Beperk, 1966) 173–77; Spieckermann, *Juda unter Assur* (see n. 10) 30–
160; P. H. Vaughan, *The Meaning of "bamâ" in the Old Testament: A Study of Etymological,
Textual and Archeological Evidence* (SOTS Monograph Series 3; Cambridge: Cambridge Uni-
versity Press, 1974); M. Weinfeld, "Cult Centralisation in Israel in the Light of a Neo-
Babylonian Analogy," *JNES* 23 (1964) 202–12, esp. 211–12; P. Welten, "Kulthöhe und
Jahwetempel," *ZDPV* 88 (1972) 19–37, esp. 32; H. G. M. Williamson, "The Death of Josiah
and the Continuing Development of the Deuteronomic History," *VT* 32 (1982) 242–48;
Wiseman, "Is it Peace?" esp. p. 325; H. W. Wolff, "Das Ende des Heiligtums in Bethel," in
Archäologie und Altes Testament (FS Kurt Galling; Tübingen: Mohr, 1970) 287–98; Würth-
wein, "Josianische Reform." The most important literary analyses of the two chapters or
longer sections of them are the works of Dietrich, Hoffmann, Hollenstein, Lohfink,
Mayes, Nelson, Rose, Spieckermann and Würthwein.

61. Hoffmann, *Reform und Reformen*, 33–38.
62. Ibid., 38–46.
63. Ibid., 47–167.
64. Basic reflections pertinent to this point concerning the gradual construction of
author-reader communication in large texts and its meaning for redaction-critical work
may be found in R. Oberforcher, *Die Flutprologe als Kompositionsschlüssel der biblischen Ur-
geschichte: Ein Beitrag zur Redaktionskritik* (Innsbrucker theologische Studien 8; Innsbruck:
Tyrolia, 1981) 11–86. A comparison will make clear, however, that Hoffmann falls short
of the differentiation of questions that is achieved here.
65. Hoffmann, *Reform und Reformen*, 323–66.

complement to those of Moshe Weinfeld,[66] which were already excellent and comprehensive. Hoffmann's lists are especially valuable for their painstaking commentary.

Starting from this broad basis, he then attempts to open up the text before him as a single and systematic affirmation. He has achieved a great measure of success. It is a joy to discover with him, again and again, new lateral relationships, allusions, resumptions, and text constructions that in the previous literature, which was anything but sparse, had never been pointed out, or at least not in such a way as to promote an understanding of the final whole.[67] I think we ought to study Hoffmann's book carefully. It offers a great deal from which we can learn.

Unfortunately I cannot describe all his results here. I would rather proceed directly to two critical comments, without withdrawing anything of what I have just said.

The first in a certain sense assumes his own standpoint and follows his main interest as he has thus far indicated it. I think that, despite his immense effort, he has still not sufficiently grasped or given an adequate account of certain parts of the text. His work needs to be carried further.

For example, he has observed that, in the description of Josiah's cultic measures in the region of Samaria, the reform program as such (2 Kgs 23:15 and 19) is so placed as to frame the prophetic legend in 23:16–18:[68]

1. Bethel (15)
    2. *Fulfillment story: 1 Kings 13* (16–18)
3. The other "high places" of the North (19–20)

An analogous phenomenon, however, can be found earlier in the description of the cultic measures in the region of Judah (see figure following this paragraph). There are listed in 2 Kings 23 a total of ten statements of reforms.[69] Of these, it is precisely the two in the middle

---

66. Weinfeld, *Deuteronomy*, 320–65. An often-remarked deficiency in these lists was the exclusion of Genesis through Numbers.

67. For the most part in the past the point of attack was the isolation of what was Deuteronomic or, within the Deuteronomic, a distribution among various strata and different hands.

68. Hoffmann, *Reform und Reformen*, 219 (diagram).

69. This numbering presupposes Hoffmann's analysis of the structure of these statements (pp. 220–23), which I think is quite good. Cf. the helpful summary on pp. 226–27 where, however, a few small inaccuracies have slipped in.

that deal with the centralization of the cult of Yahweh in Jerusalem,[70] while the first four and the last four treat the abolition of foreign cults. The natural conclusion is that neither should one look to find a historically correct sequence,[71] nor should the distinction between cultic purification and cultic centralization be erased.[72] Instead, the statement about cultic centralization should be seen as having been moved to the central position in the rhetorical structure[73]—in precise analogy, by the way, to the structural relationships in Deuteronomy 12.[74]

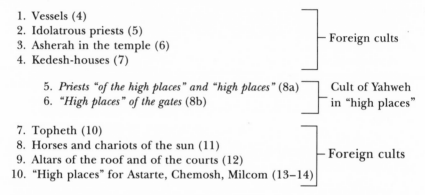

1. Vessels (4)
2. Idolatrous priests (5)
3. Asherah in the temple (6)   Foreign cults
4. Kedesh-houses (7)

    5. *Priests "of the high places" and "high places"* (8a)   Cult of Yahweh
    6. *"High places" of the gates* (8b)   in "high places"

7. Topheth (10)
8. Horses and chariots of the sun (11)
9. Altars of the roof and of the courts (12)   Foreign cults
10. "High places" for Astarte, Chemosh, Milcom (13–14)

For the overall construction of the Josiah narrative, Hoffmann has certainly given a good description of the framing (2 Kgs 22:1–2 and 23:25–30), but for the material within the frame he has fallen back

70. The related, chiastically-structured notice about the treatment of the priests of the high places in Jerusalem even serves to give this middle section a trace of narrative expansion, parallel to the much longer one in 23:16–18. On the chiasm "priests, 'high places,' 'high places,' priests," cf. Hoffmann, p. 213.

71. This is the old presupposition, at one time regarded as self-evident, that caused Jepsen ("Reform"), for example, to resort to rearrangements.

72. Hoffmann (*Reform und Reformen*, 214) also thinks that the Deuteronomistic cult-critique "never" distinguishes "cleanly between high places of Yahweh and high places of foreign gods." The cult of the high places is instead "always a cult of foreign gods." Undoubtedly, from the time of Solomon the cult of the high places is always drawn into the realm of the first commandment. Nevertheless there are cases in which other gods are referred to by name and others in which this does not happen.

73. Hoffmann is correct when he surmises that it is intended, by means of the "profusion of the actions" of Josiah to produce an "impression of total, absolute completeness of every conceivable reform action" (p. 219). Beyond that, the report, as the longest of all the collections of cultic measures in the whole work, is meant to "assemble *all* the previous cultic reforms at once in *a single* reform" (p. 251). But still, this reform has a point beyond all that, which has been given the central place.

74. Deut 12:2–3 (against foreign sanctuaries); 12:4–28 (sacrificial cult for Yahweh in a single sanctuary); 12:29–31 (against foreign cults).

upon the old literary-critical concepts "discovery report" and "reform account." In this way he gets into difficulties in trying to establish the boundaries between the two "reports" and besides, he declares the Huldah oracle, without giving any substantiation for the statement, to be "the center of the entire composition."[75] It is nevertheless evident that the present text is divided into five action units, each introduced by a "sending" or a "command" from the king (22:3, 12; 23:1, 4, and 21).

1. Introductory formula (22:1)
2. Evaluation (22:2)
    3. *Corpus (22:3–23:24—Dating in 22:3 and 23:23–24)*[76]
I.	22:3	"King Josiah sent"	*Temple, book, penitence*
II.	22:12	"the king commanded"	*Questioning of Huldah*
III.	23:1	"the king sent"	**Covenant made**
IV.	23:4	"the king commanded"[77]	*Cultic reforms*
V.	23:21	"the king commanded"	*Passover in Jerusalem*
4. Evaluation (23:25–27)
5. Concluding formula (23:28ff.)

The outermost units deal with Josiah's concern for the temple, with the book found there, with Josiah's conversion resulting from his encounter with the book (I), and with the new festival of worship established in the temple in accordance with the book (V). The center (III) tells how before Yahweh, king and people obligate themselves to this book—a counterpoise throughout to the "making of the covenant in Moab" described in Deuteronomy at the beginning of the historical work (cf. especially Deut 28:69)—whereby at the same time the content of the book is communicated. The two intermediate units (II and IV)

---

75. Hoffmann, *Reform und Reformen*, 169. He then makes the rather confusing arrangement of the next 100 pages dependent on this methodically inconsistent compositional analysis.

76. The exact counterpart to the dating in 22:3 is in 23:23, but 23:24 also belongs to the framing of the corpus because it refers back to 22:4 and 8 through the name Hilkiah and the reference to the discovery of the book. A literary-critical analysis would, of course, have a great deal to consider at this point. But if 23:24 was added relatively late, one needs to ask in this connection to what extent the person who made the addition might have considered the verse not as breaking the structure, but instead as adding clarity.

77. It would seem that 23:4 disturbs the nice alternation that would exist without this verse between the verbs *send* and *command* in 23:3, 12; 23:1, 21. Scholars can and must draw literary-critical conclusions from this fact. But at the level of the final text, a certain conformity to the other recognizable unit-beginnings is apparently sufficient. The notice about the return to Jerusalem in 23:20, however, shows that this was deliberate. It corresponds to the observation that the preceding units of activity not only begin with the king but also always end with the king in Jerusalem. Cf. Lohfink, "Bundesurkunde," 267–71.

point chiastically forward and backward in history. The oracle of Huldah announces the twofold end that is described later in the book: the
end of Josiah and the end of Judah.[78] The cultic reform causes one to
look back: to the demand of the Deuteronomic Law that now at last is to
be fulfilled (reform in Judah), and to the definitive abolition of the cultic sin that has been historically so decisive, that of Jeroboam (reform in
the North). The geographical movement of reform, incidentally, corresponds to the geographical movement of Israel in its entry into the land
under Joshua: from the middle region first to the south and then to the
north. Simply on the basis of its construction, 2 Kings 22–23 serves as a
focal point to draw the whole Deuteronomic History together.

Hoffmann's work can surely be continued, in this and similar ways,
along his own line of thought—and yet, this evidently corresponds
only halfway to his thinking. Thus I come to my second critical plea.

Hoffmann sees this analysis of the definitive Deuteronomic History
as a sort of springboard. He accuses others of being too much the priso-
ners of literary criticism.[79] But he himself wants to pursue "tradition
criticism," and that is just as much a matter of looking behind the text,
as now given, into its prehistory. Thus he regularly discusses the question whence the Deuteronomistic author could have gotten his knowledge and what measure of historical fact lies behind it. Of course,
according to Hoffmann there is not much behind it. His new insights
into the present form of the text serve him primarily as arguments to
show that no *Vorlagen* need be presumed, whether revised or even simply worked into the text. In this way he rapidly arrives at the idea of a
very independent literary work, often depending on nothing but a
knowledge of the past derived from hearsay. And on this point it is impossible to avoid taking a very critical look at his proofs. The final shape
of the Deuteronomistic History, which functions so astonishingly well,
in no way excludes the possibility that it had a complicated prehistory
and that one can even reconstruct that history, at least in part, through
an analysis of the text.[80]

In all the originality and individuality that Hoffmann has brought
to the study of the Deuteronomistic History, he has, perhaps without

---

78. It should not go unremarked that the double structure of the Huldah oracle corresponds to the double structure of the "reform account."

79. Hoffmann, *Reform und Reformen*, 18–19. He seems unjustly to lump together the
acceptance of redactional layers and the reconstruction of "source filaments."

80. Detailed criticism of Hoffmann's "tradition-critical" arguments of course can not
be undertaken here. There was an echo earlier of a minor example, in connection with
the question of the existence of a new city of Jerusalem at the time of Josiah (see above
at nn. 22–24).

being fully aware of it himself, introduced something like a new paradigm into this area of research. It would be possible, from his starting point, to make a consistent synchronic exposition of the historical books. Even if he prefers to understand himself as the representative of a diachronic stance, the synchronic point of departure that is implicit in his work should be taken up.[81] Thereby it is clear that there can be no final choosing between the two points of departure. Both questions supplement one another.[82] But up to now scholars have done far too little questioning along the synchronic line, and the diachronic question must not necessarily call forth the kind of answer that Hoffmann refers to as "consistent tradition criticism." Investigations from the diachronic standpoint that are not afraid to discover a multiple stratification of texts are always welcome.[83]

81. Analyses of the final text of the Deuteronomic History such as Hoffmann presents are only the beginning of a "synchronic" literary analysis. Quite different questions must follow, such as those proposed by R. Polzin, *Moses and the Deuteronomist: A Literary Study of the Deuteronomic History*, vol. 1: *Deuteronomy, Joshua, Judges* (New York: Seabury, 1980). The interplay between the "reporting" speech (of the author) and the "reported" speech (of Moses, various prophets and kings, of God himself) reaches here in 2 Kings 22–23 a final critical stage. Who is, finally, in the right: the king who asks for an oracle; the oracle of the prophetess; God, no longer speaking through a prophet and in fact talking only to himself in 23:27; or the author who in 23:26 confirms God's statement by anticipation and then proceeds to relate the story of its fulfillment? Or is there another "reported" speech from the beginning of the work, say Deuteronomy 4 and 30, which towers untouched above all the rest and is not extinguished by any of the narrated events; that in fact, through the author's strangely open-ended conclusion in 2 Kgs 25:27–30, is extended into a future that cannot yet be recounted? One should keep in mind that in such contexts the concept of an "author" does not refer to a historical writer and his/her subjective intention, but to an element in the thought system of the work itself: the "author" who presents him/herself in the text. Polzin (ibid., 18) expresses this as clearly as one might wish: "There may actually have been no single individual or recognizable group to whom this term refers. I use it heuristically to designate that imagined personification of a combination of literary features that seem to constitute the literary composition of the Deuteronomic History. For me, the text creates the Deuteronomist's features as much as it creates those of Moses. The Deuteronomist is the 'implied author' of this work."

82. There seems to me to be no fixed order in which the questions must be put. Both aspects condition one another reciprocally. One may well assume, in the present state of research, that a more intensive synchronic analysis of the text would make more difficult any too-facile ramblings of literary-critical fantasy. It might in many cases be much less simple to discover relevant tensions, contradictions and doublets. Those are, in fact, the observations that must ground a verifiable literary criticism.

83. One must, of course, always reckon with the possibility that a concrete text proposed for investigation has *no* "prehistory," but rather comes from a single author just as it now stands. For example, Deut 4:1–40 seems to me to show no signs of a "literary-historical structure." But such a conclusion in no way excludes diachronic inquiry. It makes sense, for one thing, to examine the text with the usual methods to see *whether* it is

This is the case, for example, with Spieckermann's analysis of the Josiah chapters, to which I will now turn.[84] Spieckermann is in search of what he often refers to as the "literary-historical structure" of the text. In the end, what he wants is the historical message. If he finds it, he exploits it right away. In the course of his analysis, as it moves through the text, he always reconstructs the historical events immediately, bringing all other historical sources into the picture as he goes.

One may question whether this representational technique furthers the clarity of the textual analysis. But it must be admitted that Spieckermann almost always deals thoroughly with previous research. For example, he offers, quite incidentally, what to my knowledge is the most extensive investigation of the problem of the *wĕqāṭal*-narratives,[85] which represent a well-known *crux* in the analysis of the so-called reform accounts between 23:4 and 23:15.[86] He differs from Walter Dietrich of the Smend school at decisive points, especially with regard to the Huldah oracle,[87] but in the end he also offers a picture of the stratification of

---

"stratified." If the answer is negative, we have still posed the diachronic question. This is what, for example, G. Braulik has done for this text in "Literarkritik und archäologische Stratigraphie: Zu S. Mittmanns Analyse von Dt 4,1–40," *Bib* 59 (1978) 351–83. A different reading of this work based on a misunderstanding of its title would have to result in a false interpretation of the work. Such a work is subject at every moment to refutation through literary-critical arguments if these can be found. But if it has once been established that a text like Deut 4:1–40 is the product of a single literary act, one is still not at the end of the possible diachronic questions. One must seek for antecedent content and forms, perhaps even texts with which this text is in dialogue. Finally, the more general context, in this case Deuteronomy and the Deuteronomic History, has a history of composition, and the place of the text in question must be located within it. All these questions are diachronically oriented and should be distinguished from synchronic text-analysis.

84. Spieckermann, *Juda unter Assur*, 30–160.

85. Ibid., 120–30. See further the literature mentioned there. To this should be added: W. Gross, "Otto Rössler und die Diskussion um das althebräische Verbalsystem," *BN* 18 (1982) 28–78, esp. 68–69 (with additional literature).

86. The phenomenon was given its first full literary-critical evaluation by B. Stade, "Anmerkungen zu 2. Kö. 10–14," *ZAW* 5 (1885) 275–97. In the period covered by this report it was used again by Hollenstein ("Literarkritische"), who was followed by others. Spieckermann reaches the conclusion that we can reckon with *wĕqāṭal*-narratives from the eighth century on, and therefore we should be very cautious in making literary-critical evaluations. One may probably agree with him on this, so far as it is a matter of the acceptance of much later, individual additions. But even allowing for the possible occurrence of this form in the seventh and sixth centuries, it remains a literary-critical finding worthy of mention when the occurrences of the form within a precisely definable piece of text pile up, while in the rest of both chapters they are completely absent.

87. For Dietrich (*Prophetie und Geschichte*, 55–58) a written source was worked over by "DtrP" and "DtrN," while for Spieckermann (*Juda unter Assur*, 58–71) it was only "DtrN." Of the authors mentioned in n. 60 above, especially Hoffmann (*Reform und Reformen*,

the text that should be classified with the orientation of the Smend school.[88] A source that recounted in sequence the repair of the temple,[89] discovery of the book, penitence of the king, the oracle of Huldah, the making of the covenant and cultic reforms in Jerusalem and in Judah is extensively evaluated and largely preserved. "DtrH" gave it a narrow frame in 2 Kgs 22:2 and 23:28, added a few highlights to the reform account, and extended the scene in 23:16–20. Then two different "DtrN"s reworked the Huldah oracle and reinterpreted it, adorned the passages on the making of the covenant with Deuteronomic style elements, inserted the Passover celebration at 23:21–23, attached another reforming deed at 23:24, and most important, created the interpretation of history at 23:25–27 that indeed elevates Josiah above all his predecessors but indicates that God's wrath because of Manasseh's sins is all the greater. Finally, there were some later and minor additions of various sorts.

My first question to Spieckermann would be whether, with his acceptance of the three Deuteronomists of the Smend school, he really does justice to what is to be found, especially in the second half of chapter 23, or whether he is not bringing a predetermined system into the text. Is it really reasonable to assume that the attempt to explain how the pious Josiah made his reforms in vain and how Jerusalem and Judah were destroyed in spite of everything was not the work of "DtrH," writing already more than two decades after the destruction of Jerusalem; neither was it of "DtrP," who expanded the work of "DtrH," but instead of a still later "DtrN," who first revised the Huldah oracle and then added a historical interpretation in 23:25–27? The mention of "*this* book of the covenant" in 23:21 sounds as if at one time it stood

---

170–89), Mayes ("King and Covenant," 38–45; *Story of Israel*, 128–30), Nelson (*Double Redaction*, 76–79), Nicholson (*Deuteronomy and Tradition*, 14–15), Priest ("Huldah's Oracle," 366–68), Rose ("Bemerkungen," 89–105), and Würthwein ("Josianische Reform," 402–96) have concerned themselves with the Huldah oracle. Cf. further Lohfink, "Kurzgeschichte," 320, n. 8 and 340, n. 53; Cross, *Canaanite Myth*, 286, n. 46. It is clear from the divergence of opinions and the way in which they are supported that the matter at hand can probably never be satisfactorily illuminated with the means at our disposal. The arguments for supposing a reinterpretative revision in light of Megiddo and the fall of Jerusalem, however, remain valid, even if we must forego the reconstruction of an older text. Spieckermann's reconstruction remains one of many possibilities.

88. The following statements are somewhat crudely general. A more precise picture can be drawn from the clearly arranged "text reconstructions" in the appendix, [*Das Deuteronomium: Entstehung, Gestalt und Botschaft*, 423–29].

89. At this point Spieckermann, *Juda unter Assur*, 179–82, offers an extremely fine discussion of the question of the relationship to 2 Kings 12 that simply puts Hoffmann's analysis (*Reform und Reformen*, 118–25) in the shade.

very close to 23:3. Neither verse betrays any knowledge of Moses. In
23:3 one reads only of the commandments, testimonies, and statutes of
Yahweh. But should these two verses be attributed to different hands
and the words about *Yahweh*'s commandments, testimonies, and statutes in 23:3 be ascribed to, of all people, that "DtrN" who in 23:25 describes the newly-discovered document not as the word of Yahweh but,
with a quite different concept, as the "Torah of *Moses*"? And in 23:3 is
one to suppose that the expression "with the whole heart and the
whole soul" (without any suffix!), which is nowhere to be found in the
Deuteronomic or Deuteronomistic work, has been inserted by the
same hand that in 23:25 makes use of the precise expression of Deut
6:5, "with all *his* heart and with all *his* soul and *with all his might*"?
Where are the weighty reasons that would compel such implausible
conclusions? In addition, must one assume a special redactional layer
for the prophet story in 23:16–18? Then, do not the very different
judgments in 23:25 and 23:26–27 about Josiah and what came after
him indicate that the first verdict was in the text and that later the
other, which narrows and even reverses it, had to be added because of
what had in fact occurred? This part of the text was certainly not composed at a single stroke. And many other observations point to a different stratification from what Spieckermann proposes. He seems to have
been too conscious from the outset of the existence of "DtrH," "DtrP,"
and "DtrN," and what sort of things is to be assigned to each of them.[90]

In contrast, I prefer to continue to attribute the verses on Josiah's
Passover to the *Vorlagen*.[91] In addition it seems to me that precisely the

90. Compare, for example, the way in which "DtrN" is introduced (Spieckermann,
Juda unter Assur, 43–46).

91. On this point I hold to my reconstruction of the source text, 22:3–23:3, 21–23.
Cf. my "Bundesurkunde" and "Kurzgeschichte." Neither Spieckermann nor more
recent authors have mentioned or discussed my observations that indicate that verses
23:21–23 are part of the primary content of 22:3–23:3. The only argument worthy of discussion that speaks against including 23:21–23 in this contemporary source is calendric:
the eighteenth year of Josiah, in which both the finding of the book and the Passover
Feast are to be located, if the text is really contemporary, would have begun in the
spring, so that there would remain no interval for the cultic reforms between the finding
of the book and the Passover. But this argument is only valid if one includes the "reform
account" in the same source (literarily) or (historically) places all the reforms after the
finding of the book and before Josiah's Passover. Both are disputable. In addition, they
presume as certain that the reckoning of years at this point commences each year with
spring. Würthwein ("Josianische Reform," 408) writes: "It is taken by all the experts who
have worked with Old Testament chronology to be certain that at the time of Josiah the
year began in the spring." But this statement proves, at the most, that Würthwein has
failed to consult some of the "experts." He gives no further indication of his sources.
Since the publication of Nebuchadnezzar's chronicle, at any rate, the question of the

text from 23:25 onward constitutes one of the places in the books of Kings where a decision between Smend and Cross has to be made, which is why one must argue here much more cautiously and with much greater reflection on possible alternatives.[92] I suspect that in the end the result will be in favor of Kuenen's old presumption of a pre-exilic and an exilic edition of the historical work.[93]

My second question to Spieckermann concerns the *Vorlage* that the oldest Deuteronomist used. (Whether one locates him before or after the Exile, in this discussion, is a matter of indifference.) Spieckermann presumes the literary unity of the verses he attributes to a *Vorlage*. I should ask him to give positive proof of this, since for a long time the contrary presupposition was the usual one.

The distinction between a "discovery report" and a "reform account" originated with Östreicher.[94] He was undoubtedly led to his theory by the disposition of material in the chronicle, but he supported it with observations based on the text. These persuaded many authors who did not follow him without reservation in his assessment

---

year's beginning has been reopened. One group of "experts" had always contended for the year's beginning in the fall, at the time of Josiah. Admittedly, 2 Kgs 23:23 was one of their arguments for it. But when one realizes how few clues we have to work with in the calendric realm, he or she ought at least to begin by mistrusting those who eliminate one possible source of information because it does not fit into their already-existing system. And the literary-critical problems ought to be approached first of all with literary-critical arguments. Another argument against the source character of 23:21–23 is the expression "since the days of the judges who judged Israel." A "period of judges" is supposed to be a Deuteronomistic construct. But the expression cannot in any way be proved to be Deuteronomistic, for the whole phrase appears only here (cf. the most comparable texts: 2 Sam 7:11 and Ruth 1:1). It would, on the contrary, be necessary to give positive proof that in Josiah's society, in which, possibly at the same time the first Deuteronomistic version of the book of Judges was being written, one really could not have so described Israel's premonarchic period.

92. On this, see the essay by G. Vanoni in the present volume [[*Das Deuteronomium: Entstehung, Gestalt und Botschaft*, 357–62]].

93. As I see the situation at the moment, I would regard as work of the exilic redaction the revision of the Huldah oracle (with the lead-in at 22:13b), perhaps some expansions in the area of the "reform account," then 23:26ff., and possibly 23:24 as well. If one removes these parts from the text, the overarching structure of 2 Kings 22–23 that was established above in the discussion of Hoffmann's work is even more clearly seen (in which case the positive Huldah oracle would point to an open future). The actual forming of the text would then have been done by the preexilic Deuteronomist, who in 23:25 already clearly described the book that was discovered as the "Torah of Moses." This allows for the introduction of questions concerning very early "nomistic" redaction, at least here at the end of the books of Kings.

94. See nn. 4, 6, 8, and 9 above for his delimitations.

of the chronicle.[95] Spieckermann disputes the principal argument, that of the difference in style between the "discovery" and the "reform" accounts. He admits this difference but considers it unimportant because occasioned by the differing objects of reference.[96] Oddly enough, he then argues at 23:16–18 for a different layer, with the reasoning that here "the listing of objects of reform" is "interrupted by an episode in narrative style."[97] He does not explain why a criterion that is valid in the one instance is invalid in the other.

It may be less satisfying for a historical examination if one concludes that the realistically probable relationship between the discovery of the Torah, the making of the covenant, and the cultic centralization (perhaps even cultic purification) was the literary creation of the first Deuteronomist, not already observable in his source material.[98] But this is something one must put up with if the textual analysis points that way. The observations with regard to 2 Kgs 23:5–14 that were made above in the discussion of Hoffmann's work weaken still further the supposition that the Deuteronomist wished to arrange things chronologically at this point.[99] This fact may have to be accepted, too, espe-

95. Among these were Alt, Gray, Jepsen, and Noth. For references, cf. Dietrich, "Josia und das Gesetzbuch," 15, nn. 9 and 10. In the period of this report: Barth, *Jesaja-Worte,* 251; Lohfink, "Bundesurkunde," 265–67; Nelson, *Double Redaction,* 76–85.

96. Spieckermann, *Juda unter Assur,* 79.

97. Ibid., 116.

98. This is also the case with theories that suppose a written source only in the case of the "reform account" and regard the description of the finding of the book, the episode with Huldah, and the making of the covenant as the work of a "Deuteronomist" (who is then usually located quite late): cf. for example Würthwein, "Josianische Reform"; Hoppe, "Origins of Deuteronomy"; Mayes, *Story of Israel* (with two variants). Realistically, I consider this position scarcely tenable. If a source can be reconstructed within 2 Kings 22–23, it lies behind the narrative (couched in such individual style) of the king's zeal for restoration of the temple, the finding of the book, the royal penitence, the questioning of the prophetess, the making of the covenant, and the celebration of the Passover. What is apparently "Deuteronomistic" in this area proves on closer inspection to be precisely non-Deuteronomistic, although very close to it. The narrative technique is quite subtle and reveals a closer kinship to narrative sections in Jeremiah than to redactionally-conceived "Deuteronomistic" texts in Deuteronomy through 2 Kings. (On this see Lohfink, "Kurzgeschichte") This does not, however, necessarily indicate the time of origination. It can also point to a similarity of original purpose or to an origin in the Shafan family circle. The "reform account," on the contrary, reveals a number of "Deuteronomistic" characteristics; in fact, they are the sort that belong within the horizon of the Deuteronomistic books of Kings.

99. I regard it as scarcely provable that he was using a written source here; see n. 98. It is, of course, possible that he had one before him. If so, it is probable that he made relatively free use of it. But it is equally possible that, especially if he was writing during Josiah's lifetime, he based his work simply on personal recollection and generally available knowledge.

cially since the author, despite lack of interest in chronological matters, still apparently attached importance to communicating facts. And historians must find him all the more appealing if they can presume that the first Deuteronomistic hand was preexilic, that is, practically contemporary with the events.

I will stop here. Spieckermann's monumental book, in which the analysis of 2 Kings 22–23 is only one component, brings together so much of the preceding discussion of Josiah and his times, and of the book of Deuteronomy, that it can very well serve as a starting point for further discussion. It must in any case occasion new discussion, for it is too much involved in the old but by no means completed debate over the question how and to what degree Noth's theory of the Deuteronomistic History can be maintained in an altered form.

This discussion and all the work that is being done related to 2 Kings 22–23 are important for research on Deuteronomy itself, for this is where the switch-points are being shifted. Here the historical location of Deuteronomy will be determined—and a great deal in the interpretation of the book depends on that. Since the book of Deuteronomy could be a part of the Deuteronomistic History, hypotheses about the redactional history of this work are also always questions about where and how the same redactional layers could be found in Deuteronomy itself. That sort of question has long been discussed with regard to the framing sections of Deuteronomy but very seldom for the central portion.[100] Also, many points concerning the language and literary technique of Deuteronomy cannot be decided from Deuteronomy alone. Finally, methodological insights, such as the fact that both diachronic and synchronic textual analyses are necessary, must be given a quite different impetus than previously, and this in the study of Deuteronomy itself.

100. This may be connected with the fact that, according to Noth, the "Deuteronomist" interpolated Deuteronomy 5–30 as a block into his work. The first questions about this were expressed in 1961 by Wolff, "Kerygma," 180–82. Then G. Minette de Tillesse ("Sections 'tu' et sections 'vous' dans la Deutéronome," *VT* 12 [1962] 29–87) first approached the question in the sense of a differentiation from Noth's position. My latest contribution to the question is "Kerygmata."

Polity of the Covenant People: The Book of Deuteronomy

S. DEAN MCBRIDE, JR.

[[229]] Our ancient predecessors in the work of biblical interpretation still have much to teach us. In his *Antiquities of the Jews* (4.176–331), written toward the end of the first century A.D. for an enlightened gentile audience, Josephus concluded a review of the pentateuchal narrative with an apologetically motivated but nonetheless insightful paraphrase of Deuteronomy. The book, he averred, preserves the divinely authorized and comprehensive "polity" or national "constitution" that Moses, on the final days of his life, delivered in both oral and written testamentary forms to the tribes of Israel assembled near Abile in the Transjordan. Most noteworthy here is Josephus' choice of the Greek term *politeia*, rather than *nomos* or the like, to describe the juridical substance of Deuteronomy; there is no reason to doubt that he understood *politeia* to represent Hebrew *tôrâ* in its characteristically Deuteronomic usage.[1] The [[230]] implications of the Greek term in this context are profound, going well beyond immediate questions of semantic field and translational equivalence. The association of Torah with *politeia* invokes the heady realm of Hellenistic philosophical debate regarding the origins and evolution of human statecraft and, above all, about whose state had attained the most sublime model of government.[2] By

Reprinted with permission from *Interpretation* 41 (1987) 229–44.

1. See especially *Antiquities* 4.184, 193, 198, 302, 310, 312. It is clear from the latter passage, in conjunction with 4.198, that Josephus differentiated the Mosaic *politeia*, which treats only the essential order of Israelite society, from other pentateuchal corpora of rules, cultic regulations, and judicial precedents (i.e., he did not confuse a "constitution" with a "lawcode").

2. The classical locus of this discussion is, of course, Plato's *Laws* (esp. Books 3–4) and Aristotle's *Politics*. Jewish apologists who preceded Josephus, notably Aristobulus and Eupolemus, had claimed preeminence for Moses as legislator, and similarly also Philo

identifying the Mosaic Torah of Deuteronomy as the ancient Israelite *politeia,* Josephus boldly advanced the case for Jewish priority in the history of civilized political thought and practice. Nor would his educated Roman audience have missed the *polemical* thrust of this. His claim undermined one of the grand, elitist pretensions of Rome, elaborately expounded by Polybius and Cicero, that its vast territorial empire was the logical outcome not simply of the efficient and often brutal use of military power but of its manifest preeminence among the world's nations in the cultivation of virtue, the exercise of rational governance, and the practical implementation of social justice.[3]

The view of Deuteronomy's central contents and ideological significance which the present essay will sketch is therefore by no means a new one, even though it has received surprisingly little attention from biblical scholars in recent decades.[4] Perhaps in our contemporary zeal to explore [[231]] and affirm the fascinating literary, tradition-historical, and homiletical dimensions of the Deuteronomic work we have lost sight of its broader social and political import; if so, we have also failed to confront directly its particular theological witness. At all events, the current bicentennial celebration of the drafting and ratification of the

---

(*Moses,* esp. 2.49–51). Josephus significantly expanded and reshaped the argument through his intentional use of the Platonic and Aristotelian concept of *politeia.* Cf. also Josephus' encomium of Moses and the Mosaic legislation in *Against Apion,* 2.145–86.

3. Cicero, *The Republic,* 1.70; 2.30, 65–66; and note especially this revealing statement of thesis in Polybius, *Histories,* 6.2.9–10: "Now the chief cause of success or the reverse in all matters is the form of a state's constitution; for springing from this, as from a fountainhead, all designs and plans of action not only originate, but reach their consummation" (*Polybius: The Histories,* trans. W. R. Paton, LCL [Cambridge, Mass.: Harvard Univ., 1923], III, 271). Cf. Carl Joachim Friedrich, *The Philosophy of Law in Historical Perspective,* 2nd ed. (Chicago/London: Univ. of Chicago, 1963) 13–34; and also his *Transcendent Justice: The Religions Dimension of Constitutionalism* (Durham, N.C.: Duke Univ., 1964) 3–20.

4. Cf. Harold M. Wiener, *Studies in Biblical Law* (London: David Nutt, 1904) 52–83 and esp. 109; Kurt Galling, *Die israelitische Staatsverfassung in ihrer vorderorientalischen Umwelt* (Leipzig: J. C. Hinrichs, 1929) esp. 56–61; and, most recently, the terse remarks of Moshe Weinfeld, *Deuteronomy and the Deuteronomic School* (Oxford: Clarendon, 1972) 164, 168–71. It is noteworthy that Baruch (Benedict de) Spinoza, one of the ostensible fathers of modern biblical criticism, enthusiastically discussed the social and constitutional significance of the Deuteronomic legislation, in Chap. 17 of his *Tractatus theologico-politicus,* published anonymously in 1670 (*A Theological-Political Treatise and A Political Treatise,* trans. R. H. M. Elwes [New York: Dover, 1951; rpt.] 214–36). The extent to which this controversial work of Spinoza may have informed the political thought of his more influential contemporary, John Locke, is moot. However, that the political import of Deuteronomy was recognized or exploited during the formative era of American constitutionalism is amply attested by three extraordinary "election sermons" reprinted in *God's New Israel: Religious Interpretations of American Destiny,* ed. Conrad Cherry (Englewood Cliffs: Prentice-Hall, 1971) 67–105.

Constitution of the United States provides an especially appropriate
occasion for us to give renewed consideration to a biblical document
that is, arguably, the Constitution's most ancient antecedent.

The Book of the Torah of Moses

Deuteronomy is set off from earlier parts of the Pentateuch by well-
known characteristics of literary style and a remarkably coherent structure. While the subject matter may generally be described as the testamentary speeches and acts of Moses, a series of four editorial
superscriptions (1:1–5; 4:44–49; 29:1 [Heb. 28:69]; 33:1) systematically
introduces the coordinated segments of the work, describing the particular character and content of each major part.[5] It is important to remember, however, that the book's most striking mark of distinction is
openly and proudly displayed from beginning to virtual end: It claims
repeatedly to embody as its central segment (4:44–28:68) a *written* de-
position of the authoritative Torah mediated through Moses to Israel.[6]
Moreover, by reason of this claim Deuteronomy stands apart as the
only individual book of Scripture whose test is expressly referred to
elsewhere [[232]] within the Hebrew Bible itself.[7] Especially in view of

5. The first modern scholar to call attention to this editorial frame was Paul Kleinert, *Das Deuteronomium und der Deuteronomiker*, Untersuchungen zur alttestamentlichen
Rechts- und Literaturgeschichte 1 (Bielefeld/Leipzig: Velhagen & Klasing, 1872) 166–67;
although Kleinert's case (pp. 136–58) for identifying Samuel as the Deuteronomist, who
succeeded to the prophetical office of Moses and represented Mosaic law in a new social
context (cf. Deut 18:15–19 and 1 Sam 8:4–22; 12) lacks literary and historical cogency,
his insight into the character of the Deuteronomic legislation exceeded that of most of
his more celebrated scholarly contemporaries and successors. In recent scholarship,
Kleinert's perception of the editorial structure of Deuteronomy has been developed by
Norbert Lohfink, "Der Bundesschluss im Land Moab: Redaktionsgeschichtliches zu Dt
28, 69–32, 47," *BZ* n.f. 6 (1962) 32–34; and Gottfried Seitz, *Redaktionsgeschichtliche Studien
zum Deuteronomium*, BWANT 93 (Stuttgart: W. Kohlhammer, 1971) 24–30. Unfortunately
without acknowledgement of this earlier "critical" work, comparable insights are explored by Robert Polzin, *Moses and the Deuteronomist: A Literary Study of the Deuteronomic
History* (New York: Seabury, 1980).

6. Compare especially the rubric in 4:44 ("This is the Torah that Moses promulgated for the Israelites") with references to "this Torah" (1:5; 4:8; 17:18, 19; 27:3, 8, 26;
28:58, 61; 29:29 [Heb. 28]; 31:9, 11, 12, 24; 32:46) and "this book of the Torah" (29:21
[Heb. 20]; 30:10, 31:26; cf. also "this book" in 29:20 [Heb. 19], 27 [Heb. 26]).

7. To be sure, most of these references are found within the larger "Deuteronomic/
Deuteronomistic" literary corpus, or otherwise reflect the Deuteronomic usage (though
not necessarily with the same degree of specificity). I take the following to be unambiguous
references to the Mosaic polity as represented in Deuteronomy: Josh 1:7, 8; 8:31, 32, 34;
22:5; 23:6; 1 Kgs 2:3; 2 Kgs 14:6 (cf. 2 Chr 25:4); 22:8, 11; 23:24, 25 (cf. also 23:2, 3); Mal 4:4
[Heb. 3:22]. Correlation is less exclusively certain or immediate in many additional cases,

these external witnesses, the book's self-consciousness regarding its own peculiar form, function, and singular importance is quite extraordinary. Before we examine the major juristic contents of the central document, several observations may provide initial support for Josephus' identification of "this Torah" as a *politeia*, an Israelite "polity" or political "constitution."

Although modern commentators often remark that the typical rendering of *tôrâ* as "law" in English translations is misleading, the alternatives usually proposed on the basis of etymological considerations, "teaching" and "instruction," are scarcely an improvement as far as the Deuteronomic usage is concerned.[8] Conception of *tôrâ* as "teaching" or "instruction" has promoted a much too facile understanding of Deuteronomy itself as essentially a didactic, moralizing, or homiletical work.[9] More importantly, neither term conveys the normative, prescriptive force of *tôrâ* in Deuteronomy. [[233]] The "words" or stipulations of "this Torah" are not simply admonitions and sage advice offered in the name of Moses to guide the faithful along a divinely charted path of life; they are set forth as sanctioned political policies, to be "diligently

---

such as the following (most of which designate the Torah as Yahweh's own): 2 Kgs 10:31; 17:34, 37; 2 Chr 14:4 [Heb. 3]; 31:21; Ps 89:30 [Heb. 31]; Ezra 7:6; Neh 8:1–3; 13:1, 3; Isa 42:4, 21, 24; 51:4, 7; Jer 9:13 [Heb. 12]; 16:11; 18:18; 26:4; 31:33; 32:23; 44:10, 23; Lam 2:9; Amos 2:4; Hab 1:4; Zech 7:12. I consider the following to be among the important pre- or proto-Deuteronomic occurrences of *tôrâ* with a comprehensive (covenantal) sense: Deut 33:4, 10; Hos 4:6; 8:1; Ps 78:5, 10.

8. Recently, e.g., A. D. H. Mayes, *Deuteronomy*, NCBC (Grand Rapids: Eerdmans/London: Marshall, Morgan & Scott, 1979) 116–17. Cf. also Barnabas Lindars, "Torah in Deuteronomy," *Words and Meanings: Essays Presented to David Winton Thomas*, ed. Peter R. Ackroyd and Barnabas Lindars (Cambridge: Cambridge Univ., 1968) 117–36.

9. E.g., Calum M. Carmichael, *The Laws of Deuteronomy* (Ithaca: Cornell Univ., 1974) 17–52, as well as his recent study *Law and Narrative in the Bible: The Evidence of the Deuteronomic Laws and the Decalogue* (Ithaca: Cornell Univ., 1985). Cf. also Dale Patrick, *Old Testament Law* (Atlanta: John Knox, 1985) 257–59. This continuing trend in the discussion of Deuteronomic traditions received impetus a generation ago from the brilliantly complementary studies of Martin Noth and Gerhard von Rad. According to Noth, the legal corpora of the Pentateuch lack jurisprudential efficacy, because they presuppose a sacral community "Israel" that survived the period of the judges only as a ghostly ideal ("The Laws in the Pentateuch: Their Assumptions and Meaning," *The Laws in the Pentateuch and Other Studies*, trans. D. R. Ap-Thomas [Philadelphia: Fortress, 1966] 1–107). Von Rad's extraordinarily influential work went much further, virtually denying the character of these corpora as genuine "law" (*Old Testament Theology* I; trans. D. M. G. Stalker [New York: Harper, 1962] esp. 195–203, 219–31); in this view, for example, Deuteronomy becomes " . . . simply and solely an artistic mosaic made up of many sermons on a great variety of subjects—here is gathered the total expression of an obviously extensive preaching activity" (p. 221). In rejecting such reductionism, we need not deny the strong features of *paraeneses* in the Deuteronomic polity as well as its framework.

observed" by Israelite king and common citizen alike (17:19; 31:12; 32:45), and on their strict observance hangs the fate of the entire nation (e.g., 28:58–68). What speaks against the rendering "law" is not some inchoate threat of legalism that might diminish the theological vitality of the Hebrew term, for while *tôrâ* in Deuteronomy is theologically cogent, it remains no less decidedly a jurisprudential concept.[10] Rather, the problem is that neither our English word "law" nor its Greek counterpart, *nomos*, is sufficiently discrete to express at once the distinctiveness and the scope which *tôrâ* exhibits, especially in Deuteronomic usage but also elsewhere. On the one hand, *tôrâ* in this usage is not an abstraction or umbrella term covering every rule, decision, and act that Israelite social authority might choose to acknowledge and enforce; on the other hand, it does connote the totality of particular categories of legislation and judicial practice appropriate to it. It is the type of law connoted by *tôrâ* that is at issue. We can name it most easily with reference to its self-declared function: "This Torah" is covenantal law, the divinely authorized social order that Israel must implement to secure its collective political existence as the people of God.[11]

In its received form, the whole Book of Deuteronomy is both about "this Torah" and literally constructed around it. Thus while the initial editorial superscription in 1:1–5 introduces the Mosaic memoirs that immediately follow in 1:6–4:40 (with a brief editorial supplement in 4:41–43), it does so already with a clear view toward the promulgation of "this Torah" (1:3, 5). The polity proper is separately introduced by the second superscription in 4:44–49. Here *tôrâ* is the regnant concept (4:44), but it is epexegetically defined by 4:45 as comprised of "the treaty-stipulations (*hā ʿēdōt* [RSV "the testimonies"]) and "the statutory rulings" (*haḥuqqîm wĕhammišpāṭîm* [234] [RSV "the statutes, and the

---

10. Particularly revealing is this remark of von Rad (*Theology* I, 222): " . . . it is obvious from what has been said that this term 'torah' cannot be rendered by our word 'law,' for its theological meaning would then be curtailed." While I do not wish to impugn von Rad's theological immense contributions, much of his discussion of Deuteronomy in particular seems bent on finding hermeneutical solution to a problem that only exists to the extent that "law" and "gospel," social order and religious faith, theology and political practice are understood *a priori* to be mutually incompatible categories. They were clearly not so for ancient Israel, as the prophetical literature attests at least as vigorously as the pentateuchal traditions.

11. A distinction between legal "policy" and juridical "technique," similar to that originally suggested by George Mendenhall ("Ancient Oriental and Biblical Law," *BA* 17 [1954] 26–31) remains cogent in my judgment. But I agree strongly that we should not consider "law and covenant ideal types in polar opposition, as Mendenhall has recently done" (Jon D. Levenson, "The Theologies of Commandment in Biblical Israel," *HTR* 73 [1980] 23).

ordinances"]).[12] Elsewhere in Deuteronomy, the term *ʿēdôt* reappears only twice (6:17, 20); in all three instances its most obvious referent is the decalogue of 5:6–21, whose fundamental demand that Israel give undivided allegiance to Yahweh is illustrated, elaborated, and eloquently motivated throughout the Mosaic speech of the following five chapters (6–11).[13] On the other hand, the compound term *haḥuqqîm wĕhammišpāṭîm* (hendiadys) is a standard Deuteronomic designation for the constitutional matters which, though fully sanctioned by divine authority, are promulgated only through the legislative agency of Moses.[14] These are the matters set forth in the ordered whole of 12:2–26:15, to which we will return below. Their presentation is immediately followed by report of a mutual swearing of oaths; this is the constitutive act per se, the ratification ceremony, formally inaugurating, or reinaugurating, the covenantal bond between Yahweh and Israel (26:16–19).[15] Then the polity proper receives a two-part conclusion: first, with Moses' charge to the tribes regarding ceremonial reaffirmation of the polity once they have entered their homeland (27); and second, with an elaborate listing of sanctions, the blessings and the curses which pertain not only to the covenantal bond in a narrow sense but to the whole constitutional legacy of Torah that must continue to define Israel's national life (28, and especially vv. 58–61). Yet there is more. A third editorial superscription in 29:1 [Heb. 28:69] informs us that what follows, apparently through 32:52, is another "covenant" altogether, initiated not at Horeb

12. On these and related terms, see esp. George Braulik, "Die Ausdrücke für 'Gesetz' im Buch Deuteronomium," *Biblica* 51 (1970) 39–66. Regarding the *ʿēdôt*, however, identification with the decalogue articles reviewed in Deuteronomy 5 appears certain. Cf. Ps 25:10; 99:7; and, reading *ʿēdôt* for *ʿēdût*, the appellations "the ark of the treaty-stipulations" (Exod 25:22; Josh 4:16, etc.) and "the two tablets of the treaty-stipulations" (Exod 31:18, etc.); cf. also Deut 10:1–5 and 1 Kgs 8:9.

13. See esp. Norbert Lohfink, *Das Hauptgebot: Eine Untersuchung literarischer Einleitungsfragen zu Dtn 5–11*, AnBib 20 (Rome: Pontifical Biblical Institute, 1963); and *The Christian Meaning of the Old Testament*, trans. R. A. Wilson (Milwaukee: Bruce, 1968) 87–102. Cf. also Felix García López, *Analyse litteraire de Deuteronome, V–XI* (Jerusalem: Pontificium Institutum Biblicum de Urbe, 1978).

14. More specifically, the "statutory rulings" can be considered constitutional articles completing "the mandate (*hammiṣwâ*) which Moses was commissioned by both Israel and God to receive at Horeb, *after* the decalogue itself had been promulgated (5:22–6:3). The most important references supporting this interpretation are: 5:1, 31; 6:1, 20; 11:32; 12:1; 26:16, 17.

15. I.e., 26:16–19 seals the Horeb covenant for the generation to whom Moses speaks (cf. 5:2–3) and embraces the statutory rulings as legislation authorized by this covenant; the "Moab Covenant" of chaps. 29–32 has another albeit related purpose. On the formulas of ratification, see esp. Norbert Lohfink, "Dt 26, 17–19 und die 'Bundesformel,'" *ZKT* 91 (1969) 517–53; and his remarks in *Great Themes from the Old Testament*, trans. Ronald Walls (Edinburgh: T. & T. Clark, 1982) 24–27.

but in the land of Moab. [[235]] Although aspects of this second covenant are strikingly similar to the first, there are some obvious differences. The main emphasis here falls on Moses' imminent departure
and how Israel can survive without his unifying leadership. What the assembled Israelites now accept on solemn oath—on their own behalf
and that of their descendants, as individuals, as separate tribes, and as
a federated nation—is full accountability for the maintenance of their
common life (29:2 [Heb. 1]–30:20). Furthermore, Moses does not leave
them leaderless: Joshua will oversee the conquest of their homeland
(31:7–8, 14–15, 23); and Moses' own guidance will remain forever with
them in the form of the written constitutional *tôrâ* (31:9–13, 24–26)
together with his prophetic witness to its efficacy (31:16–22, 27–30,
32:1–47). The rest is epilogue, including the report of Moses' valedictory blessings on the tribes (33), the brief account of his death and
Joshua's succession (34:1–9; cf. 32:48–52), and the final editorial epi-
taph extolling Moses' peerless career (34:10–12).

It should be apparent that whatever earlier or independent function the book's outer frame may once have had, it now serves admirably
to highlight the character of the central document as a constitution.[16]
Thus the Mosaic memoirs of 1:6–4:40 commence neither with a review
of Moses' call nor, most significantly, with any mention whatsoever of
Israel's deliverance from Egyptian bondage. Reference to such events
would be expected in the "historical prologue" of a treaty or formal
covenant-document, but that is manifestly not the intention of these
memoirs. Rather, the initial recollections are of the abrupt divine command to depart Horeb and to take possession through conquest of the
land that God had consigned on oath to Israel's forebears (1:6–8) and
of the civil administration quickly put into place by Moses and the
federated tribes so that these marching orders could be carried out
(1:9–18). What follows seems exquisitely designed to etch into popular

---

16. The outer frame of chaps. 1–4 and 29–32 exhibits at least two major stages of literary formation, the last of which (see esp. chaps. 4 and 29–30) can be identified as the
work of an exilic Deuteronomist. Yet there remains considerable scholarly disagreement
regarding both the extent and character of this exilic edition and the history of composition that preceded it; cf. Josef G. Plöger, *Literarkritische, formgeschichtliche und stilkritische
Untersuchungen zum Deuteronomium*, BBB 26 (Bonn: Peter Hanstein, 1967); Jon D. Levenson, "Who Inserted the Book of the Torah?" *HTR* 68 (1975) 203–33; Brian Peckham, *The
Composition of the Deuteronomistic History*, HSM 35 (Atlanta: Scholars, 1985) esp. 30–33. I am
not persuaded by recent critical efforts to distinguish multiple layers of redaction in both
outer frame and polity, e.g., Siegfried Mittmann, *Deuteronomium 1, 1–6, 3 literarkritisch und
traditionsgeschichtlich untersucht*, BZAW 139 (Berlin: Walter de Gruyter, 1975); and Rosario
Pius Merendino, *Das Deuteronomische Gesetz: Eine literarkritische, gattungs- und überlieferungsgeschichtliche Untersuchung*, BBB 31 (Bonn: Peter Hanstein, 1969).

memory the message that national failure and success are alike predict-
able: the former, when God's [[236]] decrees issued through Moses are
rejected by the body politic (1:19–46); and the latter, when they are
effectively implemented (2:1–4:40). In the "Moab covenant" of 29:1
[Heb. 28:69]–32:47, the same lesson is underscored, though now with
a crucial difference. Because Moses has promulgated the constitutional
law in its entirety, fulfilling the role of legislative mediator to which he
had been elected at Horeb (5:27–31), knowledge of God's providential
governance is accessible to every Israelite (30:11–14; 31:9–13); authoritative decision making and the responsibilities which go with it have
been democratized (30:15–20). The written Torah and the institutional
order it defines have become a surrogate for Moses himself. In short,
the contents of the outer frame bridge formidable distances: the geographical distance between Horeb, where in wilderness isolation Israel
first became God's people, and Moab, where its history as a territorial
state, surrounded by other nations, is about to begin; the temporal distance, between ancestral generations to whom divine promises were
made and the present generation for whom those promises could become actuality; and, perhaps greatest of all, the political distance between a fledgling community of liberated slaves and an institutionally
structured society, responsible for maintenance of civil order, economic well-being, and human rights for all of its citizens.

Deuteronomic Constitutionalism

As we examine the design and chief concerns of the polity itself, it will
be useful to keep in mind the following definition:

> The true nature of a constitution and of constitutionalism, its *differen-
> tia specifica* by which it contrasts with all non-constitutional regimes, is
> discovered by asking: What is the political function of a constitution?
> For its function is to realize specific political objectives. Among these
> the core objective is that of safeguarding each member of the political
> community as a political person, possessing a sphere of genuine au-
> tonomy. The constitution is meant to protect the *self* in its dignity and
> worth; for the self is believed to be primary and of penultimate value.[17]

The Deuteronomic "Book of the Torah" is a new literary genre. It
has no true peer or parallel among the legal corpora preserved in the
preceding books of the Pentateuch,[18] nor has there yet been discovered

17. Friedrich, *Transcendent Justice*, 16–17.
18. The so-called Holiness Code of Leviticus 17–26 is the closest pentateuchal parallel (and roughly contemporary with Deuteronomy in date).

an ancient Near Eastern document equivalent to it. We can recognize, to be sure, important resemblances between "this Torah" and various genres of [[237]] Near Eastern literature: the "codes" of cuneiform law, the *mešarum* acts of Mesopotamian rulers, the loyalty oaths they imposed upon their subjects and vassals, the apologies and protocols of Egyptian kings, and especially the international treaties about which so much has been written in recent decades.[19] While the Deuteronomic Torah may be deeply indebted to such traditions, however, it is identical in form, content, and purpose to none of them. With it, something quite distinctive seems to have been created, a comprehensive social charter, perhaps uniquely appropriate to the peculiar covenantal identity that Israel claimed for itself and which was the product of mature reflection on this identity.

In comparison with other biblical and ancient Near Eastern traditions of law, the *differentia specifica* of the Deuteronomic legislation is most conspicuous in its concern to empower a broad constituency of the community whose integrity and political independence it seeks to protect. Couched in the form of first-person Mosaic speech, the polity is directly addressed to "all Israel," which is conceived throughout to be both a corporate entity and a collectivity of the individual selves who comprise its membership.[20] Pertinent here too are the "motive

19. For a brief overview of most of these genres and bibliography, see Samuel Greengus, "Law in the Old Testament," *IDBSup*, 229–32. Cf. also Weinfeld, *Deuteronomy*, 146–47. While comparative study of the international treaties and *ade* agreements has shed abundant light on particular aspects of Deuteronomic language and tradition, failure to observe the conspicuous *differences* between these Near Eastern documents and Deuteronomy, especially as regards overall structure and specific juridical contents, accounts for two extreme positions. Thus there are scholars, on the one hand, who have supposed that Deuteronomy preserves the actual text of a "suzerainty treaty" made between Yahweh and Israel through the mediation of Moses (e.g., Peter C. Craigie, *The Book of Deuteronomy*, NICOT [Grand Rapids: Eerdmans, 1976] 20–32, 79–83; cf. also J. G. McConville, *Law and Theology in Deuteronomy*, JSOTSup 33 [Sheffield: JSOT Press, 1984] 3–7, 159). On the other hand, there are scholars who cite "parallels" between Deuteronomy and treaty documents of the Assyrian period to argue that the whole concept of a political covenant between Israel and Yahweh must be a Deuteronomic innovation of the eighth or seventh century (Dennis J. McCarthy, *Treaty and Covenant*, AnBib 21/21A [Rome: Pontifical Biblical Institute, 1963, 1978]; cf. Ernest W. Nicholson, *God and His People: Covenant and Theology in the Old Testament* [Oxford: Clarendon, 1986] 56–117). In my judgment, the peculiar character of Deuteronomy refutes both of these extremes: The covenant idea is ancient in Israel, underlying the centuries-long development of tradition that culminated in the reflective, comprehensive promulgation of a constitutional Torah during the later Judaean monarchy.

20. Cf. esp. "all Israel" in 5:1 and 27:9 with 13:12; 18:6; and 21:21. On the rhetorical (rather than exclusively redactional) significance of second-person singular and plural references to Israel, see Lohfink, *Hauptgebot*, 244–51. Even within the juridical corpus of

clauses" and other parenetic elements ⟦238⟧ that accompany key enactments.[21] Thus most of the unifying religious and civil institutions deemed inviolable by the polity are not simply presented as impositions of theocratic will; instead of self-authenticating oracular pronouncements or stark apodictic decrees bearing the stamp of royal office, we find this legislation making liberal appeal to the experiences and interests of an Israelite public.[22] Similarly, while restraints and severe penalties are prescribed against individuals whose actions violate basic rights to life and livelihood of other members of society, or whose words and deeds are considered threatening to the community at large, the emphasis falls less on legitimating mechanisms of social control than on assuring due process for those accused of serious crimes. Yet if these features of style and content distinguish the polity from international treaties, royal decrees, codifications of judicial precedents, and the like, they do not support characterization of the work as an anthology of covenantal preaching; it is something else and genuinely new, the charter for a constitutional theocracy.[23]

Following the editorial superscription in 4:44–49 and a terse narrative introduction (5:1aα), the polity opens with an extensive prolegomenon in three parts, each beginning with the appeal "Hear, Israel!" (5:1aβ; 6:4; 9:1; cf. 10:12). Although the chief concern throughout the prolegomenon is Israel's allegiance to Yahweh alone, attendant principles of Deuteronomic constitutionalism are rhetorically highlighted as well, clearly in anticipation of the legislation promulgated in 12:2–26:15. Thus the first part (5:1–6:3) not only reviews the fundamental

---

the polity, traditional third-person casuistic formulations are few and confined to chaps. 21–25; on the forms and import of the second-person style of legislative address, see Seitz, *Studien*, 142–83; Dale Patrick, "Casuistic Law Governing Primary Rights and Duties," *JBL* 92 (1973) 180–84; and Harry W. Gilmer, *The If-You Form in Israelite Law*, SBLDS 15 (Missoula: Scholars, 1975).

21. See now esp. Rifat Sonsino, *Motive Clauses in Hebrew Law: Biblical Forms and Near Eastern Parallels*, SBLDS 45 (Chico: Scholars, 1980).

22. Contrast, e.g., the juridical formulations in Leviticus 17 and Ezekiel 44–47. Interestingly, Plato (*Laws*, 4.722–724) castigated the typical legislative style of his day, which he called "despotic prescription," and suggested that promulgations of law should preferably be introduced with explanatory prefaces and also include statements of persuasion with the individual prescriptions themselves. Thus the Deuteronomic polity already exhibits what Plato proposed as an ideal.

23. Once again, the terminology originated with Josephus: "Our lawgiver . . . gave to his constitution the form of what—if a forced expression be permitted—may be termed a 'theocracy,' placing all sovereignty and authority in the hands of God" (*Against Apion*, 2.165, *Josephus*, trans. H. St. J. Thackeray, LCL [Cambridge, Mass.: Harvard Univ., 1926] IX, 359).

demands of the decalogue, which articulate Yahweh's sovereignty, but legitimates Moses in his role as spokesman for Yahweh. This means that Israel must accept the Mosaic legislation as covenantal policy, comparable in authority to the decalogue stipulations themselves. The second part (6:4–8:20) offers the fullest and most forceful presentation of Israel's covenant ideology to be found in the whole of Hebrew Scripture. The reciprocals of fidelity to [[239]] Yahweh's commands, imparted through Moses, and Israel's special status as the sanctified people of God are dramatized with particular reference to the military, cultural, and spiritual challenges which conquest of a national homeland will pose. In the third part (9:1–10:11 + 10:12–12:1) the basic requirements of personal and communal obedience, upon which a national future depends, are juxtaposed to Israel's prior history of recalcitrance. Particularly noteworthy here is the affirmation that egalitarian justice is the crux of theocratic government (10:17–19); the single most important contribution of Deuteronomic constitutionalism to our political heritage is the concerted effort to implement this theme.

In describing the Israelite *politeia*, even Josephus felt a need to question the organization of articles in 12:2–26:15.[24] Modern scholars, generally working on the assumption that this material originated as a lawcode or, even more narrowly, as a program for cultic reform, have resorted to a wide variety of literary, tradition-historical, and redaction-critical arguments to account both for the scope of the laws included and their present order.[25] While it is probably beyond the reach of critical analysis to demonstrate convincingly a detailed logic to the received arrangement or, otherwise, to recover the compositional history of the corpus, formulaic signals as well as subject matter suggest a remarkably coherent five-part structure.[26] Our immediate attention is drawn to what the contents of these five divisions reveal about the political objectives of Deuteronomic constitutionalism.

24. *Antiquities* 4.197. The comment, however, seems primarily offered as warrant for treating selected laws from earlier pentateuchal corpora alongside those in the Deuteronomic polity.

25. For representative critical views, see Seitz, *Studien*, 92–95, and his own extensive treatment thereafter. Cf. also Stephen A. Kaufman, "The Structure of the Deuteronomic Law," *Maarav* 1 (1978–79) 105–58; and George Braulik, "Die Abfolge der Gesetze in Deuteronomium 12–26 und der Dekalog," *Das Deuteronomium: Entstehung, Gestalt und Botschaft*, ed. Norbert Lohfink, BETL 68 (Leuven: Leuven Univ., 1985) 252–72. [[Reprinted in English translation in this volume, pp. 313–35 below.]]

26. This structure is indicated by the alternation of two temporal clauses: "When Yahweh your God has extirpated the nations . . ." (12:29; 19:1); "When you have invaded the land . . . " (17:14; 26:1). If one finds it helpful to do so, the resulting five-part design may be identified as chiastic or palistrophic. The discussion which follows parallels my brief treatment in "Deuteronomium," *TRE* 8, 533–35.

Since the beginning of the nineteenth century, the brief initial division, 12:2–28, has served as the cornerstone for critical reconstructions of the histories of Israelite cult and literature. What lends such unusual importance to this legislation is, of course, the ostensible connection between its restriction of sacrificial rites and related ceremonies to a single sanctuary and the program to repristinate and unify the official Yahwistic cultus of greater Judah which, according to 2 Kings 22–23, was enforced by King [240] Josiah in the late seventh century B.C. Whether the rigorous measures attributed to Josiah were directly inspired by the Deuteronomic text continues to be debated, but there can be little doubt that they share a patriotic zeal for Yahwism, which identified cultic diversity and theological pluralism as prime threats to national cohesiveness. Thus the keynote prescriptions in 12:2–12 make a categorical distinction between the manifold installations of worship that Israel must destroy when it conquers its homeland and the singular sanctuary, "the place Yahweh your God will choose," where Israel's social solidarity under the rule of God is to be celebrated.[27] To be sure, this legislation attests important theological nuances and, by suppressing provincial religious practices, may have encouraged spiritualization of Yahwistic worship; but we should not overlook the fact that its overt purpose is to identify the unique institutional locus of Israel's communal life.

The second division, 12:29–17:13, is likewise but more comprehensively concerned with national integrity, defining corporate institutions, rites, and judicial procedures that are to sustain all Israel as the discrete people of Yahweh. Although prominent attention is given herein to such matters as dietary restrictions (14:3–21), sacral dues (14:22–9; 15:19–23), and national religious festivals (16:1–17), the focus is not cultic in a narrow sense. For example, the division opens with legislation empowering the community to initiate preemptive action against any individuals or groups in its own midst who promote sedition (chap. 13). Again, in 15:1–18 issues of broad social and economic import are addressed, with particular concern to institutionalize restrictions on the practice of debt-slavery. Most important of all for the preservation of political stability is the judicial system legislated in 16:18–17:13. It needs to be stressed that this system is expressly

27. The antiquity of the appellation for the single sanctuary cannot be demonstrated; it is most easily understood as a Deuteronomic designation for Zion and the Jerusalem Temple, based upon Judaean royal ideology: cf. Ps 78:67–69; 132:13–14; 1 Kgs 8:15–21; 2 Kgs 23:27. For suggestions regarding earlier roots, see Moshe Weinfeld, "The Emergence of the Deuteronomic Movement: The Historical Antecedents," *Das Deuteronomium,* 76–98.

grounded in the responsibility of the *whole* society to maintain justice; hence officers of the city courts in each tribal jurisdiction are both chosen by and act on behalf of the population at large (16:18–20).[28] Judicial procedures and restraints are treated in 17:2–13. [[241]] Of special importance here is the role of the judicial council, which is attached to the single sanctuary and comprised of levitical priests and a national "judge." Their function is not to serve as an appellate court per se but, like the Roman *juris consultus*, to issue authoritative directives regarding cases that local magistrates are unable to decide and bring before them (cf. 1:17). Moreover, 17:11 may be understood to include an extraordinary reference to the Deuteronomic polity itself: "You must act in strict accord with the *tôrâ*, which they shall interpret for you, and according to the precedent they cite for you; you shall not waver right or left from the decision they announce to you."

The constitutional significance of the matters treated in the central division, 17:14–18:22, has long been recognized though perhaps not sufficiently appreciated.[29] We learn first that monarchy is a *permissible* institution of the Yahwistic theocracy, but only so long as the election and prerogatives of the king are strictly delimited (17:14–17). While it is remarkable enough to find in an ancient document such restraints imposed on the powers of a nation's chief executive officer (and these restraints are by no means insubstantial in comparison with those of the celebrated Magna Carta of medieval England), what follows articulates a principle of constitutional government that we usually think to have been an innovation of the American political experience: The *only* positively specified task of the Israelite monarch is to study the written Deuteronomic polity throughout his reign and to serve as a national model of faithful obedience to its stipulations (17:18–20). Therefore the executive neither makes the law of the land nor stands above it. But he may be involved implicitly in its official interpretation as well as enforcement, for it is not unlikely that the king was supposed to function as the national "judge" who, according to 17:9–12, convened or otherwise sat with the judicial council of levitical priests. The latter are treated in the legislation that immediately follows (18:1–8). Because of their traditional claim to hold office by virtue of divine election alone and the broad authority given them in judicial as well as

28. It is possible that the Deuteronomic scheme represents a democratization of the judicial system which, according to 2 Chr 19:4–11, was introduced into Judah by king Jehoshaphat in the ninth century B.C. Cf. Georg Christian Macholz, "Zur Geschichte der Justizorganisation in Juda," *ZAW* 84, 314–40; and Moshe Weinfeld, "Judge and Officer in Ancient Israel and in the Ancient Near East," *IOS* 7 (1977) 65–88.

29. Cf. Spinoza, *Theological-Political Treatise*, 226; and esp. Lohfink, *Great Themes*, 58–72.

cultic affairs, the levitical priests potentially exercise more power than the king over the Israelite nation.[30] It is thus a constitutionally significant restriction that levitical guilds are granted no "territorial apportionment" (*ḥēleq wĕnaḥălâ*) with the rest of Israel. As the designated bureaucracy of the covenant people, however, levitical officials [[242]] are assured support through sacral taxes which must be contributed by those who do have holdings of land (18:1–4; cf. 14:27–29; 26:12–13). The central division concludes with paragraphs that place formidable restrictions on any other persons who might claim political authority by virtue of extra-constitutional knowledge of the divine will. Those who practice various forms of magic and divination are categorically dismissed (18:9–14); and while Israelite prophecy is indeed recognized, on the precedent of Moses' own role at Horeb, to be an authoritative mode of divine communication to the covenant people, the claims of individual prophets must be measured against stringent theological and pragmatic standards (18:15–22; cf. 13:2–6).

The constitutional reasoning of the first three divisions has moved a significant distance: from provision for the single sanctuary, which focuses Israel's corporate identity as one people under God (in sharp contrast to the cultic and national factionalisms of the land's previous inhabitants); through delineation of the political structures and common obligations that bind the Israelite nation together; and to delimitation of the social authority that can be exercised legitimately even by divinely "chosen" officers. This reasoning is completed in the final two divisions, where rights and responsibilities of individual citizens are brilliantly illuminated.

The fourth division, 19:1–25:19, is the longest in the polity; its varied contents are typically described by commentators as "miscellaneous," which indeed may have to be the case if one presupposes that the Torah document is a code of laws. Yet the logic of what is included and excluded herein becomes much clearer when we recognize the broader constitutional character of the polity. Matters treated in this division bring into relief the social policies that the covenant community is sworn to protect, above all the sanctity of life and the worth of individual personhood.[31] If these statutes seem more wide-ranging,

---

30. Cf. 10:8–9; 21:5; 31:9; 33:8–10. It may be pertinent to the likely role of "levitical priests" in the transmission and crystallization of the Deuteronomic legislation that 18:1–8 (see esp. v. 5) stands at the center point of the polity's literary design.

31. Insightful perspectives on the social, ideological, and cultural significance of this legislation may be gained from the following three, quite different studies: Anton Causse, "L'idéal politique et social du Deutéronome. La fraternité d'Israel," *RHPR* 13 (1933) 289–323; Mary Douglas, *Purity and Danger: An Analysis of Concepts of Pollution and*

formally diverse, and discretely focused than legislation in the preceding divisions, so much the better to show that it is not enough for society to affirm humanitarian ideals in the abstract. The quality of justice is measured by responsible procedures and specific results. Egalitarian justice, like political life itself, can only be [[243]] practiced in a social arena where basic values collide and concrete decisions must be made between divergent human interests. So it is that most of the statutes in this division deal with issues of conflict in which individual lives, livelihoods, and personal liberties are directly at stake. The consistent witness throughout is that each member of the larger community—whether male or female, child or adult, native born or sojourner, culprit or law-abiding citizen, land owner, laborer, or refugee slave— must be treated with the dignity due someone whose life is infinitely precious. Whenever society acts, as it must, to prosecute and punish those guilty of grievous offenses or even to pursue its well-being through warfare, the worth of all living things has to be respected. In short, this division more than any other segment of the constitution shows us in sensitive detail just what it means for the covenant community to claim identity as "a people holy to Yahweh your God" (7:6; 14:2, 21; 26:19); for if holiness involves corporate apotheosis, setting Israel apart from all other nations, it does so by making sanctification of life at once the prime objective of the whole social order and the political prerogative of everyone who resides in Israel's midst.[32]

The final division, 26:1–15, is elegantly brief, prescribing two liturgical acts which identify personal well-being and shared prosperity as reciprocal objectives of covenantal politics. Thus, after the land granted by God has been conquered and settled, those who harvest its bounties must regularly bring some of the produce to "the place Yahweh your God will choose" and there both individually acknowledge and communally celebrate the continuing providence of Israel's divine sovereign (26:1–11). Every third year, when the entire tithe of the annual harvests has been set aside by landholders to provide for the levitical bureaucracy and others who are wards of the state, confession of personal fidelity to God is followed by petition for God's renewed

---

Taboo (London: Routledge & Kegan Paul, 1966) 1–57; and Jacob J. Finkelstein, "The Goring Ox: Some Historical Perspectives on Deodands, Forfeitures, Wrongful Death and the Western Notion of Sovereignty," *Temple Law Quarterly* 46 (1973) 169–290, esp. 253–55, 269–72.

32. Cf. Num 16:3, where the revolutionary import of the Deuteronomic ideology of sacral personhood and democratized political authority apparently finds expression as the watchword of Korah's "levitical" rebellion.

blessing on the nation as a whole (26:12–15). So the concluding section of the polity brings us full circle, back to the institutional center of Israel's identity, where its public theology is celebrated (12:2–28; cf. 6:20–25).

The modest aim of the foregoing discussion has been to support Josephus' identification of the Deuteronomic "Book of the Torah" as a social charter of extraordinary literary coherence and political sophistication, thereby also recognizing the work to be the archetype of modern western constitutionalism. But a confessional word may be offered in conclusion: ⟦244⟧ For Jews and Christians committed to the continuing struggle for social justice and human rights, the Deuteronomic model of theocentric humanism remains an eminently practicable legacy.

Covenant in a Century of Study since Wellhausen

E. W. NICHOLSON

[[54]] Not so long ago covenant was among the least controversial issues in Old Testament study. Arguably, indeed, it was the least controversial of all. There was virtual unanimity among scholars that God's covenant with Israel was among the most ancient features of Israelite religion and was fundamentally constitutive of its distinctiveness from the outset. Those of you who were my contemporaries as students in the 1950s will recall how we were familiarized with this in the prescribed textbooks and other recommended reading of the time, in, for example, the widely used histories of Israel by John Bright and Martin Noth, or Bernhard Anderson's popular *The Living World of the Old Testament*, in those well-known monographs by G. Ernest Wright as well as in standard works from influential British scholars, most notably H. H. Rowley. It came to us from our teachers and from books such as these as something of an "assured result" of Old Testament research long since established and accepted among scholars internationally. Indeed, you will recall that exactly at that time, in the mid-1950s, a new phase in covenant-study was launched by G. E. Mendenhall's famous essay in the *Biblical Archaeologist* which seemed to offer remarkable proof from a quite unexpected source—Hittite treaties of the Late Bronze Age—of just how assured we could be about that "assured result." There followed, into the 1960s, a seemingly endless flow of monographs, articles and notes on "treaty and covenant" further buttressing the well-established consensus. At the same time there began to appear in ever increasing numbers translations of important German works, both old and new, by such internationally renowned figures as A. Alt, A. Weiser,

Reprinted with permission from *Crises and Perspectives* (OTS 24; Leiden: Brill, 1986) 54–69.

W. Eichrodt, G. von Rad, W. Zimmerli which we could now as teachers introduce to our students and which further illustrated, if that were needed, just how universally accepted was this view of the antiquity and fundamental importance of the covenant.

But the 1960s, though they saw the appearance of still further works in support of the received view, saw also a new challenge to it, and the decade ended with the publication of L. Perlitt's remarkably vigorous [[55]] and impressively detailed *Bundestheologie im Alten Testament* which incisively shook confidence in it and argued that the notion of a covenant between God and Israel was after all a theologoumenon coined in the late pre-exilic period, just as Wellhausen had maintained in his *Geschichte Israels I* in 1878. Thus a century or so of study had brought us back to where it began, and there is now renewed controversy about an issue which had seemed long settled, just as there was in the years which followed the publication of Wellhausen's momentous work.

My purpose in this paper is to outline the history of research which has led full circle back to Wellhausen, first because it may help to explain why we are where we are currently on this subject, and second because it may also help to point the way forward. My introductory remarks have already indicated four main phases in the study of covenant since Wellhausen: the debate which followed his work, a second phase which brought about the consensus to which I have referred, a third phase which endeavoured to consolidate this on the basis of ancient Near Eastern suzerainty treaties, and, finally, the current situation in the wake of Perlitt's work.

I

The controversy which Wellhausen's work generated and which yielded a variety of conflicting views on the origin and nature of the covenant is of some interest in itself, and I shall briefly mention some of these views. But my main purpose in taking you back to that period of controversy, which persisted from the publication of his *Geschichte Israels I* to the end of the First World War, is that it sets in sharp relief the remarkable unanimity of opinion on the subject which very quickly came about in the immediately following years, and raises the question how such unanimity suddenly appeared where hitherto there had been marked division of opinion. Further, that division of opinion was not simply between critical scholarship in adherence to Wellhausen on the one side, and conservative, church apologists on the other. Critical scholarship itself was divided on the issue, and scholars who shared

Wellhausen's methods and conclusions on other important matters were opposed to each other on this one.

I mention but a few who came down on his side of the debate. He had the weighty support of B. Stade in his monumental *Geschichte des Volkes Israel* and other works, and notable, detailed studies of the covenant texts in the Old Testament by, for example, R. Kraetzschmar and J. J. P. Valeton [[56]] likewise supported him or at least substantially so. Or again, though scholars such as K. Budde and H. Gunkel argued against him that a covenant was made at Sinai, it was merely to conclude that this was a covenant between the Israelites and the Kenites or Midianites, not between God and Israel; the notion of this latter covenant, they agreed with Wellhausen, arose only as a much later development.

On the other side, however, there was no shortage of disagreement with Wellhausen's view. Stade's history of Israel in support of it was matched by R. Kittel's influential *Geschichte der Hebräer* opposing it. Within the ranks of the "history-of-religions movement" H. Gressmann differed from his close colleague Gunkel on this issue, finding, for example, that the short narrative in Exod 24:9–11—the eating of a meal in the presence of God on the holy mountain—is a covenant-making tradition of very great antiquity. Similarly, in an article which has remained influential to this day, C. Steuernagel, who identified himself with many of Wellhausen's critical views, argued that the covenant blood-ritual in Exod 24:3–8 is also of great antiquity, possibly even reflecting a covenant ceremony of the pre-settlement period. Others attacked Wellhausen's view at its heart, rejecting his understanding of early Israelite religion as a "natural bond" between God and the people. Rather, it was a religion grounded in historical events which, interpreted by Moses, pointed to the divine election of Israel which was consolidated by the making of a covenant between Yahweh and his newly appropriated people (so, for example, F. Giesebrecht in his influential monograph *Die Geschichtlichkeit des Sinaibundes*). Here in England, W. Robertson Smith too, for all his admiration of Wellhausen's work, opposed him on the matter of the covenant. He argued that from the time of Moses onwards Yahweh was no mere natural clan deity but the God of a confederation for which a covenant religion was entirely appropriate. That is, the covenant was no mere "theological idea" of a late period but performed an ancient religio-sociological function, as we may describe it, uniting diverse groups with each other and with their common God Yahweh—an understanding of the origin and nature of the covenant in the earliest period of Israel's history which, as we shall see, was later to become widely favoured.

This is a sufficient, though far from exhaustive, description of the debate which Wellhausen's work generated during the period to which

I refer. Very remarkably, however, as I have already indicated, the controversy rapidly disappeared in the years immediately following the First World War, and within little more than a decade the consensus which I mentioned earlier had established itself. [[57]]

II

A striking illustration of the shift which now took place from controversy to widespread agreement is provided by Gunkel's article on "Moses" for the second edition of *Die Religion in Geschichte und Gegenwart* in 1930. In the first edition of this article in 1913 he had written: "Um Sinai hat M(ose) dann die Stämme gesammelt und einen Bund mit den Midianitern geschlossen." ("Moses then assembled the tribes at Sinai and made a covenant between them and the Midianites.") In the second edition, however, this same sentence was changed to read: "Um Sinai hat M(ose) dann die Stämme gesammelt und durch einen 'Bund' Jahves mit ihnen sie innerlich geeinigt." ("Moses then assembled the tribes at Sinai and by means of a covenant of Yahweh with them gave them an inner unity.")

The arguments which now so widely prevailed were as follows.

1. The view already argued in the preceding period that the covenant was from the outset a necessary feature of Israelite religion as a religion founded upon historical events, a religion of "election" and not a "natural bond," now found fresh and widespread emphasis. One thinks especially in this connection of influential works by J. Hempel, A. Weiser, K. Galling, and most notably W. Eichrodt's well-known *Theologie des Alten Testaments*.

2. Crucially significant, and lastingly so, was M. Noth's famous monograph *Das System der zwölf Stämme Israels* in which he argued that Israel originated as a confederation of tribes founded upon a covenant between them and their common God Yahweh. With this work a point of stability was achieved for understanding the covenant, not as a theological *idea*, but as an *institution* which was formative and normative in Israelite society and religion from the outset.

3. Contributions from S. Mowinckel during the 1920s were also influential, first his *Psalmenstudien I–VI* (especially the second volume *Das Thronbesteigungsfest Jahwäs und der Ursprung der Eschatologie*) and then still more especially his monograph *Le Décalogue*. In these works he argued not only that the covenant was an essential feature of Israelite society and religion but also that

a "renewal of the covenant" formed a significant part of an annual cultic festival centring upon Yahweh's kingship as creator of the world and Lord of his people Israel, and he found evidence of the influence of this liturgy upon, for example, the form and contents of the Sinai pericope in Exodus 19–24. The influence of Mowinckel's ideas can be seen in works by, for example, A. Alt, A. Weiser, and G. von Rad which in turn were themselves widely influential.

⟦58⟧ Why was it that these arguments so effectively dispelled the controversy which had hitherto abounded on the matter of the nature and antiquity of the covenant? After all, as you will have noticed, they were not wholly new. The first was familiar among those who opposed Wellhausen's view in the preceding generation, and the second is clearly akin to W. Robertson Smith's suggestion made much earlier than the covenant would have performed a necessary religio-sociological function in early Israel as a tribal society.

Due weight must be given to the vigour and fresh detail in which they were now newly argued. For example, whilst it had been suggested much earlier that pre-monarchic Israel took the form of a tribal "amphictyony," it was not until Noth's epoch-making monograph that it was presented in such detail and so compellingly. But when allowance has been fully made for the powerful advocacy which these views now received, and for the new insights advanced by Mowinckel, other important trends contributed significantly, indeed decisively, to the consensus which now emerged and which was to prove so durable concerning the nature and antiquity of the covenant.

A variety of trends converged to focus increasing attention upon the distinctiveness of Israelite religion and of Old Testament faith and piety. For example, though the "history-of-religions movement" now began to go into decline, its well-known quest for the individuality (*Eigentümlichkeit*) of Israel, its culture and religion, remained as a legacy which served to emphasise the covenant as a conspicuously distinctive feature of Israelite religion. Still more influential in this connection was the emerging Neo-orthodoxy of those years. Its emphasis upon revelation "von oben nach unten" and its corresponding denigration of "natural theology" created a climate conducive to an emphasis upon Israel's history as the arena of God's self-revelation, and gave increased impetus to discerning the uniqueness of Israel's faith which from now onwards was more and more regarded as having been radically discontinuous with the religious thought-world of its environment. All this led to increased attention upon the "particularist" elements of Israelite faith such as the "saving history," "election," and "covenant." The notion that Israelite religion began as something of a "natural bond" was abandoned; indeed, nothing could have been more alien to the new theological climate of the time than such a view. In addition, darkly ominous during those years after the First World War was the beginning of a new upsurge of anti-semitism in Germany which carried with it a call for the abandonment of the Old Testament as part of the church's scriptures. Reaction to this yielded a corresponding fresh emphasis upon the abiding value of Old Testament faith and piety, including its covenant-theology. To this [[59]] may be further added that a theology of "the people of God," of which the covenant grounded in that people's confessional choice formed such an important basis, became a subject of increasing interest in a situation which had begun to give rise to racially-based German *Volkstum.*

But much more significant than these various trends, because it was much more direct, was the influence that now came from the sociology of religion which had entered its modern era largely through the work of Emil Durkheim and, of special interest for Old Testament research, Max Weber.

In broad terms, it may be said that whereas hitherto a society's religion had come to be regarded as one feature among others in its life, one social phenomenon among other such phenomena, it was now seen to be a formative and normative force, creative in forms of social life and organization. Religious beliefs and practices with their related institutions were now viewed as belonging to the very "nuts and bolts," so to speak, of a society, creating solidarity among its members and influencing powerfully many aspects of its life. As a result, attention was now increasingly focused upon the *function* of religious beliefs and commitments in the making and development of a society.

I cannot here describe in detail why Weber devoted himself to a study of ancient Israelite religion in his work *Das antike Judentum* which first appeared as articles in 1917–19 and then as the third volume of his *Gesammelte Aufsätze zur Religionssoziologie* in 1921. His primary interest was in the relation between a society's religion and its economic activity. For our purpose what is important is the predominant role he assigned to the covenant in the foundation of Israelite society and religion and in their subsequent history. From the outset Israel was an "oathbound confederation"; by means of a covenant Yahweh became partner to the ritualistic and social order of the confederation. Thus the covenant was no mere "theoretical construction," but was the basis of the cohesion which existed between the otherwise diverse groups which became known as Israel. For Israel the deliverance from bondage in Egypt was seen as a token of God's power and of the absolute dependability of his promises, and also of Israel's lasting debt of gratitude. The uniqueness of the exodus was constituted by the fact that this miracle was wrought by a god until then unknown by Israel who thereupon accepted him as its God by means of a solemn covenant. This covenant was based upon mutual pledges bilaterally mediated through Moses: Yahweh by this means gave his solemn promises to Israel and accepted Israel's pledges of obedience to his holy enactments. And since Yahweh was a partner to the covenant, all violations of these enactments were violations of the solemn agreement between him and Israel: the confederacy law was thus jealously guarded [[60]] by Yahweh. Further development of the confederacy law was carried out on a covenantal basis. Weber also argued that already in the pre-monarchic period the Levites became exponents and teachers, and thus transmitters, of the divine law. The pre-classical prophets were likewise custodians of the covenance enactments which at a later time similarly underlay the preaching of the great prophets.

The decisive role of its religion in the foundation and making of Israel as a people and a nation had long been a prominent interest among students of the Old Testament. Not surprisingly, therefore, they were a receptive audience to this new emphasis in the field of sociology upon just such a creative role of religion in societies generally. Leading figures such as Kittel and Gressmann, in programmatic essays in the 1920s on the future tasks of Old Testament research, urged attention to the insights which this field was currently offering, and they made special reference to Weber's impressive and in so many ways fascinating work. They were not hammering on closed doors. The scholarly literature in our subject during those years, and notably that which concerned itself in one way or another with the origin and significance of the covenant, contains numerous references to Weber's work. This can be seen in contributions by, for example, Alt, Weiser, Hempel, Galling, Eichrodt, and Noth. As far as I am aware, the only serious critical dissent came from W. Caspari. The view that the covenant originated at the earliest time as the means whereby the disparate elements of Israel were united and held together and bound to Yahweh their common God now became widely approved. In fact the matter can be summed up succinctly as follows: though other important influences came to bear on the issue, Weber's work was crucially decisive in swinging scholarship away from controversy on it to the view that the covenant was of the essence of Israelite religion and society from the earliest period of its history. From within the ranks of Old Testament scholars proper Noth's monograph on pre-monarchic Israel as a sacral confederation firmly established such a view and gave it the widest possible currency for a generation to come.

III

Time does not permit me to document the widespread reception of this understanding of the antiquity and significance of the covenant in the writings of scholars during the inter-war and immediate post-Second World War years. I must move ahead to the third phase of covenant research since Wellhausen, that which concerned itself with the evidence of ancient Near Eastern suzerainty treaties.

[[61]] As I mentioned earlier, Mendenhall's essay in the *Biblical Archaeologist* in 1954 launched this new phase. He accepted the dominant view of earlier research of the socio-religious and institutional nature of the covenant in Israelite origins and history. Since Israel did not emerge in the genealogical manner described in the Old Testament, it can only have been the covenant, he maintained, that constituted the basis of the relationship between the tribes. What was lacking in the discussion hitherto, however, was a concept of a covenant which would have bound together the tribes and at the same time would have formed a foundation for their belief that in this event Yahweh became the God of Israel. This difficulty is overcome, Mendenhall argued, once it is seen that the type of covenant which operated was modelled upon the Hittite treaty-form whereby a great king bound his vassals to faithfulness to himself and at the same time ordered relationships between these vassals themselves as subjects of the same overlord. Further and significantly, this particular treaty-form was contemporary with Israelite origins in the Late Bronze Age. He then went on to argue that the decalogue in Exodus 20 and other covenant texts in the Old Testament display the influence of that treaty-form.

A spate of monographs and articles by others followed, further developing and elaborating Mendenhall's tersely stated thesis, and treaty texts from the neo-Assyrian period of the first millennium were now also brought into the discussion. In addition to the influence of the treaty-form upon Old Testament covenant texts, the use of individual words and phrases in these texts was now likewise traced to the treaty literature, for example, the "father-son" relationship as applied to Yahweh and Israel, "to know" Yahweh in the sense of acknowledging his legitimate claims as Israel's suzerain, the command "to love" Yahweh, the description of Israel as Yahweh's *s⁽e⁾gullāh* "special possession"; it was suggested that even the central demand of the covenant texts for Israel's exclusive allegiance to Yahweh may have been influenced by the demand of suzerains in the treaty texts for the exclusive loyalty of their vassals.

Many were persuaded by all or much of this, and I include myself among them. But further reflection has convinced me that this phase in covenant research is one that in fact has yielded little that is of lasting value.

In his well-known study *Treaty and Covenant* D. J. McCarthy effectively disposed of the view that the Sinai pericope in Exodus 19–24 was influenced by the Hittite treaties. The resemblances are merely superficial; the pericope lacks essential features of the Hittite treaties such as a historical prologue and the curses and blessings formulae. Rather, McCarthy argued, the pericope witnesses to an ancient ritualistic covenant-making tradition in Israel which was foreign to the treaty tradition. It is [[62]] only in late texts such as 1 Samuel 12 and Joshua 24, which he classified as "proto-Deuteronomic," and most prominently in Deuteronomy itself that the influence of the treaties manifests itself, specifically the form and terminology of the neo-Assyrian treaties. M. Weinfeld in his full-length study supported McCarthy's conclusions in this respect.

But the same observation which McCarthy made about the Sinai pericope may also be made about Deuteronomy, namely, that the resemblances between it and the treaty-form as exemplified in the neo-Assyrian treaties are more apparent than real. The pronounced historical element in the prologue to Deuteronomy has nothing resembling it in these treaties, and the laws in Deuteronomy are much broader in their scope than the treaty stipulations. In the works of both McCarthy and Weinfeld the weight of the analogy in fact rests upon Deuteronomy 28, the long list of curses which resembles the similarly long lists in the Assyrian treaties and indeed seems to incorporate some formulations from these treaties.

Yet here too there is a significant difference, for Deuteronomy 28 also includes a list of blessings, a feature lacking in the contemporary Assyrian treaties. Further, it is only by an uncritical acceptance of the curse list in Deuteronomy 28 as the work of a single author, or substantially so, that it can then be argued that this author in drawing up such a long list was seeking to emulate the lists in the treaties. Indeed, there has been something of an argument in a circle in this matter: the treaty lists are appealed to for proof that the curse list in Deuteronomy 28 is a unity, or substantially so, and then Deuteronomy 28, established as a unity on this basis, is appealed to as evidence that its author was influenced by the treaty lists. But the majority of commentators are agreed that Deuteronomy 28 developed in several stages, and if, as seems likely, this is so, then neither the length of the list nor its heavy emphasis upon curse can be regarded as the planned work of a single author seeking to emulate the long curse lists in the treaties. The end result may look like such a treaty list, but neither in origin nor in its subsequent stage-by-stage expansion was it consciously intended as such. The heavy emphasis upon curse in this chapter is readily explained by the historical circumstance that it was developed and expanded during a period—the late seventh and early sixth centuries B.C.—when curse was seen to hover more and more ominously over the nation and then fell catastrophically upon it in the events of 597 and 587 B.C. Thus the threat which had accompanied the giving of Yahweh's *Torah* was sharply augmented, in both length and severity; Israel's crime was thus made to fit the foreordained punishment, and so the punishment fitted the crime.

[63] At another but, I think, no less important level, it has in any case to be asked whether the suzerain-vassal analogy would have had any appeal of an apt or desirable nature in ancient Israel. Notwithstanding all the references in the treaties to the "love" of suzerain for vassal and of vassal for suzerain, to the suzerain as "father" and the vassal as "son," such relationships were surely rarely if ever like that. Vassals did not as a rule "love" those who conquered and dominated them, and the very language of intimate and familial relationships employed in the treaties reflects, not the reality of the relationships, but the politically, strategically and economically motivated endeavour of suzerains to maintain with the least amount of trouble possible the subservience of subject states. To tell Israelites that Yahweh "loves" them in the same way as Ashurbanipal or Nebuchadrezzar "loves" his vassals, including Israel, and that they are to "love" Yahweh as vassals "love" their suzerains would surely have been a bizarre depiction of Yahweh's love for his people and of the love with which they were called upon to respond to him. The use in Deuteronomy and related texts of such imagery as the "father-son" relationship, the command to "love" Yahweh, "to know" Yahweh, and so forth, need not be seen as a borrowing from treaty texts. Rather, it is more plausibly explained as the result of borrowing on the part of both treaty scribes and the biblical authors from a common and self-evident source: the familiar settings of everyday life.

IV

The attempt to relate the Old Testament covenant to suzerainty treaties may be said to represent a dead-end in the social/functional approach; the search for a model that will explain how the covenant functioned in the religious and social life of ancient Israel here overreaches itself. More than this, it is apparent in prominent works of the treaty approach such as those by McCarthy and Weinfeld that they themselves have gone some way towards cancelling it. Both of these scholars still insist that there was a covenant in the earliest stages of Israelite history which exercised some sort of socio-religious function. But in their consideration of the influence of the treaties they have begun to understand it as having become a metaphor or analogy for the relationship between God and his people. Thus what began with Mendenhall as an attempt to buttress the received view of the socio-religious and institutional nature of the covenant, represents in its later stages something of a shift back to understanding it as a theological ideal or analogy. On a different basis a contribution from G. Fohrer in the mid-1960s represents something of the same shift. Already a few years earlier, C. F. Whitley [[64]] in a brief discussion had restated Wellhausen's main conclusion that the covenant was a late innovation in Israelite religion. Thus the course of research since Wellhausen began to turn full circle, and was completed most notably by Perlitt's work, alongside which may also be mentioned that of E. Kutsch. For both of these scholars the notion of a covenant between Yahweh and Israel was a theological concept of the late pre-exilic period, a creation of the Deuteronomic movement of the seventh century B.C. designed to meet specifically theological needs and crises which confronted Israel at that relatively late time.

Kutsch's work is the most detailed study of the word $b^e r \bar{\imath} t$ since Kraetzschmar's monograph in 1896. I do not think it is successful (see especially J. Barr's critique in the Zimmerli Festschrift). His intention is to determine the meaning of the word from its various contexts in the Old Testament. But in essence he seems to be guided by an etymological approach, a search for a *Grundbedeutung*. This he finds to be "obligation," and he concludes that a $b^e r \bar{\imath} t$ consisted of the unilateral imposition or acceptance of an obligation; *Verpflichtung* rather than *Bund* is the proper way to understand the word.

The discovery of such a "common denominator," however, shows only that it was simply that: one particular feature that was part of what it meant to make a $b^e r \bar{\imath} t$; and it is a mistake to proceed from this, as Kutsch does, to the conclusion that $b^e r \bar{\imath} t$ can then be represented simply by "obligation," as though a $b^e r \bar{\imath} t$ necessarily consisted solely of this, and this exhausted the semantic range of the word. The word itself refrains from mapping out the various distinctions which Kutsch wishes to draw between one kind of a $b^e r \bar{\imath} t$ and another. It is the context alone which determines this, and if, with Kutsch's own stated intention, we are to ascertain the meaning of the word not from its etymon, whatever that may be, but from its usage, then it is difficult to see how, as it seems, he can regard the bilateral connotation of the word in some contexts as a secondary or exceptional use of it. It seems rather than the semantic range of the word was such that it could be used indifferently for unilateral and bilateral arrangements. It seems indeed that this one word in Biblical Hebrew had to do service for a range of activities which in, say, English are covered by such terms as "agreement," "treaty," "contract," "promise," "obligation," and the like.

Whilst Kutsch's study of the word *bᵉrît* is the most detailed since Kraetzschmar's monograph of 1896, Perlitt's book is the most detailed presentation yet of the view that Israel's covenant traditions are the product of a late period and arose in response to various theological needs and crises. He begins where the theological use of the word *bᵉrît* is most expansively and intensively employed, that is, in the Deuteronomic/Deuteronomistic [[65]] corpus of the seventh and sixth centuries B.C., whence he moves to other texts to determine whether its theological usage is a product of the late period in which it is most in evidence or of earlier origin. He finds that none of these other texts witnesses to a pre-Deuteronomic origin of a covenant-theology, not even the book of Hosea where the one clear reference to a covenant between Yahweh and Israel (8:1) is a secondary, Deuteronomistic addition (6:7, he maintains, has nothing to do with such a covenant).

V

In the works of both Perlitt and Kutsch, conspicuously so in Kutsch's many contributions on the subject, there is a marked scaling-down of the significance usually attached to the covenant in the study of the Old Testament. This, together with other shifts of interest in current research, has contributed to something of an eclipse in the study of covenant recently. And in any case, a century or so of debate which was turned full circle back virtually to where it began may understandably be considered to have run itself into the ground, leavening "covenant" as seemingly rather a played-out concept for students of the Old Testament.

In the few minutes that remain to me I can state only very briefly the gains I consider to have been made in the recent stages of the debate together with a proposal which I offer as a way of helping to place the study of the covenant firmly once again on the agenda of Old Testament research.[1]

In two main respects I would align myself with Perlitt's conclusions. First, I welcome the shift away from understanding the covenant as having been originally an institution which operated in the formation of

1. I provide a fuller discussion of this and of the survey in the foregoing pages in my book *God and His People: Covenant and Theology in the Old Testament* (Oxford, 1986).

Israel as a tribal society. None of the descriptions of the making of the covenant provides any evidence that any part of its purpose was to unite the diverse tribes into a tribal league. That the tribes already belong together as "Israel" is the presupposition of each of these texts. What they concentrate on is Israel's relationship with, and commitment to, God as the people chosen by him for his own. That is, in origin the covenant had to do with an ideal or vision of what it meant to be "the people of Yahweh." I shall say something more about this below.

Second, I am persuaded that the notion of such a covenant was a relative latecomer in the history of Israelite religion. Against Perlitt, I believe that the references to it in Hosea are authentic; but on the other [[66]] hand, I do not believe that we can with any confidence trace its origins further back than the period of this prophet, and it is in any case clear that it received its most intensive and expansive treatment at the hands of Deuteronomic authors of the late pre-exilic and the exilic period.

In these two respects Perlitt's work has, in my opinion, fully vindicated the position of Wellhausen. Beyond this I find a further insight of Wellhausen which provides a basis not only for a way forward in the debate about the covenant but also for a fresh understanding of how crucial it was in the development of what is distinctive in the faith of ancient Israel. He wrote of the great prophets of the eighth century as having effected a decisive change in Israel's perception of its relationship with God by breaking the mould of a "natural bond" between them and transferring the relationship unto the plane of moral response and commitment. My proposal is that in this also Wellhausen was correct and, further, that the notion of a covenant between Yahweh and Israel arose as one of the results of the decisive change these prophets brought about. And here the sociology of religion which in earlier stages of the debate seemed to offer an attractive but ultimately misleading line of enquiry, since it diverted scholarship into a wild goose chase after a very early, socially operative covenant, still has some useful insights to offer.

I refer to the arguments of such recent writers as Peter Berger, on the basis of lines already laid down by thinkers such as Durkheim and Weber, that religion and religious concepts have as one of their most important roles the legitimation of particular sorts of social order. Now if such an analysis is applied to ancient Israel (as it has been, at least implicitly, by H. H. Schmid) one can trace a highly distinctive development, in which a phase where religion legitimates society is succeeded by one in which a new style of religious thought emerges that challenges and de-legitimates the apparently stable and divinely ordained social structures. The crucial figures in bringing about this transformation were (as Wellhausen correctly saw) the classical prophets. But if covenant-theology was also a creation of this same period, then the conclusion that the covenant idea itself is intimately bound up with the vast religious change which these prophets initiated lies close to hand.

The proposal with which I conclude, therefore, is that covenant-language served as the focal point for that desacralization of a religious society of which the prophets were the chief agents. The concept of a covenant between Yahweh and Israel is, in terms of "cash-value," the concept that religion is based, not on a natural or ontological equivalence between the divine realm and the human, but on *choice*: God's choice of his people and their "choice" of him (cf. for example Deut 26:17–19; 27:9–10; Josh 24:22), that is, their free decision to be obedient and [[67]] faithful to him. Thus understood, the covenant is a central expression of the distinctive faith of Israel as "the people of Yahweh," children of God by adoption and free decision rather than by nature or necessity. This has been obscured somewhat by too narrow a concentration on questions of terminology, and lost sight of altogether in the (fruitless) quest to find ancient parallels in the sphere of social institutions. So far from being a social institution, the covenant represents the refusal of prophets and their disciples to encapsulate Yahweh's relationship with his people in institutions, and to insist that it depends on a moral commitment on both sides which needs to be continually reaffirmed in faithful conduct, not taken for granted as though it were part of the order of nature.

Just how dominant was this element of response and freely-given commitment in the covenant concept may be seen from the "new covenant" prophecy in Jer 31:31–34, where an insistence on the non-automatic character of the covenant is maintained even in a passage which is precisely concerned to say that God's grace is in the future to be bestowed without the requirement of any human response, and that it is, indeed, guaranteed; so imbued is the author with the idea that the covenant was a two-sided affair with a no built-in guarantees that he is constrained to produce a paradoxical theory according to which God himself promises to make possible the very response which he inexorably demands.

So far from being merely one among a wide range of terms and ideas that emerged, flourished, and had their day, the covenant is, therefore, a central theme that served to focus an entirely idiosyncratic way of looking at the relationship between God and his people, and indeed, between God and the world. As such it deserves to be put back squarely on the agenda for students of the Old Testament.

Bibliography

Alt, A., *Die Ursprünge des Israelitischen Rechts*, Leipzig 1934, reprinted in his *Kleine Schriften* I, Munich 1953, 278–332; E.trs. "The Origins of Israelite Law," *Essays on Old Testament History and Religion*, Oxford 1966, 79–132.

Anderson, B. W., *The Living World of the Old Testament*, Englewood Cliffs 1957 and London 1958.

Barr, J., "Some Semantic Notes on the Covenant," *Beiträge zur Alttestamentlichen Theologie, Festschrift für Walther Zimmerli zum 70. Geburtstag*, ed. H. H. Donner, R. Hanhart, R. Smend, Göttingen 1977, 23–38.

Berger, P., *The Social Reality of Religion*, London 1969.

Bright, J., *A History of Israel*, London 1960.

Budde, K., *The Religion of Israel to the Exile*, New York and London 1899.
Die Religion des Volkes Israel bis zur Verbannung, Giessen 1990.

Caspari, W., *Die Gottesgemeinde am Sinai und das nachmalige Volk Israel*, BFChrTh 27, Gütersloh 1922. [[68]]

Eichrodt, E., *Theologie des Alten Testaments* I, Leipzig 1933, II, 1935, III, 1939. E.trs. *Theology of the Old Testament* I, London 1961 (from the sixth German edition of vol. I, Stuttgart 1959), II, London 1967 (from the fifth German edition of vols. II and III, Stuttgart 1964).

Fohrer, G., "Altes Testament—'Amphiktyonie' und 'Bund'?," *TLZ* 91, 1966, cols. 801–16 and 894–904.

Galling, K., *Die Erwählungstraditionen Israels*, BZAW 48, Giessen 1928.

Giesebrecht, F., *Die Geschichtlichkeit des Sinaibundes*, Königsberg 1900.

Gressmann, H., *Mose und seine Zeit. Ein Kommentar zu den Mose-Sagen*, FRLANT, N.F. 1, Göttingen 1913.
"Die Aufgaben der alttestamentlichen Forschung," *ZAW* 42, 1924, 1–33.

Gunkel, H., "Mose," *Die Religion in Geschichte und Gegenwart*, 1st ed., vol. IV, Tübingen 1913, cols. 516–24.
"Mose," *Die Religion in Geschichte und Gegenwart*, 2d ed., vol. IV, Tübingen 1930, cols. 230–7.

Hempel, J., *Gott und Mensch im Alten Testament. Studie zur Geschichte der Frömmigkeit*, BWANT III:2, Stuttgart 1926.

Kittel, R., *Geschichte der Hebräer* I, Gotha 1888. E.trs. *A History of the Hebrews* I, London and Edinburgh 1895.
"Die Zukunft der alttestamentliche Wissenschaft," *ZAW* 39, 1921, 84–99.

Kraetzschmar, R., *Die Bundesvorstellung im Alten Testament in ihrer geschichtlichen Entwickelung*, Marburg 1896.

Kutsch, E., *Verheissung und Gesetz. Untersuchungen zum sogenannten "Bund" im Alten Testament*, BZAW 131, Berlin and New York 1973.

McCarthy, D. J., *Treaty and Covenant*, Analecta Biblica 21, Rome 1963, 2d rev. ed., Analecta Biblica 21A, Rome 1978.

Mendenhall, G. E., "Covenant Forms in Israelite Tradition," *BA* 17, 1954, 50–76.

Mowinckel, S., *Psalmenstudien II. Das Thronbesteigungsfest Jahwäs und der Ursprung der Eschatologie*, Kristiania 1922.
Le Décalogue, Paris, 1927.

Noth, M., *Das System der zwölf Stämme Israels*, BWANT IV:1, Stuttgart 1930.
  Geschichte Israels, Göttingen 1950. E.trs. *The History of Israel*, 2d rev. ed.,
  London 1960.
Perlitt, L., *Bundestheologie im Alten Testament*, WMANT 36, Neukirchen-Vluyn
  1969.
Rad, G. von, *Das formgeschichtliche Problem des Hexateuch*, BWANT IV:26, Stuttgart
  1938, reprinted in his *Gesammelte Studien zum Alten Testament*, Munich 1958,
  9–81. E.trs. "The Form-Critical Problem of the Hexateuch," *The Problem of
  the Hexateuch and Other Essays*, Edinburgh and London 1966, 1–78.
Rowley, H. H., *The Biblical Doctrine of Election*, London 1950.
  From Joseph to Joshua: Biblical Traditions in the Light of Archaeology, London
  1950.
Schmid, H. H., *Altorientalische Welt in der alttestamentlichen Theologie*, Zürich
  1974.
Smith, W. Robertson, *The Religion of the Semites*, London 1889.
Stade, B., *Geschichte des Volkes Israel* I, Berlin 1887.
Steuernagel, C., "Der jehovistische Bericht über den Bundesschluss am Sinai,"
  ThStK 72, 1899, 319–50.
Valeton, J. J. P., "Bedeutung und Stellung des Wortes ברית im Priestercodex,"
  ZAW 12, 1892, 1–22.
  "Das Wort ברית in den jehovistischen und deuteronomischen Stücken des
  Hexateuchs, sowie in den verwandten historischen Büchern," *ZAW* 12,
  1892, 224–60.
  "Das Wort ברית bei den Propheten und in den Ketubim. Resultat," *ZAW*
  13, 1893, 245–79.
Weber, M., *Das antike Judentum, Gesammelte Aufsätze zur Religionssoziologie* III,
  Tübingen 1921. E.trs. *Ancient Judaism*, London 1952.
Weinfeld, M., *Deuteronomy and the Deuteronomic School*, Oxford 1972.
Weiser, A., *Die Bedeutung des Alten Testaments für den Religionsunterricht*, Giessen
  1925, [[69]] reprinted in *Glaube und Geschichte im Alten Testament und andere
  ausgewählte Schriften*, Göttingen 1961, 19–50.
  Glaube und Geschichte im Alten Testament, BWANT IV:4, Stuttgart 1932, [[69]]
  reprinted in *Glaube und Geschichte im Alten Testament und andere ausgewählte
  Schriften*, 99–182.
Wellhausen, J., *Geschichte Israels I*, Berlin 1878, 2d ed. published as *Prolegomena
  zur Geschichte Israels*, Berlin 1883. E.trs. *Prolegomena to the History of Israel*,
  Edinburgh 1885.
Whitley, C. F., "Covenant and Commandment in Israel," *JNES* 22, 1963, 37–48.
Wright, G. E., "How did Early Israel differ from her Neighbours?," *BA* 6, 1943,
  1–20.
  The Old Testament Against Its Environment, London 1950.
  God Who Acts, London 1952.
Zimmerli, W., *The Law and the Prophets*, London 1965.

Deuteronomy and the Central Sanctuary

GORDON J. WENHAM

[103] For nearly a century it has been almost axiomatic to hold that Deuteronomy demands centralization of all worship at a single sanctuary, and therefore that its composition must be associated with Josiah's attempt to limit all worship to Jerusalem. From time to time this view has been challenged. A. C. Welch, for instance, showed that 'the place which the LORD will choose' need not refer to a single sanctuary, but could, if other grounds warranted it, refer to a group of approved Yahweh shrines.[1] Welch also pointed out that the command to offer sacrifice on Mount Ebal (explicit in Deuteronomy 27 and implicit in chapter 11) is very odd if Deuteronomy is a programme to limit all worship to Jerusalem.

Recently J. N. M. Wijngaards has argued that Deuteronomy does not envisage centralization of worship at Jerusalem but a series of sanctuaries serving in turn as the amphictyonic shrine.[2] Deuteronomy 5–28 is essentially a liturgy for a ceremonial procession from Succoth to Shechem re-enacting the crossing of the Jordan and the conquest of Canaan. The grounds for this novel interpretation are threefold. First, Deuteronomy constantly mentions that Israel is about to cross over the

Reprinted with permission from *Tyndale Bulletin* 22 (1971) 103–18.

This paper is a revised form of one chapter of the writer's thesis, *The Structure and Date of Deuteronomy*, accepted for the degree of Doctor of Philosophy at the University of London, 1970.

1. *The Code of Deuteronomy*, J. Clarke, London (1924) and *Deuteronomy: the Framework to the Code*, OUP, London (1932). Independently T. Oestreicher came to similar conclusions in *Das deuteronomische Grundgesetz*, Gütersloh (1923).

2. *The Dramatization of Salvific History in the Deuteronomic Schools* (*Oudtestamentische Studiën* 16) E. J. Brill, Leiden (1969) 23ff.

Jordan and take possession of the land.[3] Second, the end point of the conquest is Mount Ebal, where a great covenant ceremony is held (Deuteronomy 27). Third, Hos 6:7–10 is said to reflect this cultic procession across the Jordan in amphictyonic times.[4] [[104]] Wijngaards believes that this ritual crossing of the Jordan was later transferred to Gilgal. Hence Deuteronomy 5–28 should be dated to a period before this change of scene, sometime between 1250 and 1050 B.C.[5]

Wijngaards' view rests on a number of important observations which traditional criticism takes too little account of, but it does raise new questions of its own. First, why should chapters 5–28 be supposed to give the key to Deuteronomy's origins? Classical Wellhausen criticism regarded chapters 12–26 as the core of the book with later expansions in chapters 1–4, 5–11, 27 and 28–30.[6] Subsequently it was argued that the core of Deuteronomy is to be found in chapters 5–26, 28, but that chapter 27 is a later insertion.[7] Recent form- and redaction-critical studies have shown that chapter 27 is carefully integrated into the overall structure of the book.[8] But in this case it becomes somewhat difficult to suppose that Deuteronomy 5–28 is necessarily the core of the book. Could chapter 27 not have been added at the same time as chapters 1–4, 29ff.? The second main weakness in Wijngaards' theory is the postulation of a recurring ceremonial re-enactment of the crossing of the Jordan and the conquest of Canaan. It is very dubious whether Hosea 6:7–10 can be taken as a reference to such a custom. The exact sin being condemned is obscure, but one plausible suggestion is that it refers to abuses connected with the cities of refuge.[9] However, in spite of these reservations Wijngaards is to be thanked for again drawing scholarly attention to the

3. Ibid., 22.

4. Ibid., 9ff.

5. Ibid., 109ff.

6. J. Wellhausen in *Die Composition des Hexateuchs und der historischen Bücher des alten Testaments*,[2] G. Reimer, Berlin (1889) 192ff.

7. E. W. Nicholson, *Deuteronomy and Tradition*, Blackwell, Oxford (1967) 22 is one of a number of scholars who have held this view.

8. See M. G. Kline, *WTJ* 23 (1960–1) 1–15; D. J. McCarthy, *Treaty and Covenant*, Pontifical Biblical Institute, Rome (1963) 109ff.; N. Lohfink, *Das Hauptgebot Eine Untersuchung literarischer Einleitungsfragen zu Deuteronomium 5–11*, Pontifical Biblical Institute, Rome (1963) 111f., 234.

9. Six cities of refuge are named in Joshua 20 including Ramoth-Gilead and Shechem. When a homicide fled to a city of refuge, the elders of the city had to decide whether it was a case of murder or manslaughter. Murderers had to be executed, but manslaughterers were allowed to live in the city. According to A. C. J. Phillips, *Ancient Israel's Criminal Law*, Blackwell, Oxford (1971) 101, Hosea's complaint is that (Ramoth) Gilead is actually harbouring murderers, while manslaughterers are being killed before they reach Shechem.

presence of Shechem traditions in the book of Deuteronomy and for attempting to find a period in which they could have been incorporated
into the book.

[[105]] To avoid the objections outlined above, it is necessary to
concentrate attention on the present book of Deuteronomy. This is
not to prejudge the question of the origin of the different traditions
contained in the book. But modern investigation has shown that all
parts of the book are a carefully integrated whole; therefore if we are
to discover how the final redactor understood his material, we must
examine all texts bearing on the question of the central sanctuary and
attempt to relate them to the commands to build an altar and sacrifice
on Mount Ebal. If this redactor's views can be discovered, they may, as
Wijngaards has argued, shed light on the date of composition of Deuteronomy. To this end, the history of the central sanctuary, so far as it
can be discerned from the historical books of the Old Testament, will
be reviewed. Then, secondly, the individual texts in Deuteronomy
bearing on the Ark and the central sanctuary will be examined. Finally,
an attempt will be made to answer the question: at what stage in Israel's history is it reasonable to suppose a redactor could have combined these traditions to form our book of Deuteronomy?

History of the Central Sanctuary[10]

It is disputed whether the first Israelite sanctuary was at Qadesh,[11] and
it is certainly irrelevant to a discussion of the final redaction of Deuteronomy.[12] The Ark was probably the centre of worship for the tribes before the settlement.[13] In Canaan it was clearly a focus of Israelite
worship. According to Noth the Ark was the centre of Israelite worship.
'It was the common cult object which united the association of the
twelve tribes of Israel.'[14] Noth believes that the centre to which the
Ark was first attached was Shechem; afterwards it was transferred to
Bethel, then Gilgal, then Shiloh and finally Jerusalem. The theory that
Shechem was the first central Israelite [[106]] sanctuary rests mainly on

10. Cf. the discussion by W. H. Irwin, 'Le Sanctuaire central israélite avant l'éta-
blissement de la monarchie,' *RB* 72 (1965) 161–184.

11. Y. Aharoni, *The Land of the Bible*, Burns and Oates, London (1966) 184.

12. Qadesh is mentioned in Deut 1:2, 19, 46; 2:14; 9:23, and it might be argued that
some of the traditions in Deuteronomy 1 and 2 belonged to the sanctuary of Qadesh. But
as far as the final editor of Deuteronomy is concerned, Qadesh is just a stopping place in
the wilderness.

13. R. de Vaux, *Ancient Israel*, Darton, Longman and Todd, London (1961) 298.

14. M. Noth, *History of Israel*,[2] A. & C. Black, London (1960) 91.

Joshua 24. If this does describe the founding of the Israelite amphictyony,[15] it would seem reasonable to suppose that Shechem was the first 'amphictyonic' shrine. But if Schmitt is right in supposing that Joshua 24 is really describing the renewal or a modification of the covenant, it is possible that Shechem was not the central sanctuary.[16] The possibility must be considered that Joshua may have had special motives for relinquishing his leadership at Shechem. It is relevant to recall the case of Rehoboam. Long after Jerusalem had been established as the central sanctuary Rehoboam went to Shechem to be made king. Why Rehoboam should have chosen Shechem in preference to any other sanctuary is not stated. Nevertheless, very significant patriarchal traditions are connected with Shechem. According to Gen 12:6f. ('J') it was at Shechem that God first promised Abraham that his seed should possess the land. Again it was at Shechem that God appeared to Jacob after his return to Canaan (Gen 35:1–4 'E'), and where Jacob bought a plot of ground (Gen 33:19 'E'). It is possible that Rehoboam went to Shechem to reaffirm his fidelity to the covenant in an action analogous to the Babylonian *mēsharum*-act, because Shechem was the place with which these traditions of inheriting the land were associated.[17] The *mēsharum*-act was intended as an assertion of the ruler's claim to authority. If these motives were [[107]] behind Rehoboam's action, it is possible that similar ideas inspired Joshua or at any rate the authors of Josh 8:30–35 and 24. Joshua is portrayed consistently as the

15. The theory that early Israel was an amphictyony, a league of tribes bound together by oath, first expounded in detail by M. Noth, *Das System der 12 Stämme Israels*, Kohlhammer, Stuttgart (1930), has commanded almost universal support until recently. Details of the theory have lately been questioned. G. Fohrer in *TLZ* 91 (1966) 801ff. argues that the unity of early Israel was that of the nomadic tribal clan and that the covenant was of very little importance in Israel's history. A similar position is taken by C. F. Whitley in *JNES* 22 (1963) 37–48. On the other hand, G. Schmitt, *Der Landtag von Sichem*, Calwer Verlag, Stuttgart (1964) 89ff., argues that Joshua 24 gives no hint that the tribes originally had different origins. R. de Vaux in J. P. Hyatt, ed., *The Bible in Modern Scholarship*, Carey Kingsgate Press, London (1966) 22f. insists that עם יהדה [['people of Judah']] implies consanguinity. D. B. Rahtjen in *JNES* 24 (1965) 110–114, shows that the Philistine pentapolis was closer in structure to a Greek amphictyony than was the Hebrew league. It seems to me that 'amphictyony' is a somewhat misleading description of the Israelite league, but I shall continue to use the term as a convenient designation of the constitution of Israel before the rise of the monarchy. That the Ark, the covenant and holy war were of fundamental importance in this era is shown by some of the early poetry, e.g., Exodus 15; Num 10:35f.; Judges 5.

16. G. Schmitt, op. cit., 80ff.; cf. V. Maag, 'Sichembund und Vätergötter,' *VTS* 16 (1967) 215f., who regards Joshua 24 as the foundation of the amphictyony, yet minimizes pre-existing differences between the tribes.

17. See D. J. Wiseman, *JSS* 7 (1962) 161–172.

conqueror, the one through whom the promise to the fathers was fulfilled. It would be natural to suppose that he would have wished to visit
the place where the promise had first been made, when it had been
fulfilled. Thus the traditions in Josh 8:30ff. and Joshua 24 are not conclusive proof that the first central sanctuary was located at Shechem.

The theory that Bethel was once the central sanctuary rests on
Judges 19ff. But apart from a mention that 'the ark of the covenant of
God was there (i.e., at Bethel) in those days' (Judg 20:27), it does not
seem that any special significance is attached to Bethel in these stories.
The phrase 'in those days' is vague.[18] It may be that the Ark had been
temporarily brought from Shiloh to Bethel, a sanctuary much nearer
to Gibeah, so that God could be consulted in the holy war (cf. 1 Samuel 4 and 2 Sam 11:11). The hypothesis that Gilgal was for a time the
central sanctuary is based on the actions of Samuel and Saul there, and
the so-called aetiological legends of Joshua 4ff. However, in the days of
Samuel and Saul the Ark was still, as far as we know, at Kiriath-Jearim.
It seems dubious historical method to say that the Joshua stories refer
to a central sanctuary that was used before Samuel, when there is no
explicit evidence for it.

Only in the case of Shiloh can a good case be made for it having
been the central sanctuary of all Israel. According to the book of
Joshua Shiloh was a meeting-place of the tribes, where the tent of re-
union was set up (Josh 18:1). Annual pilgrimages were made there
(Judg 21:19–21; 1 Sam 1:3). There was a house of God, a *hêkāl*, where
the Ark was kept (1 Sam 1:9; 3:3).[19] [[108]] Later writers refer to the
destruction of Shiloh, but not to the destruction of other sanctuaries
(Jer 7:12, 14; Ps 78:60). If Shechem had been the central sanctuary, its
destruction (Judges 9) might well have been mentioned too. Finally,

18. Often, five times, in Judges it refers to the days of the Judges, when no king
reigned. On any view this is too long a period in this verse. Once RSV translates it 'one
day' (Exod 2:11).

19. Fuller discussion in R. de Vaux, op. cit., 304. Recent excavations have shown that
the Iron I deposits at Shiloh are much less than for other periods and that the destruction layers previously associated with this level actually date from the time of the Assyrian
conquest. This suggests that the settlement associated with the early sanctuary was quite
small. The biblical texts do not say specifically that Shiloh was sacked by the Philistines.
The early Psalm 78 speaks simply of Yahweh abandoning Shiloh and of the suffering attendant upon the Philistine campaign. Jeremiah could be referring to the sacking of
Shiloh by the Assyrians, and saying that just as the Ark's stay there did not guarantee
Shiloh's subsequent security, so in his day its presence in Jerusalem did not guarantee
Jerusalem. M. L. Buhl and S. Holm-Nielsen, *Shiloh: The Danish Excavations at Tall Sailūn,
Palestine, in 1926, 29, 32, and 63*, National Museum of Denmark, Copenhagen (1969)
58ff. But see R. North's caution in interpreting the results of the recent excavations, *Ori-
entalia* 40 (1971) 295–296, and Y. Shiloh's views, *IEJ* 21 (1971) 67–69.

the importance of Shiloh is all the more striking when it is remembered that no patriarchal traditions are connected with it.

When David captured Jerusalem and moved the Ark there, it became the religious as well as the political capital of his kingdom. The prestige of Jerusalem as a religious centre was no doubt enhanced by the erection of Solomon's temple. Throughout the monarchy period, as the author of Kings makes clear, worship continued apparently quite legally at shrines outside Jerusalem. This had also been the case in the days of Samuel and the judges. These shrines were permissible so long as they were not intended to be substitutes for Jerusalem, the central sanctuary. But when Jeroboam and his successors in an attempt to ensure the stability of their political power set up rival shrines at Bethel and Dan, they were opposed by prophets from north and south. However 1 Kgs 13:1ff. may have been elaborated by deuteronomistic editors, its origin, it is generally agreed, represents an early prophetic protest against forsaking the central sanctuary of Jerusalem, home of the amphictyonic traditions and institutions.[20] Similarly Amos inveighs against all the northern sanctuaries. He says that the people should seek Yahweh and not Bethel (5:4f.). Insofar as he predicts that all the sanctuaries will be destroyed and that only Jerusalem will be rebuilt (9:11), it is likely that by 'seeking Yahweh' Amos meant that the northerners should again return to true Yahwism and demonstrate it by worshipping at Jerusalem. Similarly Hosea attacks many northern shrines, but is silent about Jerusalem. The book actually contains some positive statements about Jerusalem (2:2; 3:5), and though these are [[109]] generally credited to the Hosea school, it is unlikely that they would have been added if Hosea really disapproved of Jerusalem or envisaged some other shrine as the central sanctuary.[21] 2 Chr 30:11 says that even after two centuries of schism there were still some in the north who recognized the claims of Jerusalem, though this may simply reflect the Chronicler's concern to stress the importance of the Jerusalem cult.

It was Hezekiah who first tried to centralize all worship in Jerusalem and make the temple the sole sanctuary.[22] His policy failed, and

20. See N. H. Snaith, *IB* 3, 120; J. Gray, *1 and 2 Kings*,[2] SCM Press, London (1970) 318ff.; M. Noth, *Könige* (1.1–16), Neukirchener Verlag (1968) 291ff.; S. Asami, *The Central Sanctuary in Israel in the 9th Century B.C.* (Harvard Th.D. thesis 1964) 308ff. points out that this story has many linguistic affinities with the Elijah-Elisha cycles, and suggests that they both come from a 9th-century northern source. I am also indebted to Asami (pp. 148ff.) for his observations about Amos and Hosea.

21. Asami, 187ff.

22. It has been claimed that Hezekiah's attempt at centralization is the invention of the Deuteronomist. This is now generally rejected. See J. Gray, op. cit., 670; R. de Vaux, op. cit., 336; J. Bright, *A History of Israel*, SCM Press, London (1960) 265f.

Josiah reintroduced it. However, after Josiah's death worship again flourished at the high places. It was not until after the exile that Jerusalem seems to have become the sole Jewish sanctuary in Palestine.

Deuteronomy and the Central Sanctuary

We must now summarize what Deuteronomy has to say about the Ark, the central sanctuary and worship elsewhere. The Ark is not mentioned very often in Deuteronomy. Deuteronomy 10:1–5 recalls how it was made to hold the two tables of the covenant. Von Rad regards this as an attempt to demythologize the Ark, which in earlier tradition was regarded as the throne of God.[23] But as treaty documents were customarily stored near the image of the god, this interpretation would seem to read too much into the text.[24] Deut 10:8 suggests that the Ark was considered by the redactor to be the place where Yahweh made His presence known, for it puts 'carrying the ark' in parallel with 'standing before the LORD.'[25] Similar ideas are present in Deuteronomy 31. The text of Deuteronomy is to be laid up beside the Ark (v. 26). V. 15 reports a theophany at the tent of meeting. It is not ⟦110⟧ said that the Ark is kept in the tent, though it seems likely that this is what the redactor understood.[26] Deut 23:14 orders purity in the holy war 'because the LORD your God walks in the midst of your camp.' As the Ark was used in the holy war,[27] it may be that we have here another reference to the Ark. Finally assuming for the moment that 'the place which the LORD your God shall choose' is the central sanctuary, we have a number of other texts identifying the Ark with the place of God's self-manifestation.

What does Deuteronomy mean by 'the place which the LORD your God shall choose'? Is it one place or a number of places, as Welch argued? The phrases, 'in one [any] of your tribes,' and 'from all your tribes,' are not decisive by themselves. If there was no central sanctuary in the early period, as Wellhausen and Welch believed, they could be interpreted in a distributive sense.[28] However, the general agreement that Shiloh and perhaps other centres were for a time the centre of worship

23. G. von Rad, *Studies in Deuteronomy*, SCM Press, London (1953) 40. R. E. Clements, *God and Temple*, Blackwell, Oxford (1965) 95f., follows von Rad at this point, but also holds that this was the earliest understanding of the Ark's significance, p. 35.

24. R. de Vaux, op. cit., 301.

25. If this verse is to be ascribed to the final redactor, and is not a stray gloss as vv. 6, 7 appear to be.

26. R. de Vaux, op. cit., 302 for full discussion.

27. Num 10:35f.; 1 Samuel 4–6.

28. See Deut 13:13; 17:2; 18:6; 19:5, 11; 23:17, where אחד is best translated 'any.' See T. Oestreicher, *ZAW* 43 (1925) 246–249; A. C. Welch, *JBL* 48 (1929) 296.

of all Israel makes Welch's interpretation less likely. Further, many of the passages seem to imply that a central sanctuary is intended. In chapter 12 the main emphasis is that Israel must not use the numerous Canaanite cult centres for her worship. Israel must destroy all these high places and bring her burnt-offerings, sacrifices, tithes, and firstlings to 'the place' (12:6, 11). It is not clear in these verses whether a single sanctuary is meant or whether a multiplicity of Yahweh sanctuaries is intended. Vv. 15ff., however, make it clear that at least the number of Yahweh sanctuaries must be fairly small. When the Israelite who lives a long way from the sanctuary wants to eat meat, he does not have to take the animal to 'the place,' but he may kill it in his own town.[29] More explicit directions are given about tithing in Deut 14:22–29. It is again foreseen that the Israelite may be living far from the sanctuary, and he is therefore allowed to turn his tithe into cash [[111]] and bring that to 'the place.' Deut 15:19–23 specifies that the firstlings must be eaten at the sanctuary, but blemished ones should be eaten at home. Deuteronomy 16 contains the instructions about celebrating the three national feasts of passover, weeks and tabernacles. The references to the bondage in Egypt clearly indicate that these are the national festivals, so it is most natural to infer that they were supposed to be celebrated in the central sanctuary. However, Deut 16:1–8 provided Welch with one of the strongest arguments for supposing that the author intended passover to be celebrated at the local sanctuaries. V. 6 states that the passover sacrifice must be offered in the evening, v. 7 that next morning they shall turn and go to their tents. V. 8 says that for six days they are to eat unleavened bread and on the seventh there is to be a solemn assembly to the LORD your God. Welch argued that it was quite unreasonable for the writer to demand that the Israelites come up to Jerusalem twice in a week. The writer must have intended the feast to be celebrated at the local sanctuaries. The more usual explanation of this law is that the author of Deuteronomy has combined the feasts of unleavened bread and passover.[30] It is perfectly possible that unleavened bread and passover were once independent, but this does not account for the redactor's understanding of the law in its present form. If the

---

29. It should be noted that this is not necessarily a provision introduced as the result of Josiah's reform. Of the other references in *BDB* 257a to show that זבח can be used to mean 'slaughter' as well as 'sacrifice' only 1 Sam 28:24 and 1 Kgs 19:21 seem plausible. Both are pre-Josiah.

30. R. de Vaux, op. cit., 485ff.; G. von Rad, *Deuteronomy*, SCM Press, London (1966) 111ff. But H.-J. Kraus, 'Zur Geschichte des Passah-Massot-Festes in AT," *EvTh* 18 (1958) 47–67 argues that in fact the two feats were combined in the amphictyonic period, when Passover-Maṣṣot was celebrated by all Israel at Gilgal.

traditional interpretation of the text is accepted, it must be supposed
that two visits to Jerusalem in about ten days are required. For a Gali-
laean this would total some 240 miles.[31] We are thus faced with a dilemma: either the law is almost unfulfillable or it presupposes
celebration of the feast at local sanctuaries. Kraus[32] and Kline, however,
take the phrase 'to your tents' more or less literally. It 'would here refer
to the pilgrims' temporary quarters in the holy city.'[33] This would seem
to be the best solution to the [[112]] problem, and allows us to understand the law in terms of the central sanctuary. The laws about the supreme court in Deut 17:8–13 evidently imply that there is only one
chosen place. This is reinforced by a comparison with Deut 1:17, where
Moses is the supreme judge. A similar conclusion is demanded by Deut
18:6–8 on the rights of the Levites to officiate at the central sanctuary.
'The place' is mentioned in Deuteronomy 26, whose demands are just
as applicable to the central sanctuary as to local ones. Deut 31:10f. mentions a special assembly every seven years at the feast of booths. As in
16:15 this must be celebrated at the place which the Lord will choose.
There is therefore very good reason for supposing that when the author
of Deuteronomy spoke of 'the place which the LORD your God shall
choose' he intended to refer to the central sanctuary of all Israel.

Several times the phrase mentioning the central sanctuary is expanded by the addition of the phrase 'to put his name there' (לָשׂוּם אֶת
שְׁמוֹ שָׁם)[34] or 'to make his name dwell there' (לְשַׁכֵּן שְׁמוֹ שָׁם).[35] The precise
significance of these phrases is elusive. According to von Rad Deuteronomy means by these phrases not Yahweh Himself but His substitute,

---

31. Deut 1:2 allows eleven days for the journey from Horeb to Qadesh-Barnea. If
Horeb is to be located in the southern part of the Sinai Peninsula (see Aharoni, op. cit.,
182ff.) it would appear that pilgrims might average fifteen miles a day. Perhaps higher
speeds might be possible in the easier terrain of Palestine.

32. H-J. Kraus, loc. cit., 59.

33. M. G. Kline, *Treaty of the Great King*, Eerdmans, Grand Rapids (1963) 93. 'Tents'
(אהל) often does mean 'homes' in the OT (e.g., 1 Kgs 8:66; 12:16). But in Deuteronomy
its basic meaning 'tent' is normal (cf. 1:27; 5:30; 11:6). Deut 33:18f. provides an illuminating comparison with this passage. 'Going out' stands in parallel with 'your tents,' in a
context of a call to worship on their mountain (v. 19). It is not clear whether pilgrims
would have found rooms near the sanctuary, or whether a camp was set up. Two considerations favour the latter. The Passover was probably of nomadic origin (R. de Vaux,
op. cit., 489). In using tents, its original character would be preserved to some extent.
Secondly, the Samaritans still erect tents during their celebration of the Passover (L. G.
Farmer, *We Saw the Holy City*,[2] Epworth Press, London [1953] 199). Nor is it clear why
tents are only mentioned in connection with Passover. Possibly because it was the only
one of the three feasts that fell within the rainy season.

34. Deut 12:5, 21; 14:24.

35. Deut 12:11; 14:23; 16:2, 6, 11; 26:2.

His name, dwells in the sanctuary. Von Rad holds that Deuteronomy is here demythologizing the older concept that Yahweh was present on earth; instead it is insisting that Yahweh dwells in heaven and His name on earth.[36] However, de Vaux has shown that this is too sharp an antithesis.[37] Deuteronomy can say that Yahweh is among His people (23:15), and that Israel must appear and rejoice before the Lord (16:11, 16; cf. 26:10, 13). [[113]] In Deuteronomy 26 the sanctuary is described as the place where Yahweh's name dwells, yet the Israelite worships and speaks 'before the Lord,' concluding his worship with a prayer asking God to look down 'from heaven his holy habitation.' It seems that Deuteronomy regards God as present in heaven and in His sanctuary. A further passage indicates that Yahweh's name is conceived of dwelling in His sanctuary in much the same way as the names of Canaanite gods dwelt in theirs. In 12:3 the Israelites are commanded to 'hew down the graven images of their gods, and destroy their *name* out of that *place.*' And in 12:5 they are told to 'seek the *place* which the Lord your God shall choose to put his *name* there.' De Vaux has suggested that the origin of the phrase is legal rather than cultic. He compares the phrase (*šakan šumšu*) which occurs in the Amarna letters. 'Behold, the king has set his name in the land of Jerusalem; so he cannot abandon the lands of Jerusalem.'[38] 'The phrase is an affirmation of ownership, the equivalent of taking possession.'[39] But the phrase also occurs in other texts dealing with conquests, and is often associated with the erection of a stele or other victory monument.[40] An inscription of Shamshi-Adad I of Assyria reads: 'Thus I placed my great name and my (victory) stele in the land of Lebanon on the shore of the Great Sea.'[41] Likewise Yahdunlim of Mari describes himself as 'one who erects stelae, mentioning (his) name' (*mu-re-ti na-re-e na-bi šu-mi* 1:22). Later in the same inscription in the context of reducing his enemies to vassalship, he says 'he established his name' (*šu-mi-šu iš-ta-ka-an* 2:20).[42] Shalmaneser III on his expeditions to

36. G. von Rad, *Studies*, 38f.

37. R. de Vaux, '"Le lieu que Yahvé a choisi pour y établir son nom,"' in F. Maas, ed., *Das ferne und nahe Wort, Festschrift L. Rost,* W. de Gruyter, Berlin (1967) 219–228.

38. EA 287:60–3; cf. EA 288:5–7 in *ANET* 488.

39. *RB* 63 (1966) 449. His suggestion in *Festschrift L. Rost* 221 that the phrase may have been peculiar to Jerusalem cannot be sustained in the light of the other evidence presented here.

40. I am indebted to W. L. Moran for first pointing this out to me.

41. R. Borger, *Einleitung in die assyrischen Königsinschriften I,* Brill, Leiden (1961) 14f., rev. 4.12–18; quoted by A. Malamat in *Studies in Honor of B. Landsberger,* University of Chicago Press (1965) 371.

42. Published by G. Dossin, *Syria* 32 (1955) 1ff.; new translation by A. L. Oppenheim in *ANET,*[3] 556f.

the West also erected stelae probably near the sanctuaries on Mounts Carmel and Lebanon.[43] More recently it has been pointed out that this phraseology is often associated with the inscribing of a name on the foundation stones of sanctuaries. The inscription of the [[114]] name was essential to the validity of a temple.[44] If this is the background to the Hebrew phrase, we could regard 'to make his name dwell there' as the etymological equivalent of Akkadian (*šakānum šumam*) and 'to put his name there' as the semantic equivalent. The phrases in Deuteronomy would then specify that the sanctuary in question belongs to Yahweh. Perhaps there may be slight overtones of conquest in the phraseology.

Does the author of Deuteronomy intend 'the place' to be the *sole* sanctuary, as opposed to the central sanctuary, of all Israel? The evidence on this is somewhat ambiguous. Deut 16:21 forbids the erection of an Asherah beside the altar of the LORD your God. This is taken by Driver and von Rad to be a pre-centralization law.[45] But their reasons are not conclusive. The interpretation of this law depends on the historical context to which the commentator assigns it. Much more important for understanding the redactor's attitude to the central sanctuary is Deuteronomy 27. Here it is commanded that an altar is to be erected on Mount Ebal[46] and that burnt offerings and peace offerings are to be offered there. In addition, the text of the law is to be inscribed here, which is appropriate in a sanctuary. If it be supposed that Deuteronomy allows only one sanctuary and not just a central sanctuary, Deuteronomy 27 indicates that it was located near Shechem. If Noth is right in supposing that Shechem was at one time the central sanctuary, it could well be argued that Deuteronomy was written to establish or authenticate the sanctuary there. Deuteronomy 27 would be powerful evidence for believing that the first 'amphictyonic' shrine was there. This would suggest that Deuteronomy is very early indeed, and this is the conclusion that Wijngaards has drawn.[47]

---

43. A. Malamat, loc. cit., 372.

44. Cf. S. D. McBride, Jr., *The Deuteronomic Name Theology* (Harvard Ph.D. Thesis, 1969) 93f.

45. S. R. Driver, *Deuteronomy*,[3] T. & T. Clark, Edinburgh (1902) 203; G. von Rad, *Deuteronomy* 115. Driver compares this law with Exod 20:24, and von Rad says it presupposes a multiplicity of cult centres.

46. The Samaritan version has Mount Gerizim at this point. Alteration of Ebal to Gerizim by the Samaritans is as intelligible as alteration of Gerizim by their opponents. It is difficult to know which text is original. At any rate, the point is immaterial to the argument.

47. See above.

Though Wijngaards is right to emphasize the importance of Shechem in Deuteronomy it is not obvious that the redactor of Deuteronomy located the central sanctuary there. Against ⟦115⟧ the view that Shechem was intended to be the central sanctuary may be cited the failure in Deuteronomy to call it 'the place.' Neither the Ark[48] nor the tent of meeting is mentioned in connection with it. The altar erected is of an old-fashioned type (cf. Exod 20:24f.). It seems unlikely that an altar of unhewn stones was intended to be the altar of the central sanctuary. Elsewhere, in Deut 23:19, the house of the LORD is mentioned. This would suggest that Deuteronomy envisages more than a primitive altar at the central sanctuary. On the other hand it is possible that inscribing the law on stones (27:2ff.) is the deuteronomistic equivalent of erecting a victory stele. As we have seen, the phrase 'to place the name' is often associated with the erection of a stele. It could then be argued that Deuteronomy 27 is specifying not only where the covenant is to be renewed, but the location of the place which the LORD shall choose to make His name to dwell there. The arguments are finely balanced. It could be that Deuteronomy 27 specifies the sole sanctuary for Israel is to be on Mount Ebal, or it could be that the central sanctuary is located somewhere else and only a special ceremony on Mount Ebal is envisaged. Two considerations lead me to prefer the second alternative. Long after Jerusalem had become the central sanctuary for all Israel, Rehoboam went to Shechem to be made king. Secondly, the editor of Joshua evidently supposed that in the early days the central sanctuary was at Shiloh (Josh 18:1; 22:12) yet allowed Joshua to go to Shechem to renew the covenant (Josh 24:1ff.).[49]

Undoubtedly Deuteronomy 27 is the clearest clue to the provenance of Deuteronomy in the whole book. But its presence conflicts with the idea that Deuteronomy was written to centralize worship at Jerusalem. By centralization is meant the attempt to limit *all* worship to *one* sanctuary, the policy of Hezekiah and Josiah. Deuteronomy 27 clearly prescribes that sacrifice be offered on Mount Ebal and ascribes this command to Moses. This makes it implausible to regard Deuteronomy as the programme for Josiah's reformation.

A source-critical analysis of 2 Kings 22–23 confirms this conclusion. Modern commentators agree that the account of the ⟦116⟧ discovery of the law-book and the celebration of the Passover (2 Kgs 22:3–20;

48. Josh 8:33 states that the Ark was there for the ceremony commanded in Deuteronomy 27.

49. In 'The Deuteronomic Theology of the Book of Joshua,' *JBL* 90 (1971) 140–148 I have pointed out the close affinity of Joshua with Deuteronomy which makes it likely that the same man or school was responsible for editing both works.

23:1–3, 21–23) and the list of reforms (2 Kgs 23:4–20) come from at least two different sources.[50] It is therefore dubious whether the law-book actually prompted Josiah's centralization measures. The Chronicler could be correct in placing them several years before the discovery of the law-book. It is also worthy of note that, according to Kings, Hezekiah took steps to centralize worship at Jerusalem without any prompting from a law-book.

The Place of Origin of Deuteronomy

More positively, Deuteronomy 27 gives some guidance about the possible origin of the book. It could be a northern document. It could be a southern document, but then it must date from a time prior to the desertion of the northern tribes from the Davidic house. A third possibility must also be considered; that at some time northern traditions were incorporated into the Jerusalem covenant document.

Deuteronomy 27 is the strongest argument in favour of a northern provenance of Deuteronomy. We must therefore consider the validity of this argument carefully. If Deuteronomy is a northern document, it must either derive from circles that were faithful to the official royal cult or from a sectarian group. Since the approved central sanctuaries of the northern kingdom were at Bethel and Dan, it seems unlikely that a document advocating worship on Mount Ebal can be the work of devotees of the official cult of the northern kingdom. On the other hand, it is difficult to ascribe Deuteronomy to northern sectarians, since those circles in the North which valued the old traditions of Israel and opposed the official cultus looked to Jerusalem as the true centre of worship.[51] A further difficulty with supposing that Deuteronomy was written in the North in the 9th and 8th centuries B.C. is archaeological. Shechem went into a decline after the division of the monarchy,[52] and there is no proof that a significant sanctuary remained there. [[117]] The argument for a northern origin of Deuteronomy *in this era* is therefore at best an argument from silence.

Over against this negative evidence must be set the clear positive witness of 2 Kings 22f. that some form of Deuteronomy was known and used in the Jerusalem cult a long time before Josiah's day. In a meticulous study of 2 Kgs 22:3–20; 23:1–3, 21–23, N. Lohfink arrived at the following conclusions.[53] First, this account of the discovery of the law-

---

50. E.g., J. Gray, *ad loc.*; N. Lohfink, *Biblica* 44 (1963) 261ff.

51. See above, pp. 108f.

52. G. E. Wright, *Shechem: The Biography of a Biblical City*, Duckworth, London (1965) 144ff.

53. N. Lohfink, *Biblica* 44 (1963) 261–288, 461–498.

book must have been written by a royal apologist before the death of Josiah. The account is really written to demonstrate Josiah's devotion to Yahweh, not to explain the origin of the law-book. Second, the term 'book of the law' is a technical term for a covenant document, that is the liturgy of a ceremony in which the covenant obligations are read out to the people and accepted by them. Third, the account assumes that the book in question was old. Since the royal officials had a number of ways open to them to verify its authenticity, presumably they were satisfied that it was old. Fourth, since the covenant documents were kept with the Ark, some earlier form of this document was presumably brought to Jerusalem when the Ark was. Fifth, since Deuteronomy with its covenant-treaty form would serve admirably as a covenant document, it seems likely that it was some form of Deuteronomy that was discovered in Josiah's time. This makes it likely that the origins of Deuteronomy are to be sought in the amphictyonic period and that it was subsequently transmitted, preserved, and developed in Jerusalem.

The possibility that the Shechem traditions were inserted into Deuteronomy after the secession of the northern tribes has more difficulties than either of the other two. The objections to the first theory apply to it as well. In addition, if the north Israelite traditions are eliminated from Deuteronomy, that is 11:29–30; 27, the book loses a vital part of the covenant form, namely a document clause. Furthermore, it is difficult to conceive of a time when such northern traditions could have been incorporated into the Jerusalem covenant document. For if we suppose Deuteronomy 27 to be an insertion, it must have been inserted before the redaction of the deuteronomistic [[118]] history, since, as Noth has observed,[54] it is presupposed in Josh 8:30–35. Secondly, its insertion cannot be ascribed to the deuteronomistic historian. The message of the deuteronomistic redactor of Kings and possibly an earlier pre-exilic compiler is clear: all sanctuaries outside Jerusalem were sinful. The northern kingdom's refusal to worship at Jerusalem is the real cause of their downfall according to 2 Kings 17. Similarly the kings of Judah are judged by the vigour with which they took action against the high places. Thus it is most unlikely that a tradition that Moses ordered the erection of a shrine on Mount Ebal should have been inserted into Deuteronomy at this period. Nor is it likely to have been inserted in the immediately preceding reigns. Since Josiah and Hezekiah were both dedicated to the destruction of northern shrines, it seems unlikely that they would have approved the insertion of a passage into the Jerusalem covenant document legitimizing by an appeal to Moses one of the

---

54. *Überlieferungsgeschichtliche Studien I,*[2] Kohlhammer, Stuttgart (1957) 42.

northern sanctuaries.[55] Presumably a similar antipathy to northern shrines was current in Jerusalem circles even before the fall of Samaria. In short, there is no period after the division of the monarchy in which it is likely that a southern redactor would have wanted to insert northern traditions in the book of Deuteronomy.

If, however, we suppose that Deuteronomy was a southern document and that its composition antedates the division of the kingdom, none of these problems arise. We know that Rehoboam went to Shechem to be made king, though his capital was at Jerusalem. It was customary in Israel to renew the covenant at the accession of a new king, an act perhaps parallel to the Babylonian *mēsharum*-act. It has been argued that though Deuteronomy probably locates the central sanctuary elsewhere, it prescribes that one of the first duties of Israel on entering the Promised Land is to renew the covenant and offer sacrifice near Shechem. Thus Deuteronomy would be quite suitable for use as the document in such a ceremony, if it was written sometime during the united monarchy period or earlier. To judge from 2 Kings 22f. it continued in use in Jerusalem until shortly before the fall of the city.

55. In Manasseh's reign the document seems to have been lost, see 2 Kings 22.

Deuteronomy and Ugaritic Studies

PETER C. CRAIGIE

[[155]] The discovery of the Ugaritic texts proved to be of great importance for Old Testament Studies. During the last forty-five years, as the
first texts have been studied in detail and as new discoveries have been
made, more and more light has been brought to bear upon difficulties
and obscurities contained in the Hebrew text. But, as is often the case,
there has been a tendency in the wake of new discoveries to over-
estimate their importance and to go to extremes in their application in
comparative studies. There have been recently renewed warnings concerning the danger of "pan-Ugaritism";[1] the purpose of the present
paper is to assess that danger on a very limited basis.[2] A number of topics in Deuteronomy, which have been discussed in the light of Ugaritic
Studies, are examined critically in this paper, and some provisional
conclusions will be drawn as a result of the investigations. In no sense,
however, is this paper to be taken as a comprehensive evaluation of all
the parallels proposed between the Ugaritic texts and the Hebrew text;
such an evaluation would require at the very least a lengthy monograph. The topics which have been chosen reflect to a certain extent
the potential wealth and diverse value of the Ugaritic texts for Hebrew
studies. [[156]]

Reprinted with permission from *Tyndale Bulletin* 28 (1977) 155–69. This paper was first
read at Tyndale House, Cambridge, on July 16th, 1976.

1. J. C. de Moor and P. van der Lugt, *BO* 31 (1974) 3–26.

2. This paper is one of a series in which similar critical evaluations are undertaken;
see also "The Problem of Parallel Word Pairs in Ugaritic and Hebrew Poetry" *Semitics* 5
(1975) 48–58; "Three Ugaritic Notes on the Song of Deborah" *Journal for the Study of the
Old Testament* 2 (1977) 33–49.

Cooking a Kid (Deut 14:21b)

The short biblical prohibition against cooking a kid in its mother's milk has always been a source of curiosity. The context of the prohibition in Deuteronomy, provided by the laws concerning permitted and prohibited foodstuffs, might suggest that the legislation is concerned in some sense with diet, yet the precise significance is still not clear. Maimonides had this to say:[3]

> Meat boiled in milk is undoubtedly gross food, and makes overfull; but I think that most probably it is also prohibited because it is some- how connected with idolatry, forming perhaps part of the service, or being used on some festival of the heathen. . . . This I consider the best reason for the prohibition; but as far as I have seen the books on Sabean rites, nothing is mentioned of this custom.

Maimonides' suggestion made good sense, though from his time until the early twentieth century, there has been no solid external evi- dence to support the suggestion. Soon after the first discovery of the Ugaritic texts, however, it appeared that a parallel had been found at last.

In 1933, Charles Virolleaud published a study entitled "La nais- sance des dieux gracieux et beaux. Poème phénicien de Ras Shamra,"[4] in which he presented the transliteration and translation of a text which is now referred to as *CTA* 23 *UT* 52. Line 14 of this text, which was difficult to read because of surface damage to the tablet, included the following clause in Virolleaud's *editio princeps*:

ṭb[ḥ . g]d . bḥlb
"Fais [cuire un che]vreau dans le lait"

Although Virolleaud admitted that his restoration of the line was "simplement conjecturale," it was a good attempt. His translation of *ṭbḥ* was based on Arabic and modern Hebrew cognates. Virolleaud, how- ever, did not draw any parallels with Biblical texts. W. F. Albright pub- lished a study of the text in 1934, but added nothing with respect to line 14;[5] the following year, however, H. L. Ginsberg published a lengthy [[157]] study of the text,[6] in which essentially he followed Virolleaud with respect to line 14:

3. *The Guide for the Perplexed* transl. M. Friedländer, Dover Books, New York (1956) 371.
4. *Syria* 14 (1933) 128–151.
5. *JPOS* 14 (1934) 133–140.
6. *JRAS* (1935) 45–72.

ṭb[*ḫ g*]*d . bḫlb*
"Coo[k a ki]d in milk"

In a footnote, Ginsberg drew attention to the biblical parallels to the line, and in a postscript to his study (p. 72), he cited this Ugaritic text as giving confirmation of Maimonides' view of the biblical prohibition.

During the period of more than forty years since the publication of Ginsberg's study, almost all scholars (with exceptions noted below) have followed in the view that the Ugaritic text provides a background to the biblical prohibition. Only one example will be provided. In *Ras Shamra Parallels* Vol. I, Anton Schoors notes, after a careful evaluation of the history of research, that the "biblical prohibition is certainly directed against the practice described in this [Ugaritic] text."[7] For obvious reasons, the Ugaritic parallel to the Hebrew text is appealing, but we must enquire carefully concerning whether it can be substantiated. There are at least three problems related to the proposal.

1. *Text.* The first and obvious problem concerns the text itself and the question concerning whether or not Virolleaud's conjectural restoration can be maintained. Herdner (in her edition of the text in *CTA*) is more cautious than Virolleaud:

$$\textit{ṭb} . (?) [\text{g}]\text{d} . \textit{bḫlb}$$

She notes, however, in footnote, the possibility that a sign could have been omitted:

$$\textit{ṭb} (\textit{ḫ}) . [\text{g}]\text{d}$$

Herdner's caution is appropriate, for there is very little space in the line for Virolleaud's restitution, especially if a word divider is included.[8] Before resorting to restoration on the basis of omission, however, one would have to give very careful assessment of other possible readings of the text, and since a number of other readings are possible without [[158]] assuming the omission of a letter,[9] one must conclude that Virolleaud's reading of the line

7. Pp. 29–32. (Hereafter, the abbreviation *RSP* will be used for the two volumes of *Ras Shamra Parallels* L. R. Fisher (ed.), published in 1972 and 1975.) Note that J. M. Sasson, in *RSP* I 403, is more cautious with respect to the reading of the Ugaritic text.

8. Thus Ginsberg's restitution is slightly more plausible than that of Virolleaud, in that the former omits the word divider.

9. Thus it is possible to read the earlier part of the line (*contra* Herdner) as: *ġrzm g ṭb* (reading /g/ instead of a word divider), translating: "heroes of good voice" or "sweet voiced

is far from certain. This, in turn, means that two of the words which are critical for the parallel with the biblical prohibition are in doubt (viz. *ṭbḥ* and *gd*).

2. *ṬBḤ.* In spite of the problems mentions in (1) above, let us assume that Virolleaud's reading of the text is possible and on that basis consider the meaning of the word *ṭbḥ.* Virolleaud, in his original proposal, suggested the meaning "cook" on the basis of Arabic and modern Hebrew cognate terms. The most obvious sense of the word, however, both on the basis of other occurrences in the Ugaritic texts and on the basis of the classical Hebrew cognate term, would be "slaughter,"[10] and as Loewenstamm has recently demonstrated, there is in fact no good evidence to support the existence of a Ugaritic verb *ṭbḥ* = "to cook."[11] This conclusion, in turn, further undermines Virolleaud's proposed reading of the text.

3. *GD.* Continuing with the assumption that Virolleaud's reading of the text is possible, let us consider the meaning of the word *gd.* If the meaning of the Ugaritic term is "kid," as claimed, then it must be noted that the normal noun for "kid" in Ugaritic is *gdy*;[12] why then has the present form no final /y/? In fact, it is quite possible that *gd* (if the reading is accepted) does not mean "kid" at all, but "coriander," forming thereby a parallel to the word *ʾannh* ("mint") in the marginal note to the text at this point.[13]

⟦159⟧ Let us summarize the proposed parallel data to the biblical prohibition in Deut 14:21b. First, the text of the proposed Ugaritic parallel is doubtful. Second, two of the three key words in the parallel

youth." Here, *ṭb* makes sense by itself without the necessity of adding /h/. Cf. I. Trujillo, *The Ugaritic Ritual for a Sacrificial Meal Honoring the Good Gods* (Dissertation: Johns Hopkins University, 1973) 106–111; J. C. de Moor, *New Year with Canaanites and Israelites* Kampen (1972) Part II 18–19.

10. Both Gordon (*UT* Glossary #1029) and Aistleitner (*WUS* #1111) give the primary sense as "slaughter," but include the sense "cook" with respect to the supposed occurrence of the term in *CTA* 23.14.

11. S. E. Loewenstamm, *UF* 5 (1973) 209–211.

12. Plur. *gdm.* Cf. Gordon, *UT* Glossary #560; Aistleitner, *WUS* #631. Aistleitner (*WUS* #629) suggests *gd* may refer to some category of animals such as "muskdeer."

13. See A. Caquot, M. Sznycer and A. Herdner, *Textes ougaritiques* I. *Mythes et légendes* Les Éditions du Cerf, Paris (1974) 371. The authors, who had previously noted that the Ugaritic text provided a background to the biblical prohibition, have now withdrawn their earlier view; for the earlier view, see R. Labat *et al., Les religions du Proche-Orient asiatique* Fayard/Denoël, Paris (1970) 454.

are questionable as to their meaning. Third, notwithstanding the above criticisms, the proposed parallel makes reference only to "milk," not to "mother's milk" as in the biblical text. In other words, whether one accepts or rejects Virolleaud's proposal concerning the reading of *CTA* 23.14, there is very little ground for arguing that the Ugaritic text contains material relevant to the understanding of Deut 14:21b. Having said all this, Maimonides' suggestion remains as convincing today as it was so long ago, but neither Sabean nor Ugaritic texts can be adduced in support of it!

"Cult Prostitutes" (Deut 23:17–18)?

There are two distinct laws in this short portion of legislation: (a) the prohibition of young Hebrew men and women becoming cult prostitutes (Deut 23:17); (b) the prohibition of the payment of vows with money acquired through prostitution (Deut 23:18), either cultic or common prostitution.[14] The unifying theme bringing these two laws together is clearly that of prostitution, something considered to be an "abomination" in ancient Israel, whether in a secular or cultic context. It is assumed that the first prohibition, concerning cult prostitutes, is directed against a practice current in the religions of Israel's neighbours, and indeed there is evidence of such practices in Babylonian texts. The discovery of the Ugaritic texts, however, may have provided evidence of the practice from a closer geographical and cultural context. In a number of Ugaritic texts, the term *qdšm* is employed which, for the moment, may simply be translated "consecrated ones."

[[160]] Unfortunately, the Ugaritic texts do not provide great illumination as to the precise nature of the *qdšm*. The word occurs in three texts in lists of guilds or corporations and in two of these three texts it follows immediately the word *khnm* ("priests").[15] Two further texts, containing what appear to be lists of temple functionaries also contain the word in the same position, after *khnm*.[16] A tiny tablet, thought to be an inventory or census, but probably a bill of lodging, mentions both

14. The "wage of a prostitute" (*zônâh*) suggests a common prostitute. The "hire of a dog" (*keleb*), however, could refer to male prostitution in a cultic context. The Hebrew term *keleb* may not be "dog" but "male prostitute" (synonymous or similar to *qdš*). See J. Gray, *The KRT Text in the Literature of Ras Samra*[2] Brill, Leiden (1964) 64, who has made this suggestion with respect to Ugaritic *klb*. A further possible example of the term may be found in *CTA* 114 (*UT* 305) 4: *ṯlṯ . klb.* See further Aistleitner, *WUS* #1313.

15. (a) *CTA* 17 (*UT* 113) 70–75: *khnm/qdšm/nsk.ksp.* (b) *UT* 169 (= 1026) 7–8: *khnm/qdšm/pslm.* (c) in *CTA* 73 (*UT* 114) the list reads: *qd(šm)/mrʾu s(kn)*; it is possible, however, from the condition of the tablet, that *khnm* preceded *qdšm.*

16. *CTA* 75 (*UT* 81) 2; *CTA* 76 (*UT* 82) 2. Whether all the categories listed in these texts are actually functionaries of the temple, as Herdner suggests, is open to question.

khnm and *qdšm* in such a way as to suggest that the two offices were approximately equal in status.[17] And finally, a broken tablet containing a list of personal names classified according to guilds, also contains the word *qdšm*.[18] This is the extent of the sources in the Ugaritic language, and only limited conclusions can be drawn. The principal conclusion concerns the close association between *khnm* and *qdšm*, and therefore the natural assumption that the *qdšm* were associated with the temple. Little more than this can be established with any certainty.

At this point, a natural procedure would be to turn to the Hebrew texts for the illumination of the Ugaritic texts, and the legislation in Deuteronomy 23, together with certain other biblical references,[19] is relevant. The biblical evidence might suggest that the Ugaritic word *qdšm* should be translated "cult prostitutes" (male), though the nature of the evidence must make such a claim tentative. In support of the hypothesis is the fact that the content of the mythological texts from Ugarit suggest strongly that the ritual counterpart to the myth would have included the rite of *hieros gamos*; hence the indirect information about the fertility nature of the Ugaritic religion supports the translation of *qdšm* as "cult prostitutes," [[161]] there being no other obvious terms to describe the office.[20]

Recently, however, an Akkadian text from Ugarit has been introduced into the discussion by W. von Soden.[21] The text, according to von Soden, describes the promotion of a man (and his son) from the *qdšm*-class to the *maryannu* (warrior) class. Von Soden draws three conclusions from this Akkadian text, one of which is particularly relevant to the subject under discussion: it is this. Since the *qdš* can marry and have a family, he concludes that the customary translation "cult prostitute" of the cognate term *qdš* in Hebrew dictionaries is not very appropriate. Von Soden's conclusion, however, is open to debate. There is a sense, certainly in which the term "prostitute" is inappropriate. In that

17. *CTA* 77 (*UT* 63) 3: on the interpretation of this tablet, I follow R. Dussaud, *Les découvertes de Ras Shamra (Ugarit) et l'Ancien Testament* Geuthner, Paris (1937) 55; but neither Dussaud's reading of the text, nor that of Herdner (after Virolleaud), add much to our knowledge of *qdšm*.

18. *UT* 2163 (*PRU* 5, 163) 2.8.

19. E.g., 1 Kgs 14:24; 15:12; 22:47. Cf. Hos 4:14.

20. Thus T. Yamashita cautiously suggests the link between *qdšm* and the *hieros gamos*; *RSP* 1167. The suggestion of H. Gese that the *qdšm* were not cult prostitutes but probably cult prophets, has no unambiguous support in either Ugaritic or biblical texts: *Die Religionen Altsyriens, Altarabiens und der Mandäer* Kohlhammer, Stuttgart (1970) 178.

21. *UF* 2 (1970) 329–330. The text is in *PRU* 3/RS.16.132; note that von Soden's interpretation of the text is based on a reading of line 7 (critical to the whole argument) which differs from that of Nougayrol, who first published the text.

the Hebrews used the term with a feeling of abhorrence, the English word "prostitute" may convey that feeling, though clearly, to a member of the Canaanite religion or participant in the fertility cult, the word "prostitute" would be totally inappropriate. But (and this is my point) to conclude that the married status of the *qdš* meant that he could not thereby participate in the sexual rites of the fertility cult is surely to impose modern concepts and values upon ancient societies. There is no more reason why there should necessarily be a conflict between the marital status and professional activities of the *qdšm* (viz. participation in the fertility cult) than would be the case with the *khnm.* There is, in fact, a Hebrew text which may be relevant to the discussion:

> 2 *Kgs* 23:7 "And he broke down the houses of the ritual prostitutes (*qdšym*) which were in the temple of Yahweh where the women wove robes for the Asherah-figure."[22]

Although the text is ambivalent, it may be that the women referred to were the wives of the "ritual prostitutes," and that [[162]] both partners in the marriage had a specific role to play in the fertility cult.

In conclusion, the Ugaritic references to *qdšm* have added little direct information concerning the meaning of Deut 23:17–18. On the other hand, the Hebrew text may have given further insight into the meaning of the Ugaritic term, and it is perhaps salutary to remember, so long after the discovery of the Ugaritic texts, that in the earliest comparative studies Hebrew was invaluable in the interpretation of the Ugaritic materials.

Parallel Word Pairs in Deuteronomy 32

One of the most prolific areas of development in the comparative study of Hebrew and Ugaritic poetry is to be found in the matter of parallel word pairs which are common to Ugaritic and Hebrew poetry. Although the study of such pairs has been going on for more than forty years, it has been given considerable impetus by the work of M. Dahood, first in his 3-volume commentary on the Psalms, and more recently in his contributions to *RSP* I and II respectively. Dahood's purpose, which presupposes his hypothesis, is to recover from the Ugaritic and Hebrew texts "the Canaanite thesaurus from whose resources Ugaritic and Hebrew poets alike drew."[23] In the following notes, Dahood's contribution to the subject will be submitted to a limited evaluation. The first three

22. On the translation of the text, see J. Gray, *I and II Kings*[2] S.C.M., London (1970) 730, 734.

23. *RSP* I 74.

notes which follow examine critically a number of Hebrew-Ugaritic parallel word pairs, proposed by Dahood, which occur in Deuteronomy 32. The fourth note evaluates Hebrew-Ugaritic parallel word pairs in Deuteronomy 32 in the light of parallel word pairs drawn from Arabic poetry.

Deuteronomy 32:6

Dahood lists a common Hebrew-Ugaritic parallel word pair, occurring in Deut 32:6 and several other Hebrew texts, as follows (*RSP* I 170):

Ugaritic:	*hw // hw*;	"he // he"
Hebrew:	*hw² // hw²*;	"he // he"

The repetitive word pair is not in itself remarkable, but since it (and many like it) are a part of the evidence for the hypothesis [[163]] concerning a "Canaanite thesaurus," let us examine it in a little detail.

Dahood provides only one text in support of the existence of this word pair in Ugaritic: *UT* 2114:5–6 (= *PRU* 5.137, RS.19.11). The text is a short epistle, in prose style, which was apparently written in haste. De Moor and van der Lugt simply state with respect to this pair: "No poetical parallelism in Ugaritic."[24] While in a technical sense this is correct, nevertheless the judgment may be too hasty, for lines 5–7 of the epistle have a proverbial ring to them and may therefore add some credibility to the existence of the word pair in Ugaritic. A slightly better example, but still not strong, could perhaps be adduced from *CTA* 32 (*UT* 2). 16: *hw // hw* ("it // it"). This is a ritual text but a text which has a semi-poetic character in parts.[25] In summary, there is tentative, but not convincing, evidence for the existence of the word pair in Ugaritic.

There is no dispute concerning the presence of the parallel word pair in Deut 32:6. It is the kind of word pair which one would expect *a priori* in any poetry employing some form of parallelism, and in fact this particular word pair is attested in Akkadian,[26] Egyptian,[27] an Arabic[28] poetry, to name but a few. In summary, even if the Ugaritic evidence were stronger for this word, it would not constitute strong evidence for any hypothesis.

24. *BO* 31 (1974) 12.

25. Cf. B. Levine, *JCS* 17 (1963) 105–111.

26. Akk. *šu // šu* ("he // he"): Hammurabi Law Code (Prov 4:1, 9). This is distant, but clear parallelism.

27. E.g., *sw // sw* ("he, it // he, it"): Bk. of Dead 17:38–40, 42–45 etc., in the repetitive formulaic expression.

28. Arab. *huwa // huwa* ("he // he"): Qur²an 67.1–2 (hereafter abbreviated as Q). All references to Q follow the Egyptian edition of the Arabic text.

Deuteronomy 32:22

Dahood presents us with the following common parallel word pair (*RSP* I 173):

Ugaritic:	*hr* // *'arṣ*	"mountain // earth"
Hebrew:	*'rṣ* // *hr*	"earth // mountain"

(Note: the pair, in Deut 32:22, is in the reverse sequence, but Dahood also notes examples of the Hebrew pair in the same sequence as Ugaritic.)

All of Dahood's Ugaritic examples of this word pair come [[164]] from a single Ugaritic text (*UT* 608 = RS 24.251 [Ug. 5]) and all occur in the same formulaic expression. The text in question is extremely difficult to translate and interpret, and as yet no consensus is emerging, either as to the translation of the relevant lines or as to the meaning of the term *hrm*. While Dahood assumes the meaning to be "mountains," following Gordon,[29] Virolleaud derived the meaning from Arabic *haram* ("couper . . . en petits morceaux")[30] and Astour derives the sense "weaken" from Arabic *harima*.[31] While I appreciate Astour's rendering, for the overall sense which it gives to the Ugaritic text,[32] in all fairness it must probably be concluded that the precise sense of the passage is as uncertain today as it was in 1968. Dahood's translation "mountains" appears to be based primarily on the association with *arṣ* but the evidence for the existence of the word *hr* = "mountain" in Ugaritic is slender,[33] and hence we must conclude that the existence of the Ugaritic word pair is open to serious doubt.

Deuteronomy 32:14

The following word pair was suggested initially by U. Cassuto[34] and is listed by Dahood (*RSP* I 182);

Ugaritic:	*ḥlb* // *ḥm'at*	"milk // butter"
Hebrew:	*ḥm'h* // *ḥlb*	"butter // milk"

---

29. Supplement to *UT* #19.790.

30. *Ugaritica* 5 (1968) 577.

31. *JNES* 27 (1968) 31.

32. There are, nevertheless, difficulties with Astour's interpretation; see M. J. Mulder, *UF* 4 (1972) 90–91; J. C. de Moor, *The Seasonal Pattern in the Ugaritic Myth of Ba'lu* AOAT 16 (1971) 224.

33. Gordon, *UT* Glossary #789 suggests some evidence, but see Aistleitner, *WUS* #856, with respect to the relevant text.

34. In *Tarbiz* 13–14 (1942–43), reprinted in Cassuto, *Biblical and Oriental Studies Vol. 2: Bible and Ancient Oriental Texts* Magnes Press, Jerusalem (1975) 50.

(The Hebrew pair in Deut 32:14 is in the reverse sequence, though Dahood also notes Hebrew examples in the same sequence as the Ugaritic pair.)

At first sight, this common word pair is convincing, though de Moor and van der Lugt make the terse comment: "No poetical parallelism has been detected in Ugaritic,"[35] with no further explanation. The only Ugaritic textual evidence for this word pair is *CTA* 23 (*UT* 52).14, and an examination of this text may clarify the reason for the scepticism of de Moor [[165]] and van der Lugt.[36] The last part of line 14 reads as follows:

$$[g]d \ . \ bhlb \ . \ {}^{\circ}annh \ bhm^{\circ}at$$

The reading is clear, but the last two words are written on the side (margin) of the tablet. There are a number of possible reasons for this: (a) the scribe accidentally omitted the words, and inserted them in the margin; (b) the words may be an explanatory gloss with reference to *gd . bhlb*, or even (c) an alternative ritual prescription to *gd . bhlb*. In the latter two cases, *hlb* and *hm*${}^{\circ}at$ would still be approximate synonyms (in a poetic sense), but there would no longer be clear evidence for the existence of the parallel word pair. Once again, we must conclude that the evidence for the Ugaritic word pair is in doubt.

Parallel Word Pairs in Deuteronomy 32 and in Arabic Poetry

A word of explanation may be helpful before presenting the data in this section. It is a reasonable assumption that in any poetry in which parallelism is employed, regardless of the language in which that poetry is written, similar parallel word pairs will be employed. As George Adam Smith put it many years ago: " 'Deep calleth unto deep,' tree to tree, bird to bird, all the world over. The heart of the poet is full of such natural antiphons . . . We need not, therefore, seek a Babylonian or an Egyptian origin for the parallelism of Hebrew poetry."[37] The same might be said with respect to seeking a Ugaritic or Canaanite origin for the parallelism of Hebrew poetry. If the first assumption is correct, then a second would naturally follow: the parallel word pairs common to the poetry of a variety of languages would involve a high percentage of *cognate* terms if the languages under comparison were close linguistic relatives, fewer cognate terms if the respective lan-

---

35. *BO* 31 (1974) 13.

36. For further comments on this text, see "Cooking a Kid" section (above).

37. *The Early Poetry of Israel in its Physical and Social Origins* Oxford University Press, London (1912) 16–17.

guages were less close linguistically, and no cognate terms if there was no linguistic relationship. Thus the repetitive parallel word pair "brother // brother" occurs in Ugaritic, Hebrew and Finnish poetry; it comes as no surprise to find that cognate terms are employed in Ugaritic and Hebrew poetry, but not in Finnish poetry.[38] The recent [166] study of de Moor and van der Lugt (fn. 1) and J. Khanjian's contribution to *RSP* II (pp. 394–400) have demonstrated the existence of parallel word pairs in Akkadian poetry which also occur in Hebrew Poetry. The following notes list word pairs occurring in Arabic poetry and in Deuteronomy 32; as one would expect, there are many cognate terms in the Arabic parallel word pairs, but fewer than would be the case with common Hebrew-Ugaritic parallel word pairs.

(a) *Deut 32:1*
   (i) Hebrew: $šm^c$ // h^3zyn; "hear // give ear"
   (ii) Arabic: No precise parallel, though note the following:
       $sami^c a$ // $sami^c a$; "hear // hear" (Q.30.52)
       ^3adhina // ^3adhina; "give ear // give ear" (Q.84.2–5)
   (iii) Ugaritic: $šm^c$ . . . ^3udn; (*RSP* I 361), though de Moor and van der Lugt (*op. cit.*, 23) reject this example

(b) *Deut 32:1*
   (i) Hebrew: $šmym$ // $^3rṣ$; "heaven // earth"
   (ii) Arabic: $samā^3$ // $^3arḍ$; "heaven // earth" (Q.91.5–6)
   (iii) Ugaritic: $šmm$ // $^3arṣ$; "heaven // earth" (*RSP* I 356)
   (iv) The word pair occurs also in Akkadian (*RSP* II 399) and in Egyptian (*ANET* 365a, line 4)

(c) *Deut 32:2*
   (i) Hebrew: k // k; "like // like"
   (ii) Arabic: k // k; "like // like" (Q.70.8–9)
   (iii) Ugaritic: k // k; "like // like" (*RSP* I 223f.)
   (iv) Note: the parallelism of prepositions is not remarkable, but Dahood's tables include more than 30 examples; for that reason, Arabic examples are included in these notes

(d) *Deut 32:2*
   (i) Hebrew: $^c ly$ // $^c ly$; "upon // upon"
   (ii) Arabic: $^c ala$ // $^c ala$; "upon // upon" (Q.67.22)
   (iii) Ugaritic: $^c l$ // $^c l$; "upon // upon" (*RSP* I 292)

(e) *Deut 32:6*
   (i) Hebrew: h- // h-; (interrogative)
   (ii) Arabic: ^3am // ^3am; (interrogative) (Q.52:35–36)

---

38. On parallelism in Finnish epic poetry, see G. B. Gray, *The Forms of Hebrew Poetry* reprinted by KTAV, New York (1972) 39.

(f) *Deut 32:6*
   (i) Hebrew: *hw²* // *hw²*; "he // he"
   (ii) Arabic: *huwa* // *huwa*; "he // he" (Q.67.1–2)
   (iii) Ugaritic: see the discussion in III.1 (above) [[167]]
(g) *Deut 32:6*
   (i) Hebrew: *qnh* // *ʿśh* "create // make"
   (ii) Arabic: *ḫalaqa* // *jaʿala*; "create // make" (Q.76.2)
   (iii) Note: The Hebrew text has the triple sequence, "create, make, establish" of which the first two members most clearly constitute the parallel word pair. Dahood, in *RSP* I 327, cites here the Ugaritic word pair *qny* // *knn*, corresponding to the first and third elements in the Hebrew sequence. If the comparison is to be less exact, one might note also the following sequence in Arabic: "created // shaped // wrought // composed" (Q.82.7–8)
(h) *Deut 32:8*
   (i) Hebrew: *b* // *b*; "when // when" (in conjunction with the infinitive)
   (ii) Arabic: *ʾidha* // *ʾidha*; "when // when" (Q.82.1–3)
   (iii) Ugaritic: *b* // *b*; "when // when" (*RSP* I 135)
(i) *Deut 32:11*
   (i) Hebrew: *knp* // *ʾbrh*; "wing // pinion"
   (ii) Arabic: *janāḥ* // *qawādim*; "wings // pinions"[39]
(j) *Deut 32:13*
   (i) Hebrew: *mn-* // *mn-*; "from // from"
   (ii) Arabic: *min-* // *min-*; "from // from" (Q.113.2–5)
(k) *Deut 32:22*
   (i) Hebrew: *ʾrṣ* // *hrym²* "earth // mountains"
   (ii) Arabic: *ʾarḍ* // *jibāl*; "earth // mountains" (Q.78.6–7)
   (iii) On the Ugaritic word pair, see the discussion in III.2 (above)
(l) *Deut 32:30*
   (i) Hebrew: Note the numerical parallelism: 1 // 2 and 1,000 // 10,000 (myriad)
   (ii) Arabic: General similarities can be seen in Q.8.65–66, with the following examples of numerical parallelism: 20 // 100; 200 // 1,000; 200 // 2,000
   (iii) Ugaritic: *ʿalp* // *rbt*; "thousand // myriad" (*RSP* I 114)
(m) *Deut 32:38*
   (i) Hebrew: *ʾkl* // *šth*; "eat // drink"

---

39. This word pair is from line 25 of an ode by al-Mutanabbi, one of the few Arabic poets to employ a form of parallelism; for the text see A. J. Arberry, *Arabic Poetry* University Press, Cambridge (1965) 84–91.

    (ii) Arabic: ʾakala + shariba; "eat + drink" (Q.77.43; see also Q.52.19)

    (iii) Ugaritic: ʾkl // šty; "eat // drink" (*RSP* I 108)

(n) *Deut 32:39* [[168]]

    (i) Hebrew: hēmîth // ḥiyyāh; "to kill // to make alive"

    (ii) Arabic: ʾamāta // ʾaḥyā; "to kill // to make alive" (Q.53.44)

    (iii) Note: One might compare Ugaritic *mt* // *hy* ("to die // to live") cf. *RSP* I 270, but the Ugaritic verbs do not carry the causative sense present in both the Hebrew and Arabic word pairs

(o) *Deut 32:41*

    (i) Hebrew: *l* // *l*; "to (against) // to (against)"

    (ii) Arabic: *li* // *li*; "to // to" (Q.92.7–10)

    (iii) Ugaritic: *l* // *l*; "to // to" (cf. *RSP* I 240–242; several entries)

The evidence gathered above, together with similar evidence of word pairs common to Hebrew and Arabic poetry[40] appears to confirm the initial assumptions, namely that any poetry employing parallelism will tend to contain similar word pairs, and that the percentage of cognate terms in the word pairs will vary in proportion to the linguistic relationship of the respective languages in which the poetry is written. This evidence does not disprove Dahood's hypothesis, but it seriously undermines the hypothesis in its present form. Consequently, the utility of the hypothesis for Biblical textual criticism, which is rated very highly by Dahood,[41] should probably be expressed in more cautious terms.

Summary

Ugaritic studies have made considerable progress since the publication of the earliest findings in 1930. Their value for the study of the Old Testament is beyond question, and at many points they have shed new light on the Hebrew text and on the background of the world of the Hebrews. If the notes in this paper have a somewhat negative tone, then that may serve as a reminder that the use of Ugaritic in the study of the Hebrew text is not without difficulties of a practical nature. But there [[169]] are many points in the text of Deuteronomy where the Ugaritic resources have proved to be invaluable in clarifying our knowledge of the text and in increasing our knowledge of the ancient world.[42] If, indeed, the community of biblical scholars is currently suffering from a

---

40. In my article in *Semitics* 5 (1975) see footnote 2; and in a paper entitled "Parallel Word Pairs in the Song of Deborah" *JETS* 20 (1977) 15–22.

41. *RSP* I 78–86.

42. Many other Ugaritic parallels are examined in my *Commentary on the Book of Deuteronomy* (NICOT, 1976).

mild dose of "pan-Ugaritism," no doubt that will eventually pass, as did pan-Babylonianism and other afflictions of the early part of the century. And when the affliction passes, the result can only be healthy. The enthusiastic outpourings of Dahood, and the critical nagging of conservatives such as myself, may both contribute in the long run to an increased appreciation for the text of the Bible.

Wisdom Influence in Deuteronomy

C. BREKELMANS

[[28]] One of the most important books on *Deuteronomy* to appear in recent years is the study of M. Weinfeld that was published in 1972 under the title: *Deuteronomy and the Deuteronomic School.*[1] Our main concern here with this study is not with the wealth of information it offers, nor with its extensive comparisons with extra-biblical literature, nor with its many detailed studies on biblical texts. Rather, we shall deal with the new theory it offers on the origin of the *Book of Deuteronomy*. We shall also restrict ourselves almost exclusively to the *Book of Deuteronomy* itself, as Weinfeld himself in fact does in the greater part of his study, though the title suggests otherwise.

Weinfeld's main thesis is that the *Book of Dt* originated in the scribal circles of the Jerusalem court. Thus, he looks for that origin in the South, in Judah, and not in Northern Israel, as has been defended by many scholars since A. C. Welch.[2] The arguments for the northern origin, however, are not discussed by Weinfeld; he concentrates mainly on the arguments in favor of his own position. This is also the case for the different theories about the circles in which the origin of *Dt* should be sought. The theories about a possible prophetic or priestly origin of the Book are not discussed, and the only theory he tries to refute is

Reprinted with permission from *La Sagesse de l'Ancien Testament* (ed. M. Gilbert; Bibliotheca ephemeridum theologicarum lovaniensium 51; Louvain: Louvain University Press, 1978) pp. 28–38.

1. Oxford, 1972 [reprinted, Winona Lake, Ind.: Eisenbrauns, 1992].

2. *The Code of Deuteronomy: A New Theory of Its Origins*, London, 1924; idem, *Deuteronomy: The Framework to the Code*, London, 1932. For a recent survey, see F. R. McCurley, Jr., *The Home of Deuteronomy Revisited*, in *A Light unto My Path, O.T. Studies in Honor of Jacob M. Meyers*, Philadelphia, 1974, pp. 295–315.

that of von Rad who considered the rural Levites ("Landleviten") as its authors. Weinfeld rejects this thesis by drawing attention to the fact that this thesis is based on the relatively late text of *Neh* 8:7-8. It seems rather improbable that this text would indicate anything about Levitical praxis in the pre-Exilic period. Its content fits so well with the Levitical theology of the Chronicler himself. That the rural Levites were the authors of *Dt* is all the more improbable since by introducing a unique central sanctuary, the Levites "would be comparable to one cutting the branch upon which he sits"[3] and also since "so insignificant a provincial [[29]] class as the Levites" could not possibly have at its disposal such a rich variety of material as is used in *Dt* and in the dtc history.[4] By bringing in the dtc history at this point, it seems that Weinfeld tries to refute more than von Rad ever tried to prove. Nobody, as far as I know, has ever said that the dtc history was written by the rural Levites. However this may be, von Rad's theory is the only one of all the available theories that Weinfeld tries to refute. His main concern has a more positive orientation. He tries to assemble all the arguments for the thesis that the authors who were responsible for the composition of *Dt* must be sought elsewhere, namely, in the scribal circles of the royal court at Jerusalem. For this purpose, he divides his book into three parts.

In the first part, Weinfeld tries to show that the various orations of *Dt* are not of cultic origin, but were literary, programmatic compositions from the very beginning. If the character of the orations reflects a cultic ceremony, it would be reasonable, Weinfeld says, "to suppose that the clerics who took part in the ceremony were responsible for the composition of the book."[5] If, however, they are purely literary creations without any relation to the cult, the priestly or levitical origin of *Dt* becomes more uncertain. Moreover, study of the structure of ancient treaties has shown that the literary structure of the covenant in the *Book of Dt* is an imitation of such treaties and not, as von Rad tried to demonstrate, the reflection of a cultic ceremony of which we know nothing. The treaty elements of *Dt* are then discussed in a long chapter in which special attention is given to the curses and their similarity—even as far as order is concerned—with the vassal treaties of Esarhaddon. And when Weinfeld deals with the elements that determine the style of the *Book of Dt*, i.e. its public function, its didactic purpose, and its fully developed rhetorical technique, he argues that these

---

3. Weinfeld, p. 55.
4. *Ibid.*
5. *Ibid.*, p. 57.

are the same as those of the treaties. At the same time he refers to its great similarity with wisdom literature. So the conclusion of the first part is that the authors of *Dt* must be sought among circles that held public office, that had at their command a vast reservoir of literary material, that were particularly well acquainted with international treaties, that were capable of developing and had developed a rhetorical technique, that were experienced in literary composition, and that were skilled with the pen. Consequently, the authors must have been *soferim-ḥakamim* 〚'wise scribes' or 'learned men'〛.[6]

In the second part of his study, Weinfeld considers several elements such as those connected with demythologization and secularization and the relationship with wisdom literature.

〚30〛 In the third part, he brings together the terminology and the ideas that are common to both *Dt* and the wisdom literature.

Before Weinfeld, several scholars had already pointed out the similarities in form, content, style, and terminology between *Dt* and the wisdom literature.[7] In most cases, these studies were not carried out in great detail, and the conclusions of some of them were more modest in that they only spoke of some wisdom influence on *Dt*. Nor has the search for wisdom influence been restricted to *Dt*, for, as you well know, wisdom influences have recently been discovered also in narrative texts, in the laws, and in various prophets of the Old Testament.[8] Thus, Weinfeld's book can be situated within a certain tendency of Old Testament studies. But as far as *Dt* is concerned, Weinfeld goes much further in his conclusions than others have before him and, at the same time, his book is the most extensive and thorough study of the whole problematic to date. As a kind of culminating point, it is a very important work. But does it throw light on the origin of *Dt*?

Let us first consider the highly rhetorical language of the *Book of Dt*. Are the sermons in *Dt* literary compositions made at a writing desk or are they real sermons intended to be delivered? To answer this question, let us first of all try to introduce a distinction. I do not think that it is acceptable to place all the orations in *Dt* and in the dtc history on the same level. Such orations in dtc history as those of *Joshua* 23 and *1 Kings* 8 and the theological reflections in *Judges* 2 and *2 Kings* 17 are, without any doubt, literary compositions that were never meant to

---

6. *Ibid.*, pp. 177–178.

7. For a survey of the scholarly work in this field, see B. Moore, *The Scribal Contribution to Dt., 4, 1–40*, Michigan, Univ. Microfilm International, 1976, pp. 8–23.

8. For the literature on this subject, see J. L. Crenshaw, *Method in Determining Wisdom Influence upon "Historical" Literature*, in *JBL* 88 (1969) pp. 129–142.

be read at a public gathering. And, indeed, they have a well-defined function in the composition and theology of the dtc history. They were composed for that very function and to that function must their meaning be restricted. This cannot be said in the same way of the sermons such as those in Deuteronomy 5–11, whose function in the composition of the *Book of Dt* is not so clear. They may have been written at a writing desk, but that does not exclude the possibility that they were used later on public occasions, as was also the case for the international treaty texts.

The literary style of *Dt* has been compared with certain extra-biblical texts that are written in the same kind of highly rhetorical style and show many similarities with *Dt* not only in form but also in content. The main example of this seems to be the so-called vassal treaties of Esarhaddon. But before we conclude that the rhetorical style of *Dt* was borrowed, taken over, or even strongly influenced by Assyrian documents ⟦31⟧ like the vassal treaties, it seems to me that the proper method of Old Testament study requires the study of the Israelite tradition first. We have to ask if there is a possibility that the style of *Dt* is the result of that tradition. And it does seem that there was indeed a preaching tradition in Israel that prepared the way for the highly developed rhetorical style of *Dt*. It has been shown in recent years that such texts as *Exod* 12:25–27; 13:3–16; 19:3–8; 23:20–33; 32:7–14; 34:10–16; *Joshua* 24; part of *1 Samuel* 12 and so on are to be considered protodeuteronomic.[9] Thus, there is perhaps an Israelite tradition that could explain the style of *Dt*. Although there seems to be a growing tendency to accept this idea, no general agreement, of course, has yet been reached on the matter. The problem with Weinfeld is that he pays almost no attention to this tendency. In the same way, he neglects a possible evolution within *Dt* and the dtc history itself. He dismisses the whole problem of editorial strands by saying that we have no fixed criteria by which to differentiate them.[10] That there are no generally accepted criteria may be true, but one can-

9. See N. Lohfink, *Das Hauptgebot* (*An. Bib.* 20), Rome, 1963; C. Brekelmans, *Éléments déutéronomiques dans le Pentateuque*, in *Aux grands Carrefours de la Révélation et de l'Exégèse de l'Ancien Testament*, Bruges, 1967, pp. 77–91; G. Schmitt, *Der Landtag von Sichem* (*Arbeiten zur Theologie* 1:15), Stuttgart, 1964; M. Caloz, *Exode XIII 3–16 et son rapport au Deutéronome*, in *RB* 75 (1968) pp. 5–62; F. Langlamet, *"Israël et l'Habitant du Pays." Vocabulaire et Formules d'Ex. XXXIV 11–16*, in *RB* 76 (1969) pp. 321–350, 481–507; G. Schmitt, *Du sollst keinen Frieden schliessen mit den Bewohners des Landes* (*BWANT* 91), Stuttgart, 1970; J. Loza, *Exode XXXII et la Rédaction de JE*, in *VT* 23 (1973) pp. 31–55; F. E. Wilms, *Das Jahwistische Bundesbuch in Ex. 34* (*SANT* 32), Munich, 1973; J. Halbe, *Das Privilegrecht Jahwes Ex. 34, 10–26* (*FRLANT* 114). Göttingen, 1975; E. Otto, *Das Bundes-Mazzotfest von Gilgal* (*BWANT* 107), Stuttgart, 1975; D. J. McCarthy, *Treaty and Covenant* (*An. Bib.* 21), Rome, 1978².

10. Weinfeld, p. 2.

not possibly study *Dt* and the dtc history without at least giving some attention to such compositional problems. This same criticism applies to Weinfeld's lack of interest in the prehistory of *Dt*. In doing so, he is left with only one possible procedure: comparison with extra-biblical texts. The question is, however, if this is a proper methodology for the study of the Old Testament. It is possible to explain the style of *Dt* as the culmination of a long preaching tradition in Israel, which must have had its appropriate setting in the cult. This could indicate, perhaps, that the *origin* of the deuteronomic preaching style was indeed the cult. It does not prove, however, that the deuteronomic sermons themselves were cultic: they could be literary products that used the traditional style of cultic preaching, thus giving it a more sophisticated and therefore an artificial form. This is very difficult to determine. The same is the case when we ask if the sermons were written down before they were preached or if it was the other way around. The extra-biblical texts such [[32]] as the vassal treaties of Esarhaddon were, of course, first put into writing, but they were also meant to be read publicly. This could also be the case for the sermons in *Dt*, but, again, it is very difficult to decide one way or the other.

There is some probability, then, that the sermons in *Dt* were culminations of a long Israelite preaching tradition. This might be taken as an indication that we ought to look for the origin of these sermons in the same circles as those in which the preaching tradition had its origin, i.e. the priestly circles. I have no objection to calling these priests scribes. But one must, it seems to me, object rather strongly against the identification of scribes and sages. When one does so, one is not far removed from saying that all well-educated and literary people in ancient Israel were sages. It may be, as Weinfeld says,[11] that in all former theories about the origin of *Dt*, it was accepted that the orations were first delivered before they were written down and it remains possible that it was just the reverse. But I do not see that this necessarily brings with it a new theory about the circles in which Dt originated, unless one ignores all connection of these sermons with the older preaching tradition in Israel.

We come now to the treaty background of *Dt*. Weinfeld is considerably more reserved in this regard than some scholars who discover a treaty structure or treaty elements in many Old Testament texts. He states very clearly that "only Deuteronomy has preserved the classical structure of the political treaty."[12] But even when this is restricted to *Dt*

11. Weinfeld, pp. 8–9.
12. *Ibid.*, p. 66.

as such, many questions remain open. When one reads, for example, that 1:1–6a and 5:6a are the preamble of the treaty structure and that the historical prologue is to be found in 1:6b–3:29; 5; and 9:7–10, 11,[13] which are in fact the deuteronomistic introduction to *Dt* and the dtc history and the later plural insertions in cc. 5–11, one gets the impression that there was no preamble and no historical prologue in the original *Dt.* D. McCarthy, on the other hand, finds the historical-paraenetic prologue in cc. 5–11. Again, Weinfeld considers 4:1–23 as the basic stipulation of allegiance,[14] whereas McCarthy finds "all the basic elements of the covenant scheme," in 4:1–31, although he concedes that it is no covenant document in the strict sense of the word, but rather a speech that, in its basic outline, reproduces the structure of the covenant.[15] These instances are mentioned only in order to show that defenders [[33]] of a treaty structure in *Dt* have some difficulties in discovering where the respective elements of that structure are to be found. The least one can say is that many problems must still be studied in greater detail.

But for me, the comparison of *Dt* with the vassal treaties has always involved problems that have yet to be resolved satisfactorily. To present one of these problems, let me begin with a quotation from McCarthy's study on the subject. He says: "The vassal treaties sought to control the vassal state. Essentially it was a question of the sovereign extending and exercising his power in a place outside the center of his own domination."[16] Now in the Old Testament in general and in *Dt* in particular, there seems to be no place for the idea that Yahweh is extending his dominion to a place or among a people where he was not at home before. The real object of the Old Testament texts in which a treaty background has been discovered is rather the strengthening or the maintenance of the already existing relationship between Yahweh and his people, i.e., the demand of loyalty, a demand which is, of course, not restricted to the treaty texts.

When we consider the details of the structure of the vassal treaties, there is the fact that an historical prologue is missing in all the treaty texts of the first millennium B.C.[17] When Weinfeld says that this may "be simply due to a gap in our documentary evidence"[18] and at the same

13. *Ibid.*

14. *Ibid.*

15. McCarthy, p. 193.

16. *Ibid.*, p. 118.

17. The possible exceptions do not change the overall picture. See A. E. F. Campbell, *An Historical Prologue in a Seventh-Century Treaty*, in *Bib.* 50 (1960) pp. 534–5; P. Buis, *Un traité d'Assurbanipal*, in *VT* 28 (1978) pp. 469–72.

18. Weinfeld, p. 67.

time that the historical prologue was not unknown to the Assyrians but perhaps was left out as "a matter of principle,"[19] he does not seem to be impartial. It may be true, as McCarthy says,[20] that even for the Hittites the historical prologue was not indispensable to each and every treaty because it is missing in some texts, mainly those from Ugarit. But I wonder if we would ever have discovered the treaty background for various Old Testament texts if there were no historical prologue. It seems to me that what perhaps was not essential in the Hittite treaties and what is missing completely in the treaty texts of the first millennium is, nevertheless, most essential in the Old Testament. I must admit that this makes me unsure about this whole question. To this must be added that such historical prologues (to retain the treaty terminology) are already found in predeuteronomic texts like the Decalogue, *Exod* 19:3–8 and *Joshua* 24. Therefore, I should like to suggest that these prologues [[34]] represent a very specific Israelite element in all these texts and in *Dt* as well.

Another striking characteristic of the vassal treaties of the first millennium is their great emphasis on curses. The Hittites already put the curses before the blessings, and the Assyrians even left the blessings out completely.[21] Now there is no doubt that the curses in Deuteronomy 28 are much more developed than the blessings, but it remains that the blessings precede the curses, which occurs in none of the vassal treaties we know of.

Another difference from the treaty texts is the statement in Deut 26:16–19 that the covenant was made and the oath was sworn. Moreover, in this text the oath taking is bilateral, which, according to McCarthy, is quite unexpected and almost impossible in a vassal treaty.[22]

All these questions of detail leave me much in doubt about the treaty background of *Dt.* But the problem becomes even more complicated when we take into consideration that many elements of the treaty texts are also found in other texts, such as royal grants, royal decrees, boundary stones, loyalty oaths, and even law codes. This is why Weinfeld discusses the problem of whether *Dt* is to be seen as a law code rather than as a treaty.[23] Although he prefers to consider it a treaty text, he concedes that there is a mixture of covenant and law in *Deuteronomy.* As far as the royal grants are concerned, he states that the historical prologue in *Dt* adds to the treaty form the grant formulation

---

19. *Ibid.*, p. 68.
20. McCarthy, p. 144.
21. McCarthy, pp. 144 ff.
22. *Ibid.*, p. 182ff.
23. *Ibid.*, p. 146ff.

taken over from the patriarchal traditions.[24] In a more recent study on
the loyalty oaths, Weinfeld concludes that some of the political documents that were considered treaties are actually fealty oaths. This is the
case for the vassal treaties of Esarhaddon.[25] If there is external influence, therefore, it is not so certain that this influence came from the
vassal treaties rather than from other ancient oriental traditions.

One of the major arguments that the influence came from the vassal treaties is, after all, that the order of some of the curses in Deuteronomy 28, especially those in vv. 26–30, is based on the order of the
Mesopotamian pantheon. This seems very probable to me. But if the
Esarhaddon text is not a treaty but rather a loyalty oath, it can no
longer be used in an argument for the treaty background of these
curses. Moreover, if this was indeed the common order of curses in Assyrian texts, and if this was taken over in *Dt*, there is no doubt that it
betrays the strong cultural [[35]] influence of Assyria. But it is rather
dangerous to accept direct dependence on one particular text.

I have already mentioned that the main concern of the Old Testament texts in which treaty influence has been traced is the loyalty of the
people. This brings me to a well-known example of such a loyalty oath,
that of Queen Mother Naqiᵓa. To assure the succession of Assurbanipal, she imposed such an oath not only on the brothers of the future
king, but she also made agreements with "the provincial governors, the
royal representatives, the captains, the freemen, the appointees of the
entire land and with the Assyrians, with all men and women, whosoever
was party to the covenant and oath of Zakutu, which she set up with the
people of the entire land."[26] When we are looking for parallels with the
covenant traditions of the Old Testament and with the form in which
this is presented in *Dt*, I would prefer such documents more than the
international treaties and the political ideas connected with them.

However this may be, Weinfeld presupposes that only the scribes at
the royal court were fully acquainted with treaties and other official
documents. This is indeed a presupposition, and no shred of proof is
offered for it. McCarthy rejected it, saying that such knowledge was
"the property of any educated man."[27] But this again is a statement

24. *Ibid.*, p. 74.

25. M. Weinfeld, *The Loyalty Oath in the Ancient Near East*, in *Shnaton* 1 (1975) 51–122.
Cf. also McCarthy, pp. 114ff.

26. This text has been published by R. F. Harper, *Assyrian and Babylonian Letters*,
Chicago, 1913, nr. 1239. For the transliteration and translation, see L. Waterman, *Royal
Correspondence of the Assyrian Empire II*, Ann Arbor, 1931, pp. 360ff. Our translation was
taken from H. Lewy, *Nitokris-Naqiᵓa*, in *JNES* 11 (1952) pp. 282–283, note 92.

27. In his review of Weinfeld in *Bib.* 54 (1973) p. 452.

without any proof behind it. Lohfink even accepts that there was such an inflation of oaths and treaties that even the man in the street would have been acquainted with them: they were part and parcel of the culture.[28] Although such statements are difficult to prove, there may be something to them.

But in addition to such possibilities, one should not forget that there also existed a long covenantal tradition in Israel. In its forms of expression, the cultural influence of the great empire was felt in Israel,[29] but I am not so certain that this was the case for the ideas on the covenant itself. At least, it is not clear to me how one can say that this influence came almost exclusively from the international treaties. And I am not [[36]] convinced that the only circle to which *Dt* could be ascribed is that of the scribes at the royal court.

There remain the specific wisdom elements in *Dt*. At the outset, as I have stated, a clear distinction should be made between scribes and sages. Scribes were found in all educated classes of Israelite society. And those who had the title of scribe performed different functions in the administration of the kingdom, the palace, etc. For a detailed study on this question, I refer you to the recent study of B. Moore.[30] One also has to accept with Whybray that "wisdom" was not the sole possession of a professional class (if there ever was such a class).[31] It is to be expected that wisdom elements would appear in various kinds of literature since wisdom was indeed the possession of all educated classes. We ought not to think of priests, prophets, and sages in terms of watertight compartments and differentiate between them so sharply that all contact between them would have been impossible.

In this connection, I refer to *Jer* 8:8, which is one of the basic texts, and in fact the only one for the pre-Exilic period, that indicates the activity of the wise men: "How can you say: we are wise and the law of Yahweh is with us. Yet behold, the false pen of scribes has made it into a lie." According to Weinfeld, this text shows that the wise men in the period of Hezekiah and Josiah did not confine their activity only to

28. N. Lohfink, *Unsere grossen Wörter*, Freiburg-Basel-Vienna, 1977, p. 40: "Jedenfalls gehörte es damals im Bewusstsein der Judäer zu einer überlegenen Kultur von Verträgen durchwaltet zu sein . . . das könnte man dem Mann auf der Strasse nicht mehr rauben."

29. For the religious aspects of this influence, see J. McKay, *Religion in Judah under the Assyrians* (*SBT* 26), London, 1973; M. Cogan, *Imperialism and Religion* (*SBL Monograph Series* 19), Missoula, 1974.

30. B. Moore, *Scribal Contribution*, pp. 37–67.

31. R. N. Whybray, *The Intellectual Tradition in the Old Testament* (*BZAW* 135), Berlin, 1974.

wisdom compositions, but were also active in the field of the Law, i.e. they "also invaded the sphere of religious composition."[32] I think that everyone is aware of the problems of this much disputed passage.[33] The text suggests, perhaps, that the scribes who were falsifying the Law occupied themselves with the study and the exposition of the Law. But who were these scribes? That they considered themselves to be wise (adjective) does not prove that they are to be identified with the sages as members of a special professional class. It is not so clear, therefore, that this text, which is so basic for Weinfeld, is more appropriate for his theory than the text of *Neh* 8:7–8 is for the thesis of von Rad.

This text of Jeremiah not only demonstrates, for Weinfeld, the identity of the *soferim* [['scribes']] and the *ḥakamim* [['learned men']]; it also marks a turning point in the development of the function of these scribes in that it shows that they invaded the sphere of religious literature. Weinfeld's idea is reinforced by his conception of ancient wisdom before *Dt* as native shrewdness, persuasive speech, cunning, pragmatic talent, and the possession of extraordinary [[37]] knowledge. The authors of *Dt*, however, "conceive wisdom in an entirely novel manner" that indeed reflects a turning point in the Israelite conception of wisdom,[34] i.e. they invaded the field of religion and they studied the Law as indicated in *Jer* 8:8. This opinion of Weinfeld seems rather dubious. The notion that older wisdom in Israel was only practical wisdom and pragmatic talent is a bit out of date. It is generally accepted nowadays that wisdom in Egypt, Mesopotamia, and also Israel was religious from the very beginning. It is rather difficult to consider this as a dtc creation. On the other hand, the religious elements of *Dt* are quite different from those of wisdom literature. That God guides everything because he is the creator of the world, that man cannot understand the ways of God, and that man's basic attitude toward God is one of religious fear are frequent themes in wisdom literature. In some narrative texts that have been considered in recent times as belonging to wisdom, such as the Joseph story and the succession narrative, one of the characteristic elements is said to be that in them there is no direct intervention of God in the course of history. If this is indeed one of the characteristics of wisdom literature, it is clear that *Dt* is something quite different, to say nothing of the dtc history. Most scholars also acknowledge that the more specific elements of the religion of Israel were taken up in wisdom only in a very late period, in fact we meet

32. Weinfeld, p. 162.
33. For the problems of this text, see Whybray, pp. 22f.
34. Weinfeld, pp. 254ff.

them there for the first time in *Jesus Sirach* and the *Wisdom of Solomon*. But all these specific elements are very essential to *Dt* and the dtc history. The authors of *Dt*, if they were indeed sages, were a very special kind of sage. To call them sages and to place the origin of *Dt* in their circles obfuscates rather than illuminates. One gets the impression that Weinfeld creates a very special kind of sage in order to prove that the authors of *Dt* were such sages.

The only argument that remains, therefore, concerns the terminology and perhaps some of the ideas of *Dt* that also occur in wisdom literature. Both of these elements could be said to be characteristic of, or even specific to, wisdom literature. But here again the situation is rather complex. If wisdom was not the private property of the sages but the common property of all educated classes, it seems natural enough for at least some of its ideas and part of its terminology to be shared by other authors. Even the didactic style as such may have been common to wise men, preachers, and others. Form-critical studies have accustomed us to accept one special life setting for each literary form. But the clear-cut conclusions of such an approach do not always do justice to the complexity of real life. Instruction and admonition can be used in different situations by different people and it is not at all necessary for the one to [[38]] be derived from the other. For example, the call to hear occurs in the sermons of *Dt*, in the prophetic literature, and in the wisdom literature. Must we accept that this call was first made in wisdom literature and then was taken over by other forms? Hardmeier has recently shown that such a call is not a literary form at all, but a rhetorical element that can be used in various situations.[35] The same applies to the motive clauses in legal texts, which are found already in part of the Covenant Code. Motivations for certain forms of behavior are not the exclusive possession of sages. Preachers may have used them as well, without being directly dependent on the wisdom tradition.

It is impossible here to go into any detail on the question of terminology. But studies such as that of Malfroy,[36] who considers many words as specific for wisdom literature and then also finds them in *Dt*, have to be redone with more precision and critical awareness. What Crenshaw has tried to do for the historical texts[37] should also be done for other texts. We need a clear method for the approach to such problems. I am not denying that wisdom influenced *Dt*, but I am saying

---

35. C. Hardmeier, *Texttheorie und biblische Exegese. Zur rhetorischen Funktion der Trauermetaphorik in der Prophetie* (*Beitr. z. Ev. Th.* 79), Munich, 1978, pp. 302ff.

36. J. Malfroy, *Sagesse et Loi dans le Deutéronome*, in *VT* 15 (1965) pp. 46–65.

37. See note 8.

that thus far no real method for the study of these problems has been worked out.

Let me finish by pointing out that *Dt*, from the very beginning to the end, has the form of a speech of Moses. This shows that its authors considered themselves as continuing the work of Moses, as being mediators between God and the people, as explaining for their own time what God asked from the people. Now there is a long tradition in the Old Testament that saw Moses as a prophetic figure. This may already be seen in the call narrative in *Exodus* 3–4 and it is expressly stated in *Hos* 12:14. Moses is also called a prophet in Deuteronomy 18. It is generally accepted that prophets play an important role in the dtc history and some scholars even speak of a prophetic redaction of this work. Indeed, there seem to be many arguments in favor of a prophetic background of *Dt* and of deuteronomic literature.

Weinfeld's book is thought-provoking as regards the origins of *Dt*: it forces one to rethink the entire problematic. And this is not the least of its merits. So many detailed expositions of specific texts of *Dt* are given, that one cannot afford to neglect it.

Part 2

The Outer Frame:
Deuteronomy 1–3 and 31–34

Principal Observations on the Basic Story in Deuteronomy 1–3

TIMO VEIJOLA

I

[[249]] The following survey of Deuteronomy 1–3 is based on the conviction that these chapters have reached their present state as a result of a complicated literary-historical process. The attention paid to this process is an indispensable premise for the proper understanding of the structure and the contents of these chapters.[1] Still a couple of decades ago the recognition of this fact was the self-evident starting point of every study done on Deuteronomy, but this is no longer so. The new literary approaches which stress the priority of the present text have vigorously affected exegetical studies[2] as well as other literary branches of humanities and sometimes even called into question the principal right of the traditional exegetical methods on the whole. It goes without saying that we are confronted here with a new methodical achievement and its merits are undisputed in the areas where we are dealing with

Reprinted with permission from *"Wünschet Jerusalem Frieden": IOSOT Congress, Jerusalem 1986* (ed. Matthias Augustin and Klaus-Dietrich Schunck; Beiträge zur Erforschung des Alten Testaments und des Antiken Judentums 13; Frankfurt am Main: Peter Lang, 1988) 249–59.

1. An important principal view in this matter was recently expressed by L. Perlitt, "Deuteronomium 1–3 im Streit der exegetischen Methoden," in N. Lohfink (ed.), *Das Deuteronomium* (BEThL 68; Leuven, 1985) 149–163.

2. A great influence has been exerted by R. Alter, *The Art of Biblical Narrative* (London, 1981). In the study of Deuteronomy, the new approach is represented, e.g., by G. Braulik in his stylistic analysis of Deuteronomy 4, *Die Mittel deuteronomischer Rhetorik erhoben aus Deuteronomium 4,1–40* (AnBib 68; Rome, 1978) and still more clearly by R. Polzin, *Moses and the Deuteronomist. A Literary Study of the Deuteronomic History, part 1 (Deuteronomy, Joshua, Judges)* (New York, 1980).

texts which have been uniform since the beginning. It is scarcely a mere chance that the object of the new literary approaches has usually been narrative texts, most often taken from the book of Genesis and the books of Samuel,[3] where we have at least some basis for the hope of finding literary units preserved in their original form.

Generally, however, the texts of the OT have not been transmitted to us in their original form, not even in Genesis or in the books of Samuel, to say nothing of the other books. Consequently, a literary method starting from and concentrating only on the present text is faced with a number of problems. Of course, a structure can be looked for even in texts which have their origin in a gradual literary growth, but the premise is that the extent and the diachronic relationship of the original units are known.[4]

This is not the case in the "rhetorical analysis" that R. Polzin presents of the introductory speech of Moses in Deut 1:6–4:40.[5] His analysis is based on the distinction made between reporting and reported speech, with other words: he observes where the narrator himself is speaking and where he reports [[250]] the utterances of Moses.[6] Because the reporting speech plays a particularly central role in Polzin's theory he pays close attention to the parenthetical notes in Moses' speech in 2:10, 12:20–23 and 3:9, 11, 13b–14 where he supposes to perceive the voice of the narrator. According to him, the narrator in these utterances would represent the same role to his contemporaries as Moses once did to his listeners.[7] One can't get rid of the impression that we are dealing here with a very strange narrator who expresses his main concerns in this kind of marginal, ethnographic and geographic parenthesis which up till now the research has with cause considered to be the latest additions to these chapters.[8] On

---

3. Most of the texts treated by Alter are taken from these books (cf. ibid., 3–12, 27–32, 42–46, 52–56, 60–87, 93–94, 107–113, 115–130, 137–153, 160–176, 185–189).

4. An example of this necessity is given by T. Veijola, "Toisenlaista eksegetiikkaa," *TAik* 89 (1984) 247–254, cf. idem, "David in Keila. Tradition und Interpretation in 1 Sam 23,1–13," *RB* 91 (1984) 51–87.

5. *Moses and the Deuteronomist*, 29–43. Parts of this analysis are reproduced in Polzin's article "Reporting Speech in the Book of Deuteronomy: Toward A Compositional Analysis of the Deuteronomic History," in *Traditions in Transformation, To Frank Moore Cross on the Occasion of His Sixtieth Birthday* (Winona Lake, 1981) 193–211. [[Reprinted in this volume, pp. 355–74 below.]]

6. The distinction has its roots in the literary theory of the Russian "Bakhtin's Circle"; see Polzin, *Moses and the Deuteronomist*, 18–19. The same background and method is presented in Polzin's paper "The Speaking Person and his Voice in 1 Samuel," given at the Salamanca Congress of the IOSOT in 1983, published in VTS 36 (1985) 218–229.

7. Polzin, *Moses and the Deuteronomist*, 30.

8. Cf. H. D. Preuß, *Deuteronomium* (Erträge der Forschung 164; Darmstadt, 1982) 84.

the whole, the results Polzin achieves in his analysis of Deuteronomy
1–3(4) don't at all meet the high expectations which he gives at the
beginning of his book when aiming to fill the enormous gaps left by
the traditional historical-critical research, as he maintains.[9] Actually,
Polzin's analysis confirms in a negative way the fact that the study of
the total structure of the present text can only be the last step in the
multiphase exegetical work.[10] The new "literary criticism" is not a tool
which could substitute for the traditional literary criticism.

II

The different form of address to the people (*Numeruswechsel*) has
played a central as well as disputed role in the traditional literary criticism of Deuteronomy and of its introductory chapters.[11] In my opinion, it is impossible to take the constant and often surprising change of
the number in the address (2 pers. in singular or in plural) only as a
literary style device. At least in the later textual tradition it was not
conceived in this way but attempts were made as far as possible to har-
monize the number, as the almost regular variant readings in the early
translations most clearly show. It goes without saying that these variants usually lack any text-critical value. Instead of that, they are, however, an eloquent proof of the fact that the problem caused by the
different number was already felt in an early stage of the tradition.

Nevertheless, the changing number of the address in Deuteronomy is no general means which could be applied automatically. E.g.,
Deuteronomy 4, which from the literary-critical point of view is one of
the most difficult sections in Deuteronomy, cannot be properly analy-
sed only on the basis of the different number.[12] The confusion of singular and plural address is typical of the most recent levels of the text
where possibly older texts are quoted.

[251] In Deut 3:21–22 there is a late addition where Moses encour-
ages his successor Joshua. In this passage the singular address changes
unexpectedly into the plural, but without the plural parts, especially

9. Polzin, *Moses and the Deuteronomist*, 12–16. Perlitt's estimation of Polzin's stand
regarding previous studies is: "Dieses aus der Zurückweisung alles Bisherigen gewonnene
Novitätsbewußtsein hat für mich nur noch etwas Lächerliches" (BEThL 68) 153.

10. In contrast to Polzin, who places literary criticism (in the sense he uses it) before
historical criticism (ibid., 6).

11. On the history of the problem, see Chr. T. Begg, "The Significance of *Numeruswechsel* in Deuteronomy and the 'Pre-History' of the Question," *EThL* 55 (1979) 116–124.

12. This was observed already by A. Bertholet, *Deuteronomium* (KHC 5; Freiburg/
Leipzig/Tübingen, 1899) 13.

without v. 22, the address would become fragmentary. The solution to the problem is probably to be found in the manner of the writer in basing his statement on earlier texts where both the singular and the plural are used.[13]

In the other parts of Deuteronomy 1–3, however, the different number deserves serious attention as a literary-critical indicator. Nevertheless, it is usually not enough alone, but requires still other criteria as additional evidence.[14] E.g., in Deut 1:21, which is the *locus classicus* of the *Numeruswechsel* debate, the singular address is surprising, indeed, as in the preceding (v. 20) and the following (v. 22) context Israel is addressed in the plural. Furthermore, there are two additional arguments: first, the contents and the wording of v. 21 are to a great extent a repetition of v. 8, where Israel is exhorted to take up the occupation of the Promised Land; and second, the encouragement given in v. 21 and the urging of fearlessness, which is lacking in v. 8, does not have its natural location here, because it is pronounced before the spies had explored the land and brought news about it (cf. v. 29). Observations of a principally similar kind can be made also on other singular parts in these chapters (1:31a; 2:7, 24aβb, 25; 3:2).[15] From the point of the subject matter, they are combined by two common themes: the care taken by God for his people in the wilderness (1:31a and 2:7) and the encouragement pronounced by God in a military oration to his people before the conquest of the land (1:21; 2:24aβb, 25; 3:2).

In this connection, we must take into consideration that in Deuteronomy 2 there is still another singular level which is earlier and somewhat broader than the above mentioned. It consists of vv. 9aα²b, 18, 19, 26–28, 29bα, 30b, 37a, and its main purpose is to emphasize Israel's peaceful attitude towards its neighbours Moab, Ammon and Sihon, the king of Heshbon. Thus, the singular address to Israel does not necessarily prove that the author of all these passages would be one single person.

The presence of two redactional levels in the singular form does not, however, result in the unity of the remaining parts of Deuteronomy 1–3;

13. The plural suffix in the divine name אלהיכם [['your (pl.) God']] (v. 21) may depend on the neighbouring context (vv. 18,20), whereas the plural form of v. 22 can be explained by two phenomena: the first part of the verse is based on Deut 31:1–8 where a similar encouragement is given both to the people (v. 6) and to Joshua (v. 8); the second part of the verse consists of a coined expression that elsewhere occurs only in the plural (Josh 23:3,11, cf. Deut 1:30).

14. Cf. R. Smend, *Die Entstehung des Alten Testaments* (ThW 1; Stuttgart, 1978) 72.

15. To the traditional literary criticism, the secondary character of these verses, as well as that of 1:21, has been clear for a century; see Preuß, *Deuteronomium*, 46.

but also in the sections of the plural diction there are several expansions from different ages, which we are not able to discuss here. Anyway, a close analysis of these chapters will show[16] that they cannot completely be attributed to two [[252]] or three redactors, whether we follow the tripartite model DtrH-DtrP-DtrN which was developed in Göttingen[17] or the division into a pre-exilic and an exilic deuteronomistic redaction which enjoys a great popularity in the Anglo-Saxon world.[18] The number of the redactors has for certain been greater than two or three—perhaps half a dozen, apart from minor glossaic additions.

III

Nevertheless, in Deuteronomy 1–3 there is a basic story with plural address which runs through these chapters. At this point I disagree with S. Mittmann, who on the basis of an extremely sophisticated literary-critical analysis, assumes that the basic story closed with 2:8b and was continued by the proclamation of the Decalogue in Deuteronomy 5.[19] In my opinion, the conception of M. Noth, who considers Deuteronomy 1–3 in their basic form to be the beginning of the Deuteronomistic History,[20] comes nearer to the truth. However, it seems to me that the basic story was not quite so broad as Noth supposed. Deuteronomy 1 did not yet contain the instructions of Moses to the organization of the people of Israel (1:9–18),[21] and the following story about the mission of the spies with all its consequences had not yet reached its present scope (1:19–46), but still missing were specifically those parts (viz. vv. 19a*, 22bβ, 24b, 28–30, 31b, 32, 41–46) which have caused the story to be called a perversion of the Holy War[22] or the inverted

---

16. I refer to my commentary under preparation.

17. See Smend, *Entstehung*, 111–125.

18. This theory, which is in itself not new, was revived by F. M. Cross, *Canaanite Myth and Hebrew Epic* (vol. 2; Cambridge, Mass., 1975) 274–285, and has later found many adherents, e.g., R. D. Nelson, *The Double Redaction of the Deuteronomistic History* (JSOT Supplement Series 18; Sheffield, 1981) and A. D. H. Mayes, *The Story of Israel between Settlement and Exile. A Redactional Study of the Deuteronomistic History* (London, 1983).

19. S. Mittmann, *Deuteronomium 1₁–6₃ literarkritisch und traditionsgeschichtlich untersucht* (BZAW 139; Berlin/New York, 1975) 164–169. One result of Mittmann's analysis is that the Moses of the basic level proclaims the Decalogue "im geographischen 'Ungefähr'" (Perlitt [BEThL 68] 154).

20. M. Noth, *Überlieferungsgeschichtliche Studien* (vol. 3; Tübingen, 1967) 14.

21. Originally, v. 19* was a direct continuation of v. 8abα. The additional character of the passage between these verses was observed, e.g., by N. Lohfink, "Darstellungskunst und Theologie in Dtn 1,6–3,29," *Bib.* 41 (1960) 107¹, and S. E. Loewenstamm, "The Formula בעת חחיא ['at that time'] in Deuteronomy" (Hebr.), *Tarb.* 38 (1968/69) 99.

22. Lohfink, *Bib.* 41, 114.

Holy War.[23] This aspect represents a later theological interpretation of the original story. Apart from some minor additions missing in Deuteronomy 2, contrary to Noth, were the section vv. 4–8a with a favorable attitude to Edom and also the offer of peace to king Sihon (vv. 26–28, 29bα), which was formulated on the basis of the Edom passage and Num 21:21–22.[24] To the numerous later additions in Deuteronomy 3 has to be also reckoned the commandment charging the two and a half Transjordanian tribes to participate with the other tribes in the conquest of the land west of Jordan (vv. 18–20), which Noth still assumed to belong to the basic story.[25]

The remaining, original text of Deuteronomy 1–3 is, with regard to its historiographic aim, a story about the conquest of Transjordan and its distribution among the tribes of Reuben and Gad and the half-tribe of Manasseh. It looks forward to and demands as a necessary continuation an account of how the land west of Jordan was conquered and distributed among the other tribes. From this, one could perhaps infer that there was a separate story about the conquest of the land which began in Deuteronomy 1 and [[253]] ended in Joshua 22. N. Lohfink, who recently has made such a proposal, concludes the presence of a story about the conquest of the land (*Landeroberungserzählung* = DtrL) from a particular use of the root ירשׁ [['to take possession of']] in this section of the Deuteronomistic History and assumes that historically it is connected with the efforts of King Josiah to expand his rule to the former territory of the northern tribes.[26] It is, however, very doubtful that the use of one single root gives a sufficient basis for such far-reaching conclusions, all the more as it is in reality not limited only to this part of the Deuteronomistic History.[27]

23. W. L. Moran, "The End of the Unholy War and the Anti-Exodus," *Bib.* 44 (1963) 333. [[Reprinted in this volume, pp. 147–55 below.]]

24. Cf. Mittmann, *Deuteronomium*, 64–65, 80.

25. Noth, *Überlieferungsgeschichtliche Studien*, 37. The later references to the fulfillment of this commandment (Josh 1:12–18; 4:12; 22:1–6) are in their own connections secondary, post-deuteronomistic additions.

26. N. Lohfink, "Kerygmata des Deuteronomistischen Geschichtswerks," in *Die Botschaft und die Boten, Festschrift Hans Walter Wolff* (Neukirchen-Vluyn, 1981) 87–100. Cf. idem, in *ThWAT III*, 970–973.

27. Lohfink means the use of ירשׁ in *qal* in the sense "etwas in Besitz nehmen" and in *hifᶜil* in the sense "jemanden vernichten, so daß sein Besitz übernommen werden kann." For the *qal* he offers the following deuteronomistic occurrences: Deut 1:8,21,39; 2:24,31; 3:12,18,20; 10:11; Josh 1:11–15a; 18:3(?); 21:43 and "perhaps also" Josh 24:4,8 and for the *hifᶜil* the following: Exod 34:24; Num 32:21; 33:52,(53)55; Deut 4:38; 7:17; 9:3,4,5; 11:23; 18:12; Josh 3:10; 8:7; 13:6; 23:5,9,13; Judg 2:21,23; 11:23,24; 1 Kgs 14:24; 21:26; 2 Kgs 16:3; 17:8; 21:2; Ps 44:3 (Lohfink, "Die Bedeutungen von hebr. *jrš qal* und *hif*," *BZ* NF 27 [1983] 21, 29, 30). As one can see from this list, the use of ירשׁ in these two meanings

Moreover, we have to notice that the common opinion, according to which King Josiah would have extended his cultic reform to the area of the former Northern kingdom and in so doing attempt to restitute the unified kingdom from the days of David, has in recent research turned out to be untenable. In their studies, both H. Spieckermann[28] and E. Würthwein[29] have reached the conclusion that the section of the reform account dealing with this matter (2 Kgs 23:15–20) consists completely of deuteronomistic fiction and consequently does not fit as a basis for a critical historiography.

It seems more likely to me that already in their first wording, Deuteronomy 1–3 were written by the exilic deuteronomistic author, as M. Noth had supposed.[30] Their purpose is not to offer a theological legitimation for any political program, but they are a response to the crisis caused by the exile. First, Israel had to lose its land before the land could become the object of an intensive theological reflection.[31] The generation that in Deuteronomy 1–3 prepares to take into possession this "good land" (1:25,35; 3:25a) has in reality already lost it and desires to regain it after the period spent in the "wilderness" of exile.[32]

IV

What is surprising in the basic story of Deuteronomy 1–3 is the fact that in it there is no explicit allusion to the law following these chapters. Whoever reads these chapters on their basic level could not expect to pass on immediately to the Deuteronomic law. Deuteronomy 3 ends with Moses' petition to get into the Promised Land, which is refused by God (vv. 23–28), and with a notice about the location of Moses' speech (v. 29). The narrative sequel to this follows, as is well known, in Deuteronomy 31 where Moses' advanced age and God's refusal to let him enter the Promised Land (v. 2) make up the background for Joshua's appointment as leader of Israel (vv. 7,8), and shortly after that [254] there is the account of Moses' death and

---

is not typical only of the "deuteronomistic story about the conquest of the land," although, owing to the subject matter of Deuteronomy and Joshua, it most often occurs in these books.

28. *Juda unter Assur in der Sargonidenzeit* (FRLANT 129; Göttingen, 1982) 112–120.

29. *Die Bücher der Könige* (ATD 11,2; Göttingen, 1984) 460–461.

30. Noth, *Überlieferungsgeschichtliche Studien,* 91.

31. The same is true of the institution of the kingdom, see T. Veijola, *Verheißung in der Krise* (AASF, B 220; Helsinki, 1982) 92–94.

32. This possibility is considered also by Lohfink, who, however, rejects it in favour of Josiah's time (FS Wolff, 95).

burial in the place where the Israelites, according to 3:29 had remained (34:5,6). If the Deuteronomist had from the beginning really intended the historical review in Deuteronomy 1–3 to be the prologue to the following law, would he completely have failed to allude to it in these opening chapters? In respect to his habits of working elsewhere, this seems quite improbable.

Moreover, we have to pay attention to the fact that on the basic level of the Deuteronomistic History, in the historical books there is no explicit utterance supposing that Deuteronomy as "the book of law" already was a part of the Deuteronomistic History.[33] This gives new support to the previously made suggestions claiming that Deuteronomy 1–3 originally were not a prologue to the Deuteronomic law, which accordingly did not belong to the first edition of the Deuteronomistic History.[34]

On the other hand, there is admittedly in the Deuteronomistic History a great number of allusions to the law (Torah) or Moses which is supposed to be known to the readers and which they can study in case of need.[35] All of them are, however, later than the basic level, deriving earliest from the so-called Nomistic Deuteronomist (= DtrN).[36] The same is true of Deuteronomy itself, in the earliest parts of which the Torah never appears as the general notion meaning the whole of the divine commandments. In this respect, the situation is different in the younger sections of the frame and in the additions made to the corpus where the Torah appears no less than 18 times in the broad meaning signifying the law in general. All these occurrences resemble each other to a high degree. They speak either about 'this Torah' (התורה הזאת)[37] or 'this book of Torah' (ספר התורה הזה)[38] or 'the book of this Torah' (ספר התורה הזאת),[39] and the existence of the Torah as a

---

33. The only exception could possibly be 2 Kgs 22:8,11, where the discovery of Josiah's law book is related, but even here it is not supposed that the newly found "book of the law" was a part of the Deuteronomistic History. Besides, the belonging of these verses to the earliest stratum of the Deuteronomistic History has been disputed (see Würthwein, *Könige*, 447–448).

34. See G. von Rad, *Das fünfte Buch Moses* (ATD 8; vol. 2; Göttingen, 1968) 33; J. D. Levenson, "Who inserted the Book of Torah?" *HThR* 68 (1975) 221–233; Preuß, *Deuteronomium*, 84; more cautiously even Perlitt (BEThL 68) 152, 163.

35. See Josh 1:7,8; 8:31–34; 22:5; 23:6; 1 Kgs 2:3; 2 Kgs 10:31; 14:6; 17:13; 21:8; 23:24,25.

36. For this, see R. Smend, "Das Gesetz und die Völker," in *Probleme biblischer Theologie, FS Gerhard von Rad* (München, 1971) 494–509.

37. Deut 1:5; 4:8; 17:18,19; 27:3,8,26; 28:58; 29:28; 31:9,11,12,24; 32:46.

38. Deut 30:10; 31:26.

39. Deut 28:61; 29:20; 30:10; 31:26.

written document is always supposed, as is its identity with Deuteronomy. The conception is exactly the same as in the later parts of the Deuteronomistic History mentioned above.[40]

Moreover, it is worth mentioning that the same conception of the Torah appears at the beginning of Deuteronomy, as an expansion of the original superscription, in v. 5 according to which Moses "in the land of Moab began to write[41] this Torah (התורה הזאת)." The secondary superscription clearly attempts to connect the historical review beginning in v. 6 with the topic of the Deuteronomic law. Another secondary superscription of a similar kind occurs later in 4:44, where it is competing with the older superscription in v. 45.[42] The purpose of v. 44 is also to give the reader the idea about Deuteronomy as a finished [[255]] book of the Torah "which Moses laid down for the Israelites." It seems probable to me that in both superscriptions we are dealing with the same author who later in Deuteronomy as well as in the Deuteronomistic History refers to the book of the Torah as a well-known document.[43] Obviously he was also the editor who inserted Deuteronomy as the opening section of the Deuteronomistic History. Our knowledge about the redactional process of the Deuteronomistic History strongly supports the conclusion that he was the same nomistic redactor (DtrN) who is responsible for the later references—or a part of them—to the book of the Torah in the historical books.[44] The result is strengthened by the observation that in Deuteronomy 4 there is a narrow basic level[45] which creates a literary bridge between the historical review (Deuteronomy 1–3) and the following law (Deuteronomy 5ff.) and which can be attributed to this nomistic redactor.

From the inferences made above it is, however, not allowed to draw the conclusion that the Deuteronomistic Historian (DtrH) did not know Deuteronomy at all. Of course, it was his ideological background, the influence of which is discernible even in the introductory chapters, most clearly in the account of the defeat of Sihon and Og.[46]

40. Cf. G. Minette de Tillesse, "Sections 'tu' et sections 'vous' dans le Deutéronome," *VT* 12 (1962) 48–49.

41. For this interpretation of the verb באר [['write', 'make plain']] *pi^cel*, see Mittmann, *Deuteronomium*, 14–15.

42. Cf. G. Seitz, *Redaktionsgeschichtliche Studien zum Deuteronomium* (BWANT V:13; Stuttgart, 1971) 26–27.

43. It is, of course, possible and even probable that these references derive in part from later times.

44. A similar view was advanced by Preuß, *Deuteronomium*, 84.

45. It has included vv. 1a,10,11,12a,13aα,14,22.

46. Originally the story about Sihon consisted of 2:16,17,24aα[1], 30a,31a,32–36 and the story about Og of 3:1,3,4aα,6*,7.

In both cases the theological interpretation was borrowed from the military theory of the Holy War as it was advanced in the Deuteronomic laws of warfare, especially in Deuteronomy 20. Moreover, we have to take into consideration that the Deuteronomistic Historian personally participated in the development of this military theory. It is namely he who in Deuteronomy 20 makes the distinction between the far-off and nearby nations (vv. 15–17aα[1])[47] which also gives the justification to annihilate Sihon and Og (Deuteronomy 2–3). It is most probable, even certain, that the Deuteronomistic Historian has interpreted the Deuteronomic laws in a similar way elsewhere, too. From this it does not necessarily follow that Deuteronomy was already included in his work.[48] The observations made above favor instead the conclusion that in his work the law and the history were still two separate units which were literally combined first by his pupil DtrN. Thus, even in this case the law came in only afterwards (cf. Rom 5:20).

47. Cf. R. P. Merendino, *Das Deuteronomische Gesetz* (BBB 31; Bonn, 1969) 226–227. (Merendino, however, erroneously attributes also v. 17aα[2]βb and v. 18 to the same author.)

48. As Smend seems to suppose (*Entstehung*, 73).

The End of the Unholy War and the Anti-Exodus

WILLIAM L. MORAN

[[333]] In his study of Deut 1:6–3:29 N. Lohfink has shown on the basis of G. von Rad's monograph on the Holy War[1] that in the description of the rebellion in the first chapter the Deuteronomist, while employing many of the motifs of the Holy War, has profoundly transformed them.[2] In context they are "inverted": they have lost their original meaning, they serve to describe the very opposite—an Anti-Holy-War.[3] But there is more involved than a Holy War. Through a series of allusions to Exodus 13–14 the ancient traditions on the Holy War *par excellence* are inverted and the events of Kadesh-Barnea are portrayed as an Anti-Exodus.[4]

One passage, however, which we believe confirms this interpretation, if confirmation were needed, escaped Lohfink's attention. It is Deut 2:14–16. In these verses we have the real conclusion to the history of the first chapter, for they are concerned with the death of the rebellious generation. And here too, we submit, we have however

Reprinted with permission from *Biblica* 44 (1963) 333–42.

1. Gerhard von Rad, *Der Heilige Krieg im alten Israel* (Abhandlungen zur Theologie des Alten und Neuen Testaments 20; Zürich, 1951).

2. *Biblica* 41 (1960) 105–134, especially 110–114, 119–120.

3. At the suggestion of L. Alonso Schökel, to whom I am grateful for a number of criticisms, I use the term "invert" or "inversion" rather than "pervert" or "perversion" with Lohfink, since the former is not so closely associated with morality.

4. In the inversion of Holy War motifs the Deuteronomist is probably indebted to the prophets; cf. J. A. Soggin, *Vetus Testamentum* 10 (1960) 79–83; also H. Reventlow, *Zeitschrift für die Alttestamentliche Wissenschaft* 71 (1959) 37, n. 18. For the rôle of the prophets in the history of the institution, see Robert Bach, *Die Aufforderung zur Flucht und zum Kampf im alttestamentlichen Prophetenspruch* (Wissenschaftliche Monographien zum Alten und Neuen Testament 9; Neukirchen, 1962). On the broader question of the inversion of images, see Luis Alonso Schökel, *Estudios de poética hebrea* (Barcelona, 1963) 305–306.

〚334〛 briefly the same inversion of motifs which characterizes the earlier narrative. To the Anti-Holy War—the Unholy War—and the Anti-Exodus 2:14–16 provide the fitting, almost necessary, conclusion.

The Unholy War

At 2:14–16 the onward movement of the narrative is suddenly halted, the "rhythm" of command-execution which began in 2:2ff. is broken.[5] The style becomes particularly solemn. The first sentence (v. 14) is long with a slow and deliberate movement: "And the time that we marched from Kadesh-Barnea until we crossed the Wadi Zered was thirty-eight years, until had perished the entire generation, the men of war, from the camp, as Yahweh had sworn to them." Then in a short sentence marked by assonance (*wᵉgam–bām–lᵉhummām–tummām*, rhythm 4:4) and the repetition in chiastic order of words and phrases of the previous sentence (*ᶜad tom–miqqereb hammahᵃne-YHWH//YHWH–miqqereb hammahᵃne-ᶜad tummām*), one agent of destruction is identified: "And even the hand of Yahweh was upon them to rout them in panic from the camp until they had perished." But this is not all. Once more 2:16 repeats (*ᵓanšê hammilḥāmā, tmm, miqqereb*); "And when all the men of war had perished in death from among the people"—then, and only then, follows the oracle of 2:17ff., and we hear the command, to which all others have pointed, to cross the Arnon and invade Sihon's territory in a Holy War (2:24f.).

The importance the author attaches to these verses is evident, and they are clearly intended as a solemn introduction to 2:17ff.[6] In effect, the author juxtaposes two wars, the Unholy and the Holy. Through allusion we are made in vv. 14–16 to recall the former, especially the oath of 1:35, the complete fulfilment of which is so strongly stressed. Somewhere beyond the Zered this war came to a close, and only because it did—this is clearly the author's mind—could the new and holy one begin. The contrast is unmistakable.

The contrast, however, is achieved by more than allusion. 2:14–16 has often provoked comment, especially the expressions *ᵓanšê ham-milḥāmā* 〚335〛 〚'warriors'〛 (14b, 16) and *miqqereb hammahᵃne* 〚'from the midst of the camp'〛 (14b, 15a). So distinctive in fact is the vocabulary that it has been proposed that these verses are secondary,[7] and if this proposal has been commonly rejected, a problem still remains. In 1:35 where the oath against the rebellious generation is cited, the

---

5. On the "rhythm" of 2:2–9, 13, see Lohfink's remarks, *art cit.*, 128–129.

6. Cf. Martin Noth, *Überlieferungsgeschichtliche Studien* (Halle, 1943) 35.

7. So A. Dillmann, *Die Bücher Numeri, Deuteronomium, und Josua* 2. Aufl., Kurzgefasstes exegetisches Handbuch zum Alten Testament 3; Leipzig, 1886) 244.

author adheres in essentials to his source (Num 14:22–23); nothing is said of "the men of war." In 2:14b, therefore, the restrictive apposition, "the entire generation, that is, the men of war," even though it does not contradict the earlier passage,[8] is nevertheless unexpected.[9] Moreover, though the topic of war is so frequent in Deuteronomy 1–3, the expression *ʾanšê hammilḥāmā* [['warriors']] is confined to these verses. In fact, the military character of Israel is rather assumed in these chapters or only alluded to in terms like *ʿam* [['people (bearing arms)']];[10] the explicit references to weapons in 1:14 and later to warriors in 3:18[11] are quite exceptional. Why then the evident stress in 2:14–16 on the doomed generation precisely as warriors?

In *miqqereb hammaḥᵃne* [['from the midst of the camp']] the same problem reappears, for, as Steuernagel has rightly observed,[12] reference to the camp belongs with the designation of those who died as "the men of war." Again however the same absence of parallels obtains; Israel's camp is never [[336]] mentioned in Deuteronomy 1–3.[13] The expression *miqqereb hammaḥᵃne* [['from the midst of the camp']] it is true, is found in Num 14:44, and besides Deuteronomy 2 here alone in the Old Testament; since this verse belongs to the source used by the author in chapter one, dependence on the older tradition is here quite probable.[14] Dependence, however, does not explain its use; rather, it only makes the problem more acute. Why did the author fail to use the phrase in the first chapter, where

8. On the inner consistency of the author's thought see the remarks of E. König, *Das Deuteronomium* (Kommentar zum Alten Testament 3; Leipzig, 1917) 75, and H. Junker, *Das Buch Deuteronomium* (Bonner Bibel, Bonn, 1933) 30. This is even more apparent when Deuteronomy 1 is seen as the offer and rejection of a Holy War. Underlying the restriction in P (Num 14:29) of those punished to men twenty years old and up is probably the practice of military service beginning at that age; cf. the remarks of George E. Mendenhall, *Journal of Biblical Literature* 77 (1958) 60, and John A. Wilson, in *Ancient Near Eastern Texts*, edited by James Pritchard (2nd ed., Princeton, 1955) 415, n. 13.

9. Those who perished in the desert are similarly identified in the Deuteronomic additions Josh 5:4, 6 (cf. M. Noth, *Das Buch Josua* [2. Aufl., Handbuch zum Alten Testament 7; Tübingen, 1953] 39). Num 32:13 substitutes "which did evil in the eyes of Yahweh"; on the secondary character of Num 32:6–15, see Noth, *Überlieferungsgeschichtliche Studien*, 198–199.

10. Cf. L. Rost, *Festschrift Otto Procksch* (Leipzig, 1943) 145.

11. *Ḥᵃlûṣîm* [['warriors']] and *gibbôrê ḥayil* [['might men of war']] (cf. R. de Vaux, *Les institutions de l'Ancien Testament*, I [Paris, 1958] 110; II [Paris, 1960] 13).

12. C. Steuernagel, *Deuteronomium und Josua* (Handkommentar zum Alten Testament 3; Göttingen, 1900) 9.

13. Elsewhere in Deuteronomy only in one law (23:10, 11, 12, 15) and 29:10; within Deuteronomy 1–3 tents are mentioned in 1:27. On the "camp-tradition" in Deuteronomy cf. A. Kuschke, *ZAW* 63 (1951) 78.

14. On Num 14:44b as part of the original J tradition, see R. de Vaux, *A la rencontre de Dieu*, Mémorial Albert Gelin (Paris, 1961) 58–59.

in a sense it belongs, only to employ it here, unless there is reason for a decided emphasis at this point on Israel as an army?

The questions raised by the vocabulary of these verses find their answer, we believe, in the use of *lᵉhummām* [['to rout them in panic']] in 15a. For *hmm* [['rout']] also belongs to the vocabulary of war; it refers to the divinely inspired panic which is a characteristic feature of the Holy War.[15] In this sense it is found both in Deuteronomy and in the Deuteronomic History.[16] And that it should be so understood here is beyond doubt, for, as the author is at pains to make clear, its victims are members of an army, "the men of war" in "the camp." In other words, we have in 2:15 a motif of the Holy War, but one which apart from context is not free from ambiguity; *hmm* is not a panic confined to troops. This ambiguity the author removes.

In solving the problem of the vocabulary of 2:14–16 we have of course uncovered another inversion of a Holy War motif: Yahweh inspires panic, not in the enemies' ranks, as in the Holy War, but in Israel's.[17] The author has found for the inversion of the Holy War [[337]] the obviously right conclusion, for the sin the proper punishment. It was in language taken from the Holy War that the rebels had accused Yahweh of leading them out of Egypt "to give us into the hand of the Amorites, to destroy us utterly."[18] And so they were destroyed, but for some at least the hand was another and more terrible.

It may also seem not too implausible to suggest that this underlying law of talion is an additional reason for the author's borrowing *miqqereb hammaḥᵃne* [['from the midst of the camp']] for the description of the punishment. In Num 14:44 it is recorded that Moses and the Ark remained in the camp when the Israelites insisted on fighting the Amorites. Despite being warned they chose to abandon the camp and sinned a second time, leaving Moses and the Ark behind. In doing so they also chose—this we

---

15. Cf. G. von Rad, *op. cit.*, 12. Ehrlich's proposal, *Randglossen zur hebräischen Bibel*, II (Leipzig, 1909) 254, to read *laḥᵃmîtām* overlooks the numerous examples of pregnant constructions with *min* [['from']] (cf. F. Brown–S. R. Driver–C. A. Briggs, *A Hebrew and English Lexicon of the Old Testament*, 578a), of which *mût miqqereb* [['die from among']] in the following verse is one; *hmm* is construed with *min* [['from']] in Jer 51:34; Esth 9:24; Sir 48:21.

16. Deut 7:23; Josh 10:10; Judg 4:15 (on the last two texts cf. M. Noth, *Überlieferungsgeschichtliche Studien*, 56, n. 2). In general, when Yahweh is the subject of *hmm* [['rout']] (Exod 14:24; 23:27; Josh 10:1; Judg 4:15; 1 Sam 7:10; Ps 18:15 = 2 Sam 22:15; Ps 144:6; 2 Chr 15:6), it refers to war; Isa 28:28 is the only exception.

17. The inversion of the panic motif appears already in Amos 2:14–16; cf. G. von Rad, *op. cit.*, 63.

18. On *nātan bᵉyad* [['give into the hand of']], cf. von Rad, *ibid.*, 7ff., and Lohfink, *art. cit.*, 125f. The corresponding Akkadian expression, *ina qāti nadānu*, is used of a god granting victory over enemies as early as the Old Akkadian period; cf. H. Hirsch, *Archiv für Orientforschung* 20 (1963) 75 obv. III 2–6.

suggest is hinted at by the Deuteronomist—their final punishment: they were to be driven from this camp in terror and to their death.

The remaining expressions are compatible with a context of war. *Dôr* [['generation']] causes no difficulty, *ʿam* [['people (bearing arms)']] we have already noted above, and *tmm* [['perish']] is quite in place as *ʿad tummām* [['until had perished']] in Joshua (8:24; 10:20) to describe the final rout and slaughter of the enemy shows. Only "the hand of Yahweh" may raise some doubts, for though the hand and the arm of Yahweh as a god of war are frequently mentioned,[19] there is reason to believe that the author has in mind primarily death by pestilence.[20] This is suggested by a number of considerations: (1) this is a well-attested meaning of the expressions;[21] (2) in Num 14:12, which belongs to the author's source, it is pestilence (*deber*) [[338]] which Yahweh first proposes in his plan of total destruction, and when afterwards upon the intercession of Moses he relents and restricts the punishment to one generation, though it is not said how it will die, the passage is open to the interpretation that pestilence is to be understood as remaining the principal, if not only, instrument of punishment;[22] (3) in 1 Samuel 4–6, incorporated by the Deuteronomist in his history, God's hand and panic are associated, and the former is to be understood of a deadly epidemic.[23]

However, if "the hand of Yahweh" in Deut 2:15 does refer to pestilence, as seems probable, this is less a difficulty than additional support for our interpretation, for pestilence fits perfectly in the context of war. To mention only a few examples, it is Pestilence which escorts the Warrior-God (Hab 3:5).[24] Pestilence is "the sword of Yahweh"

19. Cf. H. Fredricksson, *Jahwe als Krieger* (Lund, 1949) 101–105.

20. Judg 2:15; 1 Sam 12:15; 7:13 allow for a more general application of "the hand of Yahweh to be on (*bᵉ*) someone," but for the reasons which follow the more particular meaning imposes itself.

21. Cf. Exod 9:3, 15; 1 Sam 5:6, 7, 9, 11; 6:3, 5, 9; 2 Sam 24:16, 17; 1 Chr 21:15, 17; as a more general term for sickness, Ps 32:4; 38:3; 39:11. In Ugaritic texts (C. H. Gordon, *Ugaritic Manual* [Analecta Orientalia 35; Rome, 1955], Text 54) we also find *yd ilm* as pestilence (*mtm*), and in Akkadian *qāt* DN ("hand of such and such a god") is used for various diseases (cf. R. Labat, *Traité akkadien de diagnostics et pronostics médicaux*, I [Paris-Leiden, 1955] xxiff., but on the problem of etymology discussed on xii, n. 4, see A. Goetze, *Journal of Cuneiform Studies* 2 [1948] 269f.).

22. In Num 14:37 (P) it is by plague (*maggēpā*) that the scouts die; cf. also Num 17:13f.; 25:8f.

23. *mᵉhûmā* [['panic']] occurs in 5:9, 11; in 5:6 we should perhaps read *wayᵉhummēm* [['threw them into a panic']] for MT *wayᵉšimmēm* [['wrought havoc']]. On the hand of Yahweh see p. 337, n. 3 [[above, n. 20]]. The exact nature of the Philistine affliction remains somewhat obscure, but that *ʿopel* [['hemorrhoids'?]] was mortal and reached epidemic proportions seems clear; see H. Hertzberg, *Die Samuelbücher* (Das Alte Testament Deutsch 10; Göttingen, 1960) 40–41.

24. Cf. A. Caquot, *Semitica* 6 (1956) 57f.

(1 Chr 21:12).[25] In another inversion of Holy War motifs, it is with pestilence that Yahweh first smites man and beast in Jerusalem, and indeed "with outstretched hand and strong arm" (Jer 21:5–6). And as for 1 Samuel 4–6, other motifs of the Holy War appear in this history of the Ark, and it is in their light that the hand of Yahweh and the divine panic are to be understood.[26]

An unresolved question is whether *wᵉgam* [['and also']] in v. 15 implies that the hand of Yahweh was only one of several causes of death, or whether it stresses that the cause of death was none other than the hand of Yahweh. Recent translations and the remarks of commentators [[339]] testify to the ambiguity of the Hebrew.[27] However, in view of the traditions which know of other causes of death and were certainly known to the Deuteronomist,[28] it seems more probable that in 2:15 he singled out the type of death which could be used in an inversion of a Holy War motif.

The Anti-Exodus

Deut 2:14–16 is also the end of the Anti-Exodus. Admittedly, the evidence in these verses alone is meager. It must however be considered in the light of the previous allusions to Exodus 13–14, and then Exod 14:24 assumes special significance: "In the night watch just before dawn the Lord cast through the column of the fiery cloud upon the Egyptian force (*maḥᵃne*) a glance that threw it into a panic (*wayyāhom*)." Certainly the similarity of vocabulary is striking, and since Exodus 14 was demonstrably one of the author's sources, the probability of its being drawn upon in 2:15 seems very high.[29] Besides, since the Unholy War theme of chapter one reappears in 2:14–16, consistency would demand that the Anti-Exodus theme be worked into the conclusion.

25. Pestilence and the sword are frequently associated (Lev 26:25f.; Jer 24:10; 29:17; 32:36; 34:17; Ezek 5:17; 7:15; 28:23; 38:21–22; Amos 4:10, etc.). Cf. too the angel in 2 Kgs 19:35. The parallelism of "arrows" and "hand" in Ps 38:3 is also to be noted; see the remarks of H.-J. Kraus, *Psalmen* (Biblischer Kommentar XV, 1; Neukirchen, 1961) 295.

26. Von Rad, *op. cit.*, 12, includes 1 Sam 5:11 among the examples of a Holy War panic. Another Holy War motif is that of Yahweh who fights for Israel (1 Sam 4:3, 8), as is that of the *tᵉrûᶜā* [['shouted']] (1 Sam 4:5–6)—and of course the entire story revolves around the Ark, Israel's palladium.

27. Cf. the different options in the commentaries of Bertholet, Driver, Junker, König and Steuernagel, and in the translations of the Revised Standard Version, Confraternity of Christian Doctrine, Bible de Jérusalem; Dhorme (Pléiade) deftly retains the ambiguity of the Hebrew. Ehrlich, *op. cit.*, 253–254, takes *wᵉgam* [['and also']] as concessive: the wandering lasted thirty-eight years, even though . . . (otherwise it would have been longer).

28. Cf. Num 16:31f.; 21:6; 25:3–5.

29. Exod 14:24 suggests that *maḥᵃne* in Deut 2:14–15 be understood as the army itself rather than a place; the parallel expression *miqqereb hāᶜām* [['from among the people']] in 2:16 also favors this sense.

If we do have another case of inversion in 2:15 then "the hand of Yahweh" must probably also be included. Not only is the hand of Yahweh intimately associated with the Exodus, particularly in Deuteronomy,[30] but the author's source, Exod 14:31, which concludes the prose account and by way of summary underscores the significance of the events, [[340]] tells of the people having seen "the great hand" (exploit) done by Yahweh which led them to fear and trust. Earlier in Deut 1:32 the author alluded to this verse of Exodus 14 when he contrasted the lack of trust shown by the people at Kadesh-Barnea. In describing the punishment of this sin Exod 14:31 may therefore have been of some influence.

It is however in Exodus 15 that the hand of Yahweh enjoys special prominence; to his right hand belongs the victory at the Sea of Reeds (Exod 15:6, 12). The possible significance however of this for the interpretation of Deut 2:15 can only be appreciated when one realizes the profound influence of Exodus 15 on the composition of Deuteronomy 2–3. Since this has not been recognized, we present the evidence.

1. In Deuteronomy 2 the lack of resistance by the Edomites and Moabites, and the fear of the former (Deut 2:4) find their only support among the older traditions in Exod 15:14.[31]

2. Deut 2:25b unmistakably alludes to Exod 15:14:[32]

Deuteronomy   "This day I shall begin to put the dread and fear of you on the peoples (*ʿammîm*) under all heaven, who hearing (*yišmᵉʿûn*) the report of you will tremble (*wᵉrāgᵉzû*) and writhe (*wᵉḥālû*) before you."

---

30. *Yad ḥᵃzāqā* [['mighty hand']]: Exod 3:19; 6:1; 13:9; 32:11; Deut 4:34; 5:15; 6:21; 7:8, 19; 9:26; 11:2; 26:8; 34:12; 1 Kgs 8:42; Jer 32:21; Ps 136:12; Dan 9:15; Neh 1:10. *ḥozeq yad* [['strength of hand']]: Exod 13:3, 14, 16. *yad* [['hand']] alone: Exod 3:20; 7:5, 9:3, 15; Ps 78:42. After the renovation of the Exodus miracle at the Jordan (cf. H. Wildberger, *Jahwes Eigentumsvolk* [ATANT 37; Zürich, 1960] 59–62), in Josh 4:24 all the peoples of the earth are to acknowledge "that the hand of Yahweh is mighty" (*ʾet yad* YHWH *ki ḥᵃzāqā hiʾ*). On the "hand"-motif in the later tradition, see P. W. Skehan, *Catholic Biblical Quarterly* 25 (1963) 94–110.

31. Lohfink, *art. cit.*, 130, n. 4, has already suggested the possibility of this connection. On the problem of whether the author's attitude to the peoples of Transjordan is to be explained by this dependence on sources or by contemporary political relations, see O. Bächli, *Israel und die Völker* (ATANT 41; Zürich, 1962) 40, n. 57 and the literature cited there; see also R. Bach's remarks, *op. cit.*, 50.

32. M. Noth, *Überlieferungsgeschichtliche Studien*, 34, n. 4, considers Deut 2:24aᵇ.b–25 as secondary because they anticipate 2:32ff. and employ the 2 sg. The oracle however in 2:24 is expected in the context of a Holy War, and for the shift in number cf. Judg 20:28b, another Holy War oracle. As to 2:25, it fits too well with the rest of the evidence for the use of Exodus 15 in these chapters to be secondary. See also Lohfink's observations, *art cit.*, 129–130 on 2:24–31 as an imitation of the structure of chapter one.

Exodus   The peoples (*ᶜammîm*) hear (*šamᵉᶜû*) with trembling
                          yirgᵉzû Writing (*ḥîl*) seizes the rulers of Philistia."[33]

In both passages we have the identical sequence of *šmᶜ–rgz–ḥyl* [['fear–
tremble–writhe']] to describe the effect of Israel on other peoples. Not
only is this sequence unparalleled elsewhere in the Old Testament, but
Deut 2:15 provides besides 1 Sam 31:3 the only other occurrence of
the verb *ḥāl* [['writhe']] in prose. [[341]]

   3. In Deuteronomy 2 the *Leitwort* is the verb *ᶜbr* [['pass']], occurring
twelve times in this one chapter (vv. 4, 8, 8, 13, 13, 14, 18, 24, 27, 28,
29, 30). In Exodus 15 the one and only action predicated of the people
is precisely that of *ᶜbr* [['pass']], repeated twice (15:16b), and in the
same context as in Deuteronomy 2, namely, the passing by other peoples towards and into the Promised Land.

   4. In Deut 3:1–3, as Lohfink has acutely noted,[34] the scheme
command-execution, which has been consistently used up to this
point, is not carried through. The people are told neither to cross
Og's territory (contrast 2:4, 18) nor to cross the Jabbok (contrast 2:13,
24). The avoidance of the verb *ᶜbr* [['pass']] must be deliberate, especially since its use is resumed in 3:18, 21, 25, 28 about crossing the
Jordan. Its avoidance is explained by the author's dependence on
Exodus 15, where *ᶜbr* [['pass']] is used of the movement of the Israelites
to the *Promised Land*. This attack on Og is not, but the crossing of the
Jordan is, so whereas *ᶜbr* [['pass']] is avoided in the first case, in the
second it is added (2:29) to the account of the sources (cf. Num
20:14–21; 21:21–26).

   5. As has been previously recognized,[35] Deut 3:24b is strongly reminiscent of Exod 15:11. Compare too Deut 3:24a, 25 with Exod 15:16–17:

Deuteronomy "My lord, Yahweh, you have begun to show
             your servant your majesty (*godlᵉkā*) and
             your strong hand . . .
             Please let me cross over (*ᵓeᶜbᵉrā*) and
             see the good land across the Jordan—
             this good mountain (*hāhār*) and Lebanon."
Exodus   "Terror and dread falls upon them,
             By the majesty (*godel*)[36] of your arm
             they are made like stone,

---

   33. For the translation of *yôšᵉbê* by 'rulers,' see Frank M. Cross, Jr. and David Noel
Freedman, *Journal of Near Eastern Studies* 14 (1955) 248f.
   34. *Art. cit.*, 130.
   35. Dillmann, Driver.
   36. MT *gᵉdol* [['great']], but read *godel* [['majesty']] with G. Beer, *Exodus* (HAT 3,
Tübingen, 1939) 82, and Cross-Freedman, *art cit.*, 249.

> Until your people, O Yahweh, crosses (*ya^{ca}bor*),
> Until the people you created crosses (*ya^{ca}bor*),
> And you bring them in and plant them
> on the mountain (*har*) of your inheritance."

The similarity is evident and striking: first the majesty of God (*godel*), then the theme of crossing (*^{c}br*), and finally the very distinctive designation, for which there are very few parallels, of the Promised Land ⟦342⟧ as a mountain (-range).[37] It is also in the light of Exodus 15 that we can understand why Moses speaks of only beginning to be shown God's majesty, for there it is said that this majesty terrorizes both sides of the Jordan, whereas Moses so far as seen its effects only in Transjordan (cf. Deut 2:25).

In brief, the points of contact between Deuteronomy 2–3 and Exodus 15 are too many and too specific to be explained except by the conscious and close dependence of the Deuteronomist on the ancient poem.[38]

Embedded therefore as Deut 2:15 is in a context in which constant reference is being made to Exodus 15, it is hard to see how "the hand of Yahweh" is not an echo—and an inversion—of the saving right hand so prominent in the author's source. The fact that in Deut 3:24, where the source (Exod 15:16) speaks of Yahweh's arm, the author substitutes "your strong hand," would seem to provide additional support for this view: in the author's mind it is the saving hand of the Exodus which is about to operate against Sihon and Og,[39] the hand therefore that destroys in preparing for this operation can hardly be another.

In Deut 2:15 therefore we propose the inversion of two elements of the Exodus tradition: the panic of the Egyptians inspired by Yahweh, the saving hand.

This, we submit, was the end of the Unholy War and the Anti-Exodus.

37. The parallel passages are Deut 1:7; 32:13; Ps 78:54; see the writer's remarks in *Biblica* 43 (1962) 327.

38. Cf. the additions in Josh 2:9b, 10b, 11b (Noth, *Das Buch Josua* [HAT 7; Tübingen, 1938] 29–30). 10b refers to the conquest of Sihon and Og, and is attributed by Noth to the Deuteronomist. 9b is a virtual citation of Exodus 15b–16a, interpreting the conquest in the light of the ancient poem; in view of Deuteronomy 2–3, Josh 2:9b should in our opinion also be attributed to the Deuteronomist.

39. Cf. his argument from the victories in Transjordan with Deut 7:19b. As the references in n. 4, p. 339 ⟦p. 153, n. 30⟧ show, *yad ḥ^{a}zāqā* ⟦'mighty hand'⟧ was a formula traditionally referred to the Exodus; the implications therefore of its use in Deut 3:24 are that the conquest is an extension of the Exodus (cf. Josh 4:24!). Cf. Deut 1:29ff.; 7:17ff.; 20:1, which ground confidence in Yahweh's assistance during the conquest on the experience of the Exodus.

The Structure of the
Song of Moses in
Deuteronomy (32:1–43)

PATRICK W. SKEHAN

[[153]] The question of strophic structure, in the sense of anything like
our modern stanzas of verse, in Hebrew poetry, is always a delicate
one. Nevertheless, it is here proposed to outline a pattern on which
the writer believes the song of Moses in Deuteronomy was deliberately
constructed. In the presentation, use will be made of the latest published English rendering of this song [[see pp. 160–64 below]].[1]

As is bound to be the case with a biblical passage of this length, the
very reprinting of even a carefully done rendering calls for at least a
minimum of textual and exegetical remarks. The text represented by
this version presumes, as its editors have stated, certain variations from
the current Masoretic text. A number of these departures coincide with
the text established for their own undertaking by the commission which
prepared the new Psalter of the Roman Breviary.[2] These include:

> 5a   *šiḥătu lô bᵉnê(y) mûm*, with the Samaritan and LXX texts.
> [[5a   'The degenerate children have treated him basely'.]]

Reprinted, with permission, from *Catholic Biblical Quarterly* 13 (1951) 153–63 and *Studies
in Israelite Poetry and Wisdom* (CBQMS 1; Washington, D.C.: Catholic Biblical Association,
1971) 67–77, with addition of last paragraph.

1. In *The Book of Psalms and the Canticles of the Roman Breviary* (Paterson: St. Anthony
Guild Press, 1950) 272–77 (Confraternity of Christian Doctrine edition). The only departures from this version in the present article are indicated below in footnotes 3, 5, 10.

2. *Liber Psalmorum cum Canticis Breviarii Romani*[2] (Rome: Pontifical Biblical Institute,
1945).

14f   *wayyô**kal Ya^caqōb wayyiśba^c*, added with Sam. and LXX.[3]

⟦14f   'Jacob ate and was satisfied'.⟧

22   reading the three imperfect tenses with simple coordination, and not as *wayyiqtōl* forms.[4]

The English version goes its own way in supposing:

8d   *l^emispar b^enê(y)* *El*, with LXX.

9   *ki ḥēleq Yhwh Ya^cāqōb; ḥebel naḥălātō Yiśrāēl.*

35   *l^eyôm nāqām*, with LXX.[5]

43a, b   *harnînu šāmayim ^cimmō; w^ehābu-lō ^cōz kol-b^enê(y)* *El*, cf. LXX, in particular the line *kai enischysatōsan autō pantes huioi theou.*

⟦8d   'according to the number of the sons of God'

9   'while the Lord's own portion was Jacob, his hereditary share was Israel'

35   'against the day of vengeance'

43a, b   Heb: 'Exult with him, you heavens, glorify him, all you sons (or 'angels') of God'.

       Gk: 'and glorify him, all sons of God,'⟧

⟦154⟧ These modifications envisaged by the Confraternity rendering will be recognized for the most part as moot points among textual critics for a long time past. For such reconstruction as has been done in vv. 9 and 43, the present writer is in part responsible.[6] It is difficult not to see in the MT recension of vv. 8–9, despite its many defenders, a deliberate and tendentious modification of the primitive text, similar in character to those which later produced the *tiqqūn sôf^erîm* ⟦'scribal emendations'⟧ variations in, for example, Gen 18:22. The concept of the existence together with God of such supernal beings as we now call angels was not without difficulties, both theological and apologetic, for the pious Jew living in a predominantly polytheistic world; hence the

---

3. The present writer is satisfied that these words are an exegetical gloss to v. 14, for which the Masoretic text gives the complete original; the gloss itself is drawn from the prose passage Deut 31:20. Hence the corresponding hemistich is omitted from the English text as here printed.

4. Slighter retouches occur in vv. 13, 27, 38.

5. It also supposes *b^eašpâ(h)* ⟦'quiver'⟧ in v. 41, where the present writer would keep the *mišpāṭ* ⟦'judgment'⟧ of MT. (Hence the italics for *judgment* in the English text below, where the Confraternity version has "my quiver.") Also it would end v. 43 with *ad^emat ^cammô* ⟦'his people's land'⟧; cf. LXX.

6. In v. 9, he sees in ^c*ammô* ⟦'his people'⟧ a (purposeful?) duplication from v. 8; the disappearance of *Yiśrāēl* from v. 9 (where LXX has it) is a reflex of its substitution for *El* in v. 8. The place of the caesura in v. 9 is clearly dictated by considerations of metre and parallelism, once these points are recognized.

substitution of the mortal Israelites and their Gentile neighbors for the members of God's heavenly court in this context.

This very substitution argues against taking without qualification the position[7] that the stars are directly the "sons of God" referred to in this poem. The best interpretation of vv. 8–9 is one which will allow for the prose Book of Deuteronomy as the prime source of an exegesis for the "parceling out the descendants of Adam" in the course of which Israel becomes the Lord's "portion." Such an exegesis is present in Deut 4:19–20: "lest you lift up your eyes heavenward and see the sun, the moon, and the stars, the whole host of heaven, and be misled into worshiping and serving these, which the Lord your God has apportioned to all the peoples under heaven, while you yourselves the Lord has taken and brought out of the smelting-furnace of Egypt to be his own people of inheritance. . . . " This should be compared with Deut 29:24–25: "Because they forsook the covenant of the Lord, the God of their fathers . . . and went and served other gods and worshiped them: gods which they had not known and which He had not allotted to them." It seems clear that the *bᵉnê(y)* *ᵓEl* [['sons of God']] of Deuteronomy 32 are here associated with the heavenly bodies as in some sense the *ᵓĕlōhîm* [['gods']] of the nations foreign to Israel. The whole series of passages achieves consistency if we say that the celestial bodies are taken in the prose texts as types of real spiritual beings, the guardian angels of the individual nations, who are subject to the Lord and take charge of the nations at his bidding. Israel, however, is governed by no angel, but by the Lord himself, directly. This singling out of the [[155]] Chosen People does not imply on the part of any sacred writer an endorsement of worship of the heavenly bodies even by the Gentiles: it is affirmed that the latter have heavenly patrons, but not that their worship is properly directed. The worship condemned as wrong for the Israelites in Deut 29:24–25 is not endorsed for anyone by the language of Deut 4:19.[8] The passage in Deut 32:8–9 establishes that we are dealing with a poetic representation of theological truth; the description is, it would seem, still poetic imagery, with its possible mythological background, even when embodied in passages that are otherwise prose.

A further exegesis of 32:8–9, that dates from the early second century B.C. and confirms the reading with *bᵉnê(y)* *ᵓEl* [['sons of God']], is to be found, as has often been said, in Sir 17:17: "For every nation He

---

7. So for example W. F. Albright, *From the Stone Age to Christianity* (Baltimore, 1940) 227.

8. This is the only reservation the writer would express regarding the excellent remarks of H. Junker, *Das Buch Deuteronomium* (Bonn, 1933) 37–38. See also his discussion of Deut 32:8–9, *ibid.*, 123–24.

appointed a ruler; but Israel is the Lord's portion." To this should be added, however, Sir 16:26–28, at the beginning of the same context:

> When the Lord created His works at the first,
>> and at their making assigned their portions,
> He set in order forever His works,
>> and their principalities throughout their generations;
> They neither grew faint nor weary,
>> nor did they fail of their tasks;
> None jostled its neighbor,
>> nor ever shall they disobey His word.

The language of this section is indeed very general; but the "afterwards" of 16:29, in both LXX and Syr., makes it plain that what we have cited refers primarily to the fixing of the order of the heavens in particular, after which the Lord turns his attention to filling the earth with his good things and with animal life (16:29ff.)—compare the grouping of ideas in Psalm 148. Thus the Syriac *šulṭānᵉhōn* [['rulers, authorities']] in Sir 16:27 expresses correctly the often misunderstood *archas* [['authorities, princes, rulers']] of the Greek. God assigns the heavenly bodies their principalities (cf. Gen 1:16–18, and *prytaneis kosmou* [['rulers of the world']] in Wis 13:2); so that Sir 16:27 says for all creation something very similar to what Sir 17:17 says of the world of men. We unfortunately do not have the Hebrew of more than the first hemistich of this development in Ben Sira; but the text in its surviving versions leaves no real doubt that its author has the Deuteronomy passages in mind as well as Genesis 1. The heavenly bodies govern the visible world in virtue of a divine appointment; and similarly men are distributed among a series of rulers, while Israel is uniquely reserved for the Lord, [[156]] as in Deut 32:8–9. This can square only with a reading of Deut 32:8 which has *bᵉnê(y)* *ʾEl* [['sons of God']] in the text, and an understanding of 32:9 which [[70]] allows room for these *bᵉnê(y)* *ʾEl* [['sons of God']], somehow associated with the heavenly bodies, as rulers of the non-Israelite nations.

With regard to Deut 32:43, what seems certain is that the current Hebrew text has lost one hemistich. There is no parallelism between the command to praise, in 43a, and the *kî* [['for']] clause that follows. If the reason for praise is to occupy a full verse—or even three hemistichs, as it apparently does—the exhortation to praise should certainly run through a full line. This is reflected as late as the Yerushalmi Targum, which still has "Rejoice before him, O people: praise him, his people, Beth Israel."[9] The writer will of course concede that the LXX

---

9. Cf. the London polyglot, ed. B. Walton (1657) 4, 384.

form of v. 43 is unduly expanded,[10] and that in its first four hemistichs, which represent two separate attempts at a single Hebrew line, the influence of Psalm 96:7 LXX [[97:7 Eng.]] is clear. Yet the need for a second half-line in which somebody praises God is reflected in LXX also; and the form posited above owes nothing to the Greek of any parallel place, and can hardly be explained satisfactorily except as a serious attempt at rendering some such Hebrew as is indicated. If any tendency to a conflate text has been at work, it is certainly not in the verb *enischysatōsan* [['glorify']] which ceases to give a clear meaning even as Greek, the instant we fail to discern a Hebrew turn of phrase behind it. The equivalent here proposed has in its favor analogies in Deut 32:3, in this same poem; and in Pss 29:1 [[28:1 Gk.]]; 96:7 [[95:7 Gk.]]; 97:7 [[96:7 Gk.]]. Because all the available evidence, including the Old Latin, has the adjective "all" to qualify "sons of God" (as well as with the alternative rendering, "angels of God"), it has here been retained: though in fact the metre and parallelism would be better without it, and it is at this point that a tendency to conflate may be attributed to even our oldest witnesses for this half-line.[11]

[[157]] In the light of these observations, the text is now presented in the divisions the writer believes to be original:

A. 1 Give ear, O heavens, while I speak;
           let the earth hearken to the words of my mouth!
      2 May my instruction soak in like the rain,
           and my discourse permeate like the dew,
         Like a downpour upon the grass,
           like a shower upon the crops:

      3 For I will sing the LORD's renown.
           Oh, proclaim the greatness of our God!
      4 The Rock—how faultless are his deeds,
           how right all his ways!

10. The phrase *kai tois misousin antapodōsei* [['and on the ones who hate, he will take vengeance']] is a dittography from v. 41. One may wonder whether the *wᵉnāqām yāšîb lᵉṣārā(y)w* [['and he takes vengeance on his adversaries']] of MT is not also to be explained in this way, especially in view of the preceding *yiqqōm* [['avenges']] and the occurrence of the same words in 41. Omission of this last-named unit would not destroy, but rather improve, the parallelism, and the writer has omitted it from the translation as here printed, being of the opinion that its presence in the text is somehow connected with the corresponding loss of a hemistich in this same verse of the Hebrew as now extant.

11. H. Cazelles, *Le Deutéronome* (SBJ; Paris, 1950) 123–31, allows the "sons of God" a similar place in the text of this canticle; his treatment of v. 43 does not, however, see double renderings in our current LXX to the extent supposed above.

A faithful God, without deceit,
  how just and upright he is!

5 Yet basely has he been treated by his degenerate children,
  a perverse and crooked race!
6 Is the LORD thus to be repaid by you,
  O stupid and foolish people?
Is he not your father who created you?
  Has he not made you and established you?

7 Think back on the days of old,
  reflect on the years of age upon age.
Ask your father and he will inform you,
  ask your elders and they will tell you:

8 When the Most High assigned the nations their heritage,
  when he parceled out the descendants of Adam,
He set up the boundaries of the peoples
  after the number of the sons of God;
9 While the LORD's own portion was Jacob,
  his hereditary share was Israel.

10 He found them in a wilderness,
  a wasteland of howling desert.
He shielded them and cared for them,
  guarding them as the apple of his eye.

11 As an eagle incites its nestlings forth
  by hovering over its brood,
So he spread his wings to receive them
  and bore them up on his pinions.

12 The LORD alone was their leader,
  no strange god was with him.
13 He had them ride triumphant over the summits of the land
  and live off the products of its fields,
Giving them honey to suck from its rocks
  and olive oil from its hard, stony ground; [[158]]

14 Butter from its cows and milk from its sheep,
  with the fat of its lambs and rams;
Its Bashan bulls and its goats,
  with the cream of its finest wheat;
  and the foaming blood of its grapes you drank.

B. 15 So the darling grew fat and frisky;
        you became fat and gross and gorged.
    They spurned the God who made them
        and scorned their saving Rock.
16 They provoked him with strange gods
        and angered him with abominable idols.

17 They offered sacrifice to demons, to "no-gods"
        to gods whom they had not known before,
    To newcomers just arrived,
        of whom their fathers had never stood in awe.
18 You were unmindful of the Rock that begot you,
        you forgot the God who gave you birth. -

19 When the LORD saw this he was filled with loathing
        and anger towards his sons and daughters.
20 "I will hide my face from them," he said,
    "and see what will then become of them.
    What a fickle race they are,
        sons with no loyalty in them!

21 "Since they have provoked me with their 'no-god,'
        and angered me with their vain idols,
    I will provoke them with a 'no-people';
        with a foolish nation I will anger them.

22 "For by my wrath a fire is enkindled
        that shall rage to the depths of the nether world
    Consuming the earth with its yield,
        and licking with flames the roots of the mountains.
23 I will spend on them woe upon woe
        and exhaust all my arrows against them:

24 "Emaciating hunger and consuming fever
        and bitter pestilence,
    And the teeth of wild beasts I will send among them,
        with the venom of reptiles gliding in the dust.

25 "Snatched away by the sword in the street
        and by sheer terror at home
    Shall be the youth and the maiden alike,
        the nursing babe as well as the hoary old man.

26 "I would have said, I will make an end of them
        and blot out their name from men's memories,
27 Had I not feared the insolence of their enemies,
        feared that these foes would mistakenly boast,

'Our own hand won the victory;
the Lord had nothing to do with it.'" [[159]]

28 For they are a people devoid of reason,
having no understanding.
29 If they had insight they would realize what happened,
they would understand their success and say,

C. 30 "How could one man rout a thousand,
or two men put ten thousand to flight,
Unless it was because their Rock sold them,
and the Lord delivered them up?"
31 Indeed, their "rock" is not like our Rock,
and our foes are under condemnation.

32 They are a branch of Sodom's vinestock,
from the vineyards of Gomorrah.
Poisonous are their grapes
and bitter their clusters.
33 Their wine is the venom of dragons
and the cruel poison of cobras.

34 "Is not this preserved in my treasury,
sealed up in my storehouse,
35 Against the day of vengeance and requital,
against the time they lose their footing?"
Close at hand is the day of their disaster,
and their doom is rushing upon them!

36 Surely, the Lord shall do justice for his people:
on his servants he shall have pity.
When he sees their strength failing
and their protected and unprotected alike disappearing,

37 He will say, "Where are their gods
whom they relied on as their 'rock'?
38 Let those who ate the fat of your sacrifices
and drank the wine of your libations
Rise up now and help you!
Let them be your protection!

39 "Learn then that I, I alone, am God,
and there is no god besides me.
It is I who bring both death and life,
I who inflict wounds and heal them,
and from my hand there is no rescue.

40 "To the heavens I raise my hand and swear.
        As surely as I live forever,
41 I will sharpen my flashing sword,
        and my hand shall lay hold of *judgment.*
    "With vengeance I will repay my foes
        and requite those who hate me.
42 I will make my arrows drunk with blood,
        and my sword shall gorge itself with flesh—
    With the blood of the slain and the captured,
        flesh from the heads of the enemy leaders." ⟦160⟧

43 Exult with him, you heavens,
        glorify him, all you angels of God;
    For he avenges the blood of his servants
        and purges his people's land.

It will be seen that no unit longer than a tristich has been indicated; though a case for longer stanzas can sometimes be made.[12] The
feature which makes this particular combination of couplets and tri-
stichs seem to be a necessary one is, the reader will notice, that the
whole poem splits rather readily into three parts, each of which divides
on an identical pattern into adequate logical units, which can hardly
be an accident. When one inquires what it is that has prompted the
poet to adopt as a unity, for threefold repetition, the particular number of lines he offers us, the answer is based on alphabetic considerations. The poem consists of 69 verses, or 3 × 23; that is: three times
the number of letters in the Hebrew alphabet from *aleph* to *taw*, with
the letter *pe* added again at the end to close the cycle.[13] This supposes,

12. For example, the first six verses of each of the three sections can be grouped
into a unit. The entire poem has, however, a continuous unity which makes the nexus
between these brief "stanzas" stronger sometimes in the direction of what precedes, and
sometimes toward what follows them; so it has been thought better not to jeopardize the
distinct divisions here indicated by subordinating them to longer constructions more
tentative in character.

13. This use of a 23-line structure rather than the strict 22 is well known. In the
Psalms as we have them, Psalms 74 and 94 are of 23 lines. Job 9:2–24 is a composition of
23 lines on an alphabetic pattern. Among shorter poems, Psalm 25 goes through the Hebrew alphabet and then ends with *pe*; Psalm 34 does the same, though it skips the letter
waw. In these two latter Psalms, the use of the letter *pe* is given an allegorical turn, inasmuch as both times it is used in the same verb (*pᵉdēh, pôdeh*) of "redemption." However,
a reason that may be called mechanical underlies this device, and presumably antedates
any verbal associations of the kind. In the word *aleph* are contained three consonants: the
first in the alphabet; the twelfth, *lamed*, which in the twenty-two-letter sequence begins
the second half of the alphabet; and the "extra" letter, *pe*. By going from *aleph* to *taw* and
then adding *pe*, one makes *lamed* the exact middle of the series and sums up the whole
alphabet in the name of its first letter.

of course, a well-established literary tradition; and that the composition is quite systematic, and not a lyric effusion whose length would be subject to no fixed law.[14] On another level, the prevailing 3,3 metre of the individual lines is the standard didactic metre we know from the Book of Proverbs; and it points ⟦161⟧ in the same direction.[15] The caution should perhaps be added, that this assumption of a manner of composition for the poem which implies concern not merely for its oral, but actually for its written, form, is not a good basis for supposing a late date. At Ugarit, before the middle of the 13th century B.C., the fixed order of the Northwest-Semitic alphabet which is still familiar to us for Hebrew, and (with slight variations) for all the derivative alphabets of the West, was already well known, as recent evidence proves.[16] A legitimate inference would seem to be, that a pattern of this kind could have become standard not necessarily in the thirteenth century, but just as soon as the number of letters in that alphabet was restricted, for the writing of Hebrew, to an exact 22: certainly before the year 1000 B.C.

The fact that considerations based on the alphabet had an influence on the structure of the poem does not imply, either, that the author had to construct an acrostic of any kind, and the present writer does not mean to suggest that he did so. Both twenty-two and twenty-three line compositions occur in the Bible which are without any acrostic feature that we can discern. There are in Deuteronomy 32, however, certain light traces of an alphabetic thinking, which it may be worthwhile to examine. One is the term by which in v. 1 the author characterizes his poem as *ʾimʰrê pî* ⟦'words of my mouth'⟧; the initial letters of the two words could point to the pattern we have been discussing.

---

14. The welcome study of G. Douglas Young on "Ugaritic Prosody," *JNES* 9 (1950) 124–33, does not allow adequately in its conclusions for the regularity which is a fact in biblical compositions of "hakamic" or scribal origin, such as Proverbs, Job, and certain Psalms.

15. The chief structural irregularity of the poem is the use of three, rather than two, hemistichs within a single line of verse in vv. 14 and 39; other possibilities of the kind are implied in the textual discussion of vv. (14–)15 and 43.

16. An alphabetic cuneiform tablet, announced by C. Schaeffer and C. Virolleaud earlier this year (1950), was reproduced from a photograph and printed in the *Manchester Guardian Weekly* of March 23, 1950. Its minimal date is that of the destruction of the city of Ugarit in the mid-thirteenth century B.C. Its entire content, disposed in three rows on a slanting surface, for consultation like the modern desk calendar, are the thirty characters of the somewhat amplified, and now well known, Ugaritic alphabet. The most striking feature of the arrangement is, that though extra signs are interspersed among them, the twenty-two characters which become standard in Hebrew and Phoenician are already given in the order to which we are accustomed. This establishes that the alphabet we use has retained substantially the same sequence of characters almost, and perhaps quite, from the time of the first invention of an alphabet by some western Semite before 1500 B.C.!

Another, perhaps more significant trace can be found in v. 30. No one, it seems, has had any difficulty in recognizing one of the main divisions of the poem as occurring after v. 14. That represents one-third of the complete poem before the division; and, according to the analysis here given, two-thirds to follow it, with a second major division after v. 29. It therefore becomes significant that the [[162]] first hemistich of the supposed third section, in v. 30, runs *ʾê(y)kâ(h) yirdōp ʾeḥād ʾelep* [['how could one man rout a thousand?']]: two pairs of words that begin with *aleph* and end with *pe*, the last word being in fact a homonym for the name *aleph* on which the whole structure is based. The danger of mistaking for alphabetic devices combinations selected purely for assonance, and in general of proving too much, makes it advisable to leave it at this; but these points at least should be considered.

An exegetical question which has some relation to the textual problems of vv. 8–9, and indirectly, perhaps, to the length of the poem, will now be touched on. What is the allusion in the "number of the sons of God," or, in the Masoretic tradition, the "number of the sons of Israel"? One may try[17] to attain a thoroughly modern and prosaic meaning for the line, that calls for no background either historical or legendary. Then one will interpret the passage in its current Hebrew form to mean that God, in fixing the boundaries of the nations, reserved a land for Israel in keeping with its numbers. Few, however, have thought of construing the line in this fashion. With the reading, "sons of Israel," there is a chain of thought that runs through Rashi, the Targum Yerushalmi, and Sifré, that identifies the "number" as seventy, referring to Gen 46:27 an the seventy descendants of Israel, or Jacob, who went down into Egypt. God created lands for seventy nations, to correspond to the number of individuals in His chosen people at this turning point in their history. With a little good will, the table of nations in Genesis 10 can be gotten to yield a total very close to seventy, exclusive of the immediate ancestors of the Israelites. If then there be seventy nations, as has variously been affirmed, the "number" should of course be seventy, whether angels or Israelites be the standard of comparison. Origen, who has the LXX "sons of God" tradition, and attributes the nations to the angels and the Israelites to the Lord,[18] does not deal with the "number." In favor of an early tradition for the number seventy in connection with angels, Enoch 89:59ff. is alleged; in this there is reference to seventy (and one) shepherds

17. Joseph Reider, *Deuteronomy with Commentary* (Philadelphia, 1937) 302; the more traditional Jewish interpretation is also provided.
18. In *Num. Homil. 11:5, GCS* 30, pp. 86, 20ff.

appointed by God successively over the Chosen People.[19] A recent writer[20] has jumped all the way back from this to the "seventy sons of Asherah," [[163]] that is, of the consort of the Canaanite god El, in the Ugaritic texts. Since the biblical writer has left his allusion, if any, obscure, we should like to have far more evidence than we do of a heavenly council of seventy members presided over by the Lord, in early Hebrew thinking, before we could dare to affirm that an idea of this kind is the basis for the poetic allusion in our passage. However, the tenacity of formalities and of symbolism in the ancient Orient being what it was, the analogies of Moses and the seventy elders, and of the Jewish Sanhedrin, suggest this as a distinct possibility.

The trend of thought we have just followed suggests another. The subdivisions of the full Sanhedrin which exercised a measure of its authority and fulfilled delegated functions were composed of roughly one-third of its membership, and, exactly, of twenty-three members. Why, then, was the author of Deuteronomy 32 interested in securing a threefold repetition of a twenty-three verse pattern as the basic structure of his composition? Presumably because that was his way of writing a seventy-line poem. And the length of the poem, in turn, may not have been without influence in preserving for us, through changes of text and of interpretation, the consciousness of the number seventy in the veiled allusion of v. 8.

These reflections on the external structure of the rich and vigorous poem given to us under divine inspiration as the 32d chapter of the Book of Deuteronomy may not contribute much to an intensive appreciation of its content: but they leave the writer at least with the consoling assurance that the structure itself of the composition attests that no whole line within it has been lost, nor has any single line been violently displaced within it, since it was first written; and those who would affirm the contrary do so in the face of striking evidence for the unity and integrity of the poem.

* * * * * * *

(A note from "Qumran and the Present State of Old Testament Text Studies: The Masoretic Text," *JBL* 78 [1959] 21–22): Deuteronomy 32 is a composition for which LXX presents us with variant readings at several points in its long text. Already in 1954 (*BASOR* 136, 12–15) the writer had called attention to variant readings for v. 8

19. For a brief discussion cf. C. C. Torrey, *The Apocryphal Literature* (New Haven, 1945) 111–13; note the recurrence of the number 23 in the subdivisions of the time of the seventy shepherds into shorter periods.

20. R. Tournay, in *RB* 56 (1949) 53.

($b^e n\hat{e}(y)$ $^{\jmath}El$ ⟦'sons of God'⟧), and for the concluding v. 43. Since that time, further fragments have filled out both these parts of the text: the former now reads, in full, $b^e n\hat{e}(y)$ $^{\jmath}el\bar{o}h\hat{\imath}m$ ⟦'sons of God'⟧, as the beginning of a line, with $b^e hanh\hat{\imath}(l)$ ⟦'when he gives as a possession'⟧ directly above it; Cross has placed it securely as belonging to a MS of Deuteronomy of which numerous other fragments are also extant. For the end of the song, the writer has been able (*VTS* 4 [1957] 150, n. 1) to describe the peculiar arrangement of Deut 32:37–41 in the document, as verified with the help of one more fragment. In addition, during the summer of 1958, J. T. Milik turned up a group of verses from the middle of Deuteronomy 32 in what appeared to be a phylactery (!) from the same Qumran Cave IV; it offered further Septuagintal readings: $wyqn^{\jmath}$ ⟦'he will be jealous'⟧ for $wayyin^{\jmath}a\d{s}$ ⟦'condemn, spurn'⟧ in v. 19 (LXX *ezēlōsen* ⟦'be jealous'⟧, and the added hemistich before v. 15. Thus three separate Qumran documents combine to furnish the underlying Hebrew readings for practically all of the distinctive features of the Greek text of this song.

Samuel's "Broken *Rîb*": Deuteronomy 32

GEORGE E. MENDENHALL

[[63]] The historical nihilism characteristic of so much of biblical scholarship during the past century and still existing as a legacy from the 19th century has both stultified biblical scholarship and reinforced political tendencies that are extremely dangerous to civilization today. Lacking almost entirely any sense of historical perspective, especially with regard to the Early Iron Age ca. 1200–1000 B.C., biblical academia is seemingly incapable of realizing that we have in the biblical record an incredibly detailed mass of information about this period in Palestine in contrast to all other parts of the entire Mediterranean world.

To be sure, we are faced with the same problem (and even the methods) of Homeric scholarship, namely to distinguish between that which is really ancient, and that which derives from the reuse of old traditions for much later political purposes. But it does not seem to have gotten through to the world of biblical scholars that the early 19th century methods of "source analysis" of Homeric scholarship were given up decades ago. That is a matter of little importance in comparison with the virtual monopoly that has been obtained by those whose competence and academic output has only to do with literary forms and style. One is tempted to draw an analogy between the mainstream of modern biblical and religious scholars and those 15th century Byzantine monks who could find nothing valuable to do at the very time their whole world was tumbling down other than to gaze at their own navels. There can be little doubt that much of the current output of "biblical scholarship" in literary forms is nothing but navel-gazing, and has equal value to the world of humanity in serious trouble.

Reprinted with permission from *No Famine in the Land: Studies in Honor of J. L. McKenzie* (ed. J. W. Flanagan and A. W. Robinson; Missoula, Mont.: Scholars Press, 1975) 63–74.

Fortunately, we do have in the biblical sources some very old materials that have been preserved with little change since they are in poetic form. A serious historical problem exists, however, in the identification and dating of those early sources, and even more serious is their interpretation and utilization for social and intellectual history. Albright's last attempt to date the old poetry on the basis of stylistic forms[1] is most unconvincing since it [[64]] presupposes exactly the same kind of "unilinear evolution" that he had resisted throughout his entire scholarly career, and relies entirely upon stylistic phenomena that could easily be nothing more than individual or local poetic preferences or habits. What we need instead is in the first place a serious linguistic history of that particular dialect (or collection of dialects) of Iron Age Canaanite that has far too long been termed "Hebrew." Secondly, we need a *responsible* correlation of ancient sources with ancient historical reality— an endeavor that biblical and theological scholars seem to avoid as the bubonic plague. There is good reason for this attitude, for there can be little doubt that authoritarian social structures must depend on some kind of "phony history," and scholars must produce it.

Nevertheless, the ancient poem of Deuteronomy 32 presents a most fascinating complex of problems that still have no satisfying solutions, but little seems to have been written about it since 1962. The primary problem in the historical utilization of this source is its dating. Since it is not possible in this short essay to produce all the technical customary "proofs" for dating that are currently fashionable in academic circles, I shall only concur in the conclusions of Eissfeldt and Albright that the poem belongs to the second half of the eleventh century B.C. It not only constitutes a most important witness to religious thought of that period, but also is a most important source for the entire prophetic proclamation of several centuries later.

Cornill's description of the poem as a "compendium of prophetic theology" is perfectly accurate, but it does not follow by any means that it is a product of the prophetic movement of the 9th to 7th centuries, as even Wright argued.[2] In fact, what little we know of the 9th century prophecy gives little indication of capability of such profound theology as that exhibited in Deuteronomy 32. We have no evidence until Amos that prophecy turned from its futile and even self-destructive political "activism" to a much more mature understanding both of the nature of the original Yahwist faith and the total predicament of civilization.

1. W. F. Albright, *Yahweh and the Gods of Canaan* (London: Athlone, 1968) 1–46.
2. G. E. Wright, "The Lawsuit of God: A Form-Critical Study of Deuteronomy 32," *Israel's Prophetic Heritage: Essays in Honor of James Muilenburg*, eds. B. W. Anderson and W. Harrelson (New York: Harper & Row, 1962) 26–67.

It is now generally conceded that the 8th century prophets represent a continuity of the old Mosaic Yahwism, a position that I think not only justified but essential to any rational understanding of ancient Israel's faith and history. Yet, at the same time, far too many scholars are suffering from the delusion that pre-monarchic Israel was "too primitive" to have any highly developed theology, or that we have no sources for describing that theology.

It is certainly true that Deuteronomy 32 has extremely close ties with [65] especially the 7th–6th century prophecy. Virtually all the major themes of those prophets (including even the "remnant") have their antecedents in Deuteronomy 32. But, rather than concluding that the poem was their product, it would be much more rational to argue that Deuteronomy 32 was a major source, the "bible" so to speak, of the prophetic movement. In the first place, to dispose of Wright's dating of the poem to the 9th century (followed unthinkingly by Cross)[3] there can be no doubt that the poem is actually *quoted* in the 9th century prophetic charge to Jehu (2 Kgs 9:7; cf. Deut 32:43a) and therefore was already an authoritative ancient *source* even for the rather degenerate 9th century prophets, who seem to have been interested in little but politics. The close ties between the poem and the later prophets can best be understood as a part of the nostalgia for the past that characterizes so much of the history, culture, and thought of the 7th–6th centuries. It was a re-evaluation of very old tradition, and the discovery that it had much to offer to a society on the verge of catastrophe. But as Jeremiah particularly illustrates, it was too little and too late to avert the impending doom. For it cannot at the present time be too strongly emphasized that if politics is the "art of the possible," it is public opinion that determines *what* is possible, and that public opinion is always religious: i.e., either the worship of Yahweh with its *necessary* ethical concerns, or the worship of Baal and Asherah—the symbols of power, wealth (and, to be sure, sex).

Perhaps the ideological arguments against an early date can be most easily dealt with—and disposed of. We have already mentioned the close ties to 8th–6th century prophecy and suggested a reason that fits well with everything else we know about that period. Much more important is the close tie between the content of Deuteronomy 32 and the covenant ideology of the Late Bronze Age, as it has been reconstructed by the present writer and others during the past twenty years. The traditional late dating of Deuteronomy 32 makes it possible for those who

3. F. M. Cross, *Canaanite Myth and Hebrew Epic* (Cambridge: Harvard University, 1973) 264, n. 193.

argue that the covenant form is late in Israelite thought, to ignore it and conclude that the covenant ideology either did not exist, or was merely a late theological formulation, especially connected with the deuteronomic work. As G. E. Wright has described fairly well, Deuteronomy 32 and the structure of the Late Bronze Age covenant ideology are inseparable, but he was led astray by traditional form-critical ideas about the *Sitz im Leben* (usually defined as cultic whenever we are dealing with biblical texts). If we should start instead with the question "when and where is it most likely that the structure of covenant thought would be used, in the context obviously of a catastrophic *defeat* by an unnamed enemy?" then there can be no possible alternative to that ⟦66⟧ suggested by O. Eissfeldt and others. It is a prophetic response to the catastrophic defeat at Ebenezer and the destruction of Shiloh that must have seemed at the time to destroy all confidence in the religious ideology, its social organization, and its rudimentary institutions that were barely more than a century old at the time.

The poem cannot have originated at any time other than after the destruction of Shiloh and before the radical paganization of Yahwism that began early in David's reign and ran its natural course with the accession of Rehoboam and the consequent disidentification of the northern tribes from any further connection with the pagan Jerusalem regime. In other words, the poem must come from ca. 1050 B.C. to 1000 B.C. Any time after David's successes in war against the Philistines is reflected in Psalm 78, which is certainly a "theological answer" to Deuteronomy 32. But the conclusion that Deuteronomy 32 is a "broken" *rîb*, "that is, a specific cultic form adapted and expanded" by those "other themes," is a failure to understand historical reality when it is most vividly preserved for us. It is particularly weak when Wright tried to tie the "covenant lawsuit" to an alleged "covenant renewal" ceremony for which we have very little evidence other than Joshua 24 and Deuteronomy 27, both of which are either garbled by later tradition or have other historical contexts. The misunderstanding is compounded when it is combined with the "divine assembly" concept so popular at Harvard, which undoubtedly has clarified a few otherwise obscure passages of the Hebrew bible, most of which cluster about the period of Exile (Job, 2nd Isaiah, Genesis 1, etc.), but which has also been appealed to for explanation of many passages in the Hebrew Bible where it is not relevant.

But if we delete from the discussion of Deuteronomy 32 the various themes currently fashionable among OT scholars, what have we left? In other words, the poem has nothing to do with the "divine assembly," covenant renewal, covenant "lawsuit" (whatever that may be), cultic confession and praise, and a host of other academic clichés that have been misused in order to escape historical reality.

Though it cannot now be proven, it is at least worthwhile to point out that further biblical research cannot merely assume that Deuteronomy 32 dates to the period of the divided monarchy. In the first place, there is absolutely nothing in the poem that presupposes even the existence of the monarchy. Secondly, though this cannot be used as proof at the present time, there is an impressive number of linguistic correlations in this text with the language and idioms of the syllabic texts from Byblos;[4] those correlations also cluster about Exodus 15, Judges 5, Deuteronomy 33, and [67] Genesis 49. It is partly for this reason that I cannot take seriously the various arguments from "form-criticism" that would assign a late date to this poem.

Most of the old poetry of the Pentateuch and other sources has as its theme the celebration of successes in an indubitably turbulent period all over the once "civilized" world. Deuteronomy 32, on the other hand, stands alone as a reaction to historical calamity, and therefore the usual stylistic and form-critical analyses are simply irrelevant. What we must deal with is not mere literary "form," but with the language and content—what does it say, and how does that content fit in with what we know of the theological history of OT thought? Though I should like to come back to this poem with a thorough linguistic and conceptual analysis, it does not seem probable in the near future. Perhaps others can be stimulated to do what is imperative at the present critical stage of OT history and theology.

Just a few characteristics of the poem must be pointed out. Eissfeldt has already pointed out very archaic features of the language, as has also Albright. But the theological concepts are equally archaic. Not only does the poem illustrate the most vivid structure of the Late Bronze Age covenants before the late baroque attempt on the part of the deuteronomist to revivify it, it also illustrates the stage of thought prior to the monarchic rewriting of history for political purposes. As is the case in all the archaic poetry, this poem knows nothing of Abraham and Isaac, nothing of "Israel in Egypt," nothing of the Exodus or even the so-called "Conquest," nothing even of any concept of "national state," much less the monarchy. Israel was "found" in a desert land, historically the truth, for the "mixed multitude" (Num 11:4) that escaped Egyptian servitude with Moses was not "Israel" until it was created (v. 6)

---

4. On internal evidence I maintain that these texts cannot be much later than 2000 B.C. and could well be even earlier, or at least reflect an earlier stage of Northwest Semitic.

by an act of God,[5] and it was not a territorial state in contrast to the numerous political structures of the time (v. 8) until the paganization under the monarchy. In this regard there is a curious coincidence with the evidence from the Merneptah Stele that seems to have escaped attention, for in both very old sources political-territorial boundary lines had nothing to do with the character of the human "portion of Yahweh," or the nature of the religious community. It is indeed difficult to find or reconstruct any better description of the religious ideology of ancient Israel before the so-called "wise men" of the monarchy concocted a largely phony history for political purposes by attempting to combine certain elements of the Mosaic history with the dominant religious ideology of the pagan Bronze Age, namely the "divine charter" theology associated with the Abraham-Davidic tradition. It may be that the Bronze Age pagan ideology was right, but the record of the biblical history (or of more recent [[68]] history) certainly does not justify that idea. For even the Christology of the NT constitutes the acceptance of the old pagan ideology that had been so dominant in Jewish tradition since David, and, separating it entirely from its original political function, assimilated it completely to the mainstream of the Mosaic—early Israelite theology of the kingdom (= rule) of God.

As a framework for further progress in understanding not only this particular poem, but also for the history of Israelite religion, I would offer the following suggestions and observations:

1. Historical context: over against Wright's vague 9th–7th centuries, Eissfeldt is surely correct (among others) in seeing the poem as a religious response to the destruction of Shiloh and the capture of the Ark of the Covenant. The event cannot but have called into question the entire viability of the still relatively new religious ideology of Yahwism as well as the social structure (the twelve tribe federation) that was entirely dependent upon, and the result of the former (cf. v. 6). But the breakdown of the Yahwist theology in favor of older pagan gods (Josh 24:14–15), or perhaps new faddish cults (v. 17?; cf. Judg 5:8; unfortunately both passages are obscure), cannot but have weakened the ability of the village populations to ward off the rapacious urban warlords. The entire structure of Judges emphasizes this point, but because it is so schematized and reduced to a formula, no one seems to have taken seriously the fact that in spite of the wooden Procrustes' bed of that history, it must well have been historically correct.

---

5. Note the astonishing, and correct, statement in Deut 27:9. It includes, of course, the late anachronistic use of the term "all Israel," but it is certainly correct in its emphasis of the fact that "becoming the people of God" is a function of religious conversion.

At the same time, this evidence strongly reinforces the contention of those who maintain that the Mosaic Yahwism was a radically new religious ideology incompatible with the pre-Mosaic pagan cults; it also emphasizes strongly that the attraction of those pagan cults for the Israelite tribes is due to the fact that those cults must have been traditional and socially functional in local Palestinian society before the establishment of the federation. The fact that Yahwism was established and survived at all in the face of traditionally conservative village society is perhaps the greatest miracle of all those in the Bible—but unnoticed and unappreciated because of modern pagan cults of nationalism and racism.

As a corollary, it almost inevitably follows that the author of Deuteronomy 32 is the prophet Samuel himself. The entire poem is not only a phrase-book for the later prophets, it *is* prophecy in every sense of the term. As a prophetic oracle there are virtually no remaining serious problems of form or content, and at the same time it illustrates for us the incredible potential of the early Yahwist movement in thought as well as the indubitable social achievement of unifying a very diverse population over an astoundingly large area with no centralized monopoly of force. Albright [[69]] was certainly correct in emphasizing the enormous importance of the prophet Samuel during this transition period when the old institution of Ark and Tabernacle (and its priesthood) had been almost entirely discredited. Deuteronomy 32 points out in very vigorous terms that such social institutions and their fate are the consequence of covenant obedience or disobedience, not the *cause* either of covenant or of historical event. At any rate, the fates of Shiloh and the Ark had nothing to do with the continuing dominion of Yahweh—indeed they were *caused* by him for good reason. The same theme was repeatedly to become the basis for the *prediction* of destruction of Jerusalem and Samaria by the later prophets, though only Jeremiah specifically pointed to Shiloh as an early precedent.

2. *Sitz im Leben*: though I have not made any systematic search, I have a strong impression that this term is used only in regard to the (largely vain) search for the liturgical occasion or purpose of a rigid ritual form. If so, the term is absurd when scholars attempt to apply it to prophetic oracles. What is the *Sitz im Leben* of the oracle, also from Samuel, against Saul in 1 Sam 15:22? One can add Nathan's parable to David, Amos at Bethel, Jeremiah at the Temple (Jeremiah 7), and most of the canonical prophecy. It is only the pagan Balaq who expected the pagan prophet Balaam to produce the proper oracle for a cultic occasion, though no doubt the equally pagan kings of Jerusalem and Samaria expected their court prophets to function in a similar fashion (cf. Micaiah and his non-

colleagues). The mainstream of the biblical prophetic tradition had nothing necessarily to do with public office (as also at Mari), but rather with the message received by the prophet from Yahweh, almost always in connection with some concrete historical situation. "Cult prophets" certainly existed; some of the canonical prophets certainly were or may have been associated with them (Elisha), but to say that canonical prophecy is an *office* in OT tradition is just as absurd as it would be to argue that Jeremiah's cistern is evidence that Zedekiah's bureaucracy was short of office space, and Jeremiah was simply being treated like many a junior faculty member in many universities and colleges today.

Rather than searching for some cultic *Sitz im Leben* for the oracle of Deuteronomy 32, it would be much more appropriate to look for the historic *occasion* in which the oracle fits. This is given us at considerable length in 1 Samuel 7, especially v. 3, and the rest of the chapter describes the consequences, both ritual and historical. The social occasion of Deuteronomy 32, is, then, the very understandable gathering of the survivors to consider what was the cause of the calamity, and what should be the future policy. I would guess that the oracle of Samuel was delivered [70] at a time when the debacle was at least fresh in the memory of the tribal leaders, if not very shortly after the defeat itself. (It goes without saying that the existing context, 1 Sam 7:1–2, anticipates the subsequent history of the Ark, since that had been the major theme of the preceding sections, and therefore does not necessarily give the context of the events described in 7:3–4.) It is interesting to compare the pious clichés of 1 Sam 7:3–4 with the highly developed theology of Deuteronomy 32, even though there can be little doubt that they describe the same occasion.

3. Form: since Wright has already given a fairly adequate description of the coincidence between this poem and the covenant structure, we need not be further concerned with this topic here though many side comments could and should be added. The term Wright uses, following H. B. Huffmon[6] (and for which I may myself be at least indirectly responsible) "covenant lawsuit" now seems peculiarly inappropriate, at least in application to this poem.

As I have maintained for at least two decades, this poem is probably the best indirect evidence we have for actual village court procedures in Palestine of the Early Iron Age. It is a form thus *transferred* (as is the covenant itself!) from normal political-legal procedures into the realm of religious and historical thought. But here Yahweh is *not* suing anyone for breach of covenant; instead the breach *had* taken place, the

---

6. "The Covenant Lawsuit in the Prophets," *JBL* 78 (1959) 285–95.

consequences *had* been suffered, and the issue is whether or not Yahweh would be a reliable refuge for the future. In this regard, the poem is remarkably reminiscent of the prophecies of the Exile, and to dismiss the assurances of Deut 32:36–43 as "generalized expressions of hope," as Wright did (p. 40), is to miss the point entirely. For the issue was precisely whether the nascent Yahwism with its highly developed theology was simply to give up in favor of the old Bronze Age worship of power symbols—the baals of the city states. A generation later this did happen, but in the meantime the Yahwist theology had become so well established that it never entirely died out, even though its later major spokesmen, the prophets, had no more chance of making themselves heard than Elmer Berger has in becoming president of the World Zionist Congress.

Contrary to the expectations of finding all kinds of mythological allusions that are admittedly characteristic of much of the old poetry of the Pentateuch, the poem is almost entirely historical in context except only for vv. 7–9. But except for the curious fragment of Gen 6:1–4, it would be difficult to find in the entire OT a more accurate description of the *historic* function of ancient mythology than the passage in question. To conclude, therefore, for a late date on the basis of what is not otherwise present is [[71]] hardly an adequate scholarly method, particularly when the poem is without any real parallel other than elements that were taken up by later prophetic tradition.

Consequently, the appeal to heavens and earth have nothing to do with the "divine assembly" so popular in much later times. Instead these elements of the natural world are appealed to simply as witnesses who are expected to be active in the enforcement of the findings in a court of law. The modern legal concept of a "witness" is completely misleading and irrelevant to the social function of a witness in ancient village law courts. In the absence of governmental functionaries, those who have witnessed a legal action (or even a crime) are expected to be relied upon when a remedy is needed (cf. Ruth 4). In view of the fact that both blessings and curses are mediated largely through the natural world, there should be no difficulty in understanding the appeal to heavens and earth as witnesses in a *transferred* procedure in which I have a strong impression that Yahweh is the original defendant—in other words, Deuteronomy 32 is a prophetic theodicy long before that literary form existed. The calamity of the battle of Aphek-Ebenezer, particularly after the Ark had been brought into the battle scene, can only have led to the conclusion that Yahweh had let them down, and only a vigorous reversal of the roles of plaintiff and defendant could have been effective—as it evidently was, if the connection with 1 Samuel 7 is admitted, and as the historical evidence seems to confirm.

4. The prophetic prolegomenon: (vv. 2–3) this has absolutely no connection with the "wisdom literature" tradition as Wright correctly pointed out. Instead, it is very comprehensible in the context of a village society where there exists no monopoly of force, and where there can be only a hope that wise statements will be accepted and result in action appropriate to the situation. The optimism of v. 2 can be of course, and has been, compared to Isa 55:10–11; but this passage should also be compared (or contrasted) to Isa 6:9–10. It is worthy of note that the optimistic expectations concerning the acceptance of the Divine Word coincide with the historical periods when "He sees that their power is gone. . . . "

The prophetic word, or oracle, is historically significant in two different ways: it is either accepted as policy by the religious community, or it is rejected and enforced by God Himself through the media of the natural world and the pagan nations. In this connection it is worth consideration that the verb forms in v. 2 should be considered as jussives and are usually so translated; I would much prefer the term "optative"—a wish form, for the prophets were never in a position of social power that enabled them to command. [[72]]

5. The early down-grading of Samuel: the curious inconsistencies in the narratives concerning Samuel that so exercised the ingenuity of an earlier generation of biblical scholars seem now comprehensible. For not only was Samuel notoriously in adamant opposition to the public demand for establishing a centralized monopoly of force, he also publicly rejected and renounced Saul and thereby doubtless contributed to the latter's tragic downfall. Since virtually all of our historical narratives were written during the period of the monarchy by scribes closely identified with the royal court, it is not to be expected that those scribes would be highly enthusiastic about prophetic king makers and breakers. The prophetic intervention in North Israelite politics certainly could have done nothing to alleviate the nervousness of the pagan Jerusalemite kings, particularly after Shemaiah effectively vetoed the royal stupidity of Rehoboam. For this reason, the "late source" is likely to be more historically accurate, though after nearly half a millennium, it is too far removed from the chronological scene of action to be satisfactory. The attribution of Deuteronomy 32 to Moses himself is sufficient evidence of the very deficient historical perspectives of the late history-writers.

To sum up, Deuteronomy 32 is not a "lawsuit" at all. It is a prophetic oracle essentially concerned with the interpretation of history past, and appealing for public opinion that would make the future more palatable. It is not a "broken" *rîb*, for under the circumstances following the Philistine victory, the only possible and the only necessary course of action was a rejection of the pagan ideologies that disrupted the unity upon which the independence of the tribal villages was absolutely dependent, and a reaffirmation of the Yahwist theology.

Further, as Wright has well delineated, we have no more impressive illustration of the old covenant structure of thought than this poem, at least before Deuteronomy. To be sure, we do have bits and fragments of that old theology in the canonical prophets, especially the blessings and curses formula so well described by D. Hillers, but we need a similar study of the prophetic use of historical traditions particularly since the "historical prologue" is so important in OT theology as well as Late Bronze Age suzerainty treaties in contrast to those of the Iron Age. Wright is entirely correct in saying, " . . . there is no covenant without Credo, and no Law without Gospel" (p. 52, n. 55). Unfortunately, a political monopoly of force can easily get by for a time without gospel, and the obligations that stem from gospel are usually not at all those that a political monopoly of force can effectively enforce ("apodictic" law). The widely used term "covenant law" is a contradiction in itself, since law by definition refers properly to [[73]] those social obligations enforced by social organization, while covenant obligations must underlie and even make possible social enforcement of law. Conversely, it is equally easy to construct "credo" without any obligations other than proper performance of rituals (Deuteronomy 26, a fairly late and degenerate reductionism). Virtually all the prophets have scathing denunciations of this theme, but even today dominant concepts of religion seem to include only those themes characteristic of any primitive culture: ritual reinforcement of existing social solidarities, "proper" linguistic behavior in dealing with religious themes, and observance of ritual tabus inherited from some obscure and often phony past history. This sort of fundamentalism is, and always has been, a great danger to the successful functioning of civilized society, for like primitive society in general, it has no concept of historical dynamics, of cause and effect relationships, and effectively prevents the development of a sound historical perspective, and often enough, the reinforcement of a tolerable public and private ethic as well.

The Early Iron Age must have been an extremely traumatic period for people all over the civilized world of the eastern Mediterranean, when social organizations of all kinds including empires were disintegrating, most of them to disappear forever. It may be true that the economy and social organization of early Israel appears "primitive," but it does not follow at all that the ideology of that society can be termed primitive. For there is no other period of history when the unique system of religious thought so characteristic of the Bible could have originated, and to that system Deuteronomy 32 is an invaluable witness, emphasizing the principle that "what a man sows, that shall he also reap" (Deuteronomy 32; cf. 1 Sam 15:23b).

Legendary Motifs in the Moses Death Reports

GEORGE W. COATS

[[34]] Death reports are characteristic features in the narratives about the giants among Israel's fathers: Adam, Noah, Abraham, Jacob, Joseph, Moses, Aaron, and Joshua. All of the figures appear in variegated tales depicting each in collective memory, each with distinctive traits. Yet each shares a fate in common with his fellow giants, in common as well with every other man. And the mortality of these giants demands its share in the narrative accounts of human deeds. Nevertheless, despite the common refrain of death reports among the tales of the giants, not all the death reports in biblical narrative look alike. Some are mere notices (cf. Gen 5:5). Some develop a longer report of death. But in the process only the essential data come to light (cf. Gen 50:22–25). And some decorate a longer report of essential data with motifs that at first seem incredible. Thus, the Moses death reports note not only the demise of the giant, but also his incomparable character at the time of his death. The purpose of this paper is to explore those distinctive motifs[1] in order to determine what they are, how they function, and what insight they offer into the Moses traditions generally.[2]

Reprinted with permission from *Catholic Biblical Quarterly* 39 (1977) 34–44.

1. By motif, I mean "a characteristic of a work's design; a word or pattern of thought that recurs in a similar situation, or to evoke a similar mood within a work or in various works of a genre." Cf. J. T. Shipley, ed., *Dictionary of World Literature* (Totowa, N. J.: Littlefield, Adams, 1972) 274. If one is to understand the design of various death reports, the function of motifs peculiar to some is crucial.

2. On the Moses traditions, cf. E. Osswald, *Das Bild des Mose in der Kritischen alttestamentlichen Wissenschaft seit Julius Wellhausen* (Theologische Arbeiten 18; Berlin: Evangelische Verlagsanstalt, n.d.); R. Smend, *Das Mosebild von Heinrich Ewald bis Martin Noth* (BGBE 3; Tübingen: Mohr, 1959); F. Schnutenhaus, *Die Entstehung der Mosetraditionen.* Unpublished

The working hypothesis of the paper is that the characteristic motifs in the Moses death reports are heroic. By heroic I mean motifs whose primary intention is to describe outstanding virtues and feats, either moral or physical, not in God, but in a man.[3] Of course the virtue may derive from [[35]] God. The virtue may be faithful obedience to God's word.[4] But the virtue belongs to the man. The feat may root in divine strength. But it characterizes the stature of the man.[5] In order to expand perception of this facet in the Moses traditions, I propose to isolate a series of heroic motifs in the Moses death reports, specifically Num 27:12–23 and Deut 34:1–12.[6]

I

1. The first motif in the series highlights Moses' strength at the end of his life. "Moses was a hundred and twenty years old when he died; his eye was not dim, and his natural force had not fled" (Deut 34:7).

Three members in the statement carry the weight of the motif. The first one specifies the age at the time of death. While Moses' age is not as extensive as the age of figures in the primeval history, not even as extensive as Abraham and Jacob, it must be seen as a complete and full period. The summary statement marking Abraham's death seems harmonious for Moses as well: "These are the days of the years of Abraham's life, which he lived, a hundred and seventy-five years. Abraham breathed his last breath and died in a good age, an old man and full. . . . " To die in a good age is in itself a sign of strength and suggests that particularly the excessive ages in the prediluvian lists can be understood as legendary fragments from traditions about the ancient heroes.

An age of one hundred and twenty years is in itself, however, not excessive for biblical tradition, even if it does move beyond the range of average contemporary experience. Emphasis on Moses' strength comes

---

dissertation, Heidelberg, 1958. H. Schmid, *Mose, Überlieferung und Geschichte* (BZAW 110; Berlin: Töpelmann, 1968).

3. On heroic tradition, see Jan de Vries, *Heroic Song and Heroic Legend* (trans. B. J. Timmer; London: Oxford, 1963).

4. G. W. Coats, "Abraham's Sacrifice of Faith," *Int* 27 (1973) 389–400.

5. G. W. Coats, "Moses versus Amalek: Aetiology and Legend in Exod. XVII 8–16," in *Congress Volume Edinburgh* (VTSup 28; Leiden: Brill, 1975) 29–41.

6. On the relationship between these two reports, cf. Martin Noth, *Überlieferungsgeschichtliche Studien* (2d ed.; Tübingen, 1957) 190–216. The argument must consider other texts related to a report of Moses' death, such as Deut 32:48–52, as well as Deut 31:1–23. But the primary discussion will not focus on these texts.

from the following two members. These, too, offer some problem for interpretation. The last one involves a noun with no clear biblical parallels: *wĕlō²-nās lēḥōh* [['and his natural force had not fled']]. Perhaps a related adjective, *laḥ* [['damp, moist']], provides some insight, suggesting the fresh, moist character of vital trees and fruit. At one hundred and twenty years Moses would have been as supple as a youth. But the member is formulated in the negative and does not tie down the nature of the strength imputed to Moses.[7] The other member is more helpful. Also [[36]] formulated in a negative, the sentence depends on the verb *kāhâ: lo²-kāhătâ ᶜênô* [['his eye was not dim']]. The verb is paralleled in a negative formulation by Isa 42:4, a text emphasizing the servant's legendary strength to persevere until justice reigns in the earth. Moreover, formulations without a negative show the verb as a means for denoting the opposite of strength. Zech 11:17 sets the verb in a curse, with the arm of the victim without strength, the eye without sight (*zĕrōᶜô yābôš tîbāš wĕᶜēn yĕmînô kāhōh tikheh*). And in Gen 27:1 (perhaps of more importance) the verb describes Isaac's sight at the end of his life, an old man virtually blind and ready for death. With a negative formulation, Deut 34:7 insists that Moses is not that way.

Furthermore, this formulation stands out by contrast from a parallel text, not a death report, but a Moses speech in Deut 31:2: "I am a hundred and twenty years old this day; I am no longer able to go out and come in." The Moses who speaks in Deuteronomy 31 is an old man, feeble, unable to lead his people, ready to die. In the heroic motif, however, Moses is strong, able to do what he always had done. At one hundred and twenty years he is a young man. Indeed, he appears virtually immortal.[8] And death comes, not because of natural decay, or at least not very much of it, but because the appointed time for the end of a man's life has arrived.[9] Thus Moses' strength places him in a unique

7. But cf. W. F. Albright, "The 'Natural Force' of Moses in the Light of Ugaritic," *BASOR* 94 (1944) 32–35.

8. E. Auerbach, *Moses* (trans. Robert A. Barclay and Israel O. Lehman; Detroit: Wayne State University Press, 1975) 170–171. "Moses died, not because the enormous vitality of this giant was exhausted; he appeared to be almost immortal. He died a special death: the deity summoned the loved one to it. God ordered him to die, and die he did in full vigor. The narrator has in great simplicity molded this into a powerful image."

9. Cf. the heroes of the Nibelungenlied and Beowulf. Siegfried appeared to be immortal because he had been immersed in a dragon's blood. One tiny exception to complete immersion left a small, but vulnerable spot. And there treacherous friends attacked, killing the hero in his prime. Beowulf defended his people against a dragon, although advanced to extremely old age. To be sure, he had lost some of his youthful vigor. Yet he withstood the dragon's attack. And though mortally wounded, he succeeded in slaying the attacker and saving his people.

category. The characterization appears overdrawn, unreal. Moses is almost superhuman, a figure whose attributes stretch the imagination beyond average human experience. That characterization typifies heroic legend.[10]

2. The second motif in the series singles out Moses' spirit as a spirit of authority never to be equalled in the leadership of any other single man. In ⟦37⟧ Deut 34:9 the legendary character of this motif is not obvious. The spirit motif is tied closely to Joshua as Moses' successor. And the spirit is a spirit of wisdom now filling Joshua (not the spirit of Moses). Yet the spirit fills Joshua because ($k\hat{\imath}$) Moses laid his hands on him, a symbolic act for transferring the spirit from one head to another. In Num 27:18–21 the same motif appears. Joshua is filled with the spirit. But the act of ordination in this case functions as a means for transferring *some* of Moses' authority, *mēhôdēkā* (cf. Ps 21:6; 45:4) to Joshua. The partitive *min* seems to me to be significant, for Joshua cannot carry all of Moses' authority, Moses' vigor and strength. Nonetheless, the explicit consequence of the transferral is that the congregation will now obey Joshua as they had obeyed Moses (cf. Num 27:20; Deut 34:9). The same motif appears in the addition to the quail story in Num 11:16–17, 24–30, the account of the spirit falling on seventy elders. To be sure the motif as it now stands has been converted into an etiology for ecstatic prophecy. But the primary intention of the motif lay in the transfer of authority from Moses, the head of the people, to lieutenants who would assist Moses in administration. (It is somewhat surprising that the spirit motif is absent from Exodus 18. Cf. also Deut 3:28; 31:7, 14, 23.) Thus it is significant that the partitive *min* appears again: "I shall take *some* of the spirit (*min-hārûaḥ*) which is on you and put it on them" (Num 11:17).[11] Not even seventy men can

---

10. Beowulf's struggle with the dragon occurs under the watchful eye of his aid, Wiglaf, who comes to Beowulf's aid in his time of crisis. And the struggle proves fatal. Yet the struggle is an individual feat, a display of legendary strength in the hero's old age. Cf. the work on legendary reports of battles of Jan de Vries, *Heroic Song and Heroic Legend*, 189–190, 203. For a working definition of legend, cf. R. M. Hals, "Legend: A Case Study in OT Form-Critical Terminology," *CBQ* 34 (1972) 166–176.

11. A parallel can be seen in 2 Kgs 2:9. Elisha requests, in all probability, not a double portion of Elijah's spirit, but one-half or two-thirds. And the issue is not so much a question of inheritance, a double portion as the right of the firstborn, but a reasonable portion of the master's spirit (*bĕrûḥākā*). R. A. Carlson, "Elisée—le successeur d'Elie," *VT* 20 (1970) 403. As a consequence of the emphasis on Elijah's spirit, the story seems to me to be an Elijah story, not an Elisha story, or even a story primarily about God. (Against Gerhard von Rad, *Old Testament Theology* [trans. D. M. G. Stalker, 2 vols.; New York: Harper, 1960] 2.25–26.) Num 20:22–29 has another parallel, the death report for Aaron with Eleazar designated as successor. Yet here the legendary characteristics of such texts

carry all of Moses' spirit. Again, the superhuman ability characterizes heroic legend.

3. The third motif in the series describes the relationship Moses enjoys face to face with God. That kind of intimacy had not been known previously and would not be known again (Deut 34:10). Num 12:6–8 parallels this motif closely, although the point of communication shifts from face to mouth. Moreover, that relationship stands in contrast to the prophets who must depend on visions or dreams. The point of comparison, however, is not to denigrate the prophetic office but to elevate Moses. This [[38]] point can be established clearly by the parallel motif in Exod 33:11 with a notation that such intimacy is the intimacy of friendship. The image of Moses descending from that intimacy with a shining face too awe-inspiring for average people to behold (34:29–35) doubtlessly reflects the dynamics of such a hero. But perhaps of even greater importance, in Num 12:7, is the notation that this man, whom God addresses personally, God has trusted with his entire house (cf. Gen 39:3–4, 22).

Deut 34:11–12 moves the content of this motif from the relationship Moses enjoys with God to the mighty acts Moses did in the sight of all Israel, not God, but Moses. To be sure, the signs and wonders Moses did to the Pharaoh, his servants, and his land, had been commissioned by God. In the plague cycle, the Pharaoh witnesses the signs and wonders in order to know that Yahweh is Lord. In the Sea tradition, for Israel to witness the great work of their salvation was to witness a great work Yahweh did against the Egyptians. And on the basis of that witness Israel believed in Yahweh. But she also believed *in his servant Moses.* And the heroic formulation of that tradition in Deut 34:11–12 makes those faith-provoking deeds the deeds of Moses. Again, Moses' special character, above all others, sets the pace for heroic legend.

II

Yet despite all this legendary aggrandizement, the Moses death reports carry another motif, apparently contrary to their presentation of the hero as a superhuman of very little fault. That motif shows Moses as the sinner who cannot enter the promised land. In Deut 34:4 the motif is brief, simply a note that Moses will see the land but will not cross

---

seem totally missing. There is no reference to Aaron's spirit. To the contrary, Aaron is simply stripped of his clothes. And Eleazar is invested with them (cf. the mantle of Elijah, 2 Kgs 2:13). There is no concern to give Eleazar only part of his successor's authority. There is nothing here but transfer of office.

over into it. In Num 27:13–14, however, the prohibition against Moses' entry into the land is grounded in his rebellion at Meribah (cf. Num 20:2–13). And that element appears again, strongly, in Deut 32:48–52. Moses suffers death at the edge of the promised land as punishment for his rebellion (cf. esp. Deut 32:51–52). Thus, the question: How is this negative element in the Moses death reports to be evaluated *vis-à-vis* the positive, heroic motifs so replete in the same reports?

1. It seems to be clear that the reference to Moses' death as punishment for his rebellion at Meribah of Kadesh is a late rationalization of the tradition, an effort (on the part of Deutr or P) to resolve the theological hiatus caused by the memory of a strong and capable leader who did not make it into the land. Thus the explicit references to Moses' sin at Meribah [[39]] appear only in late texts, all in some way dependent on Deutr or P.[12] A comparison between the priestly version of the Meribah story and its earlier counterpart establishes an intentional change in the formulation of the story. That act which constitutes obedience to God's command in the older form of the story becomes explicitly an act of disobedience for P. And for the disobedience, although in a relatively minor and technical move in executing God's instructions, Moses falls before reaching the land.[13]

2. Noth observes: "Of course the Deuteronomistic historian hardly came to the idea on his own that Moses . . . died as a result of divine wrath before the crossing of the Jordan and the entrance into the promised land (Deut 3:26, 27b). In this respect he was certainly bound to the received tradition, only we are no longer in a position to ascertain how the wrath of God against Moses was explained in this tradition."[14] Noth hypothesizes, however, that the older traditions knew a motivation for Moses' punishment rooted in a vicarious substitution for punishment intended for the people. In Deut 3:26 this element can be seen: "The Lord was angry with me on your account" (cf. also Deut 1:37; 4:21; Ps 106:32).[15] If the hypothesis is correct, then Moses' character takes on a decidedly different hue. As a vicarious sufferer he bears his burden in a way that increases his stature rather than diminishing it. Indeed, the vicarious element would gain its most intense ex-

12. M. Noth, *A History of Pentateuchal Traditions* (trans. B. W. Anderson; Englewood Cliffs: Prentice Hall, 1972) 170, 479.

13. For details, cf. George W. Coats, *Rebellion in the Wilderness: The Murmuring Motif in the Wilderness Traditions of the Old Testament* (Nashville: Abingdon, 1968) 53–82. Also Auerbach, 170.

14. Noth, *Pentateuchal Traditions*, 170.

15. On the vicarious death of Moses, cf. Gerhard von Rad, *Deuteronomy, A Commentary* (trans. D. Barton; London: SCM, 1966) 209–210. Also Coats, *Rebellion*, 79–81.

pression if the sufferer should bear the guilt of his people even though he himself bears no personal guilt at all (cf. Isa 53:4–9). It is thus perhaps significant that behind the rather artificial designation of Moses' sin lies a tradition that did not report any sin on Moses' part.

3. Yet Deut 34:1–12 notes neither punishment for a sin at Meribah nor a vicarious suffering in the place of the people. There is no explicit indication in this text that Moses' death should be taken as punishment. Rather, there is only a display of the land before Moses' eye and an announcement: "I have let you see it with your eyes, but you shall not go over there" (Deut 34:4). Must we not therefore reckon with a stage in the death tradition that offers no explanation at all for Moses' death? Would that kind of tradition not fit exactly with the heroic motifs so common elsewhere in the death [[40]] reports? Rather than dying a normal death, the result of natural decay, Moses disappears into the mountain to die, alone, full of the vigor of life. And his death is tragic.[16] He does not die young, as does Samson. But he dies before he reaches his goal. As a consequence his death is as untimely as the typical death of a young hero like Siegfried in the Nibelungenlied. Moreover, there is in Deuteronomy 34 no element of punishment, anymore than the death of Siegfried stands as punishment. Moses dies. And that is that.

Yet, despite the tragic element in Moses' death, there is also a comforting vision of this hero facing the fate of every man. God's oracle to Jacob promises that at the point of death "Joseph's hand shall close your eyes" (Gen 46:4). For Moses no man was present to close his eyes. Yet God was present. "So Moses the servant of the Lord died there in the land of Moab, according to the word of the Lord. And he [the Lord] buried him in the valley in the land of Moab opposite Beth-peor. But no man knows the place of his burial to this day." The legend of Elijah's death moves in the same direction, although with markedly more intense drama. He dies in a way that no man sees, not even his successor. Rather, he disappears from sight, full of life, free to face an unknown fate, his work as yet incomplete.[17] Death, I assume, is never timely. It threatens a terrifying loneliness (cf. Matt 27:45–50). It cuts

16. Hillel Barzel, "Moses: Tragedy and Sublimity," in *Literary Interpretations of Biblical Narratives*, eds. K. R. R. Gros Louis, J. S. Ackerman, and T. S. Warshaw (Nashville: Abingdon, 1974) 120–140.

17. De Vries, 216: "Heroes often die young, like Achilles, Siegfried, and Cuchulainn. In many cases their death is miraculous. Romulus is taken up into heaven . . . , and Kag Chosrev vanishes into the desert." Cf. also 2 Kgs 13:14–21. Cf. also Lord Raglan (Fitzroy Richard Somerset), "The Hero of Tradition," in *The Study of Folklore*, ed. Alan Dundes (Englewood Cliffs: Prentice Hall, 1965) 142–157.

short work as yet unfinished. But in the heroic death of Moses or Elijah death carries a confirmation of a life's work, an affirmation of God's presence.[18]

III

1. One conclusion appears firm: legendary motifs casting Moses as an incomparable figure from the past constitute the building material for the Moses death reports. These motifs obviously do not call on subsequent [[41]] generations to "go and do likewise." To the contrary they emphasize the impossibility for fitting any other man into the mold cast by Moses. Yet, the image of Moses casts a model of leadership and strength for subsequent generations. And it is that model that functions as edification. Leaders in the line of Mosaic succession can live and work successfully if only a portion of Moses' spirit, an approximation of the full model falls on their shoulders. This construction of a death report stands in sharp contrast to the Aaron death report in Num 20:22–29.

2. A second conclusion seems to me to be justified: the motif casting Moses' death at a premature moment suggests a close relationship between the legendary elements of leadership and heroic legend, not necessarily the same generic literature.[19] If this conclusion should stand, it would raise the possibility of unity with other Mosaic traditions such as the birth story (Exod 2:1–10), the marriage story (Exod 2:11–22),[20] and a battle story (Exod 17:8–16).

18. Noth, *Pentateuchal Traditions*, 170–175. He assumes that the earlier form of tradition knew something of the way Moses died and some precise information about the location of his grave. Cf. also von Rad, *Deuteronomy*, 210. But the pursuit of that original tradition seems to be misdirected. The absence of such precise information is characteristic for legendary material. And an effort to tie it down, as perhaps P did, appears to me prosaic.

19. On heroic literature in general, cf. H. M. Chadwick and N. K. Chadwick, *The Growth of Literature* (Cambridge: University Press, 1932) I, 1–376; III, 679–772. Joseph Campbell, *The Hero with a Thousand Faces* (The Bollingen Series 17; New York: Pantheon Books, 1949) 356–364. For a contrasting position, see B. W. Anderson, *Understanding the Old Testament* (3d ed.; Englewood Cliffs: Prentice-Hall, 1975) 48. "The Exodus story is not a heroic epic told to celebrate the accomplishment of Moses as the liberator of his people. The narrator's major purpose is to glorify the God of Israel, the 'divine warrior' whose strong hand and outstretched arm won the victory over his adversaries, Pharaoh and his host." That purpose is apparent in the Song of the Sea. It is not, however, the only purpose in the Exodus story."

20. Brevard S. Childs, *Exodus: A Critical, Theological Commentary* (Philadelphia: Westminster, 1974) 31. Childs observes: "The Writer is extremely restrained in his description of this intervention. He is obviously not interested in portraying Moses as a folk hero.

Two caveats to this conclusion must be considered.

a. Is such legendary aggrandizement authentic? How close are these legendary motifs to authentic tradition? At stake in the questions is the means for authentication of any tradition, particularly any legendary tradition. A means for such procedure is to establish the relationship between the legendary tradition and its historical rootage.[21] But, it seems to [[42]] me, such procedure of authentication is not consistent with legendary tendency. Insofar as the tradition itself is concerned, legend gains authenticity by virtue of its ability to influence the shape of mores and morals in subsequent generations, not by virtue of its preservation of data useful for reconstructing past generations.[22]

b. Does such legendary aggrandizement not apotheosize the hero? There is a natural aversion to such a position since for biblical tradition such exalted status must be reserved for God alone.[23] As a consequence one may observe that Moses' grave remains unknown to subsequent generations precisely in order to prevent formation of a cult around his shrine.[24] Yet, there is no evidence for such a cult. There is certainly no evidence that Moses was elevated to the position of a god or even a demigod. There is no worship directed to Moses. Thus, it seems to me that the legendary tendency in the death reports does not carry with it the baggage of deifying Moses.

Yet, one must be careful here. Moses appears as more than the average human. He stands as the perfect example of leadership. And if my thesis is correct that he dies (for his people) without the taint of rebellion from Meribah, his perfection would shine even more brightly, so brightly that we might even request a veil to cover his face. The line between heroic leader and god becomes remarkably thin. And should

---

(Contrast this reservation with the description of Samson or Jonathan in action.)" Yet, it seems to me questionable to deny heroic quality because of restraint in description. In terse style the narrative depicts Moses' intervention on behalf of the young women, a typical concern in heroic patterns. And the intervention parallels Moses' earlier intervention on behalf of his own people, the event that caused his flight from Egypt. Moreover, the intervention highlights his *strength*, since he sets himself against heavy odds, more than one unchivalrous shepherd.

21. Dewey M. Beegle, *Moses, the Servant of Yahweh* (Cedar Rapids: Eerdmans, 1972) 30. Cf. also pp. 96–122. Beegle is concerned to establish the authenticity of Mosaic tradition by reconstructing "Moses as he was and not what various periods of tradition attributed to him." Cf. p. 82. A similar concern to evaluate Moses tradition in terms of historical authenticity can be seen in the work of Auerbach.

22. Cf. de Vries, 194–209. Further exploration of this point seems to me to be a crucial hermeneutical task for research on biblical narratives.

23. Cf. Moshe Greenberg, "Moses," in *EncJud* (New York: Macmillan, 1971) 378–388.

24. Cf. Beegle, 347; Greenberg, 387.

that tendency continue to its logical conclusion, theologians would be forced to consider some thesis about Moses' two natures. Is he not after all both human and divine, marked by a special relationship with God unparalleled by any previous servant. The fact remains, however, that biblical tradition never moves the legend of Moses that far. It is easy to shift from legend to myth. But it is not necessary. And so the emphasis of the legendary motifs in the death reports remains on the human nature of Moses, an incomparable nature, but nonetheless human.

3. A third conclusion seems to me to be in order, the opposite pole of caveat b. Gerhard von Rad once wrote: "Not a single one of all these stories in which Moses is the central figure was really written about Moses. Great as was the veneration of the writers for this man to whom God has been pleased to reveal himself, in all these stories it is *not* Moses himself, Moses the man, but God who is the central figure."[25] There can be no doubt that 〚43〛 von Rad pinpoints a prime characteristic of the Moses traditions with this assertion. Commonly Moses recedes into the background as God himself takes center stage (cf. Exod 7:17). Regularly the "little historical credos" identify God's mighty acts without reference to the acts of Moses. Indeed, if Martin Noth's thesis about Moses has any validity at all, then Moses was not originally so omnipresent in the exodus, wilderness and Sinai traditions.[26] He would have been originally a minor character on a stage filled with diverse plots, advanced to top billing for human characters only after the plots were in some degree unified.

Yet, for all of its value, this extreme formulation of Moses' role in the Moses traditions misses the impact of the legendary motifs. It seems to me that a conclusion about the Moses traditions that denies the central role of Moses in all the stories does not do justice to the legendary elements in the tradition. To be sure, God was present with Moses at his death. But the central figure, the one to whom the legendary virtues belong, is the man Moses, the Servant of the Lord. This problem takes on new weight by virtue of the challenge to exegetical work on the Pentateuch laid down by Walter Brueggemann. Brueggemann attacks a one-sided exegesis, characteristically centered on the exodus, that stresses *"the helplessness of man and the grace of God.* This [one-sided exegesis] is easily and consistently translated into social irresponsibility because man is helpless and into the centrality of Church

25. Gerhard von Rad, *Moses* (World Christian Books 32; London: Lutterworth, 1960) 8–9 [italics mine]. Von Rad, *Theology*, 2.24, makes a similar comment about Elijah: "The fact is that the subject of the Elijah stories is basically not the prophet himself, but Jahweh." Cf. also Beegle, 347–348.

26. Noth, *Pentateuchal Traditions*, 156–175.

authority because it dispenses the grace needed by helpless man and granted by a gracious God."[27] Brueggemann's observation seems to me to be confirmed by von Rad's opening remarks on the Moses traditions or Noth's reduction of Moses to a minor character in one originally independent theme. The traditions, traditions that report Israel's salvation from Egyptian bondage, could not emphasize a man so much, given the context of the contemporary theological vision of man. But the fault lies not so much in the theology of the Pentateuch, with its legendary motifs tied to giants like Moses, or Abraham, or Joseph, or Balaam. The fault lies in the exegesis. My point is that the same tendency Brueggemann attacks as part of the cause for ignoring the image of man in the royal model or in wisdom also accounts for ignoring legendary traditions presenting Moses as the central figure of a heroic series. Moses is the man whom God trusted, the man with responsibility for his people. To be sure, God stands behind him. But he stands behind the royal model as well. And through that grace the man [[44]] (Moses or David) plunges ahead into a tragic, heroic, brilliant future.[28] Brueggemann might well object that in the Pentateuch God intervenes when his fallible servant makes mistakes. The creature is not really to be trusted. In contrast the royal model stands alone, free to rise or fall by his own decision. But in legendary tradition, also, God does not intervene directly.[29] Thus, biblical theology needs, it seems to me, a more extensive examination of heroic, legendary material in the OT. For in these legends may lie a vision of man valuable for an age devoid of confidence in man and a hedge on the power of men who violate the legendary image by presenting themselves as gods.[30]

27. Walter Brueggemann, "The Triumphalist Tendency in Exegetical History," *JAAR* 38 (1970) 367–380. Cf. also his book, *In Man We Trust: The Neglected Side of Biblical Faith* (Richmond: John Knox, 1972) 13–28.

28. Cf. my comments about the same points in "Moses Versus Amalek," 39–41.

29. Cf. my discussion of Joseph as a wise administrator who interprets dreams by his own skill, not as a puppet dancing on a string. "The Joseph Story and Ancient Wisdom: A Reappraisal," *CBQ* (1973) 285–297.

30. This essay was presented as a lecture to the Sixth World Congress of Jewish Studies in Jerusalem in August, 1973.

Part 3

The Inner Frame:
Deuteronomy 4–11 and 27–30

Deuteronomy 4 and the Literary Criticism of Deuteronomy

A. D. H. MAYES

⟦23⟧ Two major views have in older criticism dominated approaches to the problem of Deuteronomy: the documentary and the supplementary views.[1] According to the former, the original Deuteronomy was promulgated in different editions which were in the course of time combined. So Wellhausen[2] proposed two independent publications of the original book (which consisted of the present chaps. 12–26): one of these comprised chaps. 1–4, 12–26 and 27, while the other included chaps. 5–11, 12–26 and 28–30. Steuernagel,[3] on the other hand, distinguished three layers in chaps. 1–11, two using plural form of address and the third singular. These correspond to three editions of the original Deuteronomy, which were understood to have been promulgated in order to make the book widely known. Steuernagel's proposal represented perhaps the extreme to which this particular view could go, with its minute division of chaps. 1–11. The major difficulty with this approach is not simply that it results in editions of Deuteronomy which are very thin in content,[4] but rather that this type of division of chaps. 1–11 especially not only cuts across passages which

Reprinted with permission from the *Journal of Biblical Literature* 100 (1981) 23–51.

1. For a comprehensive survey see especially S. Loersch, *Das Deuteronomium und seine Deutungen* (Stuttgarter Bibelstudien 22: Stuttgart: Katholisches Bibelwerk, 1967).

2. J. Wellhausen, *Die Composition des Hexateuchs* (3d ed.; Berlin: Georg Reimer, 1899) 192.

3. See the introduction to C. Steuernagel's commentary, *Das Deuteronomium* 2d ed.; HKAT 1/3, 1; Göttingen: Vandenhoeck & Ruprecht, 1923), especially 20–28.

4. Steuernagel, *Deuteronomium* 9, largely guards against this objection by holding that of the three editions of Deuteronomy only one is completely preserved, and the others only insofar as their material was distinctive.

are clearly a unity, but also holds together passages which are, on more pressing grounds, to be recognized as quite distinct.[5]

⟦24⟧ The advocates of a supplementary approach propose an original Deuteronomy which has been gradually supplemented in a variety of ways through the addition of more or less extensive passages. This is the approach most widely adopted in more recent criticism, though the detailed results of study along these lines vary considerably.[6] Our concern here, however, is in the first instance with chap. 4. In the first section of the paper it is intended to establish, firstly, the unity of the first forty verses of this chapter, and, secondly, their independence over against the chapters which precede. In the following sections of the paper other passages in Deuteronomy deriving from the same hand will be proposed, and then, on the basis of the nature and content of these passages, the attempt will be made to

---

5. Chap. 4 scarcely appears in any of Steuernagel's three editions of Deuteronomy; rather, it is divided among passages which may have come in either from further independent editions or as a result of editorial work introducing material of a parenetic kind. The analysis of S. Mittmann, *Deuteronomium 1:1–6:3 literarkritisch und traditionsgeschichtlich untersucht* (BZAW 139; Berlin: de Gruyter, 1973), must also come under this criticism. See the detailed and devastating review article by G. Braulik, "Literarkritische und archäologische Stratigraphie. Zu S. Mittmanns Analyse von Deuteronomium 4, 1–40," *Bib* 59 (1978) 351–83.

6. Cf., for example, O. Eissfeldt, *The Old Testament: An Introduction* (Oxford: Blackwell, 1965) 225–32; and G. Fohrer, *Introduction to the Old Testament* (London: SPCK, 1970) 169–78. The former thinks in terms of a lawbook which now has an introduction in chaps. 1–11 where two parallel strands have been combined through being set one after the other: 1:1–4:40 and 4:44–11:32. Fohrer proposes an original introduction in 4:44–9:6; 10:12–11:32, with a secondary addition to it in 1:1–4:43; 9:7–10:11. M. Noth, *Überlieferungsgeschichtliche Studien* (Tübingen: Max Niemeyer, 1957) 13–16, understands Deuteronomy 1–3 as the introduction to the deuteronomistic history, added by the deuteronomistic historian when he took up the deuteronomic law in essentially the form in which it is now to be found in Deut 4:44–30:20. One of the most recent and most fruitful contributions to the subject is that by G. Seitz, *Redaktionsgeschichtliche Studien zum Deuteronomium* (BWANT 5/13; Stuttgart: W. Kohlhammer, 1971). Following earlier scholars such as Kleinert in 1872 (P. Kleinert, *Das Deuteronomium und der Deuteronomiker. Untersuchungen zur alttestamentlichen Rechts- und Literargeschichte* [Bielefeld and Leipzig: Velhagen & Klasing, 1872] 167), Seitz notes that the book contains a series of superscriptions which may be divided into two groups. The one group, which is the earlier since it embraces the smaller amount of material, is to be found in 4:45; 6:1; 12:1. The other is in 1:1; 4:44; 28:69 (EVV 29:1); 33:1. While not everything in Deuteronomy is to be associated with these superscriptions, since on the one hand there were important developments before the earlier superscription system came into existence, and, on the other hand, there were additions later than the superscriptions, they do mark two significant stages in the growth of the book, bringing with them major portions of the text.

describe the particular editorial layer to which they belong against a definite background and context.

I

The Unity of Deuteronomy 4:1–40

The unity of this long passage may be established on the basis of its language, its form and its content. The language has been studied most extensively by Braulik.[7] Apart from his detailed and incisive analysis of the passage into its constitutive sections, and his description of the [[25]] stylistic techniques and characteristics of the whole passage, what is perhaps of chief relevance here is his gathering together of those features of the language of the passage which indicate the presence of a single linguistic unit.[8]

In the first place, there are the stereotyped language and the motifs which appear regularly. For example, the formula of bestowal of land appears in vv. 1, 21, 38, 40, using the verb *ntn*, "give"; in vv. 14, 21, 22a, 22b, 26, using the verb *ᶜbr*, "cross over"; and in vv. 1, 5, 21, 38, using the verb *bwᵓ*, "enter." There is the frequent appearance of a clause concerning the promulgation of the law, using the verb *ṣwh* (in the Piel), "command," and having as its subject either God or Moses: vv. 2, 5, 13, 14, 23, 40. There is reference to the divine theophany at Horeb in vv. 12, 15, 33; and to the exodus from Egypt in vv. 20, 34, 37.

Secondly, there is the repetition of significant words which thus appear as catchwords throughout the passage: *bānîm*, "children," vv. 9, 10, 25, 40; *ḥyh*, "live," "life," vv. 1, 4, 9, 10, 33; *yāmîm*, "days," vv. 9, 10, 26, 30, 32, 40 (bis); *naḥălâ*, "possession," "inheritance," vv. 20, 21, 38; *nepeš* and *lēbāb*, "soul," "heart," vv. 9, 15, 29, 39; *ᶜênayim*, "eyes," vv. 3, 6, 9, 19, 25, 34. There is an obvious consistency here which points strongly to unity of authorship.

This is confirmed by a study of the form of the chapter. It breaks down into six sections, vv. 1–4, 5–8, 9–14, 15–22, 23–31, 32–40, each of which is self-contained, and all of which, except for the last, begin with a warning to obey the law, a warning which is then reinforced through reference to history.[9] All the sections, however, belong together in the context of an overall form which constitutes a credible

---

7. G. Braulik, *Die Mittel deuteronomischer Rhetorik* (AnBib 68; Rome: Biblical Institute Press, 1978).

8. *Rhetorik*, 91–100.

9. Cf. Braulik's detailed analysis, *Rhetorik*, 7–76, 77–81.

original unit. The influence of the ancient near eastern treaty tradition
is an important factor here, especially perhaps in 4:9–31. The mixture
of exhortation and historical allusion is followed by the prohibition of
making images and finally by the curse and blessing, a pattern typical
of the treaties.[10] However, it is a pattern of presentation which pervades the thought-world of the author of the chapter, rather than one
[[26]] which has been consciously and deliberately used in the formulation of the chapter. For this is a speech, characterized by rhetorical
style with its exhortation, repetition and expansiveness, which is aimed
at inculcating what is understood as the chief commandment: the prohibition of images. This chief concern appears not only in the central
section, vv. 15–22, but also in vv. 9–14 (cf. v. 12) and vv. 23–31 (cf.
vv. 23, 25). The whole is then bound together by a prologue and epilogue in vv. 1–8, 32–40, which themselves are held together by many
points of contact:[11] v. 40 takes up "statutes" and "commandments"
from vv. 1–2; the same phrase used of the law, "which I command
you," is found in this form only in vv. 2, 40; "(in order) that" as the introduction to a promise is found only in vv. 1, 40; there is emphasis on
what the eyes have witnessed in vv. 3, 34; the adjective "great" is used
frequently—vv. 6, 7, 8 and 32, 34, 36, 37, 38. Finally, the two sections
are characterized by an explicit universalism of outlook, setting Israel
in the context of other peoples.

In content the major themes of 4:1–40 form a coherent unit: the
law promulgated by Moses in vv. 1–8, the chief commandment of the
revelation at Horeb: the prohibition of images, in vv. 9–31, and Yahweh alone is God in vv. 32–40. The last section, a concluding peroration, sits most loosely to its context, and it if any part of the whole
passage could be taken as a secondary supplement. Yet it has a close
though subtle connection with the rest of the passage. This consists
not only of the language contacts already pointed out, but perhaps es-

10. Cf. D. J. McCarthy, *Treaty and Covenant* (AnBib 21A; Rome: Biblical Institute,
1978) 190–94; N. Lohfink, *Höre Israel. Auslegung von Texten aus dem Buch Deuteronomium*
(Düsseldorf: Patmos, 1965) 91–93; and Braulik, *Rhetorik*, 101–4. There are considerable
differences between them on where and how extensively the treaty form has influenced
4:1–40. Lohfink sees no influence in vv. 32–40, while Braulik holds that vv. 1–8 may only
with considerable difficulty be integrated into the treaty scheme. McCarthy rightly emphasizes that the chapter does not form a covenant or treaty structure. For another view
cf. R. P. Merendino, *Das deuteronomische Gesetz: Ein literarkritische, gattungs- und überlieferungsgeschichtliche Untersuchung zu Dt 12–26* (BBB 31; Bonn: Peter Hanstein, 1969) 57–
60, who, while admitting the presence of elements of the covenant or treaty form, argues
that the passage has a basic text, now contained within vv. 9–15, which has been expanded through successive redactional overworkings of the text.

11. Cf. Braulik, *Rhetorik*, 86–88.

pecially in the fact that its affirmation that Yahweh alone is God follows very well on the prohibition of images, given the way in which that prohibition is understood in the chapter. While the decalogue prohibition of images referred originally to images of Yahweh, it is clear that in time the prohibition was understood to refer to images of other gods, not of Yahweh.[12] Even if in 4:1–40 the reference to the revelation at Horeb and the absence of any "form" there (vv. 12, 15–16), implies that images of Yahweh are then included in the prohibition of vv. 15–18, this prohibition certainly also here as in the decalogue prohibits the worship of other gods. The expression "other gods" is strikingly absent throughout 4:1–40, a pointer in itself to the fact that the worship of other gods is included in the prohibition of making images. For the author of this passage the very attempt to make a representation of Yahweh means serving another god who is not [[27]] Yahweh.[13] Because Yahweh is imageless any attempt to make an image of him is in fact the worship of another god. To this prohibition, therefore, the affirmation that Yahweh alone is God, in vv. 32–40, is an inevitable and necessary conclusion.

A further connecting link in the content of the whole passage has been noted.[14] The reflections on past and future reach progressively further in each succeeding section: v. 3 refers to the most recent past, Israel's experience at Baal-peor; vv. 6–8, in referring to wisdom and probably also to the building of the Jerusalem temple (through which Yahweh is "near" to his people, v. 7), point forward to the near future, the time of Solomon; vv. 10–14 refer to Israel at Horeb; vv. 16–19 may be taken to refer to the images and idols set up in the monarchic period (as under Jeroboam I, 1 Kgs 12:28–30) and the foreign cults of the later monarchy (cf. 2 Kgs 21:3–8; 23:4–14; Ezekiel 8); v. 20 reaches back to the exodus from Egypt; vv. 25–28 look forward to the Babylonian exile; finally, vv. 29–31 unite both farthest past and farthest future in seeing the possibility of Israel's renewal in exile on the basis of the covenant with the patriarchs, a possibility assured by the very fact that it is with Israel alone out of all the nations that God has entered into a special relationship (vv. 32–40).[15] This passage is a single long sermon

---

12. In Deut 5:9 "you shall not bow down to them or serve them" refers back over v. 8 to "other gods" mentioned in v. 7, so forcing the "image" of v. 8 into that same context. However, as an original reference the prohibition of making images would then be quite superfluous, the worship of other gods having already been prohibited. See my *Deuteronomy* (New Century Bible; London: Oliphants, 1979) 166–67.

13. Cf. Lohfink, *Höre Israel*, 107.

14. Cf. Lohfink, *Höre Israel*, 93–96; Braulik, *Rhetorik*, 78–81.

15. Vv. 32–40 function then as a recapitulation of the whole theme of 4:1–40, bringing it to its logical conclusion. Note how reference is made to the Horeb revelation

on a single theme—the prohibition of making images[16]—which elaborately and artistically develops the implications of that theme.

If 4:1–40 is a single unit this obviously has a very significant bearing on one feature of the chapter: the change in form of address to and from second person singular and second person plural. It is in fact this phenomenon which has been so influential in proposals for the separation of sources or layers in the passage.[17] However, one objection [[28]] continues to weaken fundamentally such a use of the phenomenon: why did a later editor not conform to the style of address of the passage into which he was introducing his own material? If it is answered that for this editor the difference in form of address had no significance then the ground is largely removed for making any distinction between the passages on this basis in the first place.[18] More-

and to the exodus in these verses in the order in which they are referred to earlier in the chapter (vv. 10–12, 20).

16. See Lohfink, *The Christian Meaning of the Old Testament* (London: Burns & Oates, 1969) 94–101, for a description of this as the "great commandment," i.e., for the author of this chapter the prohibition of images is the form in which the chief commandment, to worship Yahweh alone, is expressed.

17. For a review of the work of those such as Steuernagel, Staerk, and Puuko, who have used change of address as a criterion for determining stages of growth, cf. Loersch, *Das Deuteronomium*, 39–41. For a review of those who reject this criterion and attempt to explain the phenomenon of change of address in other ways, cf. Braulik, *Rhetorik*, 146–49. It is true that those who reject the unity of 4:1–40 do not always do so on the basis of this change of address; cf., for example, K. Marti, "Das fünfte Buch Mose oder Deuteronomium" (*Die heilige Schrift des Alten Testaments* [3d ed.; Tübingen: J. C. B. Mohr, 1909] 249) who takes vv. 25–31 as an exilic addition and vv. 9–24, 32–40 as a late addition from the preexilic redactor of the deuteronomic law. However, it has already been seen that these sections cannot easily be separated; and against Marti's view (ibid., 239) that vv. 1–8 belong with chaps. 1–3 as the introduction to an edition of the original Deuteronomy see below. It will also be seen later that a single background is demanded for the whole passage. For Merendino cf. above n. 10. Mittmann (*Deuteronomium 1:1–6:3*, 115–28) has presented a detailed analysis of the chapter into a basic layer, two supplementary layers, a further redaction together with supplements which cannot be classified. His analysis is based mainly on the criterion of change of address, backed up by other less pressing observations; cf. Braulik, *Bib* 59 (1978) 351–83. Among other recent attempts to maintain this as a criterion of source division, the most extensive is G. Minnette de Tillesse, "Sections 'tu' et sections 'vous' dans le Deutéronome," *VT* 12 (1962) 29–87; this does not, however, deal with Deuteronomy 4, and in other passages the extent to which its application is successful is doubtful; see further below. For a detailed criticism of the attempt by H. Cazelles, "Passages in the Singular within Discourse in the Plural of Dt 1–4," *CBQ* 29 (1967) 213–14, to apply the criterion, cf. J. D. Levenson, "Who inserted the Book of the Torah?" *HTR* 68 (1975) 204–7.

18. The only way to meet this objection is to adopt a view such as that of Steuernagel, viz. that different editions of Deuteronomy using different forms of address were secondarily combined, and the redactor responsible for the combination felt unable to

over, the use of different forms of address has been noted in extra-biblical documents where there is no question of editing or the combination of sources.[19] This is not to deny that a certain combination of approaches is possible: so it seems to be the case that the original parenetic introduction to the deuteronomic law was formulated in the singular form of address, and that it was only later that a style of writing which used both singular and plural forms became customary.[20] But this means in effect that this phenomenon can at best be only one (and by no means a particularly strong one) of a number of criteria of literary critical division in some passages. In Deuteronomy 4 there are no other effective criteria by which any such division might be made.

This means that the change of address must be explained on stylistic grounds. Lohfink in particular has made a sustained attempt to approach the phenomenon along these lines.[21] Every change of number ⟦29⟧ is a new form of address. The singular is the standard form by which the cult community is addressed, but in the preaching of the law the desire for effect and emphasis, together with the purpose of addressing the community no longer as a unit but as a collection of responsible individuals, brought about the change to the plural. In narrative passages different rules apply: when the listeners are referred to as having participated in the events being described the plural is used. When narrative and parenesis are joined the usage becomes confused.

Lohfink's attempt to connect the change of number with the change of *Gattung* is difficult to apply consistently, mainly because of the paucity of material and the difficulty in distinguishing clearly at all times between the *Gattungen*. But it is undoubtedly true as far as Deuteronomy 4 is concerned that at least one aspect of Lohfink's explanation is correct: that the purpose of the change is for effect and emphasis.[22]

---

carry out the changes necessary for harmonization. But this view of the origin of Deuteronomy has already been rejected above for other reasons.

19. Cf., for example, K. Baltzer, *The Covenant Formulary in Old Testament, Jewish and Early Christian Writings* (Oxford: Blackwell, 1971) 33 n. 71; J. L'Hour, "L'alliance de Sichem," *RB* 69 (1962) 13. For the text referred to cf. J. A. Fitzmyer, *The Aramaic Inscriptions of Sefîre* (BibOr 19; Rome: Pontifical Biblical Institute, 1967) 16–18.

20. Cf. my *Deuteronomy*, 36–37; and Seitz, *Deuteronomium*, 309.

21. Cf. Lohfink, *Das Hauptgebot. Eine Untersuchung literarischer Einleitungsfragen zu Dtn 5–11* (AnBib 20; Rome: Pontifical Biblical Institute, 1963) 30–31, 239–58; followed by, for example, J. Lindblom, *Erwägungen zur Herkunft der Josianischen Tempelurkunde* (Scripta Minora Regiae Societatis Humaniorum Litterarum Lundensis 1970–71 3; Lund: CWK Gleerup, 1971) 15–16; cf. also P. Buis, *Le Deutéronome* (Verbum Salutis, Ancien Testament 4; Paris: Beauchesne, 1969) 30–31.

22. On this see particularly Braulik, *Rhetorik*, 149–50.

The plural address is used mostly in 4:1–28 and that should be taken as the basic form there. It is the occasional change to singular which requires comment. In 4:1 the singular is used naturally after the singular collective "Israel," but also probably deliberately in order to call attention to the beginning of the original deuteronomic parenesis in 6:4, which in its alternative possible translation ("The Lord is our God, the Lord alone")[23] has a very close thematic connection with the present chapter. Within the first section the singular address form is used in v. 3 in order to highlight the contrast between those who had followed Baal at Baal-peor, whom Yahweh destroyed, and those who remained faithful, who are here alive. In vv. 9–10 the singular is used, as in v. 1, at the beginning of a major section of the whole passage, and also, as is frequently the case throughout the chapter, in close association with "the Lord your God" (see also vv. 3, 23, 25, 29; and the change to plural address in v. 34). The sudden change directs attention to Yahweh and his particular relationship with Israel. The singular next appears in v. 19 where Yahweh's action with the peoples is highlighted in contrast with his work in Israel.[24] In v. 21 the future of Israel in the land is emphasized through the sudden change to singular address, in order to sharpen the contrast with the fate of Moses (v. 22). In vv. 23–26 the frequent change takes place mostly in connection with the phrase "the Lord your God," but also in the context of building up to the climax in v. 26—the calling of heaven and earth to witness.

[30] Apart from v. 34, the remainder of 4:1–40 (vv. 29–40) is in singular address form. The change to plural in v. 34 coincides not only with the phrase "the Lord your God," but more particularly with the climax of the challenge to Israel to recognize that Yahweh's actions with her have no parallel in the relationship between any other god and people. Throughout the whole passage, therefore, the change of address has a clear emphatic function and cannot possibly be used to weaken the strong case which can be made for unity of authorship in 4:1–40.

The Relation of 4:1–40 to Its Context

The passage is immediately marked off from what follows in 4:41–43 by the fact that the latter is no longer speech of Moses. The main question here concerns the relationship between 4:1–40 and the preceding chapters.

23. Cf. my *Deuteronomy*, 176.

24. That v. 19 cannot be removed from its context despite this change of address is also indicated by the fact that the catalogue of objects of worship in vv. 16–19 is an original list corresponding, in reverse order, with the list of the elements of creation in Genesis 1.

The introductory "And now" in 4:1 makes what follows dependent on what precedes and indicates, therefore, that 4:1–40 never existed absolutely independently of the earlier chapters. The word performs a transitional function and is frequently used to mark the turning point from history to the lessons to be drawn from history as laws governing present behavior.[25] This has encouraged the view that the relationship between 4:1–40 and the preceding chapters should be seen as an original connection.[26] So, for example, Wright considers that chap. 4 is essential to give meaning and point to chaps. 1–3, and belongs with the latter as the introduction to the deuteronomistic history.[27] Baltzer, on the other hand, finds the covenant formulary or structure behind chaps. 1–4, consisting of the following elements: (i) the setting in 1:1–5; (ii) the historical prologue in 1:6–3:17; (iii) laws in 4:1–2, 9, 15–20; (iv) sanctions in 4:24, 26, 40.[28] Kline, also working from the covenant pattern, sees 1:6–4:49 as the historical prologue to the whole of Deuteronomy which is understood to be a covenant renewal document on the pattern of the extra-biblical treaties.[29]

There is no doubt that there exists a connection between Deuteronomy and the extra-biblical treaty tradition: the relationship exists both in formal structure (especially in the succession of historical ⟦31⟧ review, laws, blessing-curse) and in many details of vocabulary.[30] Yet the precise nature of this relationship is unclear. Deuteronomy is not a covenant or treaty document; it is a speech of Moses. This, together with the fact that it contains elements such as the Song of Moses, the Blessing of Moses and the account of his death, which cannot be seen as part of the treaty form, means that it is not possible to transfer directly and immediately from the literary context of the extra-biblical treaties to that of Deuteronomy. This is true of Deuteronomy as a whole and of Deuteronomy 1–4 in particular. Furthermore, that these chapters should in themselves form a covenant formulary structure, as proposed by Baltzer, is most unlikely, if only because of the totally imbalanced nature of the structure which results. The historical prologue is so preponderant that one is forced to assume that material relating

25. Cf. Exod 19:5; Josh 24:14; and the study by H. A. Brongers, "Bemerkungen zum Gebrauch des adverbialen *we͑attāh* im Alten Testament," *VT* 15 (1965) 289–99.

26. This is quite apart from those analyses, such as Mittmann's, which trace continuity of different sources through the first four or more chapters of Deuteronomy. This kind of analysis, however, has already been seen to be unacceptable.

27. G. E. Wright, "Deuteronomy," *IB* (Nashville: Abingdon, 1953) 2.351.

28. Baltzer, *Covenant Formulary*, 41–43.

29. M. G. Kline, *The Treaty of the Great King: The Covenant Structure of Deuteronomy* (Grand Rapids: Eerdmans, 1963) 28–31.

30. See my *Deuteronomy*, 33.

to the other sections of the pattern has disappeared.[31] Arguments for
the unity of Deuteronomy, or of parts of Deuteronomy such as chaps.
1–4, which are based on the apparent covenant or treaty structure, can
be used, therefore, only with considerable caution.

In the present context of chaps. 1–4 it is clear that the arguments
against unity cannot be ignored.[32] The transition from the historical account of chap. 3 to the parenetic sermon of chap. 4 is too abrupt and
unexpected for the chapters to have an original connection; the sum-
mons to hear in 4:1 is known elsewhere in Deuteronomy (5:1; 6:4; 9:1;
20:3; 27:9) to mark the beginning of a new section; the historical account of chaps. 1–3 is not told with an eye to obedience to the law as its
necessary consequence, so that the connection between the chapters is
quite artificial;[33] the fundamental elements of Israel's history which are
used in 4:1–40 to motivate exhortation to obedience—the theophany
at Horeb (4:9–14, 33, 36), the exodus (4:20, 34, 37), and the events at
Baal-peor (4:3)—do not appear in the previous chapters.

On the other hand, 4:1–40, though not an original continuation
of the previous chapter, presupposes that chapter and was inserted
here secondarily as its continuation. This is clearly indicated not only
by the introductory "And now," but also by the slight thematic connections which do exist between chaps. 3 and 4 (3:29 and 4:3; 3:23–28 and
4:21–22). These are consciously introduced points of contact, made in
〚32〛 order to establish what is clearly, however, a quite secondary connection between chaps. 3 and 4.

II

At this stage 4:1–40 appears as an isolated addition introduced between
chaps. 1–3 and what follows.[34] It is of later origin than chaps. 1–3; and
these chapters, as generally recognized, represent the introduction to

31. Cf. McCarthy, *Treaty and Covenant*, 188 n. 1, for other objections to Baltzer's
proposal.

32. Cf. Noth, *Überlieferungsgeschichtliche Studien*, 38; McCarthy, *Treaty and Covenant*,
189–90, 194; but especially Braulik, *Bib* 59 (1978) 357–58.

33. Cf. Buis, *Le Deutéronome*, 49, 86. There is an obvious difference between the historical account of chaps. 1–3 and that of chap. 8 where history is proclaimed as the foundation of the demand for obedience.

34. The doubtful place of the chapter for Noth is indicated by his way of referring to
Deuteronomy 1–3(4); cf. his *Überlieferungsgeschichtliche Studien*, 13–14, 27–29, 38–39, where
he questions if it is to be assigned to the deuteronomist or to a later editor. For Steuernagel, too, it is one of the most difficult chapters in the literary criticism of Deuteronomy;
cf. his *Der Rahmen des Deuteronomiums. Literarkritische Untersuchung über seine Zusammensetzung und Entstehung* (Halle: Wischan & Wettengel, 1894) 34.

the deuteronomistic history, rather than the introduction to Deuteronomy.[35] The first three chapters have no essential contact with the law;[36] they simply bring the reader up to the historical point in time at which the law was proclaimed, Israel's arrival at the border of the promised land. The chapters belong primarily, therefore, to an account of the history of Israel, and only insofar as this whole account of the history is related to a law—as indeed it is related—do the first three chapters have such a relationship. The deuteronomistic history from Deuteronomy to 2 Kings is now presented as a whole standing under the judgment of the deuteronomic law. The recurring apostasy of Israel, the repeated sin of her leaders, are meant to be seen and judged in the light of the law under which they should have lived. It is unlikely that this history is the work of a single individual or school, as originally proposed by Noth. On the other hand, its fragmentation into a compilation of separate works of editing by various deuteronomistic hands of Joshua, Judges, Samuel and Kings,[37] does not do justice to the strong element of continuity which runs through the whole. More likely is the view that one should think in terms of a late preexilic deuteronomistic history which was then supplemented to bring it to its present extent.[38]

35. For the fundamental work here cf. Noth, *Überlieferungsgeschichtliche Studien*, especially pp. 14–18.

36. Seitz (*Deuteronomium*, 29) conjectures that 1:9–15, 16–17, 18 has the deuteronomic law in mind. However, it is more probable that vv. 9–18 deal simply with the administration and judicial organization of Israel, and that the section has its conclusion in v. 18.

37. Cf. Fohrer, *Introduction*, 192–95.

38. Cf. J. Gray, *I & II Kings* (2d ed.; London: SCM, 1970) 6–9, 753–54; F. M. Cross, *Canaanite Myth and Hebrew Epic* (Cambridge: Harvard University, 1973) 274–89. References to the exile of Judah, as in 2 Kgs 17:19–20, give the impression of being exilic additions to an already existing work which did not know of, and so was completed before, the destruction of the southern kingdom. Levenson (*HTR* 68 [1975] 218–21) has very plausibly proposed that the second edition of the deuteronomistic history should be linked with Deut 4:1–40 as the work of one author or redactor. He also suggests (ibid., 221 n. 40) that the deuteronomic law was introduced into the deuteronomistic history by this second redactor, so that it is only at this stage that the historical work can properly be termed deuteronomistic. This is attractive, particularly because it supplies a motive for this deuteronomistic redaction having taken place. However, it leads to certain difficulties, particularly in relation to the content of the original Deuteronomy and its relationship with the decalogue. In a paper being prepared (see provisionally my *Deuteronomy*, 161–65) it is proposed that the presence of the decalogue is presupposed by the author of Deut 4:1–40, that it was not, however, originally connected with Deuteronomy, but that it was introduced here by the deuteronomistic historian, whose hand is to be seen in Deuteronomy 1–3, within his account in 5:1–6:1; this deuteronomistic account then leads into the deuteronomic law. In other words, it was the deuteronomistic historian, as distinct from the author of 4:1–40, who introduced the deuteronomic law.

But however precisely one may decide ⟦33⟧ on this issue, it remains clear that Deuteronomy 1–3 is related in the first instance to such a history of Israel rather than to the law.

The work of this deuteronomistic historian is most clearly continued in Deut 31:1–8, 14–15, 23, where the commissioning of Joshua by both Moses and Yahweh is related in fulfillment of the command given in 3:27–28,[39] and in 34:1–6, in which is related the fulfillment of the command given to Moses in 3:27 to ascend mount Pisgah in order that he might view the land before his death.[40] This deuteronomistic account then continues into Joshua where there is related the carrying out of the task for which Moses in Deuteronomy 31 commissioned Joshua.

However, there are also important passages between the end of Deuteronomy 3 and the beginning of Deuteronomy 31 where the deuteronomistic historian is also at work. Two of these passages are the account of the giving of the decalogue in chap. 5 and the story of the breach of covenant in parts of chaps. 9–10. The latter story presupposes the ⟦34⟧ former, and identity of authorship is suggested by the common vocabulary used ("out of the midst of the fire," 5:22; 9:10; 10:4; "assembly," 5:22; 9:10; 10:4), the common style of second person plural form of address,[41] and the fact that it is only in these two parts of chaps. 5–11 that narrative rather than parenesis is the characteristic style. That the author in question is the deuteronomistic historian is

---

39. In 31:16–22 there is the introduction to the Song of Moses; it clearly constitutes a secondary intrusion into this chapter. It is unlikely that vv. 14–15, 23 should be treated as a parallel JE account to the deuteronomistic story of the commissioning of Joshua in 31:1–8 (as proposed by Levenson, *HTR* 68 [1975] 209–10). Rather, vv. 14–15, 23 function as divine confirmation of what has earlier been done by Moses. Moreover, there is a significant difference between the two passages, which indicates that they cannot be treated as parallel accounts: while in vv. 1–8 Moses commissioned Joshua both to take the land and to assign it to the tribes, in vv. 14–15, 23 only the first of these tasks is mentioned. The second appears in Josh 1:6. This, according to Lohfink ("Die deuteronomische Darstellung des Übergangs der Führung Israels von Moses auf Josue," *Scholastik* 37 [1962] 38–43), is a deliberate construction in which the deuteronomistic presentation of events proceeds step by step.

40. In 34:1 there is a priestly addition introducing the phrase "from the plains of Moab to Mount Nebo." Nebo is the name by which the priestly writer knows the mountain of Moses' death; cf. Num 33:47, and compare the priestly passages in Num 22:1; 26:3, 63; 31:12, together with the priestly Deut 32:48–52. The last mentioned passage has been inserted here in order to recover the connection between the announcement of Moses' death (Num 27:12–14) and the actual account of his death (the priestly portion of Deuteronomy 34), after these two parts of the priestly writing were separated by the insertion of Deuteronomy; cf. Noth, *Überlieferungsgeschichtliche Studien*, 190–191.

41. The decalogue, in second person singular form of address, is a quotation within the deuteronomistic account. For details see my *Deuteronomy*, 161–65, 194–96.

suggested by the fact that this account found its way here at some stage
between the original Deuteronomy, which did not include the decalogue, and the editing represented by 4:1–40, which presupposes it
but is not responsible for it.[42] Since the deuteronomistic historian is
the only known editor coming between these two stages, and since in
both Deuteronomy 1–3 and the relevant sections of chaps. 5, 9–10 historical narrative is the dominant style over against the parenesis of
both 4:1–40 and the original parenetic introduction to the deuteronomic law now edited in chaps. 6–11, it is most probably to the deuteronomistic historian that one should look for the one responsible for
the study of the Horeb covenant in chap. 5 and the breaking of it in
chaps. 9–10.

The work of the deuteronomistic historian in Deuteronomy 1–3 is
continued, therefore, in chaps. 5, 9–10, recounting the making and
breaking of the Horeb covenant;[43] it then takes up again in a significant way[44] in Deuteronomy 31, before relating the death of Moses and
the following story of Joshua. Its primary concern is with Israel's history, which it presents as standing under the judgment of Yahweh. This
is effected through the incorporation of the deuteronomic law. The
deuteronomistic editing of Deuteronomy is presupposed by the author
of 4:1–40; this passage belongs, therefore, to a second editorial stage
in the growth of the ⟦35⟧ book. Our task now is to determine the extent of this second stage and the contribution which it has made to the
book. As with the deuteronomistic historian, so the editor responsible
for 4:1–40 undoubtedly introduced isolated verses and comments; our

---

42. On both of these points see the work referred to in the previous note. In general,
one may say that the isolation of the decalogue from the deuteronomic law, both physically
in the book and also in terms of subject (the decalogue belongs with the Horeb theophany,
the deuteronomic law with the event of law proclamation by Moses), indicates that it did
not appear in the original Deuteronomy. Secondly, the major concern of 4:1–40 with the
prohibition of images is not reflected in the form of the decalogue as it appears in Deuteronomy 5, where the construction tends to emphasize the Sabbath commandment as the
most significant element; cf. Lohfink, "Zur Dekalogfassung von Dt 5," *BZ* 9 (1965) 17–32.
For a study of the historical sections in 5:1–6:3; 9:7–10:11, which connects them with Deuteronomy 1–3 and the deuteronomistic historical work, see also F. García López, "Analyse
litteraire du Deutéronome," *RB* 85 (1978) 5–49.

43. The deuteronomistic historian introduced the Horeb story both to round off his
historical reflection in the first three chapters (cf. 1:2, 6, 19), and also to provide a precise context of origin for the deuteronomic law which he intended to include in his history (cf. 5:27, 30–31). This law had its original heading in 4:45, identifying it simply as
law of Moses without relating it to Horeb or to Yahweh. For the deuteronomistic historian Moses received this law from Yahweh at Horeb.

44. Occasional deuteronomistic additions to the deuteronomic law are by no means
precluded; however, they are difficult to identify.

present concern, however, is with the more extensive passage which may with reasonable probability be seen to derive from his hand. From these the nature of this second stage as a major step in the formation of the book may be appreciated.

Deuteronomy 6:10–19

Lohfink argues that in this chapter vv. 4–25 form a unit, a literary form found elsewhere as a device for proclaiming and interpreting the chief commandment of the decalogue.[45] On the analogy of parallel, but older, forms, found in Exod 12:24–27 and 13:3–10, 11–16, the basic form may be determined as consisting of two conditional sentences: when you come into the land, you shall keep the commandment . . . when your son asks you . . . you shall answer. In the present passage this basic form is to be found in vv. 10–15, 20–25. Vv. 4–9 are taken to belong to the parenetic framework which connects what follows to the preceding chapter, while vv. 16–19 simply expand the basic form with additional warnings, without breaking that form. However, as Soggin has observed, the child's question which Lohfink sees as part of this form always appears in connection with some cultic action;[46] in Deuteronomy 6 the only such action is to be found in vv. 4–9. These verses, therefore, cannot be taken as an additional parenetic framework. That they should in fact be seen in close association with vv. 20–25 is indicated by the connection not only of action and sign but also of the situation of a father instructing his child. Furthermore, vv. 10–18(19) constitute a quite distinct form with a chiastic structure,[47] which is broken if vv. 16–19 are taken as an expansion.

In a number of respects there is sufficient contact between 6:10–19 and 4:1–40 to indicate unity of authorship. There is common allusion to the decalogue and concern with the worship of other gods (the remainder of 6:4–25 does not presuppose the decalogue); there is the same change from singular to plural form of address at decisive points ⟦36⟧ in order to introduce particular emphasis (the prohibition of the worship of other gods in v. 14, and the prohibition of testing Yahweh

---

45. Cf. Lohfink, *Höre Israel,* 56, 70–71; idem, *Das Hauptgebot,* 113–14, 157, 163.

46. J. A. Soggin, "Kultätiologische Sagen und Katechese im Hexateuch," *VT* 10 (1960) 341–47; cf. also Josh 4:6–7, 20–24. See also M. Weinfeld, *Deuteronomy and the Deuteronomic School* (Oxford: Clarendon, 1972) 34–35.

47. Cf. Seitz, *Deuteronomium,* 72–74. So against the analysis of F. García López, "Deut VI et la traditio-redaction du Deutéronome," *RB* 85 (1978) 161–200. The latter distinguishes four sections in 6:4–25, the earliest being vv. 4–9, followed by vv. 10–13, 20–25 and finally vv. 14–19.

with the general demand to keep the commandments in vv. 16–17);[48] there is the same concern that settlement in the land and familiarity with its benefits will bring failure to keep fresh the memory of it as the gift of Yahweh who demands obedience (4:25; 6:10–12); there is common reference to the oath to the patriarchs (4:31; 6:10, 18); and there is the shared thought that nations have been dispossessed in order that Israel might have land (4:38; 6:19). Finally, the two passages share a considerable stock of terminology:[49] fear (4:10; 6:13); (the gods of) the peoples (4:19; 6:14); a jealous God (4:24; 6:15); destroy (4:26; 6:15); diligently keep (4:9; 6:17); that it may go well with you (4:40; 6:18); good land (4:22; 6:18).

Deuteronomy 7:4–5, 7–15, 25–26

The two subjects treated in this chapter, the destruction of the peoples and the avoidance of the worship of their gods, are set together so abruptly in v. 16 (v. 16b is superfluous after v. 16a), that they must be considered to have been brought together here secondarily. The second of these subjects is treated in vv. 4–5, 7–15, 25–26. The separation of these verses from their context is confirmed, moreover, by the fact that v. 6 is clearly the continuation of v. 3 rather than of v. 5,[50] vv. 7–15 have a chiastic structure,[51] and vv. 25–26 again abruptly introduce the second subject, after a conclusion has been reached in v. 24.

48. In 6:4–9, 20–25 singular address form is used throughout, with the exception of a phrase at the end of v. 20. In view of the consistent use of singular address form in the older parenesis, one may suspect that this phrase is an addition.

49. It must of course be noted that the vocabulary contacts collected here are not always exclusive to the particular editorial layer to which 4:1–40 and other passages belong. The editor responsible belongs firmly within the deuteronomistic movement and is, therefore, an inheritor of the thought and vocabulary of that movement. It is sufficient for our purposes here, however, to establish that common authorship of 4:1–40 and subsequent passages is not excluded by vocabulary study, and that the latter, in conjunction with the other points mentioned, may be held to support it.

50. The declaration that Israel is holy to Yahweh is better suited as a basis not to the command to destroy the altars of the peoples but rather to the demand for utter separation from them, as in vv. 1–3. In chap. 14 also the thought of the chosen people is linked not to a demand to destroy non-Israelite sanctuaries but to laws which require complete separation from non-Israelite practices.

51. The structure is looser and not so clear here as in 6:10–18. See Lohfink, *Das Hauptgebot*, 181–82; Seitz, *Deuteronomium*, 76–77. Lohfink connects v. 6 to this structure, but the significant element here ("from all the peoples") is repeated in v. 7, so that the latter may be taken to begin the chiasm. "On the face of the earth/ground" (v. 6) and "in/on the land" (v. 13) can hardly be taken as a significant parallel, especially in view of the totally different contexts of the expression. Otherwise, the chiastic structure described by Lohfink fits within the verses marked out here.

⟦37⟧ That Deut 7:4–5, 7–15, 25–26 go back to the author at work in 4:1–40 and 6:10–19, and so also are to be considered as secondarily inserted here, is indicated by the following points: throughout 4:1–40; 6:10–19 and the present passages from chap. 7 there is clear contact with the decalogue, and, specifically, with the prohibition of images (this prohibition being here understood, moreover, as referring to images of other gods, a dominant understanding also in 4:1–40); as in the other passages, so here the effect of this editorial layer, if not indeed its purpose, is to make a bridge between the decalogue and the older parenesis and to integrate the one into the other; the situation envisaged is Israel having arrived in the land and meeting the temptations which it poses (in 6:10–19 the temptation to forgetfulness which prosperity brings; here the temptation to apostasy which contact with the peoples brings); in style there is the use of chiasm, as in 6:10–18, and also the sudden change from singular to plural address form for particular emphasis (in v. 4 the sudden change to plural in "against you" emphasizes the dramatic result of Israel's sin: Yahweh's destruction of his people; in v. 5 the major concern of the section is expressed in plural address; in vv. 7–8a the foundation of Israel's election in the love and faithfulness of God rather than in any merit on her part is emphasized; v. 12 begins a new section in plural address, stressing Israel's obedience as the basis of her prosperity; finally, v. 25a in plural address form reverts to the major concern expressed in v. 5).[52] The following detailed points connect the verses with 4:1–40 and 6:10–19: graven images, 4:16, 23, 25; 7:5, 25; as in 4:37, so 7:7–8 connect Israel's election with the exodus from Egypt;[53] which he swore to your fathers, 7:8, 12, 13; cf. 4:31; know that the Lord (your God) is God, 4:35; 7:9; statutes and ordinances, 4:1, 5, 8, 14; 7:11; which I command you this day, 4:40 (cf. 4:2, 8); 7:11; only in 4:31; 7:12 and 8:18 is the term "covenant" applied to the promise to the patriarchs.

Deuteronomy 8:1–6, 11b, 14b–16, 18b–20

The distinction between an early and late layer in this chapter is particularly clear in vv. 11–18 in connection with the meaning assigned to the word "forget." Only in v. 11b is it used with reference to the commandments. Otherwise in this section (cf. vv. 14, 17) to forget Yahweh means to assign to oneself the credit for wealth and prosperity, whereas

52. Once again, as in chap. 6, the parenetic context into which this layer has been introduced is in singular form of address.

53. 7:6 is complete in itself. Vv. 7–8 take up the theme of election from that verse and connect it with the exodus. On the connection with 4:37, cf. also L. Perlitt, *Bundestheologie im Alten Testament* (WMANT 36; Neukirchen-Vluyn: Neukirchener, 1969) 58–59.

it is in fact because of Yahweh's favor that Israel enjoys these [[38]] things.[54] A straightforward division of the chapter on the basis of this distinction may then be carried out. The older parenesis begins in v. 7,[55] and, apart from the late insertion of vv. 11b, 14b–16,[56] continues to v. 18a. The later layer, after its introduction in v. 1, uses in vv. 2–6 the literary pattern of argument from history, building up to its conclusive demand for obedience to the commandments in v. 6.[57] A further general reference to the commandments in v. 11b is followed in vv. 14b–16, 18b by a reference to the exodus and wilderness wandering interpreted as a time of humbling and testing, leading up to the blessing in conformity with the covenant with the patriarchs. The layer then concludes in vv. 19–20 with a specific warning not to worship other gods. The two layers have been brought together using the literary form of a chiasm.[58]

The connections of the late layer in this chapter with 4:1–40; 6:10–19; 7:4–5, 7–15, 25–26 are very close. In subject there is the same concern with both the commandments in general and with the worship of foreign gods in particular; in both 4:37 and 8:14b reference is made to the exodus from Egypt, and in the present section that reference clearly alludes to the decalogue. The form of argument from history, as it appears in 8:2–6, is to be found also in 4:35–40 and 7:7–11. The succession of humbling followed by blessing (v. 16) is reminiscent of the presentation of curse and blessing in 4:25–31,[59] where too the blessing is associated with God's remembering the covenant with the fathers. While the older parenesis is in singular form of address, the later layer

---

54. Cf. Seitz, *Deuteronomium*, 79.

55. Translating the first word *kî*, "when," rather than "for" (RSV); cf. the same construction in 6:10, 20. The apodosis of the sentence beginning there is then to be found in v. 11a.

56. For these as later additions, cf. also Steuernagel, *Deuteronomium*, 81. V. 17 clearly follows well immediately after v. 14a.

57. For this pattern cf. Lohfink, *Das Hauptgebot*, 125–31. It consists of three elements: (a) remember what Yahweh has done; (b) know what this implies for faith; (c) apply this knowledge through keeping the commandments.

58. Cf. Lohfink, *Das Hauptgebot*, 194–95; idem, *Höre Israel*, 76. Lohfink outlines the form as follows: v. 1, warning; vv. 2–6, wilderness; vv. 7–10, the land; v. 11, warning (the central point of the structure); vv. 12–13, the land; vv. 14–17, wilderness, vv. 18–20, warning. However, he also takes this as an indication of the unity of the chapter (the author of which he identifies as the author of the late layer in the previous chapter). This need not necessarily be the case; although the use of the chiastic form may indicate an original unit, there are clearly passages where it is deliberately used in order secondarily to bind together different literary layers; cf., for example, my *Deuteronomy*, 113 (on 1:1–5), 173 (on 5:27–6:3).

59. See also further below.

exhibits the same alternation of singular and plural which has already been observed as a stylistic device within the other passages. There is a sudden change to the plural within v. 1, when ⟦39⟧ the basic importance of obedience to the commandments is being inculcated (cf. also 7:12), and at the end, in vv. 19b, 20, the style again reverts to the plural form of address in order to emphasize the utter solemnity of the warning being given to each individual Israelite.

Other detailed points of contact between this passage and 4:1–40 and other passages already seen to be from the same author are: which I command you this day (4:40; 8:1, 11b); testing (6:16; 8:2; the same verb is translated "attempted" in 4:34); fearing (4:10; 8:6); covenant (4:31; 7:12; 8:18b—in all cases the covenant with the patriarchs); which he swore to your fathers (4:31; 6:10, 18; 7:12; 8:18b); I solemnly warn you (8:19; the same phrase translated "I call . . . to witness against you" in 4:26); you shall surely perish (4:26; 8:19); because you would not hearken (7:12; 8:20).

Deuteronomy 10:12–11:32

It has already been noted that the account of the covenant breaking is to be ascribed to the deuteronomistic historian who introduced also the covenant making story in chap. 5. The beginning of the present section is clearly marked off from the covenant breaking story by the opening "And now." The function of this phrase (as seen already with 4:1) is to connect what follows with what precedes, but just as in 4:1 so here the connection is not an original one. A story of covenant breaking is not precisely what one would expect as a historical prologue before the commandments.[60] Furthermore, since the phrase "and now" nevertheless presupposes the preceding account, the present section must be understood to be later than the deuteronomistic historian, just as 4:1–40 is from a hand later than the deuteronomistic historian at work in chaps. 1–3.

Apart from some fairly minor later additions the section seems to be a single unit.[61] Lohfink is prepared to see the unit extend as far as

60. Cf. G. von Rad, *Deuteronomy* (Old Testament Library; London: SCM, 1966) 83; Lohfink, *Das Hauptgebot,* 229. So against Seitz, *Deuteronomium,* 81–91, who takes 10:12–13 as the conclusion to the basic deuteronomic speech in 9:1–7a, 13–14, 26–29; 10:10. Vv. 14–22 are taken by Seitz to be a late addition, and chap. 11 as deuteronomistic with some later additions.

61. In 10:19 the sudden and specific demand to love the sojourner, though by no means out of keeping with general deuteronomic thinking (cf. Deut 5:15; 15:15; 16:12; 24:17–18), is surprising here. The context concerns Israel's attitude to God, motivating it by reference to her slavery in Egypt. The verse is probably a late gloss which came in by attraction to v. 18 (cf. also Lohfink, *Das Hauptgebot,* 223). 11:29–30 stand out from their

[40] 11:17,[62] a section which (with the omission of 10:19) contains five commandments, each with its justification (10:12–15; 10:16–18; 10:20–22; 11:1–7; 11:8–12), followed by blessing and curse in 11:13–17. The justifications make reference to Israel's saving history, beginning with the patriarchs (10:14–15), going on to the exodus (10:21), the deliverance at the Red Sea and the wilderness period (11:2–7), and ending with the land to be settled (11:10–12). The last justification has close links with the following blessing and curse, apart from the normal association of law with blessing and curse, for agricultural concerns are paramount in 11:13–17.

The remainder of the chapter, however, performs a summarizing function in relation to the preceding chapters which is wholly suitable as a continuation of 10:12–11:17, and as an immediate prelude to the deuteronomic law. Vv. 18–21 take up the beginning of the deuteronomic parenesis in 6:4–9, expressing much of it in plural address; vv. 22–25 take up the thought of the deuteronomic parenesis in 7:1–3, 6, 17–24; and vv. 26–32 (with the exception of the addition in vv. 29–30) hold together as a conclusion to the whole of chaps. 1–11, bringing Israel finally to the point of decision: whether or not to obey the law which now follows. Furthermore, as noted below, there is a certain correspondence between 4:1–40 and 10:12–11:32 which supports a unity of structure and of authorship in this passage.

The overall structures of 4:1–40 and 10:12–11:32 are by no means dissimilar. Both begin (4:1–8; 10:12–22) with a prologue in which general reference is made to the commandments, to Israel's history and to her exclusive worship of Yahweh, culminating in a reference to Israel of the present ("a great nation," 4:7–8; "as the stars of heaven for multitude," 10:22). Then comes a historical prologue (4:9–14; 11:1–7), emphasizing that which "your eyes have seen." This leads into a general warning against disobedience culminating in a reference to the land (4:15–22; 11:8–12). The following section (4:23–31; 11:13–25) looks to the future with its prospect of curse and blessing dependent on Israel's attitude to the law. Finally (4:32–40; 11:26–32), an epilogue brings the section to a close with general exhortation to obey the law in "the land which the Lord your God gives you."

---

context: their particular geographical concern disrupts the continuity of the context which culminates in the general warning to obey the commandments in the land. The verses have been brought in here to act as a framework, with 27:12–13, to the deuteronomic law; cf. L'Hour, *RB* 69 (1962) 166–67. In v. 31 the first word *kî* should be translated "when" rather than "for." This is the beginning of an independent section, finding its apodosis in v. 32; cf. also above n. 55 on 8:7.

62. Lohfink, *Das Hauptgebot*, 220–25; idem, *Höre Israel*, 37.

In both passages the influence of the covenant or treaty form is obvious, especially in the succession history-demand-sanction,[63] and [[41]] again in both it is a question of this pattern offering a basis and framework for a speech rather than for a covenant document. In style the speech of 10:12–11:32 also exhibits a mixture of singular and plural forms of address; though, whereas in 4:1–40 the first part of the speech was predominantly in the plural (4:1–31), with only occasional changes to singular, and the remainder in singular (4:32–40), with only one change to the plural, in 10:12–11:32 the first part of the speech is predominantly in the singular (10:12–22) with one change to the plural (10:19 being taken as an addition), and the remainder (11:1–32) is mainly in the plural, with occasional change to the singular. Yet, this difference in itself may have a stylistic purpose: that 4:1–40 and 10:12–11:32 should be seen as fully complementary parts of a framework embracing the parenetic introduction to the deuteronomic law. As elsewhere, the change in the form of address may be explained either as the result of the wish to emphasize particularly significant statements,[64] or as deliberate and to some extent haphazard changes intended to stimulate attention to what is being said.[65]

Other links with 4:1–40 and passages from the same author include the following: and now, 10:12, cf. 4:1; which I command you this day, 10:13, cf. 4:40; 8:1, 11b; the Lord set his heart in love upon your fathers and chose their descendants after them, 10:15, cf. 4:37; 7:7; you shall fear the Lord your God, you shall serve him, 10:20, cf. 6:13; the literary form of argument from history appears in 10:20–22; 11:2–8 and also in 4:35–40; 7:7–11; 8:2–6; great and terrible things which your eyes have seen, 10:21, cf. 4:9, 34; discipline, 11:2, cf. 4:36; 8:5; his mighty hand and his outstretched arm, his signs, 11:2–3, cf. 4:34; take heed, 11:16, cf. 4:9, 23; 11:16 refers to the decalogue, as does also the prohibition of making images in 4:15–18; you perish quickly off the good land which the Lord gives you, 11:17, cf. 4:26; good land, 11:17, cf. 4:21, 22; that your days . . . may be multiplied in the land . . . as long

63. Cf. Seitz, *Deuteronomium*, 82–83, 86–87, on 11:2–7 as historical prologue; on 11:8–9 as basic demand; and on 11:13–15 as blessing and curse. The land description of 11:10–12 is also a point of contact with the treaties, though in the latter context it is to be found before rather than after the basic demand.

64. This is the case with the sudden change to plural address in 10:15c–18, and the change to plural (which is then maintained for most of the remainder of the section) in 11:2.

65. This must be the case with the occasional changes to singular form of address in 11:8, 10, 12, 14, 15, 19, 20 (vv. 29–30, taken here as an addition, are also in singular form of address).

as the heavens are above the earth, 11:21, cf. 4:40; which the Lord swore to your fathers, 11:21, cf. 4:31; 6:18; the Lord will drive out all these nations . . . greater and mightier than yourselves, 11:23, cf. 4:38; behold (*rĕ'ēh*), 11:26, cf. 4:5. [42]

Deuteronomy 26:16–19; 27:9–10; 28:1–6, 15–19

It is most unlikely that there are no additions to the deuteronomic law deriving from the hand of the one responsible for the particular editorial layer with which we are here concerned. However, such additions are difficult to distinguish and the subject can properly be treated only within the context of a total treatment of the deuteronomic law.

This law comes to an end in 26:15, and there follows in 26:16–27:26 a collection of fairly easily distinguishable fragments which do not all come from the same hand. The first of these, in 26:16–19, is particularly noteworthy as being the formal declaration of the establishment of a (covenant) relationship between Yahweh and Israel.[66] Whether or not there exists behind these verses an actual covenant formula which has a pre-deuteronomistic history,[67] the language of this present section is undoubtedly late, having its closest connection with the editorial layer already marked out in earlier chapters: this day, 26:16, cf. 4:4, 8, 40 etc.; statutes and ordinances, 26:16, cf. 4:1, 8 etc.; you shall be careful to do, 26:16, cf. 4:6; 7:11; 8:1; 11:22, 32; with all your heart and with all your soul, 26:16, cf. 4:29; walk in his ways, 26:17, cf. 8:6; 10:12; 11:22; obey his voice, 26:17, cf. 8:20; the universalist thought of 26:19 is close to that of 4:6–8 (cf. also 10:21). Moreover, the express concern of the section with the exclusive relationship between Yahweh and Israel brings it right into the specific subject area which dominates the passages already considered.

The second fragment in 27:1–8 is clearly marked off from what precedes. The particular concern with Mount Ebal, and the view that this is the area to which Israel will immediately come on crossing the' Jordan,[68] connects the section with 11:29–30, which has already been seen to be a late addition in chap. 11. This section may, therefore, be taken to come from the same hand. Moreover, the verses clearly secondarily separate 27:9–10 from 26:16–19, for these two fragments have

66. For a study, see particularly Lohfink, "Dt 26, 17–19 und die 'Bundesformel,'" *ZKT* 91 (1969) 517–53.

67. So R. Smend, *Die Bundesformel* (Theologische Studien 68; Zürich: EVZ, 1963) 9; but cf. the cautious remarks of Perlitt, *Bundestheologie*, 106–7.

68. On this cf. O. Eissfeldt, "Gilgal or Shechem?" in *Proclamation and Presence* (ed. J. I. Durham and J. R. Porter; London: SCM, 1970) 90–101.

very close connections:[69] obey the voice of the Lord your God, [[43]] 27:10, cf. 26:17; commandments and statutes, 27:10, cf. 26:17; which I command you this day, 27:10, cf. 4:2, 40; 26:16. In content, too, the verses very suitably conclude 26:16–19: Israel's status as the people of God is here formally affirmed, following on the formal declaration of the establishment of the relationship in 26:16–19.

The following section in 27:11–26 is probably to be connected with 27:1–8 and so also with 11:29–30. It has the same ceremonial concern with Ebal and Gerizim, and is certainly not presupposed by the editorial layer with which we are mainly concerned.[70] Within all of 26:16– 27:26, therefore, the two basic passages, in 26:16–19 and 27:9–10, may be held to derive from the author of the layer which takes its starting point in 4:1–40, and to act, with 10:12–11:32, as a framework to the deuteronomic law.

The second part of this framework is continued into 28:1–68. This chapter of blessings and curses presents a complex picture which is the result of secondary elaboration of originally shorter units.[71] Its basis may be found in a parallel series of blessings and curses in vv. 3–6, 16– 19. The origin of these is unclear, but it is important to note that in form they are not paralleled in the forms of blessings and curses found in the extra-biblical treaties, and in content they make no reference to law or covenant. It may be that the curses of vv. 16–19 are secondarily modeled on the blessings in vv. 3–6, and that the latter originated in the custom of imparting blessings at the sanctuary. However, both blessings and curses are now connected with law and covenant, in the first instance through the introductions now provided in vv. 1–2, 15. Moreover, they are also now firmly anchored in the treaty tradition through the subsequent elaboration which has taken place in the addition by stages of the rest of the chapter, for in this elaboration direct connections can be made with the ancient near eastern tradition of treaty curses.

The stage at which these blessings and curses came into the context of Deuteronomy, to be seen as sanctions attached to the law, is,

69. It is unlikely that the reference to the Levitical priests in 27:9 is original. The following verse uses the first person singular, so presupposing a reference to Moses only in v. 9. The reference was probably added her to legitimate a particular function the Levitical priests were understood to exercise—such a function as that presupposed in v. 14. The addition may, therefore, be from the hand of the later author of the section which includes v. 14.

70. This, of course, does not immediately mean that the series of curses in 27:15–26 is late. However, the probability is, nevertheless, that they are in fact of late origin. For a study see my *Deuteronomy*, 344–46.

71. Cf. my *Deuteronomy*, 348–51.

therefore, to be determined from a consideration of the original introductions in vv. 1–2, 15 and their authorship. Here it appears that it is not to the original deuteronomic context but rather to that of the late editorial layer that we should look. The introductions are composed of phrases and expressions which have been already encountered in this layer: obey the voice of, 28:1, 15, cf. 8:20; 27:10; careful to do, 28:1, 15, cf. 4:6; 7:11; 8:1; 11:22, 32; his commandments which I command [[44]] you this day, 28:1, 15, cf. 4:2; 11:13, 22, 27, 28; 27:10; will set you high above all the nations, 28:1, cf. 26:19. If this is so, the deuteronomic law did not originally conclude with blessings and curses, these being an addition from later time. They are an addition which, moreover, seems to have been the subject of considerable expansion; this expansion would have taken place either subsequent to the first introduction of the blessings and curses into this context in vv. 1–6, 15–19, or perhaps (in part) at the time that they were introduced.

Deuteronomy 29:1–30:20 (31:1)

The limits of this section are disputed: 29:1 (in the Hebrew 28:69) is frequently understood to be the conclusion of the preceding chapters rather than the introduction to what follows. On the other hand, the appearance of the word "covenant" in this verse links it strongly to the future occurrences in this chapter (vv. 9, 12, 14, 21, 25). In fact, the verse looks both backwards and forwards:[72] the "words" to which it refers are undoubtedly the preceding laws, blessings and curses, while the description of these words as "the words of the covenant" points forward to the definition of these laws as *covenant* laws, which the following chapters are at pains to emphasize.

At the other end, it has also been argued that 29:1 should be understood as the heading to a section which extends far beyond the limit here set.[73] However, 31:1 is probably to be understood as an original concluding formula to this section, which has been modified only after the introduction of further words of Moses, especially the Song of Moses in chap. 32.[74] Moreover, the last part of this section in 30:15–20 performs a summarizing and concluding function which rounds off what precedes. The section as a whole consists of a series of speeches centered on the theme of covenant obedience. Together they constitute a sermon on the law which has been proclaimed, and they follow a coherent order: in the first (29:1–9), obedience is advocated

---

72. Cf. E. Kutsch, *Verheissung und Gesetz* (BZAW 131; Berlin: de Gruyter, 1972) 140–41.
73. Cf. Lohfink, "Der Bundesschluss im Land Moab. Redaktionsgeschichtliches zu Dt 28, 69–32, 47," *BZ* 6 (1962) 32–56, who sees the section as extending to 32:47.
74. Cf. Seitz, *Deuteronomium*, 33–34.

on the basis of what history has shown; the two parties to this covenant are then identified in the second part (29:10–15), it being made clear that it is Israel of the future as well as Israel of the present which is obligated; the third part of the section (29:16–8) moves on to indicate the curse that will inevitably follow on disobedience; in the fourth (29:29–30:14), the blessing and restoration which follow destruction are proclaimed; and finally (30:15–20), the whole is summarized. [[45]] Israel is presented with the alternatives of life and good, death and evil, and her obedience to the commandments is urgently exhorted.

It is clear that there are strong connections between the overall form of this section and forms found in the extra-biblical treaty tradition, and the attempt has been made to base the form here directly on the extra-biblical treaty form. So, for example, Baltzer[75] finds a historical prologue in 29:2–8, the basic demand in 29:9; the blessing and curse in 30:16–18, and witnesses in 30:19. Once again, however, as with 4:1–40, it is to be understood rather that the relationship between the section and the treaties is not as immediate as seems to be implied here.[76] The allusions to significant treaty elements, such as basic stipulation, blessing and curse, and witnesses, do not stand out here as formally distinct parts of a document; rather, they are embedded in the substance of a speech or sermon and form the basic framework for its construction and elaboration.

What has already been said is sufficient to establish a very close connection between 29:1–30:20 and the editorial layer already marked out; the following detailed points of contact in language and thought confirms that this connection should be thought of in terms of unity of authorship:[77] 29:2–9 has the form of the argument from history which has appeared on several occasions in this layer, cf. 4:35–40; 7:7–11; 8:2–6; 10:20–22; 11:2–8; trials . . . signs . . . wonders, 29:3, cf. 4:34; for the thought and expression of 29:5, cf. 8:4; you have not eaten . . . that

---

75. Baltzer, *Covenant Formulary*, 34–36.

76. Cf. also McCarthy, *Treaty and Covenant*, 199–205. McCarthy gives the following outline of the section in terms of the covenant form: *mise en scène* (29:1); historical prologue (29:2–9); list of parties (29:10–15); stipulation (29:16–19); curse (29:20–28); blessing (30:1–10); exhortation (30:11–14); curse-blessing (30:15–19); witnesses (30:19); exhortation (30:19b–20). But while emphasizing the treaty elements which appear here (the list of parties to the treaty comes immediately before the treaty stipulations in at least one extra-biblical text), McCarthy notes that this does not mean that we have here a covenant document: "Once again, as in Dt 4, we have a speech with rhetorical effects and touched by Wisdom themes, but one whose structure and elements show forth the covenant tradition." See also Perlitt, *Bundestheologie*, 27–29, who argues that it is not ceremonial which we find here, but preaching which uses elements of the covenant formula.

77. For some of these see also Levenson, *HTR* 68 (1975) 212–16.

you may know, 29:6, cf. 8:3; careful to do, 29:9, cf. 4:6; 7:11 etc.; 29:13 expresses the covenant formula of 26:16–19; as he swore to your fathers, 29:13, cf. 4:31; 6:18; 11:21; idols of wood and stone, 29:17, cf. 4:28; the prohibition of idols/foreign gods presupposed here is the central concern of 4:1–40 and the related passages noted; jealousy, 29:29, cf. 4:24; covenant, in 29:25, seems to be specifically the decalogue (cf. the continuation in v. 26), as also in 4:13; gods whom they [46] had not known, 29:26, cf. 11:28; allotted, 29:26, cf. 4:19; curses (*qĕlālâ*), 29:27, cf. 28:15; in 30:1–10 the blessing is presented as a state which will follow on the curse rather than as an alternative possibility to the curse, as also in 4:25–31;[78] and you call . . . to mind, 30:1, cf. 4:39; return to the Lord your God . . . and obey his voice, 30:2, cf. 4:30; which I command you this day, 30:2, 8, 16, cf. 4:2, 40 etc.; with all your heart and with all your soul, 30:2, cf. 4:29; 26:16; the uttermost parts of heaven, 30:4, cf. 4:32; for the thought of 30:6, cf. 10:16; for 30:7, cf. 7:15; commandments . . . statutes, 30:10, cf. 20:17; 28:15; very near, 30:14, cf. 4:7; in your mouth and in your heart, 30:14, cf. 11:18–19; by loving the Lord your God, by walking in his ways, 30:16, cf. 10:12; his commandments and his statutes and his ordinances, 30:16, cf. 7:11; 8:11b; you shall live and multiply, 30:16, cf. 8:1; drawn away to worship other gods and serve them, 30:17, cf. 4:19; for the thought and expression of 30:18, cf. 4:26; 8:19; I call heaven and earth to witness against you this day, 30:19, cf. 4:26; cleaving to him, 30:20, cf. 10:20.

Deuteronomy 32:45–47

It has already been seen that the work of the deuteronomistic historian, which is found in Deuteronomy 1–3, is continued in 31:1–8, 14–15, 23; 34:1–6. It has also been noted that 32:48–52 are from the hand of the priestly writer. The same hand appears in 34:7–9, while the conclusion of the last chapter is probably as late as the time of the formation of the Pentateuch.[79] The Song of Moses in 32:1–44, with its introduction in 31:16–22, 30, together with the Blessing of Moses in chap. 33, are, on the other hand, late isolated interpolations. The context does not presuppose them: the Blessing is appropriate to its context insofar as it was the custom for a father to impart his blessing shortly before his death (Genesis 27; 48; 49); the Song has been made to suit its context through being interpreted (by means of its introduction in 31:16–22) as testifying to the destructive anger of Yahweh in response to Israel's sin (31:24–29), an interpretation which is not, however, appropriate to the

78. On this see also further below.
79. See my *Deuteronomy*, 411.

Song as a whole (cf. 32:36–43). There remain to be considered 31:9–
13, 24–29 and 32:45–47.

There is a clear relationship between the first two of these three
passages: both are concerned with the law, the first with its future public proclamation and the second with its preservation as witness against
Israel in the future; both are concerned with the Levites, as the ones
who have the responsibilities of proclaiming and preserving the [[47]]
law; both make reference to the ark of the covenant of the Lord, as carried by the Levites; neither passage betrays any close relationship to its
context. There is some relationship with the editorial layer which has
been marked out in that the fundamental concern is with the law, and
also in the echoes of the treaty tradition which come through in both
passages: in the first the command for the regular public reading of the
law and in the second the laying up of the law by the ark/sanctuary
and the theme of witness, all may be taken to reflect treaty concerns.[80]
Furthermore, the concern for transmission of knowledge of the law to
future generations, and also some of the phraseology in both sections,
find parallels in 4:1–40.[81] However, it is nevertheless doubtful that
these two passages should be put in this context.[82] Nowhere else in this
editorial layer has a particular interest in the Levites and the ark appeared; nowhere else in this layer is there an interest in ritual and ceremony as expressed here; in no other part of this layer is an exclusive
emphasis placed on the sin of Israel and the consequent curse of the
law, such as appears in 31:24–29;[83] and the sections do not fit well as a
continuation of this layer as last represented by chaps. 29–30. In fact,
these two sections find their closest link with other passages already
seen to be additions to this layer: 11:29–30; 27:1–8, 11–26. Through all
these passages ritual, the Levites, and an emphasis on the curse, are
recurrent features, so that one may discern here a stage in the growth
of Deuteronomy which may be called its Levitical edition,[84] an edition
which is later than that with which we are here primarily concerned.

On the other hand, the third passage, 32:45–47, not only offers a
suitable conclusion to the layer which begins in 4:1–40, but there are

80. Cf. McCarthy, *Treaty and Covenant*, 63–64, 66.

81. Be careful to do, 4:6; 7:11; 31:12; the land which you are going over Jordan to
possess, 4:14; 30:18; 31:13; call heaven and earth to witness, 4:26; 30:19; 31:28; act cor-
ruptly, 4:16, 25; 31:29; provoking him to anger, 4:25; 31:29.

82. The view expressed in my *Deuteronomy*, 371, must, therefore, be revised.

83. Levenson, *HTR* 68 (1975) 211, associates this emphasis on the future sin of Israel
with 29:21–28. The latter passage, however, has its immediate complement in the promise of blessing in 30:1–10.

84. In addition 10:8–9 may be included among these passages.

close contacts in thought and vocabulary which suggest that the verses should be seen as deriving from that same hand: lay to heart, 32:46, cf. 4:39 (with a different verb); which I enjoin, 32:46, cf. 4:26; be careful to do, 32:46, cf. 4:6; 7:11, etc.; on 32:47, cf. 4:26, 40, etc. The teaching of the law to children is the subject also of 4:9; and the word "life" (32:47) has already been seen to be one of the catchwords which characterize 4:1–40. ⟦48⟧

III

The following passages may, therefore, be held to represent the contribution of an editor whose work marks a significant stage in the growth of Deuteronomy: 4:1–40; 6:10–19; 7:4–5, 7–15, 25–26; 8:1–6, 11b, 14b–16, 18b–20; 10:12–11:32 (omitting 10:19, 11:29–30); 26:16–19; 27:9–10; 28:1–6, 15–19, 29:1–30:20; 32:45–47. That other isolated verses may also derive from the same hand is probable; but these represent the major element of this editor's work and are, therefore, determinative for a description of the character, the concerns and the background of the work. The general character and concerns of the work have already become apparent in the course of the preceding delineation of the passages which belong to it; but there are some particular aspects which should be highlighted in order that the very reason for this edition having been composed in the first place might be appreciated.

First, within the general context of a desire to inculcate obedience to the law, the editor is in particular concerned with the possibility that Israel might worship other gods. This is expressed (as in 4:1–40) in the form of a prohibition of making images, or a command to destroy images (7:5, 25), or in the form of a direct reference to the worship of other gods (6:14; 8:19; 11:16, etc.). In any case, it is clear from the terminology used that it is the decalogue to which reference is being made, and it is what is understood to be the chief commandment of the decalogue which is being highlighted. This is not, however, the most important commandment of the decalogue as the latter is presently structured in Deuteronomy 5. There the form clearly points to the Sabbath commandment as the chief commandment.[85] So, while the editor with whom we are here concerned clearly presupposes the presence of the decalogue in Deuteronomy 5, it is unlikely that this same editor is responsible for its introduction. It is in fact probable that it is to the deuteronomistic historian that we owe the introduction

85. Cf. above nn. 38, 42.

of the decalogue: it has been introduced in the context of the provision of a historical setting for the proclamation of the deuteronomic law. On the other hand, the editor's emphasis on the decalogue prohibition of the worship of other gods, while it should certainly be seen as reflecting his understanding of the chief importance of the decalogue in a particular historical situation, also derives generally from his desire to integrate the decalogue more completely within Deuteronomy than it had been until then. It was first introduced as part of a historical account; it is now emphasized as decisively important in its own right, through its chief commandment being made the leitmotif of the introduction and conclusion to the deuteronomic law.

[49] Secondly, it is through the work of this editor that Deuteronomy became imbued with specifically covenant or treaty thought forms and terminology. Again, reference has already been made to the treaty form which lies behind and has influenced 4:1–40; 10:12–11:32; 28:1–6, 15–19 and 29:1–30:20. In addition, 26:16–19; 27:9–10 have been seen to contain the formal declaration and affirmation of a covenant relationship between Yahweh and Israel. It should be noted, however, that it is first now that Deuteronomy acquired this intimate relationship with the treaty or covenant. The deuteronomic law which the deuteronomistic historian incorporated into his work was a lawbook, a collection of laws delivered by Moses to the children of Israel before they entered the land.[86] It contained a heading, an introduction now edited within chaps. 6–11, and the deuteronomic law of chaps. 12–26. No reference was made to it as covenant law; it was simply a collection of laws understood to derive from Moses. Of course, since the treaty or covenant was a legal form, there are similarities between the form of codes of law, such as Deuteronomy originally was, and covenants or treaties;[87] both may have prologues, stipulations, and sanctions. But the situation to which each is addressed is different: the lawcode is issued by a king as the law by which his own people is governed; the treaty formally regulates relationships between different kings and their peoples. It is the latter idea which the editor introduced through presenting the law primarily as regulating the relationship between Yahweh and Israel. The deuteronomic law had been the law of Moses by which Moses regulated the life of the people of whom

86. The original heading to the deuteronomic law is probably to be found in 4:45; cf. Seitz, *Deuteronomium*, 26–27, 35–36.

87. It is undoubtedly for this reason that Weinfeld (*Deuteronomy and the Deuteronomic School*, 146–57) believes that the form of the lawcode and that of the treaty have converged in Deuteronomy.

he was leader; the editor has transformed it into the law which regulates the covenant relationship between Yahweh and Israel.

A possible reason for this transformation may be suggested. The deuteronomistic historian either intentionally or unwittingly introduced a new aspect to the status of the deuteronomic law through inserting the decalogue in the contest of his historical editing of the book: this law no longer existed as an isolated collection proclaimed to Israel by Moses; it now stood, at least historically, in some relationship to the decalogue and covenant on Sinai. It was with the question of this relationship that the editor was concerned when he introduced covenant categories into the deuteronomic law. This law is not to be seen as of secondary importance in relation to the Sinai covenant; rather, it too is covenant law, not only received from God at Sinai, but proclaimed to Israel in the context of a new covenant made in Moab (29:1). It is ⟦50⟧ primarily in order to safeguard the status of the law of Moses that the editor has presented it as covenant law.

Third, there is a close connection between the thought of this editor of Deuteronomy and the prophets of the exile. So the scornful description of the idols in 4:28 finds its closest parallel in Isa 40:19–20; 44:19–20; 46:6–7; the allusion to creation in 4:32 is unique in Deuteronomy but common in Second Isaiah (Isa 45:18–21; 46:9–10); the uniqueness of Yahweh (Deut 4:35, 39) is a basic thought of the same prophet (Isa 43:10–13; 44:6; 45:6–7, 22); on swearing by the name of Yahweh (Deut 6:13; 10:20), cf. Isa 48:1; 65:16; Jer 5:7; 12:16; on circumcision of the heart (Deut 10:16; 30:6), cf. Jer 4:4; 6:10; for Israel as a praise, a fame and an honor (Deut 26:19), cf. Jer 13:11; 33:9; on the detestable things and idols of Deut 29:17, cf. Jer 7:30; 16:18; 32:34; Ezek 6:5, 9, 13; 7:20; 11:21; 14:3; 20:16, 30; 23:7; 44:10, 12; for the phrase stubbornness of heart, Deut 29:19, cf. Jer 3:17; 7:24; 9:13; on the verb uprooted, Deut 29:28, cf. Jer 1:10; 12:14–15; 18:7; anger and fury and great wrath, Deut 29:28, cf. Jer 21:5; 32:27; restore your fortunes, Deut 30:3, a phrase particularly frequent in Jeremiah (Jer 29:14, 30:3, 18; 31:23); in Deut 32:47, trifle, there is the terminology of Isa 55:11.

The exilic background which this indicates for the editor responsible for this layer in Deuteronomy is suitable also from the point of view of the general concern of the editor. The exiles were living in a situation where the attractions of the worship of other gods would have been pressing, not least by reason of the fact that the exiles had lost possession of the land to which the worship of Yahweh properly belonged; loss of land, even if it did not mean defeat of Yahweh by the gods of Babylon, would certainly be understood to mean the end of Yahweh's relationship with his people. Now if ever it was a time for a presentation of this relationship which emphasized its dependence on obedience, and it is this presentation which the editor through using covenant or treaty forms and thought set out to effect. Yet in doing so, the editor clearly wished to avoid giving the impression that since this relationship depended on obedience, and since Israel had not been obedient, that relationship had simply come to an end. This pessimistic view is countered by means of a significant modification which the editor carried out in the treaty form which he adopted.[88] In the treaty context the curse and blessing which would follow on disobedience and obedience were alternate possibilities; the editor has made them successive stages in the history of the relationship between God and Israel. In Deut 4:25–31; 29:16–30:14 (cf. also above on 8:16) Israel is assured [51] that after the punishment and destruction which will result from her disobedience, there will follow renewed blessing and restoration if Israel returns to Yahweh. Israel in exile is being shown that her present experience is the curse which results from her disobedience; she is also being assured that through repentance and return the favor of God which belongs to that broken covenant relationship will be realized in her life and history once again.

88. This and other modifications have been discussed by Lohfink, "Die Wandlung des Bundesbegriffs im Buch Deuteronomium," in *Gott in Welt* (Festgabe für Karl Rahner; ed. H. Vorgrimler; Freiburg: Herder, 1964) 1.423–44.

The Decalogue:
Ancient Israel's Criminal Law

ANTHONY PHILLIPS

[[1]] In 1970 I published my *Ancient Israel's Criminal Law: A New Approach to the Decalogue.*[1] The main thesis of my book was the contention that the Decalogue in an original short form given at Sinai constituted pre-exilic Israel's criminal law. From both the legal and narrative material, I argued that ancient Israel distinguished between crimes and torts, the former always demanding the exaction of the death penalty by the community, the latter payment of damages to the injured party. In contrast to torts where the action lay between the individuals themselves as plaintiff and defendant, criminal offences were not the personal concern of any individual who may have suffered injury, but of the community at large upon whom the responsibility for conviction rested.[2] Failure to comply with the requirements of the Decalogue brought direct divine punishment on the community which could only ward off such action by the execution of the criminal. It was not the apodictic form of the Decalogue which indicated its Israelite origins, but its content which on entry into Canaan had to be superimposed on and integrated with the indigenous law resulting in the *Mishpatim* [['judgments']] of the Book of the Covenant, which clearly differentiate between crimes and torts, a distinction which again underlies Deuteronomy.

Reprinted with permission from *Journal of Jewish Studies* 34 (1983) 1–20.

1. A. Phillips, *Ancient Israel's Criminal Law: A New Approach to the Decalogue*, Oxford 1970 (hereafter cited as Phillips, *AICL*).

2. M. J. Buss, "The Distinction between Civil and Criminal Law in Ancient Israel," *Proceedings of the Sixth World Congress of Jewish Studies 1973* i, Jerusalem 1977, pp. 51–62 also recognises the importance of distinguishing between crime and tort in ancient Israel's law, though on many particular issues we hold different opinions.

In my book I connected this thesis with Mendenhall's assertion that the description of the inauguration of the covenant at Sinai in the Exodus narrative and its theological interpretation was modelled on the form of the Hittite suzerainty treaties.[3] Indeed I believed that I was in fact strengthening Mendenhall's argument by establishing the inner unity of the Ten Commandments. While Rogerson in his review of my book thought that this connection with the Hittite treaties was vital to my thesis,[4] Nicholson rightly surmised that my understanding of the Decalogue as Israel's criminal law code could be maintained independently of Mendenhall's [2] views.[5] It is now clear to me following the work of both McCarthy[6] and Nicholson[7] that although the suzerainty treaty form does influence the later compilation of the Sinai narrative in Exodus, as well as Deuteronomy, it only entered Israel's theology following the fall of the northern kingdom to Assyria. Consequently if the Decalogue derives from earliest times, the treaty form plays no part in its original composition and interpretation. Similarly my use of the Nothian view of the amphictynony,[8] also considered by Rogerson as vital to my thesis,[9] is in fact peripheral to my main argument, though I would with McCarthy[10] seek to caution against a too sweeping rejection of any tribal unity in pre-monarchic Israel. While Mayes[11] has shown that the amphictyonic hypothesis as elaborated by Noth can no longer be maintained, nonetheless ancient Israel was not a total disunity as the emergence of the monarchy confirms. There were common religious traditions which did single out the Hebrews from the indigenous population of Canaan and which in my view were secured by the Decalogue. It thus remains my contention that it was the Decalogue which both created Israel as a distinct community, and, though from time to time reinterpreted and remoulded, secured her survival from the earliest days of the settlement until exile in Babylon.

Two main objections have been advanced against my thesis: (i) that the Decalogue itself is a late composition,[12] perhaps Deuteronomic;[13]

---

3. G. E. Mendenhall, "Ancient Oriental and Biblical Law," *BA* 17, 1954, pp. 26–46, "Covenant Forms in Israelite Tradition," *ibid.*, 50–76.

4. J. Rogerson, *PEQ* 104, 1972, p. 157.

5. E. W. Nicholson, *Theology* 75, 1972, pp. 154f.

6. D. J. McCarthy, *Treaty and Covenant,*[2] *Analecta Biblica* xxiA, Rome 1978.

7. Nicholson, *Exodus and Sinai in History and Tradition*, Oxford 1973.

8. M. Noth, *Das System der zwölf Stämme Israels*, *BWANT* iv:I, Stuttgart 1930.

9. Rogerson, *op. cit.*, 157.

10. McCarthy, *op. cit.*, 282.

11. A. D. H. Mayes, *Israel in the Period of the Judges*, *SBT* ii/xxix, London 1974.

12. Mayes, *Deuteronomy, New Century Bible Commentary*, London 1979, pp. 161ff.

13. Nicholson, "The Decalogue as the Direct Address of God," *VT* 28, 1977, pp. 422–433.

and (ii) that the Biblical evidence itself does not warrant my assertion
that the Decalogue constituted pre-exilic Israel's criminal law, and
thereby established legal principles which distinguished her law from
that of all other ancient Near Eastern legal collections.[14] I have already
sought to defend myself against these charges, both reasserting the
early date of the Decalogue,[15] and, in studies of murder[16] and adultery,[17] the distinctive [[3]] nature of Israel's criminal law as derived
from it. Here I summarize, modify and augment my arguments.

I

If the Decalogue carried such significance as I have suggested, it is perhaps strange that reference to it is so rare in the Old Testament. While
it is set out in both Exodus 20 and Deuteronomy 5 in the accounts of
the inauguration of the covenant at Sinai/Horeb, the only other allusions to it occur in Hos 4:2 and Jer 7:9 where apparent reference
is made to some specific commandments concerned with offences
against the person. While such partial citing of particular commandments cannot be taken as conclusive evidence of the existence of the
whole collection of Ten Commandments, it does however seem to me
that in both cases deliberate appeal is being made to the Decalogue.[18]
Yet, as I argued in my essay "Prophecy and Law,"[19] in neither case does
the citing of the specific commands of the Decalogue form an integral
part of the prophetic material, nor indeed of the prophets' message as
a whole. Thus while Hos 4:1 indicates the general charge against Israel
and Hos 4:3 the direct consequences of its breach, v. 2 seems to be a
later interpretation of what conduct actually constituted lack of *emet*
[['truth']], *ḥesed* [['kindness']] and *da^cat ʾelohim* [['knowledge of God']].
For neither the rest of Hosea's prophecy, nor that of his fellow
prophet to the north, Amos, points to that state of general chaos which
would of necessity have followed the conduct described in Hos 4:2.

14. See in particular M. Greenberg, *JBL* 41, 1972, pp. 535–538; B. S. Jackson,
"Reflections on Biblical Criminal Law," *JJS* 24, 1973, pp. 8–38 = *Essays in Jewish and Comparative Legal History, Studies in Judaism in Late Antiquity* x, Leiden 1975, pp. 25–63 (hereafter cited as Jackson, "Reflections").

15. Phillips, "A Fresh Look at the Sinai Narrative" to be published in *VT* in two parts
(hereafter cited as Phillips, "A Fresh Look").

16. Phillips, "Another Look at Murder," *JJS* 28, 1977, pp. 105–126 (hereafter cited as
Phillips, "Murder").

17. Phillips, "Another Look at Adultery," *JSOT* 20, 1981, pp. 3–25 (hereafter cited as
Phillips, "Adultery"), "A Response to Dr. McKeating," *ibid.* 22, 1982, pp. 142–143.

18. H. W. Wolff, *Hosea*, Philadelphia 1974, pp. 67f.

19. Phillips, "Prophecy and Law," in *Israel's Prophetic Tradition*, eds. R. Coggins, Phillips and M. Knibb, Cambridge 1982, pp. 217–232.

Similarly while Jer 7:5b–6 indicates the course of action which Israel is to follow to avoid *Yhwh's* judgment, the specific reference to provisions in the Decalogue in v. 9 seems intrusive for nowhere else in Jeremiah is any reliance placed on breach of the Decalogue as the reason for Judah's rejection. In my view, both in Hos 4:2 and Jer 7:9 the Decalogue is being used theologically as a blanket expression to indicate total rejection of *Yhwh* which in the case of Hosea justifies the fall of Samaria, and of Jeremiah the fall of Jerusalem. Like the insertion of *berit* [['covenant']] in Hos 8:1,[20] and the use of the covenant theology in Jeremiah, this is the work of the Deuteronomistic redactors concerned to show the utter rejection of the Decalogue, in their eyes the sole covenant law of Horeb (Deut 4:13, 5:22).

Indeed what is striking in the eighth century prophetic material (apart from Hos 4:2) is the total lack of condemnation of those acts for which sanctions were prescribed and enforced by the courts. This does not [[4]] necessarily mean that such acts were never perpetrated, but we must assume that when they occurred they were dealt with under the law, the criminal suffering execution in the prescribed manner. Had the prophets been able to condemn a more obvious breakdown in law and order, they would certainly have done so. Instead, detailed examination of the prophetic traditions indicates that Amos, Micah and Isaiah rested their indictment solely on the general charge of lack of humaneness and maladministration of justice, the kind of actions already condemned in the Book of the Covenant (Exod 22:20–23:9).[21] While such conduct could never be precisely defined, nor enforced by the courts through legal sanctions, it was the prophets' contention that its very unnaturalness should have been obvious to Israel (Amos 1–2:8; Isa 1:3).[22] Their innovation was then to hold that Israel's election depended not merely on appropriate cultic practice or observance of enforceable law, but also on those general principles of natural law which of necessity could never be precisely defined but which rational men ought to be able to discern for themselves. The other prophetic tradition is that of Hosea, who condemns Israel for her lack of loyalty to *Yhwh* due to her syncretistic cult. This he interprets as apostasy. Because in Deuteronomic eyes such apostasy accounted for both the fall

20. L. Perlitt, *Die Bundestheologie im Alten Testament, WMANT* xxxvi, Neukirchen-Vluyn 1969, pp. 190ff.

21. The references to idolatry in Micah (1:7, 5:10–15) and Isaiah (2:8, 18, 26) are redactional as also is the comment on murderers at the end of Isa 1:21 (O. Kaiser, *Isaiah 1–12*, London 1972, p. 18).

22. J. Barton, "Natural Law and Poetic Justice in the Old Testament," *JTS* 30, 1979, pp. 1–4, "Ethics in Isaiah of Jerusalem," *ibid.*, 32, 1981, pp. 1–18.

of Samaria and Jerusalem, this tradition now dominates the Biblical material, though both eighth century prophetic traditions are found in the Deuteronomic laws and are brought together in Jeremiah, itself the result of Deuteronomistic redaction.[23]

But the fact that the Decalogue is only set out in full in Exodus 20 and Deuteronomy 5, and then in a form which betrays a late compilation, need not of itself cause surprise. For it must be remembered that not all ancient Israel's theological traditions had to be recalled in subsequent literature, which still depended on those traditions for its interpretation. So, as has often been pointed out, no further mention is made in the Old Testament of the Eden narrative of Genesis 3. J having established the predicament of man in the world in which God had set him, the rest of the Old Testament could be understood against that basic theological assessment of man's condition. There is then no *prima facie* reason why this should not also be true of the Decalogue if it too established the conditions for Israel's position in the world in which God had set her. Indeed it is apparent that those to whom [[5]] the prophets proclaimed judgment did not see themselves as under threat, even as late as the time of Jeremiah (6:14, 8:11). Rather, both in their excessive religious zeal and, we must assume from the prophetic silence, in their outward maintenance of enforceable law and order, the people believed that *Yhwh* was ensuring their protection as his elect (Jer 7:4). Hence the business community in the time of Amos makes no attempt to breach the sabbath requirements, thereby confirming that, in spite of every intention of continuing their dishonest business practices, outward conformity with the requirements of the Decalogue determined their actions (Amos 8:4–6).

In fact those who hold that the Decalogue is a Deuteronomic composition can give no satisfactory theological explanation for its collection at that time based on its contents. Indeed these bear very little relation to the main thrust of the Deuteronomic laws to which the Decalogue now acts as the preface. Certainly no one could have composed the Decalogue as a summary of Deuteronomic legal concern. Rather the reverse is the case, for as now presented the Deuteronomic laws are to be understood as deduced from the Decalogue. By inserting the Decalogue into the original book of Deuteronomy, the Deuteronomistic redactors give the new law collection a proper pedigree, thereby validating its legitimacy.[24] Further the redactors' deliberate alteration

23. Nicholson, *Preaching to the Exiles*, Oxford 1970; R. P. Carroll, *From Chaos to Covenant*, London 1981.

24. Deut 5:1–6:3 and 9:1–10:11 form the major insertions of the first Deuteronomistic redactors into the original book of Deuteronomy which resulted in the formation of

of the Sinai narrative (Exodus 19–24, 32–34) enabled the Deuteronomic laws associated with Josiah's reform to supersede all previous
law as the sole canonical statement of *Yhwh*'s covenant requirement.[25]
This involved the omission of (i) the Book of the Covenant by immediately introducing the tablets of the law following the giving of the
Decalogue (Deut 5:22) and (ii) the laws of Exod 34:11ff. by asserting
that only the Decalogue was written on the second set of tablets (Deut
10:4). The fact that in contrast to the Book of the Covenant, the Deuteronomic law collection almost totally omits all civil law, further indicates that its concern is with that law which can cause divine rejection,
namely the criminal law derived from the Decalogue and, following
the prophetic protest, the laws of humaneness and maladministration
of justice (Amos, Micah and Isaiah) and apostasy (Hosea).

While there is no direct evidence that the Decalogue originally
consisted of short apodictic commands, nor if it did can we be certain
of their precise [[6]] form, the fact that the Deuteronomic version
shows a deliberate theological development from the Exodus version,
which in turn in the case of the sabbath commandment has also been
subjected to later reinterpretation by the Priestly theologians, indicates
that in the text of Exodus 20 and Deuteronomy 5 we have the product
of a period of reflection and reassessment necessitated by successive
changes in Israel's theological outlook.

Clear indication of the adaptation of the Sinai Decalogue of Exodus
20 to Deuteronomic legal concern is found both in the commandments
concerning parents and coveting. So in Deut 5:16 the Deuteronomistic
redactors add to the promise of longevity the additional promise of
prosperity in the land which God gives them. This conforms with the
Deuteronomic extension of the motive clauses designed to secure obedience to the unenforceable laws of humaneness and righteousness already found in the Book of the Covenant (Exod 22:20b, 22–23, 27, 23:9)
to include the idea of prosperity for the performance of certain apparently uneconomic injunctions.[26] Though obedience to such commands
did not on the face of it look as if it could possibly bring the performer
any material blessing, *Yhwh* would in fact secure him personal gain

---

the Deuteronomistic History Work (Deuteronomy–2 Kings) for which the Deuteronomistic redactors composed Deuteronomy 1–3 as the introduction. Later a second redaction
took place which included the insertion of Deut 4:1–40 (Mayes, "Deuteronomy 4 and the
Literary Criticism of Deuteronomy," *JBL* 100/101 1981, pp. 23–51. [[Reprinted in this volume pp. 195–224 above.]]

25. Phillips, "A Fresh Look."

26. B. Gemser, "The importance of the Motive Clauses in Old Testament Law," *VTS*
i, 1953, pp. 50–66.

(Deut 14:29, 15:4–6, 10, 18, 23:20). Similarly, the reversal of house and wife in the commandment on coveting is a deliberate move by the Deuteronomistic redactors to conform with the Deuteronomic law under which for the first time women were treated as equal with men under the law (Deut 7:3, 13:6, 15:12–17, 17:2–5, 22:22). No longer could a wife be listed alongside her husband's other chattels. She herself had acquired rights under the law and was herself a member of the elect community with all the privileges and duties which that entailed (Deut 12:12, 18, 16:11, 14, 29:11, 18).

Further, by a subtle modification of the Sinai Decalogue of Exodus 20, the Deuteronomistic redactors were able to emphasise one new concern of the exilic situation which formed no part of the original Deuteronomic law collection (Deuteronomy 12–26). This they achieved by (i) introducing the exodus as an explanation for keeping the sabbath (Deut 5:15) and inserting the ox and the ass in the list of those who should do no work on it (Deut 5:14), thereby securing verbal links with both the beginning and end of the Decalogue; and (ii) running together the short apodictic injunctions of the last four commandments. As a result, the sabbath commandment was now thrust into a dominant position at the centre of the Decalogue, so underlining its new overall importance in the different circumstances facing exilic Israel.[27] In exactly the same way the Priestly theologians built on to the [[7]] sabbath commandment in Exodus 20 the connection with their creation theology in Genesis 1 in which they interpreted the sabbath as the sign that God could never repudiate his election of Israel. Since the sabbath was fixed in creation, and the only people in the world who kept the sabbath were the Jews, they too were fixed in creation. Only failure to appropriate their election could invalidate it.[28]

These examples of Deuteronomistic and Priestly reinterpretation of the Decalogue clearly show that the text was in no way sacrosanct, but as with other Hebrew law could be reinterpreted and remoulded to take cognizance of the changed legal and theological situations facing Israel, usually the result of political upheaval. What was important was that in whatever new circumstances Israel found herself the fundamental demands of the Decalogue should continue to reflect *Yhwh*'s will for his elect people.

Indeed it has been my contention that the commandments on images, the name of *Yhwh*, sabbath, parents and coveting all reflect earlier pre-Deuteronomistic remoulding of the original short apodictic

27. N. Lohfink, "Zur Dekalogfassung von Dt 5," *BZ* 9, 1965, pp. 17ff.
28. Phillips, *God B.C.*, Oxford 1977, p. 48.

commandments consequent upon a new theological position, itself the result of political change, namely the fall of the northern kingdom leading to Hezekiah's reform (2 Kings 18).

Since the first commandment prohibits relationships with all other gods, it is clear that originally the commandment on images would have been concerned solely with representations of *Yhwh*. These would have been in human form since that is how Israel thought of her God (Deut 4:16; Isa 44:13; Hab 2:18f.; Ps 115:4ff.). But the change of person in Exod 20:5 indicates that whoever expanded the commandment took the first two commandments as one and interpreted the images as those of other gods. Further, these images are now envisaged as representations from the animal world. The same picture is reflected in the laws of Exod 34:11ff., where Exod 34:17 again takes the first two commandments together and, as the context indicates, obviously refers back to the golden calf of Exodus 32, itself associated with the bull images of Jeroboam I (1 Kgs 12:28). Further, both in the expanded second commandment (Exod 20:5) and in Exod 34:17, *Yhwh* is described as jealous, a term only used of him when his claims over Israel are threatened by other gods.[29]

Both in my *Ancient Israel's Criminal Law*[30] and in a recent article,[31] I have examined the laws of Exod 34:11ff. and concluded that they reflect [[8]] Hezekiah's reform, the whole Sinai narrative Exodus 19–24, 32–34 being the work of the Proto-Deuteronomists in Jerusalem writing in the light of that reform and the threat to Judah.[32] They are responsible for the Covenant Code framework in its present form (Exod 19:3–8, 20:22–23, 24:3–8), and the introduction into the Sinai narrative of both the Book of Covenant and the tablets of the law on which they understood both the Decalogue and the Book of the Covenant to have been written (Exod 24:12), a summary of the more important provisions of which they set out on the second set of tablets (Exod 34:11ff.).[33] Further, they now introduce the Book of the Cove-

29. H. Th. Obbink, "Jahwebilder," *ZAW* 47, 1929, pp. 265ff.; R. Knierim, "Das Erste Gebot," *ibid.* 77, 1965, p. 33.

30. Phillips, *AICL*, 167ff.

31. Phillips, "A Fresh Look."

32. In my *Ancient Israel's Criminal Law*, I used the term 'JE redactor' to describe these authors. But because (i) the whole issue of what is meant by E is now in dispute (B. S. Childs, *Introduction to the Old Testament as Scripture*, London 1979, p. 122), and (ii) the thought and language of these theologians foreshadows what comes to be known as Deuteronomistic theology, it is better to link them with their successors rather than their uncertain predecessors.

33. Only when Deuteronomy was attached to the Tetrateuch to form the Pentateuch was there an attempt to reconcile the Sinai narrative with the Deuteronomic account that

nant with a new preface prohibiting molten images and stressing the necessary simplicity of Israelite sanctuaries (Exod 20:22–26). This radical theological revision of the Sinai narrative resulted from reflection on the changed political situation following the vindication of Hosea's prophecy in the Assyrian conquest. These southern theologians saw that disaster as due to Israel's apostasy symbolised in her bull images.[34] This led Hezekiah in his reform to eject from the temple even the serpent Nehushtan, although attributed to Moses (2 Kgs 18:4). It also explains the central role which the incident of the golden calf now plays in the Sinai narrative (Exodus 32),[35] commandments on molten images both prefacing the Book of the Covenant (Exod 20:23), and being repeated in the laws on the second set of tablets (Exod 34:17). These same ideas underlie the Proto-Deuteronomists' expansion of the second commandment now interpreted as prohibiting images of other gods in animal form of which Nehushtan and the bulls form examples. Later, the commandment was to be expanded further in the final Deuteronomistic redaction of Deuteronomy when astral worship associated with the last years of the Davidic monarchy (2 Kgs 21:3–6) becomes associated with it (Deut 4:19).

Following their introduction of the Book of the Covenant into the Sinai [[9]] narrative, the Proto-Deuteronomists added to the sabbath commandment the list of those who should do no work on the sabbath, their purpose being to make the commandment conform to Exod 23:12. By the use of the term holy, Israel is reminded that the sabbath is the creation of *Yhwh* on whose election alone her existence depends. Later, the Deuteronomistic redactors were to justify the sabbath commandment by reference to Israel's slavery in Egypt and *Yhwh*'s deliverance of her (Deut 5:15). Similarly, the hortatory expansions of the commandments on the name and on parents are also the work of the Proto-Deuteronomists who as in Exod 20:10 refer to God by the third person form. The reason that they did not do so in their expansion of the commandment on images was that by taking the first and second commandments together, they were conditioned by the 'before me' of

---

only the Decalogue (the Ten Words) was written on the second set of tablets (Deut 10:2, 4). So the Pentateuchal editors inserted the Deuteronomistic phrase, the Ten Words, in Exod 34:28. This explains why scholars have found it so difficult to isolate ten commandments in Exod 34:11ff. There never were nor was it ever intended that there should be Ten Words in Exod 34:11ff. (Phillips, "A Fresh Look").

34. On Jeroboam I's purpose in establishing bull images at Dan and Bethel (1 Kgs 12:28) see W. F. Albright, *From the Stone Age to Christianity*[2], Baltimore 1946, pp. 203, 229.

35. For a discussion of the origin of the story of the golden calf, see Phillips, *AICL*, 170ff.

Exod 20:3. In fact, the third person form was much more suited to their parenetic style. Further, just as the Proto-Deuteronomists introduced motive clauses into the laws of humaneness and righteousness in the Book of the Covenant (Exod 22:20b, 22–23; 23:9),[36] so they introduce such a clause into the commandment on parents. The question of longevity in the land was of course uppermost in the people's minds as they faced the Assyrian threat. Later, as we have seen, both in the Deuteronomic laws, the new motive of the promise of prosperity for obedience to apparently uneconomic laws was inserted, support for parents being considered a financial burden. The tenth commandment was also expanded by the Proto-Deuteronomists as part of their emphasis on the laws of humaneness and righteousness. By an additional *hamad* [['to covet']] clause they extended it to include all other property which an Israelite might have acquired by agreement, purchase or gain, which explains the absence of children and confirms that 'house' cannot be interpreted as 'household.' Later under the influence of Isa 5:8 and Mic 2:2 the Deuteronomistic redactors added 'field' to the list.

Let me sum up my argument so far. While the apparent reference to the Decalogue in Hos 4:2 and Jer 7:9 appears to be the work of the Deuteronomistic redactors, the prophetic silence on the Decalogue can be explained in other ways than ignorance of its existence, for their indictment does not indicate that total chaos in society which would result from its breach. Indeed the people appear fully confident of *Yhwh*'s continued election. Further, the Deuteronomistic redactors use the Decalogue theologically to give support to their law seen as superseding all previous laws in the Sinai narrative, being the complete expression of the will of *Yhwh*. The Deuteronomistic [[10]] development of the Sinai Decalogue to reflect Deuteronomic legal concern, seen again in the Priestly theologians' introduction of their creation theology into the sabbath commandment, indicates that the Decalogue was subject to continuous revision in the light of new theological ideas, themselves often the consequence of political events. This explains the expansion of the short apodictic commandments by the Proto-Deuteronomists following the fall of Samaria interpreted as due to northern apostasy, and leading to Hezekiah's reform. It is then my contention that before the Proto-Deuteronomists re-wrote the Sinai narrative Exodus 19–24, 32–34, the Decalogue existed as a series of short apodictic commandments. Can we be more precise about its origins?

36. While the laws of humaneness and righteousness are in the 'thou' form, the additions are in the plural, like the Covenant Code framework (Exod 19:3–8, 20:22–23, 24:3–8), also the work of the Proto-Deuteronomists.

II

In criticising my book, *Ancient Israel's Criminal Law*, Greenberg[37] curiously failed to recognise the debt I owed to his seminal essay, "Some Postulates of Biblical Law."[38] In this he concluded that a basic difference in the evaluation of life and property separated biblical law from other ancient Near Eastern law. While in non-biblical law an economic and political evaluation pre-dominated, biblical law was governed solely by a religious evaluation. This resulted in three main postulates: (i) biblical law being a statement of God's will made pardon or mitigation impossible: consequently both the murderer and the adulterer had to be executed; (ii) no property offence was punishable by death; (iii) vicarious punishment was ruled out.

In my book I sought to confirm these postulates by arguing that (i) all ten commandments concerned either an injury to God or to the person of a fellow Israelite, but never his property; (ii) the penalty for breach of every commandment was death, the exaction of which was mandatory, but which was never required for a property offence; (iii) while apostasy would result in the extermination of all males within a family so that the family would be entirely blotted out (2 Kgs 9:26), the substitution of someone for execution for another's crime was never permitted (Exod 21:31).

Before I seek to defend my thesis, I must rebut the suggestion of McKeating that I take "it for granted that we know how Israelite law 'worked'; how it functioned in society."[39] On the contrary, I fully recognise that the material is extremely fragmentary; much remains uncertain; some is idealistic; part could never have been enforced; all has 〚11〛 been subjected to theological considerations. Indeed the law collections, with the exception of the *Mishpatim* 〚'judgments'〛 of the Book of the Covenant (Exod 21:12–22:16), are not so much instructions to the judiciary as sermons to the nation. Rather than legal codes establishing a judicial system, these collections constitute theological literary works concerned with the maintenance of Israel's election. But since it was Israel's theology which made her a distinct people in the ancient Near East, it seems reasonable to assume that the various collections might provide sufficient evidence to indicate that at certain points Israel's law was different in principle from other ancient Near

37. See n. 13.

38. Greenberg, "Some Postulates of Biblical Law," in *Yehezkel Kaufmann Jubilee Volume*, ed. M. Haran, Jerusalem 1960, pp. 5–28. 〚Reprinted in this volume, pp. 283–300.〛

39. H. McKeating, "A Response to Dr. Phillips by Henry McKeating," *JSOT* 20, 1981, p. 26.

Eastern law. Of course we are dealing with probabilities, even possibilities, not certainties. But it now remains my assertion that the Old Testament contains enough evidence to show that Greenberg's postulates as elaborated and extended by myself can be established, even if much of my case must of necessity rest on the argument from silence.

In his criticism of Greenberg, Paul[40] and myself, Jackson argues that there were three instances when property offences resulted in the exaction of the death penalty: (i) brigandage, (ii) kidnapping and (iii) sacrilege.[41] But (i) Jackson's distinction between theft and brigandage[42] is irrelevant to the administration of early Israelite law; (ii) man-theft is not a property offence for which damages are paid (Exod 21:37ff.), but a crime which requires the exaction of the death penalty (Exod 21:16), for the offender is no ordinary thief but is specifically described as "the stealer of the life of one of his brethren" (Deut 24:7), the equivalent of a murderer; and (iii) there is no indication of a particular offence of theft of sacred objects in the Old Testament comparable to CH 6 and 8. Of the cases cited by Jackson, Achan and his family were not executed for theft, but because his action had brought them within the ban to which Jericho was already subject (Joshua 7); Jacob's order that the person with whom Laban's household gods are found should be executed merely indicates the power of the *paterfamilias* at that time (Gen 31:17ff.); and there is no indication that Joseph or his steward thought that death was the appropriate penalty for theft of his cup (Gen 44:1ff.). The possibility of such a punishment only enters the conversation because the brothers were so certain of their innocence that they were able to make such an extravagant offer. All we have in these last two accounts is stories of the pursuit of thieves on the discovery of loss of [[12]] property, not a reference to a special offence of sacrilege. It remains then my assertion that no property offence was punishable by death.

Both Jackson and McKeating have criticised Greenberg and myself for our opinion that execution for murder and adultery was mandatory, Jackson arguing that in the *Mishpatim* [['judgments']] "there is no explicit statement of general principle, whether allowing or prohibit-

40. S. Paul, *Studies in the Book of of the Covenant in the Light of Cuneiform and Biblical Law*, VTS xviii, Leiden 1970.

41. Jackson, "Reflections," 17.

42. Jackson, "Some Comparative Legal History: Robbery and Brigandage," *Georgia Journal of International and Comparative Law* i, 1970, pp. 45ff., *Theft in Early Jewish Law*, Oxford 1972, pp. 1–40, 180–181, 251–253 (hereafter cited as Jackson, *Theft*). On Jackson's interpretation of the distinction between *gnb* [['to steal']] and *gzl* [['to seize, rob']] see J. Milgrom, "The Missing Thief in Leviticus 5:20ff," *RIDA* 22, 1975, pp. 71–80.

ing composition."[43] He believes that there was a period in which composition for homicide was permitted and, following Loewenstamm,[44] points to Prov 6:32–5 "as evidence that adultery could be settled by payment of an agreed amount of compensation."[45] McKeating adopts the same view,[46] noting that there is little direct evidence of the death penalty being applied for adultery. Indeed in his view, while Deut 22:22 and Lev 20:10 command execution as a matter of course, in fact its infliction in the end rested on the attitude of the husband.

Kofer [['ransom']] is only mentioned once in the *Mishpatim* [['judgments']] when an ox known by its owner to have a propensity to gore kills a man or woman (Exod 21:30). Uniquely the owner is permitted to save his life by paying *kofer* [['ransom']] to the injured family. But this is no exception to the rule that in every case the murderer must be executed, because the ox is still stoned to death as the murderer, which explains why its flesh cannot be eaten. The biblical law of the goring ox is then in sharp contrast to LE 54-5 and CH 250-2, which are only concerned with compensating the injured party but provide no penalty for the ox. So while Babylonian law treats injury caused by a goring ox both to men and animals as a civil offence, making provision for pecuniary compensation, biblical law sharply contrasts the death of a man by an ox as a criminal offence with the death of an ox by an ox which, as in Babylonian law, leads to a civil action for damages (Exod 21:35f.). The fact that under biblical law, even death caused by an animal requires exaction of the death penalty, confirms its mandatory nature. Where there is no difference in principle, biblical and Babylonian law remain identical (LE 53; Exod 21:35).[47]

Jackson points out though that the way in which *kofer* [['ransom']] is introduced into the law of the goring ox indicates that it was a well known practice. But that does not mean that Israelite law countenanced it. Rather its absence from the *Mishpatim* [['judgments']] in the face of the absolute demands of Exod 21:12, 15–17 [[13]] indicates that in contrast to the hitherto common Canaanite practice of *kofer* [['ransom']] (2 Sam 21:4), Israelite law was making execution for murder

---

43. Jackson, "Reflections," 21ff.

44. S. E. Loewenstamm, "The Laws of Adultery and Murder in Biblical and Mesopotamian Law," *Beth Miqra* 13, 1962, pp. 55–9 (Hebrew) = E. T. in *Comparative Studies in Biblical and Ancient Oriental Literatures*, AOAT cciv, Neukirchen-Vluyn 1980, pp. 146–53.

45. Jackson,"Reflections," 34.

46. McKeating, "Sanctions against Adultery in Ancient Israelite Society with Some Reflections on Methodology in the Study of Old Testament Ethics," *JSOT* 11, 1979, pp. 57–72 (hereafter cited as McKeating, "Sanctions").

47. For further discussion see Phillips, "Murder," 109ff.

mandatory. Exceptionally, Exod 21:30 amends earlier law (Exod 21:29) to allow the owner as accessory to the goring ox to pay *kofer* ⟦'ransom'⟧. But in demanding the death of the ox as a murderer, indigenous Canaanite law is being modified due to the principles of Hebrew law.[48]

Further evidence that as a crime, murder was the responsibility of the local community to expiate, rather than of direct concern to the family of the deceased, comes from the ancient provision on the unknown murderer (Deut 21:1–9).[49] As the reference to elders indicates, this comes from a time before professional judges were appointed.[50] The nearest town to the corpse is made responsible for propitiating *Yhwh* in order that no punishment should fall on the community. Forbidden by the principles of Hebrew law to execute a substitute for the murderer, the killing of a heifer is prescribed. No blood is shed and the animal's carcass is simply abandoned. As McKeating indicates by connecting this provision with the killing of the seven sons of Saul (2 Samuel 21),[51] Canaanite ideas on fertility underlie the heifer ritual, the rite being designed to prevent drought and consequent famine, interpreted as the most frequent form of direct divine punishment. But despite this reliance on Canaanite practice, Deut 21:1–9 retains the distinctive principles of Israel's criminal law. In contrast to CH 24 and HL 6, no interest is shown in the deceased or his family; no attempt is made to identify him or contact his family; the community and not a specific individual are responsible for the heifer ritual; no mention is made of any compensation.

As I have already noted, Loewenstamm, Jackson and McKeating have cited Prov 6:35 as evidence for the payment of *kofer* ⟦'ransom'⟧ for adultery. However, they fail to recognise that *kofer* ⟦'ransom'⟧ is

---

48. Jackson also cites Exod 21:22 and Exod 21:32 as envisaging "monetary payment as the consequence of homicide" ("Reflections," 23). But the whole point of Exod 21:22 (in contrast to Exod 21:23–25) is that there is no taking of life, the assault on the pregnant woman being treated as a tort for which damages are paid. While Exod 21:32 demands the death of the murderer—the ox—the owner is treated as a tortfeasor and pays damages to the slave's master (Phillips, "Murder," 116f.).

49. For full discussion, see *ibid.*, 124ff.

50. See below, pp. 18f. Those provisions in Deuteronomy which mention elders administering justice (19:12, 21:2ff., 19f., 22:15ff., 25:7ff.), while still current law at the time Deuteronomy was promulgated, must antedate Jehoshaphat's reform (2 Chr 19:5; cp. Deut 16:18ff.). Hence the introduction of 'judges' in Deut 21:2. The compiler of the Deuteronomic legal corpus probably interpreted this ancient law as referring to the death of someone killed in battle, which explains its present position in the middle of the war laws (Mayes, *Deuteronomy*, 53, 284).

51. McKeating, "The Development of the Law on Homicide in Ancient Israel," *VT* 25, 1975, pp. 62ff.

also used of an illegal payment ⟦14⟧ designed to avoid prosecution for an offence already committed. It is to this illegal sense of a cover-up operation by the payment of a bribe or hush-money to judges to pervert the course of justice that *kofer* ⟦'ransom'⟧ in 1 Sam 12:3 and Amos 5:12 refers, as it does in Prov 13:8, where a rich man always subject to the threat of blackmail is contrasted with a poor man who has nothing with which to buy off the blackmailer. Similarly *kofer* ⟦'ransom'⟧ in Prov 6:35 describes hush-money as the parallel use of *shohad*, the normal Old Testament word for the payment of money to pervert the course of justice ('bribe'), confirms. What is being contemplated is the possibility of a cover-up operation whereby the adulterer would escape criminal prosecution by bribing the husband to keep quiet. Since the husband could in any event divorce his wife at will under family law and need give no reason, the criminal law was always liable to be treated with contempt if the bribe offered to the husband was sufficiently attractive, especially because the prosecution normally rested on him. But the sage points out that an adulterer would be very foolish to rely on such a possibility of escaping his criminal responsibility, for usually the husband's jealousy would seek vengeance in the adulterer's total ruin.[52]

Nor can I accept McKeating's view that it was only with Deuteronomy and the Holiness Code that an attempt was made to make death for adultery mandatory.[53] While it is true that no such provision appears in the Book of Covenant, neither Deut 22:22 nor Lev 20:10 are entirely new enactments. Rather, both have been expanded to bring the offending woman within the scope of criminal liability to which the adulterer had long been subject, and which results in the case of Deuteronomy in the carefully framed legislation of Deut 22:13–29. This is clear both from the singular *mot yumat* ⟦'be put to death'⟧ in Lev 20:10, and the emphasis placed on 'both of them' in Deut 22:22, who are then again specifically identified,[54] and is another example of the way in which women were brought within the scope of the law by the

---

52. See further Phillips, "Murder," 117ff., "Adultery," 17f. Prov 6:27–35 reflects postexilic law. As v. 33 indicates, the adulterer is now no longer executed. Nonetheless he is to be totally disgraced in a way from which he will never recover. This refers to the postexilic penalty of excommunication from the community (Lev 18:29), which except in cases of murder replaced the death penalty for crimes (Phillips, *AICL*, 28ff., 124ff.). Loewenstamm ("The Laws of Adultery and Murder in the Bible," *Beth Miqra* 18–19, 1964, pp. 77f. (Hebrew) = E.T. in *AOAT* cciv, pp. 171f.) rightly rejects Weinfeld's assertion that nothing can be learnt about actual legal practice from Prov 6:32–35 ("The Concept of Law in Israel and among her Neighbours," *Bet Miqra* 17, 1964, pp. 58–63 (Hebrew)).

53. McKeating, "Sanctions," 63ff.

54. Phillips, "Adultery," 6.

Deuteronomists.[55] Before this extension of the criminal law it would have been left to the husband to deal with his adulterous wife as he saw fit under family law [[15]] (Hos 2:4, Jer 3:8), though as in all family law he had no power of life or death over her.[56] Normally he would have divorced here, which as elsewhere in the ancient Near East would have included stripping the wife and driving her from the matrimonial home (Hos 2:5). This stripping cannot then be understood as an alternative punishment to death.

It remains then my view that the criminal law governing murder and adultery in Israel was unique in the ancient Near East. Both demanded community, not private, action leading to the execution of the murderer and the adulterer, and after the Deuteronomic reform of the adulteress as well. The injured party could not pardon the criminal, take any private act of revenge,[57] or settle for damages. The only thing which concerned him, as it did the community at large, was that the criminal should be tried, convicted and executed, and he was under a duty to do all that he could to effect this. Indeed he would often have been the chief witness in the prosecution. In my view, this situation could only have arisen because ancient Israel came into being through accepting a distinctive set of demands which made her a peculiar people among other ancient Near Eastern peoples. Could this have been other than the Decalogue?

Jackson rightly cautions against a synthetic view of non-Biblical ancient Near Eastern law, holding that each collection must be considered on its own.[58] But it is clear that no non-Biblical collection made the rigid distinction between criminal and civil offences based on whether the offence was against person or property. Yet it is the necessity to make this distinction which underlies the compilation of the *Mishpatim* [['judgments']] the earliest section of the Book of the Covenant (Exod 21:12–22:16) normally dated to the period of the settlement and clearly directed at the judiciary.

The *Mishpatim* [['judgments']] begin with a series of crimes all of which require the exaction of the death penalty by the community: murder (Exod 21:12); assault on parents (Exod 21:15); man-theft (Exod

---

55. See above, p. 6.

56. Phillips, "Some Aspects of Family Law in Pre-Exilic Israel," *VT* 23, 1975, pp. 349–361, "Another Example of Family Law," *ibid.* 30, 1980, pp. 240–245.

57. For my understanding of the office of *goʾel haddam* as an official of the local community, see Phillips, *AICL*, 102ff., and "Murder," 111ff. There is no evidence of the exercise of blood vengeance in Israel.

58. Jackson, "Reflections," 14.

21:16); and repudiation of parents (Exod 21:17).[59] Then follows a collection of precedents differentiating murder from assault (Exod 21:18–27). These lead on to a number of rulings on animals which include injury caused by an ox, injury caused to an ox or ass, and theft of an ox, sheep or ass (Exod 21:28–22:3). This section also deals with the killing of a thief caught breaking in. Further precedents concerning [[16]] damage or illegal appropriation of personal property including seduction of a virgin conclude the laws (Exod 22:4–16).

For all civil offences including assault, theft, damage to, or illegal appropriation of property, damages are payable by the offender to the injured party, which may be punitive (Exod 21:37ff.), the aim being to compensate the injured and deter further similar actions. Clearly, the four absolute demands of the criminal law are being differentiated from the provisions of the civil law: murder from assault, the body being treated as part of a man's personal property; man-theft from theft of property. Exceptionally, assault on parents as well as their repudiation carries the death penalty, while seduction of a virgin—in contrast to adultery (Lev 20:10; Deut 22:22)—results in damages. What situation has necessitated the compilation of the *Mishpatim* [['judgments']] and why do these four particular crimes head the list of precedents?

Canaan, of course, already possessed an established legal system long administered by the elders in the gate. Like other Canaanite practices, whether cultic or secular, this would have been taken over by the Hebrews on entry into the land, but made subject to any overriding principles of Hebrew law. Clearly, the Hebrew compiler of the *Mishpatim* [['judgments']] aims to place an absolute duty on the community to execute certain criminals for particular offences against persons, while at the same time to affirm that offences against property should be settled by payment of compensation to the injured party. Where it is unclear whether certain action results in a crime or tort, as in the case of injury leading to death (e.g., Exod 21:18f.), the compiler provides a ruling. In this way he imposes the mandatory demands of the four criminal laws (Exod 21:12, 15–17) on the administration of justice of his day.

Apart from the fact that the four criminal laws all concern offences against persons and not property, their inner connection would not be obvious were it not that the Decalogue also contains commandments on parents, murder and theft. Although *ganab* [['to steal']] in Exod

59. For this interpretation see H. C. Brichto, *The Problem of 'Curse' in the Hebrew Bible,* *JBL Monograph Series* 16, Philadelphia 1963, pp. 132ff.

20:15 carries no object, this must refer to the person of a fellow Israel-ite,[60] for as the context makes clear, the objectless commandments on murder and adultery, like that on theft, are all to be understood as committed against one's neighbour as specified in the commandment on false witness. This is even more obvious in the Deuteronomic ver-sion of the Decalogue where the four commandments are run together (Deut 5:17–20). Just as Exod 21:12 makes explicit what is meant by 'kill' in Exod 20:13, so Exod 21:16 does the same for 'steal' in [[17]] Exod 20:15. Further, interpreting *ganab* as man-theft explains the strange order of the commandments cited in Hos 4:2; third, ninth, sixth, eighth and seventh—two kinds of spoken crimes, two kinds of murder (Deut 24:7 calls the man-thief 'the stealer of life') and adultery (cp. Jer 7:9).

The *Mishpatim* [['judgments']] thus provide evidence that from ear-liest times the Hebrews imposed certain fundamental principles on the indigenous law which appear to derive from the Decalogue, namely that while certain offences against the person required the exaction of the death penalty by the community, injuries to property are a matter for the parties themselves to be settled by the payment of damages. This explains the otherwise curious phenomenon that unlike other cases of assault (Exod 21:18ff.), exceptionally assault on parents carries the death penalty (Exod 21:15), a far stiffer penalty than CH 195. It is then a mistake to describe the casuistic laws of the *Mishpatim* [['judg-ments']] as Canaanite in origin. Like the apodictic commands, they derive from the new situation in Canaan caused by the entry of the Hebrews into the land and reflect the distinctive principles of their law.

Once again it needs to be stressed that even if Exod 21:12, 15–17 do refer to three of the commandments of the Decalogue, the citing of some of the commandments does not prove the existence of the full collection of ten. Nonetheless, the sharp distinction which the *Mishpa-tim* [['judgments']] introduce between offences against persons and offences against property points to a particular theological concern which we have also seen reflected throughout the pre-exilic period in the laws on murder and adultery. Such a distinction also underlies Nathan's parable (2 Sam 12:1–14).[61]

The prophet describes how a rich man appropriates a poor man's one ewe lamb to feed a visitor. David is so incensed that he declares that the offender should be put to death like any common criminal.

60. A. Alt, "Das Verbot des Diebstahls im Dekalog," *Kleine Schriften zur Geschichte des Volkes Israel* i, Munich 1953, pp. 333–340.

61. Phillips, "The Interpretation of 2 Samuel XII 5–6," *VT* 16, 1966, pp. 242–244. Cp. Jackson, *Theft*, 144–8.

The rich man has, however, not committed a crime but the civil offence of theft of a sheep, for which damages are prescribed which even if punitive constitute an entirely inadequate remedy in view of both the callous nature of the rich man's action and his immense wealth. But when Nathan declares that David is the man, it is not to convict him of the civil offence of theft of property, but of the crime of adultery which carries the death penalty. David is only spared through the direct intervention of God.

Finally, I return to the tenth commandment, perhaps the least accepted part of my original thesis. While breach of the other commandments could have resulted in legal action, the injunction not to covet could not, for mental attitudes, however reprehensible, can only become the object of [[18]] legal concern once a move is made to implement them.[62] Many scholars have, of course, sought to establish that the verb *ḥamad* [['to covet']] carries with it not merely the idea of mental desire, but also the physical steps necessary to gratify it. This seems very unlikely and lacks etymological support both from Hebrew and cognate languages. Further there is clear evidence that to indicate change of possession, *ḥamad* must be followed by an additional verb of taking (Deut 7:25; Josh 7:21; Mic 2:2).[63] In any event the Deuteronomistic redactors by their use of the alternative *ʾawah* [['to desire']] in Deut 5:21b confirm that they understood *ḥamad* [['to covet']] in terms of desire alone.

There is general agreement that the commandment originally covered the house only. Therefore any explanation of its original purpose must take account of why the house should be so picked out. In my book, I argued that the concern of the commandment was not with the house as such, but with the status of elder which was automatically conferred on the owner of a house with the responsibility of taking part in the local community's affairs.[64] Principal among these was the administration of justice intended to be exercised by the heads of all houses.[65] Consequently, judicial matters could only have been properly administered so long as citizens remained free householders. In my view, it was the purpose of the original commandment to achieve this.

62. Jackson, "Liability for Mere Intention in Early Jewish Law," *HUCA* 42, 1971, pp. 197–207.

63. Exod 34:24 should not be considered an exception. The verse indicates that when the Israelites go up to worship at the central sanctuary, there will be no one left to desire their land because everyone else will have been expelled (Phillips, *AICL*, 149f.).

64. *Ibid.*, 151f.

65. E. W. Davies, *Prophecy and Ethics: Isaiah and the Ethical Traditions of Israel*, Sheffield 1981, pp. 92, 100ff.

In my book I argued that the original short apodictic commandment had contained a verb of taking. But with the change in the administration of justice from the elders to professional judges under
Jehoshaphat's reform (2 Chr 19:5),[66] confirmed by the Deuteronomic
law (Deut 16:18ff.), the commandment lost its purpose and was spiritualised by the insertion of the verb *ḥamad* [['to covet']]. While I still
maintain that the singling out of the house must be connected with the
status of elder which house ownership conferred, it now seems to me
more probable that when the Decalogue was originally set in its Sinai
narrative context in Exodus, the tenth commandment was already spiritualised, the verb *ḥamad* [['to covet']] being used. Clearly, soon after
the settlement the commandment would have lost its original purpose,
for in the changed [[19]] economic situation in Canaan dispossession of
property could take place legally. While sale of property followed by
purchase would not lead to any loss of status as an elder,[67] economic
pressures could result in an Israelite having to sell himself into slavery
for insolvency, so losing his legal status within the community (Exod
22:2b). Although Exod 21:2–4 specifically ensured that a Hebrew slave
could recover that status after six years slavery, the ceremony of making
slavery permanent (Exod 21:5–6) confirms that few felt able to take advantage of it. There was little point in exchanging security without freedom for freedom without security. Nonetheless, the ideal of a slaveless
property-owning society in which each family had a stake in the community's decisions remained valid and was preserved by the tenth commandment, which in effect became an early example of the laws on
humaneness and righteousness. This explains why Isaiah and Micah,
who presupposed that the administration of justice was in the hands of
professional judges (Isa 3:2; Mic 3:1–2, 9–11), continued to condemn
seizure of realty by the rich (Isa 5:8; Mic 2:2), though there is no need
to assume that illegal means were used.[68] It was part of that conduct
which was against God's will and could bring judgment on his people,

66. Albright, "The Judicial Reform of Jehoshaphat," in *Alexander Marx Jubilee Volume*,
ed. S. Lieberman, New York 1950, pp. 61–82; Knierim, "Exodus 18 und die Neuordnung
der Mosaischen Gerichtsbarkeit," *ZAW* 73, 1961, pp. 162ff.; Phillips, *AICL* 17ff.; Mayes,
Deuteronomy, 263ff.; Davies, *op. cit.*, 96f., who, however, on the strength of Ezra 10:8, 14 argues that professional judges acted alongside the local elders.

67. I cannot accept that realty could not be sold out of the family forever. Lev 25:23
is part of the idealised Jubilee law. Neither Isaiah nor Micah appeal to it, nor make any
mention of the Jubilee. There is no reason to assume that Ahab's request to purchase
Naboth's vineyard was in any sense improper (1 Kings 21). Naboth merely resorts to an
appeal to filial piety to get out of an awkward situation (H. Seebaas, "Der Fall Naboth in
1 Reg. XXI," *VT* 24, 1974, pp. 474–488).

68. Davies, *op. cit.*, 69.

for in effect it operated against the principles of natural justice. The spiritualisation of the commandment also accounts for its absence from the Deuteronomistic insertions in Hos 4:2 and Jer 7:9 which refer to specific crimes which could be prosecuted.[69] It remains then my view that the original tenth commandment concerned the person of the individual Israelite and not his property. It was with the Proto-Deuteronomists that the emphasis of the commandment changed as they added a further clause to include all other property which an Israelite might have acquired by agreement, purchase or gain, later expanded further by the Deuteronomistic insertion of field.[70]

As Greenberg sensed, I believe that there is then within the oldest legal traditions of the Old Testament clear indication of the rigid division of crime and tort based on whether the person or his property was the subject of the offence. It is this distinction which the compiler of the *Mishpatim* [['judgments']] integrates into local Canaanite legal practice, thus from the first differentiating Israel's legal collections from those of all other ancient Near Eastern [[20]] law. Can the origin of this distinction lie elsewhere than in the Decalogue?

In earliest times, the criminal law derived from the Decalogue would have been administered by the clan elders like any other ancient customary law (Lev 18:7ff.). During the settlement period it appears that there were officials appointed to maintain general oversight over and obedience to Hebrew law (Judg 10:1–5, 12:7–15; 1 Sam 7:16), though they may have exercised their authority over a much more limited area than previously thought.[71] This would have been a difficult period as the distinctive traditions of Hebrew law were imposed on the indigenous population. The *Mishpatim* [['judgments']] contain a collection of their authorised rulings. But with the advent of the monarchy, the ultimate responsibility for the administration of law passed to the king. It was his duty to uphold justice (Psalm 72; Isaiah 9, 11). Indeed I have argued that the original Book of the Covenant built around the *Mishpatim* [['judgments']], but before the Proto-Deuteronomistic revision, dates from the early days of the Davidic monarchy.[72] Throughout the pre-exilic period, legal power increasingly became centred in the monarchy as Jehoshaphat brought the administration of justice much more firmly under his authority and Hezekiah both reformed the law and attempted some centralisation of worship, which under Josiah was finally secured,

69. I would not now connect the final phrase of Hos 4:2 with Exod 22:1–2a (see Phillips, *AICL*, 152), but rather translate it 'and crime follows crime.'

70. See above, p. 9.

71. Mayes, *Israel in the Period of the Judges*, 65ff.

72. Phillips, *AICL*, 158ff., and in a review in *JTS* 27, 1976, pp. 425f.

together with a further reform of the law. But during this period, there is no indication of any attempt by the king to abolish the distinction between crime and tort based in my view on the Decalogue.

It therefore still seems most natural to accept Mendenhall's contention, though not his attempt to prove this from the Hittite suzerainty treaties, that the Decalogue created Israel as a peculiar people both in its religious and legal practice.[73] But these were not distinct parts of Israelite life, for, as well as the distinction between crime and tort based on injury to person or property, monolatry,[74] the absence of images[75] and black magic,[76] and the institution of the sabbath,[77] all derived from the Decalogue. Law through which her religion found its expression thus characterised Israel from Sinai to Babylon. It has characterised Judaism ever since.

73. See above, n. 2.
74. Phillips, *AICL*, 37ff.
75. *Ibid.*, 48ff.
76. *Ibid.*, 53ff.
77. *Ibid.*, 64ff.

Malediction and Benediction in Ancient Near Eastern Vassal-Treaties and the Old Testament

F. Charles Fensham

[1] With the rapid publication of new material from the Ancient Near East problems concerning various subjects are elucidated. Especially the admirable publications of the Ugaritic material are to be mentioned. In one of these publications under the able hand of J. Nougayrol a few fragments of treaties between a Hittite king and his vassals, are present.[1] These treaties are welcome additions to the few Near Eastern vassal-treaties at our disposal.[2] In the year 1958 two very important publications were made, one by D. J. Wiseman on the vassal-treaties of Esarhaddon and the other by A. Dupont-Sommer on vassal-treaties of the city Sefire in Aramaic.[3] With all this new material as well as the vassal-treaties of the Hittite kings discussed by Korošec in 1931,[4] but published earlier on,[5] we can move on much surer ground concerning this type of treaty. It is obvious from a comparison of these treaties that the form and even the language are closely related, which shows that

Reprinted with permission from *Zeitschrift für die Alttestamentliche Wissenschaft* 74 (1962) 1–9.

1. Cf. C. F.-A. Schäffer, *Le palais royal d'Ugarit*, IV. J. Nougayrol, *Textes Accadiens des archives sud*, 1956.

2. Cf. D. J. Wiseman, *The Vassal-treaties of Esarhaddon*, 1958, pp. 27–28 for a definition of a vassal-treaty.

3. D. J. Wiseman, *op. cit.*, and A. Dupont-Sommer, *Les inscriptions araméennes de Sfiré*, 1958 and cf. also F. Rosenthal, Notes on the Third Aramaic Inscription from Sefire-Sûjîn, *BASOR* 158, 1960, pp. 28ff.

4. Cf. V. Korošec, *Hethitische Staatsverträge*, 1931. This study of Korošec is still basic, cf. E. von Schuler, Hethitische Königserlässe als Quellen der Rechtsfindung und ihr Verhältnis zum kodifizierten Recht, *Festschrift für Johannes Friedrich*, 1959, p. 462 n. 2.

5. Cf. J. Friedrich, *Staatsverträge des Ḫatti-Reiches in hethitischer Sprache*, MVAG, 1926, pp. 1–48.

from Late Bronze into the Iron Age, from the second half of the Second Millennium to the first half of the First Millennium the form and language of Near Eastern and Old Testament vassal-treaties or covenants were, with a few minor differences, similar.[6]

[[2]] The similarity in form and contents between the Old Testament covenant and the vassal-treaties is fully discussed by G. Mendenhall in a few articles in Biblical Archaeologist which was later on published in a booklet.[7] The importance of this publication cannot be overestimated. Mendenhall was the first scholar who has discovered the parallelism between Old Testament covenant forms and the Hittite vassal-treaties. In his publication he gives a broad discussion of the background of these treaties and the similarities and differences between the various biblical and Hittite covenant forms and need not be repeated in this paper.[8] The following is, however, important for our discussion: He draws the attention to the interesting curses and blessing formula and points out that these phenomena place the covenant immediately under the sanction of the god or gods.[9] With an open eye for the Old Testament he draws a comparison between it and Deuteronomy 28. We are much obliged to Mendenhall for this comparison, because there is probably much more to it than one may expect. Mendenhall worked exclusively with the Hittite vassal-treaties. In the meantime the very interesting material from Ugarit turned up and the position becomes clearer. The purpose of this study is to investigate into the meaning and form of the malediction and benediction final clauses of Near Eastern vassal-treaties. We want to compare this with the same kind of material from the Old Testament in legal and prophetic writings.

The Final Clauses of Malediction and Benediction in Near Eastern Vassal-Treaties

Malediction

It is well known that in the Ancient Near East important written or engraved material was protected by short or extensive curse formula. E.g., the person who should try to nullify the judgments of the code of Ham-

6. Cf. Wiseman, op. cit., p. 28; Dupont-Sommer, op. cit., p. 75 against Mendenhall, Law and Covenant in Israel and the Ancient Near East, 1955, p. 30. For Sumerian and Babylonian oaths with treaties cf. S. A. B. Mercer, The Oath in Babylonian and Assyrian Literature, 1912, pp. 20–24.

7. Cf. Mendenhall, op. cit.

8. Ibid., pp. 26–31, 35ff.

9. Ibid., p. 34. Cf. Klaus Baltzer, Das Bundesformular, 1960, pp. 24–26 where a short, but important discussion is given of malediction and benediction. Baltzer emphasised the fact that these final clauses are closely connected with the lists of gods as witnesses. I am indebted to Prof. Georg Fohrer who has drawn my attention to this important book of Baltzer.

murapi or to erase the royal name, was frightened by a curse-formula.[10] This matter was regarded so important that Merikare in Egyptian Wisdom Literature instructs his son: "Do not [[3]] damage the monuments of another."[11] The same kind of curse was pronounced on the boundary-stones (*kudurru*) with lists of private property and rights.[12] The curses inscribed on tombs and sarcophages are well known.[13] In every case the gods are called on to inflict the punishment of the curse. We may, thus, expect a curse or malediction in vassal-treaties. In every instance, except the Old Testament, it is placed first, probably as a kind of deterrent against breach of treaty. The malediction is closely linked up with the whole idea of unfaithfulness or breach of promise concerning the stipulations of the treaty. The terminology used for breach of treaty is interesting. In the Hittite vassal-treaties we have various words and ideas to give expression to breach of promise. In the treaty between Muwatalliš and Alakšanduš the idea of 'breaking off' prevailed;[14] in the treaty between Muršiliš II and Duppi-Teššub we have the meaning 'not to honor';[15] in the treaty between Šuppiluliuma and Mattiwaza which was inscribed on a separate tablet, the idea 'not fulfilling' is present.[16] Of these words the idea 'breaking off' is very interesting. The Hittite word *šarra-* is used, which is well studied by Goetze.[17] His main conclusion is that *šarra-* means 'to break off parts from something' the result being that the affected thing is reduced in its value. J. Friedrich gives the meaning 'to divide', 'to make in halves'.[18] In the case of a treaty it may either mean the breaking off of certain stipulations of the treaty or breaking off the relation between the two parties. In every case the punishment of the gods of the oath is asked. In the Akkadian vassal-treaties between Muršiliš II and Niqmepa of Ugarit the term for the breach of promise is 'not to keep' (*lā inaṣār*[19]). This idea is almost identical with

10. G. R. Driver-J. Miles, *The Babylonian Laws* 1, 1952, p. 100.

11. Cf. A. Volten, *Zwei altägyptische politische Schriften*, 1945, p. 39.

12. Cf. Wiseman, *op. cit.*, p. 27.

13. E.g., the curses on Egyptian tombs are well known. For tomb robbery cf. Helck-Otto, *Kleines Wörterbuch der Ägyptologie*, 1956, pp. 131–132. Cf. the curse on the sarcophagus of Ahiram Th. C. Vriezen-J. H. Hospers, *Palestine Inscriptions*, 1951, p. 9 and for a translation Rosenthal, *Ancient Near Eastern Texts*, 1955, p. 504, from now on quoted as *ANET*. Cf. also for an extensive study of malediction and the violation of tombs André Parrot, *Malédictions et violations de tombes* 1939.

14. Cf. J. Friedrich, *Hethitisches Elementarbuch* 2, 1946, p. 19 for a transcribed text of this treaty.

15. Cf. A. Goetze in *ANET*, p. 205.

16. *Ibid.*, p. 206.

17. Cf. A. Goetze, *The Hittite Ritual of Tunnawi*, 1938, AOS, pp. 45ff.

18. Cf. J. Friedrich, *Die hethitischen Gesetze*, 1959, p. 131.

19. Cf. Nougayrol, *op. cit.*, p. 87.

that present in the Hittite treaty between Muršiliš and Duppi-Teššub, which points to a kind of common terminology used by Muršiliš for his vassal-treaties. In the vassal-treaties of Esarhaddon the terminology is much more complicated than in the [[4]] short straightforward Hittite treaties. In these treaties the idea of changing (*e-nu-u*), negligence (*e-gu-u*), transgression (*i-ḥa-tu-u*) or erasing (*i-pa-sa-si-e*)[20] is present. These words take care for much more than the simple positive or negative expressions in Hittite. If we add the more detailed stipulations from line 410 on,[21] the difference is immediately clear, but the basic idea is the same. In the vassal-treaty of Sefire in Aramaic the breach of promise is simply expressed by one idea, viz. 'to be utterly unfaithful' (*yšqr*).[22]

What is the position in the Old Testament? The first text we want to discuss is Deut 8:19. Almost the whole chapter elaborates on the benediction of Deut 8:1. But then in v. 19 in typical casuistic style the idea of forgetting God is present. In Hebrew we have the construction of the infinitive absolute which strengthens the verb *šākaḥ*. This verb has various shades of meaning in Hebrew and is used here in the sense of breach of promise because the head partner in the covenant has been forgotten. In spite of the fact that commentators in the past, did not interpret this chapter in light of a legal background,[23] we are certain that this should be the case. Mendenhall refers to the formula of Deuteronomy 28 as possibly related to the common Near Eastern curse and blessing idea.[24] In Deut 28:15 the term for breach of promise is *lōʾ šāmaᶜ* which is exactly the same as *šākaḥ*. The very same formula is found in Jer 11:3 where a curse is pronounced against a breach of covenant.[25] A very interesting parallel between the Old Testament and Hittite treaties we find in the word 'break' (*pārar*). This word is used with both parties, namely Yahweh or Israel as subject. E.g., in Jer 14:21 Jeremiah prayed the Lord not to break his covenant with his people. This is markedly foreign to the common legal conception, viz. that the major party of the covenant has no obligation whatsoever except a voluntary help in case the vassal is attacked by mutual enemies. It is, thus, impossible for the major party to break the treaty because he is not un-

20. Wiseman, *op. cit.*, p. 57.

21. *Ibid.*, p. 60.

22. Cf. Dupont-Sommer, *op. cit.*, 17, 36 '*toute infidélité du vassal Matiʾel*'. Cf. Hebrew stem *šqr* 'to deceive'.

23. Cf. S. R. Driver, *Deuteronomy*, 1902, *ad loc.*; G. E. Wright, *Deuteronomy* in *The Interpreters Bible* 2, *ad loc.*

24. Cf. Mendenhall, *op. cit.*, p. 34 and cf. also D. J. Wiseman, *op. cit.*, p. 26 n. 200.

25. For curse in the Old Testament cf. Sheldon H. Blank, The Curse, the Blasphemy, the Spell, the Oath, *HUCA* 23/1, pp. 73–83; J. Hempel in *BZAW* 81, 1961, pp. 30ff.

der any obligation. The view, that the major party, Yahweh may break the covenant, has probably developed out of certain religious trends. The fact that the covenant was still in operation was due to God's lovingkindness. The 〚5〛 people have broken it already, but through the love of God the covenant was not abolished. At any moment, however, the Lord may decide to break the covenant from his side which was already broken by the people. On the other hand strong emphasis is placed in the Old Testament on the break of covenant by Israel and Judah.[26] The stem *prr* is known from Akkadian *parāru* in the meaning 'to break';[27] from Ugaritic in the possible meaning 'break an agreement'.[28] It is possible that we have in this word some connection with the idea of *šarra-* in Hittite, although in Hittite the meaning of division or breaking in halves predominates. Important is the fact, however, that it is used for the breaking of a covenant. In taking our investigation above into account, we must not be surprised to find a difference in terminology between various vassal-treaties which were formed at different places, in different circumstances, at different times. In spite of this we have a remarkable parallel trend which may point to a common source of origin. In the Old Testament this breach of covenant is closely intertwined with the religious aspect, with the Lord and his highly developed ethical religion.[29]

The breach of treaty or covenant puts the real idea of malediction into effect. The style of this formula is the common style of Near Eastern casuistic jurisprudence, viz. the 'if'-clause with the punishment in the second part of the sentence. The pronouncement of this punishment is the malediction. In the Hittite vassal-treaties the idea of destruction is present.[30] In the treaty between Muršiliš and Niqmepa the Akkadian word *lu-ḫal-li-qu-šu* is used from the stem *ḫlq* in the sense 'disappear', 'vanish', 'perish' or stronger like 'obliterate' or 'destroy'.[31] The position in the vassal-treaty of Esarhaddon is somewhat different. If the treaty should be broken, the gods would bring calamities on the vassal in various ways, like deprivation of fatherhood and old age etc.

---

26. Cf. Deut 31:16, 20; Jer 11:10, 31:32.

27. Cf., e.g., in *ARM* II 94:26 and Bottéro et Finet, *Répertoire analytique des tomes I à V*, p. 241.

28. Cf. C. H. Gordon, *Ugaritic Manual*, 1955, p. 165. The text is unfortunately broken, but it is possible that *apr h( )* stands in an antithesis to *uṭn ndr*. Text 128:3, pp. 29–30.

29. This is fully developed and worked out by W. Eichrodt, *Theologie des Alten Testaments*, 1948, 1, pp. 232ff.

30. Cf. Goetze in *ANET*, pp. 205–206.

31. Cf. Nougayrol, *op. cit.*, p. 90 and *The Assyrian Dictionary*, 1956, pp. 36–40; F. Delitzsch, *Assyrische Lesestücke*, 1912, p. 162.

All the calamities are mentioned over scores of stipulations.[32] In the Sefire-treaty the same kind of punishment-clauses are inserted which point to material disadvantages of the infidel.[33] Interesting, however, is a ⟦6⟧ shorter malediction formula on the right side of the document. The punishment is here a turning over or upsetting of the house of the vassal, the changing from a lower to a higher state, probably meaning a reversion of social classes, and the fact that the name of the vassal shall not be continued.[34]

A few examples from the Old Testament may suffice: In Deut 8:19 strong emphasis of the infinitive absolute is used with the stem ʾābad. This verb is as close to the meaning of the Akkadian ḫalāqu as we may expect.[35] In Deut 8:19 the short formula is used, but in Deut 28:15ff. the longer form of punishment- and curse-clauses is inserted, sometimes directly parallel to the clauses of the treaties of Esarhaddon and Sefire. This longer form was also used and known in the time of the Hittites as is shown by the special curse and blessing tablet of Šuppiluliuma.[36] In some cases the Old Testament simply refers to calamities (rāʿôt) which shall overtake the Israelites, cf. Deut 31:21, Jer 11:11. Although the specific calamities are not mentioned, this type of phrase is stylistically related to the longer form of malediction. Out of this we may conclude that two forms of malediction were used in the Ancient Near East, even in the same treaty, namely a longer and shorter one. These two forms continued, as far as we may conclude from our sources, from the time of the Hittites to the time of Josiah.[37]

Benediction

With the malediction clause is in some cases used a clause of benediction.[38] This clause is encountered in all the Hittite vassal-treaties as well as the Akkadian texts of Ugarit. Traces of it are present in the vassal-treaties of Sefire. There is, however, no trace of it in the vassal-treaty of Esarhaddon. This may be explained by the rigid attitude of the Assyrians against their vassals or by the mutilated state of the tab-

32. Wiseman, *op. cit.*, pp. 59ff.

33. Dupont-Sommer, *op. cit.*, pp. 17–18.

34. *Ibid.*, pp. 87–88.

35. For the meaning of ʿābad cf. Köhler-Baumgartner, *Lexicon in vetus testament libros*, ad loc.

36. Goetze, *ANET*, pp. 205–206.

37. The idea of breach of covenant is very important in the writings of Qumrân. This is also accompanied by blessings for the obedient and curses for the infidel. Cf., e.g., *DSD* 2, pp. 1–18.

38. Curses and blessings were already used in the Old-Babylonian period. Cf. Mercer, *op. cit.*, p. 21.

lets. Where the benediction is used, it is couched in the casuistic style like the malediction-clauses.

The faithfulness of the vassal is expressed by a uniformity of vocabulary rather remarkable. The Hittite treaties of Muršiliš and Duppi-Teššub has the word 'honour' and the treaty of Šuppiluliuma and ⟦7⟧ Mattiwaza 'fulfill'.[39] In the Akkadian written treaty between Muršiliš and Niqmepa the word 'keep' or 'guard' is used from the stem *naṣāru*.[40] The very same word is also used in the fragment of the benediction of the treaty of Sefire, viz. *yṣrw* from the stem *nṣr*.[41]

In the Old Testament both in Deut 8:1 and 28:1 the stem *šāmar* is used with almost the same meaning as *nāṣar*. Very important in this case is Deut 33:9 where the blessing of Moses on Levites is mentioned and is said: 'For they observed (*šāmar*) thy word/and kept (*nāṣar*) thy covenant.' In this sentence the parallelity between the verbs *šāmar* and *nāṣar* is clear. The use of *nāṣar* with covenant is, however, very important in light of the same word in the Akkadian of Ugarit and the old Aramaic of Sefire. We have, thus, a very close parallel in vocabulary in this case between the various vassal-treaties and the Old Testament.

The benediction in the second clause is expressed in the following manner: In the Hittite vassal-treaties the idea of protection is present. In case of the treaty of Muršiliš and Duppi-Teššub a shorter clause is used which promises the protection of the gods of the oath over the vassal's person, his wife, his son, his grandson, his house and his country.[42] The tablet of Šuppiluliuma and Mattiwaza has a very important longer clause with everything mentioned in the short clause included, but then in the form of a wish prosperity is pronounced and also the idea of an everlasting kingdom for the vassal king.[43] The shorter clause is also present in the treaty between Muršiliš and Niqmepa where the stem *naṣāru* is used in the meaning 'to protect', exactly as in the Hittite treaties.[44]

In Deuteronomy 8 the blessings are enumerated almost in the same way as the malediction-clauses in longer form. In the first clause a broad formula is used, viz. 'that you may live and multiply, and go in and possess the land which the Lord swore to give to your fathers.'

---

39. Goetze, *ANET*, p. 206.

40. Nougayrol, *op. cit.*, p. 90.

41. Dupont-Sommer, *op. cit.*, pp. 87, 91.

42. Goetze, *op. cit.*, p. 206.

43. This reminds us of the idea of a kingdom ᶜad-ᶜôlām for Israelite and Jewish kings. Cf., e.g., 2 Sam 7:13, 16. For a study on ᶜôlām cf. E. Jenni, *Das Wort* ᶜôlām *im Alten Testament, ZAW* 65, 1953.

44. Nougayrol, *op. cit.*, p. 90.

This clause stands in close parallel to the Hittite clauses. In Deuteronomy 28 the same form is present and a long enumeration of benedictions in the same style as in Deuteronomy 8.

The Execution of the Punishment

This problem is only encountered at the malediction-clauses. On a breach of covenant punishment must follow. The curses of the gods ⟦8⟧ in the extrabiblical material is a deterrent, but not an actual punishment. some of the curses must come into effect somehow or else the treaty would have been of no value. In the extrabiblical treaties it is not mentioned how punishment is inflicted.[45] In the Old Testament two different views are present. The first is that the breach of covenant is directly punished by God as Supreme Judge of heaven and earth.[46] Numerous examples of this action of God are present, e.g., in Jeremiah 11 to call one instance to mind. The second view on the punishment of the breach of covenant is judgment by lawsuit. This material is fully discussed by Herbert Huffmon and need not be repeated here.[47] The former one, viz. direct punishment on the breach of covenant is probably the only one which could have been used by Near Eastern kings, because it seems strange that a king should have allowed a lawsuit to take place between him and his vassal. The Old Testament idea of a lawsuit may be picturesque language which is borrowed from common civil legal procedures.[48]

The Final Clauses of the Vassal-Treaties and Old Testament 'Heil-Unheil'

In this paragraph we just want to draw a few lines from our investigation to the common Old Testament view on '*Heil-Unheil*' ⟦'salvation/damnation'⟧.[49] The 'Heil-Unheil'-prophecies form the core of the prophetic message. The background or origin of these prophecies is a difficult Old Testament problem.[50] We are not going to give all the various views concerning it.[51] We are just referring to a few conclusions which might be

45. Mendenhall, *op. cit.*, p. 34.

46. Cf. G. Dossin, L'inscription de fondation de Iahdun-Lim roi de Mari, *Syria* 32, pp. 1–28 where Šamaš is called judge of heaven and earth.

47. Herbert B. Huffmon, The Covenant Lawsuit in the Prophets, *JBL* 78/4, 1959, pp. 285–295.

48. For the execution of law cf. É. Cuq, *Études sur le droit Babylonien, les lois Assyriennes et les lois Hittites*, 1929, pp. 353ff.

49. Hardly translatable into English. May be 'Salvation-Damnation'.

50. Cf., e.g., G. von Rad, *Theologie des Alten Testaments* 2, 1960, pp. 247ff.

51. Cf. H. Gressmann, *Der Messias*, 1929, pp. 77ff.

drawn from our study and which might throw some light on the problem. The close connection between the covenant and salvation or calamity, was emphasized by various scholars.[52] Our study brings us to the same conclusion. The idea of '*Heil-Unheil*' might go back to the final clauses of malediction and benediction in the vassal-treaties of the Ancient Near East. '*Heil*' or salvation or protection is promised to those who keep the covenant. Even the vivid description of a blissful time with numerous blessings, with an everlasting kingdom might go [[9]] back to the same clauses. But it is also true that later on other influences and material were incorporated. In spite of this, the basic background of the idea of salvation might be present in the vassal-treaties. The same is true of the idea of punishment or damnation. The '*Unheil*'-prophecies refer in many instances to a breach of covenant. Compare, e.g., Hos 4:1–3 where transgressions of the Ten Commandments are mentioned with Hos 4:5ff. where the punishment is pronounced.[53] It is clear from the Old Testament that the 'Day of the Lord' is a day of judgment, a day on which the Lord punishes everyone who transgressed against him (cf. Zeph 1:4f.).[54] It is also true that the punishment of the *yôm Yahweh* is not only directed against Israel, but also against their enemies. It is interesting to note that the promise to obliterate enemies is also part of the vassal-treaties as we hope to argue in another paper. The 'Day of the Lord' might thus be regarded as the day of the execution of punishment after the breach of covenant. The broken covenant and the calamities accompanying it, are vividly described by the prophets, especially Jeremiah and Ezekiel. The only solution for this broken covenant is the forming of a new covenant between God and his obedient remnant (cf. Jer 31:31; Ezek 34:25, 37:26).

The following summary can be given: There is a close connection in form between the Near Eastern vassal-treaties and the Old Testament covenant. In the Near Eastern treaties the breach of treaty is accompanied by maledictions and the obedience to the treaty by benedictions. Old Testament covenant-forms follow the same pattern and these forms might be the background of the whole idea of Old Testament salvation and damnation.

---

52. Cf. W. Eichrodt, *op.cit.*, pp. 232ff. and 240ff.; Th. C. Vriezen, *Hoofdlijnen der Theologie van het Oude Testament*, 1954, p. 64.

53. Cf. Huffmon, *op. cit.*, pp. 294–295.

54. Cf. on the Day of the Lord H. H. Rowley, *The Faith of Israel*, 1956, pp. 179ff. with extensive literature in the notes. Cf. also P. A. Verhoef, *Die Dag van die Here*, 1956 *passim*.

The Curses of Deuteronomy 27: Their Relationship to the Prohibitives

ELIZABETH BELLEFONTAINE

⟦49⟧ Recent studies in the field of OT law have concentrated almost exclusively upon one or other of the series of laws designated by Alt as apodictic.[1] The results of these studies suggest that the apodictic law category is not formally homogeneous and that Alt's original division of the pentateuchal laws into just two categories is an oversimplification. The present article reviews two major works dealing with two subgroups of Alt's apodictic laws and proceeds to an investigation of a third subgroup.

The first serious attack upon Alt's form-critical classification was undertaken by Erhard Gerstenberger.[2] Since Gerstenberger's thesis is generally well known, a detailed presentation need not be given here. Briefly, Gerstenberger confines Alt's term "apodictic" to the prohibitions and commands which refer to hypothetical future offenses and which lack all statement of a fixed legal consequence. These prohibitions and commands are described as non-conditional norms of everyday life, are usually formulated in the second person singular and appear mostly in negative form.[3] Their origin lies in the kinship ethos of the Semitic clans. Because of their predominately negative expression, Gerstenberger refers to them as "prohibitives." While the present

Reprinted with permission from *No Famine in the Land: Studies in Honor of J. L. McKenzie* (ed. J. W. Flanagan and A. W. Robinson; Missoula, Mont.: Scholars Press, 1975) 49–61.

1. A. Alt, "Die Ursprünge des israelitischen Rechts," *Kleine Schriften zur Geschichte des Volkes Israels* (3 vols.; München: C. H. Beck'sche, 1953; 1959) I, 278–332.

2. *Wesen und Herkunft des "apodiktischen Rechts"* (WMANT 20; Neukirchen-Vluyn: Neukirchener Verlag, 1965).

3. Some positively formulated passages are considered original although in context they may be prohibitive. These include commands to refrain from some action (Exod 23:7a),

writer does not accept all of Gerstenberger's conclusions, the term "prohibitive" will be used in this article with his definition.

Hermann Schulz accepted Gerstenberger's conclusions and proceeded to his own analysis of the biblical death laws characterized by the phrase *mōt yûmāt* [['to put to death']].[4] The death laws along with the prohibitives and the curses of Deuteronomy 27 had all been subsumed by Alt under the category of apodictic law. Schulz questioned Alt's designation and proposed that the death laws constitute a separate law form.[5]

Schulz begins by a study of the threefold prohibitive list in Exod 20:13–15 and finds a corresponding death law for each prohibitive: Exod 21:12; Lev 20:12 and Exod 21:16. The death sentence is imposed for crimes [[50]] forbidden by the prohibitives, and the prohibitives form the basic norms from which the death laws are derived. In each case the death law defines the corresponding prohibitive more precisely and brings it into the legal sphere. For example, the prohibitive, "You shall not kill" (Exod 20:13), is made legally more precise by the death law, "Whoever strikes a man so that he dies, shall be put to death" (Exod 21:12). Conversely, without reference to the prohibitive, the death law is not correctly understood.

An analysis of all the death laws reveals that each one is rooted in a corresponding prohibitive.[6] For some, the prohibitives have not been preserved, although without doubt they once existed and formed the basis for the existing laws.[7] These probable forms have been reconstructed by Schulz. In other cases the prohibitive has been assimilated to the death sentence so that the two now appear in a single statement.[8]

---

and those which extend or define more precisely a prohibitive (Lev 19:10; Deut 23:19–20), as well as positive commands which have no negative counterpart such as the observance of the Sabbath and the honoring of parents (Exod 20:8, 12; also Lev 19:32). Gerstenberger, *Apodiktischen Rechts*, 43–49.

4. H. Schulz, *Das Todesrecht im Alten Testament. Studien zur Rechtsform der Mot-Jumat-Sätze* (BZAW 114; Berlin: Töpelmann, 1969). In general, Schulz accepts throughout his work the conclusions of Gerstenberger.

5. He likewise rejects the proposal that the death laws are more accurately defined as casuistic law. The proposal was made by H. Gese, "Beobachtungen zum Stil alttestamentlicher Rechtssätze," *TLZ* 85 (1960) 147–50; R. Kilian, "Apodiktischen und Kasuistisches Recht im Licht ägyptischer Analogien," *BZ* 7 (1963) 185–202.

6. Lev 24:15b is an old death sentence with Exod 22:28a as its prohibitive basis. Exod 21:15 is related to 21:12 and is similarly rooted in Exod 20:13. Exod 22:18–20 is a death sentence list connected with the cult.

7. Exod 21:17; 21:20; 31:14a.

8. Lev 27:29; Exod 21:18.

Schulz points out that the prohibitive constitutes a norm for action but does not suffice for judging concrete cases. The death law was the initial legal formulation which brought the prohibitive into the sphere of law. Therefore, a special legal relationship exists between the death law and the prohibitive norm. Furthermore, there is a traditio-historical relationship since the death laws reflect an advanced stage of development which required a more exact definition of the criminal act and a determined legal consequence.

These connections are sustained in later texts. Schulz finds that the death laws of Leviticus 20 are based upon the corresponding prohibitives of Leviticus 18 and 19 and that they represent a later stage of development than the participial death laws of the Book of the Covenant. The participles have given way to relative clauses, and every fundamental element of the death law has been expanded. Yet the legal relationship between prohibitive and death sentence endures. New emphasis is placed upon the relationship by adding to the death law a declarative statement which contains in part the formulation of the parallel prohibitive.[9]

Schulz insists that despite the legal connection the death law is not merely a derivative of the prohibitive. The latter establishes a fundamental order of life for the community. When this order is violated a new law is needed by which the violation can be recognized and a penalty imposed.[10] The death law is to be understood as an independent legal statement with a unique structure and origin. The origin is determined by an analysis of Gen 26:6–11. The incident described is typical rather than historical and leads Schulz to conclude that the tribal community was the situation in life of the death law.[11]

A further significant point made by Schulz concerns the community and [[51]] its imposition of the death sentence. To deal with death law violations the assembly of the local community as a secular judgment community did not suffice. The community needed assurance of divine protection against possible disastrous effects released by the execution of a criminal. In cases concerning the death law it was necessary to convene the people as a cultic judicial community. Only such a sacred assembly could have jurisdiction over death law cases and be competent to pronounce the death penalty.[12]

Further details of Schulz's study of the death law need not be presented here. What is of significance are his conclusions that the death

9. Schulz, *Das Todesrecht*, 46–51.

10. In Gen 26:6–11 and Lev 24:20–23 the OT has preserved some accounts of how the death laws came to be formed.

11. Schulz, *Das Todesrecht*, 95–113.

12. Schulz, *Das Todesrecht*, 113–29.

law is a distinct law form within Israelite legal tradition, that it has a special legal relationship to the prohibitives, and that the application of the death law could be made only in a sacral setting.

Schulz's conclusions prompt us to ask similar questions of the curses of Deuteronomy 27. Is a relationship such as that between death laws and prohibitives peculiar to these forms, or does a similar relationship exist between other law forms, specifically between the curses of Deuteronomy 27 and certain prohibitives?[13] It is the proposal of this paper that such a relationship does exist; that each curse had at one time a corresponding prohibitive norm from which it was derived and which it was designed to protect and define. Since all the curses relate to crimes committed in secret, it is this aspect of any corresponding prohibitive which will be noted.

The curse list of Deut 27:15–26 is recognized as very ancient, dating from the earliest period of Israel's history.[14] The last verse, however, cannot be considered as part of the original list. It is not directed, like the preceding curses, towards a definite violation of the divine will but refers back to Deut 27:3 and speaks of "the words of this law" in general. Furthermore, it departs from the positive formulation used throughout the list ("cursed be he who . . . ") and expresses itself negatively ("cursed be who does not . . . "). The verse must be considered a later deuteronomic addition to the primitive list.[15]

The antiquity of the first curse is likewise questionable. In general the language reflects a late period.[16] The style of the verse differs from the usual curse formulation by the use of the relative construction instead of a participle after *ʾārûr*, "cursed be. . . . "[17] Therefore, despite attempts to reconstruct a simpler, original statement,[18] one hesitates

13. Another question, of course, which lies beyond the scope of this paper, is that of a possible relationship between the curses and the death laws. Schulz deals briefly with the question and concludes that they do not reveal any noticeable interdependence. Schulz, *Das Todesrecht*, 61–71; cf. 79–83.

14. G. von Rad (*Deuteronomy* [London: SCM, 1966] 167) describes the list as "the most ancient series of prohibitions preserved for us in the Old Testament." See also P. Buis, *Le Deutéronome* (VS: Ancien Testament, 4; Paris: Beauchesne, 1969) 371; H.-J. Kraus, *Worship in Israel* (Richmond: John Knox, 1966) 141–44. For opinions which date the curses in the deuteronomic period, see E. Sellin and G. Fohrer, *Introduction to the Old Testament* (Nashville; Abingdon, 1968) 143; Schulz, *Das Todesrecht*, 81.

15. Von Rad, *Deuteronomy*, 167.

16. J. Blenkinsopp, "Deuteronomy," *JBC* 6:65.

17. Von Rad, *Deuteronomy*, 168.

18. Alt considered the relative clause as a modification of an original participle and reconstructed the statement to read: "Cursed be he who sets up an image in secret." Alt, "Die Ursprünge," 314. P. Buis proposes: "Cursed be the one who makes an idol and places it in a hiding-place." P. Buis et J. LeClerq, *Le Deutéronome* (SB; Paris: Librairie Le-Coffre, 1963) 173–75.

to consider this verse as an element of the primitive list. It seems to have been composed later than the rest of the list and joined to it either before or after the list was placed in its present context. Nevertheless, the verse betrays the author's effort to compose a curse against idolatry in keeping with the viewpoint of the basic series, and so can be studied as an independent element of the ⟦52⟧ present list.

After excising the definitely late phrases in the middle of the text (v. 15) and the adjective "molten," there remains: "Cursed be the man who makes a graven image and sets it up in secret." The concluding phrase qualifies the first clause and brings it into harmony with the rest of the list. There is no prohibitive in the OT against the setting up of an image in secret. The general prohibition against images, however, is a basic tradition in Israel.[19] The prohibitive upon which the first clause of v. 15 is based is Exod 20:4: *lōᵓ taᶜᵃśeh-lᵉkā pesel* ⟦'You shall not make for yourself an idol'⟧. The correspondence is clear: *ᵓārûr hāᵓîš ᶜᵃšer yaᵓᵃśeh pesel* ⟦'Cursed is the man who makes an idol'⟧. To this first clause was added the qualifying statement regarding the secrecy of the deed. The result is an imprecation against anyone who would make an image and erect it secretly. A development of the prohibitive norm has taken place. The curse has taken up the prohibited deed, under a certain aspect, an aspect which could not be reached by the ordinary process of law, and has given it new form by means of the curse formulation. Further, by placing it under the special jurisdiction of the divinity, it has established for the prohibited deed an inescapable consequence to be determined and executed by the deity. In this way, the prohibitive norm has been made legal: it has been given the only legal character possible under the aspect of secret violation. That this character is of a sacral-legal nature is evident from the curse formula itself, from the ritual ceremony which the series describes and possibly also from its situation in life in the covenant renewal ceremony.[20]

The same relationship to a basic prohibitive norm can be demonstrated for most of the curses in the original list, and it can be argued for the others. Deut 27:16 invokes a malediction upon one who treats with contempt, that is, dishonors (*qlh*) his father or his mother. The OT has preserved no negative statement corresponding to this curse. There is, however, the positively formulated precept of Exod 20:12 commanding the honoring (*kbd*) of mother and father, as well as Lev 19:3 which employs the verb *yrᵓ* ⟦'reverence'⟧. There also exist the two

---

19. Cf. Exod 20:4, 23; 34:17; Lev 19:4; 26:1; Deut 4:15–18, 23, 25; 5:8.

20. On the question of the situation in life see Alt, "Die Ursprünge," 322–28; Krause, *Worship*, 145.

death laws of Exod 21:17 and Lev 20:9 directed against those who curse (*qll*) mother or father. Several scholars have argued for an original negative form of the parents command in the decalogue which would have read: "Do not curse (*qll*) your mother or your father."[21] Schulz in particular argues for the existence of such an original prohibitive which would have formed the basis for the existing death laws, for Lev 19:3a, and perhaps also for Exod 20:12. The latter would either have been derived from the negative precept or have existed along with it.[22]

While such a reconstruction provides a correlative basis for the death laws, it fails to do so for the curse employing, as it does, a different verb. [[53]] This holds true even if one accepts *qll* as meaning not only verbal repudiation but any expression of repudiation.[23] While the curse is understood as meaning the exact opposite of the decalogue command,[24] it could not have been derived directly from it.

More acceptable is the proposal of an original negative formulation employing the verb *qlh* and reading: "*lōʾ taqle ʾet-ʾābīka wᵉʾet-ʾimmeka*," "You shall not despise [treat with contempt, dishonor] your father or your mother."[25] The verb used here is broader in meaning than the more specific terms "curse" (Exod 21:17) and "strike" (Exod 21:15), and encompasses a wider range of actions relating to rejection of parental authority.[26] This original prohibition has not been preserved. Just as the positive command, "Honor your father and your mother," covers a broader sphere of action than the prohibitive against cursing and came to replace it, so too, it eventually displaced the negatively formulated precept against "dishonoring" parents. We may conclude, therefore, that a prohibitive correlative to the curse of Deut 27:16 originally existed and has been lost to the present text. The curse formula extends to all actions contrary to the original prohibitive and still covered by the positive precept of the decalogue when these are done in secret.

Deut 27:17 invokes a curse upon the man who removes his neighbor's landmark. The only prohibitive in the biblical legislation against the removal of a neighbor's landmark is found in Deut 19:14. Deut

21. Von Rad, *Deuteronomy*, 58; J. J. Stamm and M. E. Andrew, *The Ten Commandments in Recent Research* (SBT 2 2; London: SCM, 1967) 96.

22. Schulz, *Das Todesrecht*, 52–55.

23. As suggested by A. Phillips, *Ancient Israel's Criminal Law* (New York: Schocken, 1970) 80.

24. S. R. Driver, *Deuteronomy* (Edinburgh: T. and T. Clark, 1960) 301.

25. E. Nielsen, *The Ten Commandments in New Perspective* (London: SCM, 1968) 84, 89.

26. The legal-historical narrative of Deut 21:18–21 provides a typical illustration of such repudiation.

27:17 takes up this prohibitive and places the action under a curse. The correspondence is clear: Deut 27:17: *ʾarûr massîg gᵉbûl rēᶜēhû* ⟦'Cursed is he who moves his neighbor's boundary mark'⟧. Deut 19:14: *lōʾ tassîg gᵉbûl rēᶜᵃkā* ⟦'You shall not move your neighbor's boundary mark'⟧. There is no secrecy clause, but the deed is obviously one which would not be done openly. Judging by other references to the landmark in the biblical text,[27] such tampering remained a problem in Israel. The removal of the landmark, especially in the early period, was seen not merely as a civil offence. Since the land belonged to Yahweh and was only given in fief to the people, transfer of land was not permissible. This is the meaning of Lev 25:23 which reflects Israel's earliest attitude towards the land.[28] Removal of a landmark involved the appropriation of land granted by Yahweh to another as an inheritance; it meant violating Yahweh's proprietorship. Hence, action contrary to the prohibitive of Deut 19:14 brought the deed into the sacral sphere. The malediction of Deut 27:17 is rooted in this prohibitive and brings it into the sacral-legal sphere for the punishment of violators.

The curse of Deut 27:18 is directed against one who "misleads a blind man on the road." There is no direct parallel to the curse among the biblical prohibitives. The only precept regulating conduct toward the blind is the ⟦54⟧ second prohibition of Lev 19:14 forbidding the placing of a stumbling block before a blind man. The curse does not take up the forbidden deed as described. Nevertheless, while verbal parallelism is lacking, it is clear that the curse is similar in function and force to the prohibitive. Both the intent of the curse and the range of actions covered by it are inclusive of the action described in the prohibitive. To mislead a blind man would be to fail to lead him on a safe—and unobstructed—path and to deliberately direct him along an unsafe—perhaps obstructed—way. The curse of Deut 27:18 seems to have been phrased so as to take up not only the specific deed of Lev 19:14 but also all other similar acts of meanness against a blind man. The prohibitive, while being taken into the sacral-legal sphere, is expanded and interpreted in the broadest possible terms. Such a malediction would be necessary because the blind man would likely be unable to bear witness in court. Only the vengeance of God could reach the person who would take such unfair advantage of the handicapped.

The rights of other unfortunate members of society are safeguarded by the malediction of Deut 27:19: "Cursed be he who perverts

---

27. Prov 22:28; 23:10; Job 24:2; Hos 5:10.

28. Alt, "Die Ursprünge," 327–28; G. von Rad, "The Promised Land and Yahweh's Land in the Hexateuch," *The Problem of the Hexateuch and Other Essays* (Edinburgh: Oliver and Boyd, 1966) 85.

the justice due to the sojourner, the fatherless, and the widow." The curse is rooted in the prohibitive of Deut 24:17 where the verbal parallels are very close. The word order is the same, but the perversion of justice toward the widow is defined precisely as taking the widow's garment in pledge.[29] The prohibitive states: "You shall not pervert the justice due to the stranger, to the fatherless, or take a widow's garment in pledge." Originally the widow was probably simply named along with the stranger and the orphan, as in the curse formula, and the expansion into a separate prohibitive sentence was the result of a later need for more exact definition of the deed. This supposition is strengthened by the omission in the prohibitive of the conjunctive *waw* before *yātôm* (orphan) which appears as it does in the threefold series of Deut 27:19.

The linking of these three disinherited classes is a typical deuteronomic combination.[30] Yet the linking is not original with Deuteronomy since a similar grouping is found in the earlier tradition of Exod 22:20–23. The second verb of v. 20a is an addition. So too is the motivating clause of v. 20b, which is in the plural address and from which the plural has been transferred to v. 21.[31] By excising these additions two short, terse prohibitives remain: "You shall not wrong a stranger. You shall not afflict any widow or orphan." These prohibitives along with Exod 23:9 (cf. also Lev 19:33–34) are part of the same tradition which is expressed in more legal terms in Deut 24:17. It is this latter prohibitive, in its original shorter form, which is taken up by Deut 27:19 and recast in the form of a curse bearing the [55] consequence of divine vengeance.

The act of bestiality accursed by Deut 27:21 has a prohibitive correlative in Lev 18:23 and is placed under the sentence of death by Exod 22:18 and Lev 20:15. The verb used to describe the action is *škb* (to lie with) and designates sexual intercourse.[32] It is questionable, however, that the prohibitive of Lev 18:23 forms the basis for the curse. It belongs to a short, rather loosely unified list (Lev 18:18–23) dealing with unnatural sexual acts. It seems to have been composed expressly as an appendix to the preceding series of prohibitions on sexual relations within the family (Lev 18:7–17).[33] It bears the stamp of the priestly tradition and is more concerned with ritual cleanness than

29. Cf. Exod 22:26–27.

30. Deut 10:18 (the order is reversed); 14:29; 16:11, 14; 24:17, 19, 20, 21; 26:12, 13; 27:19. See also Jer 7:6; 22:3; Ps 94:6; 146:9; Mal 3:5; Ezek 22:7; Zech 7:10; Isa 1:17; 10:2; etc.

31. M. Noth, *Exodus* (London: SCM, 1962) 186; Gerstenberger, *Apodiktischen Rechts*, 82, note 1.

32. Cf. the list of laws with *škb* [['to lie with']] in Lev 20:11–13, 15–16, 18, 20.

33. K. Elliger ("Das Gesetze Leviticus 18," *ZAW* 67 [1955] 1–25) divides the lists thus: vv. 7–17a; vv. 1, 17b–23.

with the actual crime.[34] Bestiality was prohibited earlier than the time of the composition of this list, as is clear from the death law in the Book of the Covenant (Exod 22:18). In fact, the wording of the curse is more consonant with that of the death law than with the prohibitive of Lev 18:23.

The seriousness of this act seems to lie not merely in its unnaturalness but in its function as a cultic sexual practice. The three death laws of Exod 22:17–19 which include the death penalty for bestiality form a unit characterized by opposition to the service of gods other than Yahweh. The religious motivation behind the Israelite opposition to copulation with any kind of animal is clearer when considered in the light of the Hittite legislation on the topic. Hittite law forbids copulation with animals which are considered sacred—cows, dogs, swine—but allows it with mules and horses.[35] Neither the Assyrian law nor the Code of Hammurabi have anything to say on the matter which may suggest a tolerance of the practice. For the Israelites, the prohibition against bestiality must be understood as a protest against intercourse with animals as a cultic sexual act such as was practiced not only by the Hittites but also by the Canaanites for the purpose of promoting fertility by sympathetic magic.[36] These three death sentences of Exod 22:17–19 have as their cultic-legal principle the commandment to worship Yahweh alone. This must be seen as the prohibitive basis for the sacral-legal ritual invoking the vengeance of the deity upon one who copulates with any kind of beast. The curse of Deut 27:21 finds its prohibitive basis in Exod 20:2–3.

Deut 27:24 invokes a curse upon the man who slays his neighbor in secret. Without doubt such a man has violated the decalogue commandment: "Do not kill" (Exod 20:13). However, in describing the deeds, different verbs are employed. Whereas Exod 20:13 commands: *lōʾ tirṣāḥ* [['Do not murder']], the curse formula reads: *ʾārûr makkēh rēʿēhû* [['Cursed is he who strikes his neighbor']]. The participle *makkēh* [['strike']] also occurs in the death sentence of Exod 21:12. Schulz has [[56]] convincingly shown that this death law is based on the prohibitive of Exod 20:13, and that the participle of the death law more precisely defines the originally objectless prohibitive and brings it into the legal

---

34. Cf. the references to defilement (vv. 20b, 23a) and the appended defining clauses, "it is wickedness" (v. 17b), "it is an abomination" (vv. 22b), "it is perversion" (v. 23b). In v. 20 adultery is considered only as a ritual impurity. Cf. also vv. 19 and 23.

35. See Hittite Laws 187, 199 and 200 in *ANET* 196–97.

36. See G. R. Driver, *Canaanite Myths and Legends* (Edinburgh: T. and T. Clark, 1957) 107; J. Gray, *The Legacy of Canaan* (VTSup 7; 1965²) 81–82; H. Cazelles, *Études sur le Code d'Alliance* (Paris: Letouzey et Ané, 1946) 76.

sphere.[37] If this is so, then the curse formula must also be rooted in the prohibitive of Exod 20:13. The distinction drawn in Exod 21:12–14 between intentional and unintentional killing underlines the essential link between the death law and the prohibitive of the decalogue. It also portrays the attempt to deal within the legal sphere with all violations of the decalogue commandment. However, neither of these provisions obtain when the crime is committed in secret and the criminal is left without fear of the death penalty and without need to flee to a city of refuge. That such a criminal, though undetected, might not go un-punished is the purpose of the curse of Deut 27:24. The action forbid-den in Exod 20:13 is taken up by the curse and is more sharply defined by the specification that the crime is committed "against the neighbor" and "in secret." It also implies premeditation on the part of the killer. The imprecation of Deut 27:24 can, therefore, be viewed as the specific application of the more general prohibitive norm of the decalogue.

Deut 27:25 curses the man "who takes a bribe to slay an innocent person." It applies the prohibitive of Exod 23:8, "and you shall take no bribe" to a specific case: the successful hired assassin who has escaped suspicion. The incident is not simply a case of secret murder; that would be covered by v. 24. The acceptance of the bribe is the sole mo-tivation for the murderer's act for he holds no personal case against his victim.[38] Therefore he has no "right"—such as the law of vengeance might allow—to kill the designated person. In this view, the victim is "innocent." Thus, the weight of the curse rests upon the taking of the bribe for the purpose of assassination. The prohibitive foundation is not the prohibition against murder (Exod 20:13), but the prohibition against acceptance of bribes which leads to the violation of justice (Exod 23:8; cf. Deut 16:19).

The prohibitive foundations of the remaining three curses, Deut 27:20, 22 and 23, are not so clearly discernible. The incestuous behavior condemned by the curses is likewise forbidden by the prohibitions of Lev 18:8, 9 and 17, and is also linked with the death penalty in Lev 20:11, 17 and 14. Literal correspondence between the curses and the prohibitives is lacking. Whereas Lev 18:8, 9 and 17 use the phrase *ᶜerwôt . . . lōʾ tᵉgalleh* (you shall not uncover the nakedness of . . .), the curses are formulated *ʾārûr šōkeb ᶜim* (cursed be he who lies with. . .). The pro-hibitives belong to a series of sexual prohibitions (Lev 18:7–17) which are rooted in the earliest period of Israelite history but which are not

---

37. Schulz, *Das Todesrecht*, 7–16. Cf. Num 35:6 which has developed from Exod 20:13 + 21:12: " . . . that the manslayer who kills a person may flee there."

38. This meaning is clearly presented in the translation of the *NEB* which reads: "A curse upon him who takes a reward to kill a man with whom he has no feud."

now found in their original form.[39] The motivating clause attached to each prohibitive, as well as the [[57]] repetition of the prohibitive in vv. 7 and 15 and the definition of "sister" in v. 9, have been added secondarily to the prohibitives. The original complex consisted of a series of short, unqualified prohibitives: "You shall not uncover the nakedness of your mother. You shall not uncover the nakedness of your father's wife," and so forth.[40] While there is similarity of content with the curses, the lack of verbal correspondence suggests that we look elsewhere for the prohibitive basis of the curses.

In the series of death laws in Leviticus 20 we find a law which employs both the verb *škb* (lie with) and the expression "uncover the nakedness of": "The man who lies with his father's wife has uncovered his father's nakedness; both of them shall be put to death, their blood is upon them" (Lev 20:11). Lying with one's father's wife is deserving of the death penalty because one has violated the prohibitive, "You shall not uncover the nakedness of your father's wife; it is your father's nakedness" (Lev 18:8). The death law, while using the verb *škb* to express illicit sexual relations, has also incorporated the wording of the prohibitive and has used it to define the action for which the death penalty is imposed. In this way the crime of lying with one's father's wife receives precise legal definition as well as a determined legal consequence. The case is similar to the rest of the death laws in the series, Lev 20:11–21. While late revisions and expansions are evident, the predominant use throughout the list of the expressions "lie with" and "uncover the nakedness of" argues for an originally consistent unit which used these two expressions. We conclude, therefore, that the death laws of Leviticus 20 rest upon two sets of prohibitives: the preserved list in Leviticus 18 and another list, now lost, which employed the verb *škb* to express sexual intercourse. The lost list corresponded to the act mentioned in the principal clause of the death law, and was the crime for which the penalty was death.[41] We also accept that it is this ancient

39. Elliger, "Leviticus 18," 2.

40. R. Kilian, *Literarkritische und Formgeschichtliche Untersuchung des Heiligkeitsgesetzes* (BBB 19; Bonn: Peter Hanstein, 1963) 26–27.

41. This is against Schulz who finds the prohibitive foundation for the death laws of Leviticus 20 in the prohibitives of Leviticus 18. He claims that originally the prohibitives had a different form, possibly: "You shall not lie with your father's wife," etc. The transformation from the original to the present form resulted from the influence of the declarative statement appended to each sentence (e.g., "it is your father's nakedness," v. 8). Schulz's explanation presupposes a complex history: 1) an original primitive list which employed the term *škb* [['to lie with']]; 2) the subsequent addition of the declarative statement with the expression "it is the nakedness of"; 3) a still later stage in which the influence

list of prohibitives, corresponding in form and content, that formed the basis for the curses of Deut 27:20, 22, and 23.

Without doubt, the curse list of Deuteronomy 27 is rooted in the legal traditions of early Israel. Every act which is made the object of a curse is condemned in one way or another elsewhere in the biblical tradition. In all cases a prohibitive foundation can be demonstrated for the accursed deed.

A further confirmation of the original rooting of the curses in definite corresponding prohibitives is provided by the intent of the curse ritual itself. The curse ceremony as described in Deuteronomy 27 consists in the pronouncement of the curses by the Levites and the corresponding response of affirmation by the community. The purpose of the ceremony extends beyond the desire that every criminal may receive his due. It reflects [[58]] a genuine fear on the part of the community that one member may indeed commit a designated crime in secret and escape apprehension. In this event the whole community would be liable to the divine vengeance. Such a situation was the cause of Israel's defeat under Joshua because Achan had violated the prescriptions of the ban at Jericho (Joshua 7). Hence, in Deuteronomy 27 the imprecations uttered by the Levites, and totally assented to by the members of the assembly, were designed to invoke God's vengeance upon the guilty member alone and thereby to ensure the safety of the whole community.

The curse ritual as such does not necessarily promulgate new demands. The deeds mentioned were already known to the community as liable to the wrath of God. It was the possibility of their secret commission, of the criminal's eluding of justice and the consequent fearful results for the people, that prompted the community's solemn invocation of divine retribution upon the criminal. Each of these deeds, therefore, must have been previously prohibited and have been made the object of a curse only when the community was unable to punish the transgressor. However, insofar as the curses deal with the deeds under a new aspect—secrecy—they can be considered as new demands. Moreover, belief in the power of the curse to effect vindication would have had a

---

of the declarative statement caused the change from "You shall not lie with . . . " to "You shall not uncover the nakedness of. . . . " Schulz's argument is not convincing. His proposal would demand a long period of development and would militate against the antiquity of the present list. Moreover, in only three of the declarative sentences does the expression "uncover the nakedness of" appear (vv. 8, 10, 16). More often the reason given for the prohibitive is the proximity of consanguinity (vv. 7, 11, 12, 13, 14, 15; cf. 17b). It does not seem advisable, therefore, to suppose a more primitive list behind the core of prohibitives in Lev 18:7–17. See Schulz, *Das Todesrecht*, 46–51.

deterrent effect upon potential transgressors.[42] In the case of one who had already committed a crime and had escaped apprehension, participation in the liturgy would place him in the unenviable position of calling down divine judgment upon himself.[43]

It is the aspect of commission in secret that explains how a crime which is the object of a curse could be covered elsewhere by the death penalty (e.g., Deut 27:16, 20, 21, 23, 24). In the case of the death law, the crime is viewed as determinable and punishable within the judicial—albeit, the sacral-judicial—process. With regard to the curse, only the scrutiny of the deity could assure the execution of justice for secret crimes.

Despite its prohibitive basis, the curse, like the death law, is a unique law formulation within the legal history of Israel. The prohibitive, by its nature, is unconditional and does not envisage disobedience; hence, it has no adjoined legal consequence. In practice it is not operative within the legal sphere. The death law, as we have seen, makes its corresponding prohibitive legal by defining the act more precisely and by providing a definite legal penalty: death. In like manner, the curse brings into the legal sphere certain prohibitives whose violation in secret would escape the ordinary legal process. As previously noted, the "ordinary judicial process" with regard to the death law is the proceedings of the sacral-legal ⟦59⟧ community. But even this sacral judicial assembly cannot adjudicate hidden crimes. The community, as sacral assembly, must solemnly invoke the action of the deity in such cases. The curse provides the prohibitives with the only punishment which can reach secret sins: the inescapable consequence of the vengeance of God. In the curse the prohibitive norm under the aspect of secret violation is made legal.

We may conclude, therefore, that there exists a special legal relationship between the prohibitive and the curse. The action forbidden by the prohibitive is taken up by the curse, usually under a new or more specific aspect, refashioned in sacral-legal terms, and presented in a new law form.

The above study of the biblical legal traditions indicates the importance of this literature for understanding the total life of the ancient Israelite community. John L. McKenzie, of course, has long recognized this importance and has documented it in many of his writings. I am pleased to take up one suggestion made by him[44] and to offer him this paper as response.

42. H. Cunliffe-Jones, *Deuteronomy* (London: SCM, 1964) 151.

43. A. Phillips, *Deuteronomy* (The Cambridge Bible Commentary; Cambridge: University, 1973) 181.

44. In his review of Schulz's work (*CBQ* 32 [1970] 307–08), McKenzie suggests that the study could open up other areas of investigation to the reader.

The Covenant in the Land of Moab (Deuteronomy 28:69–30:20):

Historico-Literary, Comparative, and Formcritical Considerations

ALEXANDER ROFÉ

⟦310⟧ In choosing "The Covenant in the Land of Moab" as the subject of my address to the Louvain Colloquium, I wanted to pay a tribute to the Catholic scholars, whose contributions to the study of this pericope, and to the study of the Covenant-idea as well, have been paramount, and yet not always recognized as it deserved; I have in mind the names of Paul Karge (in spite of his apologetics), Hubert Junker, Paul Van Imschoot, D. J. McCarthy and Norbert Lohfink.

It is my opinion that the text of "The Covenant in the Land of Moab" begins in Deut 28:69 with the inscription "These are the Words of the Covenant which the Lord commanded Moses to make with the Israelites, in addition to the Covenant which He made with them at Horeb"[1] and the conclusion is to be found in Deut 30:20. Let me just recall a few points that substantiate this view: (a) The other covenant, the covenant at Horeb, is the one that starts in Deut 4:44 and goes on until 28:68; it consists of the Ten Commandments, *ᶜăśeret haddĕḇārīm*, which all the people heard at Horeb (5:2–4, 6–19), and the Precept,

Reprinted with permission from *Das Deuteronomium: Entstehung, Gestalt und Botschaft* (ed. Norbert Lohfink; Bibliotheca ephemeridum theologicarum lovaniensium 68; Louvain: Louvain University Press, 1985) 310–20.

1. To my knowledge, the first to have clearly stated this view was Don Yiṣḥāq Abravanel, in the introduction to his *Commentary on Deuteronomy* (Hebrew), reprinted: Jerusalem, 1964, p. vii.

hammiṣwāh, the Laws and the Judgements, *hahuqqīm wěhammišpāṭīm*, which Moses alone heard at Horeb and later reported to Israel (5:27–28; 6:1,4ff.).[2] This all extends as far as the end of Deuteronomy 26, and is then concluded by the Blessing and the Curse of Deuteronomy 28. (b) The reading of the Samaritan Pentateuch at 28:69, sustained by one Greek manuscript and the Ethiopic translation as well, "*And* these are the words of the Covenant etc.,*" *wě°elleh dibrēy habběrīt* . . . , favors with its diction the opinion that this verse is not the conclusion to what came before, but an inscription to what follows. (c) And dealing with introductory formulae, let us recall that the same form of inscription and then an opening running: "And Moses called all Israel saying to them" occurs in 4:44–5:1 and in 28:69–29:1. In both cases the inscription and the opening have been obliterated by the Massorah as well as by the Christian division into chapters. (d) Indeed, a covenant is made in our pericope. 29:8 runs: "Observe faithfully all the terms of this ⟦311⟧ covenant etc.," and vv. 11–12 run: "to enter into the covenant of the Lord your God etc." (e) And this covenant—I believe—ends with the end of ch. 30 where one finds, as usual in treaties and covenants, blessings and curses and witnesses to all. Yet, not everything in Deuteronomy 29–30 belongs to the Covenant of the Land of Moab; our task, in the first place, is to identify and detach the extraneous sections.

Let us start with Deut 30:1–10. I would describe this remarkable passage as a majestic fugue on the home of *šūb*. Seven times does this verb appear here (vv. 1, 2, 3, 3, 8, 9, 10), and with *šěbūt* (restoration) at v. 3 it makes eight. Different meanings are alternating each other: resolve in the heart (*wahăšēbōtā °el lěbābekā*), return to God, which is repent (*wěšābtā ⁽ad YHWH °ĕlōheykā*), the restoration of Israel by the Lord (*wěšāb YHWH °ĕlōheykā °et šěbūtěkā*) and the reversal of previous actions: *wěšāb wěqibbeṣkā*—God who scattered Israel reverses His action and gathers them; *wě°attāh tāšūb wěšāma⁽tā*—Israel who disobeyed God reverses to obedience.[3] God returns to delight in Israel (*yāšūb YHWH lāśūś ⁽āleykā*), Israel returns to the obedience of God (*kī tāšūb °el YHWH °ĕlōheykā*). All is change, inversion of the course of history and restoration

---

2. The last two verses of Deuteronomy 5, namely vv. 29–30 in Letteris edition, appear to be a late homiletic expansion: cf. A. Rofé, *Deuteronomy 5:28–6:1—Composition and Text in the Light of Deuteronomic Style and Three* Tefillin *from Qumran (4Q128,129, 137)*, in *Tarbiz* 51 (1981/2) 177–184 (Hebrew); reprinted in: *Introduction to Deuteronomy—Further Chapters*, Jerusalem, 1982.

3. This meaning of reversing an action, doing the opposite of before—as in 2 Kgs 24:11—was rightly recognized by Prof. Holladay in his dissertation 25 years ago; cf. W. L. Holladay, *The Root Šubh in the Old Testament*, Leiden, 1958, pp. 68–70.

of the happy past. The passage does not merely tell it; it expresses it with its special choice of words.

I will not try to tell how my forefathers, men of faith, who day per day expected redemption and the return to Sion, read this passage; what must they have felt every year when they chanted it from the Torah, during the days of repentance, on the eve of the New Year! What I can tell is the feeling of a great Jewish interpreter, Don Yiṣḥāq Abravanel, who knew very well, by personal experience, what uprooting, exile and dispersion meant. This is the comment of Abravanel:[4]

> This passage is still due to happen, because its promises were not yet fulfilled, neither in the first nor in the second Temple; this one is our consolation and hope, this is the overall healing to all our miseries.

Thus far, if we consider the meaning of the passage to its first audience of exiles and to further generations of later exiles. But what about the relation of this passage to its context? Here we have a problem. Indeed, Deut 29:27 speaks about uprooting and dispersion and Deut 30:1–10—about gathering and return, but the diction of this passage clearly demonstrates that it is not a following to Deuteronomy 29, but to Deuteronomy 28. First hints to this effect were already made by August Dillmann and Alfred Bertholet in their commentaries to Deuteronomy.[5] Here is some evidence: [[312]]

a. blessing and curse are not mentioned in ch. 29, which mentions only a curse, but in ch. 28 where we have blessings and curses;
b. "to obey the Lord" (30:2, 8, 10), literally "to hearken to the voice of the Lord"—it obtains in 28:1, 15, 45. As against it ch. 29 has a distinct expression: "whose heart turns aside from the Lord" (v. 17);
c. 30:3: "He will gather you from all the peoples where the Lord your God has scattered you there" corresponds to 28:64: "the Lord will scatter you in all the people." As against it 29:27 speaks differently about uprooting from the soil and throwing away to another land.
d. 30:9 "The Lord your God will grant you abundance in all your undertakings, in the issue of your womb, the offspring of your cattle, and the produce of your soil"—this catches on 28:11 which has a very similar diction.
e. Again in 30:9: "The Lord your God will return to delight in your well-being"—this corresponds to 28:63: "As the Lord delighted etc., so He will delight etc."

4. Cf. supra, note 1, ad locum.
5. A. Dillmann, *Numeri, Deuteronomium und Josua* (KEHAT[2]), Leipzig, 1886; A. Bertholet, *Deuteronomium, erklärt* (KHAT), Leipzig etc., 1899.

Only 30:7: "The Lord your God will inflict all those curses upon your enemies and foes who persecuted you"—connects with ch. 29, specifically with v. 20 which mentions the curse of the covenant (*ʾālōt habbĕrīt*). This, however, strengthens our case, because already August Dillmann, followed by Carl Steuernagel, Alfred Bertholet and George Adam Smith, in their commentaries a.1.,[6] noted that v. 7 interrupts the sequence between v. 6 and v. 8: "The Lord will circumcise your heart . . . and you will reverse and obey. . . . " I have no doubt that 30:7 should be considered a late interpolation into the passage.

Thus, in my opinion, it becomes evident that 30:1–10 are the continuation of ch. 28, or in other words this majestic fugue of repentance, restoration and return is the conclusion of the blessings and the curses. What is more: it is the conclusion of the great covenant of Horeb which constitutes the main body of the Book of Deuteronomy. This passage does not belong to the "Covenant of the Land of Moab"; it was transferred here by a scribe who wanted the consolation to follow all punishment, even the one mentioned in 29:21–27.

Turning now to ch. 29, we realize at once that the coherence of this chapter is even more troubled. Let us start with v. 13 where it is said that a covenant has been made and it includes those present as well as the absentees. The latter should not be understood as future generations, but as members of the community who, for some reason, did not participate in the ceremony.[7] Then, at v. 17, the possibility is mentioned that somebody is there, a single *ʾīš* [['man']] at first, whose heart turns away from the [[313]] Lord—such a person is defined as a poisonous root: *šōreš pōreh rōʾš wĕlaʿanāh*.

Now, this individual has some inner thoughts (v. 18: *bilbābō*—which proves all the more that he is a single person), and the thought is: "I will be safe, even though I follow my wilful heart" (*šālōm yihyeh lī kī bišrīrūt libbī ʾēlek*). Here comes a very difficult expression—*lĕmaʿan sĕp̄ōt hārāwāh ʾet haṣṣĕmēʾāh*—a real crux for interpreters! Its meaning should be construed in accordance with the next verses: at v. 19—"The Lord will not forgive him"; at v. 20:" The Lord will single him out." So, that individual expected to be forgiven and saved by the covering of the whole people, and this expectation was expressed with the words "*lĕmaʿan sĕp̄ōt hārāwāh ʾet haṣṣĕmēʾāh.*" Clearly we have here a simile, but what does it mean? I would suggest that *sĕp̄ōt* should be derived from *s.p.ʾ.*,[8] which appears in Ugaritic with the meaning 'to eat' and

---

6. Cf. supra, n. 5, and further: C. Steuernagel, *Das Deuteronomium, übersetzt und erklärt*[2] (GHAT), Göttingen, 1923; G. A. Smith, *The Book of Deuteronomy* (CB), Cambridge, 1918.

7. S. D. Luzzatto, *Il Deuteronomio*, Padova, 1876 (op. post.).

8. With a different interpretation this has been already conjectured by H. N. Tur-Sinai, in his *Pĕšūṭō šel Miqrāʾ*, Vol. 1, Jerusalem, 1962, a.1.

obtains in Biblical Hebrew as *mispō$^{\circ}$* = 'fodder' and in Rabbinic Hebrew as *s.p.y.* = 'feed'. We have a simile here from cases of drought and hunger: the sated, irrigated land will feed the thirsty, dry-land.[9] That individual expected to escape punishment hiding amidst the righteous community, but the Lord will not forgive him, the Lord will single him out and punish him.

Up to here, and down to v. 20, it is all about an individual; suddenly at v. 21 everything becomes plural and collective: all the land is devastated (21–23, 26) and the whole people is charged with idolatry (vv. 24–25), uprooted and thrown out to another country (v. 27). Then, abruptly again, at v. 28 the content of vv. 19–20 is resumed. "Concealed acts—i.e. the hidden sins of the individual—concern the Lord our God (meaning: the Lord will single out the sinner and punish him etc.), but with overt acts, it is for us and our children to apply all the provisions of this Torah." The connection of v. 28 with v. 20 was realized by the Talmud teachers (Sanhedrin 43b) who passed it over to all Jewish medieval commentators. It seems to me that Dillmann, who did not perceive it, led astray three following generations of critics.

Clearly, then, what comes in between, vv. 21–27 is interpolated. But for what purpose? Apparently a late scribe wanted to update the terms of a covenant of old. He needed to read the reality of his own times in the old scroll which he inherited from his forefathers.

It is interesting for the history of biblical research that this interpolation has been noted by rather conservative scholars only: Paul Kleinert, Hubert Junker and Norbert Lohfink.[10] Classical critics did [[314]] not recognize it, and the reason becomes clear reading in Steuernagel's commentary: they could not admit that individual retribution came first, and collective retribution was later interpolated. Indeed, the history of ideas of Ancient Israel was much more complex than it is sometimes assumed to be. In our particular case, it was not the theological interest in collective retribution that prompted the interpolator, but rather his desire to see the events of his own times foretold in his sacred scroll!

The situation just observed, that what we view as a patent interpolation was not recognized as such by the most audacious critics, stands to indicate on what unfirm, slippery ground we are stepping here.

---

9. The root *r.w.h.* about irrigating or irrigated land occurs in Isa 55:10; 58:11; Jer 31:11; Ps 65:11. For *s.m.$^{\circ}$* about dry land see Deut 8:5; Isa 35:7; Jer 48:18; Ezek 19:13; Ps 107:33.

10. P. Kleinert, *Das Deuteronomium und der Deuteronomiker*, Bielefeld und Leipzig, 1872, pp. 204–5; H. Junker, *Das Buch Deuteronomium*, in *Die Heilige Schrift in deutscher Übersetzung* (Echter Bibel), Band I, Würzburg 1955, p. 529; N. Lohfink, in *Der Bundesschluss im Land Moab. Redaktionsgeschichtliches zu Dt 28,69-32,47*, in *BZ* (N.F.) 6 (1962) 32–56.

Indeed, interpolations have been, and are being, detected in a rather cavalier, or arbitrary way, in order to make the text adhere to the critics' own preconceptions about its original form, contents an message. However, if one does not want this area of our discipline fall under utter discredit, he better try and lay down some rules about the legitimate detection of interpolations. To my mind, the presence of and interpolation, or secondary accretion, is made plausible only when three different types of evidence can be adduced: (a) a discrepancy (contradiction or fraction) in the textual sequence; (b) external signs, such as the resumptive repetition (*Wiederaufnahme*),[11] or a clear change of style; (c) a detectable intention on the side of the interpolator which can be shown to befit the purpose of late scribes. All three types of arguments can be summoned here: the break of sequence is patent, the interpolator's intention of justifying the Destruction and the Exile corresponds to similar editorial passages in 1 Kgs 9:6–9; Jer 22:8–9. As for the *Wiederaufnahme*—it is extant twice: the ending of v. 19a reoccurs at the end of v. 20 and of v. 26 (not 27!). This strange phenomenon will itself need some explanation.

Let us try to understand first the cause of the first resumption, at the end of v. 20. If it is true that a *Wiederaufnahme* may delimit a secondary insertion, then one should start by asking what could be the purpose of the alleged insertion of vv. 19b–20. One can indeed sense the difference of religious concepts vis-à-vis the preceding half verse (19a). While there one read about "the curse written in this book," here one finds an obvious restatement: "the curses of the covenant written in this book of Torah." What once was just a document, stating the terms of the covenant between the Lord and Israel, has become in v. 20 the ⟦315⟧ comprehensive book of Torah in which the covenant is included. Secondly, there is a shift in the character of the punishment: while in v. 19a it is the curse, as a semi-magical entity, that lies on, or cleaves to,[12] the sinner, in vv. 19b–20 the action is attributed to the Lord alone: He blots out the name of the sinner from under heaven, He singles the sinner out of all the tribes of Israel for misfortune. The interpolation appears to have rectified the notions of divine retribution. But the central point of the interpolation seems to lie in another

---

11. Cf. H. M. Wiener, *The Composition of Judges II,11 to I Kings II,46*, Leipzig, 1929, p. 2; C. Kuhl, *Die 'Wiederaufnahme'—ein literarkritisches Prinzip?*, in *ZAW* 64 (1952) 1–11; I. L. Seeligmann, *Hebräische Erzählung und biblische Geschichtsschreibung*, in *ThZ* (Basel) 18 (1962) 305–325, ad 314–324; S. Talmon-M. Fishbane, in *Tarbiz* 42 (1972/3) 27–41, esp. 35ff. (Hebrew).

12. Cf. LXX a.l. Its Hebrew Vorlage was extant at Qumran; cf. 1QS 2:12–17; CD 1:16–17 where Deut 29:18–20 is quoted. But read MT: the same gross image is used in Zech 5:3–4.

direction. Already at v. 17, in the words "or a woman, or a family, or a tribe," one can sense the tentative to bridge up the individual sin and punishment of vv. 17–19a, 28 with the collective ones of vv. 21–27. It goes to the credit of Nachmanides to have first related vv. 19–20 to the different subjects of v. 17:

> *The Lord's anger and passion rage against that man*—curse of the single, man or woman; *and the Lord blots out his name*—curse of the family, because every clan has a single name;[13] *and the Lord singles him out for misfortune*—to the tribe; *from all the tribes of Israel*—the rest of them.[14]

Thus, the passage enclosed by the *Wiederaufnahme*, vv. 19b–20, appears to be a secondary interpolation which tried to reconcile the original act of covenant with the first expansion in vv. 21–27. The lack of a clear discrepancy between vv. 19b–20 and the preceding verses finds its explanation in the special character of this insertion, i.e. its function as a harmonizing bridge between two contrasting passages.

To the history of the covenant concept it is relevant to determine when the main interpolation, that of vv. 1–27, was done. Two data can help in this matter: (a) Question and answer schemata of this kind seem to appear in Assyrian vassal treaties as early as the mid-eighth century, namely in the treaty of Aššurnirari the vi[th] with Mati'ilu of Bit-Aguši.[15] And one should recall here that between 841 and 738 at least three Israelite kings sent tribute to the Assyrian emperors: Jehu in 841, Joash around the year 800, and Menahem in the year 738. Thus, the question [[316]] and answer scheme about the desolation of the land, following a breach of treaty, may have entered Israelite history-writing as early as the beginning of the eighth century. (b) Yet, a better clue for its dating will be obtained by the inner analysis of the interpolated passage; let us take a look into it and see.

---

13. About the relation between name and family, cf. e.g. Deut 25:6; Ps 109:13.

14. Cf. Nachmanides' Hebrew Commentary in: *Miqrā'ōt Gĕdōlōt*, Wien, 1859. First hints were already made by Aben-Ezra (cf. *ibidem*). The point did not escape Dillmann (supra n. 5).

15. E. F. Weidner, *Der Staatsvertrag Aššurniraris vi von Assyrien mit Mati'ilu von Bit Aguši*, in *AfO* 8 (1932) 17–34; English Translation by E. Reiner, apud: J. B. Pritchard (ed.), *ANET*[3], Princeton, 1969, pp. 532–3. The first to note the relevance of this treaty for biblical studies was P. Karge in his monograph: *Geschichte des Bundesgedankens im Alten Testament* (Alttestament, Abhandl., 2). Münster i. W., 1910. The presence of the question and answer in that treaty was pointed out by Long and Weinfeld; cf. B. O. Long, *Two Question and Answer Schemata in the Prophets*, in *JBL* 90 (1971) 129–139; M. Weinfeld, *Deuteronomy and the Deuteronomic School*, Oxford, 1972.

One can easily realize that two punishments follow one another:[16] in vv. 21–26—the land; it is devastated by sulfur and salt, like Sodom, Gomorrah etc. If anything can be construed out of this description it is the impression of a nature-calamity—an earthquake, which at one recalls the earthquake of the times of Uzziah, in the mid-eighth century, which was mentioned, or hinted to, by Amos (5:11), Isaiah (5:25) and Deutero-Zechaviah (14:5). This section ends in v. 26 with a *Wiederaufnahme* of vv. 19a and 20: "all the curse written in this book"—a clear sign that the first interpolation did *not* include v. 27. As for v. 27, here only the people and its exile are mentioned. This verse must be considered, therefore, as a second expansion, aiming at introducing a mention of the exile into a text that did not contain it at first; this was certainly added after the destruction of Samaria in 722/1. That only a partial exile, not of the whole people, is contemplated is made clear by the harmonization at v. 17 "or a woman, or a family, or a tribe": the collectivity is still limited to a fraction of Israel; that only has gone into exile.

All in all, we have to reckon here with a fairly old act of covenant which was updated twice at least. By the eighth century the old act of covenant was already dated and needed to be revised. The original text of 29:15–28 only contained a warning to the individual not to try hiding himself behind the back of the community, as well as an injunction to the community to exterminate such an individual should his actions become known.

This latter point needs emphasizing, because of its importance to what will follow—the question of the original structure of our pericope. What is extant now in the second half of ch. 29 looks like one big curse of the covenant. Originally it was not; it was mainly one stipulation of the covenant: if an individual break the covenant and his act become known (*hanniglōt*), all the congregation is supposed to punish him. As usual, the expansion of the text has also affected its literary type.

Turning now to the structure of the vassal treaties of the Second Millennium, I have little to add to what was pointed out by Korošec, some 52 years ago,[17] namely that in many of these treaties—at that time only Hittite ones were known—one finds the following typical pattern: (a) inscription, (b) historical prologue, (c) a solemn declaration [[317]] of bond, (d) various stipulations, (e) witnesses (various gods and deified nature-elements, heaven and earth inclusive), (f) curse

16. As already noted by Lohfink (supra n. 10).

17. V. Korošec, *Hethitische Staatsverträge* (Leipziger Rechtswissenschaftliche Studien 60), Leipzig, 1931.

and blessing (short and nearly symmetrical).[18] Let me emphasize that Aramaic and Assyrian treaties of the First Millennium are quite dissimilar in their structure.

Since the early fifties, when Mendenhall first attempted to identify the structure of the Hittite Vassal treaties in the biblical covenant,[19] not a few tentatives have been made to draw out lines of correspondence between the two institutions. G. von Rad, D. J. McCarthy, K. Baltzer and others have tried to identify the treaty structure in the Covenant of the Land of Moab.[20] A. D. H. Mayes has recently contested this parallelism pointing out *inter alia* that "the only really essential element of such a ceremony (and so also of the form), the stipulations, is missing; furthermore, the chapter in fact fall into almost self-contained units."[21] Mayes is certainly right about the text in its present form. It is my contention, however, that once we identify the secondary passages, 29:21–27 and 30:1–10, the true character of our pericope and its correspondence to the Hittite vassal treaties come to light. Nearly all the elements of the Hittite treaties show here, and in the very same order: (a) the inscription—in 28:69; (b) the historical prologue—in 29:1–9; (c) the statement of bond—in 29:10–14, centering on v. 13: "to the effect that He establish you this day as His people and He be your God as He promised you"; stipulations—indeed, only one stipulation obtains here: the punishment of individual transgressors (29:15–19a, 28); I suspect that further paragraphs followed, but they were later transferred from here to the main body of Deuteronomy with the intention of forming a continuous book of law; (e & f) witnesses and concised curse and blessing—these show together at the end of our pericope (vv. 15–20); the deities heaven and earth have

---

18. E. F. Weidner, *Politische Dokumente aus Kleinasien* (Boghazkoei-Studien 8–9), Leipzig, 1923 (reprinted: Hildesheim-New York, 1970) 30–31, 50–51, 68–69, 74–75; J. Friedrich, *Staatsverträge des Hatti-Reiches in hethitischer Sprache* (MVAG 31), Leipzig, 1923, pp. 24–25; idem (MVAG 34), Leipzig, 1930, pp. 16–19, 80–83, 134–136; J. Nougayrol, *Le palais royal d'Ugarit* IV (MRS IX), Paris, 1956, pp. 84–101.

19. G. E. Mendenhall, *Covenant Forms in Israelite Tradition*, in *BA* 17 (1954) 50–76 = *The Biblical Archaeologist Reader*, Vol. 3, New York, 1970) 25–53. I hope the present article answers the stricture of E. Bickerman (*Couper une alliance*, in *Studies in Jewish and Christian History*, Part 1, Leiden, 1976, pp. 1–32) who maintains (ad p. 26) "qu'aucun texte de la *berith* hébreu n'est arrivé jusqu'à nous."

20. G. von Rad, *Deuteronomy, A Commentary* (English Translation), London, 1966; D. J. McCarthy, *Treaty and Covenant*[2] (AnBib, 21A), Rome, 1978; K. Baltzer, *The Covenant Formulary* (English Translation), Oxford, 1971.

21. A. D. H. Mayes, *Deuteronomy* (The New Century Bible Commentary), Grand Rapids, Michigan/London, 1981, a.1.

been transformed, as we could have expected, into passive nature-elements.

[318] Let us now attempt some conclusions from what we have seen. In the first place one can only express his satisfaction at the fact that the results of historico-literary criticism are confirmed by form-criticism applied to extra-biblical sources. To state it again: the structure of old treaties as analyzed by Korošec corresponds to that of the Covenant in the Land of Moab, *minus* those elements that our historico-literary criticism revealed to be interpolated, as 29:21–27, or just transposed from another context, as 30:1–10.[22] Both methods appear to sustain each other which seems to submit the essential validity of these two directions of research.

The Covenant in the Land of Moab, therefore, reflects an ancient pattern of covenant between the Lord and Israel. That is not to say that all its very text is old. Some elements might be so, especially the primary verses in 29:9–28. But otherwise it is very likely that original sections were substituted by more recent compositions. To be more explicit: the inscription itself—the present one befits the literary framework, namely the Deuteronomic fiction of Moses addressing Israel before their crossing over into the Land. But if it has become plausible that the origin of this pericope was in a ritual act-of-covenant between God and Israel in one of the Israelite sanctuaries of historical times, then the original inscription told us right about that and therefore it had to be substituted. The same about the historical prologue. The present one repeats the usual scheme of Deuteronomic history. A covenant act at one of the Israelite sanctuaries could have told a different history (let us recall the peculiar history told in Joshua 24!) and one that reached a later date for that. Therefore it could not survive its inclusion in the Fifth Book of Moses. The pattern, however, has been kept, along with some old elements.

How is one to account for the fact that the old structure of the treaties has been detected right here? The answer, in my opinion, lies at hand. Since the covenant was a central issue in the religion of Israel, it was reworked in the course of time again and again by generations of scribes. We cannot expect to find the old material and structure neither in Exodus 19–24, nor in Exodus 34, nor in Deuteronomy 5–28, and certainly not in the late Priestly Code. Just as old pieces of furniture are likely to be found in basements and attics, so the old treaty-pattern does not show in the main body of Deuteronomy, but appears

---

22. The passage 30:11–14 needs a detailed examination (cf. *infra*, n. 25). In any case its diction and contents make it clear that the passage is extraneous to its present context.

where one should expect to find it—in the appendix to Deuteronomy, ch. 29 and 30. The phenomenon is well known. The appendix to the Book of Joshua, in Judg 1:1–2:5, contains remnants of ancient pre-Deuteronomic accounts about the conquest. The appendix to the book of Samuel, in 2 Samuel 21–24, also preserves some ancient documents. The appendix to the Book of Judges, in Judges 17–21, was indeed compiled by a rather late redactor, but some of its [[319]] material, like the story of the idol of Micah, is relatively old. These appendices were the deposits of old, partially superseded, material.

Our conclusion is that the origins of the Covenant of the Land of Moab go back to an ancient ritual, moulded by the Israelites after the pattern of political vassal treaties of the Second Millennium. This conclusion runs against that of many distinguished scholars, in our times e.g. Lothar Perlitt and Rudolf Smend,[23] who maintain the late, seventh century or exilic origin of the covenant-concept. I would like, therefore, to add a few words of a more general character about the theological meaning of the covenant-idea and its historical framework.

From a theological point of view the covenant-concept does not fit in with the basic tenets of Deuteronomy. And the reason lies at hand. Deuteronomy is a monotheistic work; the covenant-concept is not necessarily monotheistic. In the same way as a vassal-king who accepts the treaty of a great king (*šarru rabû*) does not have to deny the mere existence of other great kings, but is only forbidden to serve them, so here: Israel, by committing himself in the covenant to serve the Lord alone, does not implicitly deny the existence of other gods. In other words, the covenant-idea is not inherently monotheistic, although there is no doubt that it can be also fitted into a monotheistic faith, as proved by both Judaism and Christianity.

This situation is confirmed by the examination of the covenant-formula. The original formula is similar to what we found in Deut 29:12: "You will be for Him a people and He will be for you a God." But the Deuteronomic authors were dissatisfied with this formula. They felt the need of modifying it according to their monotheistic creed, indeed—the need of expressing through it their monotheistic creed. Therefore they modified the usual formula as follows: "You will be to Him as people of treasure-trove (ʿam segullāh);[24] you will be supreme

23. R. Smend, *Die Bundesformel* (ThSt 68), Zürich, 1963; L. Perlitt, *Bundestheologie im Alten Testament* (WMANT 36), Neukirchen-Vluyn, 1969. Older critics were answered by P. Van Imschoot in his sober treatment: *L'alliance dans l'Ancien Testament*, in *Nouvelle Revue Théologique* 84 (1952) 785–805, and again in his book: *Théologie de l'Ancien Testament*, T. 1, Tournai, 1954.

24. M. Greenberg, *Hebrew* segulla: *Akkadian* sikiltu, in *JAOS* 71 (1951) 172–174.

above all peoples that He made (*ᶜelyon ᶜal kol haggōyīm ᵓăšer ᶜāśāh*); you will become a sacred people (*ᶜam qādōš*)"—which means: nearer to Him, consecrated like priests to His worship. These are the expressions of Deut 26:17–19, in the solemn conclusion of the main Deuteronomic covenant and lawbook; some of them re-occur in Exodus 19 and Deuteronomy 7 and 14. Thus it becomes clear, in my view, that for the Deuteronomic writers the proper way of describing the relation of Israel to the Lord is in terms expressing election, either directly by *b.ḥ.r.* or indirectly by *ᶜam śĕgullāh, ᶜam qādōš, ᶜam ᶜelyōn*, because with these terms the Lord's dominion over the whole world is reaffirmed. The term of covenant, which they inherited from [[320]] preceding writers, was for them inadequate; yet it was already so central a term in the religious conscience of Israel that it continued to express the solemn obligation of Israel to the Lord his God.

This, I believe, proves the relative antiquity of the covenant-concept (and covenant ritual) in Israel. A plausible conjecture is dating it to late pre-monarchical times. Much is to be said about this inherently non-monotheistic concept, nevertheless so important in shaping the faith of Israel. But this already belongs to a distinct paper.[25]

---

25. A more detailed version of this paper will appear in Hebrew in *Beer-Sheva*, Vol. 2 (= *Fs. Sh. Abramsky*), in preparation [[published as "The Covenant in the Land of Moab (Deut 28:69–30:20)," *Beer-Sheva: Studies by the Department of Bible and Ancient Near East*, vol. 2 (Shmuel Abramsky FS; Jerusalem: Magnes, 1985) 167–86 [Heb.]]]. For translation of biblical passages in the present essay I have generally followed the NJPS.

Part 4

The Central Core:
Deuteronomy 12–26

Some Postulates of Biblical Criminal Law

MOSHE GREENBERG

[[5]] Among the chief merits of Professor Kaufmann's work must be counted the tremendous impetus it has given to the study of the postulates of biblical thought. The debt that the present paper owes to this stimulus and to the lines of investigation laid down by Professor Kaufmann is patent; it is a privilege to have the occasion to offer it to him in grateful tribute.

I

The study of biblical law has been a stepchild of the historical-critical approach to the Bible. While the law had been a major preoccupation of ancient and medieval scholars, in modern times it has largely been replaced by, or made to serve, other interests. No longer studied for itself, it is now investigated for the reflexes it harbors of stages in Israel's social development, or it is analyzed by literary-historical criticism into strata, each synchronized with a given stage in the evolution of Hebrew religion and culture. The main interest is no longer in the law as an autonomous discipline, but in what the laws can yield the social or religious historian. It is a remarkable fact that the last comprehensive juristic treatment of biblical law was made over a century ago.[1]

The sociological and literary-historical approaches have, of course, yielded permanent insights, yet it cannot be said that they have exhausted all the laws have to tell about the life and thought of Israel.

Reprinted with permission from *Yehezkel Kaufmann Jubilee Volume* (ed. M. Haran; Jerusalem: Magnes, 1960) 5–28.

1. J. L. Saalschütz, *Das Mosaische Recht, mit Berücksichtigung des spätern Jüdischen*, 2 vols. (Berlin, 1848).

Too often they have been characterized by theorizing which ignores the realities of early law and society as we know them at first hand from the written records of the ancient Near East. Severities [[6]] in biblical law are alleged to reflect archaic notions that have no echo in either ancient civilized, or modern Bedouin law. Humane features are declared the product of urbanization, though they have no parallels in the urban codes of Mesopotamia. Inconsistencies have been discovered and arranged in patterns of historic evolution where a proper discrimination would have revealed that the laws in question dealt with altogether separate realms.

The corrective to these errors lies ready to hand. It is that considerable body of cuneiform law—especially the law collections[2]—which lends itself admirably to elucidate the meaning and background of the biblical law corpora. The detailed studies of these cuneiform collections, made chiefly by European scholars, furnish the student of the Bible with models of legal analysis, conducted without the prejudgments which frequently mar discussions of biblical law.

No clearer demonstration of the limits of literary-historical criticism can be found, for example, than that afforded by the studies made upon the laws of Hammurapi. Inconsistencies no less glaring than those which serve as the basis of analyzing strata in the Bible are found in this greatest corpus of Mesopotamian law. In this case, however, we know when, where, and by whom the laws were promulgated. We know, as we do not in the case of the Bible, that the code as we now have it was published as a whole, and intended—at the very least—as a statement of guiding legal principles for the realm of the king. When like discrepancies were pointed out in biblical laws it had been possible to defend stopping short with a literary-historical analysis by arguing that the discrepancies and inconsistencies [[7]] of the present text were not found in the original documents that went into it. Attempts to interpret the biblical laws as a coherent whole were regarded as naïve and unscholarly. It was not possible to argue this way in the case of Hammurapi's laws. The discrepancies were there from the beginning, and though, to be sure, they may well have originated in earlier collections, the fact remained that there they were, incorporated side by side in one law.

---

2. The following law collections are pertinent to the discussion of the criminal law of the Bible: the laws of Eshnunna (LE), from the first half of the 19th century B.C.; the code of Hammurapi (CH), from the beginning of the 18th century; the Middle Assyrian laws (MAL), 14th–11th centuries; and the Hittite laws (HL), latter half of the 2nd millennium. All are translated in J. B. Pritchard, ed., *Ancient Near Eastern Texts Relating to the Old Testament* (Princeton, 1955) 159ff. Henceforth this work will be referred to as *ANET*.

Two attitudes have been taken toward this problem in the code of Hammurapi. One, represented best by Paul Koschaker, is historical-critical. It aims at reconstructing the original laws which have gone into the present text and have caused the discrepancy; having attained this aim, its work is done. The other, represented by Sir John Miles, is that of the commentator, whose purpose is to attempt "to imagine how this section as it stands can have been interpreted by a Babylonian court."[3] The commentator is compelled in the interest of coherence to look for distinctions of a finer degree than those made by the literary historian. Such distinctions are not merely the recourse of a modern harmonist to escape the contradictions of the text; they are, it would seem, necessary for understanding how an ancient jurist, how the draftsman himself, understood the law.[4] It must be assumed that the laws of Hammurapi were intended as a consistent guide to judges, and had to be interpreted as they stand in as consistent a manner as possible.

The realization that careful discrimination between apparently contradictory laws is needed for this most carefully drafted ancient law corpus is highly pertinent for an understanding of biblical law. The literary-historical aim leads all too readily to a disregard of distinctions [8] in favor of establishing a pattern of development. Only by endeavoring to interpret the laws as they now stand does one guard himself against excessive zeal in finding discrepancies which involve totally different subjects rather than a historical development. Adopting the method of the commentator, then, we are thrown back much more directly upon the laws themselves. Recourse to literary-critical surgery is resisted until all efforts at making distinctions have failed.

Another virtue of the commentator is his insistence on understanding a given body of law in its own terms before leaping into comparisons with the other law systems. To do so, however, means to go beyond the individual rules; for it is not possible to comprehend the law of any culture without an awareness of its key concepts, its value judgments.[5] Yet much of the comparative work done in Israelite–Near Eastern law has been content with comparing individual laws rather than law systems or

3. G. R. Driver and J. C. Miles, *The Babylonian Laws*, 2 vols. (Oxford, 1952, 1955), henceforth cited as BL. The citation is from I, p. 99; cf. also p. 275, where Koschaker's approach is characterized and Miles' approach contrasted.

4. Contrast, e.g., the historical explanation of the discrepancies in the laws of theft given by Meek in *ANET*, p. 166, note 45 with Miles' suggestions in BL I, p. 80ff. The historical explanation does not help us understand how the draftsman of the laws of Hammurapi conceived of the law of theft.

5. The point is made and expertly illustrated in E. A. Hoebel, *The Law of Primitive Man* (Harvard, 1954); cf. especially chap. 1.

law ideologies. But until the values that the law embodies are understood, it is question whether any individual law can be properly appreciated, let alone profitably compared with another in a foreign system.

In the sequence I shall attempt to indicate some instances of the
gain accruing to the study of biblical law from the application of these
two considerations: the insistence, first, upon proper discriminations,
and second, upon viewing the law as an expression of underlying postulates or values of culture. The limitations of the sociological and
literary-historical approaches will emerge from the discussion. My remarks are confined to the criminal law, an area which lends itself well
to comparative treatment, and in which the values of a civilization
come into expression with unmatched clarity.

II

[[9]] Underlying the differing conceptions of certain crimes in biblical
and cuneiform law is a divergence, subtle though crucial, in the ideas
concerning the origin and sanction of the law.

In Mesopotamia the law was conceived of as the embodiment of
cosmic truths (*kīnātum*, sing. *kittum*). Not the originator, but the divine
custodian of justice was Shamash, "the magistrate of gods and men,
whose lot is justice and to whom truths have been granted for dispensation."[6] The Mesopotamian kind was called by the gods to establish
justice in his realm; to enable him to do so Shamash inspired him with
"truths."[7] In theory, then, the final source of the law, the ideal with
which the law had to conform was above the gods as well as men; in
this sense "the Mesopotamian king . . . was not the source of the law
but only its agent."[8]

6. Inscription of Yaḥdun-lim of Mari, *Syria* 32 (1955) 4, lines 1ff. I owe this reference
and its interpretation to Professor E. A. Speiser, whose critique of this part of my discussion has done much to clarify the matter in my mind; cf. his contribution to *Authority and
Law in the Ancient Orient* (*Supplement to the Journal of the American Oriental Society*, No. 17
[1954]), especially pp. 11ff.

7. Cf. CH xxvb 95ff.: "I am Hammurapi, the just king, to whom Shamash has granted
truths." We are to understand the laws of Hammurapi as an attempt to embody this cosmic ideal in laws and statutes. (After writing the above I received a communication from
Professor J. J. Finkelstein interpreting this passage as follows: "What the god 'gives' the
king is not 'laws' but the gift of the perception of *kittum*, by virtue of which the king, in
distinction from any other individual, becomes capable of promulgating laws that are in
accord or harmony with the cosmic principle of *kittum*").

8. Speiser, *op. cit.*, 12; this Mesopotamian conception of cosmic truth is a noteworthy
illustration of Professor Kaufmann's thesis that "Paganism conceives of morality not as an
expression of the supreme, free will of the deity, but as one of the forces of the transcendent, primordial realm which governs the deity as well" (תולדות האמונה הישראלית) [[*History
of the Religion of Israel*]], I/2, p. 345).

However, the actual authorship of the laws, the embodying of the cosmic ideal in statutes of the realm, is claimed by the king. Hammurapi repeatedly refers to his laws as "my words which I have inscribed on my monument"; they are his "precious" or "choice" words, [[10]] "the judgment . . . that I have judged (and) the decisions . . . which I have decided."[9] This claim is established by the name inscribed on the stele, and Hammurapi invokes curses upon the man who should presume to erase his name.[10] Similarly in the case of the laws of Lipit-Ishtar: Lipit-Ishtar has been called by the gods to establish justice in the land. The laws are his, the stele on which they are inscribed is called by his name. The epilogue curses him "who will damage my handiwork . . . who will erase its inscription, who will write his own name upon it."[11] While the ideal is cosmic and impersonal, and the gods manifest great concern for the establishment and enforcement of justice, the immediate sanction of the laws is by the authority of the king. Their formulation is his, and his too, as we shall presently see, is the final decision as to their applicability.

In accord with the royal origin of these laws is their purpose: "to establish justice," "that the strong might not oppress the weak," "to [[11]] give good government," "stable government," "to prosper the people," "abolish enmity and rebellion"[12]—in sum, those political benefits which the constitution of the United States epitomizes in the phrases, "to establish justice, ensure domestic tranquillity, promote the general welfare."

---

9. CH xxivb 76f., 81; xxvb 12f., 64ff., 78ff., 99; xxvib 3f., 19ff.

10. Ibid., xxvib 33f. It is not clear, in the face of this plain evidence, how it can still be maintained that the relief at the top of the law stele depicts Shamash dictating or giving the code to Hammurapi (E. Dhorme, *Les religions de Babylone et d'Assyrie* [Paris, 1949] 62; S. H. Hooke, *Babylonian and Assyrian Religion* [London, 1953] 29). The picture is nothing more than a traditional presentation scene in which a worshiper in an attitude of adoration stands before, or is led by another deity into, the presence of a god; it may be inferred from the context (i.e., the position of the picture above the code) that the figures of this highly conventionalized scene represent Hammurapi and Shamash. See the discussion in H. Frankfort, *The Art and Architecture of the Ancient Orient* (1954) 59 (note that Frankfort does not even go so far as Meek who sees in the scene "Hammurabi in the act of receiving the commission to write the law-book from . . . Shamash" [*ANET* 163]). For this and similar representations see J. B. Pritchard, *The Ancient near East in Pictures* (Princeton, 1954), nos. 514, 515, 529, 533, 535, 702. Miles aptly sums up the matter of authorship of the laws thus (BL 39): "Although [Shamash and Marduk] . . . are mentioned a number of times, they are not said to be the authors of the Laws; Hammurabi himself claims to have written them. Their general character, too, is completely secular, and in this respect they are strongly to be contrasted with the Hebrew laws; they are not a divine pronouncement nor in any sense a religious document."

11. Epilogue to the laws of Lipit-Ishtar, *ANET* 161.

12. See the prologue and epilogue of the laws of Lipit-Ishtar and Hammurapi.

In the biblical theory the idea of the transcendence of the law receives a more thoroughgoing expression. Here God is not merely the
custodian of justice or the dispenser of "truths" to man, he is the fountainhead of the law, the law is a statement of his will. The very formulation is God's; frequently laws are couched in the first person, and
they are always referred to as "words of God," never of man. Not only is
Moses denied any part in the formulation of the Pentateuchal laws, no
Israelite king is said to have authored a law code, nor is any king cen-
sured for so doing.[13] The only legislator the Bible knows of is God; the
only legislation is that mediated by a prophet (Moses and Ezekiel).
This conception accounts for the commingling in the law corpora of
religious and civil law, and—even more distinctively biblical—of legal
enactments and moral exhortations. The entire normative realm,
whether in law or morality, pertains to God alone. So far as the law
corpora are concerned there is no source of norm-fixing outside of
him. Conformably, the purpose of the laws is stated in somewhat
different terms in the Bible than in Babylonia. To be sure, observance
is a guarantee of well-being and prosperity (Exod 23:20ff.; Leviticus 26;
Deut 11:13ff., etc.), but it is more: it sanctifies (Exod 19:5; Leviticus 19)
and is accounted as righteousness (Deut 6:25). There is a distinctively
religious tone here, fundamentally different in quality from the political benefits guaranteed in the cuneiform law collections.

In the sphere of the criminal law, the effect of this divine authorship
of all law is to make crimes sins, a violation of the will of God. "He who
acts wilfully (against the law) whether he belongs to the native-born
⟦12⟧ or the aliens, is reviling the Lord" (Num 15:30). God is directly involved as legislator and sovereign; the offense does not flout a humanly
authored safeguard of cosmic truth but an explicit utterance of the
divine will. The way is thus prepared to regard offenses as absolute
wrongs, transcending the power of men to pardon or expunge. This
would seem to underlie the refusal of biblical law to admit of pardon or
mitigation of punishment in certain cases where cuneiform law allows it.
The laws of adultery and murder are cases in point. Among the Baby-
lonians, Assyrians, and Hittites the procedure in the case of adultery is
basically the same. It is left to the discretion of the husband to punish
his wife or pardon her. If he punishes his wife, her paramour also is
punished; if he pardons her, the paramour goes free too. The purpose
of the law is to defend the right of the husband and provide him with
redress for the wrong done to him. If the husband, however, is willing
to forego his right, and chooses to overlook the wrong done to him,

13. The point is made in Kaufmann, *op. cit.*, I/1, 67.

there is no need for redress. The pardon of the husband wipes out the crime.[14]

In biblical law it is otherwise: "If a man commits adultery with the wife of another man, both the adulterer and the adulteress must be put to death" (Lev 20:10; cf. Deut 22:22, 23)—in all events. There is no question of permitting the husband to mitigate or cancel the punishment. For adultery is not merely a wrong against the husband, it is a sin against God, an absolute wrong. To what extent this view prevailed may be seen in few extra-legal passages: Abimelech is providentially kept from violating Abraham's wife, Sarah, and thereby "sinning against God"—not a word is said about wronging Abraham (Gen 20:6). Joseph repels the advances of Potiphar's wife with the argument that such a breach of faith with his master would be a "sin against God" (39:8f.). The author of the ascription of Psalm 51—"A psalm of David, when Nathan the prophet [13] came to him after he had gone in to Bath-sheba"—finds it no difficulty that verse 4 says, "Against thee only have I sinned." To be sure the law also recognizes that adultery is a breach of faith with the husband (Num 5:12), yet the offense as such is absolute, against God. Punishment is not designed to redress an injured husband for violation of his rights; the offended party is God, whose injury to man can pardon or mitigate.

The right of pardon in capital cases which Near Eastern law gives to the king[15] is unknown to biblical law (the right of the king to grant asylum to homicides in extraordinary cases [cf. 2 Samuel 14] is not the same). Here would seem to be another indication of the literalness with which the doctrine of the divine authorship of the law was held in Israel. Only the author of the law has the power to waive it; in Mesopotamia he is the king, in Israel, no man.

III

Divergent underlying principles alone can account for the differences between Israelite and Near Eastern laws of homicide. The unexampled severity of biblical law on the subject has been considered primitive, archaic, or a reflex of Bedouin vendetta customs. But precisely the law of homicide cannot be accounted for on any such grounds.

In the earliest law collection, the Covenant Code of Exodus, it is laid down that murder is punishable by death (Exod 21:12ff.). If homicide is

14. CH 129; MAL 14–16; HL 198; cf. W. Kornfeld, "L'adultère dans l'orient antique," *Revue biblique* 57 (1950) 92ff.; E. Neufeld, *Ancient Hebrew Marriage Laws* (London, 1944) 172ff.

15. HL 187, 188, 198, 199; cf. LE 48.

committed by a beast—a goring ox is spoken of—the beast must be
stoned, and its flesh may not be eaten. If it was known to be vicious
and its owner was criminally negligent in failing to keep it in, the
owner is subject to death as well as the ox, though here the law allows
the owner to ransom himself with a sum fixed by the slain person's
family (vv. 28ff.). This is the sole degree of culpability in which the
early law allows a ransom. It is thus fully 〖14〗 in accord with a later
law of Numbers (35:31) which states, "You shall not take a ransom for
the life of a murderer who is guilty of death, but he shall be surely put
to death." A ransom may be accepted only for a homicide not committed personally and with intent to harm. For murder, however, there is
only the death penalty.

These provisions contrast sharply with the other Near Eastern laws
on homicide. Outside of the Bible, there is no parallel to the absolute
ban on composition between the murderer and the next of kin. All
Near Eastern law recognizes the right of the slain person's family to
agree to accept a settlement in lieu of the death of the slayer, Hittite
law going so far as to regulate this settlement minutely in terms of the
number of souls that must be surrendered as compensation.[16] Bedouin
law is no different: among the Bedouin of Sinai murder is compen-
sated for by a tariff reckoned in camels for any life destroyed.[17] The
Qurᵓan is equally tolerant of composition: "Believers," it reads (2:178),
"retaliation is decreed for you in bloodshed: a free man for a free man,
a slave for a slave, and a female for a female. He who is pardoned by
his aggrieved brother shall be prosecuted according to usage and shall
pay him a liberal fine."

In the Babylonian law of the goring ox, otherwise closely paralleling
that of the Bible, no punishment is prescribed for the ox.[18]

On both of these counts biblical law has been regarded as exhibit-
ing archaic features.[19] To speak in terms of legal lag and progress,
however, is to assume that the biblical and non-biblical laws are stages
in a single line of historical development, a line in which acceptance
〖15〗 of composition is the stage after strict talion. This is not only incapable of being demonstrated, the actual history of the biblical law of

16. HL 1–4.
17. A. Kennett, *Bedouin Justice* (Cambridge, 1925) 49ff.
18. LE 54; CH 250, 251.
19. Strict retaliation of life for life is "primitive," a "desert principle"; cf. Th. J. Meek,
Hebrew Origins (New York, 1936) 66, 68; A. Alt, *Die Ursprünge des israelitischen Rechts*, in *Kleine
Schriften zur Geschichte des Volkes Israel* (München, 1953) 305ff.; A Kennett, *op. cit.*, 49; on the
goring ox, cf. BL I, 444; M. Weber, *Ancient Judaism* (Glencoe, 1952) 62. For the widely held
theory of the development of punishment which underlies this view see BL I, 500.

homicide shows that it followed an altogether different principle of development from that governing Near Eastern law.

A precise and adequate formulation of the jural postulate underlying the biblical law of homicide is found in Gen 9:5f.: "For your lifeblood I shall require a reckoning; of every beast shall I require it. . . . Whoever sheds the blood of a man, by man shall his blood be shed; for in the image of God was man made." To be sure, this passage belongs to a stratum assigned to late times by current critical opinion; however that may be, the operation of the postulate is visible in the very earliest laws, as will be seen immediately. The meaning of the passage is clear enough: that man was made in the image of God—the exact significance of the words is not necessary to decide here—is expressive of the peculiar and supreme worth of man. Of all creatures, Genesis 1 relates, he alone possesses this attribute, bringing him into closer relation to God than all the rest and conferring upon him highest value. The first practical consequence of this supremacy is set forth in 9:3f.: man may eat beasts. The establishment of a value hierarchy of man over beast means that man may kill them—for good and sacrifice only (cf. Lev 17:4)—but they may not kill him. A beast that kills a man destroys the image of God and must give a reckoning for it. Now this is the law of the goring ox in Exodus: it must be stoned to death. The religious evaluation inherent in this law is further evidenced by the prohibition of eating the flesh of the stoned ox. The beast is laden with guilt and is therefore an object of horror.[20]

Babylonian law on the subject reflects no such theory as to the guilt the peculiar value of human life imposes on all who take ⟦16⟧ it. Babylonian law is concerned with safeguarding rights in property and making losses good. It therefore deals only with the liability of the owner of the ox to pay for damages caused by his ox. The ox is of no concern to the law since no liabilities attach to it. Indeed, one could reasonably argue that from the viewpoint of property rights the biblical law is unjust: is it not unduly hard on the ox owner to destroy his ox for its first offense? Ought he to suffer for an accident he could in no way have foreseen and for which he therefore cannot be held responsible?

This view of the uniqueness and supremacy of human life has yet another consequence. It places life beyond the reach of other values. The idea that life may be measured in terms of money or other property, and *a fortiori* the idea that persons may be evaluated as equivalences of other

---

20. The peculiarities that distinguish this biblical law from the Babylonian are set forth fully by A. van Selms, "The Goring Ox in Babylonian and Biblical Law," *Archiv Orientální* (18 (1950) 321ff., though he has strangely missed the true motive for stoning the ox and tabooing its flesh.

persons, is excluded. Compensation of any kind is ruled out. The guilt of the murderer is infinite because the murdered life is invaluable; the kinsmen of the slain man are not competent to say when he has been paid for. An absolute wrong has been committed, a sin against God which is not subject to human discussion. The effect of this view is, to be sure, paradoxical: because human life is invaluable, to take it entails the death penalty.[21] Yet the paradox must not blind us to the judgment of value that the law sought to embody.

The sense of the invaluableness of human life underlies the divergence of the biblical treatment of the homicide from that of the other law systems of the Near East. There the law allows and at times fixes a value on lives, and leaves it to the kinsmen of the slain to decide whether they will have revenge or receive compensation for their loss in money or property. Perhaps the baldest expression of the economic valuation of life occurs in those cases where punishment of a murderer takes the form of the surrender of other persons—a slave, a son, a wife, a brother—"instead of blood," or, [[17]] "to wash out the blood," or to "make good" the dead person, as the Assyrian phrases put it.[22] Equally expressive are the Hittite laws which prescribe that the killer has to "make amends" for the dead persons by "giving" persons in accord with the status of the slain and the degree of the homicide. The underlying motive in such forms of composition is the desire to make good the deficiency in the fighting or working strength of the community which has lost one of its members.[23] This seems to be the meaning of Hittite Law 43: "If a man customarily fords a river with his ox, another man pushes him aside, seizes the tail of the ox and crosses the river, but the river carries the owner of the ox away, they (i.e., the authorities of the respective village or town) shall receive that very man." The view of life as a replaceable economic value here reaches its ultimate expression. The moral guilt of the homicide is so far subordinated to the need of restoring the strength of the community that the culprit is not punished but incorporated;[24] this is the polar opposite of the biblical law which requires that not even the flesh of the stoned homicidal ox may be eaten.

21. From the comment of Sifre to Deut 19:13a it is clear that this paradox was already felt in antiquity.

22. Driver-Miles, *The Assyrian Laws* (Oxford, 1935) 35.

23. *Ibid.*, 36; Kennett, *op. cit.*, 26f., 54f.

24. This interpretation follows Goetze's translation (*ANET*, 191, cf. especially note 9). Since no specific punishment is mentioned, and in view of the recognition by Hittite law of the principle of replacing life by life (cf. HL 44) there does not seem to be any ground for assuming that any further punishment beyond forced incorporation into the injured community was contemplated (E. Neufeld, *The Hittite Laws* [London, 1951] 158).

That the divergence in law reflects a basic difference in judgments of value, rather than stages in a single line of evolution, would seem to be borne out by examining the reverse of the coin: the treatment of offenses against property. Both Assyrian and Babylonian law know of offenses against property that entail the death penalty. In Babylonia, breaking and entering, looting at a fire, night trespass—presumably for theft—and theft from another's possession are punished by death; Assyrian law punishes theft committed by a wife 〚18〛 against her husband with death.[25] In view of this, the leniency of biblical law in dealing with all types of property offenses is astonishing. No property offense is punishable with death. Breaking and entering, for which Babylonian law prescribes summary execution and hanging of the culprit at the breach, is punished in biblical law with double damages. If the housebreaking occurred at night the householder is privileged to slay the culprit caught in the act, though this is not prescribed as a punishment (Exod 22:1f.).[26]

This unparalleled leniency of biblical law in dealing with property offenses must be combined with its severity in the case of homicide, just as the leniency of non-biblical law in dealing with homicide must be taken in conjunction with its severity in dealing with property offenses. The significance of the laws then emerges with full clarity: in biblical law life and property are incommensurable; taking of life cannot be made up for by any amount of property, nor can any property offense be considered as amounting to the value of a life. Elsewhere the two are commensurable: a given amount of property can make up for life, and a grave enough offense against property 〚19〛 can necessitate forfeiting life. Not the archaicness of the biblical law of homicide relative to that of the cuneiform codes, nor the progressiveness of the

25. CH 21, 25; LE 13 (cf. A. Goetze, *The Laws of Eshnunna, Annual of the American Schools of Oriental Research* 31 [New Haven, 1956] 53); CH 6–10; MAL 3. Inasmuch as our present interest is in the theoretical postulates of the law systems under consideration, the widely held opinion that these penalties were not enforced in practice, while interesting in itself, is not relevant to our discussion.

26. The action of v. 1 occurs at night; cf. v. 2 and Job 24:16. V. 2 is to be rendered: "If it occurred after dawn, there is no bloodguilt for (killing) him; he must make payment only (and is not subject to death); if he can not, then he is to be sold for his theft" (but he is still not subject to death—contrast CH 8). For the correct interpretation see Rashi and U. Cassuto, *Commentary on Exodus* (Jerusalem, 1951), ad loc. (Hebrew); Cassuto points out (*ibid.*, 196) that this law is an amendment to the custom reflected in CH's laws of theft—a fact which is entirely obscured by the transposition of verses in the Chicago Bible and the Revised Standard Version. Later jurists doubtless correctly interpreted the householder's privilege as the result of a presumption against the burglar that he would not shrink from murder; the privilege, then, is subsumed under the right of self-defense (Mechilta, ad loc.).

biblical law of theft relative to that of Assyria and Babylonia, but a basic difference in the evaluation of life and property separates the one from the others. In the biblical law a religious evaluation; in non-biblical, an economic and political evaluation, predominates.

Now it is true that in terms of each viewpoint one can speak of a more or a less thoroughgoing application of principle, and, in that sense, of advanced or archaic conceptions. Thus the Hittite laws would appear to represent a more consistent adherence to the economic-political yardstick than the law of Babylonia and Assyria. Here the principle of maintaining the political-economic equilibrium is applied in such a way that even homicides (not to speak of property offenses) are punished exclusively in terms of replacement. It is of interest, therefore, to note that within the Hittite system there are traces of an evolution from earlier to later conceptions. The Old Kingdom edict of Telepinus still permits the kinsman of a slain man to choose between retaliation or composition, while the later law of the code seems to recognize only replacement or composition.[27] And a law of theft in the code (par. 23) records that an earlier capital punishment has been replaced by a pecuniary one.

In the same way it is legitimate to speak of the law of the Bible as archaic in comparison with postbiblical Jewish law. Here again the jural postulate of the biblical law of homicide reached its fullest expression only later: the invaluableness of life led to the virtual abolition of the death penalty. But what distinguishes this abolition from that just described in the Hittite laws, what shows it to be truly in accord with the peculiar inner reason of biblical law, is the fact that it was not accompanied by the institution of any sort of pecuniary compensation. The conditions that had to be [[20]] met before the death penalty could be inflicted were made so numerous, that is to say, the concern for the life of the accused became so exaggerated, that in effect it was impossible to inflict capital punishment.[28] Nowhere in the account of this process, however, is there a hint that it was ever contemplated to substitute a pecuniary for capital punishment. The same reverence for human life that led to the virtual abolition of the death penalty also forbade setting a value on the life of the slain man. (This reluctance either to execute the culprit or to commute his penalty created a dilemma which Jewish law cannot be said to have coped with successfully.)[29]

27. O. Gurney, *The Hittites* (London, 1952) 98.

28. Mishnah Sanhedrin 5.1ff., Gemara, ibid., 40b bottom; cf. Mishnah Makkoth 1.10.

29. To deal with practical exigencies it became necessary to invest the court with extraordinary powers which permitted suspension of all the elaborate safeguards that the law provided the accused; cf. J. Ginzberg, *Mishpatim Le-israel, A Study in Jewish Criminal Law* (Jerusalem, 1956), part I, chap. 2; part II, chap. 4.

Thus the divergences between the biblical and Near Eastern laws of homicide appear not as varying stages of progress or lag along a single line of evolution, but as reflections of differing underlying principles. Nor does the social-political explanation of the divergence seem to be adequate in view of the persistence of the peculiarities of biblical law throughout the monarchial, urbanized age of Israel on the one hand, and the survival of the ancient non-biblical viewpoint in later Bedouin and Arab law on the other.

IV

Another divergence in principle between biblical law and the non-biblical law of the ancient Near East is in the matter of vicarious punishment—the infliction of a penalty on the person of one other than the actual culprit. The principle of talion is carried out in cuneiform law to a degree which at times involves vicarious punishment. A creditor who has so maltreated the distrained son of his [[21]] debtor that he dies, must lose his own son.[30] If a man struck the pregnant daughter of another so that she miscarried and died, his own daughter must be put to death.[31] If through faulty construction a house collapses killing the householder's son, the son of the builder who built the house must be put to death.[32] A seducer must deliver his wife to the seduced girl's father for prostitution.[33] In another class are penalties which involve the substitution of a dependent for the offender—the Hittite laws compelling a slayer to deliver so many persons to the kinsmen of the slain, or prescribing that a man who has pushed another into a fire must give over his son; the Assyrian penalties substituting a son, brother, wife, or slave of the murderer "instead of blood."[34] Crime and punishment are here defined from the standpoint of the pater-familias: causing the death of a child is punished by the death of a child. At the same time the members of the family have no separate individuality vis-à-vis the head of the family. They are extensions of him and may be disposed of at his discretion. The person of the dependent has no independent footing.

As is well known, the biblical law of Deut 24:16 explicitly excludes this sort of vicarious punishment: "Parents shall not be put to death for children, nor children for parents; each shall be put to death for his

30. CH 116.
31. CH 209–210; cf. MAL 50.
32. CH 230.
33. MAL 55.
34. HL 1–4, 44; see also note 22 above.

own crime." The proper understanding of this requires, first, that it be recognized as a judicial provision, not a theological dictum. It deals with an entirely different realm than Deut 5:9 and Exod 20:5, which depict God as "holding children to account to the third and fourth generations for the sins of their parents."[35] This is clear from the verb יומת, "shall [[22]] be put to death," referring always to judicial execution and not to death at the hand of God.[36] To be sure, Jeremiah and Ezekiel transfer this judicial provision to the theological realm, the first promising that in the future, the second insisting that in the present, each man *die* for his own sin—but both change יומת [['shall be put to death']] to ימות [['shall die']] (Jer 31:29; Ezek 18:4 and passim).

The law is almost universally considered late. On the one hand, it is supposed to reflect in law the theological dictum of Ezekiel; on the other, the dissolution of the family and the "weakening of the old patriarchal position of the house father" that attended the urbanization of Israel during the monarchy.[37] This latter reasoning, at any rate, receives no support from the law of the other highly urbanized cultures of the ancient Near East. Babylonian, Assyrian, and Hittite civilization was surely no less urbanized than that of monarchial Israel, yet the notion of family cohesiveness and the subjection of dependents to the family head was not abated by this fact.

A late dating of the Deuteronomic provision is shown to be altogether unnecessary from the simple fact that the principle of individual culpability in precisely the form taken in Deut 24:16 is operative in the earliest law collection of the Bible. What appears as a general principle in Deuteronomy is applied to a case in the Covenant Code law of the goring ox: after detailing the law of an ox who has slain a man or a woman the last clause of the [[23]] law goes on to say that if the victims are a son or a daughter the same law applies (Exod 21:31). This clause, a long-standing puzzle for exegetes, has only recently been understood for what it is: a specific repudiation of vicarious punishment in the

35. Ibn Ezra in his commentary to Deut 24:16 already inveighs against the erroneous combination of the two dicta; the error has persisted through the centuries (cf., e.g., B. D. Eerdmans, *The Religion of Israel* [Leiden, 1947] 94).

36. Later jurists differed with regard to but one case והזר הקרב יומת [['if anyone else comes near, he shall be put to death']] (Num 1:51; 3:10; 18:7) according to Gemara Sanhedrin 84a (cf. Mishnah Sanhedrin 9.6); but the scholar to whom the Gemara ascribes the opinion that יומת here means by an act of God (R. Ishmael) is quoted in the Sifre to Num 18:7 as of the opinion that a judicial execution is intended (so Ibn Ezra at Num 1:51). The unanimous opinion of the rabbis that Exod 21:29 refers to death by an act of God (Mechilta) is a liberalizing exegesis; see the ground given in Gemara Sanhedrin 15b.

37. J. M. Powis Smith, *The Origin and History of Hebrew Law* (Chicago, 1931) 66; Weber, *op. cit.*, 66.

manner familiar from cuneiform law. There a builder who, through negligence, caused the death of a householder's son must deliver up his own son; here the negligent owner of a vicious ox who has caused the death of another's son or daughter must be dealt with in the same way as when he caused the death of a man or woman, to wit: the owner is to be punished, not his son or daughter.[38] This principle of individual culpability in fact governs all of biblical law. Nowhere does the criminal law of the Bible, in contrast to that of the rest of the Near East, punish secular offenses collectively or vicariously. Murder, negligent homicide, seduction, and so forth, are punished solely on the person of the actual culprit.

What heightens the significance of this departure is the fact that the Bible is not at all ignorant of collective or vicarious punishment. The narratives tell of the case of Achan who appropriated objects devoted to God from the booty of Jericho and buried them under his tent. The anger of God manifested itself in a defeat of Israel's army before Ai. When Achan was discovered, he and his entire household were put to death (Joshua 7). Again, the case of Saul's sons, who were put to death for their father's massacre of the Gibeonites in violation of an oath by YHWH (2 Samuel 21). Now these instances are not a matter of ordinary criminal law but touch the realm of the deity directly.[39] The misappropriation of a devoted object—חרם—infects the culprit and all who come into contact with him with the taboo status of the חרם (Deut 7:26; 13:16; cf. Josh 6:18). This is wholly analogous to the contagiousness of [[24]] the state of impurity, and a provision of the law of the impurity of a corpse is really the best commentary on the story of Achan's crime: "This is the law: when a man dies in a tent every one that comes into that tent, and every thing that is in the tent, shall be unclean" (Num 19:14). Achan's misappropriated objects—the story tells us four times in three verses (Josh 7:21, 22, 23)—were hidden in the ground under his tent. Therefore he, his family, his domestic animals, and his tent, had to be destroyed, since all incurred the חרם [['accursed', 'taboo']] status. This is not a case, then, of vicarious or collective punishment pure and simple but a case of collective contagion of a taboo status. Each of the inhabitants of Achan's tent incurred the חרם [['taboo']] status for which he was put to death, though, to be sure, the actual guilt of the misappropriation was Achan's alone.

38. Cassuto, commentary ad loc.; P. J. Verdam, "On ne fera point mourir les enfants pour les pères en droit biblique," *Revue internationale des droits de l'antiquité* 2/3 (1949) 393ff. (See postscript.)

39. Recognized by Verdam, *op. cit.*, 408, and already by S. R. Driver in his commentary to Deuteronomy (*ICC*, 1909) 277.

The execution of Saul's sons is a genuine case of vicarious punishment, though it too is altogether extraordinary. A national oath made in the name of God has been violated by a king. A drought interpreted as the wrath of God has struck at the whole nation. The injured party, the Gibeonites, demand life for life and expressly refuse to hear of composition. Since the offending king is dead, his children are delivered up.

These two cases—with Judg 21:10f. the only ones in which legitimate collective and vicarious punishments are recorded in the Bible[40] —show clearly in what area notions of family solidarity and collective guilt are still operative: the area of direct affronts to the majesty of God. Crimes committed against the property, the exclusive rights, or the name of God may be held against the whole family, indeed the whole community of the offender. A principle [[25]] which is rejected in the case of judicial punishment is yet recognized as operative in the divine realm. The same book of Deuteronomy that clears parents and children of each other's guilt still incorporates the dictim that God holds children to account for their parents' apostasy to the third and fourth generation (5:9). Moreover it is Deut 13:16 that relates the law of the חרם [['taboo']] of the apostate city, ordaining that every inhabitant be destroyed, including the cattle. For the final evidence of the concurrent validity of these divergent standards of judgment the law of the Molech worshiper may be adduced (Lev 20:1–5): a man who worships Molech is to be stoned by the people—he alone; but if the people overlook his sin, "Then I," says God, "will set my face against that man, and against his family. . . . " (See postscript.)

The belief in a dual standard of judgment persisted into latest times. Not only Deuteronomy itself, but the literature composed after it continues to exhibit belief in God's dooming children and children's children for the sins of the parents. The prophetess Huldah, who confirms the warnings of Deuteronomy, promises that punishment for the sins of Judah will be deferred until after the time of the righteous king Josiah (2 Kgs 22:19f.). Jeremiah, who is imbued with the ideology of Deuteronomy, and who is himself acutely aware of the imperfection of the standard of divine justice (31:28f.), yet announces to his personal enemies a doom that involves them and their children (Jer 11:22;

---

40. The massacre of the priestly clan at Nob (1 Sam 22:19) and the execution of Naboth's sons (2 Kgs 9:26) are not represented as lawful. Both cases involve treason, for which it appears to have been customary to execute the whole family of the offender. This custom, by no means confined to ancient Israel (cf. Jos. Antiq. 13.14.2), is not to be assumed to have had legal sanction, though it was so common that Amaziah's departure from it deserved to be singled out for praise (2 Kgs 14:6).

29:32). And both Jeremiah and the Deuteronomistic compiler of the Book of Kings ascribe the fall of Judah to the sins of Manasseh's age (Jer 15:4; 2 Kgs 23:26f.; 24:3f.). Even Job complains that God lets the children of the wicked live happy (21:7ff.). Thus there can be no question of an evolution during the biblical age from early to late concepts, from "holding children to account for the sins of parents" to "parents shall not be put to death for children, etc." There is rather a remarkable divergence between the way God may judge men and the way men must judge each other. The [[26]] divergence goes back to the earliest legal and narrative texts and persists through the latest.

How anomalous the biblical position is can be appreciated when set against its Near Eastern background. A telling expression of the parallel between human and divine conduct toward wrongdoing is the following Hittite soliloquy:

> Is the disposition of men and of the gods at all different? No! Even in this matter somewhat different? No! But their disposition is quite the same. When a servant stands before his master . . . [and serves him] . . . his master . . . is relaxed in spirit and is favorably inclined (?) to him. If, however, he (the servant) is ever dilatory (?) or is not observant (?), there is a different disposition towards him. And if ever a servant vexes his master, either they kill him, or [mutilate him]; or he (the master) calls him to account (and also) his wife, his sons, his brothers, his sisters, his relatives by marriage, and his family . . . And if ever he dies, he does not die alone, but his family is included with him. If then anyone vexes the feeling of a god, does the god punish him alone for it? Does he not punish his wife, his children, his descendents, his family, his slaves male and female, his cattle, his sheep, and his harvest for it, and remove him utterly?[41]

To this striking statement it need only be added that not alone between master and servant was the principle of vicarious punishment applied in Hittite and Near Eastern law, but, as we have seen, between parents and children and husbands and wives as well.

In contrast, the biblical view asserts a difference between the power of God, and that of man, over man. Biblical criminal law foregoes entirely the right to punish any but the actual culprit in all civil cases; so far as man is concerned all persons are individual, morally autonomous entities. In this too there is doubtless [[27]] to be seen the effect of the heightened stress on the unique worth of each life that the religious-legal postulate of man's being the image of God brought about. "All persons are mine, says the Lord, the person of the father as

41. Gurney, *op. cit.*, 70f.

well as that of the son; the person that sins, he shall die" (Ezek 18:4). By this assertion Ezekiel wished to make valid in the theological realm the individual autonomy that the law had acknowledged in the criminal realm centuries before. That God may impute responsibility and guilt to the whole circle of a man's family and descendants was a notion that biblical Israel shared with its neighbors. What was unique to Israel was its belief that this was exclusively the way of God; it was unlawful arrogation for man to exercise this divine prerogative.

The study of biblical law, then, with careful attention to its own inner postulates has as much to reveal about the values of Israelite culture as the study of Psalms and Prophets. For the appreciation of this vital aspect of the biblical world, the riches of cuneiform law offer a key that was unavailable to the two millennia of exegesis that preceded our time. The key is now available and the treasury yields a bountiful reward to those who use it.

POSTSCRIPT. To note 38: Professor I. L. Seeligmann calls my attention to the fact that this interpretation was earlier advanced by D. H. Müller, *Die Gesetze Hammurabis* (Wien, 1903) 166ff. A. B. Ehrlich's interpretation (in his *Randglossen,* ad loc.) taking בן [['son']] and בת [['daughter']] to mean "free man" and "free woman" in contrast with עבד [['servant']], אמה [['maidservant']] of v. 32 may now be set aside, ingenious as it is (though forced as well: the suggested parallels John 8:35 and Prov 17:2 [Seeligmann] deal with matters of inheritance and ownership where son [not "free man"!] and slave are apt contrasts; not so here. Note also the particle או [['or']] in Exod 21:31, indicating the verse to be an appendix to the foregoing, rather than connecting it with the new clause, v. 32, beginning with אם [['if']]).

[[28]] To p. 21. This interpretation of Lev 20:5, understanding the guilt of the family before God as due merely to their association with the Molech-worshiper, is open to question. The intent of the text may rather be to ascribe the people's failure to prosecute the culprit to his family's covering up for him; see Rashi and Ibn Ezra. In that case "his family" of 5a is taken up again in "all who go astray after him" of 5b, and the family is guilty on its own.

"Moses My Servant": The Deuteronomic Portrait of Moses

PATRICK D. MILLER

[[245]] No single figure so dominates the pages of the Old Testament as does Moses. Historical reconstructions of the actual role played by Moses in the origins of Israel vary considerably along a spectrum from those who see the biblical record as essentially accurate in ascribing a leading and formative place in Israel's history to Martin Noth's famous conclusion that Moses came into the story "because his grave site lay on the path of the Israelites who were occupying the land."[1] The portrait of Moses that is drawn in the Pentateuch is obviously the result of a complex stream of tradition, story, and legislation whose final shape is more readily discernible than the process by which it came into being. That final portrait, with all its complexities and, indeed, contradictions (even within the Book of Deuteronomy itself), testifies to the significance of the figure of Moses in the history of Israel's religion and stakes a claim for his continuing authoritative place in the religious faith of those communities that live by these Scriptures.[2]

[[246]] Within the Book of Deuteronomy Moses is not only the central figure but is virtually the only figure. Indeed the only persons who

Reprinted with permission from *Interpretation* 41 (1987) 245–55.

1. M. Noth, *A History of Pentateuchal Traditions*, trans. B. W. Anderson (Englewood, N.J.: Prentice Hall, 1972) 173.

2. One has only to note such chronologically extreme examples as the arrest of Stephen because he spoke "blasphemous words against Moses and God" and would "Change the customs which Moses delivered to us" (Acts 6:11, 14) and the more contemporary denominational conflicts over the issue of "Mosaic authorship," a matter of long-standing debate in part because of the significance of the figure of Moses and his authority.

speak in the book are Moses and God.[3] That very fact serves to lift up the role of Moses in Deuteronomy and thus in the tradition that builds upon it. The voice of Moses blends with the voice of God and in fact takes over frequently for God in speaking to the people. Moses is the leader of Israel, as the rehearsal of past events in chapters 1–3 reminds the reader. In Deuteronomy as a whole, however, the total focus is on Moses' role as the mediator of the divine word, the spokesman for God to the people. He has that function and distinction in a way that no other figure has. Indeed the people explicitly set him as the only one who can listen directly to God, and the Lord approves that special place for Moses (5:22–32).

The book begins by identifying all its words as "the words that Moses spoke to all Israel" (1:1) and two verses later makes clear that "Moses spoke to the people of Israel according to all that the Lord had given him in commandment to them" (1:3). Thus Moses' words are co-terminous with God's words; and the book introduces Moses, not as the hero or leader of the people in their wanderings as is very much the case in Exodus and Numbers, but solely as the bearer of the divine word, which is in Deuteronomy the *torah*, the law.

That is made clear in a *third* introductory verse (1:5), which serves to indicate to the reader that the identification of Moses as the transmitter or bearer of the divine law is not quite sufficient. According to verse 5 Moses did not simply speak the law, that is, repeat the words he had received from God (however the mode of reception); he "undertook to explain this law. . . . " In his communication of the word of God, Moses functions as *teacher*.

I

The reader who moves out from this introduction will be struck by the fact that a significant feature of the Deuteronomic profile of Moses is his teaching activity. While Moses is typically understood as law-giver—and Deuteronomy underscores that role—in this book the act of transmitting the law is a teaching task. The Lord *tells* or *speaks* all the commandments, the statutes, and the ordinances to Moses, who in turn *teaches* them (4:5, 14; 5:31; 6:1). Such language is not accidental. In chapter 5 where there is self-conscious identification of how the people will receive the divine words, the statutes and commandments

---

3. The significant role of the narrative voice in Deuteronomy and the Deuteronomistic History has been elaborated by Robert Polzin in *Moses and the Deuteronomist* (New York: Seabury Press, 1980).

of God, and the role that Moses is ⟦247⟧ to play, the Lord says: "Go and say to them, 'Return to your tents.' But you, stand here by me, and I will tell you all the commandments and the statutes and the ordinances which you shall *teach* them, that they may do them in the land which I give them to possess" (5:30–31). In 6:1, as Moses begins now to transmit the instruction of God, this understanding of his responsibility as a teaching one is reiterated.

Such a view of Moses' role as transmitter of the divine law is found nowhere else in the Pentateuch. He is everywhere seen as the mediator of the divine law, but Deuteronomy alone presents that activity as an act of instruction and teaching, spelling out the laws and statutes, explaining them as clearly as possible, interpreting what they mean for Israel. The unusual verb *be³er* that is usually translated in 1:5 as "explain" or "expound" occurs in 27:8 referring to Moses inscribing the law on the tablets of stone as clearly as possible that they may be easily perceived. It is that same sort of making clear for the sake of understanding that belongs to the teaching task as defined by Moses' activity. In distinction from a giving of the law that is mere promulgation that could be done by a spokesman, teaching the law means it "is to be explained and applied by Moses to the particular situation of the Israelites."[4]

Yet this teaching of the word of the Lord is not only the communication of information or explanation. It is a *teaching to do*. Result or purpose constructions regularly follow references to Moses' teaching, as in 5:31 "... the ordinances which you shall teach them *that they may do them in the land which I give them to possess*" (4:1, 5; 6:1; cf. 4:10; 31:12). That is why the book has such a hortatory character to it and why it has many more motivation clauses than any other body of biblical law. It is often described as preached law, but in the categories of the book itself and its depiction of Moses, it is described as more a precisely *"taught* law." The teaching that Moses does is in no sense the neutral communication of material, like a mechanical copier; it is an intense effort to elicit from his audience a response of obedience. Moses seeks at every turn to convey, explain, and also stir the heart to respond to the divine instruction, to follow the way that is set forth.

Yet another feature of the teaching of Moses is a concern for the passing on of the tradition to the next generations, who will not have seen the fire and heard the voice, nor experienced the Lord's provision and discipline along the journey, nor heard Moses' exposition of God's will. For that reason Moses insists that the teaching not end with his own activity but go on in persistent and intense fashion (4:9–10;

4. Peter Craigie, *The Book of Deuteronomy* (Grand Rapids: Eerdmans, 1976) 92.

6:7, 21–25; 31:3) both in the ⟦248⟧ family (6:7) and in the sacral gatherings of the whole community (31:13), so that each new generation may come to know and come to obey.

The future-oriented character of Moses' teaching is reflected in a special way in chapter 31 where he teaches the people a song, that is, the song that appears in Deuteronomy 32. This is not the law but a witness against the people for time to come. As they sing in the future the song that Moses has taught them, they will bear witness against themselves about their failure to keep the law of the Lord Moses taught them.

II

If there is any facet of Deuteronomy's portrait of Moses that stands out in a way comparable to his depiction as teacher of the law, it is the image of Moses as *prophet*. Elsewhere in the Pentateuch Moses is portrayed as the recipient of a prophetic call (Exodus 3–4) and the Book of Hosea testifies to the early understanding of Moses as a prophet, but Deuteronomy lifts this role to such a prominence that it becomes definitive for all the subsequent history of prophecy. Moses is both model for any future prophet (18:15, 18) and the greatest of all prophets (34:10–12).

To see Moses as the greatest of the prophets, however, is not to shift away from the perception of him as recipient and teacher of the divine law. Indeed the central characteristic that identifies Moses as the ideal prophet is his function as the mediator of the divine word. That is indicated explicitly by 18:18 as well as by the reference in verses 16–17 to chapter 5 where Moses was given the role of mediator by both the people and God. By depicting Moses primarily as such a spokesman, the whole Book of Deuteronomy implicitly underscores the identification of prophecy with the communication of the divine word that is commanded. This is consistent with the Deuteronomic emphasis on the priority of the Word of God as the vehicle of divine presence and rule. Moses is the prophet par excellence not only because of the great signs and wonders (see 13:1) that the Lord empowered him to do (so 34:10–12) but primarily because of his faithful speaking the word and will of God to the people. Indeed, as chapter 34 indicates, no other prophet like Moses has arisen, or been raised up by the Lord, if one uses the criterion of mighty deeds and signs and wonders as a basis for comparison. But one *can* expect that the Lord will raise up a prophet (or prophets) who, like Moses, will faithfully convey God's word to the people and in so doing represent God's rule in the new order that God is creating in and out of this people.

One of the issues that arises when one looks closely at Deut 18:15–22, where Moses is described as the prototype of prophecy and defines it for the future by his example, is whether Moses alludes in these [[249]] verses to a single, individual prophet whom God will call or raise up sometime in the future or to a line of prophetic figures such as is actually seen in the Old Testament. In light of both the history of prophecy at the time this book took shape as well as the inclusion of the law of the prophet in this charter for Israel's leaders, it is likely that the Deuteronomic law envisioned not one future prophet but prophets (plural) like judges, kings, and priests. The language "God will raise up for you a prophet like me" does suggest, however, that this was an occasional position of authority and not a regular continuing office, a figure raised up by the Lord when a new word needed to be spoken.

Chapter 18:15–22 does, however, seem still to stand in some tension with chapter 34:10. "The Lord *will raise up* for you a prophet like me" (18:15) contrasts rather sharply with "And *there has not arisen a prophet since* in Israel like Moses." The tension, as suggested above, is partly resolved by distinguishing between speaking the word commanded by the Lord (future prophets like Moses) and great signs and wonders (none like Moses). There is something else happening here, however. Chapter 34 was added to Deuteronomy after the formulation of the law of the prophet in chapter 18. When that took place, it served to elevate Moses' role not only as a spokesman of the Lord but also as wonder-worker, as prophetic mediator of the Lord's power, so that the absolute claim was made that no prophet like Moses has arisen since. Once that claim is made, to wit: *down to the present* (the time of the narrator) there has been no prophet like Moses, one can hardly see 18:15–22 simply in terms of a continuing line of prophets through Israel's history. The only way to resolve the contradiction or tension between chapters 18 and 34 is by projecting into the future the announcement that God will raise up a prophet, a projection that eventually happened in Judaism and Christianity (John 1:21, 25; 6:14; 7:40). That shift from many prophets to one prophet in the future is, therefore, created in some sense by the Book of Deuteronomy itself and by its understanding of Moses as the ideal prophet with whom all other prophets are to be compared but with whom no other prophet compares.

In some streams of tradition, the expectation is for the coming of a prophet like Moses; in some it is, like the anticipation of the coming of Elijah, an expectation of the return of Moses himself. It is not surprising that such a hope was associated with Jesus of Nazareth, either indirectly through John the Baptist (John 1:21) or directly as Jesus was seen as a new Moses (so the Gospel of Matthew) or as the prophet God had raised up (Acts 3:22–25). When Acts 3:22 is compared with Acts 3:26, one sees how Jesus is identified with the anticipated prophet both as having been "raised up" by God and as the Lord's servant (see below). The words of Deuteronomy [[250]] are now understood to have their fulfillment and reality beyond the history of Israelite prophecy in one who, like Moses, is the Lord's servant, proclaimer and indeed embodiment of the Word of God, and who was "raised up," not merely as prophetic spokesman but as the realization of God's delivering power to which the prophetic word continually attests, the inaugurator of that new order that is the Kingdom of God.[5]

The Deuteronomic portrait of Moses with its focus on him as primarily teacher and prophet, and that by virtue of his receiving and communicating the divine word—the commandments, statutes, and ordinances—to the people, is not without some bearing on the issue of Mosaic authorship, a matter that has come to be associated with the factual question of whether or not Moses was the historical author of all the material in the Pentateuch. It is, of course, highly unlikely that we have here an accurate historical report of words and actions by Moses on the plains of Moab before the settlement. The creation of the Book of Deuteronomy appears to have been a complex, prolonged process, most of which probably took place at a much later time. What was in the minds of the now unknown persons who over a period of time composed Deuteronomy can only be a matter of speculation. However, it is likely that the ascription and reception of this book as Mosaic was done in a most serious fashion and that the portrait of Moses as the teacher-prophet who alone received the divine word from the Lord and expounded it to the people served to enhance the seriousness with which the book would be received by the community.

Deuteronomy was meant to be—and was received as—instruction about God's way that was rooted in, grew out of, and was consonant with the covenant stipulations and the divine activity that created Israel as a people. While in many ways the traditions and statutes were updated, they were regarded as part and parcel of that primary foundational formulation of the relationship between God and Israel. One assumed that this instruction, which grew out of the Mosaic instruc-

5. For a helpful and extended discussion of the relation between Jesus as prophet and Jesus as Word of God, see Karl Barth, *Church Dogmatics* IV/3 (Edinburgh: T. & T. Clark, 1961) 38ff.; and for a brief presentation of some of the relationships between the Deuteronomic Moses and Jesus see Elizabeth Achtemeier, *Deuteronomy, Jeremiah* (Philadelphia: Fortress, 1978) 45–47.

tion, belonged with it, and fresh explication of the law of God in a new time did not mean that it is new law. Rather it was a part of the whole and properly carried the authority of Moses. The introductory verses of the book, reinforced constantly by the rest of the chapters, say in effect to readers of any time: Read these words as the Lord's instruction taught and explained by the prophet Moses, and you will know what force and authority they are to have.[6]

III

[[251]] While the picture of Moses as prophet is not peculiar to Deuteronomy and even there rests explicitly on only two texts (chaps. 18 and 34), it is in some respects the most comprehensive way of characterizing the Deuteronomic portrait. We have already seen that those characteristics that identify him as prophet are also those that belong to his role as transmitter/teacher of the law (one who speaks to the people all that the Lord commands). The two other prominent features of the "Mosaic" portrait are also consonant with the prophetic experience and understanding as we see it elsewhere: *intercessor* and *suffering servant of God.*

Moses' intercessory activity in behalf of the people is described in 9:7–29 and 10:10–11, a reflex of Exodus 32–34 and some of the stories in Numbers. It is also recalled in a general fashion by Jeremiah (15:1) and Psalm 90, which is the one psalm ascribed to Moses, presumably because of its petitions on behalf of the people.[7] The intercessions of

6. The following remarks by Hartmut Gese are instructive for thinking about the place of Moses as the transmitter and teacher of the law:

> Once we recognize that the events of tradition history took place in living settings, we will conclude that we can identify those areas of life that correspond to the areas of tradition. We can, for example, connect the priestly teaching of Torah or law with the priestly realm of tradition, and so forth. The strands of tradition which were formed in this manner often reveal specific concepts of authorship. In complete contrast to our concept of authorship, the traditional material is not considered "intellectual property." As the transmitters receive and hand on, they are also responsible contributors to the process, but they are not authors. It is in keeping with the nature of the material that the founder of such a school of tradition is regarded as the author. Accordingly we can understand that the Mosaic Torah must be regarded as revelation given to Moses, even when its formulations and the structure of its content date from a later time. When the Pentateuch says, "Moses spoke," this expresses a real truth which cannot be properly dealt with by the objection, raised by our limited way of thinking, that this is unhistorical ("The Biblical View of Scripture," *Essays on Biblical Theology* [Minneapolis: Augsburg, 1981] 21).

7. See in this regard D. N. Freedman, "Who Asks (or Tells) God to Repent?" *The Bible Review* 1/4 (1985) 56–59.

Moses is reminiscent of the intercession of another prophet, Amos (7:1–6), and has several features in common with it.

1. Like Amos (and indeed like the suffering servant of Isaiah 53:12) Moses prays for divine mercy for the people in the full knowledge of their sin and disobedience. In both cases the sin of the people is not a single rash action against the will of God but a persistent pattern of disobedience—at Horeb (v. 8), Taberah, Massah, Kibroth-hattavah, and Kadesh-barnea (vv. 22–24). Both prophets know the extent of the people's sin but dare to appeal to the mercy of God no matter how extensive the history of rebellion and stubbornness may be. It is almost characteristic of the intercessors of the Old Testament that their passionate intercession is most clearly present when the sin is greatest (cf. Abraham's pleas for Sodom and [[252]] Gomorrah). It is as if they know that the mercy of God is equal to and indeed more intense than the judgment of God.

2. The intercessor appeals to various aspects of the Lord's character and concern in order to motivate and urge a positive response to the prayers in behalf of the people. For Amos, the appeal is rooted in the prophet's knowledge of God's special concern for the weak and defenseless ("How can Jacob stand? He is so small!"). Moses makes several appeals:

a. He appeals to the nature and quality of the relationship. Israel is God's chosen people, God's peculiar treasure or possession ("your people and your heritage"—9:26, 29). So Moses urges that God not destroy the relationship that has been created.

b. Moses appeals to the redemptive work of God, the saving act by which God redeemed Israel from slavery (9:26). It is as if Moses says, "Do not bring to nought the work you have done in this people."

c. Moses then draws upon the basis of God's election of Israel mentioned earlier in the chapter (v. 5), the oath which the Lord swore to Abraham, Isaac, and Jacob (see the parallel verse in Exod 32:13). Here a reminder of God's own faithfulness serves as ground for Moses' plea for mercy.

d. Finally, Moses appeals to the reputation of the Lord's power in the world, which is really a call for the vindication of God's power before the people.

In all of this there is at base Moses' appeal to the integrity of the Lord who is one, that is, to the oneness of the Lord's purpose. God is not divided within himself either in being and manifestation or in purpose. It is an understanding of the Lord as one and as one who is consistent in dealing with the people that grounds Moses' cry for God's mercy to the people.

3. The result of Moses' intercession is the same as that of Amos—the rather startling word that the Lord listened to Moses' prayer and heeded it (cf. Exod 32:14, "And the Lord repented of the evil which he thought to do to his people"). It is startling because it suggests that a change of mind is possible for God and indeed happens, a notion that cuts against our ideas both of divine consistency and the nexus of cause and effect that seems to operate in all matters. Furthermore, the various efforts on Moses' part to motivate God to turn from judgment to mercy may seem inappropriate if we have learned that the essence of prayer is "Thy will be done." Yet the Scriptures persistently testify that the heart of God is moved by the importuning prayers of chosen servants and that a dimension of the divine consistency is precisely the continuing inclination of God toward a merciful dealing with humankind and especially those who are God's people. [[253]] What is clear from the motivating appeals of Moses is that the prayer is not for an arbitrary or inconsistent action on God's part. It is a prayer for God to act according to the divine will and purpose as it has been manifest over and over again—a purpose that is faithful, redemptive, forgiving, grounded in perduring relationships, and constantly being vindicated before the public audience of peoples and nations. The prayer with all its appeals, and as it pushes God, is precisely "in tune" with who God is and how God acts. It anticipates later prayers in behalf of a sinful humanity ("Father, forgive them . . . ," Luke 23:24) and the hearkening response of God that will withhold appropriate judgment for the sake of mercy, yea even take the judgment for the sake of mercy ("Truly this was the Son of God!"—Matt 27:54).

In yet another prayer of Moses (3:23–28) we see the Deuteronomic profile of Moses as a type or model figure anticipatory of later figures in the biblical tradition. Here we get a glimpse of Moses as God's suffering servant, an image that is not writ large in the book but appears at three places (1:37; 3:23–28; and 4:21–22). At one point in Deuteronomy (32:51–52) Moses' not being allowed to enter the promised land is attributed to his breach of faith with God. But that is clearly a Priestly text that has entered into the Deuteronomic literature and is not a part of the Deuteronomic tradition about Moses. The dominant view of Deuteronomy is that Moses was the Lord's faithful servant whose death outside the promise was due to the Lord's anger on account of the people. Frequently in Deuteronomic literature Moses is designated as servant of the Lord (Deut 3:24; 34:5; Josh 1:1, 2, 7, 13, 15; 8:31, 33; 9:24; 11:12, 15; 12:6; 13:8; 14:7; 18:7; 22:2, 4, 5). In the three passages from Deuteronomy cited above, Moses is clearly identified with the people in the punishment that is placed upon them, but the judgment on Moses is for *their* sin (1:34–37). Moses does not share the fearful perspective of the people, but he shares existence with them and so must suffer with them. In 3:22 as well as 4:21–22 the emphasis is even more on Moses' chastisement as representative of and for the people: Moses is prohibited from entering the land on account of the sin of the people who are allowed to enter. We do not have here a full-blown notion of the salvation and forgiveness of the many brought by the punishment of the one, but we are on the way to that. It is in the line of that innocent suffering one who is designated the Lord's servant and of whom it is said, as the people could have said of Moses:

> Surely *he* has borne our sicknesses
>   and carried our pains. . . .
> *He* was wounded for our transgressions,
>   bruised for our iniquities. . . . ⟦254⟧
> The Lord has laid on him the iniquity of us all (Isa 53:4–6).

Deuteronomy does not see Moses' failure to enter the land as a meaningless accident or even simply a personal judgment upon him; but this happening, like all happenings, is by the purpose and power of God. Of all people, Moses merited the promise. Not to receive it can only be in the divine will. So for the sake of the people Moses bears the judgment. The one identifies with and gives his life for the many. The texts of Deuteronomy nowhere say that Moses' death outside the land is *in order that* the people might live in the land, but 4:21–22 especially put these two realities close together. The sentence that ties all these passages together is: "The Lord was angry with me on your account." That repeated "on your account" is an echoing anticipation, a beginning point in that stream of innocent servants who receive the judgment that rightly belongs on others. It is the word that is meant to echo beyond these texts, reminding all hearers that the special way in which judgment becomes grace in the work of this God is when the Lord's own servant receives the judgment "on your account."

IV

So the Book of Deuteronomy paints a portrait of Moses that anticipates those other servants of God who will communicate and teach the word of the Lord and will stand with the people and in their place before God. We are told that this leader of Israel is a model or type of those to come ("a prophet like me") but also that none can compare with him ("There has not arisen a prophet since in Israel like Moses").

Whatever tension there may be between those two perspectives, both are to be maintained. The reader of Deuteronomy learns something fundamental about those who are God's servants, chosen agents of the will and word of the Lord. But what Moses gave Israel is non-repeatable. The Book of Deuteronomy says that all that is needful for your life as a community under God, guided and blessed by the Lord, is found in these words that Moses spoke and taught as charged by the Lord. Nothing more is needful (4:2 and 12:32 Eng.).

That is why the commissioning of Joshua and the death of Moses are important matters in Deuteronomy bringing the Torah to a close.[8] A leader is needed to guide the people safely into the promised land. That is not Moses, for explicit and implicit reasons. The explicit reasons have been noted above—God was angry with Moses on account of the people. The implicit reason, however, is that Moses' work is truly done. The people [[255]] have now the word of the Lord which Moses taught, and that will be their guide in the land that the Lord has promised. Israel is to live now by the Torah that Moses has taught and in a very real sense does not need Moses. The "closing" of the Torah is co-incidental with the death of Moses in a real sense. He now moves off the scene, and Israel henceforth will not be led by a great authority figure but by the living word of the Torah that Moses taught and that goes always with the people in the ark (10:1–5), God's word in the midst of the people. Joshua is commissioned as leader, but it is clear that he is not Moses. Moses is the "servant of God"; Joshua is "the servant of Moses" and is not called "servant of God" although Moses will be so designated throughout the Book of Joshua. At the commissioning of Joshua it is made clear (and indeed emphatically so in the Hebrew text) that it is the *Lord* who goes over before Israel and will be with Israel (31:3, 7–8). Joshua will be the human leader of the people in battle and will allot the land, but he is not the authority figure who spoke face to face with God. If such a figure moved onto the scene, then the whole weight and purpose of the instruction that Moses gave as charged by the Lord would be undermined. There may be figures "like" Moses, but no new Moses. One sees, therefore, the significance of the portrayal of Jesus as in some sense a new Moses whose word claims to stand with all the authority of Moses' words and indeed even to transcend them (which, of course, is quite different from contra-dicting or negating them as if often presumed).

8. For an important treatment of the death of Moses in the Deuteronomic and Priestly traditions, but along different lines than those laid out here, see Thomas W. Mann, "Theological Reflections on the Denial of Moses," *JBL* 98 (1979) 481–94.

Before Moses leaves the scene, however, he speaks to the people in song and poetry (Deuteronomy 32; 33). The first of these chapters is a song of judgment, which the Lord has Moses teach the people so that they may have it in their hearts and on their lips when in time to come they wander far from the Lord's instruction. The second is a poem of blessing upon all the tribes of Israel, anticipating their life in the land and the provision and place that God will give them. So it is that as the people are sent on their way by Moses but without him, they carry not only the divine instruction that he has taught them but also a word of warning and a word of blessing as a final testament of Moses for the time when the people come into their "inheritance," the good land which the Lord their God has granted them.

The Sequence of the Laws in Deuteronomy 12–26 and in the Decalogue

GEORG BRAULIK

For Deuteronomy[1], the Decalogue embodies the substance of the "covenant" that YHWH made with Israel at Horeb (in 5:2–3 with Moses as the people's partner; in 29:1 [Heb. 28:69] without him), directly linking covenant and Decalogue together (4:13; 9:9, 11). According to the deuteronomic theory, the Ten Commandments were the only words that God addressed to the whole assembly (5:22). Though this fact is the source of their unsurpassable dignity, the revelation still needed a mediator: Moses (5:5). YHWH wrote the "ten words" on two tablets of stone (4:13; 10:4); but because of the people's protest, which YHWH accepted, Israel from then on received all further expressions of YHWH's will only through the mediation of Moses (5:23–31). Moses, for his part, then delivered this Torah, after it was written down, to the priests (cf. 10:4 with 31:9), so that it could be preserved in the ark of the covenant together with the tablets of the Decalogue (cf. 10:5 with 31:26). For future proclamation of divine words in particular situations, YHWH would raise up another prophet like Moses (18:15–18).

Deuteronomy explains Moses' mediatorial role in two ways. According to 5:31, YHWH in person had already communicated to him "all the commandments and the statutes and the ordinances" (*kol hammiṣwa*

Translated and reprinted with permission from "Die Abfolge der Gesetze in Deuteronomium 12–26 und der Dekalog," in *Das Deuteronomium: Entstehung, Gestalt und Botschaft* (ed. Norbert Lohfink; Bibliotheca ephemeridum theologicarum lovaniensium 68; Louvain: Louvain University Press, 1985) 252–72. Translation by Linda M. Maloney.

1. This paper was originally delivered as a seminar paper at the Thirty-third Colloquium Biblicum Lovaniense, 17 August 1983, Louvain, Belgium.

haḥuqqîm wĕhammišpāṭîm) that he was to teach Israel. But according to 4:14 (cf. v. 5), Yʜwʜ had only ordered Moses to teach the people "statutes and ordinances" (*ḥuqqîm ûmišpāṭîm*, without the article) and not to repeat a separate law of Yʜwʜ in addition to the Decalogue.[2] The reports of the event at Horeb tie this additional divine revelation to Moses (or rather his responsibility to teach it) directly to Yʜwʜ's promulgation of the Decalogue, both as to place (5:31) and time (4:14). They seem to suggest and even to urge an understanding of the "statutes and ordinances" as an informative (5:31), or even more, an authoritative (4:14) interpretation of the Decalogue, in the sense of a set of directions for its fulfillment in given, concrete situations. The Decalogue is obligatory always and everywhere, while the laws are valid only in Israel's own land (4:5; 12:1).[3] Does Deuteronomy in fact endorse this kind of understanding of the promulgation of laws as an "interpretation" of commandments already given by Yʜwʜ?

In fact, the use of the plural pairing, "statutes and ordinances" (*haḥuqqîm wĕhammišpāṭîm*) is the first indication of the way the relationship between the Decalogue and individual laws in Deuteronomy is to be explained. The oldest instances are found in Deuteronomy, so that we may conclude that the use of this expression is something proper to that book. In the second speech of Moses it is introduced only as a structural signal (with the exception of some out-of-sequence usages.[4] Thus it stands as a frame around the deuteronomic paranesis (5:1 and 11:32), and in 12:1 and 26:16 it frames the codex of special rules. This means that when Moses recites "statutes and ordinances" (5:1), they contain (in spite of the new beginning at 6:1) first of all the Decalogue itself, which is placed at their head (5:6–21), and then paraneses, in which the text of the beginning of the Decalogue plays a central role and is expanded in the form of paraphrases (6:10–15; 7:8–11); in fact, there is even a paraphrase of a paraphrase of the Decalogue, with commentary (8:7–20).[5] Within the deuteronomic legal corpus, however,

---

2. The emphasis here is on the "what" of the Mosaic teaching of the law. Similarly, 4:13 emphasizes the writing down of the Decalogue, but in contrast to 5:22 is silent about a delivery of the two tablets to Moses.

3. Cf. G. Braulik, "Weisheit, Gottesnähe und Gesetz: Zum Kerygma von Deuteronomium 4,5–8," in *Studien zum Pentateuch: Fs. W. Kornfeld* (ed. G. Braulik; Vienna, 1977) 165–95, at 171–72.

4. N. Lohfink, *Das Hauptgebot: Eine Untersuchung literarischer Einleitungsfragen zu Dtn 5–11* (AB 20; Rome, 1963) 56–57.

5. N. Lohfink, "Die These vom 'deuteronomistischen' Dekaloganfang: Ein fragwürdiges Ergebnis atomistischer Sprachstatistik," in Braulik, *Studien*, 99–109, at 101–4. The paraphrase of the Decalogue in 4:15–20 is also a part of the "statutes and ordinances" that Moses teaches (vv. 1 and 5).

they also include other laws, as well as casuistic developments of most of the commandments in the Decalogue (13:1-5 [Heb 2-6], 6-11 [Heb 7-12], 12-18 [Heb 13-19]; 17:2-7; 19:11-13, 16-19; 21:1-9, 18-21; 22:13-21, 22, 23-27; 24:7).

The question about the reference to the Decalogue is sharpened if this double expression ultimately refers only to 12:1-26:16.[6] In a strict sense, Moses merely announces at 5:1 that he intends to present some "statutes and ordinances." But in 11:32 he is not looking back; instead, he is pointing forward. It is the "title" in 12:1 that really introduces the "statutes and ordinances," using this double expression; the statement of promulgation, which we would expect to find, is completely missing. Yet in 26:16 it is not Moses, but YHWH who commands, despite the fact that elsewhere the one who utters the laws is always a human being and not, as with the Decalogue, God in person. Thus if the phrase *statutes and ordinances* is meant to designate the deuteronomic codex (12:1-26:16) as an explanation of the Decalogue, the relatively few casuistic expansions mentioned above would not seem sufficient to justify the structured usage of this double expression. If it did not signal a further relationship of the deuteronomic codex to the Decalogue beyond these few instances, the term "statutes and ordinances" would include more laws that reveal no relationship to the Decalogue than laws that give it concrete shape. This kind of incongruity, in face of the exact systematization within the book, is improbable from the outset.

F. Horst in particular attempts to explain the redactional function of the double expression in 12:1 as an indication of the existence and distribution of two types of legal material.[7] According to this study, the *ḥuqqîm* are "charter rights of YHWH" located in chaps. 12-18, while the *mišpāṭîm* are the civil law in chaps. 19-25. It seems that the privileged, or charter, commands described by Horst are an independent collection

---

6. If the "statutes and ordinances" are limited to the legal corpus, however, the striking selection of verbs of promulgation associated with this expression will need explanation. In the "heading" at 4:45, in 6:1, which also functions as a kind of title for what follows, as well as in 5:1, and 11:32, where the term serves as a structural signal, but in other places also, we do not find *ṣwh* [*Piel*], as in the majority of promulgation statements. That this would have been possible is clear from 7:11. On this point, see G. Braulik, "Die Ausdrücke für 'Gesetz' im Buch Deuteronomium," *Bib* 51 (1970) 39-66, at 62. This peculiar feature may indicate that in the "statutes and ordinances," Moses is not only giving an authoritative promulgation of laws, but also proclaiming paranesis, i.e., that which we find in chaps. 5-11, the first section framed by this expression. For particular remarks on 5:1 and 11:32, cf. Lohfink, *Hauptgebot*, 275.

7. F. Horst, *Das Privilegrecht Jahwes* (*Rechtsgeschichtliche Untersuchungen zum Deuteronomium*) (FRLANT 45; Göttingen, 1930) 120-23 (= *Gottes Recht: Gesammelte Studien zum Recht im Alten Testament* [Theologische Bücherei 12; Munich, 1961] 17-154, at 150-54).

of ten legal statements, in other words, a second Decalogue, but this remains completely hypothetical and has nothing in common, as far as content goes, with the Decalogue of Horeb. Furthermore, a division of "statutes" and "ordinances" into two mutually exclusive group designations that refer to particular sets of laws or indicate their order with respect to one another is at least doubtful. This is first, because of the way in which the double expression is used elsewhere in Deuteronomy, and second, because of the interpretation of "charter law" and "civil law" that is characteristic of the deuteronomic legal corpus as we have it.

The most recent overview of research in Deuteronomy by H. D. Preuss[8] shows how many problems are encountered by all the studies devoted to the structural principles of Deuteronomy 12–26. It appears that we have so far progressed very little beyond the equally unsatisfactory[9] divisions proposed by J. Wellhausen.[10] So, according to Preuss, "a fully illuminating explanation of the complete sequence of texts and text groupings in Deut 12–25 has not yet been found."[11] But he sees a possible solution in the evidence that the sequence of laws is related to that of the Decalogue, although Deuteronomy may be interested in nothing more than the most general sort of arrangement.[12] "For the fact that Deut 12–25 is oriented, at least in some parts and in a general sense . . . toward the sequence of laws in the Decalogue appears to be a central

---

8. H. D. Preuss, *Deuteronomium* (Erträge der Forschung 164; Darmstadt, 1982) 108–12. A synopsis of the most important efforts at division and ordering of the material can be found in G. Seitz, *Redaktionsgeschichtliche Studien zum Deuteronomium* (BWANT 93; Stuttgart, 1971) 92–93.

9. *Die Composition des Hexateuchs und der historischen Bücher des Alten Testaments* (Berlin, 1963) 353–63. Seitz (*Studien*; see n. 8 above) does not mention Wellhausen at all; Preuss (*Deuteronomium*, 108) cites only the older arrangement in *Composition*, 203ff., which Wellhausen himself later regarded as inadequate and which he revised at the end of the third edition through an "extensive listing of the content of the genuinely deuteronomic law," *loc. cit.*

10. Preuss, *Deuteronomium*, 108. However, a short article that Preuss does not mention and a monograph deserve special mention. H. M. Wiener ("The Arrangement of Deuteronomy 12–16," *Journal of the Palestine Oriental Society* 6 [1926] 185–95) saw the present ordering of the laws as determined by two principles: the religious interest of the author, and associations resulting for that author not from any kind of legal theory but naturally and even necessarily from the circumstances of the time and experience of the immediate situation. C. M. Carmichael has suggested a completely new possibility in *The Laws of Deuteronomy* (Ithaca and London, 1974): among other things, the legal material is said to be organized, from Genesis through Numbers, into narrative sequences according to associative characteristics. It is true that this extensive study is "as regards tradition and redaction criticism (and often literary criticism as well) as quixotic as it is uncritical, and as a suggested solution will certainly not carry us farther" (Preuss, *Deuteronomium*, 109–10).

11. *Ibid.*, 112.

12. *Ibid.*

conclusion of recent scholarship that awaits further verification and testing."[13]

The conclusion I have here cited may give the impression of being based on a number of studies on this topic. However, apart from a very few publications that contain marginal observations on the subject, there exist in fact only assertions in the form of theses that lack any adequate argumentation.[14]

The function of the Decalogue as the structural principle of Deuteronomy was extensively described, for the first time, by F. W. Schultz in 1895. In the foreword to his commentary on Deuteronomy he wrote: "In Deuteronomy . . . the Law . . . is itself, in a certain sense, a commentary," because in it Moses "by means of the order in which he treats them, has placed each section of the Torah in close relationship to one of the commandments of the Decalogue. In this way he has made the Decalogue the key to the rest of the Law, but equally and at the same time has made the rest of the Law an interpretive expansion on the Decalogue."[15] But for Schultz this commentary does not begin with the deuteronomic codex; it starts immediately after the text of the Decalogue in chapters 6–11.[16] Because of his artificial arrangement of texts,[17] but also because of his defense of Mosaic authorship, Schultz received little recognition and practically no acceptance. Only in 1979 was he again brought to critical attention by S. A. Kaufman.

13. Preuss, *Deuteronomium*, 111–12.

14. So, for example, H. Breit, *Die Predigt des Deuteronomisten* (Munich, 1933), esp. pp. 31–34, was convinced, in agreement with Calvin and especially Luther, that the message of Deuteronomy was based on the Decalogue (p. 33). M. Noth, *Überlieferungsgeschichtliche Studien: Die sammelnden und bearbeitenden Geschichtswerke im Alten Testament* (3d ed.; Tübingen, 1967) 101, left it at the very important conclusion that it appeared to the Deuteronomist that "the special relationship between God and the people," i.e., the covenant, was "founded on the communication of the Decalogue, for which the Deuteronomic law following 5:28 represents the authentic divine interpretation." According to A. Phillips, *Ancient Israel's Criminal Law. A New Approach to the Decalogue* (Oxford, 1970) 182, "The Deuteronomic law . . . in main constitutes an expansion of the criminal law of the Decalogue."

15. Schultz, *Das Deuteronomium* (Berlin, 1895) iii. This commentary is not noted by Preuss, *Deuteronomium*.

16. Schultz, *Deuteronomium*, 13–24, develops the following arrangement: commandments I–II (prohibition of other gods and of images) = Deuteronomy 6–11; III = 12–13; IV = 15:1–16:17; V = 16:18–18:22; VI = 19:1–21:9; VII = 21:10–23; VIII = 22; IX–X = 23–25. Within these correspondences, Schultz believes that he can also discover that from chap. 12 on Moses "with remarkable regularity" proceeds in such a way "that he always adduces exactly three parts as belonging to one commandment, and that as he proceeds to expand further on one of the three, he makes three subdivisions" (*Deuteronomium*, 16).

17. See C. Steuernagel's opinion in *Die Entstehung des deuteronomischen Gesetzes* (Halle, 1896) 10.

In a brief article that was even overlooked by Kaufman, A. E. Guilding suggested that not only Deuteronomy 13–15 (sic) but also the Book of the Covenant (Exod 20:22–23:17) and the collection in Leviticus 10–23 were "an orderly exposition of the Decalogue, which is the basis of the whole legal system."[18] What is original here is that, starting with the fifth commandment (regarding parents), Guilding organizes the ten commandments in pairs and orders each pair to a group of laws in the corresponding chapters of Exodus or Deuteronomy.[19]

Not published and practically unobtainable is an excursus in H. Schulz's dissertation[20] in which he gives reasons for his opinion concerning the influence of the Decalogue on the order of the deuteronomic laws. According to Schulz, "the whole of the deuteronomic legal material in chapters 12–15 is built on the schematic arrangement of the Decalogue. In spite of a variety of enrichments . . . the fundamental tripartite division among Yhwh and the cult, parents and family, and the social and moral realm remains demonstrable, though a strong division in the last of the three areas is no longer maintained."[21]

This initiative was developed further in 1979 by S. A. Kaufman, in the most extensive contribution to this subject to date.[22] But while Schulz accepted the "Decalogue-pattern" as formative only in its larger outlines and supposed later editing and additions, Kaufman supports the thesis that the deuteronomic law comes from a single redactor who structured his collection of laws down to the last details, according to the model of the complete Decalogue.[23] Kaufman dispenses with literary-

18. A. E. Guilding, "Notes on the Hebrew Law Codes," *JTS* 49 (1948) 43–52, at p. 43.

19. For the deuteronomic law the arrangement is as follows (pp. 47–49, 52);

> Honor to parents, no murder: 16:18–22:8 (sic);
> No adultery, no stealing: 22:13 (sic)–24:7 (sic);
> No false witness, no coveting: 24:10 (sic)–25:16.

20. H. Schulz, "Das Todesrecht im Alten Testament" (diss. in typescript, Marburg, 1966) 151–57. There is a brief reference to it in the publication with the same title in BZAW 114 (Berlin, 1969) 65; see also O. Kaiser, *Einleitung in das Alte Testament: Eine Einführung in ihre Ergebnisse und Probleme* (4th ed. Gütersloh, 1978) 118.

21. Schulz, *Todesrecht* (BZAW) 66–67. In addition, the deuteronomic law is framed by the Decalogue, whose program it seeks to represent paradigmatically, and the series of curses, composed in relation to the Decalogue, in 27:15–26 (pp. 67–68). This latter was programmatically composed for liturgical purposes, as a conclusion of the whole legal teaching in Deuteronomy and consciously related back to 5:6ff. (p. 70).

22. S. A. Kaufman, "The Structure of the Deuteronomic Law," *MAARAV* 1/2 (1978–79) 105–58; see esp. p. 112 and n. 43.

23. Kaufman, "Structure," 112. On the correspondences between the sequence of individual parts of the law and the commandments of the Decalogue, see the survey on pp. 113–14. Starting from these fixed points, Kaufman examines the intermediate and border zones and, in effect, arranges the whole of the legal material, without exception, in a single series corresponding to the commandments of the Decalogue.

critical and redaction-critical differentiations within the deuteronomic law. The delimitation and interpretation of the individual laws are not given a grounding within the text. Differences between texts are too quickly smoothed over and remain unevaluated. But, in spite of its methodological and exegetical deficiencies, the effort in this study to explain the sequence of laws in the deuteronomic codex (more precisely, in Deut 12:1–15:16) and its relationship to the Decalogue as its structural model constitutes a challenge to research in Deuteronomy. Furthermore, a thorough discussion appears urgent because for other collections of laws from the ancient Orient a system has already been demonstrated.

Following the investigations especially of H. Petschow on the system of the laws in the Codex Hammurabi and the Laws of Eshnunna,[24] we already know the most important techniques in ancient Oriental codification of laws. These principles of arrangement do not, of course, correspond to the point of view of Roman or of modern European legal systems. They have already been verified in parts of the deuteronomic legal corpus.[25] Kaufman recognizes his indebtedness to these studies,[26] and they also form the background to my own analysis. Characteristic are, first, the division of the legal material according to categories oriented more or less to spheres of life, objects, or particular states of affairs; and second, that within the principal themes, the laws are grouped according to five principles of arrangement.[27] In addition, special importance is attached to the phenomenon of attraction, whereby

24. H. Petschow, "Zur Systematic und Gesetzestechnik im Codex Hammurabi," *Zeitschrift für Assyriologie* 57 (1965) 146–72; "Zur 'Systematik' in den Gesetzen von Eschnunna," *Symbolae juridicae et historicae M. David dedicatae*, v. 2 = *Iura orientis antiqui* (Leiden, 1968) 131–43.

25. N. Lohfink, "Die Sicherung der Wirksamkeit des Gotteswortes durch das Prinzip der Schriftlichkeit der Tora und durch das Prinzip der Gewaltenteilung nach den Ämtergesetzen des Buches Deuteronomium (Dt 16,18–18,22)," in *Testimonium Veritati: Fs. W. Kempf* (ed. H. Wolter; Frankfurt/M, 1971) 143–55, esp. 147–48 [reprinted in this volume, in English translation, pp. 336–52]; V. Wagner, "Der bisher unbeachtete Rest eines hebräischen Rechtskodex," *BZ* 19 (1975) 234–40 (missing from Preuss, *Deuteronomium*, and not mentioned by Kaufman, "Structure").

26. Kaufman, "Structure," 115–18, esp. 117–18.

27. Petschow ("Gesetzestechnik," 170–71), finds the following scheme of systematization:

1. "chronological," i.e., "according to the actual or possible order of events";
2. "according to the objective importance of the matters regulated or the social position of the persons affected or the value of the object";
3. "according to the frequences of the cases";
4. "as juxtaposition of event and counter-event";
5. "in as homogeneous a sequence as possible in the case of objectively and legally identical situations."

legal material is inserted according to key words or associative ideas.
However, these basic principles of organization partly divide laws that,
juristically considered, belong together, and order them in varying subject groups. The resulting law book appears to us unsystematic.

In Israelite law, however, beyond the individual paragraphs and
their ordering, there may well have been, to a greater extent than elsewhere in the ancient Orient, a feeling for stylistic composition of
whole groups of laws. In what follows, this will be evident again and
again in regard to the material in chapters 12–26. It may be that the
stronger rhetorical shaping is connected with the fact that these texts
were regarded as "covenant law" and were intended to be read in public, within cultic assemblies.

In what follows I will presuppose the delimiting of the laws suggested by Norbert Lohfink in the German "Common Translation"
[*Einheitsübersetzung*]. This was created for the practical purposes of a
vernacular edition of the Bible, but it is clear that the following criteria
are also employed there: a new topic; the new beginning of a casuistic
law (through *kî* in the general instance and *ʾim* in the particular instance); a change of form (e.g., between casuistic, seemingly casuistic,
and apodictic); framing; and concluding formulae (such as the so-
called *biʿarta* formula). This delimitation is different in part from the
scope of the laws as determined by Kaufman, which formed the basis of
his study.

My essay is based on investigations by means of which Norbert
Lohfink and I are preparing a joint commentary for the Hermeneia Series.[28] As my introductory remarks have indicated, the question of the
relationship of the Decalogue to the legal code will not be imposed on
the text from without but is provoked by Deuteronomy itself through
the specific use of the double expression *ḥuqqîm ûmišpāṭîm*. The following reflections presuppose the principles of systematization in ancient
Oriental law discovered by Petschow. In addition, they proceed in critical fashion from Kaufman's principal thesis concerning the commandments of the Decalogue as structural pattern for the deuteronomic
collection of laws but without entering into a discussion of all the particular arguments. It is rather the purpose of this article to sketch the
disposition of the deuteronomic code of laws and the influence of the
Decalogue on the arrangement of its individual laws or sub-codes.
What is at issue is a systematization at the level of final redaction. This

---

28. Cf. also the multi-copied notes for N. Lohfink's lectures on "Das Privilegrecht
Jahwes im Buch Deuteronomium: Vorlesungen über Dtn 12–16 und 26," held at the
Philosophisch-Theologische Hochschule St. Georgen, Frankfurt am Main, 1983.

does not exclude the possibility either of an originally independent existence of individual laws, or of previous redactions with differing purposes. Moreover, there was always the possibility that, within ancient Oriental principles of systematization, or subsequent to the body of laws framed in accordance with the structure of the Decalogue, additional material could be introduced by means of digressions. In addition, there are a number of anomalies in the deuteronomic law that probably can be explained only on the diachronic level, since on the synchronic level they must remain in place, and they disturb the logic of the edifice. Thus they have to be tolerated as tensions whose existence is conditioned by the history of their development. Nevertheless, the present study will attempt to clarify the structure of the existing text of chapters 12–26 and to make the Decalogue visible therein as a kind of large-scale or general framework for its composition and arrangement.

Our conclusions may be summarized as follows: chapters 12–18 correspond to the Decalogue only in some rather vague and generalized respects:

First Commandment: The one temple and the one God of Israel, 12:2–13:19.

Second Commandment: Taking the name in vain, 14:1–21. YHWH's holy people in its ritual difference from the peoples of other gods.[29]

Third Commandment: Keeping the Sabbath holy, 14:22–16:17. Cult and brotherhood in sacred rhythm—Israel's gathering together at the three pilgrimage feasts.

Fourth Commandment: Honoring parents, 16:18–18:22. Offices in Israel.

It is only beginning with chapter 19 that one can discern most exact correspondences to the fifth through tenth commandments. Kaufman has established these by means of a number of telling observations that need not be summarized here. In distinction to chapters 12–18, however, there are two places in chapters 19–25 where blocks of legal material are thematically woven together. The two transitions are to be found in the border areas between the blocks of laws ordered to the fifth and

29. In contrast, Kaufman, "Structure," 122–29, relates Deut 13:1–14:27 to the second commandment (according to the Catholic numbering). But this relationship—"a cornerstone of the entire structure" (p. 124)—is much too remote. The second commandment is thus interpreted as forbidding the swearing of false oaths in the name of YHWH. He also fails to consider that chap. 13 reveals a very close relationship with the first commandment and that 14:22–27 must be related to the block of laws that follows (see below, p. 325).

sixth commandments (22:1–12) and those belonging to the sixth and seventh commandments (23:16–24:5). Such transitions between groups of laws must have been possible in principle, since the Codex Hammurabi also offers at least one example.[30]

Fifth Commandment: Preserving life, 19:1–21:23. Deliberate killing (with digressions).

Transition from the topic "preserving life" to that of "sexuality," 22:1–12. The topic of "sexuality" is first introduced at 22:5 with the motif of "crossing over," while the subject of "killing" is last clearly evident at 22:8.

Sixth Commandment: Rape and Family, 22:13–23:14 [Heb 15]. Concentrates completely on the area of sexuality.

Transition from the topic of "sexuality" to that of "property," 23:15[Heb 16]–24:5. The "property" theme appears for the first time at 23:15–16 (escaped slaves), while the theme of "sexuality" is found for the last time at 24:5 (excusing the newly-married from military service).

Seventh Commandment: Property, (23:15–25)24:6–7. The theme of property will be taken up again at 24:19–22 and 25:4, but at 24:8 the next topic ("judgment") begins.

Eighth Commandment: [Truth in the face of] judgment, 24:8–25:4.

Ninth/Tenth Commandments: Coveting 25:5–16. The closing frame of the legal corpus begins at 25:17, looking back to themes from Deuteronomy 12, and the two rituals in 26:1–15 are deliberately conceived as a conclusion to the body of laws.

In what follows, I will illustrate these theses as they apply to 12:2–18:22, that is, in the area where there are only vague correspondences to the Decalogue, and then with regard to one of the two transitional texts, namely, 22:1–12.

The superscription at 12:1 makes two decisive juristic statements: one concerning the area of validity (the land "given" by YHWH) and a second concerning the length of the laws' application (as long as Israel lives in this land). At the same time, the two ordering principles of the legal sections that follow in 12:2–16:12 are probably indicated. YHWH's charter rights, that is, the prescriptions about worshiping YHWH alone in 12:2–14:21, are determined by the location of the one sanctuary. Thus the spatial dimension is dominant. The cultic and social obligations in 14:22–15:23, however, hold for periodically recurring times and culminate in 16:1–17 with the three annual pilgrimage feasts at the central sanctuary. Thus, here, the temporal dimension dominates.

30. Petschow, *Gesetzestechnik*, 164 n. 107.

In detail, 12:2–31 gives, structurally speaking, the first clear unit: Israel is on the verge of entry into its land, which will be centered on one single sanctuary. The command to destroy foreign places of worship (vv. 2–3) and the prohibition of Canaanite cultic practices (vv. 29–31) frame four laws dealing with the sacrificial cult at the unique sanctuary of Israel. The paragraphs in this central part are shaped in thematic and linguistic parallelism; the successive laws are also connected in a special way with one another and do not compete with each other. The divergent passages within individual laws, introduced with for (*kî*) or but (*raq*), develop the juristic concretizations in each case. Thus vv. 4–7 prescribe a single place for worshiping YHWH. Verses 8–12 go on to fix the time when this prescription will go into effect. Verses 13–19 make a distinction, consequent on the centralization of the cult, between sacrifice and profane slaughter. Verses 20–28 contain a legal interpretation: they limit the possibilities for this secular slaughter and regulate the treatment of blood, both in profane slaughtering and in the offering of sacrifices at the central sanctuary. All these laws are thematically connected with that one place, so that the local aspect is determinative. Before the temporal aspect relating to it is taken up at 14:22, another motif, dominant in chap. 12, demands development: that of uniqueness. The Canaanites have many gods, and they are worshiped in many sanctuaries. Israel will have but one sanctuary, where it will worship its one and only God YHWH. So it is logical to find in chap. 13 those laws that insure an exclusive veneration of YHWH.

Deuteronomy 12:29–31 thus functions as a structural hinge. This paragraph at the end of chap. 12 is connected primarily to 13:2–3, thus closing the frame around the theme of the single sanctuary. At the same time, however, this prohibition on Canaanite religious practices introduces several themes that will be treated in 13:1–18 [Heb. 2–19] and 14:1–21. For example, the motif of "following other gods" in 12:30 is contained in the first law in chap. 13 (see v. 2), the motif of idol worship in all three laws in chap. 13 (see vv. 2, 6, and 13). With the words *abominable, sons,* and *burn . . . in the fire,* 12:31 presents the key expressions for the final law in chap. 13 (see vv. 12, 14, and 16) and the first two in chap. 14 (see vv. 1 and 3). Thus the motifs and formulations of 12:30–31 are taken up in order and concretized in specific laws. It is true that chap. 13 is no longer concerned with the adoption of cultic forms, but instead with the gods themselves. However, these are not the gods of the destroyed peoples of Canaan; they are the gods of the surrounding nations, that is, all "other gods," as such. The motif of "rites of other nations" is taken up in 14:1–21. These verses treat of the rejection of these rites by Israel, a difference in ritual that makes Israel a contrast society.

The three "casuistic" laws in 13:1–18 are collected under the point of view of Israel's exclusive loyalty to YHWH. They are particularly true to type in having their closest analogical relationship, in regard to both form and content, in the "Hittite regulations for service," which also apply to the exclusive loyalty and relationship of service to an overlord. In chap. 13 the whole matter of YHWH's right to unique worship is explicated on the basis of three extreme social situations: in vv. 1–5, temptation to falling away through prophets, who have the highest competence in this area and command charismatic authority and even miraculous signs; in vv. 6–11, temptation by family members and friends, that is, in the realm of the first and strongest religious experiences and intimacy; in vv. 12–18 the defection of a large group ("city") from Israel's socioreligious consensus. These three extreme cases are mutually revealing, are shaped by their subject matter into a unity, and therefore are also attuned linguistically to one another. In addition, whole passages in 13:1–18 are paraphrases of the beginning of the Decalogue.

To the one God for Israel corresponds the unique relationship of the people to YHWH. This relationship sets Israel apart, as "children of YHWH" and "holy people," from all other nations. The next unit of law, in 14:1–21, is devoted to this theme. Like 13:1–18, this section in 14:1–21 is connected to 12:31. The verbal links between the two emphasize the special interest of this group of laws. In three paragraphs, 14:1–21 makes explicit Israel's special status in terms of abstention from particular customs and particular foods. Verses 1–2 forbid mourning rites, vv. 3–21a certain foods, and v. 21b a certain way of preparing food. Despite their differing length, they are a single unit. This is especially clear from the formal arrangement. Verses 2 and 21 frame the food prohibitions, while vv. 1 and 21 present an additional, doubled framing determined by motif, which leads into the sphere of life and death, the realm of the ancient Oriental fertility cult and ancient Oriental otherworldly religion. The motif of the "children of YHWH" corresponds to the kid and its mother, and the forbidding of mourning rites corresponds to the prohibition on eating carrion. But as children of YHWH, the Israelites are YHWH's people, *ʿam*, which really means YHWH's family. Again the reader is faced with a closed group of laws.

This completes a chain of associations that began in chap. 12. At this point, then, the arrangement can take up the other thematic tension that was indicated there, namely, that of place and time. Chapter 12 groups laws of centralization under the aspect of space, that is, a place chosen by Y_HWH_. In 13:1–14:21 there is a kind of associative digression. Now, the section 14:22–16:17 begins again with the central sanctuary and, through the arrangement of its laws, unfolds the time aspect. In contrast to chap. 12, where because of the unique legitimate site for worship the laws cannot refer to more than one place, 14:22–16:17 has a variety of times as its direct principle of connection. The bridge between this block and the immediately preceding laws begins with the key word 'eating' (ʾkl). It ties the last two laws in the first block of legal material dealing with charter rights (12:2–14:21), namely those prohibiting certain foods in 14:3–21, to the first two laws in the second block of this material (14:22–16:17), namely the orders concerning tithes in 14:22–29. The similarity of content is especially clear if one understands the tithe as "service" (in the sense of "serving" or "regaling" someone at table).[31]

The group of laws in 14:22–15:23 forms the first unit. Common to these laws is the fact that they are all concerned with the elimination, in the context of sacred rhythms, of class distinctions arising in Israel. This applies even to the first law about eating the tithe at the central sanctuary, which adds the statement that the Levites are also to be invited. It is true that the tithe has already been mentioned in chap. 12. But it is only at this later point that its particular modalities are regulated. This shows that it is *not* to be brought to the central sanctuary every year. Instead, according to 14:28–29, in every third and sixth year within the seven-year cycle, the tithe is to be presented in the place where one lives, for the benefit of the poor. But with this statement the question of place has become secondary, and the ordering from the point of view of time comes to the fore. The introduction of time suggests that, in light of the key words 'annually' and 'every three years', the reader can now turn to the final year of the whole cycle and treat what has to happen "every seven years." So 15:1–6 speaks of the release of debts that is due in that seventh year, and vv. 7–11 logically follow, with their statement that, in spite of the forgiving of debts due in the seventh year, one should still allow credit to poor Israelites. The law about freeing those enslaved for debt after six years of slavery, that is, in the seventh year, also comes in at this point because of the number seven. Probably this does not refer to the fixed final year of the seven-year cycle, but to the seventh year of each individual's enslavement, indicating that such manumissions could, in fact, occur in any year. It is then reasonable, after this digression occasioned by the reference to a period of time, to return to the ordinances that apply every

31. N. Airoldi, "La cosidetta 'decima' israelitica antica," *Bib* 55 (1975) 179–210.

year. Thus the law concerning the sacrifice of the firstlings follows. It is to be brought each year to the central sanctuary—and with this law the line of argument returns to the point where it began in 14:22.

The laws in 14:22–15:23 are, at the same time, an example of grouping according to the social status of the subjects touched by them. Thus, according to 14:22–27, at the time of the annual tithing at the sanctuary the Israelite and his household should eat a meal and rejoice; in this, the "Levite" is not to be neglected (v. 27). Next, 14:28–29 directs that in every third year the tithe for the "Levites, the sojourners, the orphans and the widows" is to be presented in the individual towns. The release of debts required in every seventh year is, according to 15:1–6, to be accorded to every "needy kinsman," and 15:7–11 directs that he should also be offered credit at all times, while 15:12–18 demands the liberation of "enslaved kinspeople" in the seventh year of their enslavement. Finally, 15:19–23 directs that the individual and his household (v. 20) are to eat the firstling of the herd each year at the sanctuary. This links the social ring back to its beginning, for 14:23 already dealt with the firstlings of cattle, sheep and goats and with the family meal at the chosen place.

If the tithe is brought to the central sanctuary during the Feast of Booths, the offering of the firstlings described in 15:19–23 may also be connected with the autumn festival pilgrimage (note the connection in 14:23). But this brings the series of laws to the concluding pilgrimage feast. Therefore in 16:1–17 a new group of laws with a temporal determination can begin with the spring festival and give regulations for the paschal *matzoh* bread, the Feast of Weeks, and the Feast of Booths. Verses 16–17 form a kind of summary conclusion. The theme of "Yнwн's charter rights" has been carried through in its temporal and spatial dimensions, and in this ordering, the laws dealing with the central sanctuary are the corner posts of the arrangement: first the group in chap. 12, then (after the first digression) the laws concerning the annual tithe in 14:22–27, next (after the second digression) the laws in 15:19–23 about the bringing of the firstlings, and finally the group of laws in chap. 16. The so-called "laws of centralization" are thus not arbitrarily inserted, but instead are strategically distributed. The theme of centralization is found later in only two of the laws concerning offices: in 17:8–13, the directions for the judicial court at the central sanctuary; and in 18:1–8, where the rights of the rural Levites at the sanctuary are regulated. Both these laws, of course, are now embedded in new structural arrangements within the deuteronomic charter proposal.

Can 12:2–16:17 be coordinated, as to structure and content, with the first three commandments of the Decalogue? The preceding sketch of the arrangement of laws within this charter of rights shows that the redaction, including its digressions, seems to follow some other principles of systematization. Beyond this, 14:1–21 in particular can only be related in a very roundabout process of reasoning to the commandment regarding the divine name. Therefore as far as redactional criticism is concerned, no original connection of chapters 12–16 with the first three commandments of the Decalogue can have been intended. But this does not exclude the possibility that a later rereading of this text integrated it in the conceptual structure that organized the whole codex in light of the Decalogue. It is only in this sense that what has been said above (see pp. 320–22) can be valid.

Norbert Lohfink has already analyzed the arrangement of 16:18–18:22 in detail.[32] As his analysis shows, the individual laws were redacted into a unified charter mainly through associative attraction.

Relating this part of the law to the fourth commandment of the Decalogue appears problematic, not least because of modern exegesis of the command to honor one's parents.[33] Nevertheless, Philo of Alexandria (*De Decalogo* 31.165) already thought that the commandment "regarding respect for parents at the same time points toward many important laws, such as those . . . concerning rulers and the ruled."[34] So it is possible that a redactional reinterpretation of the laws regarding office in 16:18–18:22 could have been made on the basis of the Decalogue-structure of the whole legal codex.[35]

I now proceed to a closer analysis of 22:1–12 as an example of the structuring of a transitional area between two blocks of laws. The text, when taken as a whole, is still generally regarded as an unsystematic collection of the most disparate sorts of regulations.[36] These are usually interpreted as humanitarian laws and old taboos for warding off foreign

32. Lohfink, "Sicherung," esp. pp. 147–58.

33. On this, see R. Albertz, "Hintergrund und Bedeutung des Elterngebots im Dekalog," *ZAW* 90 (1978) 348–74.

34. Cited according to Philo of Alexandria, *Die Werke in deutscher Übersetzung*, vol. 1 (2d ed.; ed. L. Cohn et al.; Berlin, 1962) 371–409, at 406.

35. Schultz, *Deuteronomium*, 19–21, sees an extension of the command regarding parents in 16:18–18:22; Guilding, "Notes," 52, cites Philo. Kaufman, "Structure," 133, states with regard to the laws of office, without further qualification: "These rules proclaim the authority figures just as the Fifth Commandment proclaims the authority of the parents within the family."

36. See, for example, A. Phillips, *Deuteronomy* (Cambridge Bible Commentary; Cambridge, 1973) 146; J. A. Thompson, *Deuteronomy. An Introduction and Commentary* (London, 1974) 233.

religious practices.[37] But how did the redactor who put them at this place in the codex and in this sequence want them to be understood?

As far as content is concerned, 21:1–23 assembles some rather different laws under the theme of premature death;[38] in 22:13–29 all the laws concern forbidden relationships between man and woman. Both these redactional units are structured chiastically.[39] In addition, they are connected with one another by means of a number of linguistic similarities.[40] These systematic arrangements indirectly isolate 22:1–12 as a compositionally independent intermediate text, since its content unites differing regulations, and it is not chiastically structured. Finally, it is noteworthy that the rules of ancient Oriental codification, as summarized by Petschow in his five principles of arrangement, are followed in 21:15–21 and 22:13–29, but not in 22:1–12.[41]

While the casuistic rules in chap. 21 and in 22:13–29 are almost completely dominated by the third person, both the apodictic and the casuistic laws in 22:1–12 are all addressed in the second person, with the exception of v. 5. Nevertheless, the heterogeneous material in this collection is not gathered under a single perspective.[42] Instead, it combines two groups of laws. Thus, vv. 1–3, 4, 6–7, and 8 constitute four paragraphs concerning the preservation of animal and human life. They are within the scope of the fifth commandment of the Decalogue. On the other hand, in vv. 5, 9–11, and 12 one finds three (or five) paragraphs forbidding certain types of mixing. With these, one is already in the realm of the sixth commandment. This interpretation will be further clarified below. In any case, the intermediate text 22:1–12 does not lend itself to division into thoroughly separate and sequential parts that can in turn be related to the preceding and following blocks of laws.[43] It is, instead, characteristic of this text that its two groups

37. So, e.g., Phillips, *Deuteronomy*, 146.

38. C. M. Carmichael, "A Common Element in Five Supposedly Disparate Laws," *VT* 29 (1979) 129–42.

39. G. J. Wenham and J. G. McConville, "Drafting Techniques in Some Deuteronomic Laws," *VT* 30 (1980) 248–52.

40. *Ibid.* 252 n. 9.

41. See Wagner, "Rest," 236–37.

42. Even A. D. H. Mayes, *Deuteronomy* (New Century Bible Commentary; Grand Rapids, Mich., 1981) who places 22:1–12 under a single title (p. 305), must ultimately admit two different aspects to the redaction to support a thematic ordering of the prohibitions in vv. 5, 9–11. The laws are said to be placed in sequence "out of a concern for the integrity of all forms of life and the preservation of the distinction of the created order" (p. 306). Verse 12 would then be attached here only because of the law which precedes it (p. 309).

43. This against Kaufman, "Structure," who relates 19:1–22:8 to the fifth commandment in the Catholic numbering (pp. 134–37) and 22:9–23:19 to the sixth commandment (pp. 137–39). 22:5 "seems intrusive and may well be displaced from its original position

of laws are interleaved within one another. The confusion of sexes through exchange of clothing in v. 5 is inserted within the realm of "preservation of life," continued by vv. 6–7 and 8. Looking at it from the other side, one sees that allowing the mother bird to live (vv. 6–7) as well as the precautions against a fatal accident in v. 8 intrude into the field of "preventing mixtures" introduced by v. 5. If it were merely a matter of the attraction of associated material, then the things that belong together thematically would be arranged in direct sequence. But evidently the two groups of laws have been redactionally interleaved, so as to give a sharper profile to the transition from one subject to another. Incidentally, the same technique can also be observed in 23:17–24:5 for the tradition from the theme of "sexuality" to that of "property."

If it is true that this technique is also used in 22:1–12 to dovetail two groups of laws with differing content, at the same time a subtle joining by means of key words serves to shape a self-contained intermediate text.[44] In detail, this happens as follows: the law concerning neighborly assistance in v. 4 is shaped, both syntactically and in its formulations, in a way that is largely parallel to v. 1, the beginning of the law about runaway stock and lost property. Whereas v. 1 speaks of oxen and sheep, v. 4 mentions ass and ox; but the ass, which, as a beast of burden, replaces the sheep of v. 1, has been used in v. 3 to begin the list of other lost property, in whose regard one may no more be indifferent than in the case of the lost oxen and sheep of v. 1. Thus v. 4 is connected to v. 1 as well as to v. 3, but differs from both in two respects: first, it reverses the order of the animals, naming first the ass of v. 3 (*ḥămôr*) and only after that the ox (*šôr*) of v. 1. Second, it uses the expression "fallen down by the way" (*npl* [*Qal*] *badderek*), which corresponds to the helpful gesture of raising the animal.[45] Both actions, however, are formulated in syntactic parallelism to v. 1. By these common features and differences, v. 4 is certainly distanced from its model in Exod 23:5, but it becomes a connecting link between vv. 1–3 on the one side and vv. 6–10 on the other, for the expressions *ḥămôr/šôr/npl* [*Qal*] *badderek* serve as key words in an (ornamental) chiastic structure

among other laws of forbidden mixtures in vv. 9–10" (p. 136). But the clothing motif in v. 5 is an element of a chiastic structure that extends through vv. 5–12 on the level of content and thus constitutes a bridge between the blocks of laws (p. 136; on this point see n. 47 below).

44. On some of the references that follow, cf. Seitz, *Redaktionsgeschichtliche Studien*, 166, 174–75, 250–51.

45. The opposition of *npl* [*Qal*] and *qwm* [*Hiphil*] in the absolute infinitive with finite verb-form is found only here in the OT.

and are repeated, reversing the order of v. 4, in vv. 6, 8 and 10.[46] Thus, v. 4 could have been given its concrete shape by the redactor of the transitional text as we have it. The prescriptions for clothing in vv. 5 and 11 are connected to one another by the negated verb *lbš* [*Qal*] ⟦'to wear'⟧, which is used only at these two places in Deuteronomy.[47] Finally, the repeated words that overlap the various laws—*bayit* (v. 2) and *bayit ḥādāš* (v. 8), *śimlâ* (v. 3) and *śimlat ʾiššâ* (v. 5)—give a feeling of unity. But since both these expressions are only picked up in variations, their repeated use is distinguished from those repetitions within the structure that we mentioned earlier. Despite their differing content, vv. 8 and 9 follow easily on one another within the topic "building a new house and planting a vineyard" (cf. Deut 20:5–7, 28:30).[48] But formally, v. 9 belongs with vv. 10–11.[49] Verse 12 is attracted to v. 11 by the subject of "clothing."[50]

Despite all that has been said, 22:1–12 does not stand as an independent block of text between two others, but as a bridging text it is also linked, both in what it says and the way it says and the way it formulates it, to the laws that precede and follow it. Thus *npl* [*Qal*] is used in Deuteronomy, apart from 22:4 and 8, only in 21:1 to refer to one who has "fallen" in open country, namely a murder victim. When 22:4 calls for the raising of a collapsed animal, apparently one should also think, in the context, that its life is to be preserved thereby. But in any case, someone's fall from an unprotected house roof (v. 8) would bring about blood guilt, which is designated in Deuteronomy only here and at 19:10 with *dāmîm*.[51] Thus *npl* [*Qal*] and *dāmîm* connect the laws in 22:4, 8 with the field of the fifth commandment in the Decalogue.[52] As far as the law of neighborly help in vv. 1–3 is concerned, the asso-

46. I am grateful to C. Locher for this observation.

47. In contrast, the chiasmus established by Kaufman ("Structure," 136) for vv. 5–12 is undifferentiated: clothing (v. 5), animals (vv. 6–7), house (v. 8), field (v. 9), animals (v. 10), clothing (vv. 11–12).

48. Perhaps it is for this reason that 'field', which would fit better with 'sowing', as apparently preserved by the parallel law in Lev 19:19 from the ancient prototype, is replaced by 'vineyard'; thus Seitz, *Redaktionsgeschichtliche Studien*, 250–51.

49. It could fit within a chiastic arrangement on the topical level: mixing of plants (v. 9), mixing of animals (v. 10), mixing of (animal) wool and (vegetable) flax (v. 11).

50. Kaufman, "Structure" (see n. 22 above) 136, sees a possible connection between the edges of the roof, where a parapet is to be erected (v. 8) and the edges of the cloak, where tassels are to be attached (v. 12).

51. The frequent use of *dam* in chap. 19 and in 21:1–9 is particularly noteworthy.

52. Compare Deut 22:8 with the directions about careless killing in Exod 21:33–34 within the context of laws about killing and other bodily harm in 21:12–36.

ciation of death or destruction would have been close to hand with the mention of 'lost goods' (*ʾăbēdâ*) that 'have been lost' (*ʾbd*). Finally, there is also a connection between 22:2 and 21:12: the strayed animal and the woman prisoner of war are to be brought into the interior of one's house (*ʾel tôk bêtekā*). These two places represent the only occurrences of this prepositional expression in the Old Testament.

For the discussion of a redactional ordering of individual laws toward particular commandments of the Decalogue, a key role should be ascribed to vv. 6–7. They forbid, when a bird's nest is seized, that the 'mother sitting upon', that is, together with, '(her) young' (*ʾēm ʿal bānîm*) 'be taken', that is, be killed for one's own nourishment. The expression, following Gen 32:11 and Hos 10:14, represents complete destruction. This prohibition thus belongs to the "commentary" on the fifth commandment of the Decalogue. It is true that nearly all commentators[53] up to the present[54] connect the protection of the mother bird with the commandment concerning parents, the fourth of the Decalogue. In this connection they point to the promise in Deut 22:7, "that it may go well with you, and that you may live long," the same thing that is promised for honor done to human parents in 5:16. This same promise, with the two verbs *yṭb* [['to go well']] and *ʾrk* [*Hiphil*] [['to be long']] is otherwise found only at 4:40. It is true that in the latter verse it occurs in an extended form, but it still represents the only genuine parallel to 22:7. For only in 4:40 and 22:7 is Israel the addressee and subject of *ʾrk* [*Hiphil*] [['to be long']], whereas in 5:16 "days" is the subject. In addition, the motivation of the commandment about parents in 5:16 reverses the order of the verbs in contrast to 4:40 and 22:7, mentioning first the lengthening of the days of life and afterward, well-being. But I may add that the formula appears in connection with individual commands requiring "respect for life, or for the bearer of life."[55] The law that regulates the taking of a bird's nest in 22:6–7 can thus be connected only with the fifth commandment of the Decalogue.[56] But then Guilding's thesis, that the commandments of

---

53. An exception is, e.g., P. C. Craigie, *The Book of Deuteronomy* (The New International Commentary on the Old Testament; Grand Rapids, Mich., 1976) 288–89. He has nothing to say about v. 7b.

54. Most recently O. Keel, *Das Böcklein in der Milch seiner Mutter und Verwandtes: Im Lichte eines altorientalischen Bildmotivs* (Orbis biblicus et orientalis 33; Fribourg, 1980) 44.

55. R. P. Merendino, *Das deuteronomische Gesetz: Eine literarkritische, gattungs- und überlieferungsgeschichtliche Untersuchung zu Dt 12–26* (Bonner biblische Beiträge 31; Bonn, 1969) 256.

56. On the purpose of this regulation, see Craigie, *Deuteronomy*, 288–89.

the Decalogue are always commented in pairs, in this case the fourth and fifth commandments, loses its only basis in 22:1–12.[57] The laws in vv. 1–3, 4, 6–7, and 8 belong within the subject matter of the commandment against killing.

In contrast, the laws in 22:5, 9–11, 12 belong to the subsequent field of the sixth commandment. It is possible that they cover an ancient holiness code.[58] Then the redactor could have placed them before the other sexual regulations for that reason. In any case, together with the cultic-sexual rules concerning acceptance into the assembly of Yʜᴡʜ (23:1–8), the purity of the armed camp (23:9–14), and the prohibition of cult prostitution (23:17–18), they form a redactional "frame" around the laws for marriage and family (22:13–30). One detail of the prohibition of transvestism signals its belonging to the field of the sixth commandment, namely the expression *śimlat ʾiššâ* [['dress of a woman']] since *śimlâ* [['dress, apparel']] specifically with regard to women's clothing is used otherwise only at 22:17 (note *ʾiššâ* in v. 16),[59] the legal procedures to be followed when a wife is accused of having had premarital intercourse. The taboos against certain combinations in vv. 9–11 reveal a connotative relationship "to religious, and especially sexual mixing."[60] Thus the "vineyard" mentioned in v. 9 is also a topos in the language of love. Consequently, the forbidden sowing may have been conceived by the redactor in its sexual aspect (cf. Sir 26:20). According to Deut 22:10, ox and ass are not even to be employed in a common task, whereas the parallel in Lev 19:19 forbids only the inter-

57. Against Guilding, "Notes," 47–48, esp. 48. Oddly enough, he limits the block of text that is supposed to correspond to the commandments about parents and about killing to 16:18–22:8, whereas the next block begins only at 22:13. In this way, vv. 9–12 are, without explanation, left out of consideration.

58. This is the import of many explanations given for these verses. The text itself speaks explicitly of the transvestism in v. 5 as "an abomination for Yʜᴡʜ" (*tôʿēbâ*); on this point see W. H. P. Römer, "Randbemerkungen zur Travestie von Deut. 22,5," in *Travels in the World of the Old Testament: Fs. M. A. Beek* (ed. M. S. H. G. Heerma Von Voss et al.; Studia Semitica Neerlandica 16; Assen, 1974) 217–22. The common sowing and harvest "become holy," that is, they are withdrawn from normal use, and are forfeit to the sanctuary. The wearing of tassels demanded by v. 12 is (re)interpreted in Num 15:37–41 in terms of faith in Yʜᴡʜ.

59. In the nearer context, 21:13 speaks expressly of *śimlat šibyâ*, and 22:3 and 24:13 of *śimlātô*.

60. C. Steuernagel, *Das Deuteronomium* (2d ed. HAT I/3,1; Göttingen, 1923) 132. In addition, C. M. Carmichael, "Forbidden Mixtures," *VT* 32 (1982) 394–415, surmises a sexual meaning. But he bases its origin on "cryptic remarks of Jacob about the actions of his sons" (p. 411). These are imaginative speculations, but can scarcely be maintained exegetically.

breeding of two different kinds of animal. It is noticeable that this prohibition of any bastardizing of animals and of other mixing in Leviticus
precedes the law about the misconduct of another man's concubine
(19:20–21). In Deut 22:12 the words *kĕsût* 'cloak' and *ksh* [*Piel*] 'cover',
which are missing in the parallel at Num 15:37–41, may betray the redactor's intention: they refer to the covering of nakedness, for *kĕsût*,
which is found only here in Deuteronomy, describes, as in Exod 22:26,
the blanket that is worn by the poor as a cloak (*śimlâ*, cf. Deut 24:13)
over the naked body, as in Job 24:7 and 31:19 and metaphorically in
26:6. But *ksh* [*Piel*] [['cover']] is used in Deuteronomy otherwise only at
23:13 for the covering up of excrement. So the tassels may simply have
weighted and drawn down the corners of the square cloak, in order "to
protect the body, and especially the private parts, from being uncovered."[61] Consequently, a rationalization like that in Num 15:38–40 appeared unnecessary.

The preceding analyses of the disposition of the text reveal clear
distinctions between the systematization of the "charter rights" (12:2–
16:17) and the "constitutional provisions" (16:18–18:22) on the one
hand and the structure that shapes the transitional section in 22:1–12.
In addition, the ordering of the prescriptions in the "penal and civil
code" (chaps. 19–25) diverges from the preceding parts of the codex
also in the way in which the groups of laws are brought into approximately relationship with the individual commandments of the Decalogue. Besides this, the laws from chap. 21 to chap. 25 are those least
affected by deuteronomic language. There is an intention behind them
whose interest is not primarily covenant theology or paranesis, but
clearly and simply jurisprudence. It is also here most frequently, within
the legal corpus, that reference is made to material from the book of
the covenant (Exodus 21–23). Only within chaps. 19–25 are the so-
called *biᵓarta* laws[62] correctly arranged in relation to the respective
commandments of the Decalogue.[63] This observation already permits
one to conclude that probably, in the history of development of the
deuteronomic legal corpus, chaps. 12–18 lay to hand for the redactor
who wanted to understand the deuteronomic codex according to the
Decalogue and then to give a juristic expansion, in light of the

61. This was already noted by Schultz, *Deuteronomium*, 559; see also pp. 559–60 on
corresponding Jewish views and customs; most recently Phillips, *Deuteronomy*, 147.

62. Against F.-L. Hossfeld, *Der Dekalog: Seine späten Fassungen: Die originale Komposition
und seine Vorstufen* (Orbis biblicus et orientalis 45; Fribourg, 1982) 279–80, esp. n. 247.

63. Thus the laws in 19:11–13, 16:21; 21:1–9, 18–21 are related to the fifth commandment, 22:13–21, 22, 23–27 to the sixth, and 24:7 to the seventh.

Decalogue, to this book of laws, which was regarded as incomplete. Thus the laws were only secondarily integrated into this concept and for that reason can only be interpreted with difficulty on the basis of the Decalogue as model. But the laws regarding offices can only have been edited into a unified group during the Exile.[64] This means that the deuteronomic collection of laws can only have been expanded and structured in imitation of the Decalogue during the Exile or afterward. This says nothing about the age of the laws that were included. But probably the laws in chaps. 21–25, from a redaction-critical standpoint, must be said to constitute the newest part of the deuteronomic codex.

The older laws were thus mainly directed to cultic and social matters. During the Exile an ordering of offices that served to establish a division of power (and thereby was critical of the state) was added, and afterward a still more detailed code of laws was included. The "charter of YHWH's rights" in chaps. 12–16 and 26, which is thus both historically and theologically the core of the deuteronomic collection of laws, now forms a kind of "frame" around the whole. In the intention of the final redaction, the system of the whole body of laws is to be interpreted on the basis of the order of the Ten Commandments. The individual laws thus appear as concretizations of the Decalogue. This need not necessarily agree with a modern historical-critical exegesis of the Decalogue. The double expression "statutes and ordinances" (*ḥuqqîm ûmišpāṭîm*) in fact signals a commentary of the Decalogue through the deuteronomic legal corpus, since its structure, at the level of final redaction, is oriented to the order of the commandments of the Decalogue.

There can be no doubt that much of what has been sketched above as a series of theses is in need of further detailed investigation. But if the results here presented are correct, the following theologically important consequence, among others, emerges: The Decalogue and the legal codex are embraced, in Deuteronomy, by YHWH's covenant with Israel. Therefore the Decalogue was "never understood as an absolute law of moral conduct"[65] in Israel. But the deuteronomic redaction has decided that the Decalogue may never be divorced from the law that interprets it. This relationship of the Decalogue to the individual laws as its context is, of course, as the parallels in Exodus 20 already show, temporally determined. But since then there can be, for hermeneutics, no retreat from the principle of such a connection between the Decalogue and the individual laws as the regulations for its accomplish-

---

64. Lohfink, "Sicherung," 149.

65. G. von Rad, *Theologie des Alten Testaments I: Die Theologie der geschichtlichen Überlieferungen Israels* (6th ed.; Munich, 1968) 207.

ment. In the law, the Decalogue finds its "positive content" and thus is enabled "to furnish positive norms for the conduct of life."[66] Conversely, the deuteronomic collection of laws systematized on the basis of the Decalogue can, according to the prologue to the Decalogue (5:6) only be realized under the precondition of that freedom for which YHWH has redeemed his people.[67]

66. Against G. von Rad, *Theologie,* 208, who with these words denies that the Decalogue can be "a directive for moral life" (*loc. cit.*). F. Crüsemann has most recently held the same position: *Bewahrung der Freiheit: Das Thema des Dekalogs in sozialgeschichtlicher Perspektive* (Munich, 1983) 8–13, 81–82.

67. A continuation of this article is to appear under the title, "Zur Abfolge der Gesetze in Deuteronomium 16, 18–21,23: Weitere Beobachtungen," probably in *Bib* 69 (1988). [[This article was published in *Bib* 69, pp. 63–92.]]

Distribution of the Functions of Power: The Laws Concerning Public Offices in Deuteronomy 16:18–18:22

NORBERT LOHFINK

⟦55⟧ In 1748 Charles Baron de Montesquieu published a book titled *De l'Esprit de Loi*. This was the first time anyone had systematically worked out a theory of organizational distribution of the functions of the power of the state. Since then, distribution of functions of power has been accepted as one of the basic principles of most democratic constitutions. The decisive thing about this theory is the separation and counterbalancing of the various functions of the state, all of which must be regulated by a fundamental law. The number of separated functions and their precise demarcations may vary, but the classic trinity is the legislature, the executive, the judiciary. Montesquieu, who got his ideas from observation of what obtained in England at that time, illustrated these ideas with examples from classical antiquity. As far as I can see, he failed to notice that he might also have cited an example from the Bible.

The Church of Jesus Christ is not a state. Good arguments can be adduced that it should be, in reality, a *communio* of congregations, supervised in such a way that they are able to live according to the principle of unanimity. Even such congregations must have something resembling law, but whether such an issue as distribution of functions of power need to be raised is open to question. The charisms of the early Christian congregations were something different.

There are also arguments, however, for an organized structure in the nature of a "greater Church," and, *de facto*, such "greater churches"

Reprinted with permission from "Die Sicherung der Wirksamkeit des Gotteswortes durch das Prinzip der Schriftlichkeit der Tora und durch das Prinzip der Gewaltenteilung nach den Ämtergesetzen des Buches Deuteronomium (Dt 16,18–18,22)," in *Great Themes from the Old Testament* (trans. Ronald Walls; Chicago: Franciscan Herald, 1981) 55–75.

[[56]] exist. They are seen, preeminently, in the ecclesial entities of today. Even in a departmentalized society, they manifest many similarities with the state, and we cannot ignore the fact that their laws show tendencies to assimilate to state parallels. The Roman Catholic Church, in particular, according to a statement of the canon lawyer Klaus Mörsdorf, "has developed fully the concept of the unity of power." The origins of this concept are various. It can hardly be disputed, however, that in the course of this development great pressure was exerted in the direction of assimilation to state models, particularly in ages when the concept of the absolutist state was dominant. Today the demand is constantly made, especially by American canonists, with perhaps only partial success, that Catholic canon law be reformed in accord with the principle of the distribution of functions of power. There are real prospects of introduction of an independent executive jurisdiction, though not in the highest instances.

Obviously, we face the question: Are not tendencies to assimilate to state models again at work, rather than the effort to find genuinely ecclesial constitutional forms? If imitation of the state model of distribution of power functions is too external, can the written word of God (for example) and the full emergence of charisms be assured the place they ought to have in the Church of Christ? And so the further question arises: Might we not be able to find, in the Bible itself, possibilities for the distribution of power functions that are proper to the Church, and need not be imitated? They would have, it is true, an element of historical relativity, but they would provide the right starting point for our discussions.

Most Catholic canon lawyers still see unrestricted discussion of a thoroughgoing distribution of functions of power within the Church as fraught with theological problems. Their theology pushes them, rather, in the direction of centralization of power, which is linked with the traditional Catholic rationale of the structure of the Church. This theology posits a legislative act of the historical Jesus, by which he conferred powers upon the Church he founded. Through this posited act, the monarchical papacy and the unified authority of the Church were established [[57]] once and for all, and no one has the right to alter any of it—at least not at the highest level, although at lower levels some compromises may be allowed. Moreover, in the theory of ecclesial authority an important part is played by the concept of the representation of the *one* Christ, who combined in himself all the offices of the Old Testament dispensation of salvation (one is accustomed to speak of the offices of teacher, priest, and pastor, associated respectively with prophet, priest, and king). Finally, it may be that vestiges of the neo-Platonist idea of emanation still operate underground. If, in the last analysis, the Church is ruled by God, then God's will must necessarily flow down from above, step by step, as it were; hence at least at the apex of the human order there must be a single channel, directed by God himself, and only at lower levels could the streams of God's will begin to branch into subsidiary channels. Were things otherwise, the divine guidance of the Church would not be assured, according to this conceptual model.

Today, however, the theory of the formal institution of the monarchical papacy by the historical Jesus is exegetically untenable. Furthermore, in the New Testament the fulfillment of all the Old Testament offices in Jesus was intended to be a Christological affirmation, and Jesus was thereby designated the all-embracing, unsurpassable, eschatological mediator of the new covenant. From this affirmation, should this mediator be succeeded by something in the form of a Church—and such a development is indeed necessary—nothing can be deduced concerning the differentiation of offices within the Church. One can share in the power of Christ, in the latter or in the former respect. On the latent notion of emanation, one may say conclusively that we are not under any obligation to neo-Platonism. Is the intellectual problem really altered if, instead of saying God guides only one free being infallibly (the pope) and all others only through him, we say that he guides many free beings infallibly?

We are not committed, therefore, to a theology that insists upon unification of the functions of power. We are on a better theological tack if we proceed from the idea of a Church that is instituted not in juridical detail but in its essence, and is irrevocably bound by the word [[58]] of God, and possesses the assurance that it will preserve that word unfalsified throughout the ages. But this Church will have the right—the duty, indeed—to form its official structure to suit the circumstances of history. Part of this historical accommodation will consist in refraining from capriciously tampering with structures that are in place and functioning. But one does not have to justify this sort of well-founded conservatism in law by reference to the historical Jesus; it is simply human common sense. And on the very same plane belongs accommodation to those forms of law that each epoch finds best and most suited to it. It is precisely in this context that we must place the current question about greater distribution of the functions of power—a very proper question.

If one wishes to discover typically ecclesial possibilities of such distribution, it is useful (to say the least) to keep one's eyes open to such models as may be found in Holy Scripture. And because we are concerned with a Church that has in many aspects accommodated to the state, it may be wise to look at the Old Testament, for in those days Church and state had not yet become differentiated. Obviously, we will not find a model there that can be simply transposed; but we may perhaps learn to what things we must always pay heed concerning the distribution of the functions of power, as this would operate within the community of the faithful.

With this in mind, we shall present and discuss the laws concerning offices in Deuteronomy. They may well form a draft of a constitution that is based upon the distribution of functions of power, although scholars have not hitherto really observed this fact.

The Deuteronomic Laws Concerning Offices

The first part of the Deuteronomic law book (Deut 12:2–16:17) is devoted to the regulation of the cult. It deals with the central sanctuary of Israel, the exclusiveness of the cult of Yahweh in Israel, clean and unclean foods, and the obligations attached to various holy seasons.

[59] A new theme is introduced abruptly at Deut 16:18: judges and officials. Here begins the law concerning offices, and this interests us in the following details. A kind of ideal for judges is set out (16:19f.); then, following an introductory section (16:21f–17:1), containing a few apodictically formulated cultic precepts, comes the casuistically conceived description of a model process, with its inbuilt rule of the two witnesses (17:2–7). All of this is attached, by association, to the prescription for setting up local courts in 16:18. The main thread is picked up again in 17:8 and developed: as well as local courts, there is to be a central court of justice (17:8–13). At the end of this law, the death penalty is decreed for nonacceptance of the verdict of this central court (17:12f.).

> [16:18] You are to appoint judges and scribes in each of the towns that Yahweh is giving you, for all your tribes; these must administer an impartial judgment to the people. You must not pervert the law; you must be impartial; you must take no bribes, for a bribe blinds wise men's eyes and jeopardizes the cause of the just. Strict justice must be your ideal, so that you may live in rightful possession of the land that Yahweh your God is giving you.
>
> You must not plant a sacred pole of any wood whatsoever beside the alter that you put up for Yahweh your God; nor must you set up a standing stone, a thing Yahweh your God would abhor. To Yahweh your God you must sacrifice nothing from herd or flock that has any blemish or defect whatsoever, for Yahweh your God holds this detestable.

If there is anyone, man or woman, among you in any of the towns
Yahweh your God is giving you, who does what is displeasing to Yahweh
your God by violating his covenant, who goes and serves other gods and
worships them, or the sun or the moon or any of heaven's array—a
thing I have forbidden—and this person is denounced to you; if after
careful inquiry it is found true and confirmed that this hateful thing
has been done in Israel, you must take the man or woman guilty of this
evil deed outside your city gates, and [[60]] there you must stone that
man or woman to death. A man may be put to death only on the word
of two witnesses or three; and no man may be put to death on the word
of one witness alone. The witnesses shall be the first to raise their hands
against him in putting him to death, then all the people shall follow.
You must banish this evil from your midst.

If a case comes before you which is too difficult for you, a case of
murder, legal rights or assault, or any dispute at all in your towns, you
must make your way to the place Yahweh your God chooses, and approach the Levitical priests and the judge then in office. They will hold
an inquiry and give a decision for you. You must abide by the decision
they pronounce for you in that place which Yahweh chooses, and you
must take care to carry out all their instructions. You must abide by the
verdict they give you and by the decision they declare to you, swerving
neither right nor left of the sentence they have pronounced for you. If
any presumes to disobey either the priest who is there in the service of
Yahweh your God, or the judge, that man must die. You must banish
this evil from Israel. And all the people shall hear of it and be afraid
and not act presumptuously a second time. [17:13]

The central court of justice of Deuteronomy was not, as one often
reads, a court of appeal, which could reverse the verdict of a court of
first instance. Rather, it was supposed to uphold—not overthrow—the
judgments made by normal means in the local courts over particular
cases. It was superior to the local courts because it had a sacral character. Thus the law concerning the central court of justice provides for
the presence, alongside the "judge" (17:9, 12), of the "Levitical priest"
(17:9), that is, "the priest who is there in the service of Yahweh your
God" (17:12).

Because formerly the king had been the highest judge, the "system
of justice" theme is followed by the theme of kingship (Deut 17:14–
20). The Deuteronomic law concerning kings is based upon the presupposition [[61]] that Israel, having completed occupation of the
land, will want to install a king (17:14). First it determines the qualifi-
cations of kingship: the king must be chosen by Yahweh and he must
be an Israelite (17:15). There follows a kind of picture of the ideal king
(17:16–17). This leads to the prescription that the king possess a copy

of the Deuteronomic law, must have it always by him, and read from it daily (17:18–20).

> [17:14] When you reach the land that Yahweh your God gives you, and take possession of it and live there, if you say to yourself, "I will appoint a king over me like all the surrounding nations," it must be a king of Yahweh's choosing whom you appoint over you; it must be one from among your brothers that is appointed king over you; you are not to give yourself a foreign king who is no brother of yours.
>
> Ensure that he does not increase the number of his horses, or make the people go back to Egypt to increase his cavalry, for Yahweh said to you, "You must never go back that way again." Nor must he increase the number of his wives, for that could lead his heart astray. Nor must he increase his gold and silver excessively. When he is seated on his royal throne he must write a copy of this Law on a scroll for his own use at the dictation of the Levitical priests. It must never leave him and he must read it every day of his life and learn to fear Yahweh his God by keeping all the words of this Law and observing these laws. So his heart will not look down on his brothers and he will swerve neither right nor left from these commandments. If he does this, he will have long days on his throne, he and his sons, in Israel. [17:20]

By an association of ideas, the theme of kingship is followed by the theme of the ministers of the cult (Deut 18:1–8). The priests had already been mentioned in the law concerning the central court, and in the law concerning the king. Their chief function is the offering of sacrifice, from which they derive their livelihood. The law concerning the priesthood [62] starts off with the principle that priests may not own heritable land, but must live from the parts of the sacrifices that belong to Yahweh (181f.). All Levites from the rural towns, who had lost their livelihood as a result of the centralization of worship, are guaranteed the right of participating in the service of the central sanctuary and of sharing correspondingly in the portion of the sacrifices (18:6–8).

> [18:1] The Levitical priests, that is to say the whole of the tribe of Levi, shall have no share or inheritance with Israel: they shall live on the foods offered to Yahweh and on his dues. This tribe is to have no inheritance among their brothers; Yahweh will be their inheritance as he promised them.
>
> These are the priests' dues from the people, from those who offer an ox or a sheep in sacrifice; the priest is to be given the shoulder, the cheeks, and the stomach. You must give him the first fruits of your corn, your wine, your oil, as well as the first of your sheep's shearing. For Yahweh your God has chosen him out of all your tribes to stand

before Yahweh your God, to do the duties of the sacred ministry, and to bless in Yahweh's name him and his sons for all time.

If the Levite living in one of your towns anywhere in Israel decides to come to the place Yahweh chooses, he shall minister there in the name of Yahweh his God like all his fellow Levites who stand ministering there in the presence of Yahweh, and shall eat equal shares with them, no count being taken of the claims he has on the Levitical families for the goods he has sold. [18:8]

A kind of transition is then made to the law concerning prophets, which we find in Deut 18:9–22. At times in the ancient East, activities in the sanctuaries included such things as rites of child sacrifice and various forms of soothsaying and sorcery; all of this is forbidden (18:9–12). The positive intention of these practices was the desire to find, in specific life situations, individual contact with the deity. For [[63]] Israel, too, this motive was recognized and a means was provided, but one that was not under the control of the priesthood. The prophets take their place beside the priests (18:13–15). Then follows the etiology of these men, who are inspired afresh from time to time by Yahweh for the sake of his people. The office of the prophet is seen as having been instituted at Horeb, in association with the giving of the law (18:16–18). Within the framework of this etiology is recorded Yahweh's promise and his commandment. The promise: Those who do not obey the words of the prophets, Yahweh himself will judge (18:19). (It is different in disobedience to the verdict of the central court, when Yahweh does not take part in punishment but delegates its execution to Israel.) The commandment: Prophets who are not commissioned by Yahweh, or prophets who speak in the name of other gods, are to be punished by death (18:20). There follows a criterion which enables one to recognize a prophet who has no genuine commission from Yahweh: the nonoccurrence of what he foretold (18:20–22).

[18:9] When you come into the land Yahweh your God gives you, you must not fall into the habit of imitating the detestable practices of the natives. There must never be anyone among you who makes his son or daughter pass through fire, who practices divination, who is soothsayer, augur or sorcerer, who uses charms, consults ghosts or spirits, or calls up the dead. For the man who does these things is detestable to Yahweh your God: it is because of these detestable practices that Yahweh your God is driving these nations before you.

You must be entirely faithful to Yahweh your God. For these nations whom you are dispossessing may listen to soothsayers and diviners, but this is not the gift that Yahweh your God gives to you; Yahweh your God will raise up for you a prophet like myself, from among yourselves, from your own brothers; to him you must listen. This is what you yourselves asked of Yahweh your God at Horeb on the day of the Assembly. "Do not let me hear again," you said, [[64]] "the voice of Yahweh my God, nor look any longer on this great fire, or I shall die"; and Yahweh said to me, "All they have spoken is well said. I will raise up a prophet like yourself for them from their own brothers; I will put my words into his mouth and he shall tell them all I command him. The man who does not listen to my words that he speaks in my name shall be held answerable to me for it. But the prophet who presumes to say in my name a thing I have not commanded him to say, or who speaks in the name of other gods, that prophet shall die."

You may say in your heart, "How are we to know what word was not spoken by Yahweh?" When a prophet speaks in the name of Yahweh and the thing does not happen and the word is not fulfilled, then it has not been spoken by Yahweh. The prophet has spoken with presumption. You have nothing to fear from him. [18:22]

The next section of the law treats the cities of refuge, and the law concerning offices is thus completed. It comprises the law concerning the judicial system, the king, the priests, and the prophets. The persons or classes of persons who are dealt with are judge, official, priest, king, prophet.

A Coherent Constitutional Scheme

Recent biblical scholarship agrees on the thesis that all the laws concerning offices are not of the same antiquity and that all intrinsically manifest several strata, so that at least part of the text, as we now have it, was not originally formulated with the intention of forming a component of a set of laws concerning the various offices in Israel. But for the most part the matter is left there, and one refrains from asking further whether the four laws about offices belonged together at least from a certain stage in their development onward, and from that point were [[65]] intended to be read as a single system of pronouncements. This problem for the history of redaction is posed in what follows.

Obviously, it is possible that when the laws were gathered together, the dominant idea was that this was a kind of museum of ancient unrelated, individual laws. But it is equally possible that they had come to be understood as a self-consistent piece of legislation. That the latter possibility is more probable can be shown, and serves as a preliminary to the explication of the date of the decisive comprehensive redaction of this group of laws.

If anyone had regarded the whole Deuteronomic law as a unity, that person would have been the editor, or—for the law undoubtedly has many strata—the last reviser of the law concerning the king. He demands that the king possess a copy of "this *torah.*" Nowhere else within Deuteronomy 12–26 is this *corpus* itself designated comprehensively as *torah.* On the contrary, the term *torah* recurs in the sections of the Book of Deuteronomy which are placed around the older middle section (Deuteronomy 5–28) and which belong to the total redaction of the book. It always denotes the whole middle section—paraenesis, laws, blessing, and curse, all of these. Wherever the word *torah* appears, it is this section that is designated a unity, and the laws concerning offices stand at the center of this unity.

The techniques that were used in the ancient East to arrange material in a comprehensive collection of laws have nothing in common with modern principles of presentation of laws. Linking often occurs from sheer association of ideas. In the process, it may happen that in the middle of the treatment of theme A, a new them, B, emerges. In such a case, theme A suffers temporary interruption; theme B is first dealt with, then theme A is continued. If the sequence A, B, A2 occurs, one may count on it that, in the eyes of the author of the sequence, the laws that are grouped under B are so closely related that they can be driven, like a wedge, into the equally well related laws of group A. The Deuteronomic laws concerning offices, which start with the laws concerning the judicial system, provide just such an example. In contrast to [[66]] the laws which follow, they are more concerned with a collection of things—the judicial system—than a group of persons. However, three different groups of persons appear within them: judges, officials, and priests. Clearly, this leads to thoughts about the different groups of persons, and thus we arrive at the themes "king," "priest," "prophet." And at 19:1, with the law concerning cities of refuge, we are back at our original material, the judicial system, for the "cities of refuge" theme leads to the special procedure in cases of manslaughter or murder. After a short paragraph on the shifting of boundaries (19:14), the list of laws on the judicial system continues with a paragraph on the principle of the two witnesses (19:15) and one paragraph on the punishment for perjury under oath in court (19:16–21).

The sequence A, B, A2 is clearly evident. The laws concerning the constitution of the courts in Deut 16:18–17:13 have two aspects. In themselves, they form the beginnings of a series of laws concerning Israel's judicial system; these continue in 19:1. At the same time, however, they treat of persons and offices in Israel, thus stimulating the treatment of a series of laws about offices. And so we have to regard them as the first in that series. From the point of view of a legal system, therefore, all the laws concerning offices belong together.

It might be objected—if it is a question of the systematic treatment of all the important offices in Israel—that a matter of such great importance as the supreme military command is never mentioned. On close examination, however, this objection turns into confirmation. In the view of Deuteronomy, a distinction must be made between the mercenary troops, who are directly subject to the king, and the conscript army of the whole people. The mercenary force is given only passing mention in the law concerning the king, when it is decreed that the king must not acquire too many horses (17:16), for the number of horses indicates the size of the royal charioteer force. The leadership of the army is regulated by Deuteronomy in the law on calling up the army (Deut 20:1–9). At the calling up, two groups of persons take part: the priest and the scribes. "Priest" (in the singular) most probably indicates the figure known to us from 17:12, who delivers the battle sermon. The scribes, a [[67]] group of officials known to us from 16:18, form the troops. When these units have been formed, they place officers over them (20:9).

According to the theory of Deuteronomy, there is no permanent officer corps for the conscript army. This corps is reconstituted for each war, as is the host. In contrast, those who have to live permanently in relation to the army are treated in the laws concerning offices, although in that context their sporadic operations on the occasion of the calling up of the army are not mentioned. We cannot expect to find, on Deuteronomic presuppositions, explicit law concerning a supreme military hierarchy.

The list of laws concerning the most important offices in Israel is complete, and so we have good reason to assume that the chief redaction of this section of the Deuteronomic law was intended to be a comprehensive piece of legislation concerning the principal functions of power in Israel.

Dating the Chief Redaction of the Constitution

To date the chief redaction of the section, one must look for the most recent strata that stretch through several laws. We may ignore more recent glosses and additions in only one law, because there cannot be any design behind them that comprehends the entire group of laws. In what follows below, a few reasons will be indicated for thinking we must set this redaction in the period at the beginning of the exile—that is, late in the first half of the sixth century B.C.

The Torah, which is stressed in the law concerning the king, is written on a roll (*sefer*) and kept safe by the "Levitical priests." This connects it with the Deuteronomic Chronicle, which belongs to the beginning of the exilic period. According to the law concerning priests, every rural Levite had the right to offer sacrifice in Jerusalem. According to 2 Kgs 23:9, this right was not granted to the rural Levites by the reform of Josiah (621 B.C.). It is commonly concluded from this fact that the Jerusalem priesthood engineered this omission in executing the [[68]] Deuteronomic law on its own vital interest. It is more likely, however, that this passage was not yet in the law at this time, and now expresses a further-reaching claim of the one-time rural Levites. On the other hand, the passage must be dated before the end of the exilic period, for by then the great compromise between the Zadokites and the Levites was beginning to take shape, and Deuteronomy knows nothing of this.

The rule at the end of the law concerning prophets, and distinguishing between authentic and false prophets of Yahweh, may well be ancient, but it turns attention forcibly to the problems that exercised Jeremiah and his school.

If, on the basis of such observations, one accepts the beginning of the exile as the time when the decisive redaction of the group of laws concerning offices was made, and if one links this redaction with the Deuteronomic revision of the historical traditions of Israel, the draft of a constitution which developed as a result is not the description of an existent reality but a utopian theory. Much that is in the draft may have been adumbrated during the time of the monarchy in Judah. But the laws concerning offices are also the result of a critical encounter with the constitutional arrangement in the time of the monarchy. Much in the draft may have asserted itself after the exile, when Deuteronomy again became accepted as law; but at least one element had forever been severed from the total system: after the exile, there was never a restoration of monarchy. As the lack of one element affects all other elements in a system, the constitutional theory in Deuteronomy was never concretely realized. It remained a utopian theory.

Distribution of the Functions of Power as the Key Concept of the Constitution

What, then, was the essential principal of this theory? My thesis is that something like the notion of the distribution of functions of power was its guiding force. We will demonstrate this thesis step by step.

[[69]] Certainly we find no official structure in Deuteronomy in which all functions are gathered up and held in a single hand. The model of the nomadic community, in which the sheik is everything—leader, teacher, priest, lawgiver, judge—already lay far in the past, and the princely absolutism of early modern times (or papal centralization of power) was hidden in the future. We are dealing, rather, with a system in which various functions are distributed among various groups of people. The fact that these functions included those that no longer fall within the competence of the modern state, such as the sacrificial cult and the creation of contact with the deity, should pose no problem for the historically minded observer—especially if transference to the Church of the secular notion of the distribution of functions of power is a matter for debate.

Of as little account, too, should be the fact that the separate functions are in part distributed to others, and combined, in a way that is not customary today. Even today, however, the distribution of functions need not automatically be understood in the civil-juridical sense. It might well be that in a system wherein functions are distributed, a specific authority is regarded as supreme, allowing all the rest to flow from it by delegation, and as always capable of redefining or totally recalling them to itself. But neither is this the case with the Deuteronomic draft constitution.

In the conditions that prevailed in the ancient East, that sort of supreme authority was associated solely with the king. We think, for example, of the rule of the pharaohs in Egypt. In the Deuteronomic laws concerning offices, however, the monarchy is in the middle of the list, not at its head. Nor is it said anywhere that the king defines functions or installs officials. According to Deut 16:18, Israel itself provides its judges and officials, and its king as well (17:15). The priests and the judge at the central court are simply there—there is no indication whence they came. Presumably the text has in mind hereditary office. The prophet is called from time to time by Yahweh himself (18:15). And we inquire about the functions of the king, only one function is named: he must read the Torah daily and live exactly according [[70]] to its prescriptions (17:18–20). Thus he never had the right to alter its regulations on the distribution of functions among the various offices, in order, for example, to enlarge his power at the expense of others.

This leads to the last requirement, if we are to speak about a distribution of functions in the modern civil-juridical sense. The functions must be distributed among *different* authorities—that is, no one authority is simply a delegation from a superior authority—and delegation of the separate, distributed powers must be made in accord with an antecedent constitutional law that exists for these powers. Precisely such a law is found in the laws concerning offices in Deuteronomy.

There is no need for astonishment, however, if we do not find that this law exists separately, as a kind of fundamental law, but see it

embedded in a codex which claims to contain all of Israel's laws. This
fact is connected with another: after Deuteronomy, Israel had no con-
tinuously active legislature. Deuteronomy takes no account of the necessity of creating new laws and altering old ones. Israel had received
the laws at Sinai—once and for all; hence they are valid for all time,
and are never to be changed (Deut 13:1). Yahweh was the legislator.

On such presuppositions, obviously, it is not necessary to distinguish between constitutional and other law. The laws concerning
offices, which form only one part of the Deuteronomic book of laws,
can nonetheless be regarded as genuine constitutional law. Even the
last condition is fulfilled: we are able to speak of a genuine distribution
of the functions of power.

However, when we speak about this distribution it is important to
take account of more than the formally juristic viewpoint. When in
modern times systems of the distribution of functions of power have
been introduced, it was, as a rule, against a very concrete background.
There had formerly been abuse of power, concentrated in a single
hand. As a rule, also, people were striving toward a concrete political
goal: a balance of powers.

In a well-functioning state, no one group or individual should be
allowed to become too powerful, and a balance of powers automatically
[71] engenders mutual control of powers. Montesquieu describes all
this in great detail, and the fathers of the American Constitution were
imbued with this spirit. Historically, we see the reaction against princely
absolutism, but it is important to ascertain whether the same thing was
happening in the draft constitution of Deuteronomy.

There, too, a balance of powers was being brought about. In practice, the formerly much wider powers of the king and the priests were
circumscribed in favor of the judges and the prophets. In earlier times
the king had also been supreme judge. Thus the law concerning the
king by association of ideas follows the law concerning judges. But this
is a purely historical association. In the laws concerning offices, the
king no longer is the supreme judge; and nothing is gained by allowing older circumstances to color our interpretation of these laws—as
sometimes happens in exegesis.

In earlier days the priests had served the oracle, thereby creating
individual contact with the deity. Because of this, the law concerning
prophets became associated with the law concerning priests, which it
now followed. This, too, is a purely historical association. In this law
concerning offices there is no mention of priestly oracles, and individual contact with the deity is clearly the concern of the prophets.

Another prominent function of the king was the conduct of battles. For this purpose, the kings of Israel and Judah had their standing armies. All that remains of this in our legislation is the remark in 17:16, that the king shall not possess too many horses. Warfare, as we saw, was thought of in terms of the people's army; and in the passage in Deuteronomy devoted to this the king is not mentioned.

Small space is given in 17:17 to the harem and the property of the king. It delimits another function the king possessed, which we must not underestimate. He was a symbol. By a large harem and ceremonial display of splendor, he was a sign of the prosperity of the state.

In reality, only two things are left for the king: administration (so obvious as to require no mention) and the exemplary reading of the Torah. The king is now no more than administrator and model Israelite.

Where the monarchy was weakened, the judges became stronger. [72] Now the legal system is seen as an autonomous authority, no longer under the king and his governors in the garrison cities. The central court, however, is in the hands not only of judges but priests as well. The priests have three functions: exercising sacral-judicial power, offering sacrifice, and custody of the Torah. According to Deut 31:9–13, the last function includes the office of teaching the Torah to the rising generation.

The function of making contact with the deity is taken away from the priests; this now belongs exclusively to the prophets. The prophets are designated the successors of Moses, for their origin lies where Moses received the Torah, on Mt. Sinai. This makes them the born interpreters of the Torah (the law), which is unchangeable, but times change; this Yahweh sends the prophets to tell men what the ancient law means in new situations. In a certain sense, the prophets replaced the legislature. Certainly they are not representatives of the people, but representatives of God. They are regarded as charismatic personalities, not as cultic officials; hence they are hard to manipulate. They embody a counterbalance to all other authorities.

On the whole, therefore, we may put it like this: An earlier and greater concentration of power in monarchy and priesthood is scaled down and an attempt is made to create a balance of power between four different authorities: the judiciary, the king, the temple priesthood, and free charismatics. We may describe the distribution of functions of power as the guiding principle of this constitution for offices, although there is no sign of any historical continuity leading to our modern forms of such distribution of functions, and there are many differences in detail from modern systems.

The Torah and Free Charisms

The Deuteronomic draft constitution may well prove important for discussion of possible distributions of functions of power in the Church's system of ministries in virtue of the fact that it places this ⟦73⟧ constitution firmly in the context of the word of God. However, its full significance appears when we become aware of the danger of following secular tendencies in the present battle for distributing functions in the Church, and when we pose the question whether there might not be special forms of distributing functions that are proper to the essence of the Church, in contrast to the state. Deuteronomy is well aware that it is not just *any* law book but the law book of the historically chosen people of Yahweh. Its system of the distribution of functions, too, is conceived in these terms. Two elements in particular emerge from this: in the Deuteronomic draft constitution, the Torah always has pride of place, and at a strategically important point there is a legally secured place for the eruption of free charism that eludes legal definition. In virtue of the fact that all offices are subordinate to the Torah, God rules in Israel through the revelation he had given in the course of Israel's earlier history, for this revelation is present in the Torah as scripture. Inasmuch as the prophets have a legally assured sphere of influence, God reserves for himself the possibility of exercising his sovereignty over this people in ever new ways, as occasions arise.

What does this mean in detail? First, the law concerning kings subordinates the king complete to the Torah. According to 17:18–20, he must possess a copy of the Torah and keep it always by him, reading from it daily, so that he learns to fear Yahweh and to observe all the words of the Torah. Like every other Israelite (17:20), he is thus totally subject to the Torah.

A second incidental statement concerning the Torah is contained in the law about the king. Because the original Torah is in the custody of the Levitical priests (17:15; cf. 31:9), it follows, from Deut 31:10–13, that custody of the Torah implies the obligation to teach it and hand it on to the rising generations in Israel. The ministry of priests is thus tied to the Torah—not exactly as is the ministry of the king, it is true, but insofar as it commands them to guide the people.

The judicial system in Israel also is related to the Torah. Deut 17:11 presupposes that the verdict given by the central court is identical with the Torah, although what exactly is meant by this ⟦74⟧ may be somewhat obscure. Here we have an older text, dealing with inquiry directed to God, that has been applied to the Torah, and this could not have been brought about without internal tensions. We can at least expound the text by saying that the expanded version indicates that when judgment is pronounced, the spirit of the Torah ought to break through. This applies also to the local court. The word *Torah* is not used in this context, but the model process that is described concerns trespass of the First Commandment of the Decalogue, which is the very heart of the Torah.

The prophets likewise are bound to the Torah—but are perhaps less subordinate than parallel to it. In 18:16 is an etiology of the prophetic office, which is connected with Deut 5:23–31, where we learn how Moses was installed as mediator of the Torah. At that time Yahweh had foretold that Israel would never in future lack a prophet, and in the law concerning the prophets, Moses is twice described as the first of the prophets (18:16f.). The parallel between prophet and Torah is not so strongly stressed as to make us expect that Yahweh will expand the Torah with new laws, through the operation of the prophets. Rather, the prophets seem to be thought of as a means of concretizing and actualizing the will of God, as set out in general terms in the Torah. At all events, in another part of the Deuteronomistic historical writings (2 Kgs 17:13) they are even described as mediators of the law. Even though we do not cite this text in our interpretation of the Deuteronomic law concerning prophets, in the Deuteronomic draft constitution the prophets—those free and unpredictable charismatics—in all their dignity and significance are directly compared with the Torah.

The emergence of prophets is provided for. Paradoxical though it may sound, the sphere of operation that was juridically provided for them is one of the offices in the distributively structured constitutional system. But more is involved than with the other offices, for the prophets, like the Torah, have precedence over the other offices. From another point of view, less is involved, because as free charismatics they are not a legally definable entity in the strict sense. And so, conversely, 〚75〛 their role is not canceled by the fact that with the other definable entities there is a real distribution of functions of power.

Through the priority of the written Torah and the legally provided sphere of operation for the free action of God through his charismatics, the Deuteronomic law concerning offices hints at what must be heeded when we undertake a specifically ecclesial distribution of functions of power—if we do not wish to fall into the trap of following purely civil models, as happened in former times when unification of powers was sought. Having recognized this danger, however, the fundamental problems, which we find exercising many Catholic canonists, must be cleared up. It must at least be felt possible to admit a distributed system of offices right up to the highest level, should, in a particular period, the faithful feel the need of it and it is commended by reason.

In the end, however, we are left with the question we touched on by way of introduction: Is the assimilation of the Church to state models not, on the whole, much more questionable than is commonly supposed, and is the Church, in the New Testament sense, not best understood in terms of "congregation," and ought not its legal system reflect that understanding?

Part 5

New Directions in
Recent Research

Reporting Speech in the Book of Deuteronomy:
Toward a Compositional Analysis of the Deuteronomic History

ROBERT POLZIN

The Deuteronomic History

[[193]] That corpus of the Hebrew Bible that stretches from the Book of Deuteronomy through 2 Kings is called the Deuteronomic History. It consists of seven books: Deuteronomy, Joshua, Judges, 1–2 Samuel, and 1–2 Kings. The analysis that follows concerning the reporting speech of the Book of Deuteronomy will attempt to uncover the various points of view that make up its compositional structure. The term, "composition," therefore has to do with the relationships of various points of view, on a number of levels, that make up a literary work. I will assume from the start that the Deuteronomic History is a unified literary work; I do not base this assumption upon previous historical critical analyses. By the term "Deuteronomist" I mean that person or persons, functioning in an authorial or editorial role, and responsible for the final form of the Deuteronomic History. There may actually have been no single individual or recognizable group to whom this term refers. I use it heuristically to designate that imagined personification of a combination of literary features that seem to constitute the literary composition of the Deuteronomic History. For me, the text creates the Deuteronomist's features as much as it creates those of Moses. The Deuteronomist is the "implied author" of this work.[1]

Reprinted with permission from *Traditions in Transformation: Turning Points in Biblical Faith* (F. M. Cross Festschrift; ed. Baruch Halpern and Jon D. Levenson; Winona Lake, Ind.: Eisenbrauns, 1981) 193–211.

* It is with pleasure and gratitude that I dedicate this article to Frank M. Cross.

1. I understand "implied author" in a somewhat different way than Wayne Booth does in *The Rhetoric of Fiction* (Chicago: University of Chicago, 1961).

One way to get at a useful framework within the text is to attend to the various shifts that occur within the text and within the various levels of the text. These shifts often indicate the implied author's devices for framing his work and, once identified, can help us understand how he may be said to manipulate and program his readers' responses. The various points of view realized in the text are represented there in a ⟦194⟧ number of ways that are interrelated, and an attempt to articulate a framework is the first step in analyzing what a text or its author seems to be saying. Much of what is written, its "author" does not subscribe to. He may, for example, be offering up a position to ridicule. A framework helps us articulate what an author's stated position is, as distinct from statements he transmits for various other reasons.[2]

If we begin with V. N. Voloshinov's demonstration of the crucial importance of "reported speech" in language analysis,[3] we are immediately able to segment the Deuteronomic History into two basic units which, although not quantitatively balanced, are amazingly complementary from a compositional point of view. It has long been emphasized that basic to the viewpoint of the Deuteronomist is "that system of prophetic prediction and its exactly observed fulfilment which pervades the whole work of this writer."[4] If we apply this obvious aspect of the Deuteronomist's position to his work *in toto*, we see that a compositional device occurring innumerable times within it—that is, first the word of God is reported by a prophet, then a description of events follows with the explicit statement that these events happened "according to the word of God" (or a statement similar in meaning)—appears to be operating in the relationship between the two largest segments of the work. The first segmentation of the Deuteronomic History results in separating the Book of Deuteronomy from Joshua–2 Kings. We thereby see that Deuteronomy, in that it is almost totally a number of Mosaic speeches, functions as an expression of the prophetic word of God, and that Joshua–2 Kings mainly recounts events that constitute "its exactly observed fulfilment."

The balanced nature of this first division is seen when one applies Voloshinov's distinction between reporting and reported speech to the two basic sections of the Deuteronomic History. The Book of Deuteronomy contains thirty-four chapters. Almost all the book consists of re-

2. My goal, therefore, is to begin the task of literary interpretation programmatically outlined by B. Uspensky in *A Poetics of Composition* (Berkeley: University of California, 1973).

3. *Marxism and the Philosophy of Language* (New York: Seminar, 1953).

4. G. von Rad, *The Problem of the Hexateuch and Other Essays* (New York: McGraw-Hill, 1966) 208–9.

ported speech, mostly in direct discourse and mostly of Moses, whereas only about fifty-six verses are reporting speech, the Deuteronomic narrator's, which forms the context for Moses' direct utterances. On the other hand, Joshua–2 Kings is predominantly reporting speech, that of the narrator, with a significantly smaller amount of reported speech scattered throughout. (Here, however, the disproportion between reporting and reported speech is not so great as in Deuteronomy.) In Deuteronomy, reported speech of its hero is emphasized; in Joshua–2 Kings, the [195] reporting speech of its narrator is dominant. It is as though the Deuteronomist is telling us in Deuteronomy, "Here is what God has prophesied concerning Israel," but in Joshua–2 Kings "This is how God's word has been exactly fulfilled in Israel's history from the settlement to the destruction of Jerusalem and the Exile."

Another significant aspect of the relationship between Deuteronomy on one hand and Joshua–2 Kings on the other is seen in the internal arrangement of reporting and reported speech within each of the two segments themselves. In Joshua–2 Kings it is not enough to chronicle Israel's continual disobedience and the countless disastrous events that resulted from such disobedience. As von Rad has detailed for us with regard to 1–2 Kings,[5] the narrative systematically singles out the reported speech of prophets who periodically arise to announce to various individuals the punishing word of God. Thus, for example, intermittent recurring reported prophetic speech interrupts the narrative at least eleven times in 1–2 Kings, apparently to reinforce what appears to be the general point of view of Joshua–2 Kings taken as a whole: how Israel's history is dependent upon the word of God that is the Book of Deuteronomy. In Joshua–2 Kings, the reporting narrator is intermittently supported in his basic story of Israel's history by the occasional reported words of various prophets. The preponderant reporting narrative of the narrator and the intermittent reported speech of a number of prophets within the narrative help to articulate the same evaluative point of view.

When we look at the Book of Deuteronomy, the relationship between the reporting narration and reported prophetic speech is reversed. Reported prophetic speech absolutely predominates, with reporting narration at a minimum and on occasion a confusing interruption. We will discuss this last point in the third section of this paper, but for now it is enough to underline how the respective roles of narrator's words and prophetic word in Deuteronomy form a mirror image of their roles in Joshua–2 Kings. In Deuteronomy the unobtrusive

5. *The Problem*, 205–21.

reporting speech of the retiring narrator reinforces and supports here
and there the preponderant reported speech of the greatest prophet of
them all, Moses. In Joshua–2 Kings, lesser prophets occasionally appear to reinforce by their reported speech the now preponderant and
highly visible reporting speech of the narrator.

If we first divide up the Deuteronomic History into Deuteronomy
on one hand and Joshua–2 Kings on the other, the concept of reported speech, primarily in the form of direct discourse, allows us to
see that in the first section, according to quantity and distribution,
Moses' words are to the narrator's words as, in the second section, the
narrator's words [196] are to the words of a number of lesser prophets. The significance of this first compositional relationship is great.

The distribution of reported speech and its reporting context has
helped form a preliminary criterion that allowed us both to segment
the text into its two largest main sections and to discover a couple of
complementary relationships between these sections. This criterion
can now be used to help us articulate a central problem confronting
any attempt at a literary interpretation of the Deuteronomic History:
wherein does the ultimate semantic authority of this complex lie? By the
phrase, "ultimate semantic authority," we mean the basic ideological
and evaluative point of view of a work,[6] the unifying ideological stance
of a work's "implied author." Do we find it in the speech of the narrator, forming the slight frame of the Book of Deuteronomy and the
main body of Joshua–2 Kings, or is it present in the reported speech
both of Moses, forming the bulk of Deuteronomy, and of other mouth-
pieces of God scattered throughout the rest of the history?

Another way to express the problem is this: there are two kinds of
speech in the Deuteronomic History, the word of the narrator and the reported words of those individuals who form part of his story. What is immediately obvious from even a superficial reading of the text (and to be
expected) is that among the figures in the story preeminent place is given
to the figure of God himself, and that the preeminent speech the Deuteronomic narrator reports is speech purported to be from God himself.
Therefore, is the implied author's stance to be found in the words of the
narrator or in the words of God found in the narrative? Or, as a third possibility, is it found somehow synthesized both in the narration that quantitatively predominates and in the quoted words of God that are
quantitatively much less dominant in the Deuteronomic History?

All three of the possibilities just mentioned assume that the Deuteronomic History is indeed a *monologue,* that is, its ideological evaluation is carried out from a single dominating point of view which

6. Cf. M. Bakhtin, *Problems of Dostoevsky's Poetics* (Ann Arbor: Ardis, 1973).

subordinates all others in the work. The Deuteronomic History, viewed as the juxtaposition of two principal utterances, that of its narrator and that of God, is constructed as an utterance within an utterance: the reported word of God is found within the reporting word of the narrator. Stated in these terms, the ideological composition of this work appears to be overtly monologic, since the immediate obvious message of the narrator is, "God has said 'such and such' to Israel, and the events of Israel's history have happened in the way I am now describing them: as a fulfilment of God's word." This is the narrator's obvious conclusion [197] about the history of Israel. He says to the reader, "In terms of what God and myself say, 'I and the Father are one.'"

Bakhtin summarizes the characteristics of a novel that is basically monological in structure; his words are equally valid for a work such as the Deuteronomic History:

> How and in what elements of the verbal whole is the author's ultimate semantic authority realized? For the monologic novel this question is very easily answered. Whatever types of word the novelist-monologist may introduce and whatever their compositional distribution may be, the author's interpretations and evaluations must dominate all others and must comprise a compact and unambiguous whole.[7]

Viewed from this perspective, the central authority figure of the history is God and, consequently, the prophets of God within the narrative who are described as reporting His words. In addition, since the history purports to show how this divine speech has been verified in history, we may say that the narrator's general position may be understood as one that is in agreement with the ideological positions of the central authority figures of his story. It is apparent therefore that if the Deuteronomic History is viewed as the intersection of two words, God's and the narrator's, the overall picture presented therein is one in which, concerning the ideological plane, the narrator's word is presented as subordinate to God's word which the narrator reports. The Deuteronomic History is not the intersection of two equally weighted

---

7. Ibid., 168. For those who question the validity of putting the genres of novel and history together in the same semantic boat in regard to the concept of monologic dialogic structure, it should be noted here that, apart from the ambiguities of calling the Deuteronomic History "history," this study proceeds in wholehearted agreement with the views of Hayden White (*Metahistory* [Baltimore and London: Hopkins, 1973]) and Roland Barthes ("Historical Discourse" in *Structuralism: A Reader*, Michael Lane, ed. [London, 1970] 145–55) on the nature of historical discourse and its relation to literary interpretation. Both authors underline, from different perspectives, the similarities between the interpretive elements and imaginative constructions found in historiographic works and those found in other genres such as the novel.

words, but the conjoining of God's word to the narrator's word in a dominant to subordinate relationship respectively.

When we inquire further into the overtly monologic structure of the history on the plane of ideology, we find that the question is not quite so simply answered. For even if we can say that the narrator clearly intends to subordinate his position to the word of God which he reports to us, we still must inquire what precisely does God say within the work, and how precisely is His word said to be fulfilled in it? For clearly even a [[198]] monologue may contain a variety of ideas and viewpoints that may or may not compete with one another with equal weight or authority. This raises the question of whether the history, as an overt monologue in which the Deuteronomist has subordinated his narrator's voice to God's voice as its echo, actually may contain a *hidden dialogue* within the word of God itself and/or within the "subordinate" word of the narrator. There is not just one utterance of God but a number of them reported to have been said by God throughout the historical period covered by the narrative. There is not just one utterance of the narrator interpreting God's word, but a number of them.[8]

Therefore the possibility exists that, whatever may be the obvious monologic composition of the Deuteronomic History taken as a unity, a closer reading of the text may reveal a hidden dialogue between competing voices within the various utterances of God both in themselves and as interpreted by the Deuteronomic narrator. Bakhtin describes theoretically what would be the case if a work were indeed a true dialogue:

> The weakening or destruction of the monological context occurs only when two equally and directly object-oriented utterances come together. Two equally and directly object-oriented words within a single context cannot stand side by side without dialogically intersecting, regardless of whether they corroborate one another or on the contrary contradict one another, or have any other sort of dialogical relationship (the relationship of question and answer, for example). Two equal-weighted words which speak to the same subject, once they have come together, must become oriented one to the other. Two embodied thoughts cannot lie side by side like two objects—they must come into inner contact, i.e., must enter into a semantic bond.[9]

An attempt to answer such a basic question as whether we have in the history a monologue or a dialogue, in the sense employed by Bakh-

---

8. Indeed, the basic issues that I am raising here have been set out by Wayne Booth in *The Rhetoric of Fiction*. Booth's discussion, in the manner with which he exemplifies his conclusions with countless examples from modern western literature, complements the more methodologically oriented analyses of Bakhtin more than thirty years earlier.

9. Bakhtin, *Problems*, 156.

tin, ought not, at first, to be based upon the historical-critical approaches of modern biblical scholarship. From a methodological point of view, historical criticism is ill-suited for beginning attempts at understanding the important questions that an interpretation of the Deuteronomic History involves, however necessary such approaches are for an adequate understanding. Therefore, the present study begins at a point that is operationally prior to the kinds of historical critical stances [[199]] that up to now have divided biblical scholars on the structure of the Deuteronomic History, e.g., the question of the existence and description of at least two editions of work. For, whatever might be the Deuteronomic History's genesis, what we are now asking is where does a close compositional reading of this work place it within the dynamic poles of a dialogue on one hand and a monologue on the other? Whatever the answer may turn out to be, no help is at this preliminary point relevant, since both the predominantly dialogic and a predominantly monologic ideology could conceivably be the final result of either one or more editions of the Deuteronomic History. At the same time, I fully recognize that historical-critical analyses are methodologically useful, indeed necessary to refine further and even, in some cases, to alter preliminary approximations of a dialogic or monologic composition of our text.

It does seem clear that even with regard to the overtly monologic nature of the Deuteronomic History, it would be too simplistic to say that the ultimate semantic authority is to be found solely in the words of God reported in the history, or solely in the words of the narrator that form the controlling narrative. For clearly, even though the narrator assumes that his words are subordinate to God's words, by the very fact that he "takes over" what God has said and uses it for his own purposes, to this extent he is subordinating God's words to his own. Therefore, it seems that we would be more faithful to an intuitive first impression of the work to assume that ultimate semantic authority, be it predominantly monologic or dialogic, will be found somehow synthesized in the narration that quantitatively predominates, but by authorial plan is subordinate, and in the quoted words of God that are quantitatively subordinate, but by authorial plan dominant.

Another way of describing the position just stated would be to say the following: the ultimate semantic authority of a work, the implied author's "intention,"[10] a text's basic ideological perspective, can be realized not

---

10. Confer on this point Bakhtin (*Problems*, 160–61) and Uspensky (*A Poetics*, 8–16). I should point out here that when I write of the implied author's *intention*, I use this term in its phenomenological sense. The intentionality of the text is as much my own reconstruction as the implied author of a text is.

only by a narrator's direct word, but as Bakhtin puts it, " . . . with the help of the words of others, created and distributed in a specific way as belonging to others."[11] Moreover, if it is possible to find the author's voice in the words of others, conversely, it is also possible to find in the author's words, or in those of his narrator, reflections of points of view that are subordinate or even contrary to his basic ideological position. In other words, the specific composition of a work on the ideological plane is not always concurrent with its composition [[200]] on less basic levels such as the phraseological level of reporting reported speech.

The above point is especially relevant to our discussion of the compositional structure of the Deuteronomic History in general and of its two basic sequential sections in particular.[12] An adequate explanation of the Deuteronomic History's framework must begin to delineate which of its utterances are single-voiced and which are double-voiced, on a number of compositional planes. Moreover, on the basic plane of a work's ideology, a proposed framework ought to be able to describe which of the text's utterances or words express its dominant ideological voice(s), which its subordinated or dependent ideological voice or voices, and which utterances express both kinds of voices. Furthermore, the framework constructed ought to illuminate the various relationships between competing voices of whatever level in the text, and between various levels themselves, that is, the concurrence or not of the compositional structure of different planes.

The basic requirements of an adequately constructed framework are further complicated by the object we are investigating. The Deuteronomic History is an especially complex arrangement of messages within a message, so that it would be especially helpful to construct a satisfactory description of how its internal messages interrelate to form that message we call the Deuteronomic History.

Moses and the Deuteronomic Narrator as Hero and "Author" of the Book of Deuteronomy

1. Concerning the attribution of utterances in Deuteronomy, most of the book is a series of direct quotations of Moses. Within this body of Mosaic utterances, in one instance, 27:1–8, Moses and the elders of Israel speak as one in direct discourse, and in another instance in the

11. *Problems*, 155.
12. The Russian structuralists have already worked out many of the implications of the fact that "within a single utterance there may occur two intentions, two voices." Cf. Bakhtin, *Problems*, 153ff.

same chapter, 27:9–10, Moses and the Levitical priests are quoted in direct discourse. In all other cases in the reporting of Moses' words, Moses speaks alone. In addition, the Deuteronomic narrator, like Moses, is able to quote God in direct discourse: five times toward the end of the book, 31:14b; 31:16b–21; 31:23b; 32:49–52; and 34:4b.

The book is more than just Moses' utterances within the narrator's utterances: Moses' utterances continually quote, with direct discourse, other utterances, as for example throughout chapters two and three which are mostly various quotations within a quote. Here Moses is 〚201〛 quoted by the narrator as quoting a number of others. Each of these cases can be described as an utterance (of the person quoted by Moses) within an utterance (of Moses) within an utterance (of the narrator).

It is sometimes more complicated than this. For example, 1:28 has the narrator quoting Moses quoting Israel quoting Israel's scouts at Kadesh Barnea. And in 2:4–5; 32:26; and 32:40–42, we find the narrator quoting Moses quoting Yahweh quoting Himself, all in direct discourse. In such cases, we have examples of an utterance within an utterance within an utterance within an utterance.

The varying complexities of quotes within quotes that make up most of Deuteronomy is further enhanced by a complicated temporal scheme relating the quotes to their context. At first, Moses' words look mostly to past events and past statements, as in the first address of Moses in 1:6–4:40. Then in his second address, 5:1b–28:68, Moses starts to turn his attention to the future, and a much larger proportion of other people's utterances found within this address expresses what they will, should, or should not say in the future, e.g., 6:20–25; 7:17; 9:4. Then in the third address of Moses, 29:2–31:6, whenever Moses quotes anyone directly, it is their *future* utterances he quotes, coinciding with this address's almost complete orientation toward the distant future. Finally, the group of Moses' sayings that ends the book's collection of his utterances, 31:7–33:29, also emphasizes the future in its quotes, as 31:17b and 32:37–42 show.

The temporal relations of Moses' inclusion of utterances within his own utterances is occasionally even more complex, as for example in 9:26–29. In this pericope the narrator is quoting Moses who, in the valley of Beth-Peor, is quoting what he (Moses) had said at Horeb to the effect that he had prayed that the Egyptians would not say "such and such" at some time subsequent to the events at Horeb.

One of the immediate results of this exceedingly complex network of utterances within utterances is the deliberate representation in Deuteronomy of a vast number of intersecting statements, sometimes in agreement with one another, sometimes interfering with one another. This enables the book to be the repository of a plurality of viewpoints, all working together to achieve an effect on the reader that is multi-dimensional. We should not be surprised that such a sophisticated work has come down to us from the first millennium B.C. This complex intersecting of viewpoints deserves to be taken seriously and analyzed carefully by the modern reader.

The immediate hero of the book is Moses as the spokesman of God. The only other person who is quoted by the narrator is God. (We have already mentioned that Moses speaks with the elders of Israel in 27:1–8, and that he speaks with the Levitical priests in 27:9–10.) Thus there are [[202]] only two direct voices[13] which the narrator asks us to attend to in the book: Moses' and God's. Deuteronomy may be described therefore as the speech of the Deuteronomic narrator in which he directly quotes only two figures in the story, predominantly Moses and sometimes God.

As far as Moses is concerned, none of the words of God which he quotes are described as also having been heard by the people, except for the Decalogue (5:6–21). In fact, in chapter five, Moses makes the point that only when God spoke the Decalogue was He heard by the people: all the other words of God were deliberately avoided by the people as directly heard words, and were to be transmitted indirectly to them through Moses' reporting. As for the narrator, he like Moses directly reports God's words. In 31:14b he relates, in direct discourse, God's words to Moses; he does so again in 31:16b–21; 32:49–52; and 34:4b. He also directly reports God's words to Joshua in 31:23b. *In all these cases, he is a privileged observer and reporter of God's words, just as he describes Moses describing himself to be in chapter five.* The point is unavoidable that only two personages in the book directly hear and relate God's words (apart from the Decalogue): Moses and the Deuteronomic narrator.

13. I use the term "voice" sometimes to refer to a text's own distinction between reporting and reported speech. In this instance the expression plane of a narrative itself distinguishes the voice or words, say, of its narrator from those of various characters in the story. At other times I use "voice" to refer to distinguishable perspectives on the ideological plane of the text. In this instance I am concerned with the implied author's ideological position as I have reconstructed it from the interrelationships discovered between the utterances of narrator and characters in the text. This stance of the implied author may be complex enough to warrant talking about two or more ideological voices and the specific order of subordination and/or equality apparent among them. Distinction of voice on the expression plane is the construction of a text's author. Distinction of voice on the ideological plane is the construction of the interpreter: this construction is what we call "the implied author."

2. If only Moses and the narrator are privileged to hear God's word in the book, and even though Moses reports the bulk of God's words found therein, only the words of God that are reported by the narrator are *immediately* reported there. The preponderance of God's words found in Deuteronomy are on another level, a secondary or mediate level. That is, the narrator quotes Moses as quoting God. One might begin therefore one's analysis of the book by articulating a problem similar to the one made above concerning the entire Deuteronomic History. There it was asked whether the ideological position of the Deuteronomist as implied author is to be found in the words of God or in the words of the Deuteronomic narrator. Here we may ask an [[203]] analogous question. How reliable a narrator do we have here, and how is his voice related to the voice of the book's implied author?

The emphasis in Deuteronomy is on the legislative and judicial word of God, and the conveyors of this word are two: Moses and the narrator. In interpreting the book, do we understand Moses' word as subordinate to the narrator's, or is the narrator's word subordinate to that of Moses? The narrator might be said to be the main carrier of the implied author's ideological stance since he alone conveys to us Moses' conveying of the words of God that constitute most of the book. But if so, one notices that, as vehicle for the book's ultimate semantic authority (he alone can tell us what Moses says that God says to the reader of the book), the narrator seems at great pains to impress upon his reader that it is Moses, and Moses alone, who possessed the type of reliable authority to convey accurately and authoritatively the direct words of God that form most of the book. We find ourselves in a dilemma: we are asked by the narrator to accept his assertion that "there has not arisen a prophet since in Israel like Moses, whom the LORD knew face to face . . . " (34:10), at the same time as it is only the Deuteronomic narrator who knows Moses face to face! If the path to God is through Moses, the path to Moses is through the text's narrator. Does the reader interpret the reported words of Moses by means of the reporting context: "Moses was God's greatest prophet, therefore believe *him* when he says . . . "? Or does one interpret the reporting words of the narrator by means of the reported words of Moses: "Moses said such and such, therefore believe *me*, as narrator, when I say . . . "?

In our brief introductory remarks to the Deuteronomic History above, we made the assumption that ultimate semantic authority in the work, that is, the implied author's main ideological stance, probably should be looked for both in the words of God and in the words of the narrator. We can apply this assumption to the Book of Deuteronomy

itself by stating that the ultimate ideological stance of the book ought
to be looked for both in the reporting words of the narrator, its "author's" spokesman, and in the reported words of Moses, its hero. We
may note that in Deuteronomy we find both the narrator and Moses
utilizing the formula that is the basic constituent of the whole history:
"God said 'such and such'; therefore this event happened precisely to
fulfill His word." For example, Moses is quoted as saying:

> "And the LORD heard your words and was angered, and he swore, 'Not
> one of these men of this evil generation shall see the good land which
> I swore to give to your fathers . . . ' " (1:34–35).

In the next chapter, Moses is then quoted as saying: [204]

> "And the time from our leaving Kadesh-Barnea until we crossed the
> brook Zered was thirty-eight years, until the present generation, that
> is, the men of war, had perished from the camp *as the LORD had sworn
> to them*" (2:14, emphasis added).

We find the Deuteronomist employing the same compositional device
in the narrator's portions of Deuteronomy. Thus the narrator says:

> And the LORD said to Moses, "This is the land of which I swore to
> Abraham, to Isaac, and to Jacob, 'I will give it to your descendants.' I
> have let you see it with your eyes but you shall not go over there"
> (34:4).

to which he immediately adds in 34:5:

> So Moses the servant of the LORD died there in the land of Moab,
> *according to the word of the LORD* (emphasis added).

These pericopes illustrate very well how elements of the ultimate semantic stance of the Book of Deuteronomy (as of the whole history), to
which is subordinated everything else in the text, are to be found both
in the utterances of the narrator and in the utterances of Moses as
hero of the book.

We may expect to find characteristics of the narrator's speech in
the hero's speech, and vice-versa, on any or all compositional planes of
the book. Both words will be "double-voiced," and to this extent the
question must be raised about Deuteronomy which was previously
raised about the whole Deuteronomic History: if it is clear that this
book is an overt monologue (its narrator is clearly stating, "As far as
our basic stance is concerned, Moses and I are one."), to what extent
may we characterize the book, in its compositional structure, as a hid-

den dialogue or even as a hidden polemic? Are there competing and equally weighted points of view represented in Deuteronomy on a number of compositional planes? Concerning the ideological plane of the book, the four pericopes quoted above show that it is probably misguided to attribute dominant viewpoints solely to the narrator or solely to Moses. It is possible, I believe, to determine by careful rhetorical analysis elements of the text that can be said to belong to the ultimate ideological stance of the book, just as one can discover and describe other elements that are clearly subordinate to this viewpoint.

The Reporting Speech of Deuteronomy:
The Narrator's Direct Utterances

The reporting context of Deuteronomy comprises only about fifty-six verses: 1:1–5; 2:10–12, 20–23; 3:9, 11, 13b–14; 4:41–5:1a; 10:6–7, 9; 27:1a, 9a, 11; 28:69; 29:1a; 31:1, 7a, 9–10a, 14a, 14c–16a, 22–23a, 24–25, 30; [[205]] 32:44–45, 48; 33:1; 34:1–4a, 5–12. The remainder of the book is composed of utterances of various individuals, mostly Moses, reported in direct discourse.

1. What is the position of the Deuteronomic narrator and what is his voice like?[14] The obvious relation of reporting to reported speech shows that, on the phraseological plane at least,[15] Moses' words are to some extent subordinated to the narrator's. Although the narrator has deliberately put himself in the background and Moses in the foreground, the narrator's word, for very specific reasons, remains visibly separate on the surface of the text. Since the book's surface is constructed mostly in two voices, and since the implied author could have chosen completely to merge his narrator's voice with the voice of his hero, as seems to be the case in the Book of Qoheleth, it is clear that Deuteronomy emphasizes, even on the phraseological plane, a distinction between the word of Moses and the word of the narrator. What are the implications of such an arrangement?

The most obvious functions of the narrator's words are that they situate the words of Moses in time and space (when, where, and in what circumstances Moses spoke the words reported by the narrator), and that they define the preeminent position Moses held as leader and legislator of his people. It is also clear that the narrator does not attempt

14. Here "voice" is used to refer to the expression plane of our narrative; it is not a reconstruction as "voice" on the ideological plane would be.

15. In Uspensky's perspectival scheme the phraseological, spatial-temporal and psychological levels are on a text's surface or plane of expression; the ideological level refers to the deep structure or composition of a text.

to interpret the words of Moses to any great extent in the Book of Deuteronomy. This is to be expected since the other main section of the history, Joshua–2 Kings, so clearly and so often indicates that it functions as the Deuteronomist's main interpretation of the word of Moses found in Deuteronomy. The *overt* function of the narrator's direct utterances in Deuteronomy is to represent to his readers the word of Moses as preeminent, and Moses himself as the greatest prophet in Israel's history.

On the other hand, there are clear indications, even within the brief scope of fifty-six verses, that the content and distribution of the narrator's direct utterances serve to exalt his importance as one who is as necessary to his contemporaries as Moses was to his, and to legitimate that self-serving claim by means obvious and subtle. We now want to explain how, within the narrator's apparently monologic utterances, there are in fact two ideological perspectives that interfere with one another to such an extent that the narrative carries within itself (just as Moses' utterances do) a hidden tension concerning the preeminence of Moses.

〚206〛 Most of the narrator's words provide a suitable frame for the words of Moses in that the former do not distract the reader, either by their quantity or in their emotional power, from attending to the preponderantly powerful words of the book's hero. Examples of the narrator's respectful reticence are found in 1:1–5 and 4:41–48 in the first Mosaic address, 5:1a and 28:69 (Hebrew versification) in the second address, and 29:1a in the third.

But there are other words of the narrator which in fact serve to "break frame,"[16] either by distracting the reader from Moses' main message through the insertion of a number of apparently pedantic, explanatory side-remarks, or else by simply interrupting Moses' words without apparent reason, such as within Moses' third short address: "So Moses continued to speak these words to all Israel, saying . . . " (31:1). What do these narrative "interruptions" of Moses' speech mean?

A typical explanation of these occasional frame-breaks points to some sort of editorial activity aimed at (haphazardly) bringing the text up-to-date, either by explaining archaic terms for contemporary readers or by artificially adding others words of Moses that the editor felt were sufficiently important. If it cannot be decided whether these verses indicate the activity of an author or rather of an editor, an argu-

---

16. Erving Goffman, *Frame Analysis. An Essay on the Organization of Experience* (Cambridge, MA: Harvard University, 1974).

ment for their not being crude or haphazard interruptions of the text can still be articulated. Historical-critical explanations of these verses as crude editorial additions may be considered premature, since it can be plausibly argued that such frame-breaks perform an integral and important function in the text. Rather than indications of sloppy editorial tampering, these breaks in the text serve to represent the narrator's subtle but powerful claim to his audience to be the sole authentic interpreter of Moses' words. Let us look at some of these passages.

2. In Moses' first address, 1:6–4:40, the text abruptly shifts from Moses' utterance to the narrator's comment, and back again, five times. For example in chapter two, Moses is recalling to the Israelites how they had avoided passing through Edom at the command of the LORD, and had turned toward Moab. Then the text suddenly shifts to another voice:

> The Emim formerly lived there [Moab], a people great and many and tall as the Anakim; like the Anakim they were also known as Rephaim, but the Moabites all them Emim. The Horites also lived in Seir formerly, but the sons of Esau settled in their stead: as Israel did to the land of their possession which the LORD gave to them (2:10–12).

Four other interruptions, similar in pedantic tone and content, appear [[207]] in this first address: 20:20–23; 3:9, 11, 13b–14. What strikes one immediately is how relatively minor appear to be those points of Moses' speech that the Deuteronomist feels important enough to interrupt with explanatory background information from his narrator. Somehow, what Moses at this point is saying is especially important to the Deuteronomist's audience, and so the text is interrupted with information whose contemporary importance is indicated within these interruptions by phrases such as, " . . . even to this day" (2:22); "is it [Og's bedstead] not in Rabbah of the Ammonites?" (3:11); and " . . . Havvoth-jair, as it is to this day" (3:14). Given these verses' nature as explanations of relatively minor aspects of Moses' speech, why are they there at all, if we are to assume that they are not disruptive to the text?

As Uspensky brings out[17] and Booth amply illustrates,[18] shifts such as these often indicate an author's device for manipulating and programming his readers' responses. Specifically then, even if we might have lost, over the ages, historical information that would help us see the importance that the content of these interruptions might have had

17. *A Poetics*, 148.
18. *The Rhetoric of Fiction, passim.*

to the Deuteronomist and his audience, it still must be pointed out here that frame-breaks of this kind are a frequent device by which an author/editor, even of an ancient work, may *involve* his readers more in his message. In the case of Deuteronomy, this would involve shifting the reader back and forth a number of times between the "that day" of Moses and the "this day" of the Deuteronomist. By breaking frame five times, the Deuteronomist may very well be forcing the reader to shift back and forth a number of times between narrated past and narrator's present.

We are suggesting that the Deuteronomic narrator is pictured here as subtly reinforcing the *difference* between Moses' audience and his own audience so that the latter, while attending focally to Moses' powerful authority and message, is subsidiarily and intermittently kept aware of the distance between the two audiences. These frame-breaks force the Deuteronomic audience to shift from a subsidiary awareness that they are descendants of these earlier Israelite, and therefore distant hearers of Moses' teaching, to a momentary focal awareness of this situation, and then back again to the continuing focal awareness of the earlier context of the story.

By chapter four, principally by means of these five breaks, the reader of the Deuteronomist's day has begun to *feel,* inchoately and almost without being aware of it, what he will by the end of the book consciously apprehend, that the book's author, through his narrator, is as important to him as Moses was to those earlier Israelites.

[208] We can be more specific than this. The function of these frame-breaks appears to be a chief means by which the narrator begins to program his audience to realize that he is indeed the Moses of his generation. In this first address Moses looks to the past and invokes it as the interpretant for his audience's present and future. If we look at the utterances of Moses to make a point, we will see that the perspective of Moses' first address involves a shifting back and forth between "the day that you stood before the LORD your God at Horeb" (4:10) and the "this day" when "I set before you . . . this law in Moab" (4:8). Moses uses "that day" at Horeb to help him cement "this day's" interpretation of that law. We are suggesting that just as Moses is described as doing this explicitly in his first address, so also the Deuteronomist, by taking Moses' "this day" and transforming it into "that day" (1:3) when Moses set forth the law, uses it to cement "this day's," that is, the Deuteronomist's interpretation of Moses' law, namely, the history from Joshua to 2 Kings as recounted by his narrator.

The deliberate comparison made between how Moses taught and how the Deuteronomic narrator teaches is all the more impressive when we consider that he here implies it by subtle compositional means rather than by bald and bold statements. Were we to look closely at Moses' addresses, we would see that this same comparison between Moses and the narrator is much more boldly stated. The difference is instructive. Given the overt message of the history, "Moses was the greatest prophet of God: I the narrator am just his interpreter," if the narrator is to convey to his audience an analogous status in regard to Moses as interpreter of the Law, he will be more inclined to represent such a point of view more or less clearly through *Moses'* utterances, while leaving to his own utterances more subtle ways of manipulating his audience in the same direction.

The implication of the foregoing analysis is that parts of the narrative which serve either as a frame for the Mosaic utterances or as a statement of Moses' eminence are to be distinguished from other parts of that narrative which break frame in order to prepare the reader to accept authorial claims for eminence, or at least for a status equal in his own generation to Moses' status in the latter's generation.

3. The frame-breaks that interrupt Moses' second address (5:1b–28:68) also function as interruptions designed to put the narrator on the same level as Moses, and even to *limit* the authority of Moses. The first interruption occurs in 10:6–9. Here, after the narrator relates information about Israel's itinerary and about Aaron's death in verses six and seven, we read:

> *At that time* the LORD set apart the tribe of Levi to carry the ark of the covenant of the LORD, to stand before the LORD to minister to him and [[209]] to bless in his name *to this day*. Therefore Levi has no portion or inheritance with his brothers; the LORD is his inheritance, as the LORD your God said to him (10:8–9; emphasis added).

There are a number of features worth noting in this frame-break, besides the function it has of jolting the reader back to a focal awareness of another time and circumstance. In verse eight, the italicized words recall the typical Mosaic device of using "that day" to clarify "this day"; only in this example it is not clear who is supposed to be employing the device. Second, the list of levitical functions, to carry the ark, to stand before the LORD to minister to him, to bless, seems to be a summary of God's words, here apparently rendered in indirect discourse which continues on into verse nine. Then, in verse 9b, "as the LORD your God said to him" suddenly shifts the report into direct discourse again, as the phrase, "the LORD your God" shows. Verses eight and nine sound very much like a continuation of Moses' speech in verse five. On the other hand, the phrases, "At that time . . . to this day," are ambiguous enough to make us wonder whether in fact verses eight and nine are a continuation of the frame-break of verses six and seven.

The very ambiguity of verses eight and nine serves to underline what we have been noticing all along: the utterance of Moses and the utterance of the narrator are in many respects indistinguishable. Both employ the device, "God said such and such; such and such an event fulfils God's word." As we have already noted, 1:34–35 and 2:14 have Moses speaking this way, and 34:4–5 has the narrator speaking in exactly the same way. Again, as we have seen, since both use the "that day . . . this day" device in their utterances, verse eight could have been spoken by Moses just as well as by the narrator. We should point out here that verse 9b, if attributed to the narrator, would be a rare instance in Deuteronomy of the narrator's speech employing "quasi-direct discourse."[19] Here, the presence of "as the LORD your God said to him" does not indicate the narrator's utterance (since he never uses the second person to indicate the audience for whom he is writing) but rather Moses' reported speech in some kind of direct discourse. Verses eight and nine are a good example of how the voices of Moses and narrator echo one another.

Chapter twenty-seven contains three narrative interruptions:

Now Moses and the elders of Israel commanded the people . . . (27:1a)
And Moses and the levitical priests said to all Israel . . . (27:9a)
And Moses charged the people the same day . . . (27:11)

It is possible to regard chapter twenty-seven as an obvious and awkward ⟦210⟧ interruption of Moses' second address only if one forgets that the whole book shows signs of an intricately planned composition. What is important here is that Moses speaks in conjunction with the elders of Israel and with the levitical priests. If we have faith in the deliberate compositional complexity of the book, we are led to see the frame-breaks of 27:1a, 9a as further diminishing the uniqueness of Moses' authority at a key place in the text.

The frame-break of 27:11 is similar to the frame-break within the third address, 31:1. Both appear to continue the Deuteronomist's practice of shifting the reader back periodically to the narrator's present in order to reinforce the reader's experience that it is the narrator who is the vital link between Moses and the "this day" of the reporting speech.

Within the narrator's direct utterances, it is by means of the distribution of the frame-breaks we have just discussed that the unique status of Moses, emphasized in the other parts of the reporting narrative,

19. Cf. Voloshinov, *Marxism*, 137–59.

is undermined. The narrator's utterances are spoken in two ideological voices which interfere with one another: an overt, obvious voice that exalts Moses and plays down its own role, and a hidden voice that will soon exalt itself at the expense of Moses' uniqueness.

4. In summary, our analysis of the distribution and content of the various "authorial" interruptions by the narrator in Moses' three addresses indicates a subtle but effective strategy on the part of the Deuteronomist gradually to diminish the unique status of his hero at the very same time as the retrospective elements of Moses' own utterances are enhancing that status. Already by the end of Moses' first address, during which we hear Moses deftly rehearsing past events and utterances to prepare his audience to heed "the statutes and the ordinances which I teach you" (4:1), the Deuteronomist by means of five narrative interruptions of apparently inconsequential nature is beginning to accustom his audience to listen to his narrator's voice, a voice that also rehearses past events and utterances as a means of inclining his audience to heed what *he* is teaching them.

In Moses' second address, a series of narrative interruptions furthers the process of diminishing Moses' unique status at the same time as it is being augmented by the account of his magisterial actions and utterances. In 10:6–9 the normal signals that up to now have so clearly separated reported from reporting speech in the book are so muted that it is not possible to say for sure whether verses eight and nine are the reporting utterance of the narrator or the reported word of Moses. The effect of this compositionally is to reinforce in yet another way what has been accomplished by the previous frame-breaks. Once again brought back by 10:6–7 to a brief focal awareness that it is the narrator who is transmitting the words of Moses, not Moses speaking directly, the reader of 10:8–9 now experiences the narrator's utterance and the hero's word as ⟦211⟧ indistinguishable in tone, style, and content: the voice of the Deuteronomic narrator merges for a brief moment with Moses.

By the time we reach the last word of the narrator in the book, 34:5–12, we are well disposed to interpret this first explicit and direct evaluation of Moses' unique status in the proper perspective. The soft, still voice of the narrator has deftly drawn attention to itself throughout the book with such subtle persistence that when we come to the words that frame the end of the narrative, and read therein:

And there has not arisen a prophet since in Israel like Moses, whom the Lord knew face to face . . . (34:10) we are tempted to disagree and to say in reply:

> On the contrary, the LORD our God *has* raised up for us a prophet like
> Moses from among us, and God *has* put His words in his mouth, and
> he *has* spoken to us all that God commands him. And whoever of us
> do not give heed to God's words, which this latter prophet speaks in
> His name, God will require it of us.

This dissenting reply to 34:10, which comes to us somehow through
the book itself, is expressive of another voice which has entered into a
gentle but effective dialogue with the first. The author's narrative
frame-breaks have allowed us to introduce this other voice.

The dissenting reply I have just quoted above is actually adapted
from the words of *Moses* in 18:15–18. We are thus led into a consideration of the reported speech of Moses. Here too, as 18:15–18 illustrates,
what appears to be the monologic word of the greatest prophet of
them all perhaps contains a hidden dialogue between two "Mosaic"
voices, to some degree in conflict. The first, most obvious Mosaic voice
functions in exactly the same way as 34:10 does in the reporting context: to exalt the hero of Deuteronomy and to subordinate its "author."
At the same time, a second Mosaic voice speaks in the book to exalt
the narrator at the expense of Moses' uniqueness, just as the frame-
breaks do within the reporting context. The main question there as
here is whether these two voices are of equal weight.

Divine Speech in
Deuteronomy

CASPER J. LABUSCHAGNE

[[111]] The book of Deuteronomy contains 30 passages phrased as words spoken by God, divine speeches (henceforth DS). They are distributed as follows: 10 DSs in Deuteronomy 1–3; 8 DSs in Deuteronomy 4–11 and 2 DSs in Deuteronomy 12–26 (= 10 DSs in Deuteronomy 4–26), and once again 10 DSs in Deuteronomy 27–34. It is not difficult to identify them, for, except in one instance, they are all ushered in by introductory formulas (henceforth DSF) qualifying them as divine speech.

The only exception, which is unique in the Pentateuch, is in a poetic passage, the Song of Moses in Deuteronomy 32. As I have shown elsewhere,[1] the overall structure of the song is such that the poet alternates several DSs with his own comments. The first DS in the Song is the monologue in vv. 20–27, the only one in Deuteronomy.[2] This divine self-resolution is followed by the poet's comments in vv. 28–31, easily recognizable by the fact that in the second part of this passage (vv. 30–31) the poet refers to God in the third person and uses the name YHWH and the term 'our Rock'. This passage, which is a well-balanced literary

Reprinted with permission from *Das Deuteronomium: Entstehung, Gestalt und Botschaft* (ed. Norbert Lohfink; Bibliotheca ephemeridum theologicarum lovaniensium 68; Louvain: Louvain University Press, 1985) 111–26.

1. See C. J. Labuschagne, *The Song of Moses: Its Framework and Structure*, in I. H. Eybers, F. C. Fensham, C. J. Labuschagne, W. C. van Wyk, A. H. van Zyl (ed.), *De Fructu Oris Sui, Essays in Honour of Adrianus van Selms* (Pretoria Oriental Series, 11), Leiden, 1971, pp. 85–98.

2. For the monologues in the Pentateuch see my paper read at the 11th Congress of the IOSOT at Salamanca 1983, C. J. Labuschagne, *The Literary and Theological Function of Divine Speech in the Pentateuch*, in *VTSuppl* (forthcoming).

unit in itself,[3] is followed by a second DS in vv. 32–35, which can be identified as such by the use of the first person singular in the second part of the speech (vv. 34–35). The following verse, v. 36, does not belong to the DS, for here the poet expresses his hope that YHWH will give his people justice, and he refers to YHWH in the third person singular. The last DS in the Song (vv. 37–42) is introduced by *wayyō᾽mèr*, and is followed by the final comment of the poet in v. 43.

Returning to the disguised DS in vv. 32–35, I might refer to the literary form to which Meir Weiss drew our attention 20 years ago,[4] the so-called 'performative speech' (in German 'die erlebte Rede') also known as the 'interior monologue'. It differs from the ordinary direct speech because it lacks an introductory formula. In this literary device the [[112]] author writes from the viewpoint of the subject, or character in question and uses direct speech. In my opinion, a more suitable term would be 'subjective speech'. There are several examples of such 'subjective speech' in the Pentateuch, but this is the only instance where it is employed with regard to God.[5] The lack of the introducing DSF here can easily be explained as being in accordance with the composition technique in the Song where the poet's comments also have the form of 'subjective speech'.

Once one has identified the DSs, it is relatively easy to determine and delimit precisely the words to be regarded as divine speech. There are, however, two problems: first, the question whether the words phrased in the 3rd person singular in Deut 1:8b, 36; 2:12, 21 and 5:11–16 belong to the *oratio recta*; and second, the problem whether the so-called 'ethnographic notices' in Deut 2:10–12 and 20–23 should be considered part of the DS in which they occur. In order to determine the exact scope of the DSs, we have to solve these two problems.

As to the first, it is important to note that the use of the 3rd person singular in divine speech is not exceptional; it occurs many times elsewhere in the Pentateuch (e.g., in Gen 9:16; 16:11; 18:19; 19:13f.; 21:17; Exod 3:12; 4:5; 19:21f., 24; 20:7, 10–12; 24:1; 30:11–16, 34–38; 31:15; 34:10, 14, 23f., 26). As a matter of fact the greater part of the DSs in the book of Leviticus is phrased in the 3rd person singular, and so is a

---

3. This passage consists of 34 words, a number that is used frequently in the Pentateuch as a composition device. See further below, and cf. the paper referred to in the previous note.

4. See M. Weiss, *Einiges über die Bauformen des Erzählens in der Bibel*, in *VT* 13 (1963) pp. 456–475, esp. 460ff.

5. Cf. Gen 26:7, 9; 32:31; 41:51, 52. See also R. Gordis, *Quotations as a literary Usage in Biblical, Oriental and Rabbinical Literature*, in *HUCA* 22 (1949) pp. 157–219, and R. Gordis, *Kohelet—The Man and his Work*, New York, 1951, pp. 95–101.

large section of the Decalogue in both versions (Exod 20:7, 10–12; Deut 5:11, 12, 14–16), which no commentator, so far as I am aware, would want to delete as secondary additions. On the whole Deuteronomy commentators seem to be at a loss with regard to the 3rd person wording in the DSs, e.g., S. R. Driver[6] considers 1:8b an 'addition'; P. C. Craigie, and before him C. Steuernagel[7] prefer the reading of the Samaritan Pentateuch and the LXX, which is phrased in the 1st person. Others skip the problem without comment.[8] As to 1:36 neither Driver nor Craigie give any comment, leaving the 3rd person wording as it is. The two references in 2:12 and 21 are situated in the two 'ethnographic notices', which we shall discuss presently. The 3rd person wording in the Decalogue is tacitly accepted by all commentators as an integral part of the direct address of God.

[[113]] The real question is of course whether 3rd person wording may be used as a criterion for determining the scope of direct speech. In my opinion it should not. The considerable number of examples given above, including the Decalogue and the book of Leviticus, proves that 3rd person wording in the *oratio recta* was an accepted practice for biblical writers. These passages can all be explained as a kind of 'subjective speech' in a direct speech i.e., phrased from the viewpoint of the listener. They are part and parcel of the *oratio recta*.[9] If this is correct, we have no reason to disavow the legitimacy of the 3rd person singular passages in the DSs in Deuteronomy, or elsewhere in the Pentateuch. I shall support my argument by adducing additional evidence further below.

This brings us to the second problem: the question as to the legitimacy of the so-called 'antiquarian notices' (Driver), or better, the 'ethnographic sections' in 2:10–12 and 20–23. Since we cannot discuss the whole problem in any detail here, it must suffice to say that all the 'ethnographic', 'geographic', 'prehistoric' and 'historic' notices in 1:2, 3; 2:10–12, 20–23; 3:9, 11, 13b, 14; 10:6–7 and 11:30 belong to the same category, and that the point at issue is whether we regard this

---

6. S. R. Driver, *Deuteronomy in The International Critical Commentary*, Edinburgh, 1895, p. 14.

7. P. C. Craigie, *The Book of Deuteronomy* in *The New International Commentary on the Old Testament*, Grand Rapids, 1976, p. 96; C. Steuernagel, *Deuteronomium und Josua*, in *HAT*, Göttingen, 1900, p. 3.

8. See e.g., K. Fr. Krämer, *Numeri und Deuteronomium* in *Herders Bibelkommentar, Die Heilige Schrift für das Leben erklärt*, II/1, Freiburg, 1955, p. 234 and J. Ridderbos, *Het Boek Deuteronomium*, in *Korte Verklaring der Heilige Schrift*, Kampen, 1963, p. 59.

9. See note 4 of my paper cited in note 2 above. The reasons for the use of 3rd person singular in a direct speech is a subject for further study.

type of information as loose, disconnected notices inserted here and there by one or several successive interpolators, or whether such notices should be considered integral parts of the text. I myself am convinced that such notices belong structurally to the text into which they have been integrated.

For a detailed discussion of these matters, I must refer to my forthcoming commentary on Deuteronomy. I restrict myself here to the two 'ethnographic notices' about which there seems to be general agreement among commentators that they should be regarded as (late) explanatory notes, which have been inserted into the text. This may be so, but whoever 'inserted' these notices must have done it in such a way that the structural balance of the text was not disturbed.

Both notices are enveloped in divine commands: in 2:9–13 it is between God's command to Moses with regard to territory God has assigned to the Moabites, phrased in 2nd person *singular* (v. 9) and God's command to the people, in 2nd person *plural* wording, to get ready and cross the border, the Zared (v. 13a); in 2:17–24 the notice is situated between God's command to Moses with regard to territory assigned to the Ammonites, phrased in 2nd person *singular* (vv. 18f.) and God's command to the people, in 2nd person *plural* wording, to get ready and cross the border, the Arnon (v. 24).

In both cases the 'ethnographic notice' serves to bridge the gap created by the contrast between the command to Moses and that to the people. Neither in v. 13 nor in v. 24 is there any word that has this bridging [[114]] function between the 2nd person *singular* and 2nd person *plural* commands. In 1:37–40 there is a divine decision concerning Joshua and the young generation phrased in 2nd person *plural* between God's address to Moses and his command to the people; however the emphatic $w^{e\jmath}att\grave{e}m$ [['As for you']] (v. 40) marks the change to 2nd person *plural* command. In 2:3–5 the contrast between God's command to the people in 2nd person *plural* (v. 3) and the command to Moses in 2nd person *singular* (v. 4) is bridged by the peculiar phrasing of the words $w^{e\jmath}\grave{e}t\text{-}h\bar{a}^c\bar{a}m$ *ṣaw.* [['And command the people']].

My conclusion is that the 'ethnographic notices' simply cannot be missed in their context. Therefore they should be regarded as an integral part of their context. They are certainly not late interpolations inserted haphazardly into the text. In their present context they are meant to be part of the DSs in which they are situated, and cannot be missed there.

Another problem, peculiar to the DSs in Deuteronomy 1–3, is the question as to the exact function of the two forms of address: 2nd person *singular* and 2nd person *plural.* More precisely, is there any system in the use of the two forms in the DSs? Before we address ourselves to this problem, it is important to note that there is on the whole no doubt concerning the identity of the addressed, except in 2:24b, 25. Contrary to the rule that Moses is addressed by God in the 2nd person *singular*, and the people (including Moses) in the 2nd person *plural*, here in 2:24b, 25 the people are addressed in the *singular* form. This can be explained as a stylistic device to emphasize the importance of the divine command to Israel to begin with the occupation of the promised land. The sudden change of number here can be compared with the abrupt transition from *plural* to *singular* in 2:7, where the change of number also indicates the end of God's message Moses had to bring over to the people.

If we examine the very conspicuous 2nd person *plural* imperatives, we can detect the system: God addresses the people directly when it concerns the five crucial turning-points during the journey from Horeb to the Arnon:

1. 1:6–8   the command to set out in order to occupy the land (*dibbèr* [['spoke']] and *lēʾmōr* [['saying']] are for extra emphasis)
2. 1:40   the command to turn back and set out for the wilderness
3. 2:3   the command to turn definitely towards the north
4. 2:13a   the command to cross the Zared (*lēʾmōr* [['to say']] is for extra emphasis)
5. 2:24   the command to cross the Arnon.

God addresses Moses with regard to things that concern him personally (1:37f.; 3:26–28) and when he is charged to convey a specific, already formulated message to the people (1:42; 2:4ff.) and also with regard to the relations with Moab (2:9) and Ammon (2:17ff.; *lēʾmōr* [['saying']] is for emphasis) and with regard to the occupation of the land of Sihon (2:31) [[115]] and of Og (3:2). The people are included in the address by the use of 2nd person *plural* in 1:6–8 (the only instance the preposition *ʾēlênû* [['to us']] is used in a DSF) where God commands them to set out from Horeb. In 1:35ff., where God announces his decision about entrance into the land, the people are once more included in the address. Finally, the people are addressed in 2:24b, 25, where God commands them (in the 2nd person *singular*!) to begin with the occupation of the promised land. Our conclusion is: there is a system and the exception to the rule serves the purpose of emphasis.

The 10 DSs in 1–3 show a distinct structure: the most crucial divine commands are marked by the three phrases beginning with *rab-lākèm/*

lāk, ⟦'enough'⟧, in 1:6; 2:3; 3:26. They form the framework of the over-all structure of chapters 1–3. The other seven DSs are situated between them in a 3 + 4 pattern. We get the following scheme:

A. 1:6–8 *DS to people and Moses at* HOREB: *"Enough . . . !"*
   I   1:35f.   DS to people and Moses about entrance into the land
      II   1:37ff.   DS to Moses and people about entrance into the land
         III   1:42   DS to Moses about the people's decision to attack
B. 2:2ff. *DS to Moses and the people at* SEIR: *"Enough . . . !"*
         IV   2:9   DS to Moses with regard to Moab and his land
      V   2:17ff. DS to Moses about Ammon and his land
   VI   2:31   DS to Moses concerning Sihon and his land
VII   3:2   DS to Moses concerning Og and his land
C. 3:26–28 *DS to Moses about himself and Joshua at* PISGAH: *"Enough . . . !"*

This is a beautiful example of the use of a series of 10, of which many other examples can be given, some of which I have already drawn attention to.[10]

We shall now examine the DSFs. In my first publication on the sub-ject of divine speech in the Pentateuch,[11] I dealt with the Deuteronomy material very summarily. Since then I have addressed myself more thor-oughly to this material and studied the DSFs and the DSs with regard to their number, their distribution in distinct series, their pattern and their function. The revised Synopsis, in which I account for every DSF, shall be presented and discussed presently. I find it very useful to study formulas as these in synopsis. It was by means of such a synopsis that I first discovered the pattern of the DSFs in the Tetrateuch.

It is necessary to distinguish between introducing and referring DSF, the latter of which have been studied by D. E. Skweres.[12] We shall first ⟦116⟧ deal with these briefly and supply additional informa-tion concerning their use in Deuteronomy: *ṣiwwāh* ⟦'commanded'⟧, *nišbaᶜ* ⟦'swore'⟧, *dibbèr* ⟦'promised'⟧, and *ʾāmar* ⟦'said'⟧. Significantly enough the verb *ṣiwwāh* is exclusively used as a referring DSF, never as a formula introducing DS like in Gen 2:16 and 3:17. The verb *nišbaᶜ* ⟦'vowed'⟧, on the other hand is used twice (with *lēʾmōr* ⟦'saying'⟧) to

10. See C. J. Labuschagne, *The Pattern of the Divine Speech Formulas in the Pentateuch—The Key to its Literary Structure,* in *VT* 32 (1982) pp. 268–296, esp. pp. 279ff. In Deuteron-omy 1–3 YHWH *ʾĕlōhênû* ⟦'the Lord our God'⟧ occurs 10x and likewise 10x in 4–6; in the 'we-sections' there are two series of 10 verbs in 1st person plural, the first in 1:19; 2:1, 8, 13b–15 and the second in 2:32–36; 3:1, 3–17, 29; the Decalogue is divided into 10 com-mandments and the name YHWH occurs 10x in it. For the series of 10 DSs and DSFs see the Synopsis below.

11. See my article cited in the previous note, pp. 279f.

12. D. E. Skweres, *Die Rückverweise im Buch Deuteronomium,* in *Analecta Biblica* 79, Rome, 1979.

introduce DS (1:34; 34:4b). Another difference between the two verbs is that *ṣiwwāh* [['commanded']] is frequently (15x) used with a variety of epitheta accompanying the divine name, such as *ʾĕlōhay* [['my God']], *ʾĕlōhênû* [['our God']] (1 + 4 = 5x), *ʾĕlōhêkā* [['your (sg.) God']], and *ʾĕlōhêkem* [['your (pl.) God']] (7 + 3 = 10x), while *nišbaᶜ* [['swore']] lacks all such epitheta. As to their frequency: *ṣiwwāh* [['commanded']] with Yₕwₕ as subject occurs 34 (2 × 17) times in Deuteronomy (with Moses as subject 52 times = 2 × 26) 23 times with the name Yₕwₕ and 11 times without, 15x with epitheta and 8 times without. I mention these numbers explicitly, for we shall come across them time and again. The book of Deuteronomy is full to the brim of number symbolism! The verb *nišbaᶜ* [['swore']] with Yₕwₕ as subject occurs 31 times in Deuteronomy, of which 11 times with the divine name, 11 times with *lātēt lᵉ* [['to give to']], 11 times in the phrase (*ka*)*ʾᵃšer nišbaᶜ* (*Yₕwₕ*) *laʾᵃbōtêkā* [['as he swore to your fathers']] which attests to the frequent use of the number 11, occurring very often, particularly in Genesis, as I have shown elsewhere.[13]

I need not discuss the contents of these '*Rückverweise*' any further now, since Skweres has dealt extensively with this subject. I confine myself here to discussing the statistics of the two other verbs used in the referring DSFs, *ʾāmar* [['to say']] and *dibbēr* [['to promise']]. At this stage, we must consult the synopsis. We note the following:

 a. There are 10 references to God's speaking from the fire, *mittôk hāʾēš*, of which 8 instances contain some form of the verb *dibbēr* [['to promise']] and 2 instances refer to '*his words*' (4:36) and '*his voice*' (5:24). These series of 10 and 8 are typical of Deuteronomy—we shall find them again and again.

 b. The term *par excellence* for introducing direct speech, *lēʾmōr* [['to say']], occurs 10 times with God as the speaker: 5x with *verba dicendi* and 5x without (the latter are 1:34; 1:37; 2:5; 9:23; and 34:4b).[14]

 c. The partly stereotyped phrase *kaʾᵃšer dibbēr* (*Yₕwₕ*) [['as he promised']] is found in two series of 8: the first series (marked *kaʾᵃšer¹⁻⁸*) occurs

---

13. In addition to the article cited in note 10 above, see also C. L. Labuschagne, *Additional Remarks on the Pattern of the Divine Speech Formulas in the Pentateuch*, in *VT* 34 (1984) p. 91–95, where more examples of the 7 + 4 pattern are adduced. It is most significant that this pattern (7 + 4 = 11) occurs in the book of Genesis containing the promises to the fathers, and that the number 11 can be found frequently in connection with the verb *nišbaᶜ* [['to swear']] in Deuteronomy. This cannot be a coincidence. The significance of the (undoubtedly symbolic) number eleven is a subject for further study. It is interesting to note that the eleven instances of *nišbaᶜ* connected with the divine name Yₕwₕ are divided into 7 + 4 (seven instances in chapters 1–11 and four in the rest of the book—see the Synopsis).

14. With Moses as speaker it occurs 15x (8x in chapters 1–3 and 7x in 4–31). With the people as speakers it occurs another 15 times.

in chapters 1–11; ⟦117⟧ the other series (marked *ka⁻ᵃšèr*¹′⁻⁸′) occurs in chapters 12:1–31:13. In the two series together, 8 instances contain the name YHWH (marked YHWH¹⁻⁸) and 8 do not (marked *dibbèr*¹⁻⁸ ⟦'promise'⟧), and the preposition *lāk* ⟦'to you (sg.)'⟧ (marked *lāk*¹⁻⁸) is used 8 times, in the ratio: 3x in the first series and 5x in the second. A peculiarity of the first series is that it has the preposition *lākèm* ⟦'to you (pl.)'⟧ (1:11 and 11:25) in the first, and again in the last instance.

This intricate, but nevertheless well-balanced, structure of the partly stereotyped phrase clearly shows that the words were carefully weighed, selected and counted in order to get these structures and series. It did not surprise me, when I assessed the total number of words in them (i.e., the smallest syntactical units) to find that the first series has 34 (2 × 17) words (see 1–11: Total Ref. DSF = 34), and that the second series yields 26 words (see 12:1–31:13: Total Ref. DSF = 26). Here we encounter once more the numbers 17 and 26 (and their multiples—see above where we discussed *ṣiwwāh* ⟦'commanded'⟧). They both represent the divine name YHWH: 26 is the sum of the letter value (Y = 10 + H = 5 + W = 6 + H = 5 = 26) while 17 is the sum of the digits (1 + 0 + 5 + 6 + 5 = 17).

For a fuller discussion of these divine numbers and their significance I refer to my paper read at the congress of the IOSOT in Salamanca.[15] Here I must restrict myself to saying that I discovered that certain parts of the Tetrateuch (Genesis and the 'Deuteronomistic sections' of the Tetrateuch) and the book of Deuteronomy are literally teeming with these numbers in one way or the other. The use of these divine numbers (and their multiples) is the hallmark, the distinguishing characteristic of Deuteronomy and, in my opinion, of the Deuteronomistic redaction of the Tetrateuch. I realize that this has enormous consequences for the study of the whole Pentateuch problem, but at this stage of my investigation of the divine speech material I have to refrain from drawing any further conclusions.

d. Let us continue our discussion of the synopsis and turn to the 10 remaining phrases referring to God's speaking, which form the last series of Ref. DSFs starting at 5:24b (marked *dbr/⁻mr*¹⁻¹⁰ ⟦'tell/say'⟧). They cover a variety of situations in which God has reportedly spoken. When I constituted the synopsis I naturally scanned the concordances, looking for the *verba dicendi* with YHWH as subject. Having accounted for all phrases occurring in the series I have just described, there were *nine* left, which was suspect, because I expected another series of either *eight* or *ten*. Realizing that the special merit of a series is that it sustains itself, I continued the search until at last, I found the tenth in Deut 26:17, the *Hiphᶜil* of the verb *⁻āmar* ⟦'say'⟧ with *Israel* as (the grammati-

---

15. See note 2 above.

cal) subject: *ʾèt-YHWH hèʾᵉmartā hayyôm lihyôt lᵉkā lēʾlōhîm* "You have made ⟦118⟧ YHWH say today that he will be God to you." I was quite sure that this was the missing reference to God's speaking only when I discovered that in transitive *Hiphᶜil* forms the *grammatical* subject is not necessarily the *logical* subject of the verb, and that the biblical writers considered the logical subject as the real subject, i.e., the actual performer of the action.[16] Therefore YHWH must be regarded as the *logical* subject of the verb here: Israel makes him say and accepts his declaration, but it is YHWH who declares that he'll be her God. In the long debate on this passage, and especially on the meaning of the *Hiphᶜil* of *ʾāmar* ⟦'say'⟧,[17] I have chosen for the literal meaning and find YHWH's declaration in v. 17 and that of the people in vv. 18f. There YHWH is the *grammatical* subject of the verb: "He has made you say today . . . ," but it is Israel who is the *logical* subject, who declares that she'll be God's special people as he had said. If one chooses for the meaning 'proclaim', then of course we get the converse: Israel's declaration in v. 17 and YHWH's in vv. 18f. But this does not make the passage any clearer or the syntax any smoother, for in both declarations there is a change in person, which, in my opinion, serves the purpose of emphasis.

Having accounted for every DSF referring to God's speaking, we now turn to the introducing formulas and to the DSs. The Synopsis shows that the 10 DSs in chapters 1–3 are ushered in by 8 DSFs containing the verbs *dibbèr* ⟦'tell, promise'⟧ and *ʾāmar* ⟦'say'⟧ (numbered 1–8) and by *lēʾmōr* ⟦'saying'⟧ in the 2 instances where there are no *verba dicendi*. The total number of words (underlined) in the DSFs is 31; and the DSs yield 463, which add up to 494, which is a multiple of the divine number 26 (19 × 26). The 8 instances of the preposition *ʾēlay* ⟦'to me'⟧, of which the second one occurs in a referring DSF, seem to have the function of joining the introducing and the referring DSFs together.

The second series of 10 DSs we find in chapters 4–26. The first 8 occur in chapters 4–11 (marked DS⁴⁻¹¹ (marked DS¹⁻⁸) and the other 2 in the 'law section' chapters 12–26 (marked DS⁹ᐟ¹⁻¹⁰ᐟ²).

Of the first series of 8 in chapters 4–11, six are introduced by *verba dicendi* with *ʾēlay* ⟦'to me'⟧ (both marked 1–6) and two are ushered in

---

16. The fact that this phrase belongs to the DSFs clearly shows that the actual performer of the caused action was considered to be the real subject of the verb, in spite of the fact that the grammatical subject is someone else. Another example in Deuteronomy can be found in 7:19 where YHWH is the grammatical subject of the verb *yṣʾ* ⟦'liberate'⟧ and Israel the logical subject and performer of the action of going out; see the arguments in my forthcoming commentary on Deuteronomy in the Dutch series *De Prediking van het Oude Testament.*

17. See *THAT*, I, Sp. 214; *TWAT*, I, Sp. 353f. For a detailed study of the passage, see N. Lohfink, *Dt. 26:17–19 und die Bundesformel*, in *Zeitschrift für katholische Theologie*, 91 (1969), pp. 517–553.

by *lē᾽mōr* [['saying']] (marked *lē᾽mōr*⁶:⁸-*lē᾽mōr*⁷ is part of the fuller DSF). The total number of words (underlined) in these 8 DSFs introducing DS is 21, which brings [[119]] the total number of words in the DSFs of chapters 1–11 to 52 (i.e., 31 + 21), once again a multiple of the divine number 26 (2 × 26). The DSs in these series of 8 yield 358. Together with the DSFs they have 379 words. As we have noted before, the total number of words constituting the 8 *ka᾽ᵃšèr dibbèr* [['as he promised']] phrases, amounts to 34, a multiple of the divine number 17 (2 × 17).

The first of the 2 DSs in the 'law section' (marked DS⁹/¹ in 17:16) is introduced by the only Ref. DSF having an introducing function, which is phrased conspicuously differently and is accompanied by *lākèm*, [['to you (pl.)']] obviously for the sake of emphasis. The second DS (marked DS¹⁰/²) is introduced by the 7th regular introducing DSF in the series of eight, which contains the 7th *᾽ēlay* [['to me']]. The total number of words in this 10th DS is 51, once again a multiple of the divine number 17 (3 × 17). The grand total of words in the DSFs and DSs together in the 'law section' is 63 (a number that seems to have been associated with law).[18] When we assess the grand total of words in the DSFs and DSs in chapters 4–26, we get 379 + 63 = 442, which is a multiple of *both* 17 *and* 26 (17 × 26)! Finally, in the whole book so far, chapters 1–26, the words constituting the DSFs are 58 (31 + 21 + 6 = 58), the number that represents the numerical value of *kᵉbôd* [['glory']] *YHWH*, which occurs several times.[19]

The last series of 10 DSs begins in 31:2 where the first DS is ushered in by the remarkable formula *wᵉYHWH ᾽āmar ᾽ēlay* [['and the Lord said to me']] (phrased so to make it emphatic?), the 8th and last in that series of 8 DSFs, here accompanied by the 8th *᾽ēlay* [['to me']] (marked *᾽ēlay*⁸′). Is it a coincidence that the DSF and the DS have 8 words? The function of this second series of 8 prepositions (marked *᾽ēlay*¹′⁻⁸′) is evidently to form a bracket joining all the material in the chapters 4:1–31:13 together, a function similar to that of the stereotyped phrases in the books of Exodus–Numbers, as I have illustrated elsewhere.[20]

The second DS in the series is in 31:14, the beginning of the concluding chapters of the book, 31:14–34:12. Here again we may note

---

18. It is well known that the Mishnah and Talmud have 63 tractates, but it is worthwhile to note that the first pericope of the 'law-section' in Deuteronomy (12:1–3) is made up of 63 words and so is the last pericope (26:16–19).

19. See C. Schedl, *Baupläne des Wortes, Einführung in die biblische Logotechnik*, Wien, 1974, pp. 50, 192. Cf. also my paper referred to in note 2 above, footnote 10. For further examples of 58 representing the *kᵉbôd* [['glory']] *YHWH* see Deut 5:28b–31 where the DS consists of 58 words and 9:26b–29 where the prayer of Moses is likewise made up of 58 words.

20. See the article cited in note 10 above, *op. cit.*, esp. pp. 270ff.

the bracketing function of the series of 10, which join the concluding section of the book to the preceding sections. As a matter of fact the last 3 instances of the series of 34x *ṣiwwāh* [['command']] and the last two occurrences of the series of 10x *lē⁻mōr* [['saying']] have the same bracketing function. I have already remarked that the DS in 32:32–35 lacks an introducing DSF. Would an extra *wayyō⁻mèr* [['and he said']] here have disturbed the numerical balance of the nine [[120]] introducing formulas in this series, which have exactly 26 words? And was this the reason for the use of the literary device of the 'subjective speech' in the Song of Moses? Moreover, was it because of this numerical balance that the 4th instance of the DSFs with *wayyō⁻mèr* [['and he said']] referring to Moses in the 3rd person (34:4a) reads *⁻ēlāw* [['to him']] (one word) instead of *⁻èl-mōšèh* [['to Moses']] (two words)? Was it for the sake of getting 26 words that the DSFs in 32:48 are so exceptionally long? And does this type of numerical structure explain the variety in wording and in length of the so-called stereotyped phrases occurring in series: *ka⁻ᵃšèr dibbèr* [['that he told']] (2 words); *ka⁻ᵃšèr dibbèr lākèm* [['as he promised you (pl.)']] (3 words); *ka⁻ᵃšèr dibbèr YHWH ⁻ēlay* [['as the Lord promised me']] (4 words); *ka⁻ᵃšèr dibbèr YHWH ⁻ᵉlōhêkā lô* [['as the Lord your God promised him']] (5 words) and *ka⁻ᵃšèr dibbèr YHWH ⁻ᵉlōhê ⁻ᵃbōtêkā lāk* [['as the Lord God of your fathers promised you']] (6 words)? What is more, doesn't this account for the remarkable baroque-like language so typical of Deuteronomy, with its extraordinary ability to expand and contract itself and to be kneaded in the numerical structures? And finally, does the numerical system explain the inclusion of the 'ethnographic notices' in the DSs in chapter 2, and does it also account for the remarkable structure of 1:1–5 with its presumably suspect 'geographic notice' in v. 2?

We do not know the answers to all these questions yet, but so much is certain, that we can state that the evidence for number symbolism and numerical structures as determining factors with regard to the wording, the phrasing and the scope of literary compositions in Deuteronomy is conclusive.

The fact that the grand total of words constituting all DSs in the whole book of Deuteronomy is 1,343, a multiple of the divine number 17 (79 × 17) attests to the use of this type of number symbolism in the entire book.[21] What we found in the subsections of the book, supports this conclusion.

What I have put forward up till now is only the tip of the iceberg. There is an overwhelming amount of evidence to show that the use of

---

21. Cf. remark (c) in note 39 of the article cited in note 2 above.

the divine numbers is a vital part of the composition technique employed by the Deuteronomist(s). The words constituting the DSFs and the DSs themselves were carefully weighed and meticulously counted in order to fit them into patterns conforming to the rules of this numerical system, dominated by the divine name numbers 17 and 26. The purpose of the writer(s) seems to have been to let the divine name manifest itself in the words expressing divine speech, by means of the divine numbers and their multiples.

If we look beyond the tip of the iceberg, we find that the whole book of Deuteronomy is literally teeming with these numbers, not only in the texts referring to divine speech, but also elsewhere throughout the book. In my analysis of the first eleven chapters (to be published in the [[121]] forthcoming commentary in the Dutch series *De Prediking van het Oude Testament*) I have not come across a single section that totally lacks a numerical structure. When, as a result of my study of the DSFs in the Pentateuch I first came to realize that the biblical writers meticulously *counted* not only the formulas (7 + 4 etc., and 7 + 7 etc.) but also the *words* of these formulas in order to let them fit into premeditated patterns and to make them conform to the rules of numerical structures. I was convinced that we have to take their counting seriously if we want to understand the anatomy of their writings. This is how I learned to appreciate the worth and excellence of the method for analysing biblical texts advanced by the Austrian scholar Claus Schedl.[22] This method, known as logotechnical analysis (*Logotechnik*), involves the counting of the smallest syntactical units and assessing their number in the main clauses, subordinate clauses, sentences, pericopes and larger literary units. Up to the present time, for some reason or other this method, which is extremely objective and accurate, has not yet been appreciated, let alone employed by biblical scholars. In my opinion, this method is a very helpful, essential and indispensable tool for analysing biblical texts.

A logotechnical analysis enables us to detect concealed structures in the text that were not discovered up till now by traditional methods of literary analysis. Let me give two examples:

First, Deut 3:21–22: this pericope has 34 (2 × 17) words. A superficial logotechnical analysis shows that it consists of two parts: a) v. 21, Moses' address to Joshua, phrased in 2nd person singular, which yields 26 words, and b) v. 22, Moses' address to the people, phrased in 2nd person plural, which has 8 words (26 + 8 = 34). A deeper analysis shows that there are four main clauses:

---

22. See his book referred to in note 19 above.

1. $w^e{}^{\jmath}\bar{e}t$-$y^eh\hat{o}s\hat{u}^{a c}$ ṣiwwêtî bā${}^{\jmath}$ēt hahî${}^{\jmath}$ lē${}^{\jmath}$mōr   (6)
2. ^{c}ênêkā hārō${}^{\jmath}$ōt ${}^{\jmath}$ēt kol   (4)
3. kēn ya${}^{c a}$śeh YHWH l^{e}kol-hammamlākōt   (5)
4. lō${}^{\jmath}$ tîrā${}^{\jmath}$ûm   (2)

⟦1. I also charged Joshua at that time, saying,
2. "You Have seen with your own eyes all;
3. so shall the Lord do to all the kingdoms.
4. Do not fear them."⟧

which are made up of 17 words. There are three subordinate clauses introduced by ${}^{\jmath a}$šèr ⟦'that, which'⟧ and kî ⟦'for, because'⟧:

1. ${}^{\jmath a}$šèr ^{c}āśāh YHWH ${}^{\jmath e}$lōhêkèm liš^{e}nê hamm^{e}lākîm hā${}^{\jmath}$èllèh   (7)
2. ${}^{\jmath a}$šèr ${}^{\jmath}$attāh ^{c}ōbēr šămmāh   (4)
3. kî YHWH ${}^{\jmath e}$lōhêkèm hû${}^{\jmath}$ hannilḥām lākèm   (6)

⟦1. "that the Lord your God has done to these two kings;
2. into which you shall cross over.
3. for it is the Lord your God who will battle for you."⟧

which yield once again 17 words.[23]

Second, Deut 1:34–40: this pericope is made up of 95 words grouped in seven *p^esukîm* ⟦'verses'⟧ as follows: ⟦122⟧

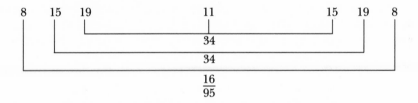

This is a typical example of the menorah-structure, of which there are several instances.[24] The first DS, in vv. 35–36, about entrance into the land, addressed to the people and phrased in 2nd person *plural*, consists of 34 words: the introduction to the second DS and that part of

---

23. The *four* main clauses and the *three* subordinate clauses show the 4 + 3 = 7 pattern; this pattern is repeated in the verbal forms: *four* verba finita and *three* participia.

24. So far as I know C. Schedl was the first to focus attention upon this remarkable structure when he discovered it in Deut 5:14. See C. Schedl, *op. cit.*, p. 172. For more examples I must refer to my forthcoming Deuteronomy commentary.

the DS phrased in 2nd person *singular*, addressed to Moses, are made up of 26 (11 + 15) words (vv. 37–38); the entire second DS consists of 5 words expressing God's refusal to let Moses enter the land and 34 expressing his approval of the entrance of Joshua and the young generation into the land (together = 39 = *YHWH* *ʾeḥād*). Finally it may be noted that the concluding part of this address, v. 39, is phrased in 2nd person *plural*, which means that the people are once again included in the address. The further analysis of the pericope will take us too far; it might suffice to say that the main clauses together are made up of exactly 68 words, a multiple of 17 (4 × 17).

I have selected these two examples more or less at random, but every pericope could have been selected to illustrate how the numerical system, based on the divine numbers 17 and 26 and their multiples, works.

It stands to reason that the use of these numbers as a vital part of the composition technique employed in Deuteronomy has now been firmly established. The weight of the evidence proves beyond any doubt that the book of Deuteronomy was not written in an offhand way, but was carefully constructed according to premeditated schemes and structures dictated by number symbolism. The creating of this literary masterpiece is comparable to the making of a vast crossword puzzle or to the weaving of a Persian carpet. This regards not only the smaller literary units and subsections, but also the larger sections, in fact the whole book. The last redaction must have been more thorough and painstaking than we ever thought. The whole book is pervaded by this numerical system representing symbolically the presence of God. It bears witness to the extreme care with which the authors surrounded their writing about God's speaking.

This sheds new light on the command in Deut 4:2 and 13:1 not to add nor detract from "the word I command you." The real purpose of this so-called 'canonical formula' is a twofold one: first, to protect the law [[123]] against tampering with it, and second, to preserve the intricate, latent-theological structures of the text, which obtained a sacred character.

It is in this light, in my opinion, that the difficult text in Deut 29:28 should be interpreted:

hannistārōt lᵉ YHWH ʾᵉlōhēnû wᵉhanniglōt lānû ûlᵉbānênû ʿad-ʿōlām láᶜᵃśôt ʾēt-kol-dibrê hattôrah hazzōʾt

The hidden things are for YHWH our God, but the revealed things are for us and our children for ever, that we may do all the words of this law.

Here again the plain meaning of the text refers to its immediate context where it is spoken of national disaster as a consequence of disobedience. But at the same time it has another message: the concealed things, the esoteric knowledge with regard to the written text of the law, the sacred numerical structures, are for the benefit of God, to his glory, but the text of the law in its straight, plain language is for the benefit of the people. It is a coded message to the ordinary people, to the uninitiated, who do not know the hidden intricacies of the text, to obey the law in its plain meaning.

The key to the code is in the two words *hannistārōt* ⟦'the hidden things'⟧ and *wehanniglōt*, ⟦'the revealed things'⟧ both written defectively (a fact signalized in the massora). Their Gematria yields the following:

> *The sum of the digits of their letter value:*
> h = 5 + n = 50 + s = 60 + t = 400 + r = 200 + t = 400 = 26
> w = 6 + h = 5 + n = 50 + g = 3 + 1 = 30 + t = 400 = 26
> *The sum of the digits of their alphabet value:*
> h = 5 + n = 14 + s = 15 + t = 22 + r = 20 + t = 22 = 26
> w = 6 + h = 5 + n = 14 + g = 3 + 1 = 12 + t = 22 = 26

The discovery of hidden things gives birth to true knowledge. May this knowledge lead us to real understanding.

Synopsis of Divine Speech in Deuteronomy

1–3

1:3   kₑkōl ᵓašèr ṣiwwāh ¹Yₕwₕ ᵓōtô ᵓalēhèm

1:6ff.   *Yₕwₕ ᵓᵉlōhēnû dibbèr¹ ᵓēlēnû bᵉḥōrēb lē̤mōr¹*
                                DS¹ 48 (DSF 6 + DS 48 = 54)

1:8   ᵓèt-hā̤āreṣ ᵓašèr nišbaᶜ Yₕwₕ la̤abōtêkèm lᵉᵓabrāhām
      lᵉyiṣḥāq ûlᵉyaᶜaqōb lātēt lāhèm ûlᵉzarᶜām ᵓaḥᵃrêhèm

1:11   ka̤ašèr¹ dibbèr¹ lākèm   (*Ref. DSF* 3)

1:19   ka̤ašèr ṣiwwāh² Yₕwₕ ᵓᵉlōhēnû ᵓōtānû

1:21   ka̤ašèr² dibbèr Yₕwₕ¹ ᵓᵉlōhê ᵓabōtèka lāk¹   (*Ref. DSF* 6)

⟦124⟧

1:34ff.   (wayyiqṣōp wayyiššābaᶜ) *lē̤mōr²*   DS² 34 (DSF 1 + DS 34 = 35)

1:35   ᵓēt hā̤àreṣ haṭṭōbāh ᵓašèr nišbaᶜtî lātēt la̤abōtêkèm

1:37ff.   (gam-bî hit̤annap Yₕwₕ biglalkèm) *lē̤mōr³*
                                DS³ 47 (DSF 1 + DS 47 = 48)

1:41   kₑkōl ᵓašèr-ṣiwwānû³ Yₕwₕ ᵓᵉlōhēnû

1:42   *wayyō̤mèr² Yₕwₕ ᵓēlay¹*   DS⁴ 13 (DSF 3 + DS 13 = 16)

2:1   ka̤ašèr³ dibbèr Yₕwₕ² ᵓēlay²   (*Ref. DSF* 4)

2:2ff.	*wayyō⁾mèr*³ Yhwh *⁾ēlay*³ *lē⁾mōr*⁴	DS⁵ 55 (DSF 4 + DS 55 = 59)
2:9ff.	*wayyō⁾mèr*⁴ Yhwh *⁾ēlay*⁴	DS⁶ 66 (DSF 3 + DS 66 = 69)
2:14	ka⁾ašèr nišbaᶜ Yhwh lāhēm	
2:17ff.	*wayᵉdabbēr*⁵ Yhwh *⁾ēlay*⁵ *lē⁾mōr*⁵	
		DS⁷ 121 (DSF 4 + DS 121 = 125)
2:31	*wayyō⁾mèr*⁶ Yhwh *⁾ēlay*⁶	DS⁸ 13 (DSF 3 + DS 13 = 16)
2:37	wᵉkōl ⁾ašèr-ṣiwwāh⁴ Yhwh ⁾ᵉlōhēnû	
3:2	*wayyō⁾mèr*⁷ Yhwh *⁾ēlay*⁷	DS⁹ 22 (DSF 3 + DS 22 = 25)
3:26ff.	*wayyō⁾mèr*⁸ Yhwh *⁾ēlay*⁸	DS¹⁰ 44 (DSF 3 + DS 44 = 47)
	1–3: Total: DSF 31 + DS 463 = 494 (19 × 26)	

4–11

4:5	ka⁾ašèr ṣiwwanî⁵ Yhwh ⁾ᵉlōhāy	
4:10	*bè⁾ᵉmōr*¹ Yhwh *⁾ēlay*¹	DS¹ 21 (DSF 3 + DS 21 = 24)
4:12	wayyᵉdabbēr Yhwh ⁾ᵃlêkèm mittôk hā⁾ēš¹	
4:13	⁾ašèr ṣiwwāh⁶ ⁾ètkèm laᶜaśōt	
4:14	wᵉ⁾ōtî ṣiwwāh⁷ Yhwh bāᶜēt hahî⁾	
4:15	bᵉyôm dibbèr Yhwh ⁾ᵃlêkèm bᵉḥōrēb mittôk hā⁾ēš²	
4:21	wayyiššābaᶜ lᵉbiltî ᶜobrî ⁾èt-hayyardēn	
4:23	⁾ašèr ṣiwwāh⁸ Yhwh ⁾ᵉlōhêkā	
4:31	⁾èt-bᵉrît ⁾ᵃbōtêkā ⁾ašèr nišbaᶜ lāhèm	
4:33	qôl ⁾Elohim dabbēr mittôk ha⁾ēš³	
4:36	ûdᵉbārāw šāmaᶜtā mittôk ha⁾ēš⁴	
5:4	dibbèr Yhwh ᶜimmākèm bāhār mittôk ha⁾ēš⁵	
5:2, 5ff.	(Yhwh ⁾ᵉlōhênû kārat ᶜimmānû bᵉrît bᵉḥōrēb . . .) *lē⁾mōr*⁶	
		DS² 189 (DSF 1 + DS 189 = 190)
5:12	ka⁾ašèr ṣiwwᵉkā⁹ Yhwh ⁾ᵉlōhêkā	
5:15	ᶜal-kēn ṣiwwᵉkā¹⁰ Yhwh ⁾ᵉlōhêkā	
5:16	ka⁾ašèr ṣiwwᵉkā¹¹ Yhwh ⁾ᵉlōhêkā	
5:22	dibbèr Yhwh . . . mittôk hā⁾ēš⁶	
5:24a	wᵉ⁾èt-qōlô šāmaᶜnû mittôk hā⁾ēš⁷	
5:24b	kî yᵉdabbēr¹⁾ ⁾Elohim ⁾èt-hā⁾ādām	
5:26	qôl ⁾Elohim ḥayyîm mᵉdabbēr mittôk-hā⁾ēš⁸	
5:27a	⁾ēt kol-⁾ašèr yō⁾mar²⁾ Yhwh ⁾ᵉlōhênû	
5:27b	⁾ēt kol-⁾ašèr yᵉdabbēr³⁾ Yhwh ⁾ᵉlōhênû ⁾ēlêkā	
5:28ff.	*wayyō⁾mèr*² Yhwh *⁾ēlay*²⁾	DS³ 58 (DSF 3 + DS 58 = 61)
5:31	wa⁾ᵃdabbᵉrāh⁴⁾ ⁾ēlêkā ⁾ēt kol-hammiṣwāh	
5:32	ka⁾ašèr ṣiwwāh¹² Yhwh ⁾ᵉlōhêkèm ⁾ètkèm	
5:33	⁾ašèr ṣiwwāh¹³ Yhwh ⁾ᵉlōhêkèm ⁾ètkèm	
6:1	⁾ašèr ṣiwwāh¹⁴ Yhwh ⁾ᵉlōhêkèm	
6:3	ka⁾ašèr⁴ dibbèr Yhwh³ ⁾ᵉlōhê ⁾ᵃbōtêkā lāk² (*Ref. DSF 6*)	
6:10	⁾el-hā⁾ārèṣ ⁾ašèr nišbaᶜ la⁾ᵃbotêkā lᵉ⁾abrāhām lᵉyiṣḥāq	
	ûlᵉyaᶜᵃqōb lātēt lāk	

6:17   ᵓašèr ṣiwwᵉkā[15]
6:18   ᵓèt-hāᵓārèṣ haṭṭōbāh ᵓašèr-nišbaᶜ Yʜwʜ laᵓᵃbotêkā
[[125]]
6:19   kaᵓᵃšèr[5] dibbèr Yʜwʜ[4]   (*Ref. DSF* 3)
6:20   ᵓašèr ṣiwwāh[16] Yʜwʜ ᵓᵉlōhênû ᵓètkèm
6:23   ᵓèt-hāᵓārèṣ ᵓᵃšèr nišbaᶜ laᶜᵃbōtênû
6:24   wayᵉṣawwênû[17] Yʜwʜ
6:25   kaᵓᵃšèr ṣiwwānû[18]
7:8   ᵓèt-haššᵉbuᶜāh ᵓᵃšèr nišbaᶜ laᵓᵃbōtêkèm
7:12   ᵓèt-habberît weᵓèt-haḥèsèd ᵓᵃšèr nišbaᶜ laᵓᵃbōtêkā
7:13   ᶜal-hāᵓᵃdāmāh ᵓᵃšèr-nišbaᶜ laᵓᵃbōtêkā lātēt lāk
8:1   ᵓèt-hāᵓārèṣ ᵓᵃšèr-nišbaᶜ Yʜwʜ laᵓbōtêkèm
8:18   ᵓèt-bᵉrîtô ᵓᵃšèr-nišbaᶜ laᵓᵃbōtêkā kayyôm hazzèh
9:3   kaᵓᵃšèr[6] dibbèr Yʜwʜ[5] lāk[3]   (*Ref. DSF* 4)
9:5   ᵓèt-haddābār ᵓᵃšèr nišbaᶜ Yʜwʜ laᵓᵃbōtêkā lᵉᵓabrāhām
       lᵉ-yiṣḥāq ûlᵉyaᶜᵃqōb
9:10   ᵓᵃšèr dibbèr Yʜwʜ ᶜimmākèm bāhār mittôk hāᵓēš[9] ...
9:12a *wayyō ᵓmèr*[3] Yʜwʜ *ᵓēlay*[3′]   DS [4] 19 (DSF 3 + DS 19 = 22)
9:12b ᵓᵃšèr ṣiwwîtim[19]
9:13f. *wayyō ᵓmèr*[4] Yʜwʜ *ᵓēlay*[4′] *lē ᵓmōr*[7] DS[5] 23 (DSF 4 + DS 23 = 27)
9:16   ᵓᵃšèr ṣiwwāh[20] Yʜwʜ ᵓètkèm
9:23   (bišᵉlōaḥ Yʜwʜ ᵓètkèm ...) *lē ᵓmōr*[8] DS[6] 7 (DSF 1 + DS 7 = 8)
9:25   kî ᵓāmar[5)] Yʜwʜ lᵉhašmîd ᵓètkèm
9:28   ᵓel-hāᵓārèṣ ᵓᵃšèr dibbèr[6)] lāhèm
10:1f. (*bāᶜēt hahî ᵓ*) *ᵓāmar*[5] Yʜwʜ *ᵓēlay*[5] DS[7] 27 (DSF 3 + DS 27 = 30)
10:4   ᵓᵃšèr dibbèr Yʜwʜ ᵓᵃlēkèm bāhār mittôk hāᵓēš[10] ...
10:5   kaᵓᵃšèr ṣiwwanî[21] Yʜwʜ
10:9   kaᵓᵃšèr[7] dibbèr Yʜwʜ[6] ᵓᵉlōhêkā lô   (*Ref. DSF* 5)
10:11a *wayyō ᵓmèr*[6] Yʜwʜ *ᵓēlay*[6′]   DS[8] 14 (DSF 3 + DS 14 = 17)
10:11b ᵓèt-hāᵓārèṣ ᵓᵃšèr nišbaᶜtî laᵓᵃbōtām lātēt lāhèm
11:9   ᶜal-hāᵓᵃdāmāh ᵓᵃšèr nišbaᶜ Yʜwʜ laᵓᵃbōtêkèm lātēt lāhèm
       ûlᵉzarᶜām
11:21 ᶜal-hāᵓᵃdāmāh ᵓᵃšèr nišbaᶜ Yʜwʜ laᵓᵃbōtêkèm lātēt lāhèm
11:25 kaᵓᵃšèr[8] dibbèr[2] lākèm   (*Ref. DSF* 3)

       4–11: Total: DSF 21 + DS 358 = 379
       1–11: Total DSF: 31 + 21 = 52
       1–11: Total *Ref. DSF* = 34

12–26
12:20 kaᵓᵃšèr[1′] dibbèr[3] lāk[4]   (*Ref. DSF* 3)
13:6   ᵓᵃšèr ṣiwwᵉkā[22] Yʜwʜ ᵓᵉlōhêkā

13:18	kaᵓašèr nišbaᶜ laᵓabōtêkā	
15:6	kaᵓašèr2′ dibbèr⁴ lāk⁵	(*Ref. DSF* 3)
17:16	wᵉ Yʜwʜ ᵓāmar⁷⁾ lākèm	DS⁹ᐟ¹ 6 (DSF 3 + DS 6 = 9)
18:2	kaᵓašèr3′ dibbèr⁵ lô	(*Ref. DSF* 3)
18:17ff.	*wayyō⁾mèr*⁷ Yʜwʜ *ᵓēlay*7′	DS¹⁰ᐟ² 51 (DSF 3 + DS 51 = 54)
18:18	ᵓēt kol-ᵓašèr ᵓaṣawwènnû²³	
18:20	ᵓēt ᵓašèr lōᵓ-ṣiwwîtîw²⁴ lᵉdabbēr	
19:8a	kaᵓašèr nišbaᶜ laᵓabōtêkā	
19:8b	ᵓēt-kol-hāᵓārèṣ ᵓašèr dibbèr⁸⁾ Yʜwʜ lātēt laᵓabōtêkā	
20:17	kaᵓašèr ṣiwwᵉkā²⁵ Yʜwʜ ᵓèlōhêkā	
26:3	ᵓèl-hāᵓārèṣ ᵓašèr nišbaᶜ Yʜwʜ laᵓabōtênû lātēt lânû	
26:13	ᵓašèr ṣiwwîtānî²⁶	
⟦126⟧		
26:14	kᵉkōl ᵓašèr ṣiwwîtānî²⁷	
26:15	kaᵓašèr nišbaᶜtā laᵓabōtênû	
26:16	hayyôm hazzèh Yʜwʜ ᵓèlōhêkā mᵉṣawwᵉkā²⁸	
26:17	ᵓèt-Yʜwʜ hèᵓᵉmartā⁹⁾ hayyôm	
26:18	kaᵓašèr4′ dibbèr⁶ lāk⁶	(*Ref. DSF* 3)
26:19	kaᵓašèr5′ dibbèr⁷	(*Ref. DSF* 2)

12–26: Total: DSF 6 + DS 57 = 63
4–26: Total DSF and DS (379 + 63) = 442 (17 × 26)
1–26: Total DSF: 31 + 21 + 6 = 58

27:1–31:13

27:3	ᵓèrèṣ . . . kaᵓašèr6′ dibbèr Yʜwʜ⁷ ᵓèlōhê ᵓabōtêkā lāk⁷	
		(*Ref. DSF* 6)
28:8	yᵉṣaw²⁹ Yʜwʜ ᵓittᵉkā ᵓèt-habbᵉrākāh	
28:9	kaᵓašèr nišbaᶜ lāk	
28:11	ᶜal-hāᵓadāmāh ᵓašèr nišbaᶜ Yʜwʜ laᵓabōtêkā lātēt lāk	
28:45	ᵓašèr ṣiwwāk³⁰	
28:68	ᵓašèr ᵓāmartî¹⁰⁾ lᵉkā	
28:69	ᵓašèr ṣiwwāh³¹ Yʜwʜ ᵓèt-mōšèh	
29:12a	kaᵓašèr7′ dibbèr⁸ lāk⁸	(*Ref. DSF* 3)
29:12b	wᵉkaᵓašèr nišbaᶜ laᵓabōtêkā lᵉᵓabrāhām lᵉyiṣḥāq ûlᵉyaᶜaqōb	
30:20	ᶜal-hāᵓadāmāh ᵓašèr nišbaᶜ Yʜwʜ laᵓabōtêkā lᵉᵓabrāhām lᵉyiṣḥāq ûlᵉyaᶜaqōb lātēt lāhèm	
31:2	wᵉYʜwʜ⁸ ᵓamar ᵓēlay8′	DS¹ 5 (DSF 3 + DS 5 = 8)
31:3	kaᵓašèr8′ dibbèr Yʜwʜ⁸	(*Ref. DSF* 3)
31:7	ᵓèl-hāᵓārèṣ ᵓašèr nišbaᶜ Yʜwʜ laᵓabōtām lātēt lāhèm	

12:1–31:13: Total *Ref. DSF* = 26

31:14–34:12

31:14a *wayyō>mèr*[1] Y*HWH* *>èl-mōšèh*[1]   DS[2] 11 (DSF 4 + DS 11 = 15)

31:14b wa*>a*ṣawwènû[32]

31:16ff. *wayyō>mèr*[2] Y*HWH* *>èl-mōšèh*[2]   DS[3] 140 (DSF 4 + DS 140 = 144)

31:20 *>èl-ha>a*dāmāh *>a*šèr nišba*c*tî la*>a*bōtāw

31:21 *>èl-hā>ārèṣ >a*šèr nišba*c*tî

31:23a *way*e*ṣaww*[33] *>èt-y*e*hôšu*a*c* bin-nûn

31:23b *wayyō>mèr*[3]   DS[4] 16 (DSF 1 + DS 16 = 17)

31:23c *>èl-hā>ārèṣ >a*šèr nišba*c*tî lāhèm

32:20ff. *wayyō>mèr*[4] ⎤
32:26 (*>*āmartî) ⎦ DS[5] 95 (including *>āmartî*): (DSF 1 + DS 95 = 96)

32:32–35> DSF! DS[6] 37 (DSF 0 + DS 37 = 37)

32:37ff. *w*e*>āmar*[5] ⎤
32:40 (w*e*>āmartî) ⎦ DS[7] 68 (inc. *>āmartî*) = 4 × 17 (DSF 1 + DS 68 = 69)

32:48ff. *way*e*dabbēr* Y*HWH* *>èl-mōšèh*[3] *b*e *c*èṣèm hayyôm hazzèh lē*>*mōr[9]
                                        DS[8] 77 (DSF 8 + DS 77 = 85 = 5 ×17)

33:27 *wayyō>mèr*[7]   DS[9] 1 (DSF 1 + DS 1 = 2)

34:4a *wayyō>mèr*[8] Y*HWH* *>ēlāw*   DS[10] 15 (DSF 3 + DS 15 = 18)

34:4b zōt hā>ārèṣ *>a*šèr nišba*c*tî l*e*>abrāhām l*e*yiṣḥāq ûl*e*ya*c*a*qōb
        lē*>*mōr[10] (DS is part of DS[10]!)

34:9 ka*>a*šèr ṣiwwah[34] Y*HWH* *>èt-mōšeh*[4]

27–34: Total: DSF 26 + DS 465 = 491
1–34: Grand total: DSF 84 + DS 1,343 (79 × 17) = 1,427

⟦61⟧ One of the more perplexing problems in the study of the Hebrew text of Deuteronomy is the frequent change in the use of second
person singular and plural forms in verbs and pronominal suffixes, the
so-called *Numeruswechsel.* Deuteronomy 12 is a useful focus for a fresh
look at this phenomenon with its division into two parts, one in the
plural (12:1–12) and the other in the singular (12:13–31). There are
four short "singular" insertions in "plural" contexts (12:1, 5, 7, 9) and
two instances of the reverse (12:16 and 13:1, which is the proper conclusion of the literary unit). With the change in 12:13 between the two
sections, there are seven instances of the *Numeruswechsel* here, one of
which has a singular verbal form sandwiched between two plurals in
the space of four lexical items (12:4b–5a). This paper will attempt to
demonstrate that all seven occurrences are to be explained by an aspect of the received textual tradition which has received virtually no
attention within the mainstream of scholarly discussion, namely its
metrical structure.

Modern discussion of the *Numeruswechsel* is oriented around the
work of G. Minette de Tillesse (1962) and N. Lohfink (1963). Minette de
Tillesse explained the phenomenon in terms of a redactional process in
a detailed study of Deuteronomy 5–12. H. Cazelles (1967) subsequently
included Deuteronomy 1–4 in a similar analysis. Lohfink, on the other
hand, chose to explain the phenomenon on stylistic grounds in his study
of Deuteronomy 5–11. The attempt of his student G. Braulik (1978) to
explain the same phenomenon in Deuteronomy 4 on stylistic grounds

Reprinted with permission from *Proceedings of the Ninth World Congress of Jewish Studies*, division A: *The Period of the Bible* (Jerusalem: World Union of Jewish Studies, 1986) 61–68.

has precipitated a lively debate. Meanwhile, the larger problem has led to at least three doctoral dissertations in recent years:[1] an enormous work by C. Begg (1978), one by Y. Suzuki (1982), and another by W. R. Higgs (1982). Begg presents a masterful survey of pertinent literature from the time of de Wette (1805) to the present and suggests what appears to be a combination of the two perspectives in his focus on the use of the second person singular in the quotation of earlier material. Suzuki offers an elaboration of the redactional point of view arguing for several levels of scribal activity marked by changes in both person and number beyond that of the so-called *Numeruswechsel* per se. Higgs affirms the use of the *Numeruswechsel* for purposes of redactional literary analysis on statistical grounds.

[62] My work on the metrical structure of the Hebrew text of Deuteronomy has its starting point in the work of Braulik (1978) in which the text of Deuteronomy 4 was scanned using the familiar word-stress system of the Ley-Sievers approach. Finding his discussion provocative but not entirely persuasive, I sought to find a more sensitive system of metrical scansion. The search led to the combination of perhaps the oldest approach, the so-called Alting-Danzian system (1654–1771), with the recent work of the Polish linguist J. Kurylowicz (1972), sometimes described as the system of "Syntactic-Accentual Meter."[2] The Alting-Danzian system is based on the counting of "morae" to assess the relative length of respective units. It is essentially a means of assessing one aspect of the familiar concept of parallelism on quantitative grounds. The counting of syntactic-accentual units, on the other hand, is a means of describing the rhythmic "beats" within a text in terms of meter. The combination of these two approaches in scanning the Hebrew text has led to a number of surprising insights into the literary structure of familiar texts.

To clarify the method of analysis which follows, it is useful to offer a brief definition of the term "mora" and to summarize a number of rules for counting both morae and syntactic-accentual units. A "mora" is the shortest measurable unit of sound in a given language and thus a subdivision of the syllable. By the end of the 17th century the system of

---

1. C. T. Begg, "Contributions to the Elucidation of the Composition of Deuteronomy with Special Attention to the Significance of the *Numeruswechsel*," 5 vols. (Leuven, 1978); Y. Suzuki, "The '*Numeruswechsel*' in Deuteronomy" (Claremont, 1982); and W. R. Higgs, "A Stylistic Analysis of the *Numeruswechsel* Sections of Deuteronomy" (The Southern Baptist Theological Seminary, Louisville, 1982).

2. On this literature see my discussion in *Bib* 65 (1984) 384–85, and *CBQ* 46 (1984) 671–72. The term used here is that of T. Longman, "A Critique of Two Recent Metrical Systems," *Bib* 63 (1982) 230–54.

mora-counting had evolved into the "*systema trium morarum.*" In the hands of H. Grimme, at the turn of the 20th century, syllables were classified as containing from one to four morae each.[3] E. Isaacs (1918) subsequently argued for a simplification of the system back to two categories.[4] Colleagues working in modern languages where the quantity of the vowel is significant in poetic scansion have confirmed the correctness of Isaacs' observations. For our purposes all syllables are classified as either short or long according to the following rules:

1. Short vowels which are counted as one mora include the standard short vowels *i e a o u* and the reduced vowels, i.e., the vocal shewa and the composite shewas.
2. Long vowels which are counted as two morae include the unchangeable long vowels *î ê ô û* and normally the changeable long vowels *ē ā ō* as well.
3. The *furtive patah* is counted as one mora.
4. Postaccentual *qameṣ* in nonverbal situations is considered short and counted as one mora.
5. The shewa under the labial consonants (b m p) following the conjunction is considered vocal and is counted as one mora. Elsewhere such shewas are considered silent (no count).
6. Final stressed *seghol* before *he*, when accompanied by a disjunctive accent, is considered long and counted as two morae.
7. Vowels within a final *kaph* or *nun* are not counted. A preceding silent shewa is opened (counted as one mora). ⟦63⟧
8. The final *qameṣ* in the second person singular of verbal forms in the perfect tense is counted as long (two morae) when the form in question has a disjunctive accent mark. Elsewhere it is considered short (one mora).

The counting of syntactic-accentual units is based on a close reading of the Masoretic accentual system. The boundaries of such units are normally marked by the appearance of one of the 18 disjunctive accents (*distinctive vel domini*) as listed on the insert to *Biblia Hebraica Stuttgartensia* (BHS). Departures from this system involve the appearance of *ṭiphâ* when the following *ʾatnāh* or *sillûq* does not fall on a metrical boundary, or the use of *ʾazlâ* followed by a conjunctive accent other than *geresh*.

3. H. Grimme, "Abriss der biblisch-hebräischen Metrik," *ZDMG* 50 (1896) 529–84; 51 (1897) 683–712; and "Gedanken über hebräische Metrik," *Vierteljahrsschrift für Bibelkunde* 1 (1903) 1–14.

4. E. Isaacs, "The Metrical Basis of Hebrew Poetry," *AJSL* 35 (1918) 20–54.

In the following analysis the first column of numbers in the right hand margin is the mora-count for that line. The second column is the number of disjunctive accents marked in the translation by the appearance of a slash (/) or its equivalent. A double slash (//) marks the presence of both *ʾatnāḥ* and *sillûq*. The triple slash (///) marks the presence of the *setumah* and *petuḥah* paragraph markers in the Masoretic system and the abnormal spacing between verses which appears in some manuscripts and here in both BH and BHS (at the end of 12:3, 7, 14). The symbol (ʃ) marks the two occasions where a disjunctive accent has been added *metri causa* (in 12:5, 31). The third column is the sum of the syntactic-accentual "beats" for that particular unit. It will be observed that these numbers tend to fall into concentric patterns within respective "strophes" (or larger metrical units, whatever the proper term may be).

12:1	These / are the statutes and the ordinances /	14	2	
	Which you shall be careful to do / in the land /	15	2	5
	which Yhwh has given /	8	1	
	The God of *your fathers / to you to possess (it)* //	15	2	5
	All the days / that you live / upon the earth. //	21	3	
2	You shall surely destroy /	8	1	
	all the places /	8	1	6
	Where the nations served there /	13	1	
	Whom you / are dispossessing / their gods //	20	3	
	Upon the high mountains / and upon the hills /	20	2	4
	And under / every green tree. //	10	2	
3	(And) you shall tear down their altars /	11	1	
	(And) You shall smash / their pillars /	12	2	4
	and their Asherim — /	7	1	
	You shall burn (them) with fire /	8	1	
	And the images of their gods /	12	1	
	You shall hew (them) down //	7	1	6
	And you shall destroy their name /out of the place /	14	2	
	that one. /// ⟦64⟧	3	1	
4	You shall not do so / to Yhwh / your God //	18	3	
5	But / rather the place /	9	2	7
	Which Yhwh your God will choose / from all your tribes /	19	2	
	To put His name / there // for His tabernacling ʃ	13	3	5
	You shall seek / *and you shall go there.* //	13	2	

6	And you shall bring there / your burnt offerings /	15	2	
	And your sacrifices / and your tithes /	15	2	4
	And / the offerings of your hands //	9	2	
	And your votive offerings /	5	1	
	and your freewill offerings /	7	1	6
	And the firstlings of your herd / and your sheep //	15	2	
7	And you shall eat there /	6	1	
	before /Yhwh your God /	12	2	6
	And you shall rejoice / in all / that you undertake /	11	3	
	You / and your households //	9	2	4
	Which *He has blessed you / Yhwh your God. ///*	14	2	
8	You shall not do / according to all /	9	2	5
	That we are doing / here / today //	15	3	
	Each (one) whatever is right in his own eyes //	13	1	
9	For you have not come / as yet //	12	2	
	To the rest / and to the inheritance /	14	2	7
	Which Yhwh *your God* /	10	1	
	is giving you. //	6	1	
10	And you shall cross over / the Jordan /	9	2	
	And you shall dwell in the land /	9	1	
	Which Yhwh your God causes you to inherit //	16	1	
	And He will give you rest from all your enemies /	17	1	7
	round about /	5	1	
	And you shall dwell in safety //	6	1	
11	And it shall be the place /	10	1	
	Which Yhwh your God will choose for you /	15	1	
	to make His name tabernacle / there /	9	2	5
	Thither you shall bring /	9	1	
	All / that I / command you ⟨today⟩ //	19	3	
	Your burnt offerings and your sacrifices /	12	1	5
	your tithes /	7	1	
	And the offerings of your hands /	7	1	
	and all / your votive offerings /	9	2	
	Which you have vowed to Yhwh //	10	1	7
12	And you shall rejoice / before / Yhwh your God	16	3	
	You / and your sons / and your daughters /	16	3	5
	And your men-servants / and your maid-servants //	12	2	
	And the Levite / who is in your gates /	14	2	
	For he has no / portion or inheritance /	14	2	5
	with you. // ⟦65⟧	3	1	

13	*Take heed /*	5	1
	that you do not offer / your burnt offerings //	11	2
	At every place / that you see //	11	2 } 8
14	*But at the place / which Yhwh will choose /*	15	2
	in one of your tribes /	8	1
	There / you shall offer your burnt offerings //	11	2
	And there you shall do / all /	8	2 } 6
	That I / am commanding you. ///	11	2
15	*However, whatever your soul-life desires /*	7	1
	You shall slaughter / and you shall eat flesh /	12	2
	According to the blessing of Yhwh your God /	11	1 } 6
	Which He has given you / within all your gates //	7	2
	The unclean and the clean / they may eat of it /	17	2
	As of the gazelle / and as of the hart //	10	2
16	*However, the blood /* you shall not eat //	12	2 } 8
	Upon the earth you shall pour it / like water. //	15	2
17	*You are not /*	5	1
	to eat within your gates / the tithe of your grain /	15	2
	And your wine and your oil /	11	1 } 8
	And the firstlings of your herd / and of your flock //	15	2
	And any of your votive offerings / which you vow /	12	2
	And your freewill offerings /	6	1
	and the offerings of your hand //	9	1
18	*But / before Yhwh your God /*	14	2 } 6
	you shall eat them / in the place /	11	2
	Which He will choose / Yhwh your God / (it) /	14	3
	You and your son and your daughter /	11	1
	and your man-servant and your maid-servant /	8	1 } 6
	and the Levite /	6	1
	Who is within your gates //	7	1
	And you shall rejoice / before Yhwh your God /	17	2
	in all that you undertake //	8	1 } 8
19	*Take heed / that you do not forsake the Levite //*	16	2
	all of your days / on the ground. ///	5+5	2
20	*When Yhwh your God enlarges your territory /*	18	1
	just as He said to you /	7	1 } 3
	And you say: /	6	1
	"I will eat flesh!" / because your soul-life desires /	16	2
	to eat flesh //	8	1
	According to all that your soul-life desires /	6	1 } 5
	You shall eat flesh. //	7	1

21	*If it is far from you /*	6	1	
	The place / which He shall choose / Yhwh your God /	17	3	
	to put His name there /	9	1	7
	And you shall sacrifice /	6	1	
	from among your herd and from your flock / [[66]]	11	1	
	Which Yhwh has given / to you /	9	2	
	just as / I have commanded you //.	8	2	7
	And you shall eat / within your gates /	11	2	
	According to all that your soul-life desires. //	7	1	
22	*Indeed / just as the gazelle is eaten / or the hart /*	22	3	5
	So / you may eat of it //	8	2	
	The unclean ⟨among you⟩ and the clean /	13	1	3
	One as well as the other / they may eat of it. //	9	2	
23	*Only be courageous / not / to eat the blood /*	12	3	5
	For the blood / is the soul-life //	11	2	
	And you shall not eat the soul-life / with the flesh //	15	2	
24	*You shall not eat it //*	8	1	7
	Upon the earth you shall pour it / like water //	15	2	
25	*You shall not / eat it //*	8	2	
	That it may go well for you /	7	1	
	and for your sons after you /	10	1	4
	When you do what is right / in the eyes of Yhwh. //	18	2	
26	*Only your holy things / which are due from you /*	14	2	
	and your votive offerings /	6	1	6
	You shall take and you shall go / to the place /	14	2	
	which Yhwh shall choose. //	7	1	
27	*And you shall offer your burnt offerings /*	13	1	
	the flesh and the blood /	9	1	6
	Upon the altar / of Yhwh your God //	11	2	
	And the blood of your sacrifices / shall be poured out /	12	2	
	Upon the altar / of Yhwh your God /	11	2	4
	And the flesh / you shall eat. //	10	2	
28	*Be careful and you shall obey / all / these words /*	23	3	
	Which I / am commanding you //	11	2	7
	That it may be well for you //	7	1	
	and for your sons after you /	10	1	
	for ever /	5	1	
	When you do / what is good and right /	14	2	5
	In the eyes / of Yhwh your God. ///	13	2	
29	*When Yhwh your God cuts off /*	13	1	3
	The nations / whom you are going there /	16	2	

	To dispossess them / from before you //	13	2	
	And you shall dispossess them / and you shall dwell /	16	2	5
	in their land. //	4	1	

30	*Take heed / that you be not ensnared / after them /*	16	3	5
	After / they have been destroyed from before you //	15	2	
	And that you do not inquire after their gods / saying: /	17	2	
	"How did they serve / these nations /	18	2	
	their gods — /	7	1	7
	That I also may do likewise / even I?" // ⟦67⟧	11	2	

12:31	*You shall not do so / to Yhwh / your God //*	16	3	
	For every abomination to Yhwh /	10	1	7
	Which He hates / they have done / for their gods /	17	3	
	Yea f even their sons / and their daughters //	15	3	5
	They 'burn in the fire' / for their gods. //	15	2	

13:1	*The whole matter /*	8	1	
	which I / command you /	13	2	5
	That you shall be careful / to do //	12	2	
	You shall not add to it /	10	1	3
	And you shall not detract / from it. ///	9	2	

Sections with second person singular forms are marked in the above translation with italics.

The four most interesting examples of the *Numeruswechsel* in Deuteronomy 12 are in 12:5, 7, 9 and 16 where it clearly functions as a "boundary marker" within concentric metrical structures which scan respectively /7:5/4:6:6:4/5:7/ (in a "plural" context) and /8:6:6:8//8:6:6:8/ (in a "singular" context). The *Numeruswechsel* in 12:13 marks the boundary between the "plural" and "singular" sections of the chapter. The other two examples are in 12:1 and 13:1 which function as an envelope around the literary unit as a whole. The last of these appears in a concentric structure which scans /3:5/5:7:7:5/5:3/ (12:29–13:1). The "plural" insertion here consists of two lexical items which appear shortly before the end of the unit but not precisely at the boundary, much like the situation in 12:1 where two "singular" terms are inserted. The effect in each case is to signal the commencement or the end of a major structural unit in the organization of the book as a whole.

The metrical configuration /4:6:6:4/ or /6:4:4:6/ in 12:2–3, 6–7 and 25–27 has an interesting distribution. The /5:5/ unit in 12:1 is balanced structurally by the repetition of the /5:5/ metrical unit in 12:12 which concludes the "plural" half of the chapter. The /6:4:4:6/ unit in 12:2–3 thus becomes a sort of opening "refrain" in its function. It is repeated in the center of the first elaborate concentric structure of 12:4–9 and again in the center of the second to last such structure in 12:23–28. In another study I hope to demonstrate a similar phenomenon in Deuteronomy 13–14 where the opening metrical unit, this time a /4:8:8:4/ unit, becomes a "refrain" which appears three more times in the next section of the "central core" of Deuteronomy.

A second "refrain" appears in the /7:5:5:7/ and /5:7:7:5/ elements found at the conclusion of each half of Deut 12:1–13:1 and again within the /3:5:7:7:5:3/ structure in 12:20–22. A broken version of this "refrain" also frames the /4:6:6:4/ structure in both 12:4–9 and 12:23–28. The use of the term "refrain" here is deliberate to suggest the field of music which may have much more to do with the actual Hebrew text of Deuteronomy than we are used to thinking.

⟦68⟧ Books in antiquity were written for the ear and not the eye. Deuteronomy is perhaps the most liturgical book in the Hebrew Bible and thus we ought not to be surprised to find in it an elaborate set of aural signals to facilitate its transmission in recitation. If the text was composed to be recited, and if that text is still in a metrical form, it follows that it may also have been composed with music as an essential aspect of the tradition itself. In this regard we would do well to look more closely at what T. Georgiades has shown for the ancient Greeks. As he put it, "For the ancient Greeks, music existed primarily as verse. The Greek verse line was a linguistic and simultaneously a musical reality. The connecting element, common to both language and music, was rhythm."[5] He went on to argue that it is quite inaccurate to translate the term μουσική as music. The two terms designate quite different things. The term μουσική represents a form of musically determined verse from which both our familiar concepts of "music," "prose" and ultimately "poetry" come. For him, "The ancient Greek line was a singular formation for which there is no analogy in Western Christian civilization. It was, if you will, music and poetry in one, and precisely because of this it could not be separated into music and poetry in two tangibly distinct components."[6] Is it not possible that a somewhat analogous situation existed in ancient Israel? And if so, it may be that the book of Deuteronomy is a peculiarly useful text in our quest to redefine the terms "prose" and "poetry" in biblical studies.

5. T. Georgiades, *Music and Language*, trans. by M. L. Göllner (Cambridge: Cambridge University Press, 1982) 4.

6. *Ibid.*, 6.

INDEX OF AUTHORITIES

Index of Scripture References

Old Testament

411

Deuterocanonical Books

New Testament

Other Sources